Encyclopedia of Modern American Extremists and Extremist Groups

Encyclopedia of **MODERN AMERICAN EXTREMISTS** and **EXTREMIST GROUPS**

Stephen E. Atkins

An Oryx Book

GREENWOOD PRESS
Westport, Connecticut • London

11/6/03

Library of Congress Cataloging-in-Publication Data

Atkins, Stephen E.
   Encyclopedia of modern American extremists and extremist groups / Stephen E. Atkins.
      p.   cm.
   Includes bibliographical references and index.
   ISBN 0–313–31502–7 (alk. paper)
   1. Radicalism—United States—Encyclopedias.   2. Cults—United States—Encyclopedias.
   I. Title.
   HN90.R3 A75   2002
   320.53'03—dc21   2001057729

British Library Cataloguing in Publication Data is available.

Library of Congress Catalog Card Number: 2001057729
ISBN: 0–313–31502–7

First published in 2002

Greenwood Press, 88 Post Road West, Westport, CT 06881
An imprint of Greenwood Publishing Group, Inc.
www.greenwood.com

Printed in the United States of America

The paper used in this book complies with the
Permanent Paper Standard issued by the National
Information Standards Organization (Z39.48–1984).

10 9 8 7 6 5 4 3 2 1

Contents

Chronology of Events

1958	Mark L. Prophet starts the Church Universal and Triumphant	ham, Alabama, by the Ku Klux Klan kills four black girls
	Edward Fields founds the National State's Rights Party in Georgia	1964 February 15 — Sam Bowers starts the White Knights of the Ku Klux Klan
June 19	J. B. Stoner, a member of the Ku Klux Klan, bombs Bethel Baptist Church in Birmingham, Alabama	March — Malcolm X leaves the Nation of Islam and forms the Muslim Mosque
July 27	George Lincoln Rockwell starts an organization in Arlington, Virginia, that becomes the American Nazi Party	June 21 — Members of White Knights of the Ku Klux Klan murder three civil rights workers, Jim Chaney, Andy Goodman, and Michael Schwerner near Philadelphia, Mississippi
December	Robert Welch starts the John Birch Society	
1960	William Potter Gale establishes a paramilitary group, the California Rangers	July 3, 1964 — Civil Rights Act of 1964 passes
	Robert Allen "Al" Haber revitalizes the Student League for Industrial Democracy and renames it Students for a Democratic Society	July 11 — Members of the Ku Klux Klan kill Lieutenant Colonel Lemuel Penn in Colbert, Georgia
	Robert DePugh forms the Minutemen	1965 February 21 — Malcolm X assassinated by adherents of the Nation of Islam
April 3	First American Nazi Party rally takes place in Washington, D.C.	March 25 — Civil rights worker, Viola Liuzzo, killed by members of the Ku Klux Klan
1961 June 11–15	Student activists from Students for a Democratic Society issue the Port Huron Statement, recasting the SDS as a radical student organization	October 31 — Daniel Burros, a neo-Nazi, commits suicide after newspaper exposes his Jewish background
July	Formation of an international alliance of neo-Nazi groups in the World Union of National Socialists	1966 January 10 — White Knights kill Vernon Dahmer, an NAACP leader, near Hattiesburg, Mississippi
1962 July 8	Robert Shelton forms the United Klans of America	October 15 — Huey Newton and Bobby Seale form the Black Panther Party in Oakland, California
1963 June 12	Civil rights leader, Medgar Evers, is assassinated by Byron de la Beckwith	1967 — Sheldon Emry establishes the Lord's Covenant Church in Phoenix, Arizona
		Members of American Nazi Party change name and form the National Socialist White People's Party
September 16	Bombing of Sixteenth Street Baptist Church in Birming-	August 25 — Dissident member of the American Nazi Party, John Pat-

ler, assassinates George Lincoln Rockwell in Arlington, Virginia

October 28 — Huey Newton and a friend engage in a gunfight with Oakland police, and Newton is injured

October 30 — New York police raid Queens Minutemen group and seize illegal weapons

1968 — David Berg starts Teens for Christ youth group

April 4 — Sniper assassinates Martin Luther King, Jr., in Memphis, Tennessee

April 6 — Eldridge Cleaver, a leader in the Black Panther Party, and Bobby Hutton engage in a gunfight with police in Oakland, California; Hutton is killed

June 18 — Rabbi Meir Kahane and associates found the Jewish Defense League and hold the first official meeting in Manhattan, New York City

June 29 — Attempt to bomb the home of a Jewish activist in Mississippi leads to the death of Kathy Ainsworth and arrest of Thomas Tarrants

July 28 — Group of American Indian activists organize the American Indian Movement (AIM) in Minneapolis, Minnesota

August 27 — Chicago police drive demonstrators out of Lincoln Park during Democratic National Convention

September 8 — California jury convicts Huey Newton of manslaughter

1969 — Environmental activists start Greenpeace in Vancouver, British Columbia

Henry Lamont Beach and William Potter Gale form the Posse Comitatus movement

March 20 — Chicago Eight indicted in a Chicago federal court for conspiracy to cross state lines to promote a riot

June 27 — Police raid on Stonewall Inn in New York City's Greenwich Village launches the Gay Liberation Movement

July — Gay activists form the Gay Liberation Front

August 9–10 — Charles Manson and his supporters commit the Tate-LaBianca murders

October 8–11 — "Days of Rage" in Chicago at the Democratic National Convention

November 9 — Indian activists occupy Alcatraz Island and claim it as part of a native homeland

December 8 — Police raid on Black Panther headquarters kills Fred Hampton and Mark Clark

December 21 — Gay activists start Gay Activist Alliance

December 27–31 — Weather Underground members decide to conduct a terrorist campaign at a meeting in Flint, Michigan

1970 — William Pierce starts the neo-Nazi organization the National Alliance

Arch Roberts founds the Committee to Restore the Constitution

Militant wing of Minutemen forms Secret Army Organization to carry out terrorist campaign

March 6 — Weather Underground bomb detonates in Greenwich Village townhouse killing three bomb assemblers

May 29 — California Court of Appeals reverses conviction of Huey Newton on manslaughter charge

Chronology of Events

August 17	Black militants kill judge in an attempt to rescue George Jackson
November	Jewish Defense League opens a terrorist campaign against Soviet officials
November 26	American Indian Movement (AIM) seize Mayflower II
1971	Else and Alex Christensen organize the Odinist Fellowship
	Jim Ellison establishes the paramilitary survivalist the Covenant, the Sword and the Arm of the Lord
	Geronimo Pratt forms the Black Liberation Army
January 5	Angela Davis arraigned for trial on charges of murder, kidnapping, and criminal conspiracy
May 20	Ervil LeBaron founds the Church of Lamb of God
June 11	Indians end their occupation of Alcatraz Island
August 15	Five disgruntled Republicans start the Libertarian Party in Denver, Colorado
November	Radical leftists organize New American Movement
1972	Black nationalists organize the Black Liberation Army
	Eugenio Parente-Ramos forms the Communist Party USA/ Provisional on Long Island, New York
	British animal rights activists form the Animal Liberation Front
	Iceland recognizes Asatru (Belief in the Gods) as a formal religion
	Two Catholic priests, Paul Marx and Matthew Habiger, found Human Life International
	Members of Secret Army Organization, an offshoot of the Minutemen, blow up theater in San Diego, California
January 26	Members of the Jewish Defense League bomb the Manhattan office of entertainment promoter Sol Hurok killing his secretary
February 23	Militant wing of the Canadian Edmund Burke Society start the Western Guard
June 4	California jury acquits Angela Davis on all charges
August 8	Joel LeBaron excommunicates Ervil LeBaron from the Church of the First Born of the Fullness of Times
August 20	Followers of Ervil LeBaron kill Joel Franklin LeBaron, the leader of the Church of the First Born of the Fullness of Times
1973	John Africa founds MOVE in Philadelphia
	Austin J. App publishes *The Six Million Swindle* in which he denies the Holocaust by claiming most of the Jews escaped to the Soviet Union
	David Duke forms the Knights of the Ku Klux Klan
	Ben Klassen starts the Church of the Creator in Lighthouse Point, Florida
	Robert Millar founds the Christian Identity community of Elohim City in eastern Oklahoma
January 15	U.S. Supreme Court decision on abortion rights in *Roe v. Wade*
January 28	American Indian Movement members occupy Wounded Knee, South Dakota

March 5	Donald DeFreeze escapes from Soledad State Prison in California
March 26	Donald DeFreeze and allies form the Symbionese Liberation Army
October	Michael Harrington forms the Democratic Socialist Organizing Committee
November 6	Symbionese Liberation Army members assassinate Marcus Foster, the Oakland superintendent of schools
1974	William Pierce forms the National Alliance
	Puerto Rican nationalists form the Fuerzas Armadas de Liberación Nacional Puertorriqueñas (FALN) in New York City to carry out armed struggle for Puerto Rico's independence
	Gary Lex Lauck forms the Neo-Nazi National Socialist German Workers Party—Overseas Organization
February 4	Symbionese Liberation Army members kidnap Patricia Hearst
April	Richard Girnt Butler moves his Christian Identity church to Hayden Lake, Idaho
May 17	Los Angeles police kill Donald DeFreeze and five other members of the Symbionese Liberation Army in a gunfight in Los Angeles
September 11	Eduardo Arocena organizes the anti-Castro force Omega 7
1975	Robert K. Brown starts publication of the survivalist journal *Soldier of Fortune*
	Edward Abbey publishes *The Monkey Wrench Gang*
	Ervil LeBaron forms the Church of the Lamb of God

January 24	FALN members explode bomb at Fraunces Tavern in New York City
February 25	Elijah Muhammad, the head of the Nation of Islam, dies
June	Jewish Armed Resistance, the terrorist wing of the Jewish Defense League, launches a bombing campaign in the United States
June 26	Federal government charges Leonard Peltier with the murders of two FBI agents in Pine Ridge, South Dakota
August	Willis Carto starts publishing *Spotlight*
September 18	FBI agents capture major leaders of the Symbionese Liberation Army
October 4	United Freedom Front stages first bank robbery in Maine
1976	John R. Harrell founds the Christian-Patriots Defense League as a paramilitary survivalist group
	Arthur Butz publishes his book, *The Hoax of the Twentieth Century*, in which he denies the existence of the Holocaust
	Donald V. Clerkin establishes the neo-Nazi Euro-American Alliance in Milwaukee, Wisconsin
1977	James K. Warner founds and becomes first director of the Christian Defense League
	Donald Andrews forms the Nationalist Party in Canada
	Anita Bryant starts anti-gay crusade in Florida under the name Save Our Children
	Louis Farrakhan breaks with the leadership of the Nation of Islam and forms a new organization but retains the name Nation of Islam

April 28	Skokie, Illinois wins lawsuit banning Frank Collins and his group of American Nazis from holding a demonstration
May 10	Ervil LeBaron's death squad assassinates veteran polygamist leader Rulon Allred
June	Paul Franklin Watson founds the Sea Shepherd Conservation Society
September	1,000 members of People's Temple relocated to Jonestown, Guyana, South America
	William Pierce publishes the anti-Semitic, anti-government novel *The Turner Diaries*
1978	May 19th Communist Organization organizes
	Malcolm Ross publishes the anti-Semitic work *Web of Deceit*
May 25	First bombing by the Unabomber occurs at the University of Illinois at Chicago
June	Richard Girnt Butler forms the Aryan Nations
June 24	Members of Frank Collins's National Socialist Party of America march in downtown Chicago ending the Skokie controversy
August	Filiberto Ojeda Rios starts Puerto Rican independence terrorist group the Macheteros (Machete Wielders)
August 24	Macheteros kill Puerto Rican policeman at Naguabo Beach in Puerto Rico
November 2	Members of Black Liberation Army and May 19th Communist Organization plan and execute prison escape of Assata Shakur, a leader of the Black Liberation Army
November 15	Congressman Leo Ryan and his delegation arrive at Jonestown, Guyana, South America, to inspect the People's Temple
November 18	913 members of the People's Temple commit suicide or are murdered at Jonestown, Guyana, South America
November 27	Dan White murders San Francisco Mayor George Moscone and gay activist Harvey Milk
1979	Julon Mitchell, Jr., founds the Nation of Yahweh and assumes the name Yahweh ben Yahweh (God, son of God)
	Willis Carto founds the Institute for Historical Review to promote Holocaust denial
July 16	Glen Miller forms White Patriots Party out of the remnants of the North Carolina Knights of the Ku Klux Klan
	Paul Franklin Watson rams his ship *Sea Shepherd* into an illegal whaling ship, the *Sierra*, in Portuguese territorial waters
November 3	Members of the Ku Klux Klan kill five members of the Communist Workers Party in Greensboro, North Carolina
December	The FBI crushes a conspiracy to invade the Caribbean island of Dominica to set up a white supremacist state
December 3	Attack on bus by Macheteros kills two American sailors in Puerto Rico
December 20	David Duke organizes the National Association for the Advancement of White People
1980	Ingrid Newkirk and Alex Pacheco begin the People for the Ethical Treatment of Animals
	Joseph Scheidler starts the Pro-Life Action League
	Bill Wilkerson founds the Invisible Empire, Knights of the Ku Klux Klan

April 3	Five environmental activists form the radical environmental group Earth First!
May 15	Alabama jury convicts Jesse Benjamin "J. B." Stoner for the 1958 bombing of the Bethel Baptist Church in Birmingham, Alabama
September 11	Omega 7 assassinates Cuban UN official Felix Garcia Rodriguez
1981	Jorge Mas Canosa forms the Cuban American National Foundation
January 12	Members of Macheteros bomb eleven fighter planes at Muñiz Air National Guard Base in Puerto Rico
March 20	Two members of the United Klans of America kill Michael Donald, a black teenager, in Mobile, Alabama
October 20	Members of Black Liberation Army, May 19th Communist Organization, and Weather Underground rob Brink's armored car killing three
1982	Willis Carto forms Populist Party
	Ty Hardin forms the Arizona Patriots
June	Jim Burford starts his American Nazi Party in Chicago
August 12	First Mention of the Army of God comes in a kidnapping of an abortion provider, Dr. Hector Zevallos, and his wife in Edwardsville, Illinois
December	First attack by American Animal Liberation Front occurs at the Howard University Medical Science Building in Washington, D.C.
1983	Tom Metzger starts the White Aryan Resistance
	Robert Jay Mathews founds the violent white supremacist group The Order
January 1	Matt Koehl recasts the National Socialist White People's Party and renames it the New Order
February 13	U.S. Marshals' attempt to serve an arrest warrant on Gordon Kahl leads to the death of two marshals and the wounding of four others
April	Michael Ryan establishes Ryan Survivalist Commune in Rulo, Nebraska
June 3	Shootout between police and fugitive Gordon Kahl ends in Kahl's and county sheriff's deaths near Smithville, Arkansas
September 12	Victor Manuel Gerena, a member of the Macheteros, steals $7 million from a Wells Fargo depot in West Hartford, Connecticut
October 28	The first operation of The Order is to rob a pornographic bookstore in Spokane, Washington
November	Members of the May 19th Communist Organization bomb the U.S. Capitol
December 31	Last FALN bombings in New York City wound three policemen
1984	Clark Reid Martell forms first American skinhead group, Romantic Violence, in Chicago
June 18	Members of The Order assassinate Jewish talk-show host Alan Berg in Denver, Colorado
July 4	William Potter Gale and forty-four delegates start the Committee of the States which attacks the constitutionality of the federal income tax law
July 15	Members of The Order rob Brink's armored car of $3.6 million near Ukiah, California

October	Police raid and arrest Wilhelm Ernst Schmidt, a Posse Comitatus leader, for conspiracy to overthrow the government		November	David Dorr and his wife, Deborah, formed Order II
November 4	Law enforcement agents arrest leaders of the United Freedom Front		November	Terry Long assumes leadership of the Canadian Aryan Nations
November 19	Michael Bray and Thomas Spinks organize and begin a series of bombings at abortion clinics in Virginia and Maryland		December 24	David Lee Rice, a supporter of the Duck Club, kills prominent Seattle lawyer and his family
December 7	Federal law enforcement officers kill Robert Jay Mathews in a shootout on Whidbey Island, Washington		1986	Federal authorities arrest seven leaders of the Committee of the States
1985	Anonymous group of women artists and writers form the Guerrilla Girls		January	Randall Terry starts the radical anti-abortionist Operation Rescue with a demonstration in Binghamton, New York
February	Trial starts against Ernst Christof Friedrich Zundel in Toronto, Canada for making "false news"		November 9–10	Sea Shepherd activists sink two whaling ships and sabotage a whale-processing factory in Reykjavik, Iceland
March 7	Gordon Lee Baum founds the Council of Conservative Citizens		1987	David Berg reorients the Children of God and changes the name to the Family of Love
April 15	David Tate kills a Missouri state trooper on his way to the Covenant, the Sword and the Arm of the Lord compound			Scott Graham and Tony McAleer found Canadian racist skinhead organization Aryan Resistance Movement
April 18	Federal agents raid the Covenant, the Sword and the Arm of the Lord compound and end its operations			Louis McKey and Rick Sieman found the Sahara Club in Southern California to oppose environmentalists
May 11	Police capture Marilyn Buck and Linda Sue Evans, leaders of the May 19th Communist Organization		January	Klan members and civil rights demonstrators clash in Forsyth County, Georgia
May 13	Philadelphia police bomb MOVE headquarters killing eleven and destroying sixty-one buildings		February 27	Witness spots Unabomber planting a bomb in Salt Lake City, Utah
October 11	Jewish Defense League activists kill western director of the American-Arab Anti-Discrimination Committee, Alex Odeh, with a booby trap bomb in Santa Ana, California		March	Gay community forms ACT UP in New York City
			April 16	Animal Liberation Front firebombs animal diagnostic laboratory at the University of California at Davis
			September	Jeffrey Lundgren establishes a commune near Kirkland, Ohio

October 2	Jury convicts members of the Committee of the States of conspiracy to threaten government officials
1988	Paul Hall, Jr., starts publication of the Christian Identity newspaper the *Jubilee*
January	Fred Leuchter travels to Poland to study gas chambers at the death camps and publishes a report denying the existence of the gas chambers
April 7	Jury acquits defendants in the Fort Smith Sedition Trial in Arkansas
July	Father Norman Weslin forms the radical anti-abortion group the Lambs of Christ
November 13	Three skinheads with affiliation to the White Aryan Resistance kill Ethiopian immigrant Mulugeta Seraw in Portland, Oregon
December	Lyndon LaRouche receives prison terms for conspiracy, mail fraud, and tax evasion
1989	
April 17	Jeffrey Lundgren and Mormon blood-atonement cult murders Avery family
May 13	FBI arrests David Foreman for his involvement with an eco-terrorist group
August 22	Drug dealer murders Huey Newton in West Oakland, California
October 24	Randy Weaver sells sawed-off shotguns to a federal undercover agent
November	Wolfgang Droege starts the Canadian neo-Nazi Heritage Front
1990	George Burdi forms the racist band RAHOWA (Racial Holy War)
	Marijuana activists organize the Green Panthers
	Michael McGee organizes the New Black Panther Party
	Coalition of gays and lesbians form Queer Nation
January 4	Police arrest Jeffrey Lundgren and family for murdering the Avery family
April	Three Protestant fundamentalist leaders start B'nai Noah (Children of Noah)
May	Car bomb almost kills two Earth First! leaders
May 11	Elizabeth Clare Prophet's date for the end of American society and possibly the world
October 22	Tom Metzger and the White Aryan Resistance loses lawsuit and court institutes judgment of $12 million against them
November 5	Palestinian-Arab gunman charged with assassinating Rabbi Meir Kahane in downtown New York City
1991	Dave Barley moves America's Promise Ministries to Sandpoint, Idaho
May 17	George David Loeb, a minister in the Church of the Creator, kills a black sailor in Jacksonville, Florida
June	Fred Phelps launches his anti-gay crusade
July 15	Massive Operation Rescue operation opens in Wichita, Kansas
December	Kirk Lyons starts the CAUSE Foundation as a legal defense group to defend right-wing extremists
1992	Leaders of the Nation of Yahweh sent to prison on racketeering and conspiracy charges
	John McGee III and Carl Anthony Bennett form the black separatist group Stream of Knowledge, Albuquerque

	LeRoy Schweitzer starts the Freemen movement
August 21	Federal agents bungle survey of Randy Weaver property at Ruby Ridge, Idaho; a U.S. marshal and Sammy Weaver are both killed
August 22	Federal sniper kills Vicky Weaver
August 31	Randy Weaver surrenders to federal authorities
October 23–25	Meeting of anti-government activists at Estes Park, Colorado, starts the militia movement
November	Aryan Republican Army robs its first bank in its campaign to establish a white homeland
1993	Marshall Applewhite and the Heaven's Gate UFO cult reappear on the national scene
February 28	BATF agents raid the Branch Davidian compound in Waco, Texas
March 10	Michael Griffin, an anti-abortion activist, kills Dr. David Gunn in Pensacola, Florida
April 19	Final assault on the Branch Davidian compound in Waco; more than eighty cult members die
May	Survivalists form the Washington State Militia
July 15	Police arrest members of the Fourth Reich Skinheads for conspiracy and bombings in Southern California
August 6	Ben Klassen, the leader of the Church of the Creator, commits suicide
August 19	Shelly Shannon, an anti-abortion activist, wounds Dr. George Tiller in Wichita, Kansas
1994	J. Michael Hill and Steven J. Wilkins found the League of the South
	Richard McLaren forms the Republic of Texas in Fort Davis, Texas
	Linda Thompson starts the American Justice Federation to support the activities of the militia movement
January 1	Trochmann family forms the Militia of Montana
February	Jury convicts Byron de la Beckwith of the murder of Medgar Evers
February 25	Israeli government outlaws Kahane Chai
April	George Burdi founds Resistance Records in Detroit, Michigan
April	Norman Olson and Ray Southwell organize the Michigan Militia
July 29	Paul Hill assassinates Dr. John Bayard Britton and James Barrett outside an abortion clinic in Pensacola, Florida
October 5	Swiss police find first mass suicides of the Solar Temple Cult in Switzerland
October 5	Paul Hill first person convicted of violating the federal Freedom of Access to Clinic Entrances Act
December 30	John Salvi murders two abortion clinic receptionists and wounds five other persons in the Boston, Massachusetts, area
1995	Jeff Berry starts the Church of the American Knights of the Ku Klux Klan in Indiana
	Don Black brings up a white supremacist Web site, Storm-front

March	Anti-government activists form the Freemen and set up a common law government
	Two neo-Nazi skinhead brothers kill their parents and other brother
April 19	Timothy McVeigh blows up the Alfred P. Murrah Federal Building in Oklahoma City, Oklahoma
April 19	Arkansas executes Richard Snell for killing an Arkansas highway patrol trooper and a pawnbroker
June 28	Police kill Michael Hill, prominent common law advocate, in a license dispute
September 18	Richard McLaren informs governor of Texas of the claims of the Republic of Texas
September 19	The *New York Times* and the *Washington Post* publish the Unabomber manifesto
November 11	Washington State Militia goes public
November 18	Aryan Nations skinheads kill an African immigrant in Denver, Colorado
November 25	Members of the Nazi Low Riders beat to death a homeless black man in Lancaster, California
December 1	Republic of Texas movement proclaims the legal existence of the Republic of Texas
December 7	Three active-duty soldiers affiliated with the National Alliance murder a black couple in Fayetteville, North Carolina
December 23	Swiss police discover the second group of mass suicides of the Solar Temple Cult
1996	Matthew Hale forms the World Church of the Creator in East Peoria, Illinois
	Neal Horsley builds the Web site, the Nuremberg File, listing all abortion providers and their supporters
	Radical American environmentalists start the Earth Liberation Front
January 18	Peter Langan, the leader of the Aryan Republican Army, is arrested in Columbus, Ohio, after a gunfight
February 15	Negative media publicity about his role in the white supremacist movement causes Larry Pratt to resign as administrative aid in Patrick Buchanan's presidential campaign
March 22–26	Members of Heaven's Gate cult commit mass suicide
March 25	Freemen at Justus Township, Montana, refuse to surrender to government authorities, beginning a siege
April 6	Federal authorities arrest Theodore Kaczynski, alias the Unabomber, in Montana
June 13	Freemen at Justus Township, Montana, surrender to federal authorities after 81-day siege
July	Federal authorities in Arizona arrest members of an anti-government group, Viper Militia, for planning bombings
July 12	Three Phineas Priests rob a bank in Spokane, Washington
July 27	Bombing at the Centennial Olympic Park in Atlanta, Georgia, marks first appearance of Eric Rudolph
July 27	Federal agents arrest leaders of the Washington State Militia on conspiracy charges
October 8	Federal agents capture three Phineas Priests trying to rob a bank in Portland, Oregon
November	Willis Carto loses lawsuit and control of the Institute of Historical Review

Chronology of Events

November	Police raid on the headquarters of the Communist Party USA/Provisional produces a stockpile of weapons
November 29	John Salvi commits suicide in his prison cell
1997	
January 16	Eric Rudolph bombs an abortion clinic in the Atlanta area
February 15	Kehoe brothers engage in a firefight with Ohio state troopers and escape arrest
February 21	Eric Rudolph bombs a gay nightclub in the Atlanta area
March 22–26	Members of the UFO cult Heaven's Gate commit mass suicide
March 22	Canadian police find last five suicides of the Solar Temple Cult
April 27	Richard McLaren's faction of the Republic of Texas seizes hostages in Fort Davis, Texas
May 3	Richard McLaren and supporters surrender to federal and state authorities in Fort Davis, Texas
November 9	Neo-Nazi skinheads of Romantic Violence vandalize Chicago-area synagogues
November 22	Death of founder Jorge Mas Canosa hurts effectiveness of Cuban American National Foundation
December 10	Julia "Butterfly" Hill starts her tree sitting on a giant redwood in northern California
1998	
January 22	Ted Kaczynski pleads guilty to two bombing deaths and receives four consecutive life sentences
January 29	Eric Rudolph bombs an abortion clinic in Birmingham, Alabama
June 7	Three white supremacists drag James Byrd, Jr., to death in Jasper, Texas
July	Three members of the Aryan Nations assault Victoria Keenan and her son, Jason Keenan, after Keenan's car backfires
August	Davis Wolfgang Hawke establishes the American Nationalist Party by bringing up its Web site
August 21	Mississippi court sentences Sam Bowers to life imprisonment for the murder of Vernon Dahmer
October 7	Two Wyoming men assault and kill Matthew Shepard in a case of gay bashing
October 17	Arsonists from Earth Liberation Front start fire at ski buildings in Vail, Colorado
October 23	James Kopp assassinates an abortion provider, Dr. Bernard A. Slepian, at his home in Amherst, New York
1999	
February 26	Two Alabama men murder a gay man, Billy Jack Gaither
March	William Pierce and the National Alliance purchase the neo-Nazi record company, Resistance Records
July 3	Benjamin Smith, a member of the World Church of the Creator, starts a campaign of shooting which leads to two dead and eight others wounded
August 10	Buford Furrow, a member of the Aryan Nations, shoots two adults and three Jewish children and kills Filipino American postal worker in Granada Hills, California
August 11	President Clinton offers clemency to fourteen FALN inmates on the condition that they renounce terrorism

September 10 — Eleven FALN prisoners accept President Clinton's conditions and leave prison

September 15 — Larry Ashbrook, a self-proclaimed Phineas Priest, kills seven members of the Wedgwood Baptist Church in Fort Worth, Texas

November 30 — Black Bloc demonstrates against globalization at the World Trade Organization in Seattle, Washington

2000

Irving trial in London, England, clears Deborah Lipstadt of libel for challenging Irving as a Holocaust denier

February — Department of Housing and Urban Development brings suit against Ryan Wilson, a member of the neo-Nazi United States of America Nationalist Party, for the violation of federal fair-housing laws for the harassment of Bonnie Jouhari

April 28 — Shooting spree by Richard Baumhammers kills five minority members in the Pittsburgh, Pennsylvania, area

July 22 — Danforth report clears federal government of wrongdoing in Branch Davidian siege

September 8 — Richard Girnt Butler and Aryan Nations lose lawsuit threatening the existence of the Aryan Nations

September 20 — Waco court affirms that the fire at the Branch Davidian compound not government's fault

2001
February 18 — Khalid Muhammad, leader of the New Black Panther Party, dies in Marietta, Georgia

March 8 — Computer entrepreneur buys Aryan Nations compound at Hayden Lake

March 29 — French police arrest James Kopp in Dinan, France

May 21 — Earth Liberation Front start fires in Oregon and Washington

June 11 — Federal authorities execute Timothy McVeigh for Oklahoma City bombing

August 17 — Yahweh ben Yahweh, leader of Nation of Yahweh, released from prison

December 5 — Ohio police arrest Clayton Lee Waagner for sending 550 anthrax hoax letters to abortion clinics

Introduction

The term extremism is loosely thrown about to describe the movements, groups, and organizations that take the most unusual, even bizarre, positions on economic, political, religious, and social issues. Even in the dictionaries and books that use the term, the efforts made to define extremism are disappointing and limited. Extremism is defined as the advocacy of extreme positions by movements, groups, and organizations. An extremist is an individual who advocates the extreme position of a movement, group, or organization. Use of the terminology of extreme left and extreme right originates from the practice during the French Revolution of seating parties to the left or right of the presiding officer. Although there is a close identification of the extreme left and the extreme right with extremism in general, this association is more apparent in politics than it is in other arenas of life. Arizona Senator Barry Goldwater's oft-quoted statement "Extremism in the defense of liberty is no vice," denotes the strength of this belief. Perhaps the best explanation of the ingredients necessary in the creation of an extremist comes from Kerry Nobel, a leader of the paramilitary, the Covenant, the Sword and the Arm of the Lord (CSA). In his view it took a "philosophical or theological premise, based upon discontent, fear, unbelief, hate, despair, or some other negative emotion" to produce an extremist.

For the purposes of this book, an extremist movement, group, or organization is one that deviates from normal economic, political, religious, or social standards. Individuals who pursue policies or practices that are far outside the societal norm of personal behavior are classified as extremists. Although criminals fall into this definition, they rarely operate for more than personal gain or from psychological compulsion. Extremists have an agenda that transcends personal gain and psychological compulsion. They have a mission to protest or even transform the status quo. Nevertheless, a close relationship exists between extremism and criminal activities. Most extremists have legal difficulties at one time or another either as a result of crimes committed in carrying out their beliefs or because of petty crimes against persons or property. Many extremists advocate violence, but others avoid it at all cost. Some extremist groups and individuals have engaged in terrorist acts. The best explanation is the logical statement that all terrorists are extremists, but not all extremists are terrorists.

Extremist groups and individuals examined in this book fall into several distinct categories. The largest category is political extremism. Groups or individuals who espouse a fundamental transformation or the overthrow of the U.S. government fall into this category. Both left-wing and right-wing extremist groups and individuals fall into this category. Those who preach race hatred or anti-Semitism also qualify. Holocaust denial is a part of the anti-Semitic agenda. Some of these groups or individuals also preach violence against feminists, homosexuals, and immigrants.

The second largest category is religious extremism. Religious groups espousing radical religious or social views can fall into the extremist camp. Some of these religious bodies have become cults with charismatic leaders who use mind-control techniques to control their followers. Others have a worldview that may include beliefs in unidentified flying objects (UFOs) and superior extraterrestrial beings. Several of these cults have been involved in mass suicide attempts. Among the cults classified as extremist are the Children of God, Heaven's Gate, Solar Temple, and several UFO cults.

A third category is the economic and social extremists. These groups and individuals combine a strong political orientation with concern about transforming society. Again, members of this category cross the political spectrum from left to right. Among the groups are the Libertarian Party, New American Movement, and several of the separatist movements. Many of the survivalists fall into this category because of their belief in the need for a radical transformation of society. This category of extremist is more reluctant to take direct action or use violence. Groups tend either to want to transform society or to retreat from society.

The concentration and orientation of extremist groups have changed in the past fifty years. In the period from 1960 to 1975, most extremist groups had a distinctive leftist orientation. These leftist groups had ideas of transforming American society to produce what they considered a more just world. Mixed into this ideological stance was op-

position to the Vietnam War. Out of the political vortex of the 1960s came the Students for a Democratic Society (SDS). Disillusionment with the direction of American politics led many of the leftists to opt for revolutionary action. The breakup of the SDS served as a catalyst for the formation of various revolutionary organizations, including the Weather Underground, the Symbionese Liberation Army, and the May 19th Communist Organization. Black separatist movements also proliferated, led by disenchanted African Americans who had become disillusioned by what they believed were the failures of the civil rights movement and the lack of equality. The splintering of the Black Panther Party produced the New Afrika Movement and the Black Liberation Army. Violence by these leftist groups in the 1960s and early 1970s resulted in a backlash against them and radical social change.

Since the mid-1970s, the most active extremist groups have had a radical right orientation. Several of these groups, such as the Ku Klux Klan and the American Nazi Party, had been active before the 1970s, but they were either more regional in strength or were marginal organizations. A series of events beginning in the 1970s and continuing into the 1990s caused a number of radical right organizations to organize, beginning with the Minutemen and the Posse Comitatus Movement. First anti-communist and then anti-government sentiments united members of these groups. Civil rights agitation and bad economic conditions in the Farm Belt and Rust Belt produced a generation of white males who felt disenfranchised and were willing to blame the federal government for their woes. Efforts toward gun control have reinforced this paranoia about the federal government. Many of these individuals are military veterans who believe that the United States was changing into a society that was leaving them on the outside. Various conspiracy theories about the United Nations and multinational corporations have been added to this mix, and the result has been the proliferation of militia and survivalist groups.

A new strain of anarchism appeared in the 1990s. Anarchism is the philosophy that the state must be destroyed and replaced by a society without laws and restrictions. Anarchists, the terrorists of the late nineteenth and early twentieth centuries, assassinated a number of state leaders. This violent phase of anarchism withered away in the middle of the twentieth century lost in clashes among communism, fascism, and capitalism. A new strain of anarchism has developed which is a revolt against the political system and modern society. Ted Kaczynski and his Unabomber campaign is an example of the new anarchism. Another example is the anarchist group Black Bloc, which demonstrates against corporations and globalization.

Extremists and extremist groups are often in the news, but serious research on extremism has attracted little scholarly attention. Less than a dozen researchers are active in this field, and several of them are journalists whose research on news stories has resulted in in-depth articles and books. Another factor retarding research on extremists is the element of personal risk involved in dealing with individuals with volatile personalities and an inclination for violence. For example, Denver radio talk show host Alan Berg lost his life by challenging white supremacists. Morris Dees of the Southern Poverty Law Center has been threatened numerous times, and extremists exploded a bomb at the center in the 1980s. Finally, many of the extremists have access to lawyers who are sympathetic to their causes, and the threat of a lawsuit drives away many researchers.

The intention of this work is to identify and define the most influential and significant extremists, extremist organizations, and extremist events in the United States in the past half-century. The subjects that predate 1950 have been included as background information for more recent subjects. More than 75 percent of the material deals with the period since 1980 and includes subjects not carried in any other work of this type. Foreign terrorists that operate in the United States and Canada have been excluded be-cause the scope of this book is on domestic extremism. For that reason, the 1993 World Trade Center bombing and the September 11, 2001, terrorist attacks are not treated. Each citation, which varies from 200 to 1,500 words, is intended to be as factually accurate as possible. Personal data is sometimes lacking because some individuals refuse to divulge personal information for a variety of reasons. In an earlier book on terrorism, I found terrorists eager to promote themselves with inflated biographies. Extremists tend to go to the opposite extreme. They distrust authority and believe that the government will use personal information against them. Consequently, extremists make it difficult to find such data, even dates and places of birth.

Regardless of the difficulty of finding information, a collective profile of the extremists and extremist groups covered in this book makes fascinating reading. Extremists come from all segments of society. Among left-wing groups, leadership comes predominately from two segments of American society—students or former students from elite schools and former convicts. Many white leftists attended prestigious universities where they engaged in radical campus politics. Black activists tend to come from poor families and attend less prestigious schools, but a significant number of them have served prison terms and have been in court as the result of a variety of offenses. Leaders of right-wing groups range from physicist William Pierce to television repairman Tom Metzger. Many right-wing extremists are farmers or small businessmen, but a significant number are career military men. William Potter Gale and Bo Gritz both reached the rank of colonel in the U.S. Army. Many of these extremists come from families who share their views, but others come out of more tolerant environments. My conclusion, after researching these biographies, is that there are no accurate predictors of future extremist behavior.

Some of the terms used in this book need some elaboration. Often in the course of a citation certain terms have special meaning.

Among these are movement, group, and organization. A movement implies that several groups or organizations exist within it. These entities may or may not cooperate with each other, but they participate in a common struggle. A group is made up of individuals who coalesce together around a person or a set of ideas. It is a more general term than an organization, which has a set organizational structure, often with officers and sometimes even a constitution and by-laws. Extremists tend to belong to more than one movement, group, or organization, occasionally at the same time. These shifts of allegiance by individuals may be confusing, but extremists tend to be fickle and confrontational. Feuds are common among extremists, and after a falling out, the dissidents either form another competing group or organization, or they join a different one.

Material for this book came from a variety of sources. The information in each entry is based on the written source cited in the bibliography following the entry and in some cases also in the bibliography at the end of the book. The bibliography provides a list of works used in this study. Books on specific subjects were consulted, but books covered only a limited number of the subjects. The best source on extremism is a publication of the Southern Poverty Law Center, *SPLC Intelligence Report*. Material from the Anti-Defamation League also proved invaluable. Among the Internet sources, the Nizkor Project provides excellent articles on Holocaust denial. Often the only sources were journal and newspaper articles. There are two good ways to consult newspaper articles: Lexis-Nexus Academic and Newsbank. Each has a different mix of newspapers, but both provide wide coverage. Most academic and large public libraries subscribe to one or the other of these databases. Items in boldface indicate that a full essay on the topic can be found in the text. Research for this book has taken over three years, and I used both databases at various times. A recent U.S. Supreme Court decision, *New York Times Company v. Tasini*, over the use of freelance writer's materials in these databases, has resulted in the removal of some of the articles in these databases. This issue is still in litigation. Consequently, articles used in this book may no longer be available in either database.

ACKNOWLEDGMENTS

This book is dedicated to my wife, Susan Jordan Atkins; my children, Stephanie Starr Atkins and Jordan Eugene Atkins; my dog, Miss Molly; and my two cats, Dudley and Rocky. My wife deserves my thanks for her understanding when I was unable to talk to her when she wanted to communicate. I also appreciate my new study and the wall-to-wall bookshelves. My children deserve my thanks because of their constant interest in my research subjects; Miss Molly, for her companionship during those long days and nights while I checked citations; and my cats, for not killing each other even though they detest each other. Additional thanks go to my research assistant, Chelsa Bliskey, for trying to locate through the Internet elusive birth dates and other personal data on people who do not wish to reveal such information. I also want to acknowledge assistance from the Southern Poverty Law Center, Montgomery, Alabama.

A

ACT UP (AIDS Coalition to Unleash Power)

ACT UP (AIDS Coalition to Unleash Power) is a militant AIDS awareness organization which sponsors demonstrations to promote its cause. Members of the gay community formed the group in March 1987 in New York City to make the American public confront the issue of AIDS. ACT UP is a unique organization because, according to critic Stanley Aronowitz, "it is a movement of and by the victims not merely for them." Larry Kramer was one of the founders as was Mark Kostopoulos. Kramer has continued to play an active role on the national scene. Almost immediately after founding ACT UP, the leadership adopted guerrilla tactics to gain maximum publicity. Starting with a protest at the New York Stock Exchange over the pricing of the drug AZT, ACT UP has engaged in a series of direct confrontation operations. Some of these confrontations have become violent, the most famous being the interuption of trading on the New York Stock Exchange on September 14, 1989 and the disruption of a sermon by John Cardinal O'Connor at St. Patrick's Cathedral in New York City on December 10, 1989. More than 2,000 protesters demonstrated at President George Bush's Kennebunkport vacation home in September 1991. A nationwide boycott of Philip Morris Corporation for its financial support of North Carolina Senator Jesse Helms's campaign against gays ended in May 1991 when the company doubled its annual contribution of $1.3 million to AIDS research and education. By the early 1990s, ACT UP had a network of more than ninety chapters in most of the major cities in the United States. The leadership of ACT UP concluded an unofficial alliance with another militant direct action gay group, **Queer Nation**. Among ACT UP's accomplishments has been forcing the Federal Drug Administration to overhaul its approval process and expedite the introduction of medicines to help AIDS sufferers. Another activity has been pressuring drug companies to lower drug prices for AIDS medicine. ACT UP has been less active since the mid-1990s because more attention and resources have been devoted to AIDS research at the national level. By 1997 only twelve functioning chapters existed. These chapters, however, still lobby against the pharmaceutical industry for the high prices of life-prolonging medicines and for lower prices to combat the AIDS epidemic in Africa.

When the national ACT UP movement started gearing down, the chapter in San Francisco broke away from the national movement. The San Francisco area had two ACT UP chapters, ACT UP–Golden Gate and ACT UP–San Francisco. The Golden

Actor Billy Baldwin addresses an event titled ACT UP Voices '96, organized by the AIDS activist group ACT UP, near the San Diego Convention Center where the Republican Party was holding its national convention on August 13, 1996. Baldwin, who told the group he had lost two cousins to the deadly disease, is standing near a photo of Mark Kostopoulos, a founder of ACT UP. (AP Photo/John McConnico)

Gate chapter emphasized AIDS treatment issues, but the San Francisco group resorted to confrontational tactics, which caused fellow AIDS activists to disapprove of the chapter. The espousal by its leadership that HIV does not cause AIDS and that AIDS is a conspiracy by the pharmaceutical industry was the final straw. Larry Kramer denounced and disowned ACT UP–San Francisco. Michael Bellefountaine and Ronnie Burk, two of the group's leaders, denounce the use of AIDS drugs and have been active in sponsoring violent demonstrations against

what they characterize as the AIDS establishment. In the fall of 2000, activists from ACT UP–San Francisco dumped used cat litter on the head of the San Francisco AIDS Foundation and sprayed Silly String on the city's public health director. These activists have been found guilty of disturbing the peace and violating restraining orders, but fines and jail terms have not deterred them from using confrontation tactics against those they deem to be their opponents. **See also** Gay Liberation Movement; Queer Nation.

Suggested readings: Stanley Aronowitz, *The Death and Rebirth of American Radicalism* (New York: Routledge, 1996); Frank Bruni, "ACT UP Doesn't Much, Anymore: A Decade-Old Activism of Unmitigated Gall Is Fading," *New York Times* (March 21, 1997), p. B1; John Leo, "The AIDS Activist with Blurry Vision," *U.S. News & World Report* 109 no. 2 (July 9, 1990), 16; Dan Levy, "A Decade of AIDS Activism Changed America—and ACT-UP," *San Francisco Chronicle* (March 22, 1997), p. A1; Jean Marbella, "Outcasts Among AIDS Activists; Group: ACT UP San Francisco Uses Shock Tactics to Convey a Radical Message," *The Sun* (Baltimore, Md.) (February 28, 2000), p. A2; Sheryl Gay Stolberg, "AIDS Groups Revive a Fight, and Themselves," *New York Times* (March 18, 2001), sec. 4, p. 4; Tim Vollmer, "AIDS Dissidents' War on Drugs," *San Francisco Chronicle* (October 22, 2000), p. 1.

Ainsworth, Kathryn Madlyn "Kathy" (1941–1968)

Kathy Ainsworth, born Kathryn Capomacchia on July 31, 1941, in Chicago, Illinois, was part of a **Ku Klux Klan** bombing operation which resulted in her death in a gunfight with police. Her father, a circus juggler, and her mother, a vaudeville dancer, divorced when Ainsworth was a child. Mother and daughter moved to Miami, Florida. Ainsworth's father doted on her as a child, but she favored her mother. Her mother worked as a domestic in the homes of some of Miami's richest families. Ainsworth graduated with honors from Coral Gables High School. Although she had several scholarship offers in Florida, Ainsworth attended conservative Mississippi College in Clinton, Mississippi. Several of her teachers and classmates, who were staunch segregationists, reinforced her mother's racist beliefs. Ainsworth joined the **White Knights of the Ku Klux Klan** and the Americans for the Preservation of the White Race. She took a job at a health club in Jackson, Mississippi, where she met Ralph Ainsworth, the club manager. They married in August 1967. An apolitical person, he disapproved of her Klan activities, but she remained active in the Klan. She found a job teaching fifth graders at the Lorena Duling Elementary School in Jackson, Mississippi. Ainsworth quietly went about her teaching without her colleagues being aware of her association with the Klan.

Shortly after her marriage, Ainsworth became an active participant in a series of Klan bombings. At the home of Sidney Crockett Barnes, father of her college roommate Bonnie Barnes, she met **Thomas Albert Tarrants**. Tarrants, a member of the inner circle of **Samuel Holloway Bowers**'s White Knights of the Ku Klux Klan, was responsible for conducting a bombing campaign against prominent Jews and black civil rights leaders. In the summer of 1968, Ainsworth assisted Tarrants in planting bombs in synagogues and homes of Jews in central Mississippi.

On June 29, 1968, Tarrants picked up Ainsworth and drove to Meridian, Mississippi, to bomb the home of Meyer Davidson, a prominent member of the Jewish community. Unbeknownst to them, the federal authorities had been informed of the prospective bombing from two Klan members: Allon Wayne Roberts and Raymond Roberts. When Tarrants left the car to plant the bomb shortly after midnight, the police opened fire. Tarrants returned the gunfire and ran toward the car. A stray bullet hit Ainsworth in the neck and she died instantly. In a running gun battle Tarrants suffered serious injuries and was captured. Ainsworth was buried in Magee, Mississippi, in a funeral attended by many Klansmen. Ainsworth has entered the pantheon of extremist heroes. Among the groups honoring her for her sacrifice have been **Tom Metzger**'s **White Aryan Resistance** and the Ku Klux Klan. **See also** Bowers, Samuel Holloway; Tarrants, Thomas Albert; White Knights of the Ku Klux Klan.

Suggested readings: Lance Hill, "Justice for None," *Times-Picayune* [New Orleans] (February 21, 1993), p. E6; Jack Nelson, *Terror in the Night: The Klan's Campaign Against the Jews* (New York: Simon and Schuster, 1993); Don Whitehead, *Attack on Terror: The FBI Against* *the Ku Klux Klan in Mississippi* (New York: Funk and Wagnalls, 1970).

American Fascism

Modern American fascism is a variant strain of post–World War I European fascism. Two manifestations of European fascism were Benito Mussolini's in Italy and Adolf Hitler's in Germany. Other European countries developed their own versions of fascism ranging from Oswald Mosley's British fascism to the Action Française and the Croix de Feu in France. Even the United States had William Dudley Pelley's **Silver Shirts** and the German American Bund in the late 1930s. The Silver Shirts, who wore flamboyant silver shirts, blue corduroy knickers, and gold stockings, never had more than 15,000 members in its heyday, but it was still influential. Many members later became active in postwar right-wing extremist groups. An early spokesperson for American fascism was **Charles Coughlin** and his hate radio.

Both American and European fascism united staunchly against communism. Fascists also shared national and racial prejudices against non-Europeans. Strongly nationalistic, fascists distrusted any ethnic group or nationality different from themselves in appearance and customs. Fascists were also anti-democratic, anti-materialistic, anti-liberal, anti-feminist, and anti-modern. Leaders proclaimed the need "for a new spirit and a new era" and glorified violent action. These ideas appealed to a generation of Americans and Europeans suffering from the economic and social dislocation of the Great Depression of the 1930s.

Fascism experienced overwhelming defeat as an ideology during World War II, but it revived in the outbreak of the Cold War between the United States and the Soviet Union. Unreconstructed Nazis were recruited by the American intelligence community for intelligence work. Some of these Nazi operatives moved to the United States and were granted citizenship. These new citizens and their colleagues attempted to restore respectability to fascism by rehabilitating the image of the Nazi and Mussolini regimes. They developed allies in this effort from France, Great Britain, and Germany, who were eager to lend moral support. Soon efforts to improve the reputation of the Nazi regime were initiated. One tactic was to deny the worst excesses of the concentration camp system. Later, this denial included questioning the existence of the Holocaust. American fascists tried to reprogram themselves as national populists.

American fascism has been successful in repackaging itself and its message in various populist movements since World War II. Two veterans of the German American Bund, Harold Keith Thompson, a successful New York businessman, and **Francis Parker Yockey**, a neo-Nazi philosopher, were key figures in making fascism respectable in American right-wing circles. **Willis Carto** followed in this tradition by forming the **Liberty Lobby** to spread American fascism. The leading exponent of American fascism, however, has been **Lyndon Hermyle LaRouche**. He and his followers have made the transition from communism to a modern American brand of fascism which incorporates the leadership principle with anti-democratic tendencies to overturn the American system of government. Other supporters of fascism have been **Ku Klux Klan** groups and the neo-Nazi **Aryan Nations**. Fascism has merged so closely with these movements that it no longer goes by that name; white supremacy and neo-Nazism have replaced it in the lexicon of the radical right. **See also** Carto, Willis; Coughlin, Charles; Liberty Lobby, LaRouche, Lyndon Hermyle; Silver Shirts; Yockey, Francis Parker.

Suggested readings: Dennis Eisenberg, *The Re-Emergence of Fascism* (New York: A. S. Barnes, 1967); Charles Higham, *American Swastika* (Garden City, N.Y.: Doubleday, 1985); Dennis King, *Lyndon LaRouche and the New American Fascism* (New York: Doubleday, 1989); Martin A. Lee, *The Beast Reawakens* (Boston: Little, Brown, 1997); Southern Poverty Law Center, "Neither Left nor Right," *SPLC Intelligence Report* 97 (Winter 2000): 41–46.

American Indian Movement (AIM)

The American Indian Movement (AIM) was the most militant, most active American Indian organization to challenge the Indian policies of the U.S. government. A new generation of Indian leaders, unhappy about the federal government's termination program ending the special legal status of Indian tribes and the transfer of control from the federal government to the states, emerged out of their contact with the civil rights movement, and they were ready to take militant action. Around 250 Native American Indians from various Indian tribes met in Minneapolis, Minnesota, on July 28, 1968, to form a new organization to represent their interests. Among these interests were plans to stop discrimination against Indians, eliminate negative stereotyping of Indians, and end police brutality against Indians. Unlike other Indian organizations in the Twin Cities area, the new group elected an all-Indian board of directors and appointed an Indian administrative staff. Most of the original founders and leaders of AIM were from the Chippewa tribe, and the majority of them were from Indian reservations in Minnesota. The most prominent leaders were **Dennis Banks** and Clyde Bellecourt. AIM leaders later recruited **Russell Means**, a Sioux. These charismatic leaders had themselves experienced enough difficulties and legal troubles that they could relate to the experiences of other Indians. Means became especially important to AIM because, as a Sioux, his presence ensured that AIM could attract Indians outside of Minnesota.

AIM modeled its organization and many of its tactics after those of the **Black Panther Party**. In areas with large Indian populations, AIM members formed police-monitoring patrols to counter police brutality. Instances of police brutality charges dropped dramatically after the institution of these patrols. The popularity of AIM led to the establishment of chapters in most American cities. Although these efforts helped improve the self-image of American Indians, the leaders of AIM decided to conduct more militant actions. One of these actions was participation in the occupancy of Alcatraz Island in San Francisco Bay on November 9, 1969. The symbolic occupation of Alcatraz by a coalition of American Indian groups turned into a complete occupancy, and AIM members demanded clear title to the island. Indian occupiers held the island until June 11, 1971, and garnered considerable publicity. Two other operations were the 1972 occupation of the headquarters of the Bureau of Indian Affairs in Washington, D.C., and the standoff with federal officials at Wounded Knee, South Dakota, in 1973. On several other occasions, AIM leaders held protests against the murders of Indians and demanded justice.

The federal government was slow to mobilize against the American Indian Movement, but by the early 1970s the government had begun to respond. The conflict reached a peak in a battle at Wounded Knee on the Oglala Sioux reservation between the leadership of the federal-sponsored Sioux tribal government and Sioux militants. AIM intervened after some traditional Sioux elders requested their help on February 6, 1973. AIM activists occupied several buildings on the reservation on the night of January 28, 1973. FBI agents were sent onto the reservation. A standoff developed between the government and AIM. This standoff lasted seventy-one days with the government becoming increasingly determined to crush or at least neutralize AIM. Two Indians were killed and a federal marshal was paralyzed before the siege ended. Hundreds of charges were filed against AIM leaders for their role, but only fifteen minor convictions resulted. In another confrontation in 1975, AIM members engaged in a firefight with federal agents and Sioux tribal police during which one AIM member and two federal agents were killed. Leonard Peltier, an AIM leader, was convicted of murder in April 1977 and given two life sentences. A jury acquitted the other defendants.

In the aftermath of Wounded Knee, the American Indian Movement lost much of its appeal to mainstream American Indians. Because most of the leadership of AIM came from the Chippewa and Sioux tribes, other tribes felt left out. Violent confrontations also alienated the more conservative Indian leaders. Efforts of the federal government to isolate the leaders of AIM from moderate Indian leaders were aided by a disinformation campaign. The FBI's counterintelligence program (COINTELPRO) was redirected from the **Ku Klux Klan** and the Black Panther Party and used to discredit AIM leaders by spreading false rumors and leaking sensitive information. The passage of the Indian Self-Determination Act of 1975 ended much of the Indians' dissatisfaction with the federal government. As membership dropped in AIM so did the clout of AIM leadership. Both Dennis Banks and Russell Means remain important figures in the Indian rights movement, but AIM now functions as a lobbying organization for Indian civil rights. Sporadic efforts have been made to rekindle militancy among younger American activists, but tribal leaders have been successful in cooperating with the federal government to limit their appeal. **See also** Banks, Dennis; Means, Russell.

Suggested readings: Alvin M. Josephy, Joane Nagel, and Troy Johnson, eds., *Red Power: The American Indians' Fight for Freedom*, 2d ed. (Lincoln: University of Nebraska Press, 1999); Peter Matthiessen, *In the Spirit of Crazy Horse* (New York: Viking, 1983); John William Sayer, *Ghost Dancing the Law: The Wounded Knee Trials* (Cambridge, Mass.: Harvard University Press, 1997); Paul Chaat Smith and Robert Allen Warrior, *Like a Hurricane: The Indian Movement from Alcatraz to Wounded Knee* (New York: New Press, 1996); Rex Wyler, *Blood of the Land: The Government and Corporate War Against the American Indian Movement* (New York: Everest House, 1982).

American Knights of the Ku Klux Klan (See Church of the American Knights of the Ku Klux Klan)

American Nationalist Party (ANP)

Andrew Britt Greenbaum is the founder and leader of the American Nationalist Party (ANP), the most recent extremist group to be formed in the United States. Greenbaum, then a high school student, and a student friend started the Knights of Freedom (KOF) in 1996 in the Boston suburb of Norwood, Massachusetts. Greenbaum adopted the name of Davis Wolfgang Hawke. He marketed the Knights of Freedom as a pro-white, rather than a racist, organization. In 1998 Hawke renamed his group the American Nationalist Party and in the process changed the orientation of the group to a neo-Nazi racist organization.

Unlike most other extremist groups, the American Nationalist Party conducts the majority of its business on the Internet. In August 1998, when Hawke brought up his Web site for the American Nationalist Party, he was a junior at Wofford College in Spartanburg, South Carolina, where he was majoring in history and German. He adopted the name of Bo Decker to be used on his Web site to spread his neo-Nazi ideas. Hawke claims to have a larger, more influential organization than he has. He maintains that the ANP has around 10,000 members, but the Southern Poverty Law Center estimates that his dedicated followers number no more than 150. The organization lists Jeff Kay, vice president; Dallas Knight, deputy director; Patricia Lingerfelter, chief party secretary; and Matthew McKenna, security services and storm trooper. A member can join the party for $5 in monthly dues. With leaders who are less than thirty years of age, recruiting efforts are directed toward teenagers. Most of Hawke's recruitment pitch is a glorification of Adolf Hitler and the German Nazis.

Hawke's biggest handicap as the leader of the American Nationalist Party is his Jewish heritage. Although his family is Jewish, Hawke claims that he is the product of an affair between a German man and his mother. His mother has publicly denied the existence of any such affair in newspapers and to the Southern Poverty Law Center. According to Jewish law, however, he is nevertheless Jewish because descent is determined through the mother. Under Nazi racial law during the Third Reich, Jewish descent was traced back through several generations. Hawke hides behind his pro-Nazi views and attacks the U.S. government as a Zionist Occupational Government (**ZOG**). His refusal to participate in rallies and demonstrations and restrict his activities solely to the Internet has produced a backlash. This backlash was apparent after he scheduled a march in Washington, D.C., on August 7, 1999, and did not appear for the march. Criticism of his leadership has been harsh since this failed demonstration, and his dream to make the American Nationalist Party a major neo-Nazi mass movement is a tenuous one. **See also** Anti-Semitism; Internet-Based Extremists, Neo-Nazis; ZOG (Zionist Occupational Government).

Suggested readings: Francis X. Clines, "Neo-Nazis Are No-Shows at Their March," *New York Times* (August 8, 1999), sec. 1, p. 22; Brian Levin, "Some Hatemongers Don Glossy Veneers," *USA Today* (August 5, 1999), p. 15A; Sylvia Moreno, Spencer S. Hsu, and Sewell Chan, "Neo-Nazis Bow Out of March," *Washington Post* (August 8, 1999), p. C1; Southern Poverty Law Center, "Knight of Freedom," *SPCL Intelligence Report* 94 (Spring 1999): 36–39; Southern Poverty Law Center, "A Mother's Sorrow," *SPLC Intelligence Report* 94 (Spring 1999): 38.

American Nazi Party (ANP)

Various neo-Nazi groups have operated under the American Nazi Party (ANP) label in the United States. Two early American neo-Nazi parties were the prewar German American Bund and Dudley Pelley's **Silver Shirts**, but both vanished during World War II. James Madole formed the National Renaissance Party (NRP) as a Nazi party in 1949, but his difficult personality and the party's location in New York City marginalized it. The most famous and most controversial was **George Lincoln Rockwell**'s American Nazi Party. Rockwell formed the American Nazi Party in 1959 with the help of several right-wing sympathizers, but he alienated them by his financial demands and ideological disagreements. His party headquarters was located in a large, white house in Ar-

lington, Virginia, near Washington, D.C. Rockwell followed the führer principle of complete control over all activities of the party. He incorporated the ANP in March 1960 in Virginia, and the corporate charter gave him unlimited power in the party. Followers came and went, but Rockwell remained the same. Despite his efforts to publicize its activities, Rockwell's American Nazi Party always had financial and membership problems. His plans to make the party grow by conducting a proactive campaign against the Jews only produced an agreement among Jewish leaders to ignore Rockwell and the ANP. This policy infuriated Rockwell and made him look for an alternative way to build his party. Shortly before his death in 1967, Rockwell decided that the Nazi party's appeal was too limited in the United States, and he began reorienting it to reflect a more moderate white supremacist stance. This reorientation alienated many members of his party, but it had nothing to do with Rockwell's assassination in 1967 by John Patler. Rockwell's successor, **Matt Koehl**, was not able to sustain Rockwell's control of the party. Within five years, Rockwell's American Nazi Party was no longer a viable organization.

The next version of the American Nazi Party was started by Frank Collins. Collins, who had been expelled from Rockwell's party after the FBI leaked news about his Jewish background, returned to Chicago in the late 1960s and started his own version of the party, which he called the National Socialist Party of America (NSPA). His headquarters was in the Marquette Park section in southwestern Chicago. Collins adopted Rockwell's strategy of attempting to gain media attention and possible recruits by taking controversial actions. After Chicago authorities refused to allow him to march in Chicago by requiring outlandish bonds to cover expenses, Collins tried to demonstrate in the neighboring city of Skokie, which had a large Jewish population including many Holocaust survivors. This proposed march attracted widespread opposition in Skokie and caused a national controversy. Collins

Members of the American Nazi Party march across the street from the Greater Mount Hope Baptist Church on Chicago's south side, August 19, 1966. The church was the scene of a meeting between Martin Luther King, Jr., and civil rights workers at which plans were announced for further marches into white neighborhoods. (AP Photo/stf)

and his party never marched in Skokie, but the members did conduct a small demonstration in downtown Chicago. Soon afterward, Collins found himself in legal trouble and discredited in the neo-Nazi movement. **Harold Covington**, a rival in the party, found compromising photos of Collins with young boys. He turned this evidence over to the Chicago police, and Collins was arrested on child molestation charges. Collins was expelled from the American Nazi Party, convicted of the charges, and sent to jail. Covington replaced Collins as head of the party in 1980, but he operated it out of his headquarters in Raleigh, North Carolina. He had served as leader of the ANP for less than a year when rumors that he was an undercover informant for the government surfaced. After resigning his leadership po-

sition, Covington went underground for several years. These misadventures ruined any attempt of this version of the American Nazi Party to be successful.

The most recent, and long lasting, incarnation has been the American Nazi Party founded by Jim Burford in June 1982 in Chicago, Illinois. Burford, owner of a Chicago military surplus mail-order business, started this group as the successor to George Lincoln Rockwell's American Nazi Party and the National Socialist White Peoples Party (NSWPP). Most of the activities of this small party revolve around its publications. The ANP publishes two periodicals, *The Public Voice* and the *ANP Newsletter*, and provides access to pro-Nazi and pro-Hitler literature on a mail-order basis. The leaders of the ANP celebrate the birthday of Adolf Hitler in a yearly public demonstration. A small demonstration is used to publicize the ANP and to recruit new members. Despite its name identification, the American Nazi Party remains a benign collection of Nazi admirers with no serious program or agenda. Nazi sympathizers may join the ANP, but they tend to drift away to other more active groups. **See also** Covington, Harold; Neo-Nazis; Rockwell, George Lincoln; Skokie March Controversy.

Suggested readings: Anti-Defamation League, *Danger: Extremism: The Major Vehicles and Voices on America's Far-Right Fringe* (New York: Anti-Defamation League, 1996); David Hamlin, *The Nazi/Skokie Conflict: A Civil Liberties Battle* (Boston: Beacon Press, 1980); William H. Schmaltz, *Hate: George Lincoln Rockwell and the American Nazi Party* (Washington, D.C.: Brassey's, 1999); Frederick J. Simonelli, *American Fuehrer: George Lincoln Rockwell and the American Nazi Party* (Urbana: University of Illinois Press, 1999).

America's Promise Ministries/Lord's Covenant Church

The America's Promise Ministries/Lord's Covenant Church, a Christian Identity church whose members conduct an active anti-Semitic propaganda campaign, was founded by Sheldon Emry in 1967 in Phoenix, Arizona. Emry used his church as a forum to broadcast his militant anti-Semitic views. In the late 1960s, Emry also formed America's Promise radio program to spread his Christian Identity doctrine. This radio program was broadcast on more than twenty-five radio stations nationwide. Emry's pamphlet, *Billions for Bankers, Debts for People*, which blames the Federal Reserve System for all of the nation's economic ills, has become a staple for reading by right-wing extremists eager to blame Jews and liberals for the nation's problems. At the time of his death in 1985, Emry was one of the leading Christian identity ministers in the United States. His church then went through a series of ministers until Dave Barley, Emry's son-in-law, finally assumed control in 1987 and moved the church to

Sandpoint, Idaho, in 1991. From this new site, Barley concentrates on exposing what he calls the international Jewish conspiracy. He has been receptive to the **Holocaust denial movement** and its leaders. Barley has also been active in reaching out to other anti-government groups forming in the mid-1990s. He is one of the founders of the Idaho Citizens Awareness Network (I-CAN) which operates as an anti-government group with strong ties to militia and **Aryan Nations'** organizations. Barley's America's Promise Ministries has about forty active members in Sandpoint, but his monthly newsletters and Internet contacts make Barley influential in the Christian Identity movement. His church received unwanted publicity in 1998 when three of its members were arrested for robbing banks and bombing an abortion clinic in the state of Washington. The leader of this group, Jay Merrill, is a protégé of Barley. **See also** Anti-Semitism: Christian Identity; Holocaust Denial Movement, Internet-Based Extremists.

Suggested readings: Anti-Defamation League, *Danger: Extremism: The Major Vehicles and Voices on America's Far-Right Fringe* (New York: Anti-Defamation League, 1996); Michael Barkun, *Religion and the Racist Right: The Origins of the Christian Identity Movement* (Chapel Hill: University of North Carolina Press, 1997); Mary Leonard, "Hate Groups Embracing a Theology," *Boston Globe* (August 14, 1999), p. A1; Mike Wilson, "Reputation for Racism Taints Church's Welcome," *St. Petersburg Times* (March 22, 1997), p. 1B.

Andrews, Donald Clarke (1942–)

Donald Andrews, a leader of the Canadian white supremacist movement, was born in 1942 in Yugoslavia under the name Vilim Zlomislic. The Nazis killed his father, and his mother was deported to Germany to perform war work in German factories. Andrews lived in an orphanage during and after the war. Despite rumors that he had died, his mother persisted and finally located him at the orphanage in 1952. By then she had married a Canadian citizen named Andrews and had moved to Canada. Andrews went with his mother to Canada and assumed the name of his stepfather. Because he had suffered a serious injury to his thigh during the war, he spent several years in and out of Canadian hospitals for surgical corrections. Although he was a good student in high school, he lacked the funds to go to a university. Instead, Andrews studied public health at the Ryerson Polytechnical Institute on a grant. This course work allowed him to pursue a career as a public health inspector.

Although Andrews had been raised as a communist in an orphanage in Yugoslavia, he rebelled against communism in his new environment. He was one of the founders of the anti-communist Edmund Burke Society, and, after its demise, the head of the militant racist **Western Guard**. After spending a few years in the Edmund Burke Society, Andrews found it too moderate and turned instead to building a more activist organization. He continued his career as a public health inspector and as the head of the Western Guard, until he was arrested for plotting an arson attack on an Israeli soccer team in 1975. His eight-month jail sentence caused him to lose his public health job. After his release from jail, Andrews worked at several temporary jobs, including driving a taxi, selling insulation, and money lending. His investments in local real estate enabled him to own several rooming houses in Toronto.

Since a condition of his release from prison was to avoid contact with the Western Guard, Andrews formed a new political group, the Nationalist Party, in early 1977. Originally called the National Citizens Alliance, the name was changed to the National Party in June 1977. Andrews also started a newsletter in 1978 entitled the *Nationalist Report*. Always a small organization, it never had more than 150 members. It operated out of small cells of from six to eight members, with Andrews directing its activities. His manipulative and dominating personality, however, caused two of his most prominent followers, James Alexander McQuirter and **Wolfgang Droege**, to leave the Nationalist Party and join the Canadian

Ku Klux Klan. Several Canadian **neo-Nazis** considered Andrews anti-German because of his Yugoslavian background and his refusal to be slavishly pro-German. The Nationalist Party never became a major force in the Canadian **white supremacist movement**, but it serves as a training ground for racists refining their racist beliefs before they migrate to more radical organizations. **See also** Droege, Wolfgang; Western Guard.

Suggested readings: Stanley R. Barrett, *Is God a Racist? The Right Wing in Canada* (Toronto, Canada: University of Toronto Press, 1987); Warren Kinsella, *Web of Hate: Inside Canada's Far Right Network* (Toronto, Canada: HarperCollins, 1994).

Anglo-Israelism (See Christian Identity)

Animal Liberation Front (ALF)

The Animal Liberation Front (ALF), the most militant of the American animal rights groups, has its roots in Great Britain where a small body of activists, the Hunt Saboteurs, opposed hunting and hunters by resorting to disruptive tactics. Two activists, Ronald Lee and Clifford Goodman, decided in 1972 to resurrect a nineteenth-century antivivisection group, the Band of Mercy. After a series of anti-hunting incidents, this group changed its tactics to direct action on animal rights issues and renamed itself the Animal Liberation Front. When the group used violence against animal research facilities, furriers, and farming, Scotland Yard classified the ALF as a terrorist organization. The ALF is organized into two segments—a public organization for publicity, fund-raising, and propaganda, and a covert wing of tightly organized cells of activists willing to carry out attacks on property and rescue animals. The British group has around 2,500 active members, but only about 50 members are radical enough to carry out violent attacks. Because of the success of the British ALF operations, American animal rights supporters formed a branch in the United States.

The Animal Liberation Front in the

United States has pursued tactics similar to those of the British organization. Because the ALF has no office, staff, or board of directors, it is not legally an organization in the United States. Nevertheless, the ALF functions as a direct action group using sometimes illegal means to rescue animals from animal experimentation laboratories, fur farms, and any other site members believe mistreats animals. The first indication of its existence in the United States came in December 1982 when the ALF was named for its role in the rescue of cats from the Howard University Medical Science Building in Washington, D.C. Although the ALF leadership remains secret for protection against federal and state police, a support group, the Animal Liberation Support Group, was formed in 1988 to provide a legal defense for ALF activists engaged in direct action. This support group claims that it has a membership of around 10,000. For publicity and a media outlet, the ALF uses its contacts in the less militant but influential People for the Ethical Treatment of Animals (PETA). Leaders of PETA, **Ingrid Newkirk** and **Alex Pacheco**, have encouraged this contact. This symbiotic relationship has worked well over the years benefiting both the ALF and PETA.

The American version of the ALF conducts operations much as its English counterpart. Small, independently operated cells with no visible command structure launch operations. For security reasons, cells have no knowledge of the operations of other cells. An ALF Web site states that "someone joins the ALF simply by doing ALF actions"; there is no official membership. This lack of operational control has made undercover penetration by the police and other government agencies ineffective. Although the ALF has conducted about 60 percent of the 300-odd animal rights incidents in the last twenty years, the level of violence by the American organization has been much lower than it is in Britain. The firebombing of the unfinished Animal Diagnostic Laboratory at the University of California at Davis on April 16, 1987, which resulted in 4.5 million in damages, was its most destructive operation. Representatives of the ALF never claimed responsibility for this act, but police officials have been able to uncover evidence of its involvement. Despite numerous violent operations, only two individuals, Roger Thoen and Virginia Bollinger, have been arrested and convicted for activities involving the ALF. The U.S. Justice Department estimates there were 313 break-ins, arson incidents, vandalism, or thefts between 1979 and 1993, and the total has risen since 1993. See **also** Animal Rights Movement; Newkirk, Ingrid; Pacheco, Alex; People for the Ethical Treatment of Animals.

Suggested readings: Jim Adams, "Animal-Rights Vandals Hard to Stop Because of Free-Speech Protections and Its Loose Organization," *Star Tribune: Newspaper of the Twin Cities* (June 23, 1999), p. 2B; Lawrence Finsen and Susan Finsen, *The Animal Rights Movement in America: From Compassion to Respect* (New York: Twayne, 1994); Harold D. Guither, *Animal Rights: History and Scope of a Radical Social Movement* (Carbondale: Southern Illinois University Press, 1998); Janet Wells, "Animal Activists Raise the Stakes in Eco-Attacks," *San Francisco Chronicle* (April 21, 2000), p. A1.

Animal Rights Movement

The animal rights movement has introduced a new dimension to extremism in the United States. Supporters of this movement believe that animals are sentient beings able to experience pain and pleasure. As sentient beings, animals have rights. They should not serve at the pleasure of humans to eat, wear, or conduct medical experiments on regardless of the possible benefits to humans. Belief in animal rights has developed over the course of the last two centuries. Early adherents were active in the antivivisection movements in Great Britain and the United States. Two events came together to produce the modern animal rights movement: the development of violent tactics to protest animal cruelty in Great Britain and the publication in America of Peter Singer's book *Animal Liberation* in 1975. Both events redirected the earlier emphasis on peaceful opposition to animal cruelty to a different level of awareness.

Various animal rights organizations have emerged in the last two decades to advance their causes. The Animal Liberation Movement is the most extreme wing of the animal rights organizations, and its members have been willing to use violence to free animals from laboratories, breeding farms, feedlots, and slaughterhouses. Since the belief in the sanctity of an animal's life leads to a personal commitment to a vegetarian lifestyle, both animal rights and animal liberation groups have a limited membership appeal. Nevertheless, both the more moderate animal rights movement and the more radical Animal Liberation Movement have been able to attract enough activists and supporters to cause federal and state authorities to become concerned about them. Among the more hard-core independent animal rights organizations are **Ingrid Newkirk** and **Alex Pacheco's People for the Ethical Treatment of Animals** (PETA), Animal Rights Mobilization (ARM), In Defense of Animals (IDA), and the International Society for Animal Rights (ISAR). Of these organizations, PETA is by far the largest and most influential. PETA also serves as a forum and outlet for the radical **Animal Liberation Front** (ALF). The ALF has no organizational structure and exists only as a shadow umbrella for a small body of activists carrying out commando raids against institutions and agencies they deem dangerous to animals.

In such a large and diverse movement as animal rights, publicity and media exposure are always important. The most influential publication is the *Animals' Agenda*. Published by the Animal Rights Network, it specializes in connecting animal rights to other significant social issues. Another significant publication is the newspaper *Animal People*. This publication is filled with news about events in the animal rights world. For most public exposure, however, the animal rights movement turns to national media outlets—magazines, newspapers, and television. On occasion, events have been staged for the benefit of the national media and for maximum distribution of their point of view.

Studies of the animal rights movement have resulted in a distinct profile of its supporters. According to Harold D. Guither, in his *Animal Rights: History and Scope of a Radical Social Movement* (1998), they are well educated, and a significant number of them have graduate degrees. Racial composition reveals a membership that is predominantly white (93–97 percent). Supporters also tend to be above the national norms in income. Women constitute between 68 and 78 percent of the activists. Most of the supporters tend to be younger; a significant number are under thirty years of age. Most members hold professional positions in urban areas. Their political beliefs fall in the moderately liberal or liberal areas; a significant portion of movement supporters classify themselves as independents. In a choice between the two major political parties, a majority vote Democratic. Many are actively fighting for these issues on the national, state, and local political scene.

The success of the animal rights movement can be demonstrated by the size and importance of the organizations formed or mobilized to fight it. Among the opponents of the animal rights movement are the Farm Animal Welfare Coalition (FAWC), Animal Industry Foundation, American Farm Bureau, National Pork Producers Council, National Cattleman's Beef Association (NCBA), United Egg Producers, Fur Farm Animal Welfare Coalition, National Association for Biomedical Research, National Rifle Association (NRA), National Animal Interest Alliance (NAIA), and Putting People First (PPF). This impressive array of lobbying clout has been able to pressure the U.S. Congress to pass a variety of laws directed against the animal rights movement. Perhaps the most significant of this legislation was the Animal Enterprise Protection Act of 1992, which makes crimes against animal research and production facilities a federal crime with stiff penalties. **See also** Animal Liberation Front; Newkirk, Ingrid; Pacheco,

Alex; People for the Ethical Treatment of Animals.

Suggested readings: Marc Bekoff, ed., *Encyclopedia of Animal Rights and Animal Welfare* (Westport, Conn.: Greenwood Press, 1998); Lawrence Finsen and Susan Finsen, *The Animal Rights Movement in America: From Compassion to Respect* (New York: Twayne, 1994); Harold D. Guither, *Animal Rights: History and Scope of a Radical Social Movement* (Carbondale: Southern Illinois University Press, 1998); Brad Knickerbocker, "Animal Activists Get Violent," *Christian Science Monitor* (December 2, 1999), p. 5; Mark Murphy, "Fur Flies over Radical Animal Rights Tactics," *Boston Herald* (November 7, 1999), p. 16; Kermit Pattison, "ALF: Belief in Cause Justifies Militancy," *Saint Paul Pioneer Press* (April 11, 1999), p. 1A; Lois Therrien, "Cruelty in the Lab: The Growing Outcry Against Animal Research," *Business Week* (December 10, 1984), p. 146D; Alex Tizon, "The Great Ape Legal Project," *Seattle Times* (March 19, 2000), p. A1.

Anti-Abortion Movement

The anti-abortion movement provided the forum for moderates and extremists in the pro-life movement to protest against legalized abortion. As long as abortion was illegal, the opposition was mute. When the 1973 U.S. Supreme Court decisions *Roe v. Wade* and *Doe v. Bolton* (companion case with Roe which concludes that states may not make abortions unreasonably difficult to obtain) made abortion legal, the abortion debate turned nasty. Before the Supreme Court decisions, leadership in the anti-abortion movement had come from the Catholic Church, and most of its supporters were Catholics in the professions: medicine, law, and social work. After these court decisions, the movement started to attract a more diverse body of supporters. In the process, the anti-abortion movement changed from mild protest to direct action.

The immediate post-1973 anti-abortion movement concentrated on the tactics of legislation and moderate protest. Tactic number one was to attack the abortion issue on the legislative front. Anti-abortion legislators introduced legislation to overturn the Supreme Court decisions. Even though these attempts were unlikely to be successful, the legislators were persistent. Over the years this tactic has proven to be only marginally successful because government funding for abortion education and literature has been curtailed. Next, anti-abortion forces turned to state legislatures where their chances were much better. Over the next quarter of a century, state legislation restricting abortion rights started the trend for judicial review. The appointment of conservative justices to the Supreme Court has given the anti-abortion camp confidence that they could whittle away at the 1973 decisions. They have been partially successful in restricting some aspects of abortion. This tactic of progress by slow stages, however, has taken too much time in the eyes of those anti-abortion activists who espouse direct action.

Direct action, the movement's second tactic, has been much more visible if no more successful. Among the organizations to become active after 1973 was the National Right to Life Committee (NRLC), which lobbied politicians and threatened to boycott companies that produced abortion supplies and drugs that induced abortions. More militant groups soon formed, including John Ryan's Pro-Life Direct Action League and **Joseph Scheidler**'s Pro-Life Action League. Members of these groups were more confrontational, but they avoided outright violence. By the late 1970s, fundamentalist Protestants began joining these Catholic-led groups bringing with them new leaders and new tactics. These new converts believed that, since none of the mainline organizations appeared to be curtailing abortions, new tactics were needed. Anti-abortion activists began to resort to dirty tricks and sabotage. When these tactics proved ineffectual, groups formed to undertake even more violent measures.

The anti-abortion movement turned violent during the mid-1980s. Arson and bombings of abortion clinics increased from two in 1983 to thirty in 1984. Most of these violent acts were perpetrated by individuals acting alone; however, a number of new organizations came to the front to direct the violence. Much of the violence was in reaction to lack of support coming from the Reagan administration, which anti-abortion activists had considered their ally in the White House. In 1986 **Randall Terry** started **Operation Rescue**, a national organization whose goal was to direct mass demonstrations against abortion clinics and abortion providers. The mass demonstrations of Operation Rescue garnered headlines, but the abortions continued. As violence escalated in a series of mass demonstrations and assaults on abortion clinics, the anti-abortion movement began losing the public relations war. Moreover, law enforcement agencies became concerned about the escalating violence. By the early 1990s, mass demonstrations were receiving little public support, and Terry left Operation Rescue. Operation Rescue has been replaced by Operation Save America, led by Flip Benham, and it still conducts protests against abortions.

As the mass demonstrations lost steam, some of the most violent activists resorted to assassination. The extreme wing of the anti-abortion movement had by now built a moral justification for the murder of abortion providers. They cited biblical justification for murder to save the unborn. These activists were also frustrated by the election of a pro-choice president, Bill Clinton. A number of groups formed to fight the anti-abortion battle. Among the most militant of these new organizations were Father **Norman Weslin**'s **Lambs of Christ**, Reverend Matthew Trewhella's Missionaries to the Pre-Born, and Donald Treshman's Rescue America. In 1993 an anti-abortion activist, Michael Griffin, assassinated Dr. David Gunn in Pensacola, Florida. Soon afterward, a number of other doctors were shot in Florida and Kansas. On December 30, 1994, John C. Salvi murdered two abortion provider workers and wounded five others in the Boston, Massachusetts area. Then, James Kopp assassinated the abortion doctor, Bernard A. Slepian, at his home in Amherst, New York on October 23, 1998. These as-

sassinations caused some dissension with the anti-abortion movement because of adverse publicity.

During the same period, anti-abortion activists resorted to bombings and arsons. According to government officials, the number of bombings and arsons more than doubled from 1991 to 1996. The most notorious of these bombers was **Eric Robert Rudolph**. Rudolph initiated a series of bombings beginning with the Centennial Olympic Park bombing on July 27, 1996 and lasting until January 29, 1998. Few bombers or arsonists have been caught by law enforcement authorities. The violence also disturbed many in the anti-abortion movement because of a possible public backlash. The number of these attacks has diminished in the last five years.

Other tactics have been adopted by anti-abortion activists. In 1996, Neal Horsley, a Georgia anti-abortion activist and head of the Creator's Rights Party, built a Web site called the Nuremberg Files. This Web site lists all abortion providers in the United States and their addresses. His intent is to draw attention to abortion providers and their supporters, and provide a list of individuals to be prosecuted after abortion is declared illegal. Efforts through the courts to shut down this Web site have proven unsuccessful with the courts maintaining that Horsley has first amendment rights to attack abortion providers.

The latest anti-abortion activist tactic has been to direct the anthrax scare against abortion clinics. Clayton Lee Waagner, a North Dakota anti-abortion activist, mailed 550 anthrax hoax letters in October and November 2001 to abortion clinics around the United States. He placed white powder inside the letters and signed them **Army of God**. Police arrested Waagner on December 5, 2001 in Springdale, Ohio after a store employee recognized him using a Kinko's computer. At the time of his arrest he was driving a stolen Mercedes automobile and had a pistol. **See also** Bray, Michael; Hill, Paul Jennings; Human Life International; Kopp, James C.; Lambs of Christ; Operation

Rescue, Terry, Randall; Salvi, John C. III; Scheidler, Joseph; Weslin, Norman U.

Suggested readings: Patricia Baird-Windle and Eleanor J. Bader, *Targets of Hatred: Anti-Abortion Terrorism* (New York: Palgrave, 2001); Dallas A. Blanchard, *The Anti-Abortion Movement and the Rise of the Religious Right* (New York: Twayne, 1994); Frederick Clarkson, "Anti-Abortion Extremism; 'Patriots' and Racists Converge," *SPLC Intelligence Report* 91 (Summer 1998): 8–12; Frederick Clarkson, "Anti-Abortion Violence: Two Decades of Arson, Bombs and Murder," *SPLC Intelligence Report* 91 (Summer 1998): 13–16; Barbara Hinkson Craig and David M. O'Brien, *Abortion and American Politics* (Chatham, N.J.: Chatham House, 1993); Eunice Moscoso, "Anthrax Hoax Fugitive Arrested," *Atlanta Journal and Constitution* (December 6, 2001), p. 15A; James Risen and Judy L. Thomas, *Wrath of Angels: The American Abortion War* (New York: Basic Books, 1998); Eloise Salholz et al., "The Death of Doctor Gunn," *Newsweek* (March 22, 1993), p. 34; Rickie Solinger, ed., *Abortion Wars: A Half Century of Struggle, 1950–2000* (Berkeley: University of California Press, 1998); Sam Howe Verhovek, "Anti-Abortion Site on Web Has Ignited Free Speech Debate," *New York Times* (January 13, 1999), p. A1; Jerry Zremski, "Anti-Abortion Radical Fringe Considers Doctor's," *Buffalo News* (October 26, 1998), p. 1A.

Anti-Semitism

Anti-Semitism has become an integral part of the ideology of American right-wing extremism. The United States has always had a strain of anti-Semitism, which originated from political and religious ideas inherited from Europe. Traditional anti-Semitism had a strong Protestant religious base, although Catholics also shared many of the same beliefs. After the Holocaust during World War II and the struggle against Nazi Germany, traditional anti-Semitism appeared to be lessening. Americans watched with considerable interest the creation and prospering of the State of Israel. American Jews took an active role in the foreign and domestic policies of the Democratic and Republican parties.

In the last thirty years, however, a gener-

ation of extremists has discovered that anti-Semitism can be used to attract followers. **Willis Carto**, with his **Liberty Lobby**, and **George Lincoln Rockwell**, with his **American Nazi Party**, were the earliest to exploit the new anti-Semitism. **Neo-Nazis** have long attacked Jews and denied the Holocaust in an effort to sanitize the Nazi regime. Carto founded the **Institute for Historical Review** in 1978 to carry out his anti-Semitic agenda by denying the existence of the Holocaust. Over the last two decades, the Institute for Historical Review has been the leading force in advancing anti-Semitism in the United States. Anti-Semitism has also appeared in two other types of groups: Christian Identity and anti-government groups. Christian Identity theorists reject the role of Jews in the Bible and identify them as a product of Satan. Anti-government groups accuse Jews of controlling the Federal Reserve System and the banks. In all of these cases, anti-Semitism has attracted new adherents. **See also** Carto, Willis; Christian Identity; Holocaust Denial Movement; Institute for Historical Review; Rockwell, George Lincoln.

Suggested readings: Mark Abley, "Sage of Anti-Semitism," *Gazette* [*Montreal*] (July 11, 1998), p. B3; Alan Davies, ed., *Antisemitism in Canada: History and Interpretation* (Waterloo, Ont., Canada: Wilfrid Laurier University Press, 1992); Leonard Dinnerstein, *Antisemitism in America* (New York: Oxford University Press, 1994); Jeffrey S. Gurock, ed., *Anti-Semitism in America*, (New York: Routledge, 1998), 2 vols.; Chester L. Quarles, *The Ku Klux Klan and Related American Racist and Antisemitic Organizations: A History and Analysis* (Jefferson, N.C.: McFarland, 1999).

Applewhite, Marshall Herff (1931–1997)

Marshall Applewhite, the leader of the UFO cult **Heaven's Gate**, was born in 1931 in Spur, Texas. His father, a Presbyterian minister, traveled around Texas establishing Presbyterian churches. After attending a variety of schools in Corpus Christi and San Antonio, Texas, Applewhite attended Austin University in Sherman, Texas, where he majored in philosophy. Following his gradua-

A man presumed to be Marshall Applewhite, a leader of the Heaven's Gate cult, is shown in an undated image made available on March 28, 1997. Thirty-nine believers renounced lust and followed a self-castrated music teacher to a heaven where blood relations and physical love had no place. (AP Photo/APTV)

tion in 1952, he attended the Union Theological Seminary in Richmond, Virginia, and studied to be a Presbyterian minister. He decided instead to pursue a career as a professional singer. With his wife, Ann Pearce, whom he had married in 1952, Applewhite moved to New York City to study as an opera singer. In 1954 he was drafted into the U.S. Army, and served in Austria and New Mexico. After leaving the army in 1956, he studied for an advanced degree in music at the University of Colorado in Boulder. In 1960 Applewhite found a position on the music faculty at the University of Alabama in Tuscaloosa. His marriage, which had been in trouble, ended in 1965. Applewhite then moved to the University of St.

Thomas, a private Catholic college in Houston, Texas, where he taught choral music and sang roles with the Houston Grand Opera. In 1972 Applewhite had a nervous breakdown. While he was in the hospital recuperating, he met his future companion in the Heaven's Gate cult, Bonnie Lu Nettles, a nurse at the hospital. She was an active member of the Houston Theosophical Society where she met regularly with a group who made contact with dead spirits. She left her husband and four children to follow Applewhite in a nomadic life traveling around the United States.

Applewhite and Nettles formed a UFO cult. To them the term UFO meant more than an "unidentified flying object"; to them it referred to the transportation of beings from other planets and galaxies and their interaction with humans. Their UFO cult was known by several names over time: Total Overcomers Anonymous, the UFO Society, the Christian Arts Center, the Human Individual Metamorphosis (HIM) movement, and finally Heaven's Gate. During this time, Applewhite served four months in a Saint Louis jail for credit-card fraud and auto theft. Applewhite and Nettles declared that they were representatives of the "Level Above Human" who would take believers to heaven on a UFO. In their travels to California in the spring of 1975, they began to make converts with the claim that they were the two witnesses of the Bible's Book of Revelations. This claim led to the nickname, "The Two." They told their new adherents that they must change their names to shed their human identities. Applewhite became "Bo" and Nettles "Peep" in reflection of their role as shepherds of the believers. Next, they insisted that their followers must rise above human shortcomings and give up drinking alcohol, using drugs, and engaging in sexual activities. In less than a year, the cult had attracted around 200 adherents in the San Francisco area. Because of unfulfilled prophecies, their activities began to attract negative publicity. Applewhite and Nettles went underground and closed the cult to new members. Despite their disappearing act, the cult continued to attract new members. In 1985 Nettles died of cancer.

Applewhite reappeared on the public scene in 1993 when he attempted to revitalize his UFO cult. By now, he had changed his cult name to "Do" and renamed the deceased Nettles "Ti." His message that human beings must give up all earthly pleasures and be ready to leave this planet on a UFO for a new and better world remained the same. The difference was that, by 1993, Applewhite began to use new technologies to spread his message. He produced a series of videos and broadcast them to the public over satellite television. A little later, Applewhite started using the Internet to spread his message. He also established a

company, Higher Source Contract Enterprises, to design Web sites for local businesses. This business was modestly successful with an annual income of close to $111,000, and all profits went into financing the operations of the cult.

Applewhite was convinced that the appearance of the Hale-Bopp comet in 1996 masked a spacecraft that would enable the members of the Heaven's Gate to ascend to heaven. He convinced the other cult members that now was the opportunity for them to shed their human bodies and make the journey to heaven. At the time there were thirty-eight members in Heaven's Gate. Following Applewhite's instructions, members packed suitcases, put on new Nike clothes, and made sure that they had some money and loose change for the trip. Over a period of several days between March 22 and March 26, 1996, three shifts committed suicide by mixing phenobarbital sleeping pills, in applesauce or pudding, with vodka. A plastic bag was then placed over the member's head. Only the last two members were not shrouded and retained their plastic bags. Exactly when Applewhite committed suicide is uncertain, but he was not one of the last two because, according to the autopsy report, a plastic bag had covered his face. Applewhite left a videotaped message indicating that the suicides were timed to the appearance of the Hale-Bopp comet and the arrival of Easter. An examination of his body by the medical examiner revealed that Applewhite had undergone a castration operation. Applewhite's death ensured the end of the Heaven's Gate cult. A few isolated survivors remain, but there is no charismatic leader left to replace Applewhite. **See also** Cults; Heaven's Gate.

Suggested readings: William M. Alnor, *UFO Cults and the New Millennium* (Grand Rapids, Mich.: Baker Books, 1998); James R. Lewis, *The Gods Have Landed: New Religions from Other Worlds* (Albany: State University of New York, 1995); Sarah Moran, *The Secret World of Cults: From Ancient Druid to Heaven's Gate* (Godalming, U.K.: CLB International, 1999); Rodney Perkins and Forrest Jackson, *Cos-*

mic Suicide: The Tragedy and Transcendence of the Heaven's Gate (Dallas, Tex.: Pentaradial Press, 1997); Armando Villafranca and Ron Nissimov, "A Long, Twisting Road to the Gate; Troubled Signs Marked Much of Cult Leader Marshall Applewhite's Adult Life," *Houston Chronicle* (April 20, 1997), p. A1.

Arizona Patriots

The Arizona Patriots, an early extremist anti-government militia group, has been imitated by later anti-government groups. Ty Hardin, a movie and television actor, founded the Arizona Patriots in 1982 following a dispute with the Internal Revenue Service (IRS) over taxes. Hardin had left Hollywood after charging that Jews controlled the movie industry. His unhappiness with the IRS and the federal government caused him to talk with other malcontents in central Arizona. Most of his recruits came from Prescott and Flagstaff, Arizona. Hardin also formed a tax-protest school, the Common Law Institute, to fight the federal government over tax policies. Subscribers to the institute paid $530 for a packet of material to help them avoid taxes. He edited a monthly newsletter, *The Arizona Patriot* that contained anti-government literature.

Although the Arizona Patriots never attracted a large number of supporters, members made ambitious plans to take over the Arizona state government. In June 1984, members of the Arizona Patriots issued a collective indictment against all federal and Arizona state officials charging them with dereliction of official responsibilities. At the same meeting, members planned an operation to assassinate Arizona's governor, Bruce Babbitt, a federal judge, and several Arizona state policemen. Training sessions for members to carry out these missions were held on **Jack Oliphant**'s farm near Kingman, Arizona. An undercover operation culminated in a 1986 raid during which eight members of the Arizona Patriots were arrested and charged with various offenses including conspiracy to assassinate public officials. Oliphant and Foster Thomas Hoover were the

most prominent of those arrested and imprisoned. Oliphant and Daniel Taylor Arthur were sentenced to five-year jail terms. Other members received lesser sentences including probation and community service. After these arrests, the Arizona Patriots disbanded, but members drifted into other anti-government and neo-Nazi organizations. **See also** Militia Movement; Oliphant, Jack.

Suggested readings: Anti-Defamation League, *Danger: Extremism: The Major Vehicles and Voices on America's Far-Right Fringe* (New York: Anti-Defamation League, 1996); Thomas J. Knudson, "Right-Wing Group Accused of Bank Robbery Plot," *New York Times* (December 17, 1986), p. A24; Cheri Seymour, *Committee of the States: Inside the Radical Right* (Mariposa, Calif.: Camden Place Communications, 1991); Mark Shaffer, "Did Arizona Militia Leader Aid Bomber?" *Arizona Republic* (June 10, 2001), p. A12; Mark Shaffer, "Extremism Blooms Easily in Arizona Desert," *Arizona Republic* (July 2, 1996), p. A5; Brent L. Smith, *Terrorism in America: Pipe Bombs and Pipe Dreams* (Albany: State University of New York Press, 1994).

Armed Forces of the National Liberation of Puerto Rico (See Fuerzas Armadas de Liberación Nacional Puertorriqueña [FALN])

Army of God

The Army of God is a catchall term for those involved in the radical wing of the **anti-abortion movement**. The first mention of the Army of God occurred on August 12, 1982, when an abortion doctor, Dr. Hector Zevallos, and his wife, Rosalee Jean, were kidnapped in Edwardsville, Illinois. The kidnappers, Don Ben Anderson, Mathew Moore, and Wayne Moore, claimed that they were acting as members of the Army of God. The Army of God name attached to a warning in subsequent events, convinced the FBI and local police that a violent act was imminent. This happened in 1985 when shots were fired at the home of Supreme Court Justice Harry Blackmun shortly after

Larry Murray, with the ATF, points to "Army of God" envelopes addressed to Reuters America News Service, NBC News Bureau, the *Atlanta Journal and Constitution*, and WSB Television during a press conference in Atlanta on Monday, June 9, 1997. Authorities released new pieces of information and evidence from the bombings in Atlanta during the news conference. (AP Photo/Ric Feld)

he received a note with the signature of the Army of God. The Army of God has often claimed responsibility for violent acts against abortion providers. Many police authorities doubted the existence of the Army of God until the discovery of the *Army of God Manual*. This 100-page manual instructs activists on how to bomb abortion clinics and how to prevent access to abortion clinics by force. A copy of this secret manual surfaced in the case of Shelley Shannon, an Oregon housewife, who was convicted of shooting Dr. George Tiller in Kansas City. Authorities found a manual buried in her garden. The manual also includes an interview with the Army of God's alleged leader, who goes by the fictitious name Freedom Fox. See also Anti-Abortion Movement.

Suggested readings: Patricia Baird-Windle and Eleanor J. Bader, *Targets of Hatred: Anti-Abortion Terrorism* (New York: Palgrave, 2001); Sarah Moran, *The Secret World of Cults: From Ancient Druids to Heaven's Gate* (Godalming, U.K.: CLB International, 1999); Christina Nifong, "Anti-Abortion Violence Defines 'Army of God,'" *Christian Science Monitor* (February 4, 1998), p. 3; James Risen and Judy L. Thomas, *Wrath of Angels: The American Abortion War* (New York: Basic Books, 1998); Judy L. Thomas " 'Army of God' Abortion Foes Surfaced in St. Louis in '80s," *Kansas City Star* (February 4, 1998), p. 1; Jerry Zremski, "Anti-Abortion Radical Fringe Considers Doctor's Coldblooded Killing Justifiable," *Buffalo News* (October 26, 1998), p. 1A.

Aryan Brotherhood

The Aryan Brotherhood is a white supremacist prison organization with close ideological ties to the **Aryan Nations**. The first report of a white supremacist gang in a penitentiary surfaced in California's San Quentin Prison in the 1960s. By 1973 it is estimated that the Aryan Brotherhood had forty members at San Quentin and nearly 500 members throughout the California prison system. By the 1980s, the Aryan Brotherhood had spread to most of the prisons in the United States. This group has no recognized national leadership, but individual leaders have emerged in most penal institutions. It is a secretive and violent organization with the motto "Kill to get in, die to get out." Membership is smaller than in some of the other prison gangs, but the Aryan Brotherhood makes up in violent reputation for its numbers. Racial gangs in prison are common, and many white prisoners join the Aryan Brotherhood for protection from other gangs. These members also provide a source of funds, and some of these prisoners respond to membership by becoming enthusiastic activists. Members also exhibit an intense hatred of blacks and Jews. Many of them also belong to Christian Identity churches, especially **Richard Girnt Butler**'s church in **Hayden Lake**, Idaho. Recruitment of inmates to Christian Identity was a cause championed by former convict **Robert Miles**, who sent thousands of newsletters to prisoners monthly. To increase contact between the Aryan Nations and the Aryan Brotherhood, in 1987 supporters of the Aryan Nations began publishing a prison newsletter entitled *The Way*. Aryan Brotherhood members have been reported by prison officials as engaging in incidents of extortion, drug operations, prostitution, and murder. Major identifying marks for a member of the Aryan Brotherhood is a tattoo of a swastika and an SS lightning bolt, or a tattoo of a shamrock with the letter "AB" and three sixes.

The tendency toward violence by members of the Aryan Brotherhood has led to at least eight killings in and out of prison in recent years. Highest profiled among these murders was the dragging death of James Byrd, Jr., in Jasper, Texas, in 1998. Two of the three charged in the murder claimed membership in the Aryan Brotherhood during their stays in Texas prisons. In another famous murder case, a member of the Aryan Brotherhood gunned down Marine Lance Corporal Tarron Dixon, a black veteran of the Persian Gulf War, on the streets of Houston, Texas, in 1991. The assailant and his companions all received lengthy prison sentences for murder. Another crime of note was the mauling to death of a San Francisco woman, Diane Whipple, in January 2001 by a fighting dog bred to fight and trained by two members of the Aryan Brotherhood: Paul Schneider and Dale Bretches. **See also** Aryan Nations; Butler, Richard Girnt.

Suggested readings: Anti-Defamation League, *Danger: Extremism: The Major Vehicles and Voices on America's Far-Right Fringe* (New York: Anti-Defamation League, 1996); Marianne Costantinou, "Bad Company," *San Francisco Chronicle* (June 10, 2001), p. 12; Larry A. Hammond and Debra A. Hill, "Aryan Brother's Legacy Is Safer Prison System," *Arizona Republic* (February 6, 2000), p. J1; William Hermann, "30 Nabbed in Aryan Brotherhood Raids," *Arizona Republic* (April 11, 1996), p. A1; Kelsey Kauffman, "Prisons, Race, and Society," *Christian Science Monitor* (December 3, 1999), p. 11; Maria L. La Ganga and John M. Glionna, "Killer Dog Linked to Ring Run by Inmates," *Los Angeles Times* (January 31, 2001), p. 1; Dennis Wagner, "Prison Officials on Aryan Death List," *Arizona Republic* (February 4, 2001), p. A1.

Aryan Nations

The Aryan Nations is the paramilitary wing of the Christian identity movement. **Richard Girnt Butler**, the head of the Christian Identity movement, founded the Aryan Nations in the mid-1970s soon after he moved his Christian Identity church, the Church of Jesus Christ Christian, to a twenty-acre complex in **Hayden Lake**, Idaho, in April 1974. Butler had been the successor to the ministry of **Wesley Swift**, the founder of the modern Christian Identity movement. Butler established the Aryan Nations as a way to gain recruits and train them for a campaign to win a white homeland in the Pacific Northwest.

Founder of the Aryan Nations, Pastor Richard G. Butler, right, announced on July 2, 1999, at a press conference held at the Aryan Nations headquarters in Hayden, Idaho, that the group would not march in Coeur d' Alene, Idaho, on July 2, 1999. (AP Photo/Jeff T. Green)

The Aryan Nations combines militant white supremacy and **anti-Semitism** into a movement that promises direct action. In the summer of 1984, Colonel Gordon "Jack" Mohr taught survivalist tactics, and members studied the book *The Road Back*, which describes how to foment a revolution including sabotage and bombing. Members then declared themselves at war with the American government. Despite the revolutionary rhetoric, the leadership of the Aryan Nations did little to capitalize on this surge of enthusiasm. In 1996 members of the Aryan Nations published a manifesto in the language of the original Declaration of Independence and declared their independence from the United States. Blaming what they called the **ZOG** (Zionist Occupational Government) of the United States of America for usurping Aryan liberties, the authors proclaimed themselves part of a free and sovereign nation. Nothing has come of this manifesto because federal authorities never responded to it. Moreover, the leadership of the Aryan Nations has done nothing to implement any portion of the manifesto.

The primary activity of the Aryan Nations is the recruitment of new members. All types of media outlets are used, including publications, radio programs, videos, and more recently the Internet. One source of potential recruits is American jails and prisons. Beginning in 1979, the leadership of the Aryan Nations undertook a prison outreach program. A newsletter, *The Way*, is a prime recruiting tool for prison inmates. Many Aryan Nations members, who are in prison serving time for various offenses, help in the recruitment of promising inmates. The Aryan Nations also has a close working relationship with its prison offshoot, the **Aryan Brotherhood**.

Despite the militancy of its doctrine and rhetoric, only fringe elements of the Aryan Nations have resorted to direct revolutionary action. The most prominent example was **Robert Jay Mathews**'s **The Order**, or the Silent Brotherhood. Although evidence indicates that Mathews was more an Odinist (believer in Nordic gods) than a Christian Identity adherent and a lukewarm supporter of the Aryan Nations, several members of the Aryan Nations joined with Mathews in his efforts to produce a social revolution in the United States by destabilizing the federal government. Mathews's death in a gunfight with federal authorities in 1985 produced a martyr for the white supremacist movement, but he had had no imitators. Instead, individual members have resorted to violence following the concept of leaderless resistance. Perhaps more important, however, has been that Butler has been a man of words, not action. He is elderly and suffers from serious health problems. Consequently, most of the active leaders and followers of the Aryan Nations have been drifting off and joining other, more action-oriented groups. The search for Butler's successor as leader of the Aryan Nations was a lengthy process,

and his appointment of Newman R. Britton was a surprise with Britton's health so uncertain.

Butler had to relinquish ownership of the Aryan Nations compound in autumn 2000. Members of his personal staff had assaulted a woman, Victoria Keenan, and her son, Jason, in 1998 outside the Aryan Nations compound. A September 8, 2000, civil court judgment against Butler and the Aryan Nations, brought on by the Keenans of $6.3 million forced Butler into bankruptcy. At the bankruptcy auction, the winners of the lawsuit bought the Aryan Nations compound and the rights to the name Aryan Nations and the Church of Jesus Christ Christian for $250,000. Butler moved the Aryan Nations organization into Hayden, Idaho, to a home bought for him by Vincent Bertollini, a financial supporter of the Aryan Nations and Butler. Some of his former Aryan Nations members have abandoned the organization and joined the Church of True Israel in Noxon, Montana. Butler lost control of the Aryan Nations in the summer of 2001. His age, declaration of bankruptcy, and movement into a house in Hayden, Idaho weakened his control over the organization. Then his chosen successor, Newman Britton, died from complications from melanoma cancer on August 18, 2001 in Escondido, California. Butler had a variety of potential candidates to succeed him, including August Kreis, a **Christian Identity** minister from Pennsylvania; Danny William Kincaid, Ohio leader of the Aryan Nations; and Harold Ray Redfeairn, a former Ohio leader of the Aryan Nations. Butler selected Redfeairn in late September 2001 to become the new head of the Aryan Nations. Redfeairn, a native Ohioan from the Dayton area, was a convicted felon. He spent six years in an Ohio prison from 1986 to 1992 after being convicted of robbery and the attempted murder of a Dayton police officer in 1985. The headquarters of the Aryan Nations is now located in a rural compound in Ulysses, Pennsylvania, which is about 90 miles northeast of Pittsburgh. Butler remains the spiritual leader of the Aryan Nations, but

Redfeairn now determines its policies. **See also** Aryan Brotherhood; Aryan Republican Army; Butler, Richard Girnt; Mathews, Robert Jay; Order, The.

Suggested readings: Betty A. Dobratz and Stephanie L. Shanks-Meile, *"White Power, White Pride!" The White Separatist Movement in the United States* (New York: Twayne, 1997); Brad Knickerbocker, "White Separatists Plot 'Pure' Society," *Christian Science Monitor* (April 20, 1995), p. 1; Mary Beth Lane, "Authorities Wary as Ohioan Takes over Aryan Nations," *Columbus Dispatch* (October 3, 2001), p. 1B; Brent L. Smith, *Terrorism in America: Pipe Bombs and Pipe Dreams* (Albany: State University of New York Press, 1994); Southern Poverty Law Center, "Aryans Without a Nation," *SPLC Intelligence Report*, 100 (Fall 2000): 30–34; Southern Poverty Law Center, "The Last Outpost," *SPLC Intelligence Report* 101 (Spring 2001): 46–50.

Aryan People's Republic (See Kehoe, Chevie O'Brien)

Aryan Republican Army (ARA)

The Aryan Republican Army (ARA), a small white supremacist group, engaged in a series of bank robberies from the early 1990s to 1996. **Mark Thomas**, a part-time truck driver and farmer, and head of the Pennsylvania Aryan Nations, formed the Aryan Republican Army in early 1992. He recruited two young white supremacists, Richard Lee Guthrie and **Peter Kevin Langan**, to carry out his bank robbery scheme. These robberies were to provide funding to white supremacist groups to further the goal of establishing a white homeland in the Pacific Northwest. Guthrie and Langan convinced two other white supremacists, Kevin McCarthy and Scott Stedeford, to join their team. A fifth member, Michael Brescia, joined later. From the beginning, the leaders of the ARA modeled their operations after those of **Robert Jay Mathew's The Order**. Starting in November 1992 and continuing until December 1996, the ARA, operating under the code name of Mid-Western Bank Bandits, robbed twenty-two banks in seven

Midwestern states and stole more than $250,000. Not only were the banks tempting targets, but the ARA liked to retaliate against what they considered the Jewish-controlled banking system. Langan and Guthrie planned and led the robbery team. They picked small banks with only superficial protection and left behind pipe bombs and explosives to delay pursuit. While most of these explosives were duds, the police were never certain until the bomb squads dismantled them. The team wore bulletproof vests and used police radios to aid their escapes. They also taunted the FBI by renting cars under the names of FBI agents and ridiculing the efforts of the agents to catch them in newspaper letters.

The Aryan Republican Army's crime spree ended in December 1996. As the robbers accumulated more funds to be distributed to other white supremacist groups, the leaders of the ARA gained confidence. Langan tried to recruit more members to expand operations. One of the potential prospects informed on Guthrie to the police. Guthrie was captured and told the police where to find Langan. After a gunfight, the FBI captured Langan. Guthrie pleaded guilty for his part in the robberies in July 1997 and then several days later committed suicide. Langan received a fifty-five-year prison sentence for assaulting federal officers. Thomas pleaded guilty in February 1997 and turned states evidence in return for a lesser sentence of twelve and a half years in prison. The sentencing of all five members of the Aryan Republican Army ended the organization's political career. **See also** Aryan Nations: Langan, Peter Kevin; Thomas, Mark.

Suggested readings: Sharon Cohen, "They Said They Wanted a Revolution," *Ottawa Citizen* (January 6, 1997), p. C11; Richard Leiby, "The Saga of Pretty Boy Pedro: How a Wheaton Kid Became a Neo-Nazi Bank Robber, and One Confused Human Being," *Washington Post* (February 13, 1997), p. B1; Bill Morlin, "Devoted to Making Nation 'Ungovernable': Group Patterns Its Organization After the Irish Republican Army," *Spokesman-Review* [*Spokane, Wash.*] (December 29, 1996), p. 1; Judy Pasternak, "A Bank-

Robbing 'Army' of the Right Is Left in Tatters," *Los Angeles Times* (January 15, 1997), p. A1; Robert Ruth, "More Evidence Ties 'Bandits' to Hate Groups," *Columbus Dispatch* (November 10, 1996), p. 5D; Jo Thomas, "Bank Robbery Trial Offers a Glimpse of a Right-Wing World," *New York Times* (January 9, 1997), p. A12.

Aryan Resistance Movement (ARM)

The Aryan Resistance Movement (ARM) is the most active of the racist **skinhead** organizations in Canada. Scott Graham and Tony McAleer founded the Aryan Resistance Movement in 1987. Its original headquarters was in Mission, British Columbia, about eighty miles east of Vancouver. The Aryan Resistance Movement took both its name and inspiration from **Robert Jay Mathews's** insurrection and his organization **The Order**. Mathews's martyrdom in a shootout with U.S. federal agents in 1985 made him a figure of adoration by racist skinheads. Although the ARM's original area of operations was near Vancouver, the headquarters were moved to Surrey, British Columbia, in 1992, which coincided with Greg James's taking over control of the organization. James believes that only a violent fascist revolution in Canada can achieve his goal of a white supremacist society. Evidence from Canadian police sources indicates that the ARM has received financial assistance from the Libyan government of Muammar Qaddafi. Most of the ARM's propaganda and position papers are in the form of handouts, but the ARM also publishes a magazine, *The Spokesman*. More important than the printed materials for the advance of its ideology is the group's affiliation with Tony McAleer's computerized Canadian Liberty Net. This source allows ARM materials to be distributed worldwide over the Internet. **See also** Mathews, Robert Jay; Skinheads.

Suggested readings: William Boei, "Abortion Supporter 'Targeted by Right Wing,'" *Vancouver Sun* (December 10, 1994), p. 1; William Boei, "Hate on the Rise," *Vancouver Sun* (June 5, 1993), p. 1; Roger Gillespie, "Dial-a-Racist Phone System Thriving in Canada," *Gazette* [Montreal] (April 12, 1993), p. A9; Kathleen Kenna, "Racists Come out of Closet to Spread Message of Hate," *Toronto Star* (March 6, 1990), p. A19; Warren Kinsella, *Web of Hate: Inside Canada's Far Right Network* (Toronto, Ont., Canada: HarperCollins, 1994).

Asatru (Belief in the Gods)

Asatru (Belief in the Gods) is a modern adaptation of a pagan religion of the ancient Northern Europeans. Followers of Asatru have adapted pre-Christian pagan rituals and a belief in the gods of the Vikings in a new religion. Iceland recognized Asatru as a formal religion in 1972, and Svienbjorn Beinteeinsson formed an Asatru organization in Iceland in 1973, the Asatruarmenn. John Yeowell then started the Committee for the Restoration of the Odinic Rite in Great Britain, also in 1973. The movement made it to the United States shortly after the founding of the other groups. Stephen McNallen launched the Viking Brotherhood in Texas in 1974. Shortly afterward, McNallen changed the name of the group to the Asatru Free Assembly (AFA) to reflect the religious nature of the organization. At first, McNallen's AFA and Else Christensen's Odinist movement resembled each other in beliefs and practices, but soon serious differences of opinion and ritual between the groups made each go separate ways. McNallen's AFA designed Asatru as a practicing religion with strong ritualistic and spiritual dimensions. Odinism moved more toward politics and contained a distinct racial message. The AFA leadership renounced racism after members of **neo-Nazi** groups tried to infiltrate the organization. Tensions over the race question and organizational overload caused McNallen and his chief supporter, Robert Stine, to disband the AFA in 1987.

Two successor groups appeared to replace the defunct AFA. The first was the Asatru Alliance founded in 1987 by Mike Murray in direct response to the shutdown of the AFA. In his youth, Murray had been active in **George Lincoln Rockwell's American**

Nazi Party. After becoming disillusioned by Rockwell's successors, he joined Else Christensen's Odinist Fellowship. Again not satisfied, he joined the Asatru Free Assembly in 1980. Murray was very impressed with McNallen's organization, and the Asatru Alliance is modeled on it. He has even rejected efforts of the American Nazis to merge with his group. Despite its trouble with racist outsiders, the Asatru Alliance has been growing steadily. Recruiting efforts are handled partly through contacts made in its newsletter, *Vor Tru*.

The Ring of Troth moved beyond the AFA to make Asatru into a full-fledged religion. Edred Thorsson started the Ring of Troth soon after the demise of the AFA. He moved the organizations into the Neo-Pagan/Wicca community of believers and soon attracted a number of adherents from other New Age movements. Rituals and practices of the Ring of Troth are outlined in Thorsson's book, *Book of Troth* (1992). Thorsson's former affiliation with the Temple of Set and Satanism caused a controversy among the members of his new organization, and vicious infighting led to Thorsson's replacement as head of the Ring of Troth in 1991. His chief accuser, Rob Meek did not replace him because of legal problems over Meek's murder of his wife, Anne Harrington. Since 1995 William Bainbridge has been the acting head. The Ring of Troth has made only modest gains in membership in recent years, and it may have to merge with another group.

McNallen reappeared on the Asatru scene with another organization in 1996, the Asatru Folk Assembly. Again, McNallen has concentrated on the Northern European nature of the worship of the gods. He was unhappy about the generalist orientation of the Ring of Troth and its alliance with the New Age movement. Moreover, he wants his new group to ally more closely with the traditional Asatruism of Murray's Asatru Alliance. McNallen remains leery of the Nazi fellow travelers who have joined the Asatru movement, and he has taken steps to control membership.

The Asatru movement remains small. Total membership of the various groups is probably about 500 activists with perhaps another 500 fellow travelers. Active membership of the Asatru Alliance fluctuates from between 100 and 125; the Ring of Troth attracts about 100 to 125 members; another 100 to 125 individuals belong to various independent Asatru groups; and, finally, about 150 to 200 individuals are interested but refuse to join any organized group. Most Asatruers are white, male, and young. **See also** Odinism.

Suggested readings: Betty A. Dobratz and Stephanie L. Shanks-Meile, *"White Power, White Pride!": The White Separatist Movement in the United States* (New York: Twayne, 1997); Toni Heinzi, "Growing Prison Religion Stirs Concern," *Omaha World-Herald* (February 28, 1999), p. 1A; Jeffrey Kaplan, *Radical Religion in America: Millenarian Movements from the Far Right to the Children of Noah* (Syracuse, N.Y.: Syracuse University Press, 1997); James R. Lewis, ed., *Magical Religions and Modern Witchcraft* (Albany: State University of New York Press, 1996); Southern Poverty Law Center, "The New Barbarians: New Brand of Odinist Religion on the March," *SPLC Intelligence Report* 89 (Winter 1998):15–16.

B

Banks, Dennis (1930–)

Dennis Banks, one of the principal leaders of the militant **American Indian Movement** (AIM), is a Chippewa Indian who was born in 1930 on the Leech Lake Reservation in Minnesota. At the age of five, Banks was sent away to the Pipestem Indian School. After attending schools in both North and South Dakota, he joined the U.S. Air Force in 1953. Tours of duty took him to Japan and Korea. After his military service, Banks moved to Minneapolis where he was arrested for burglary in 1964. He spent a year in prison. After his release from prison, Banks found himself again in trouble with the law for forgery. During his second term in jail, he studied the tactics and philosophy of the civil rights movement and the **Black Panther Party**. Determined to go straight, Banks found a job with the Honeywell Corporation recruiting Indians to make residential heating equipment. Despite his prison record, Banks had a good working relationship with Honeywell until he started criticizing its defense contracts for producing antipersonnel weapons.

Banks was one of the leading participants in the meeting that founded the American Indian Movement in 1968. His intent was to protect American Indians from discrimination and police brutality and to protect traditional ways. Soon one of AIM's principal spokespersons, Banks was active in the seizure of the sailing ship *Mayflower II* on Thanksgiving Day in 1970 to protest the seizure of Indian lands. He was also involved in the protests against the murder of Wesley Bad Heart Bull and the Wounded Knee standoff, both in 1973. Federal authorities arrested him for assault with a deadly weapon and rioting. After conviction on these charges, he jumped bail and fled to California. California governor Jerry Brown refused to honor an extradition request from South Dakota authorities. Banks found asylum in March 1983 with the Iroquois tribe, the Onondaga Nation, in New York. Later in 1983, Banks surrendered to South Dakota authorities. He served one year of a three-year sentence in a state prison. Since his release, Banks has been active in protests against the violation of Native American ancestral burial grounds by archaeologists and collectors. In 1988 he published his autobiography, *Sacred Soul*, in Japanese. He refused to have it published in English. Banks has also acted in several movies, including *Last of the Mohicans* and *Thunderheart*. **See also** American Indian Movement; Means, Russell.

Suggested readings: Peter Matthiessen, *In the Spirit of Crazy Horse* (New York: Viking Press, 1983); Phil McCombs, "Bury His Hate at Wounded Knee," *Washington Post* (December 7,

Darryl Cherney sings during a rally prior to a hearing in U.S. District Court in Oakland, California on December 10, 1999. Cherney and the late Judi Bari, both members of Earth First!, sued the Oakland Police Department and the FBI for unlawful arrest after a car bomb explosion in May 1990. (AP Photo/Randi Lynn Beach)

1995); Paul Chaat Smith and Robert Allen Warrior, *Like a Hurricane: The Indian Movement from Alcatraz to Wounded Knee* (New York: New Press, 1996); Rex Wyler, *Blood of the Land: The Government and Corporate War Against the American Indian Movement* (New York: Everest House, 1982).

Bari, Judi (1950–1997)

Judi Bari, one of the main leaders of the radical environmentalist group **Earth First!** was born in 1950 and raised in a Baltimore, Maryland, family with strong socialistic leanings. Bari's activities in the anti–Vietnam War movement led to her dropping out of college in the 1960s. After serving as a union organizer and labor activist in the U.S. Postal Service and in several factories, she moved to Santa Rosa, California, in 1979, where she participated in abortion rights demonstrations and protests against U.S. government policies in Latin America. Between protests, Bari worked as a carpenter and raised two daughters.

Bari's job as a carpenter and woodworker led her to join Earth First!, which was founded by five political activists in 1980 to defend the environment against those who they thought were exploiting it. At the time Bari joined Earth First! it was engaged in a violent campaign against logging, including tree spiking and the destruction of logging equipment. Bari found this policy self-defeating and soon advocated a more non-violent approach, hoping to recruit loggers to the cause. She became one of the leaders of the social justice wing of the movement. Her attempt to reorient the organization from efforts to save the environment regardless of the consequences to direct political action put her in opposition to leader **David**

Foreman, the founder and principal spokesperson of the movement. He resigned from Earth First! in 1989 over philosophical differences in the future direction of the movement.

Bari became one of the new leaders of Earth First! Her fiery personality and experience as a union organizer made her a target for anti-environmentalists. In May 1990 Bari and a colleague, Darryl Cherney, were seriously wounded when a car bomb exploded under their seats while Bari was driving. She suffered severe injuries, including a broken spine and a paralyzed foot. Her pelvis was cracked in ten places. Bari and Cherney believed that the police were more interested in discrediting them than in finding the bombers. The police arrested Bari and Cherney for illegally transporting explosives. When these charges were finally dropped because of the lack of evidence, the Oakland police fed a local newspaper misleading information about the case implicating Bari and Cherney in illegal activities. Bari and Cherney sued the FBI and the Oakland police in 1991 for false arrest. Bari's injuries made her less active in the environmental movement, but she retained her drive and influence until she became ill with breast cancer. She died on March 2, 1997, at her Mendocino County, California, home from complications of the cancer. Her legal action against the authorities was still pending at the time of her death, but in 1999 Cherney won damages. Bari's legacy was the formation of an aggressive but nonviolent environmentalist organization willing to confront its enemies both in the field and in the courts. **See also** Earth First!; Foreman, David.

Suggested readings: Glenn Chapman, "Activists Win Fight to Have Case Heard," *Oakland Tribune* (September 25, 1999), p. 1; David Harris, *The Last Stand; The War Between Wall Street and Main Street over California's Ancient Redwoods* (New York: Times Books, 1996); Glen Martin, "Earth's Still First Five Years After a Mysterious Car Bomb Ripped Her Body Apart," *San Francisco Chronicle* (June 11, 1995), p. 6; Jesse McKinley, "Judi Bari, 47, Leader of Earth First Protest on Redwoods in 1990," *New York Times* (March 4, 1997), p. D23; Christopher

Reed, "Force of the Green Fuse," *Guardian* [London] (March 5, 1997), p. 15; Noël Sturgeon, Ecofeminist Natures: Race, Gender, Feminist Theory and Political Action (New York: Routledge, 1997); Michael J. Ybana, "She May Be Broken, but She Remains Unbowed," *Los Angeles Times* (January 24, 1997), p. E1; Susan Zakin, *Coyotes and Town Dogs: Earth First! and the Environmental Movement* (New York: Viking Press, 1993).

Barrett, Richard (1943–)

Richard Barrett, a militant racist agitator and leader of the **American Nationalist Party**, was born in 1943 in Washington Heights in Manhattan, New York City. His family lived in Manhattan for several years before they moved to East Orange, New Jersey. At an early age, he displayed hostility toward those different from him, especially minorities and immigrants. After a tour of duty in Vietnam, Barrett obtained a degree from Rutgers University. Later, he was to renounce his degree from Rutgers University because a professor there publicly supported the Viet Cong. In 1966 Barrett moved to Jackson, Mississippi, and became a figure in politics working with old-line segregationists Senator James O. Eastland and Senator Theodore G. Bilbo. His extreme racial views found a home in Mississippi. In 1974 he earned a law degree from Memphis State University. As well as practice law in Mississippi, he decided to run for public office. In 1979 Barrett ran for governor of Mississippi, but he finished last among the six candidates. Combining his skills as a lawyer with his strong racist views, he started working in 1987 with the Forsyth County Defense League, an organization which defends members of the Ku Klux Klan and other extremist group members being prosecuted for using violence against civil rights marchers.

In the late 1980s, Barrett decided to form the Nationalist Party with headquarters in Learned, Mississippi. His party's platform is the disenfranchisement of minority groups. Barrett wants to send Jews to Israel, Puerto Ricans to Puerto Rico, Negroes to Africa, and Asians to Asia. Besides attracting the traditional white supremacist base, Barrett has made efforts to recruit **neo-Nazi skinheads** into his party. He has also developed close ties to other white supremacist groups. Barrett's friends include **Edward R. Fields** and **Jesse Benjamin Stoner**, both leaders in the **National States' Rights Party**. Over the years, Barrett has participated in a number of demonstrations: from one in 1989 to protest the Martin Luther King holiday in Mississippi, to one in 1994 advocating pardoning **Byron de la Beckwith** after he had been convicted of killing civil rights leader Medgar Evers. Barrett has been active in developing public-access television programs advancing his white supremacist viewpoint. His most recent activity in 2001 has been campaigning for the retention of the Confederate flag on the Mississippi state flag. **See also** Fields, Edward R.; Ku Klux Klan; Skinheads; Stoner, Jesse Benjamin.

Suggested readings: Anti-Defamation League, *Danger: Extremism: The Major Vehicles and Voices on America's Far-Right Fringe* (New York: Anti-Defamation League, 1996); William F. Doherty, "Judge Nullifies City's Parade Permit Rule," *Boston Globe* (July 7, 1998), p. A1; Paul Hendrickson, "Unsealing Mississippi's Past," *Washington Post* (May 9, 1999), Magazine, p. W08; Ellis Henican, "White Supremacy, 1989-Style; 'We're Red, White and Blue,' " *Newsday* (January 25, 1989), Part II, p. 3; Ellen Uzelac, "White Supremacists Find Eager Recruits Among 'Skinheads' " *St. Louis Post-Dispatch*, (January 8, 1989), p. 5B; Curtis Wilkie, "Mississippi Supremacist's Solution: Resettle Blacks, Mexicans and Jews," *Houston Chronicle* (April 17, 1994), p. A12.

Baumhammers, Richard Scott (1965–)

Richard Baumhammers is a person with legal training whose intolerant racial views led him to kill five racial and religious minority members and wound a sixth in an April 2000 shooting spree. He was born on May 17, 1965, in Rochester, New York, into a Latvian immigrant family. His father and mother are successful dentists who teach at the University of Pittsburgh's School of Den-

tal Medicine. After graduating in 1984 from Mt. Lebanon High School in Mt. Lebanon, Pennsylvania, Baumhammers attended Kent State University in Ohio. He graduated in 1989 and entered law school at Samford University in Birmingham, Alabama. After leaving law school in 1991, he earned a postgraduate legal degree at the University of the Pacific's McGeorge School of Law in Sacramento, California. His academic specialty was international law with concentrations in immigration and import-export law. Baumhammers's only attempt to pass the Pennsylvania bar exam ended in failure. In 1995 Baumhammers moved to Atlanta, Georgia, where he lived on an allowance from his parents and never practiced law. After several years in Atlanta, Baumhammers moved back to Mt. Lebanon and lived with his parents.

In the late 1990s, Baumhammers became involved in white supremacist politics. While attending Kent State University as an undergraduate, he had a run-in with black students and was removed from the university dormitory for uttering racial slurs. In 1999 he attempted to form a racist organization, the Free Market Party. This party's platform included the elimination of non-European immigration into the United States. Baumhammers tried to recruit members and allies for his new party, but he was unsuccessful. He subscribed to several white supremacist e-mail lists and Web sites. Among these sites were **Stephen Donald "Don" Black**'s Stormfront, **William Pierce**'s **National Alliance**, and **Tom Metzger**'s **White Aryan Resistance**.

Baumhammers went on a shooting spree in the Pittsburgh area on April 28, 2000. He shot a Jewish neighbor, Anita Gordon, and set her house on fire. After firing a few gunshots at the Beth El Synagogue, he attacked two natives of India, killing Anil Thakur and wounding Sandip Patel. Less than an hour later he murdered Ji-Ye Sun and Thao Pham at a Chinese restaurant. His killing spree ended with the death of a black karate student, Garry Lee. Shortly after the last shooting, the police arrested Baumhammers. In a subsequent search of his parents' home, the police found white supremacist literature and evidence that Baumhammers had a history of mental illness.

Baumhammers's trial for the five murders was delayed because of competency hearings on his mental health. Doctors testified in a May 2000 hearing that Baumhammers suffered from paranoid schizophrenia. A judge determined at that time that Baumhammers was incompetent to stand trial and sent him to a state mental hospital for evaluation and treatment. On September 15, 2000, authorities ruled that Baumhammers was competent to stand trial. In a May 2001 trial Baumhammers was convicted on five counts of first-degree murder and racial hate crimes. The court sentenced him to death by lethal injection. Baumhammers remains in jail awaiting the mandatory appeals process for a death penalty to be completed. **See also** Black, Stephen Donald; Metzger, Tom; Pierce, William; White Supremacist Movement.

Suggested readings: Erick Bailey and Eric Slater, "Gunman in Rampage Kills 5 Near Pittsburgh," *Los Angeles Times* (April 29, 2000), p. A1; Robert Dvorchak, "Cold Blooded Killer's 20-Mile Trail Leaves 5 Dead," *Pittsburgh Post-Gazette* (April 29, 2000), p. A1; Eric Lichtblau, "Racial Writing Linked to Rampage," *Los Angeles Times* (April 30, 2000), p. A16; Jim McKinnon, "Death for Baumhammers," *Pittsburgh Post-Gazette* (May 12, 2001), p. A1; Dennis B. Roddy, "What Force Drove Baumhammers?" *Pittsburgh Post-Gazette* (April 27, 2001), p. A1.

Beach, Henry Lamont (1903–)

Henry Beach, one of the founders of the **Posse Comitatus Movement**, was born in 1903. In the 1930s, he joined William Dudley Pelley's fascist organization, the **Silver Shirts**. After World War II, Beach worked as a dry-cleaning executive until he retired in the late 1960s. In 1969 he formed the first Posse Comitatus group in Portland, Oregon. His association with co-founder William Potter Gales started at this time. Beach's actual name for the group was Sheriff's Posse Comitatus (SPC) or the Citizens' Law Enforcement Research Committee (CLERC).

He based his organization on the premise that there was no higher political authority in the United States than the county sheriff. His interpretation depended on the post–Civil War Posse Comitatus Act passed during the Grant administration in which the U.S. Congress barred the federal military from intervening in local police matters. Consequently, Beach argued that citizens have no obligation to pay federal income taxes, make social security payments, or acquire driver's licenses. Moreover, those government officials who committed criminal acts or violated their oath of office were to be hanged at the most populated intersection of streets in the township at high noon.

Beach's interpretation of the law of the land and his call for vigilante justice brought the attention of federal authorities to him and his movement. In the 1970s, Beach distributed Posse Comitatus literature around the country. Because of the militancy of its attitude toward federal and state governments, the chapters operated in extreme secrecy making estimates of their membership difficult to trace. At one time, Beach claimed that there were 100,000 members in the movement. While this figure undoubtedly is high, members in key regions around the nation in the South, Southwest, and Pacific Northwest joined the Posse Comitatus in large numbers. An FBI investigation of the Posse Comitatus organization in 1975 found seventy-eight chapters in twenty-three states. The largest and most notorious of these chapters was **James Wickstrom**'s in Tigerton Dells, Wisconsin. As the movement became more popular, Beach's role in the Posse Comitatus diminished. Other leaders emerged and pushed Beach into the background of the movement he had started. **See also** Kahl, Gordon; Militia Movement; Minutemen Movement; Posse Comitatus Movement; Silver Shirts; Wickstrom, James.

Suggested readings: James Corcoran, *Bitter Harvest: Gordon Kahl and the Posse Comitatus: Murder in the Heartland* (New York: Viking Press, 1990); Jerrold K. Footlick and William J. Cook, "Return of the Posse?" *Newsweek* (May 26, 1975), p. 54; Neil A. Hamilton, *Militias in*

America: A Reference Handbook (Santa Barbara, Calif.: ABC-CLIO, 1996); James Ridgeway, *Blood in the Face: The Ku Klux Klan, Aryan Nations, Nazi Skinheads, and the Rise of a New White Culture* (New York: Thunder's Mouth Press, 1990).

Beam, Louis (1946–   )

Louis Beam has been an active promoter for the white supremacist cause for more than two decades. He was born on August 20, 1946, in Texas and raised in Lake Jackson, Texas. After a tour of duty as a helicopter gunship gunner in Vietnam, he attended and received a degree from the University of Houston. Beam joined the Knights of the Ku Klux Klan in 1976. His mentor in the Klan was **David Duke**. Soon Beam was selected as the Grand Dragon of the Texas White Knights of the Ku Klux Klan. Using his military experience, Beam instructed his fellow Klan members in guerrilla war tactics. His followers established five secret camps in Texas and trained around 2,500 individuals. Beam's goal was to have a private army, the Texas Emergency Reserve, trained in the event of a racial war. This force was to assume control of the state of Texas and banish all minorities from it. He first came to public attention in 1981 for leading the Klan assault against Vietnamese shrimpers on the Texas Gulf Coast. To illustrate his opposition to the Vietnamese shrimpers, Beam publicly burned a shrimp boat as an object lesson. Soon afterward, a Vietnamese-owned shrimp boat was firebombed. A lawsuit against the Klan, initiated by **Klanwatch** lawyers, ended with Beam's arrest and conviction of using federal lands to train Klan members. Beam has long been a devoted follower of David Duke, but in the 1980s he found Duke too moderate and migrated to the **Christian Identity** movement and the **Aryan Nations**. His importance in the Aryan Nations stems from his establishment of the computerized Liberty Net and his "assassination point system." The Liberty Net was used to transmit Aryan Nations propaganda over the Internet. Beam's assassination point system gives rated points to activists who kill important people—politicians, law enforcement agents, civil rights leaders, journalists, and so on. This point system is outlined in his book *Essays of a Klansman* (1983).

Beam earned a reputation as being one of the more outspoken, more violent leaders in the **white supremacist movement**. Beam's attacks on the federal government and his contacts with **Robert Jay Mathews**'s **The Order** resulted in his flight to Mexico to avoid arrest by federal agents. His militant stances led to his arrest in Mexico after a gunfight, and he was extradited to the United States. A Mexican officer was killed and Beam's wife was critically wounded in the shootout. He was one of the key defendants in the 1988 Sedition Trial held in Fort Smith, Arkansas, in which the U.S. government tried white supremacist leaders for conspiracy. Several of the leaders of the white supremacist movement turned state's evidence to avoid prosecution and testified against Beam. Although Beam was acquitted of all charges, the trial caused him to become more circumspect about his public remarks. Since the trial, he has served as the Aryan Nations ambassador-at-large to other white supremacy organizations. He started a newsletter, *The Seditionist*, in the early 1990s and began to advance the tactic of **leaderless resistance** in fighting the federal government. Beam bought land near **Hayden Lake**, Idaho, and it appeared for a while that he was being groomed to succeed **Richard Girnt Butler** as head of the Aryan Nations. Butler, however, elected another figure as his successor, and Beam is no longer as active in the Aryan Nations as before. He continues to run a small business in the Hayden Lake area which specializes in camping and survival gear. **See also** Aryan Nations; Butler, Richard Girnt; Estes Park Meeting; Leaderless Resistance; Militia Movement; Order, The.

Suggested readings: Richard Abanes, *American Militias: Rebellion, Racism and Religion* (Downers Grove, Ill.: InterVarsity Press, 1996); Neil A. Hamilton, *Militias in America: A Reference Handbook* (Santa Barbara, Calif.: ABC-

The U.S. Supreme Court refused to hear the appeal of white supremacist and convicted killer Byron de la Beckwith, shown in 1994 with his wife, Thelma, in Batesville, Mississippi. Beckwith was convicted on February 4, 1994, for the June 12, 1963, sniper shooting death of Mississippi NAACP Field Secretary Medgar Evers. Prosecutors tried Beckwith a third time thirty years after two all-white juries deadlocked in 1964. Beckwith's attorney argued that his client's constitutional rights to a speedy trial and due process had been denied. (AP Photo/ File)

CLIO, 1996); Matt Krasnowski, "Supremacists' 'Lone-Wolf Tack' Poses New Peril," *San Diego Union-Tribune* (August 29, 1999), p. A1; Jim Nesbitt, "Hate Groups Keep Actions of Loners at Safe Distance," *Plain Dealer* [Cleveland] (July 8, 1999), p. A1; James Ridgeway, *Blood in the Face: The Ku Klux Klan, Aryan Nations, Nazi Skinheads, and the Rise of a New White Culture* (New York: Thunder's Mouth Press, 1990); Richard A. Serrano, "Many Fear Hate Groups Finding Fertile Ground in U.S. Military," *Houston Chronicle* (February 11, 1996); William K. Stevens, "Klan Official Is Accused of Intimidation," *New York Times* (May 2, 1981), sec. 1, p. 9.

Beckwith, Byron de la (1920–2001)

Byron de la Beckwith, one of the leading racist extremists in the United States, assassinated civil rights leader Medgar Evers. He was born on November 9, 1920, in Colusa near Sacramento, California. His father was a moderately successful California businessman, and his mother came from a wealthy Mississippi plantation family. His father died from alcohol-related illnesses in 1926. After discovering that the family was bankrupt, his mother moved back to her hometown of Greenwood, Mississippi, where she raised Beckwith with the help of a number of bachelor uncles. When Beckwith's mother died, the family selected a cousin to act as his legal guardian. The uncles all spoiled the young Beckwith who was such a poor student that he was sent to several schools in Tennessee before he returned to Greenwood High School to graduate in 1940 two classes behind his peers. He attended Mississippi State University until low grades caused him to drop out of school. Shortly after the attack on Pearl Harbor, in 1941, he joined the U.S. Marine Corps. He served with the Second Marine Division and was wounded at Tarawa in the Pacific Theater. While recuperating from his wound in the states, he married a Southern belle, Mary Louise Williams, in 1945. Beckwith left the Marine Corps in 1946 with the rank of Staff Sergeant. He returned with his wife to Greenwood and, in the next decade, worked at several jobs before becoming a successful salesperson.

Beckwith always considered himself a part of the Southern aristocracy, and the U.S. Supreme Court decision ending segregation of schools and then public facilities propelled him into Southern politics. He had been raised by his family to consider blacks as inferior and close to animals. The court decision on schools in 1954 and subsequent ones

in 1955 struck at the heart of the Southern white superiority system. Shortly after the original court decision, prominent white Southerners formed the Citizens' Council to fight desegregation. Beckwith joined the Citizens' Council and made it a central focus of his life. On June 12, 1963, Beckwith shot and killed Medgar Evers, a leading official of the National Association for the Advancement of Colored People (NAACP), in Jackson, Mississippi. Police were slow to identify Beckwith as the assassin, but a fingerprint on the rifle and some other evidence pointed to him. Police arrested Beckwith twelve days after the shooting. His stay at the Rankin County Jail allowed the white citizens to treat him as a hero. While in jail, the **White Knights of the Ku Klux Klan** recruited Beckwith as a member and recruiter. The trial was held in Jackson, Mississippi, in late January and early February 1964. Beckwith had reason to believe that he would be acquitted in any trial because no white person had ever been convicted of killing a black person in the state of Mississippi. Despite overwhelming evidence, the jury deadlocked over a verdict, and a mistrial was declared. The lack of a guilty verdict distressed the black population of Mississippi, but the failure to produce an innocent verdict disquieted Beckwith and his supporters. A second trial was held in April 1964. This time the defense team called in special investigators from the Mississippi Sovereignty Commission to conduct background checks on potential jurors to ensure an innocent verdict. Again the trial ended in a mistrial. After two failures, the state was reluctant to gamble on a third trial.

After the mistrials, Beckwith became a full-fledged member of the White Knights of the Ku Klux Klan. **Samuel Holloway Bowers** was the imperial wizard, and Beckwith acknowledged publicly that he felt honored to be associated with him. In August 1965, Beckwith was appointed by Bowers to be Klan kleagle, or general organizer, for the White Knights. Beckwith used his fame as Medgar Evers's assassin to be a successful recruiter. In 1966 he testified at the congressional hearings held in Washington, D.C., on Klan activities in the South, but like other Klansmen he refused to answer any questions citing the Fifth Amendment protection clause. Soon afterward, Beckwith started to work on the White Knights' publication *The Southern Review*. In 1967 Beckwith decided to use his popularity to run for lieutenant governor of Mississippi. His hopes of counting on Klan support met with disappointment when he finished fifth in a six-candidate race. Increased surveillance by federal agents began to curtail both Beckwith's Klan activities and the operations of the White Knights. Bowers went to jail over his role in authorizing the murder of the three civil rights activists, and he had to relinquish control of the White Knights.

When the White Knights had to go underground during Bowers's absence, Beckwith started to look at other white supremacist groups as a substitute. Beckwith began to blame the Jews for fomenting the civil rights movement. In September 1973, an FBI informant learned that Beckwith was planning to plant a bomb at the home of an official of the Jewish Anti-Defamation League in New Orleans, Louisiana. On September 27, 1973, police arrested Beckwith for carrying a bomb into New Orleans. He was charged with three federal crimes involving dynamite and weapons. After being acquitted of these charges in a federal court, the state of Louisiana tried him for the illegal transportation of explosives in May 1975. Beckwith was convicted of this crime and sentenced to five years' imprisonment and a $1,000 fine. After losing appeals, Beckwith spent three years, from 1977 to 1980, at the Louisiana State Penitentiary in Angola. Prison authorities kept him in solitary confinement during most of his prison sentence to protect him from other inmates. In prison, he continued his conversion to **Christian Identity** beliefs.

After his release from prison in 1980, Beckwith remained on the fringe of the **white supremacist movement**. He knew most of the key leaders, and they held him in high esteem. After marrying again, Beckwith moved to his new wife's home in Tennessee.

In 1992 Mississippi authorities reopened the Medgar Evers murder case. After lengthy extradition proceedings and a series of failed appeals, Beckwith stood trial in a state court in Hinds County, Mississippi. The trial took place in late January and early February 1994. A jury returned a verdict of guilty, and he was sentenced to life imprisonment. Beckwith died at the University of Mississippi Medical Center on January 21, 2001, from complications of heart disease. In racist and white supremacist circles, Beckwith is considered a martyr to the cause of white supremacy. **See also** Bower, Samuel Holloway; Ku Klux Klan, White Knights of the Ku Klux Klan.

Suggested readings: Michael Dorman, "Evers and Beckwith: A Reporter's Recollections," *New York Times* (December 17, 1996), p. B9; Claudia Dreifus," The Widow Gets Her Verdict," *New York Times* (November 27, 1994), sec. 6, p. 69; Eric Harrison, "Beckwith Is Convicted of Killing Medgar Evers," *Los Angeles Times* (February 6, 1994), p. A1; Reed Massengill, *Portrait of a Racist: The Real Life of Byron de la Beckwith* (New York: St. Martin's Griffin, 1996); Adam Nossiter, "Like a Racist from Central Casting, the Man Accused of Killing Medgar Evers Seems to Have Stepped out of a Bad Dream," *Atlanta Journal and Constitution* (March 3, 1991), p. M1; David Stout, "Byron de la Beckwith Dies; Killer of Medgar Evers Was 80," *New York Times* (January 23, 2001), p. B6; Curtis Wilkie, "Beckwith Trial Stirs Mississippi Ghosts; Some Fear for Supremacist's Rights," *Boston Globe* (January 16, 1994), p. 1.

Berg, Alan (See Mathews, Robert Jay; Order, The [The Silent Brotherhood])

Berg, David Brandt (1919–1994)

David Berg, the founder and longtime leader of the religious cult Children of God, was born in 1919 in Oakland, California. Both of his parents were Christian evangelists, but his mother, Virginia Brandt Berg, was the more successful one. His childhood was lonely as he traveled the religious circuit with his parents. Berg moved to Miami,

Florida, when his mother started a church affiliated with the Christian and Missionary Alliance. Later, his parents moved back to California. Berg graduated from Monterey Union High School, in Monterey, California. In 1941 Berg was ordained as a minister in the Christian and Missionary Alliance. Shortly after the attack on Pearl Harbor, in 1941, Berg was drafted into the U.S. Army, and he served as a conscientious objector with the U.S. Army Corps of Engineers at Fort Belvoir, Virginia. The army granted him a disability discharge because of a heart condition. He married Jane Miller in 1944 and they had four children. After the army, Berg attended several colleges on the G.I. bill, but he never obtained a college degree. He held jobs with several radio and television evangelists before returning to the ministry. After a short career as a minister at a rural Arizona church, he moved back to California in 1968 to help his mother with a coffeehouse ministry in the Los Angeles area. While preaching as a minister in the Los Angeles suburb of Huntington Beach, he became disillusioned about contemporary Christianity and decided to break with the mainstream Christian movement. Consequently, in 1968, he founded an outreach organization, Teens for Christ, to attract wayward youth and hippies. This group soon changed its name to Children of God. Berg believed that God had picked him to be the successor to the Old Testament's King David. As the charismatic leader of this new group, Berg was able to persuade members to give up material possessions, live a communal lifestyle, and devote all their energies toward converting new recruits. His views were close to a type of Christian socialism that critiqued modern capitalism for its spiritual deficiencies. Besides rejecting most of American society, Berg criticized Europe and Israel accusing them of Western decadence. He was an admirer of Muammar Qaddafi, head of the state of Libya.

Berg preached this new message of spiritual redemption in Southern California among hippies and was able to convert a significant number of followers. In 1969, however, Berg claimed to have had a revelation of a coming major earthquake in Southern California and ordered the Children of God to move to other parts of the United States to seek converts. Berg remained in Southern California until 1971 when he left for London, England, after he predicted that the comet Kohutek would cause a major earthquake in California and the devastation would culminate in the end of America. When the comet Kohutek turned out to be a dud, Berg blamed members of the Children of God and outsiders for misinterpreting his prophecy on the comet. As Berg became more remote from the membership of the Children of God, he controlled the organization through a series of letters called "Mo Letters." In these letters he gave guidance to the members on all types of subjects both personal and spiritual. Berg considered himself a messenger from God, but he never claimed infallibility. He allowed the possibility that he might misinterpret God's messages.

As the Children of God movement continued to attract new adherents, Berg made a series of controversial decisions that threatened its relationship with civil authorities both in the United States and abroad. In the mid-1970s, Berg issued a statement that extramarital sex was permissible among members of the Children of God. Shortly afterward, he initiated a policy called "flirty fishing," which allowed female members to engage in sexual relations with men to convert them to the Children of God. Berg's justification, published in his "Mo Letters," was that "if the Son of God could give up his life for the cause, surely women could give their bodies." News of this practice caused a sensation among political and religious leaders in the United States. This practice was complicated by Berg's refusal to allow women to use birth control techniques, which ensured that the birthrate among members would be high. Another letter from Berg included his permissive views on sex with minors. Subsequent rumors of child abuse and sexual improprieties caused unwanted attention from civil authorities and made members of the Children of God to become more defensive in their dealings with outsiders. In 1976 Berg made a major shift in operations by purging 300 of the top leaders of the Children of God, including his daughter, Linda Berg. He also changed the name of the organization from the Children of God to the Family of Love. Opposition to the practices of the cult by American political and religious leaders led to Berg's transferring most of the operations out of the United States.

Berg reoriented the Family of God again in 1987. A combination of the fear of AIDS and a significant increase in the number of cases of venereal disease among members caused Berg to reconsider the practice of flirty fishing. He also forbade sex with children by members of the cult to protect the cult from legal prosecutions being instituted against his organization around the world. In the midst of these changes, Berg changed the name of the organization again from the Family of Love to the Family. Berg's influence also seemed to lessen with each change. His age and lifestyle contributed to his decreasing control. He had abandoned his first wife and had been consorting with other women. His second wife, Maria, and his son, Jonathan Berg, became more influential in the reorganized group. By the early 1990s the Family had over 15,000 members in seventy countries, but increasingly authorities in many of these countries were showing concern about possible child abuse by its members. These charges led to arrests of cult members in Argentina, Australia, England, France, Paraguay, and Spain, but convictions have been rare. Berg remained in seclusion for the last two decades of his life. He died in November 1994, but the exact date and place are unknown. His widow, Maria, has assumed control of the organization. **See also** Cults; Children of God/The Family.

Suggested readings: Angella Johnson, " 'Flirty Fishin' and Free Love in Child of 60s That Gave Birth to The Family," *The Guardian* [London] (November 25, 1995), p. 2; James R. Lewis, *Peculiar Prophets: Biographical Dictionary of New Religions* (St. Paul, Minn.: Paragon House, 1999); Timothy Miller, ed.,

America's Alternative Religions (Albany: State University of New York Press, 1995); Gustav Niebuhr, " 'The Family' and the Final Harvest," *Washington Post* (June 2, 1993), p. A1; Roy Rivenburg, "25 Years Ago, the Children of God's Gospel of Free Love Outraged Critics," *Los Angeles Times* (March 21, 1993), p. E1; Gayle White, "David Berg, Founder of '60s' Jesus Freaks, Dies in Seclusion at 75," *Atlanta Journal and Constitution* (November 26, 1994), p. B12; Miriam Williams, *Heaven's Harlots: My Fifteen Years As a Sacred Prostitute in the Children of God Cult* (New York: Eagle Brook, 1998).

Black, Stephen Donald "Don" (1953–)

Don Black, the leading computer specialist and Web master for the **white supremacist movement**, was born in 1953 in Huntsville, Alabama. His father was a conservative construction contractor. At the age of seventeen, Black showed an early orientation toward extremist groups by joining **Matt Koehl**'s **neo-Nazi** group, the National Socialist White People's Party (NSWPP). He also worked for **Jesse Benjamin Stoner**'s candidacy for Alabama governor before he graduated from Athens High School in Athens, Alabama. In a mysterious incident, Black was shot and seriously wounded during the Stoner campaign by Jerry Ray, the brother of James Earl Ray of Martin Luther King assassination fame, supposedly for trying to steal the membership list of the **National State's Rights Party**. Black received a degree in history from the University of Alabama in 1974. His strong and vocal racist views, however, caused him to be thrown out of the Reserve Officers Training Corps after three years in the program. After college, he worked as a medical technician. In 1975 he worked in the headquarters of **David Duke**'s Knights of the Ku Klux Klan. Later, in 1977, Black became a key advisor to Duke. Black succeeded Duke as the head of the Knights of the Ku Klux Klan after Duke's sudden resignation as head in 1980. He continued Duke's strategy of making the Klan respectable by toning down the rhetoric while affirming the Klan's racist and anti-Semitic doctrine. In the summer of 1979, Black ran for mayor of Birmingham, Alabama, but he lost to an Afro-American politician and finished fourth in a field of five. Early in 1981, Black started courting other white supremacists at a gathering at the **Aryan Nations' Hayden Lake** compound. Everything changed for Black in late 1981 when he was implicated in a plot to invade the Caribbean island of Dominica to establish a white racist state. Federal undercover agents received a tip about the plot, and Black was arrested with nine other activists. At a subsequent trial, Black received a three-year prison sentence, which he began serving in December 1982. During his absence, the Knights of the Ku Klux Klan split: one part remained loyal to Black; the other part, led by Stanley McCollum, formed another group. Soon afterward, **Thomas Arthur Robb** replaced McCollum and gained control over the Knights of the Ku Klux Klan, leaving Black out as an outsider.

Soon after Black was released from prison in 1985 he started to look for a new role in the white supremacist movement. His stay in prison had left him unable to reestablish himself as a force in any of the various **Ku Klux Klan** groups. Several times in the late 1980s he ran unsuccessfully for public office. During this time, he married David Duke's ex-wife, Chloe, and moved to Florida. While in prison, Black had learned how to use and program computers. He capitalized on this knowledge and now makes a living as a computer consultant and Web master from his home in Palm Beach, Florida. In 1995 Black brought up a Web site, Stormfront, which now serves as the primary site for white supremacist Internet communications. His logo is "White Pride World Wide." Stormfront serves as a "White National Resource Page" with access to a variety of anti-Semitic, neo-Nazi, and white supremacist literature. Black's computer skills have made him one of the prime distributors of racist literature in the United States and abroad. **See also** Duke, David; Ku Klux Klan; Internet-Based Extremists.

Suggested readings: Anti-Defamation League, *Danger: Extremism: The Major Vehicles and Voices on America's Far-Right Fringe* (New York: Anti-Defamation League, 1996); Tyler Bridges, *The Rise of David Duke* (Jackson: University Press of Mississippi, 1994); Julie Etchingham, "Welcome to the World of Net Racists," *Times* [London] (January 13, 2000), p. 1; Tara McKelvey, "Father and Son Target Kids in a Confederacy of Hate," *USA Today* (July 16, 2001), p. 3D; Thomas O'Dwyer, "Networks of Hate," *Jerusalem Post* (August 6, 1999), p. 6A.

Black Bloc

The Black Bloc, an international anarchist organization, specializes in violent demonstrations to protest globalization. This organization of anarchists first appeared in Hamburg, Germany, in 1987 under the name the Autonomen. Autonomen's first operation was to challenge local Hamburg authorities to protect the homeless. Later members of this group attacked German **neo-Nazis** and participated in anti-nuclear demonstrations. Now the official name for this group is the Revolutionary Anti-Capitalist Bloc, but it has earned the nickname the Black Bloc from the color of the anarchist movement and the black clothes worn by followers during demonstrations. The Black Bloc made its first appearance in the United States in anti–Gulf War protests in 1991, but its activities were submerged within other anti-war groups. It first made national headlines during the violent demonstrations against the World Trade Organization (WTO) in Seattle, Washington, on November 30, 1999. Small cells of activists dressed in black clothes and ski masks operated behind officially approved demonstrations to commit violent acts, including widespread destruction of property. Cells of from five to ten individuals called affinity groups caused most of the violence. Seattle police estimated that between 200 and 300 members of the Black Bloc conducted hit-and-run operations at the WTO. Black Bloc leaders coordinated their activities with cellular phones. Seattle police believe that Black Bloc supporters caused the bulk of the $17 million in damages to businesses in Seattle.

Since the WTO meeting in Seattle, the Black Bloc has been active conducting demonstrations in both the United States and Canada. In April 2000 supporters of the Black Bloc renewed demonstrations in Washington, D.C., to protest the economic policies of the World Bank in promoting globalization. Their battle cry was, "Whose streets? Our streets!" Again around 200 Black Bloc followers caused most of the violence. On this occasion, leaders used black and red flags to signal their followers to increase or decrease the intensity of the violence. Next, Black Bloc activists showed up in Quebec City, Canada, in April 2001 at the Summit of the Americas. In Quebec, they were protesting corporate globalization and capitalism's pursuit of profit at the expense of workers and the environment. European supporters of the Black Bloc conducted demonstrations in London in May 2001 and in Genoa, Italy, in July 2001.

Authorities in the United States and elsewhere have had difficulty in identifying backers of the Black Bloc. The group appears only at public protests. It is known that there is no organizational structure, no headquarters, no meetings, and no official memberships. The unofficial center of the Black Bloc in the United States is Eugene, Oregon, but activists come from New York City and elsewhere in the United States and Canada. Prior planning for demonstrations is conducted via Internet communications, and followers agree on tactics to be used on that occasion. Black Bloc supporters adhere to a moral code that maintains that the destruction of private property is permitted, but personal injury and damage to personal property is to be avoided. Activists challenge the police at the demonstrations and destroy corporate property without remorse. American corporations targeted by the Black Bloc include Banana Republic, Gap, Levi's, McDonald's, Old Navy, and Starbucks. Black Bloc spokespersons accuse these corporations of exploiting workers and pursuing policies which damage the environment.

Suggested readings: Darryl Fears, "For the Men in Black; Anarchy Makes Sense," *Washing-*ton Post (April 17, 2000), p. A6; Allison Hanes, "Anarchy in the Air As Summit Draws Near," *Gazette* [Montreal] (April 13, 2001), p. A1; Kate Jaimet, Mike Trickey, and James Barter, "On the Plains of Abraham," *Ottawa Citizen* (April 21, 2001), p. A1; Glen McGregor, "Who Are Those Masked Men?," *Ottawa Citizen* (March 24, 2001), p. B1; Kim Murphy, "Anarchists Deployed New Tactics in Violent Seattle Demonstrations," *Los Angeles Times* (December 16, 1999), p. A3.

Black Helicopters

Most anti-government extremist groups believe that the presence of unmarked black helicopters flying around the United States is part of a secret conspiracy to suppress American freedoms and liberties. They interpret these flights as part of an international conspiracy to promote the **New World Order**. Beginning in 1971 and continuing until 1994, Jim Keith, a leading advocate of the black helicopter thesis, reported over 450 sightings of black helicopters operating in suspicious circumstances. According to Keith, some of these helicopter sightings are associated with cattle mutilations. He posits the thesis that these dead cattle are part of a testing of biological weapons by the U.S. government. Moreover, Keith charges that these black helicopters contain foreign troops and equipment which have been brought to the United States to conduct these illegal operations. The adherents of this conspiracy theory also believe that the black helicopters are part of a plot to form a national police force, which, along with agreements with foreign powers, would allow the U.S. government to be turned over to the United Nations. They distrust the United Nations because they consider it to be a part of the plot for the New World Order to subjugate the United States to foreign powers.

According to this conspiracy theory, the black helicopters and illegal operations are part of an effort to establish a series of concentration camps for American right-wing dissidents. Adherents of this theory point to

President Ronald Reagan's order to build twenty-three concentration camps under the code name Operation Rex 84. Reagan's stated intent was to build camps to handle illegal aliens and potential domestic subversives in event of a national emergency. Anti-government activists charge, however, that these facilities and holding sites could be used to hold perceived enemies of the U.S. government or the United Nations. Another agency that these anti-government groups fear is the Federal Emergency Management Agency (FEMA). Since this agency's headquarters is in the top secret National Security Agency at Fort Meade, Maryland, they distrust its intentions.

Most of these ideas can be dismissed as systemic paranoiac fears of anti-government dissidents. In each of their charges, however, there is a grain of truth. The U.S. government does have a large number of unmarked helicopters for military training and anti-drug smuggling operations. An anti-drug exercise conducted by Delta Force in February 1999 near Kingsville, Texas, attracted national attention when four black helicopters flew over Kingsville before disembarking armed troops. Government records show that the federal government has the authorization to set up holding camps to be used in case of national disasters or political insurrections. No evidence exists that such camps have ever been established. Efforts have been made to form law enforcement agencies that function on a national basis. The United Nations does conduct peacekeeping operations around the world, and it could be argued that the United States is not immune from intervention by a peacekeeping force in case of war or insurrection. These anti-government activists have linked all of these events to buttress their theory of an international conspiracy directed against them. See also Militia Movement.

Suggested readings: Jim Henderson, " 'Then We Could Hear Gunfire and Grenades Going Off': Delta Force Training Exercise Shakes Up Kingsville," *Houston Chronicle* (February 21, 1999), p. 1; Jim Keith, *Black Helicopters over America: Strikeforce for the New World Order*

(Lilburn, Ga.: IllumiNet Press, 1994); Richard Leiby, "Heard About the Black Helicopters and Detention Camps?" *Washington Post* (May 18, 1995), p. E1; David Pugliese, "Area 51: Tucked Away in the Nevada Desert Sits a Cornerstone of American Paranoia," *Ottawa Citizen* (March 21, 1999), p. C3; Michael Taylor, "Extremists Bracing for New World Order," *San Francisco Chronicle* (April 25, 1995), p. A7.

Black Israelite Nation (See Nation of Yahweh and Stream of Knowledge)

Black Judaism (See Nation of Yahweh; Stream of Knowledge)

Black Liberation Army (BLA)

The Black Liberation Army (BLA), the paramilitary outgrowth of the **Black Panther Party**, was formed when the Black Panther Party ran into organizational troubles in 1971.

It adopted a program of revolutionary action. Unlike the party, the BLA was not an organized group with a central command and a chain of command. Instead, it was an underground movement of independent groups. **Mutulu Shakur**, an acupuncturist with the Lincoln Detox Clinic in the south Bronx in New York City, became the operational head of one of the more active BLA units. Shakur had been active as a leader in the Republic of New Afrika (RNA) movement as early as 1968. His associate Assata Shakur had no leadership role, but BLA members acknowledged her to be one of their spiritual leaders. She had grown up in Queens before becoming a revolutionary in the Black Panther Party. In 1977 she was convicted for the May 2, 1973, murder of a state trooper on the New Jersey Turnpike. Her compatriots broke her out of jail on November 2, 1979, and she went underground. In 1984 Assata Shakur fled to Cuba where she remains.

The goals of the Black Liberation Army were to prepare the way for a separate black homeland in the southern United States. In the mid-1970s, the BLA joined another revolutionary group, the **May 19th Communist Organization** (M19CO), under the leadership of **Marilyn Jean Buck** and began to conduct military operations including armored car robberies. The BLA divided into two sections: the action force and the secondary team. The job of the action force was to plan and carry out the operations. The secondary team was to find safe houses and getaway vehicles. On April 22, 1980, the BLA robbed a Purolator armored car in Inwood, Long Island, and collected $529,000. The next robbery, which involved a Brink's armored car, took place on June 2, 1981, in the Bronx. This robbery netted the BLA $292,000, but one guard was killed and another wounded.

These robberies were the prelude to plans for a major operation. Members of the BLA, M19CO, and the **Weather Underground** carried out a Brink's armored car robbery on October 20, 1981, in Nyack, New York. The attempt was botched from the beginning by the killing of a guard. Although the robbers managed to take $1.6 million, the murder of two state troopers and the capture of several of the robbers cost the BLA much of its leadership. Marilyn Buck evaded capture until May 11, 1985. Mutulu Shakur went underground in California, but he was captured in February 1986 in West Los Angeles. Buck received a prison sentence of fifty years and Mutulu Shakur, sixty years for their roles in the 1981 Brink's holdup. They were the last of dozens of defendants to be sentenced for this crime. See also Black Panther Party; Buck, Marilyn Jean.

Suggested readings: Marlene Aig, "Brink's Heist Lives On in Police Memorials," *Los Angeles Times* (November 24, 1991), p. A45; John Castellucci, *The Big Dance: The Untold Story of Kathy Boudin and the Terrorist Family That Committed the Brink's Robbery Murders* (New York: Bobb, Mead, 1986); Charles E. Jones, ed., *The Black Panther Party: Reconsidered* (Baltimore, Md.: Black Classic Press, 1998); Robert D. McFadden, "Brink's Holdup Spurs U.S. Inquiry on Links Among Terrorist Groups," *New York Times* (October 25, 1981), sec. 1, p. 1; Robert D. McFadden, "Fugitive in $1.6 Million Brink's Holdup Captured," *New York Times* (May 12, 1985), p. A19; Assata Shakur, *Assata: An Autobiography* (Chicago: Lawrence Hill Books, 1987); Brent L. Smith, *Terrorism in America: Pipe Bombs and Pipe Dreams* (Albany: State University of New York Press, 1994); Ronald Smothers, "Brink's Robbery Casts Shadows from the Past," *New York Times* (October 31, 1981), sec. 2, p. 31.

Black Muslim Movement (See Farrakhan, Louis; Nation of Islam)

Black Panther Party (BPP)

The Black Panther Party (BPP), a militant black nationalist party in the United States, was active from the mid-1960s to the early 1970s. **Huey P. Newton** and **Bobby Seale** formed the party on October 15, 1966, in Oakland, California. The purpose of the party was to advance the status of the black community by defending it from the white power structure. Newton and Seale drafted a ten-point plan which incorporated several controversial features, including the refusal of blacks to fight in Vietnam. They divided up the leadership positions: Seale became the chairman of the Black Panther Party, and Newton, the minister of defense. They went into the black community and started recruiting members. At the same time, members of the party started acquiring firearms to defend themselves. Headquarters of the party was in downtown Oakland. Each Saturday the BPP had an official meeting, and within a few weeks membership was between thirty and forty. To raise funds, the party sold Mao Tse-tung's *The Red Book* on the Berkeley campus of the University of California. They used the money to buy shotguns. Members of the BBP started to monitor the activities of the Oakland police, and tension grew between the police and the party. Next, the party published a newspaper, the *Black Panther*, with **Leroy Eldridge Cleaver** as the editor. By 1967 this newspaper had a circulation of around 125,000 copies per week. The selling of newspapers and speaking engagements allowed the party to make enough money to survive.

The high profile of the Black Panther Party soon had its members in trouble with law enforcement. After a demonstration at the state capital in Sacramento, Seale and a number of the rank-and-file members of the party were arrested, and in August 1967 they were sentenced to six months in jail for disturbing the peace. On October 28, 1967, Newton was seriously wounded, and a police officer was killed in a shootout between the Black Panther leader and the Oakland police. Newton recovered from his wounds, but the authorities wanted to charge him with first-degree murder. A national campaign to free Huey Newton was soon launched. Leadership of the party decided to ally with the Peace and Freedom Party to help in Newton's defense. On February 17, 1968, a big rally was held at the Oakland Auditorium with Stokely Carmichael, a leader of the civil rights organization Student Non-Violent Coordinating Committee (SNCC), as the keynote speaker. Other prominent SNCC leaders, James Foreman and H. Rap Brown, also showed up for the rally. This rally raised $30,000 for Newton's defense. On April 6, 1968, Panther leaders Eldridge Cleaver and Bobby Hutton engaged in another gunfight with the police in which Hutton was killed.

Despite these incidents, the Black Panther Party started expanding into other cities. David Brothers established a Black Panther Party branch in Brooklyn, New York, and Lamumba Shakur soon afterward started one in Harlem, New York. Other branches opened up in Chicago, Denver, Los Angeles, New Haven, Newark, Philadelphia, Omaha, and San Diego. The FBI targeted the BPP for its counterintelligence program (COINTEL-PRO) and started spreading misinformation and rumors. Internal dissension had always been a problem in the party, and it increased with so many leaders in jail or under indictment. Slowly the leadership of the BPP crumbled in response to pressure from federal and state authorities and internal dissen-

sion among its top leaders, Newton, Seale, and Cleaver. A friendly critic of the BPP and a former member, Ollie A. Johnson III, in *The Black Panther Party: Reconsidered*, attributed the collapse of the party to the leadership being corrupted, rhetoric outstripping capabilities, dogmatism, unclear separation between administrators and activists, and failure to promote business activity. The Black Panther Party had ceased to function by the early 1970s. **See also** Black Liberation Army; Cleaver, Leroy Eldridge; Newton, Huey P.; Seale, Bobby.

Suggested readings: Jim Haskins, *Power to the People: The Rise and Fall of the Black Panther Party* (New York: Simon and Schuster Books for Young Readers, 1997); Charles E. Jones, ed., *The Black Panther Party: Reconsidered* (Baltimore, Md.: Black Classic Press, 1998); Hugh Pearson, *The Shadow of the Panther: Huey Newton and the Price of Black Power in America* (Reading, Mass.: Addison-Wesley, 1994); Bobby Seale, *Seize the Time: The Story of the Black Panther Party and Huey P. Newton* (New York: Random House, 1970).

B'nai Noah (Children of Noah)

B'nai Noah, or the Children of Noah, is a recent anti-Christian movement whose leaders, although not Jews, closely identify with the Jewish religion. Three southern Protestant fundamentalist ministers founded B'nai Noah in 1990 after years of biblical study. J. David Davis, Vendyl Jones, and Jack Saunders decided, based on their biblical studies, that religious truth resides in the seven Noahide commandments. These commandments, found in the Babylonian Talmud, include prohibitions against blasphemy, idolatry, sexual sins, murder, theft, and eating of the limb of a living creature, and a requirement for courts of justice. According to Talmudic tradition, these commandments are just as binding on Gentiles as on Jews. To assist them in understanding the Noahide commandments, the leaders of B'nai Noah have requested and received advice on interpreting the commandments from Jewish rabbis.

The B'nai Noah launched itself as a movement at an international conference in 1990. This First International Conference of B'nai Noah was held in Fort Worth, Texas, in April 1990. At this conference, the Noahide groups formed the Union of the Vineyard of the Children of Noah (Agudat Karem B'nai No'ach) as an international missionary effort. The leadership of the B'nai Noah concluded an alliance with the orthodox rabbinical leadership in Israel. Shortly afterward, many of the B'nai Noah churches began to de-Christianize their churches, including removing such Christian symbols as steeples and crosses. This action came about because members of the B'nai Noah consider these Christian symbols a form of idolatry which violates the most important of the Noahide commandments.

The existence of an alliance with Judaism and the members' missionary work among Christians has been controversial. Christian denominations find the new movement both threatening and unsettling. Members of the B'nai Noah have suffered reprisals in the form of ostracism from family members and friends, as well as loss of employment. **Christian Identity** churches have found the new movement even more threatening. They consider the B'nai Noah movement to be further proof of the existence of an international Jewish conspiracy to abolish Christianity in all of its forms. Consequently, Christian Identity ministers have declared open war on the B'nai Noah movement.

Suggested readings: J. David Davis, *Finding the God of Noah: The Spiritual Journey of a Baptist Minister from Christianity to the Laws of Noah* (Hoboken, N.J.: Ktav Publishing House, 1996); Jeffrey Kaplan, *Radical Religion in America: Millenarian Movements from the Far Right to the Children of Noah* (Syracuse, N.Y.: Syracuse University Press, 1997); Fred Mogul, " 'Judaism for Gentiles' Spreads from the Church Without a Steeple," *Jerusalem Post* (April 28, 1992), p. 1; Rhonda Robinson, "Noah Docks in Athens," *Jerusalem Report* (November 28, 1996), p. 28.

Boudin, Kathy (1943–   )

Kathy Boudin, one of the leaders of **Weather Underground** and the **May 19th Communist Organization** (M19CO), was born on May 19, 1943, to wealthy parents. Her father was a prominent left-wing lawyer. She attended exclusive private schools—the Little Red School House and the Elizabeth Irwin High School—in the New York City area. Boudin went to Bryn Mawr College in Pennsylvania, were she was a pre-med major. She earned a reputation for radical political activity before graduating in 1965 magna cum laude. She briefly attended law school at Case Western Reserve University Law School in Cleveland, Ohio. She worked in Cleveland from 1965 to 1967 organizing low-income blacks and whites. While in Cleveland, Boudin became attached to the radical wing of the Students for a Democratic Society (SDA). In 1968 she, along with two other authors, wrote a book, *The Bust Book*, which served as a handbook for political prisoners.

When Weather Underground was formed in 1969, Boudin became one of its original members. A war council of Weather Underground met on December 27–31, 1969, in Flint, Michigan, to plot strategy. It was decided there that a select cadre of 100 members would go underground and fight for a social revolution. Cells of four or five members were formed to initiate revolutionary activity. Boudin's group included Ted Gold, Diana Oughton, Terry Robbins, and Cathy Wilkerson. This cell set up an explosives factory in the basement of Wilkerson's father's house in Greenwich Village, New York City. A mistake was made while manufacturing a bomb in March 1970, and the resulting explosion killed Gold, Oughton, and Robbins. Boudin and Wilkerson escaped uninjured.

Boudin avoided revolutionary activity for the next nine years. She lived under various aliases in Weather Underground safe houses. In 1978 the Weather Underground split into two factions: Prairie Fire Collective and the May 19th Communist Organization. Members of the Prairie Fire Collective advocated returning to society and giving up the revolution. Rather than surface and stand trial on relatively minor charges, Boudin decided to stay underground. She joined the M19CO, to continue the revolution, in 1979. The M19CO concluded an alliance with the **Muluta Shakur**–led **Black Liberation Army** and its robbery campaign to raise money for a black homeland. In April 1980, Boudin started attending the Paralegal Institute in Manhattan, New York, under an assumed name to become a legal assistant. She graduated with a legal assistant certification on August 31, 1980. In the meantime, Boudin and a fellow member of the M19CO, David J. Gilbert, had a son in August 1980. After the birth of her son, she started drifting away from radical activity, but Gilbert kept pushing her to become more engaged.

Boudin's role in the BLA's robbery of a Brink's armored car on October 20, 1981, in Nyack, New York, was relatively minor. Her role and Gilbert's was to rent the vehicles for the robbery and getaway and participate in the switch between vehicles. The robbery was bungled when a guard was killed. After the transfer of the $1.6 million to a U-Haul, Nyack police officers intercepted the U-Haul with Boudin and Gilbert in the front seats. When the rear of the truck was opened, a gunfight took place in which two Nyack policemen were killed and another one was wounded. Both Boudin and Gilbert were captured.

An impressive list of lawyers defended her case at the April 1984 trial. Boudin refused to plead mitigating circumstances. Her lawyers made a deal: Boudin pleaded guilty to one count of murder and one count of robbery. On April 26, 1984, Boudin was given a sentence of from twenty years to life. She is still serving her sentence. **See also** Black Liberation Army; Buck, Marilyn Jean; May 19th Communist Organization; Shakur, Mutulu.

Suggested readings: John Castellucci, *The Big Dance: The Untold Story of Kathy Boudin and the Terrorist Family That Committed the Brink's Robbery Murders* (New York: Dodd, Mead, 1986); James Feron, "Kathy Boudin, in Reversal, Pleads Guilty to '81 Holdup and Slayings," *New York Times* (April 27, 1984), p. A1; Ellen Frankfort, *Kathy Boudin and the Dance of Death* (New York: Stein and Day, 1983); Margot Hornblower, "Kathy Boudin Clings to Radicalism While Facing Trial in Brinks Murders," *Washington Post* (February 21, 1984), p. A1; Wendall Jamieson, "Tear Down the Walls: Weathermen, 1970," *Daily News* [New York] (October 25, 1998), p. 69.

Bowers, Samuel Holloway (1924–)

Sam Bowers, the leader of the violent **White Knights of the Ku Klux Klan** of Mississippi in the 1960s, was born on August 6, 1924, in New Orleans, Louisiana. His family had been prominent in Mississippi politics; his grandfather served four terms in Congress. The family moved frequently around the South because his father was a salesperson. His parents were divorced when Bowers was fourteen years old. Bowers attended high school at Fortier High School in New Orleans where his teachers and fellow students described him as an intelligent but indifferent student. Bowers left high school before graduation and joined the U.S. Navy shortly after the attack on Pearl Harbor. He served until 1945, obtaining the rank of machinist mate first class. After obtaining a high school diploma by passing an equivalency test, he went to college first at Tulane University and then at the University of Southern California, where he majored in engineering. After graduation, Bowers and a college buddy, Robert Larson, opened a pinball and vending business, Sambo Amusement Company, in Laurel, Mississippi. He also acquired the local movie house in Laurel. A compulsive loner and a confirmed bachelor, Bower devoted most of his energy to **Ku Klux Klan** activity. In 1955 Bowers joined the Original Knights of the Ku Klux Klan of Louisiana. By the early 1960s, he had decided this group was too moderate and too passive. At a meeting of the Original Knights in Brookhaven, Mississippi, on February 15, 1964, he persuaded 200 members to join a more militant organization, his White Knights of the Ku Klux Klan.

Bowers assumed the leadership of the White Knights of the Ku Klux Klan in April

Former Imperial Wizard of the Ku Klux Klan Samuel H. Bowers of Laurel, Mississippi, is escorted by lawmen from the Forrest County Courthouse, in Hattiesburg, Mississippi, on Friday, August 21, 1998, following his conviction on murder and arson charges stemming from the 1966 firebombing death of black Hattiesburg businessman Vernon Dahmer Sr. (AP Photo/Rogelio Solis)

1964. He was active both in forming the organization and in writing its constitution. After assuming the title of imperial wizard, Bowers began to recruit members primarily from among the poorly educated, lower class, blue-collar workers in the Laurel area. Bowers made certain that he retained control of the White Knights by restricting membership to Mississippi. Because he identified the Klan so closely with his belief in Christianity, Bowers exhorted his followers to be pre-pared to kill for Christ to preserve the natural order of segregation. He came to subscribe to the **Christian Identity** views of **Wesley Swift**: a race war is imminent with whites in a battle against blacks, Catholics, communists, and Jews. His militancy toward the civil rights movement had attracted a membership of between 5,000 and 6,000 supporters by 1965. Only about 1,200 of these members, however, were hard-core believers who were willing to carry out violent acts. It was with his complicity that the members of his Klan organization, with the help of the Philadelphia, Mississippi, police, murdered three Council of Federated Organizations (COFO) civil rights workers on June 21, 1964: Jim Chaney, Andy Goodman, and Michael Schwerner. Bowers made it plain that all sanction 4 operations, or murder, had to be approved first by him. In particular, Bowers wanted to eliminate Schwerner. Other violent incidents inspired by Bowers were the burnings of twenty-six black churches, the bombing of a synagogue, and the firebomb murder of Vernon Dahmer, the leader of the National Association for the Advancement of Colored People (NAACP). Dahmer's home was firebombed on January 10, 1966, and he died twelve hours later of fire-related injuries.

The illegal activities of the White Knights landed Bowers in trouble with federal and state authorities. Bowers was tried twice in federal courts and once in a state court for complicity in Dahmer's murder, but the all-white juries refused to convict him. Twice all-white juries voted 11 to 1 for conviction, but the failure to reach a unanimous verdict caused mistrials. Bowers and five co-conspirators were tried in 1967 for the violations of the civil rights of the murdered COFO civil rights workers and found guilty. While still out on appeal of his prison sentence, Bowers planned a bombing campaign against Jews and black leaders with **Thomas Albert Tarrants**. He never stood trial for these bombings. After two years of appeals in federal courts, Bowers went to prison in 1970 and served almost six years of his ten-year sentence at McNeil Island Prison in Steilacoom, Washington. While in jail, Bowers studied religion. His organization, the White Knights of the Ku Klux Klan, faded away with Bowers in prison. Bowers never repudiated his role as a Klan leader, but he kept a low political profile after his release from prison. He returned to Laurel and ran his amusement business.

Bowers's low profile did not prevent authorities from reopening the Vernon Dahmer case. The conviction of **Byron de la Beck-**with in 1994 for the murder of Medgar Evers after nearly thirty-one years sparked interest in other outstanding cases. Dahmer's relatives pressed for a new trial for years before gaining support from Reverend Kenneth Fairley's Citizens for Justice. Together with other political allies they persuaded Mississippi State authorities to reopen the case. An investigation found new information, and on May 28, 1998, Bowers and two of his associates, Charles R. Noble and Devours Nix, were arrested. Bowers stood trial for the Dahmer killing in the Forrest County Court in Hattiesburg, Mississippi, in August 1998. Bowers's lawyer, Travis Buckley, had previously been tried for his role in the killing of Dahmer, but he escaped conviction. Witnesses indicated that Bowers had ordered the Dahmer murder but that he was not present at the scene of the firebombing. After a five-day trial, a jury convicted Bowers for the crime on August 21, 1998. His sentence was life imprisonment. Bowers will be eligible for parole in ten years when he will be in his mid-eighties. **See also** Ainsworth, Kathryn Madlyn; Ku Klux Klan; Tarrants, Thomas Albert; White Knights of the Ku Klux Klan.

Suggested readings: Seth Cagin and Philip Dray, *We Are Not Afraid: The Story of Goodman, Schwerner and Chaney and the Civil Rights Campaign for Mississippi* (New York: Bantam Books, 1989); Jack Nelson, *Terror in the Night: The Klan's Campaign Against the Jews* (New York: Simon and Schuster, 1993); Stephanie Saul, "Taking a New Look? Pressure on Miss. to Reopen a Case Many Want to Bury," *Newsday* (April 5, 1999), p. A7; Patsy Sims, *The Klan* (New York: Stein and Day, 1978); Wyn Craig Wade, *The Fiery Cross: The Ku Klux Klan in America* (New York: Simon and Schuster, 1987); Don Whitehead, *Attack on Terror: The FBI Against the Ku Klux Klan in Mississippi* (New York: Funk and Wagnalls, 1970); Curtis Wilkie, "Ex-Klan Leader Is Convicted of Murder in a Fourth Trial," *Boston Globe* (August 22, 1998), p. A1.

Branch Davidians

The Branch Davidians cult and its leader, David Koresh, were at the center of one of

Fire engulfs the Branch Davidian compound near Waco, Texas, on April 19, 1993. Eighty Davidians, including leader David Koresh, perished when federal agents tried to drive them out of the compound. A few weeks earlier four agents from the Bureau of Alcohol, Tobacco, and Firearms were slain in a shootout at the site, and six cult members were found dead inside. (AP Photo/Ron Heflin, file)

the most controversial events in recent American history. This cult had a complex history. Victor T. Houteff, a Bulgarian emigrant, joined the Seventh-Day Adventist Church (SDA) in 1918, but by the early 1930s he had begun to question SDA doctrine. His critiques were published in a multivolume series of books, *The Shepherd's Rod*. Church leaders found his teachings heretical, and he was removed from the fellowship of the Seventh-Day Adventist Church. Houteff formed his own church, the Davidians. After a lengthy search of possible sites, he selected Waco, Texas. Land on an old World War I army base just outside of Waco was purchased in 1935 and named the Mount Carmel Center. On this 189-acre tract, Houteff planned to build a church, a school, and living quarters for his followers.

By 1937, nearly seventy-five church members lived at Mount Carmel, and within another ten years there were almost two hundred. Houteff ruled the Davidians with a firm hand, and many members left because of his harsh treatment and the hardships of living at the compound. He also controlled news coming in and out of Mount Carmel. The Davidians were always short of funds, and in the early 1950s Houteff had the cult sell off some of its land. By the mid-1950s, Houteff's health was failing and he died on February 5, 1955.

A brief power struggle for control of the Davidians ensued after Houteff's death. Several of his longtime supporters wanted to succeed Houteff, but none was acceptable to the majority of members. A compromise candidate was Houteff's wife, Florence Houteff, and she was selected as the next head of the Davidians. One of her first acts was to proclaim that April 22, 1959, was the date when all prophecies of the Book of Revelations would be fulfilled. In the meantime, Benjamin Roden laid claim to the leadership of the Davidians maintaining that he was "the Branch" who had summoned members to Waco. Despite this assault, Florence Houteff remained the head and moved the Davidians to a 941-acre farm about nine miles east of Waco in December 1957. The failure of the prophecy to be fulfilled on April 22, 1959, proved catastrophic to the Davidian cult. Members had traveled from all over the country after selling their property and preparing for the day of judgment. Florence Houteff survived as its leader until 1962 when she resigned and moved to California. She left a religious body in complete disarray.

Benjamin Roden assumed the leadership of the Davidians and renamed the cult the Branch Davidians. He had been trying to gain control of the Mount Carmel organization for years. In the meantime, he had traveled to Israel and other places in the United States proselytizing people with his theological views. Roden and his wife, Lois, used a combination of bullying and court cases to gain control of the Davidians. Once in control, he remained head of the Branch Davidians until his death in 1978. Lois succeeded him, and in a controversial decision she elevated the role of women in the movement by interpreting the Holy Spirit to be female. Her son, George Roden, considered himself to be his mother's successor, but he had the disadvantage of suffering from a Tourette syndrome–like affliction. His mother had little patience with her son and welcomed David Koresh as a relief preacher in 1981. They became lovers. Lois died in November 1986 of old age. Her death left a leadership void that resulted in a lengthy battle for control of the Branch Davidians between George Roden and David Koresh.

George Roden's erratic behavior allowed Koresh to challenge him for the leadership of the Branch Davidians and win. Roden challenged Koresh by disinterring a former member's body and displaying it, showing his authority. Koresh and his followers engaged in a gunfight with Roden at the Mount Carmel compound in November 1987. In a subsequent trial, Koresh and his followers were acquitted of property invasion after it became apparent that Roden had mental problems. Roden went to jail for contempt of court for an earlier offense.

As soon as Koresh had been acknowledged the leader of the Branch Davidians, his behavior became even more extreme. He believed himself to be the second Messiah and the interpreter of the Christian apocalyptic prophecy in the Book of Revelations. He also believed it his duty to have children by the members of his flock. To prepare for the millennium, the members of the church began stockpiling food, weapons, and ammunition.

Former members of the Branch Davidians had alerted federal authorities in the early 1990s to possible violations of the law at the compound. Rumors had been circulating about possible child abuse and possession of illegal weapons. Federal officials mindful of the failure to prevent the Jonestown mass suicides in 1978 decided to investigate. Shortly afterward, a deliveryman reported dropping off two cases of hand grenades and explosives. This news coincided with reports that AR-15 and M-16 rifles were being converted to full automatic capacity at the compound. Bureau of Alcohol, Tobacco and Firearms (BATF) agents planned a search and arrest operation at the Branch Davidians compound for February 28, 1993. Their strategy was to use surprise, speed, and overwhelming force to capture Koresh and his adult male followers.

The federal raid was botched from the beginning and soon deteriorated into a stalemate. A church member learned of the intended raid and warned Koresh about it several hours before it was to be launched. Koresh also received a warning by phone. Even the news media was tipped off about the raid. Although BATF officials knew that they had lost the element of surprise, the decision was made to conduct the raid anyway. Seventy-five agents arrived at the Branch Davidian compound. After demanding access to the compound, a firefight broke out, and BATF agents found themselves outgunned by the Branch Davidians. Four BATF agents were killed and twenty wounded in comparison to six Branch Davidians killed and four wounded. Koresh received several wounds in the arm and abdomen.

Negotiations between Koresh and federal agents continued for the next fifty-one days. Several times the agents believed that Koresh was about to surrender the compound, but each time he reneged. Koresh seemed more concerned about theological problems than survival. On April 19, 1993, federal agents conducted a tank and tear gas assault on the compound. During the assault the compound caught fire at three places. Final casualties from the fire and gunshot wounds among the Branch Davidians were placed at eighty dead and numerous injuries.

The actions during the Branch Davidian siege and the aftermath are still controversial. Numerous hearings and investigations have taken place. Documentaries have been made blaming the government for the outcome of the siege. In the middle of the charges and countercharges, a jury trial convicted eight of the Davidians on weapons charges in 1994. The most important of the investigations was conducted by former Republican Senator John Danforth. His report, issued on July 22, 2000, after a ten-month investigation, cleared the federal government of wrongdoing. Prior to this report, survivors had sued the federal government for the reckless tactics and negligence of its agents. A trial opened in June 2000 in Waco, Texas. After months of testimony and listening to tapes with Koresh and government agents, U.S. District Judge Walter Smith, Jr., absolved the federal government of responsibility for the Branch Davidians' deaths on April 19, 1993. On September 20 2000, the judge issued a lengthy report of his findings which concluded that the government was not at fault in the conduct of the initial raid, nor in the final assault. Despite this judg-

ment, the controversy over the Branch Davidians and the April 19 assault continues. **See also** Cults; Koresh, David.

Suggested readings: Brad Bailey and Bob Darden, *Mad Man in Waco* (Waco, Tex.: WRS Publishing, 1993); William H. Freivogel and Terry Ganey, "Secrecy Led to Public Mistrust," *St. Louis Post-Dispatch* (July 23, 2000), p. A1; Clifford L. Linedecker, *Massacre at Waco: The Shocking True Story of Cult Leader David Koresh and the Branch Davidians* (London: True Crime, 1993); Tim Madigan, *See No Evil: Blind Devotion and Bloodshed in David Koresh's Holy War* (Fort Worth, Tex.: Summit Group, 1993); Reavis, Dick J., *The Ashes of Waco: An Investigation* (Syracuse, N.Y.: Syracuse University Press, 1995); Armando Villafranca, John C. Henry, Letitia Stein, and Tony Freemantle, "Investigation Clears Feds in Waco Tragedy," *Houston Chronicle* (July 22, 2000), p. A1.

Bray, Michael (1952?–)

Michael Bray was the first anti-abortion protest leader to resort to violence. Factual information about his birth date is lacking, but he was probably born in 1952. His father was a career naval officer with an Annapolis degree from the class of 1951. Bray grew up in Bowie, Maryland, near Washington, D.C., where he was an Eagle Scout, football player, and Maryland state-wrestling champion. He attended the Naval Academy at Annapolis, but poor grades and a bad attitude led to his dismissal from the academy at the end of his first year. After leaving the academy, he traveled extensively both in Germany and the United States. After briefly flirting with the Church of Jesus Christ of Latter-Day Saints and a year of college work at the University of Maryland, Bray entered Rockmont College, a small Bible school in Denver, Colorado. He was fascinated by his theological studies, and, after graduation from Rockmont, he studied at the Denver Theological Seminary. While at Rockmont College, he met and married Jayne Green in 1976.

Bray's first job after graduation was as a lay pastor for youth activities at his former church, the Grace Lutheran Church in

Bowie, Maryland. While at the seminary, Bray had come to embrace an activist fundamentalist approach to ethical issues, which included a strong opposition to abortion. These views soon caused him difficulties with the more liberal pastor at his church. After leading a revolt against the minister, Bray was fired. He was popular enough at Grace Lutheran Church to attract eight families to come with him when he formed a more conservative church.

Part of Bray's difficulty with the Lutheran Church hierarchy was his deep involvement in anti-abortion politics. He had become acquainted with Thomas Spinks, a home improvement contractor, at anti-abortion protests. The two men discussed ways to stop abortion and decided that bombing abortion clinics was the most direct way. Because Bray needed intelligence to carry out these bombings he joined John O'Keefe's Pro-Life Non-Violent Action Project (PNAP). O'Keefe's organization specialized in civil disobedience sit-ins at abortion clinics, but, since most of its members were Catholics, O'Keefe welcomed Protestant supporters. Bray scouted out the clinics during demonstrations and then told Spinks where to plant the bombs. He was always careful not to tie the bombings to O'Keefe's PNAP sit-ins. Over the next several months in 1984, Bray, Spinks, and another recruit, Kenneth Fields, an accountant and small business owner, planned and carried out five major bombing attacks before being caught. Despite Bray's efforts not to tie the bombings and the sit-ins together, Spinks bombed the Metro Medical and Women's Center Clinic in Wheaton, Maryland, on November 19, 1984, shortly after such a demonstration. By this time police in several states had started to suspect Spinks and he was arrested. For a reduced charge, Spinks testified in court against Bray. Bray was convicted in May 1985 of two counts of conspiracy and one count of possessing unregistered explosive devices. He was sentenced to ten years in prison. An appeals court reversed this verdict on a technicality, and in a plea bargain Bray received a six-year sentence. He spent nearly four years in prison. Moreover, his actions ended the attempt of John O'Keefe and his followers to keep anti-abortion activities nonviolent.

After his release from prison on May 15 1989, Bray became one of the leading advocates of anti-abortion violence. Although he is now a pastor with the Reformation Lutheran Church in Bowie, Maryland, he continues to advocate and justify bombings of clinics and assassinations of abortion providers. His book, *A Time to Kill: A Study Concerning the Use of Force and Abortion*, in 1994 is the official position on anti-abortion violence. His friendship with **Paul Jennings Hill** and his Defensive Action group has continued after Hill received a death sentence in Florida for the murder of an abortion doctor and bodyguard. Although Bray avoids taking part in violence, he advocates physical attacks on abortion doctors to end abortion. He has been accused of being the author of the *Army of God Manual*, but he neither accepts nor denies authorship. Bray publishes the militant anti-abortion newsletter *Capitol Area Christian News*. Bray, a follower of **Christian Reconstruction** theology, believes in a society based on Christian morality. Because of this, he considers himself at war with modern society. **See also** Anti-Abortion Movement; Hill, Paul Jennings; Lambs of Christ; Salvi, John C. III; Weslin, Norman U.

Suggested readings: Patricia Baird-Windle and Eleanor J. Bader, *Targets of Hatred: Anti-Abortion Terrorism* (New York: Palgrave, 2001); Dallas A. Blanchard, *The Anti-Abortion Movement and the Rise of the Religious Right: From Polite to Fiery Protest* (New York: Twayne, 1994); Mark Juergensmeyer, *Terror in the Mind of God: The Global Rise of Religious Violence* (Berkeley: University of California Press, 2000); James Risen and Judy L. Thomas, *Wrath of Angels: The American Abortion War* (New York: Basic Books, 1998).

Brink's Armored Car Robbery

The Brink's armored car robbery carried out by **Robert Jay Mathews**'s organization, **The Order**, in 1984 was the most successful operation undertaken by the **white supremacist movement**. Mathews and his band of twelve followers were in the middle of a series of robberies and counterfeiting schemes to raise funds to establish a white homeland in the Pacific Northwest. Most of their earlier robberies had been modestly successful, netting in the range of from a few hundred dollars to the twenty thousands. Mathews knew that a 1981 May 19th Communist Organization, and **Black Liberation Army/Weather Underground** robbery of a Brink's armored car had garnered $1.6 million for left-wing radicals. Moreover, Mathews was aware that a Brink's supervisor in California, Charles Ostrout, was a white supremacist sympathizer. After visiting Mathews in Metaline Falls, Idaho, and meeting him in California, Ostrout agreed to help in the robbery by providing a map of the route of the Brink's armored car delivery. Another Brink's employee, Ron King, agreed to help in the planning. After a scouting trip, Mathews and Denver Parmenter decided that a hill near Ukiah, California, was the best place for the robbery.

All of the inside information and intense advanced planning made the robbery almost anticlimatic. Mathews and eleven of his followers—Andrew Barnhill, Randy Duey, Jim Dye, Randall Evans, Richard Kemp, Robert Merki, Denver Parmenter, Bruce Pierce, Bill Soderquist, Richard Scutari, and Gary Yarbrough—gathered at local motels in Ukiah on July 15, 1984, to make final preparations. The next day, on the morning of July 16, the robbery took place without incident. In the confusion of the robbery, however, two weapons were left at the site of the robbery. One of these weapons was later traced to Barnhill, and federal agents instigated a manhunt to find him. Plans to meet and coordinate travel plans fell through in the excitement, but most of the participants made it to Reno, Nevada, where they counted the $3.6 million from the robbery.

Almost as soon as the money was counted, dissension broke out among the members of The Order. Several of the members resented Mathews's leadership, and the issue of splitting the money brought this dissension to a head. Bruce Pierce took $800,000, asserted pressure on Mathews, and left to form another group. Mathews was relegated to be the coordinator of operations rather than its outright leader. Each of the other participants received $40,000, but they remained with Mathews. The bulk of the money was left to Mathews to be distributed to other white supremacist groups.

The Brink's robbery proved to be the beginning of the end for The Order. Federal agents had found Barnhill's gun, but they also found Kemp's fingerprints on the abandoned van near the scene of the robbery. The big break in the case, however, occurred when an associate of Mathews, Tom Martinez, made a deal with federal authorities to avoid going to prison on counterfeiting charges. He told the surprised federal agents about The Order and its operations. In December 1984, Mathews was dead and the rest of the members of The Order were under arrest. Several of them turned state's evidence and received suspended sentences. The others were charged under the Racketeer Influenced and Corrupt Organization (RICO) statute for conspiracy for the commission of 176 acts including the Brink's robbery. About half of the money stolen in the robbery was never recovered. **See also** Lane, David; Mathews, Robert Jay; Order, The.

Suggested readings: Kevin Flynn, *The Silent Brotherhood: Inside America's Racist Underground* (New York: Free Press, 1989); Robert L. Jackson and Ronald J. Ostrow, "Law in War on Far-Right Sect: White Supremacists Tied to Western Crime Spree," *Los Angeles Times* (January 21, 1985); Stephen Singular, *Talked to Death: The Life and Murder of Alan Berg* (New York: Beech Tree Books, 1987).

Brock, Robert (1925–)

Robert Brock is one of the leading black separatists in the United States. He was born in 1925 in Louisiana, but he was raised in the Watts area of Los Angeles. His father was a longshoreman and his mother worked in hospitals. After leaving school in Watts, Brock entered the U.S. Army. His military career was undistinguished, then he became a merchant seaman. Leaving this job in the early 1950s, Brock attended Southwestern Law School in Los Angeles where he studied constitutional law. He left law school without a degree, but he has maintained a lifelong interest in legal affairs.

In 1956, Brock and other like-minded individuals founded the Self-Determination Committee, based in Los Angeles. The purpose of this group was to make a case for reparations for 246 years of black slavery. His activities there led him to be named president of the Cosmopolitan Brotherhood Association, a black nationalist group founded in 1945. Representing these two organizations, Brock assumed a leadership role in the slavery reparation movement. Patrik Jonsson of the *Christian Science Monitor* claimed that proponents of reparation believed that "the U.S. government owes about $8 billion to the millions of slave descendants who exist today." Brock established a different figure, by claiming that each of the 49 million descendents of slaves should receive $500,000 each, or more than $3 trillion. Brock made his impact on the national scene during the 1965 Watts riots, outspokenly critical of police actions.

In the 1980s, Brock began to lobby for a black homeland and started making connections with white supremacists engaged in planning for a white homeland. He agreed with their position that Jews, Hispanics, and other ethnic minorities should be repatriated outside the United States. In 2000, Gail Gans, director of the Civil Rights Information Center for the Anti-Defamation League, charged that Brock "has the distinction to be the only known black participant in the white supremacy movement." Brock has also been active in the Holocaust denial movement and a frequent contributor of writings to **Liberty Lobby** publications. In 1990, he founded United for Holocaust Fairness, a group that tried to unite white and black anti-Semites. He has also participated in activities of various Christian identity

groups. Most of Brock's activities since 1990 have been lobbying for black reparations.

In October 1994, Brock filed a lawsuit against the IRS seeking tax exemptions on behalf of the 49 million descendents of slaves, but this suit went nowhere. Tatsha Robertson in the *Boston Globe* reported in October 2000 that Brock still travels around the country making the claim that the IRS owes a "black tax rebate," of $43,209 and that for a $50 check he will file a claim for reparations for them. Brock's campaign for reparations has attracted considerable support in the black community and political supporters in the U.S. House of Representatives have introduced bills on reparations since 1989.

Suggested readings: Anti-Defamation League, *Danger: Extremism: The Major Vehicles and Voices on America's Far-Right Fringe* (New York: Anti-Defamation League, 1996); Darrell Dawsey, "Reparations Sought for Black Americans," *Los Angeles Times* (December 10, 1990), p. B1; Peter Flaherty, "New Era of Reparations Looms for U.S.," *Baltimore Sun* (August 5, 2001), p. 5C; Jeffrey Ghannam, "Repairing the Past," *ABA Journal* (November 2000), p. 1; Patrik Jonsson, "Movement to Pay Slavery Reparations Gains," *Christian Science Monitor* (January 12, 2001), p. 2; Tatsha Robertson, "Reparations Pitch Draws Hope, Scorn," *Boston Globe* (October 17, 2000), p. A1.

Buck, Marilyn Jean (1947–)

Marilyn Buck, the leader of the **May 19th Communist Organization** (M19CO) and a member of the **Black Liberation Army** (BLA), was born on December 13, 1947, and grew up in Austin, Texas. Her father was a prominent Episcopalian minister and a veterinarian. She attended a private school, Saint Stevens, in Austin. In September 1965, she enrolled in the gifted program at the University of California at Berkeley. Buck found the political environment in Berkeley stimulating, and she soon joined the Students for a Democratic Society (SDS). After a year at Berkeley, she returned to Austin and attended the University of Texas. She was less interested in her studies than her SDS activities. Consequently, in 1967, she moved to Chicago to work at the SDS national headquarters. When the SDS disintegrated in the early 1970s, Buck started her migration into other groups beginning with a loose affiliation with the **Weather Underground.**

Buck became a key member of the BLA. The only white member, her role was to plan and arrange a series of safe houses for the group to use after the commission of an operation. Buck was arrested and convicted in a federal court in San Francisco, California, in 1973 for buying weapons and ammunition for the BLA. Her sentence was for ten years in prison, and she was sent to the Federal Correctional Institution at Alderson, West Virginia. In 1977 she escaped while on a week-long furlough in New York City. Soon afterward, she became the head of the M19CO. This group carried out a series of terrorist bombings and robberies. Among them was an armored car robbery at the Livingston Mall, in New Jersey, in 1978, and a holdup at Bamberger's in Paramus, New Jersey, in 1979. Buck was an active participant in the 1981 Brink's armored car robbery at the Nanuet Mall in Nyack, New York. She was the driver of one of the getaway cars in the robbery. In a gunfight in which a guard was killed, she accidentally shot herself in the leg, which left her with a permanent limp.

Buck spent the next fourteen years underground working with several of her companions in extremist organizations. She traveled to various cities, including the Bronx, New York; New Haven, Connecticut; and Baltimore, Maryland, and lived in safe houses. An informant tipped off the FBI about her presence in New York City, and FBI agents followed Buck and Linda Sue Evans, a fellow member of the M19CO, until they captured both of them on May 11, 1985, in Dobbs Ferry, New York. In a trial held in New York City in the summer of 1988, Buck received a fifty-year prison sentence for her role in the 1981 Brink's armored car robbery and the deaths of a Brink's guard and two Nyack police officers. In 1990 an additional ten years was added to her sen-

tence for her M19CO role in the bombing of several government buildings, including the November 1983 bombing of the U.S. Capitol. **See also** Black Liberation Army; Boudin, Kathy.

Suggested readings: John Castellucci, *The Big Dance: The Untold Story of Kathy Boudin and the Terrorist Family That Committed the Brink's Robbery Murders* (New York: Dodd, Mead, 1986); Gabriel Escobar, "Term Levied in Bombings of Government Buildings," *Washington Post* (November 17, 1990), p. B4; Clifford D. May, "The Law; Terrorist or Insurgent? Diplomacy and the Law," *New York Times* (May 27, 1988), p. B5; Robert D. McFadden, "F.B.I. Asserts Fugitives Had a Network of 'Safe Houses,'" *New York Times* (May 13, 1985), p. B1; Robert D. McFadden, "Fugitive in $1.6 Million Brink's Holdup Captured," *New York Times* (May 12, 1985), sec. 1, p. 1; Joseph B. Treaster, "Marilyn Buck: A Fugitive and Long a Radical," *New York Times* (October 23, 1981), p. B5.

Burdi, George (1970–)

George Burdi, one of Canada's most extreme white supremacists, was born in June 1970. His father is a self-employed businessman in Woodbridge, Ontario. Burdi, a bright student, was well liked by his teachers and fellow students. In 1985 he enrolled in a Toronto Catholic boys' school, the De La Salle College School. While Burdi was always attracted to the doctrine and pageantry of Nazism, it was a girlfriend who introduced him to the **neo-Nazi Ernst Christof Friedrich Zundel.** Soon Burdi had made friends with some of Canada's most notorious white supremacists. Burdi also started lifting weights seriously and taking steroids. In 1989 he graduated from the De La Salle College School. After high school, Burdi enrolled at the University of Guelph where he took political science courses. While in college, he became a follower of **Ben Klassen's Church of the Creator** (COTC). Klassen was such an influence on Burdi that he traveled to North Carolina to have private discussions with him. Burdi soon tired of school and decided to work full-time for his political beliefs. Although Burdi championed the causes of the COTC, it was not until September 1992 that he had any official position with the COTC when he was appointed to the COTC's leadership council. In the meantime, Burdi and the leader of the neo-Nazi **Heritage Front, Wolfgang Droege,** had become fast friends and allies.

Burdi's influence in the white supremacist movement has come from his music group RAHOWA (Racial Holy War) and **Resistance Records.** In the fall of 1990, Burdi and three other COTC members formed the white power rock group RAHOWA, and he began performing under the name of George Eric Hawthorne. Performing songs extolling white supremacy, he soon became a staple on the white supremacist concert stage in Canada and the United States. In April 1994, he founded Resistance Records to distribute his and other white supremacists' music. Because the United States lacks hate-speech laws, Burdi located Resistance Records in Detroit, Michigan. Burdi has had frequent legal problems, including charges of assault. In 1999 Canadian authorities charged him with violation of the Canadian law against promoting hatred. His one-year sentence of community service prohibited him from performing with RAHOWA or having any involvement with Resistance Records. Burdi sold Resistance Records to **Willis Carto,** the head of the **Liberty Lobby,** who was forced for financial reasons to sell it to **William Pierce. See also** Church of the Creator; Droege, Wolfgang; Heritage Front; Klassen, Ben; Pierce, William; Resistance Records; Zundel, Ernst Christof Friedrich.

Suggested readings: Mike Blanchfield, "Neo-Nazi Jailed for a Year; Supremacist Kicked Woman in the Face, Broke Her Nose," *Ottawa Sun* (May 12, 1995), p. C1; Warren Kinsella, *Web of Hate: Inside Canada's Far Right Network* (Toronto, Ont., Canada: HarperCollins, 1994); Brian Lysaght, "Hate Music Is Latest Export from Detroit, *Chicago Sun-Times* (March 30, 1995), p. 40; Keith Schneider, "Hate Groups Use Tools of the Electronic Trade," *New York Times* (March 13, 1995), p. A12; Keith Schneider, "Skinhead Leader Finds Avenues to Spread Hate Message," *Houston Chronicle* (March 19, 1995), p. A1; Stephan Talty, "The Method of a Neo-Nazi Mogul," *New York Times* (February 25, 1996), sec. 6, p. 40.

Burros, Daniel (1937–1965)

Daniel Burros was a **neo-Nazi** and a leader in the New York **Ku Klux Klan** whose 1965 suicide made national headlines. He was born on March 5, 1937, in the Bronx borough of New York City. Both of his parents were Jews of Eastern European background. Although his father was not a religious man, his mother made sure that Burros had religious training and went through his bar mitzvah. His father was a machinist and a veteran of both the U.S. Navy and the U.S. Army, who had been wounded in the trenches in France during World War I. Burros grew up in a Jewish neighborhood of Richmond Hills, New York. Although he was always a good student in school, he was pugnacious and always fighting. He attended John Adams High School where he continued to get good grades. By the end of his junior year, however, he had gained a reputation as a radical right-wing sympathizer. Burros had become infatuated with all things German, including the Nazis and Adolf Hitler. During his senior year, Burros joined the National Guard. Shortly after graduation from high school, Burros resigned from the National Guard and enlisted in the U.S. Army for a six-year tour of duty. He volunteered for paratrooper training and served in a unit in the 101st Airborne Division. His unit was sent to Little Rock, Arkansas, to help integrate its Central High School in 1958. Soon afterward, Burros decided to leave the military. While he idealized the military life, he was a loner and unsympathetic toward desegregation. His fellow soldiers considered him a misfit, and he made several halfhearted attempts at suicide. After a negative psychiatric examination, the army released him from the remainder of his military obligation.

After his return to New York City, Burros started his career as an extremist. His first civilian job was in the Queens Borough Public Library printing cataloging cards. He bored his colleagues with his pro-Nazi views. These opinions soon caught the attention of the special branch of the New York City Police Department that deals with extremists. After flirting with membership in the fascist British National Party, Burros moved to Arlington, Virginia, in June 1960 and became a member of **George Lincoln Rockwell**'s **American Nazi Party**. Burros's main duty in the American Nazi Party was running its printing press. His best friend in the party, John Patler, was a printer by trade. Burros often feuded with other members of the party, who thought Burros was too radical in his calls for the extermination of all Jews. On July 3, 1960, Burros was arrested along with Rockwell for their participation in a riot on the Washington Mall. When Rockwell was sentenced to a thirty-day commitment for a psychiatric examination, Burros and his fellow members were devastated by Rockwell's absence. After Rockwell won his release by cooperating with the psychiatrists, Burros was arrested for defacing property at the Anti-Defamation League office in Washington, D.C. He paid a $100 fine and received a six-month suspended sentence. Burros had been working as a multilith operator for the Chamber of Commerce, but he lost this job after his boss learned about his membership in the American Nazi Party. Despite the jealousy of many of his comrades, Burros managed to work his way up in the hierarchy of the party to become the third ranking party member. By late 1961, however, Burros had become restless with Rockwell's leadership. Burros and Patler decided to leave the party and move to New York City.

Almost as soon as Burros and Patler arrived in New York City, they formed the American National Party with Patler acting as the national chairman and Burros as the national vice chairman. Burros was also the editor of its magazine, *Kill! Magazine*. Membership in this party never exceeded a dozen, but Burros was in his element as a leader directing demonstrations in an effort to attract media attention for the party. He also often informed on other extremist groups to the New York City police. After almost a year of activity, the American National Party ceased to exist when Patler left it to return to Rockwell's American Nazi Party. (Patler assassinated Rockwell in 1967.) Burros remained in New York City and became a devoted fan of Francis Parker Yockey and the ideas expressed in his book *Imperium* (1949).

The next group Burros joined was the National Renaissance Party (NRP), formed by James H. Madole who was its head. Party headquarters was located in Madole's Manhattan apartment. Madole hated Rockwell, but his party espoused many of the same anti-Semitic and racial ideas. Burros was soon a member of Madole's security troop. Despite this honor, Madole never trusted Burros and feared that he was a Rockwell spy. Burros and Madole planned a demonstration against a civil rights protest and were both arrested for conspiracy. Each of them received a one- to two-year prison term in Sing Sing State Prison in Ossining, New York; however, they were released in less than two weeks on appeal. Shortly after his release from prison, Burros left the NRP. Burros now considered himself an **Odinist**.

Burros next decided to join the Ku Klux Klan. His enthusiasm for the Klan grew after he attended a showing of the movie *Birth of a Nation*. He had previously been an acquaintance of veteran Klan organizer **Roy Everett Frankhauser, Jr.** Frankhauser convinced Burros to become a member of the **United Klans of America** (UKA) in 1965. Because the UKA needed Northern supporters, Burros was appointed grand dragon of New York and also king kleagle, or organizer, for New York State. Burros liked the organization, the uniform, and the ideas of the Klan.

Burros had been able to hide his Jewish background by ignoring it and becoming a fierce anti-Semite. As Burros assumed a more prominent position in extremist politics, the stakes became higher if the information were made public. His parents knew of his rejection of his Jewish heritage and his belonging to various neo-Nazi and Klan groups, but they kept silent. Government agents had found out about the deception early on, but they had also kept the information confidential. His protection ended during the House Un-American Activities Committee's probe into Ku Klux Klan activities. A government agent leaked the information to a newspaperman. A *New York Times* reporter confronted Burros about his Jewish background, and Burros tried to persuade him not to publish the story, but the *New York Times* ran the story on October 31, 1965. Burros was staying at Frankhauser's home in Reading, Pennsylvania, when the story appeared. When he learned about the story, Burros committed suicide by shooting himself in both the chest and the head. His Klan colleagues eulogized him as a "good Jew" because he had turned against his heritage and joined the Klan. His death became a national news story for several weeks as commentators discussed his life and motivations. **See also** American Nazi Party; Frankhauser, Roy Everett, Jr.; Ku Klux Klan; Rockwell, George Lincoln; United Klans of America.

Suggested readings: A. M. Rosenthal and Arthur Gelb, *One More Victim* (New York: New American Library, 1967); David Waghalter, "The Best of Both Worlds," *Jerusalem Report* (May 21, 2001), p. 46.

Butler, Richard Girnt (1918–)

Richard Butler is the head of the white supremacist Christian Identity Church and the **Aryan Nations**. He was born on February 23, 1918, in the small town of Bennett, Colorado, about twenty miles east of Denver. His father, a machinist by training, moved the family to Denver when Butler was an infant. His family moved to California when Butler was thirteen. After graduating from high school, he attended Los Angeles City College where he studied science and aeronautical engineering. His first job was with the Consolidated Vultee Air Craft Company. This company sent him to Bangalore, India, in 1941 to design fighter planes. He was given the honorary rank of captain. While in India, he was exposed and attracted to the Indian caste system. After the attack on

Pearl Harbor in 1941, Butler returned to the United States and served in the U.S. Air Force teaching hydraulics. After the war ended, Butler returned to Southern California to work in his family's aeronautical engineering business. He also worked at Lockheed Company as an aerospace engineer, and while there he invented a device to change aircraft tires. From the royalties earned from this invention, Butler became financially independent.

Butler had long been attracted to conservative anti-communist movements. His first political activity was with the Christian Anti-Communist Crusade. He was also active in the 1961 ballot initiative to ban communists from teaching in California schools. **William Potter Gale**, a former senior army officer and leader in the **Christian Identity** movement, introduced him to his mentor, Dr. **Wesley Swift**. Swift had developed the theology of modern Christian Identity and preached it in his church in Los Angeles. Butler's exposure to this movement led him to join this church and adopt its brand of white supremacy. Butler studied under Swift for approximately ten years and was ordained by him into the Christian Identity Church. During this decade, Butler's father died leaving him with enough money to devote himself solely to his new cause. During his course of study, Butler traveled to the South where he spread the Christian Identity message to the members of the **Ku Klux Klan**. Swift died in 1970 leaving Butler as his successor as minister to the Los Angeles church. Butler proved to be an uninspiring preacher, and his new ministry began to fail. He also had a falling-out with his former mentor Gale in 1973.

After experiencing these setbacks, Butler decided to transfer his Christian Identity church to **Hayden Lake**, Idaho, in April 1974 and start a new phase in his career. More than a dozen families moved with him to his twenty-acre compound in northern Idaho. Soon he launched a vigorous recruiting drive to gain new members. His first action was to form an anti–federal government Posse Comitatus chapter, but the effort proved unsuccessful. Other members expelled Butler within two years for trying to dominate the chapter. Rather than depend on another established group, he formed the Aryan Nations in June 1978. Among his goals for this new organization was the establishment of a white homeland in the Pacific Northwest. Butler's overwhelming ambition was to become the leading figure in the **white supremacist movement**. Consequently, he started holding annual national meetings in 1979. Leaders from around the country gathered in Hayden Lake and conferred on the progress of the movement. His success as a leader of the Christian Identity movement comes from his skill as a negotiator and conciliator among the various leadership factions in the white supremacist movement. His activities led to his indictment in the 1988 **Fort Smith Sedition Trial**, in Arkansas, for advocating the overthrow of the U.S. government, but he was acquitted of all charges.

Butler became less active in the late 1990s. His increasing age and infirmities have restricted many of his activities. Many of his more important leaders have migrated to other more active groups. In 1998 Butler named Newman R. Britton, a longtime supporter, to be his successor. This decision ended a decade-old controversy over who was to succeed him. Finances for Butler's enterprises improved with an infusion of money from two wealthy Northern California businessmen, Carl F. Story and Vincent Bertollini. His success ended, however, with the loss of a civil suit on September 8, 2000. Members of his personal security staff assaulted a woman, Victoria Keenan, and her son, Jason, in 1998 outside of the Aryan Nations compound. The $6.3 million judgment forced Butler into bankruptcy, and he lost the Hayden Lake compound. Bertollini bought Butler a small home in Hayden, Idaho, but the loss of the compound has been catastrophic to Butler. Most of his followers have migrated to other white supremacist groups and Butler's reputation and influence have been severely damaged. After his chosen successor, Neuman Britton died in August 2001, Butler decided to turn operational control of the Aryan Nations over to Harold Ray Redfeairn. Redfeairn moved its headquarters to Ulysses, Pennsylvania. Butler remains the spiritual head of the Aryan Nations. **See also** Aryan Nations; Christian Identity; Swift, Wesley.

Suggested readings: Associated Press, "Aryan Leader Fights Back; Cites Prejudice After Losing Home, Some Followers," *Newsday* (February 7, 2001), p. A16; Rafael S. Ezekiel, *The Racist Mind: Portraits of American Neo-Nazis and Klansmen* (New York: Penguin Books, 1995); Kevin Flynn and Gary Gerhardt, *The Silent Brotherhood: Inside America's Racist Underground* (New York: Free Press, 1989); Neil A. Hamilton, *Militias in America: A Reference Handbook* (Santa Barbara, Calif.: ABC-CLIO, 1996); Richard Higgins, "Neo-Nazi Area to Be Museum of Hate," *Boston Globe* (March 8, 2001), p. B4; Jim Hughes, "North Idaho Residents Learn to Despise Hate," Denver Post (June 17, 2001), p. A4; Kim Murphy, "Last Stand of an Aging Aryan," *Los Angeles Times* (January 10, 1999), p. A1; Southern Poverty Law Center, "Elder Statesman: A Life of Hate, and the Future in the Balance," *SPLC Intelligence Report* 91 (Summer 1998): 22–25.

C

Carto, Willis (1926–)

Willis Carto, a longtime supporter of anti-Semitic causes and the founder of the **Liberty Lobby**, was born in 1926 in Fort Wayne, Indiana. After graduating from high school in Fort Wayne, he joined the U.S. Army and served in the Pacific Theater during World War II. While there is no evidence that Carto attended college, he did take a few courses at the University of Cincinnati Law School. Carto found a job in San Francisco, California, as a bill collector with Household Finance. By the early 1950s, he had become attracted to right-wing causes. Among the organizations he associated with were the Congress of Freedom, an organization that combined racist and anti-communist activists, and his own creation Liberty and Property. He also became a devoted follower of **Francis Parker Yockey** and the ideas Yockey expressed in his book *Imperium* (1949). Yockey combined Oswald Spengler's decline of the West thesis with a glorification of Adolf Hitler and Nazism. Carto adopted Yockey's basic ideas and **anti-Semitism** as his personal philosophy. To advance these views, Carto published a right-wing magazine, *Right*, from 1955 to 1960. He intended this publication to unify the various right-wing organizations in the United States around the issue of race. It also advanced an anti-communist and anti-Semitic agenda.

Carto also became active in the new **John Birch Society**, but he found it too moderate on race issues. After an argument with **Robert Henry Winborne Welch, Jr.**, over the direction of the John Birch Society, Carto left. In 1957 Carto founded the Liberty Lobby, which was intended to be a forum for the radical right and a way to keep the Republican Party under the control of pro–Barry Goldwater forces. Carto also published a newsletter, *Liberty Letters*. Almost from the beginning, Carto nurtured the **Holocaust denial movement** by publishing materials denying the Holocaust ever took place. He started the **Institute for Historical Review** (IHR) in 1979 and its publication, the *Journal of Historical Review*. Carto also published the *IHR Newsletter*. Later in 1980, he formed a shadow company, the Legion for the Survival of Freedom, Inc., to serve as an umbrella organization over his other holdings.

Carto helped launch the populist movement of the 1980s. In 1980 he published a series of articles in his *Spotlight* newspaper and collected them in a book titled *Profiles in Populism*. Carto defined populism as a combination of economic and political nationalism, free enterprise capitalism, a conspiracist view of history, and racism. His interpretations of populism and his efforts to publicize them led to the formation of the

Populist Party in 1982. His guidance helped recruit a number of leaders of the racist right into the party. After a meager showing in the 1984 presidential race, the Populist Party disintegrated into factional disunity. Carto responded from his ouster from the party in 1985 by forming a rival Populist Party with David Duke as its presidential candidate in the 1988 presidential election. Carto, who operated from behind the scenes, always worked to advance the political and racial agenda of the Liberty Lobby.

Carto retained control over both the Liberty Lobby and the IHR until 1993. Senior staff members at the IHR fired him from the institute for alleged financial improprieties. The stakes were control over $10 million in stock certificates bequeathed to the Legion for the Survival of Freedom by Jean Farrel. Carto and his former associates have launched suits and countersuits against each other. Carto's loss of an earlier lawsuit and a big financial settlement to a Holocaust survivor, who had claimed the $50,000 reward for proving that he had been a victim of the Holocaust, was also a factor in dissatisfaction among staff members at the IHR. In a November 1996 court case, Carto was convicted of illegally diverting millions of dollars from IHR and other corporations. He was ordered to pay IHR $6.43 million and the Liberty Lobby $2.65 million with 10 percent interest from 1991 onward. Carto appealed the judgment. To avoid paying the final judgment, Carto filed bankruptcy papers for both the Liberty Lobby and himself in May 1998. After Carto lost control of the IHR, his Liberty Lobby started to publish a rival journal, *The Barnes Review*. Carto also bought a controlling interest in the white supremacist music company, Resistance Records, only to have to sell it to his old rival, William Pierce of the National Alliance. Carto has spent the last several years attacking colleagues in the neo-Nazi and white supremacist movements. As a result of these attacks, his newsletter, *Spotlight*, has lost nearly one-quarter of its circulation. His flamboyant lifestyle has also alienated his colleagues. Despite his legal and political dif-

ficulties, Carto is still an influential figure in the American anti-Semitic and Holocaust denial movements. He remains a major distributor of pseudo-academic materials through his Noontide Press and *The Barnes Review*. **See also** Holocaust Denial Movement; Institute for Historical Review; Liberty Lobby; Yockey, Francis Parker.

Suggested readings: Anti-Defamation League, *Danger: Extremism: The Major Vehicles and Voices on America's Far-Right Fringe* (New York: Anti-Defamation League, 1996); Doreen Carvajal, "Extremist Institute Mired in Power Struggle," *Los Angeles Times* (May 15, 1994), p. A3; Michael Granberry, "Revisionists' Founder Sued for $7.5 Million," *Los Angeles Times* (October 28, 1996), p. 1; Frank P. Mintz, *The Liberty Lobby and the American Right: Race Conspiracy, and Culture* (Westport, Conn.: Greenwood Press, 1985); Greg Moran, "Decision on Estate Fails to End Bitterness;" *San Diego Union-Tribune* (November 16, 1996), p. B1; Southern Poverty Law Center, "Paying the Price," *SPLC Intelligence Report* 97 (Winter 2000): 53–56.

CAUSE Foundation

The CAUSE [Canada, Australia, United States, South Africa, Europe] Foundation, the leading neo-Nazi legal defense institute, was founded by Kirk Lyons in December 1991. Lyons's law practice handles high-profile legal cases involving neo-Nazis, white supremacists, and cults. His first important case was the Fort Smith Sedition Trial in 1988. In this trial, he contributed to the defeat of government charges of conspiracy against fourteen of the leading white supremacist leaders in the United States. He impressed the leaders on trial there with his legal expertise and his commitment to the cause of white supremacy. Later, he was active in Richard Girnt Butler's Aryan Nations. The countries included in the CAUSE acronym are places considered by Lyons to be strongholds of white supremacy that are in danger of being overwhelmed by nonwhites. Lyons formerly had been associated with the Patriots' Defense Foundation, but he closed down this foundation when he moved operations from Dallas, Texas, to North Carolina in 1991. CAUSE served as an information clearinghouse for extremists in the United States and abroad.

Lyons was the most prominent member of the CAUSE Foundation. He established ties with other defense lawyers specializing in high-profile political cases. In the early 1990s, he developed a close working relationship with a Canadian lawyer, Doug Christie, who also defends right-wing extremists. In 1992 Lyons traveled to Germany on a fund-raising tour to help a client, Fred Leuchter, and establish a CAUSE-affiliated center there. Jürgen Rieger, a neo-Nazi lawyer, established ties with CAUSE that remain today. After the Southern Poverty Law Center labeled it a hate group, Lyons disbanded the foundation in 1998 and established the Southern Legal Resources Center as its replacement. Much of the activity in the new center has been directed toward conducting legal battles to retain the Confederate flag on state flags. **See also** Aryan Nations; Butler, Richard Girnt; Fort Smith Sedition Trial; White Supremacist Movement.

Suggested readings: Martin A. Lee, *The Beast Reawakens* (Boston: Little, Brown, 1997); Lyn Riddle, "Suits Keep Rebel Flag Defender Scurrying," *Atlanta Journal and Constitution* (April 30, 1999), p. 1B; Southern Poverty Law Center, "In the Lyons Den," *SPLC Intelligence Report 99* (Summer 2000): 18–23.

Children of God/The Family

The religious cult Children of God and its successor the Family have been controversial both in the United States and abroad. A fundamentalist preacher, **David Brandt Berg**, founded a youth movement, Teens for Christ, in 1968. Berg's goal was to attract young converts from the hippie community to his increasingly anti-Christian religious views. Shortly after its founding, the Teens for Christ name was changed to the Children of God. Berg's success among wayward young adults and hippies in Southern California was spectacular. Part of his success

came from his new group's mandate that full-time members commit themselves totally. Adherents were charged to give up all material possessions, live in communes, and devote their lives to missionary work. This type of commitment appealed to many young people in the 1960s.

Berg, a charismatic leader, made most of the major decisions for the Children of God. His leadership role was reinforced by his belief that God had selected him to be the successor of the Old Testament's King David. The youthful members of the Children of God called Berg "Moses David" or "Father David." Berg attacked established churches as being ineffective in fulfilling the needs of modern worshipers, and he urged a return to the early church in which all believers lived together and shared all possessions. He based much of his teaching on his interpretation of the Book of Revelations, and he preached the coming of the anti-Christ and the Apocalypse. Many of his teachings were also anti-government, anti-Semitic, and anti–world government. Berg was an admirer of Muammar Qaddafi, the chief of state of Libya, and his followers cast Qaddafi as a Messiah-like figure. In 1969 Berg predicted that a major earthquake was about to hit Southern California, and he warned his supporters to disperse to other localities. Members of the Children of God became nomads who traveled in packs around the United States preaching Berg's message of salvation. In 1970 Berg took about 200 of his followers to an abandoned ranch near Thurber, Texas, where they formed a large commune. Another large commune remained at an old mission building on Skid Row in Los Angeles. Berg closed his two large communes in the United States in September 1971 and advised his members to form into smaller communes before re-forming them in other countries. He believed that the United States would soon fall to communism, and he wanted to preserve his cult. His adherents spread to every continent and established communes at hundreds of sites. By January 1973, Berg declared that his group had 2,400 full-time members in 140 colonies in forty countries. Berg kept control over his missionaries by sending out a steady stream of letters called "Mo Letters," which gave guidance on all matters both personal and spiritual.

In the mid-1970s, Berg made a series of decisions that threatened the ability of the Children of God to continue to function in the United States and in other countries. First, Berg decreed that extramarital sex was permissible among the members of the Children of God. In May 1976 he advanced the idea of using female members to convert men to the cult by engaging in sexual relationships with them. This practice was called "flirty fishing." Complicating the use of this practice was Berg's absolute prohibition against the use of birth control techniques. News of the practice of flirty fishing hit the American media. A nationwide controversy developed among political and religious leaders, and these leaders attacked this practice. The subsequent increase in the number of births among members of the Children of God only increased the hostility of outsiders. Finally, rumors began to surface about possible child abuse and sexual abuse of minors by members of the cult. These rumors led governments in Argentina, Australia, France, Great Britain, Paraguay, and Spain to arrest members on various moral charges. While most of those arrested were released after cult members refused to cooperate with authorities and the charges proved impossible to substantiate, questions about the conduct of members of the cult continued. In 1977 Berg made major changes in the organization of the Children of God. First, he purged 300 of the top leaders and replaced them with others. Then, he renamed the cult the Family of Love. By this time, most of their missionary work in the United States had ceased. By April 1981, the renamed Family of Love had colonies in seventy-six countries, including some Muslim countries, and its membership was nearly 9,000.

The worldwide missionary activities of the Family of Love continued until another reorientation took place in 1987. In the next decade, Berg gradually relinquished control over the group allowing member groups considerable autonomy. In 1987 Berg decided to reassert central control over the cult. The twin scourges of AIDS and venereal disease caused the leadership to call off flirty fishing. Child sex and incest were also banned. A central office, World Services, was established to oversee operations. Leaders other than Berg had assumed importance, including his son, Jonathan Berg, and his second wife, Maria. By July 1988, the Family of Love had over 12,000 members, but more than half of the membership were children. Despite his efforts to reassert his influence, Berg's life of seclusion made it difficult. His health was failing and he died in November 1994. Maria Berg replaced her husband as the official leader of the cult.

Because many of the cult members believed that the Apocalypse was approaching and Christ would reappear, they began returning to the United States in the early 1990s. Even the fact that Berg's prediction of 1993 as the date of the Apocalypse had proven false had not deterred the faithful. These members of the Family have established more than twenty communal homes around the United States. They work hard to project a clean-cut, friendly family image. Members still conduct missionary work but in a less controversial fashion using street preaching as their main recruiting tactic. They no longer place as much emphasis on recruiting but in raising their large families in their faith. Leaders now emphasize building the commitment to the Family among its followers' children. The common practice is to integrate children into all the activities of the cult at the age of twelve and have them assume adult responsibilities. **See also** Berg, David Brandt; Cults.

Suggested readings: James R. Lewis, *Cults in America; A Reference Handbook* (Santa Barbara, Calif.: ABC-CLIO, 1998); James R. Lewis and J. Gordon Melton, eds., *Sex Slander and Salvation: Investigating the Family/Children of God* (Stanford, Calif.: Center for Academic Publishing, 1994); Timothy Miller, ed., *America's Alternative Religions* (New York: State University of New York Press, 1995); Evan Moore, "Children of

God Cult Returns as the Family/Religious Groups Says It Has Changed Its Ways," *Houston Chronicle* (October 10, 1993), p. A1; Sara Moran, *The Secret World of Cults: From Ancient Druids to Heaven's Gate* (Godalming, U.K.: CLB International, 1999); Gustav Niebuhr, " 'The Family' and the Final Harvest," *Washington Post* (June 2, 1993), p. A1; Roy Rivenburg, "25 Years Ago, the Children of God's Gospel of Free Love Outraged Critics," *Los Angeles Times* (March 21, 1993), p. E1.

Children of Noah (See B'nai Noah)

Christian Defense League (CDL)

The Christian Defense League (CDL), an extremist anti-Semitic group organized to build a white Christian movement, was founded by **James K. Warner** in 1977. Warner had been an active member of **George Lincoln Rockwell**'s **American Nazi Party** in the 1960s before breaking with him and joining the **National State's Rights Party**. After moving to California in the mid-1960s, Warner formed a mail-order book service, the Sons of Liberty, to distribute anti-Semitic and racist publications. He also launched in 1971 the New Christian Crusade Church in Hollywood, California. In 1976 Warner moved his operations to Louisiana and joined **David Duke**'s Knights of the Ku Klux Klan. Following a consistent pattern of joining an extremist organization and then finding fault with it, Warner left the Klan to establish his own group.

Warner started the Christian Defense League as a vehicle to express his views on the danger of what he perceives to be a Jewish world conspiracy. Acting as its president, national director, and editor of the newsletter, *The CDL Report*, Warner runs the organization as his personal propaganda outlet. The national headquarters is located in Arabi, Louisiana. Membership in the CDL remains small, but this does not bother Warner. He has also reestablished the New Christian Crusade Church in Louisiana and claims a religious tax-exempt status with the Internal Revenue Service. From the CDL and his church, Warner continues to attack Jews and Israel. He subscribes to the **Christian Identity** doctrine that the white race descends from Adam, and the other races, especially the Jews, are products of Satan's union with Eve. Consequently, he was an early and vocal convert to the **Holocaust denial movement**. In 1984 the CDL established an office in Washington, D.C., and named it the Americans First Lobby. Warner also started a new magazine, *World Economic Review* (WER), to serve as a forum for his increasing interest in world affairs. Warner continues to spread his extremist views on world events from the CDL's various publications. **See also** Anti-Semitism; Christian Identity; Holocaust Denial Movement.

Suggested readings: Anti-Defamation League, *Danger: Extremism: The Major Vehicles and Voices on America's Far-Right Fringe* (New York: Anti-Defamation League, 1996); Bob Harvey, "Hate Groups Use Religion as Disguise," *Ottawa Citizen* (May 1, 1993), p. C5; Frank D. Roylance, "Internet Gives Youths Path to Hate Groups," *Baltimore Sun* (April 22, 1999), p. 11A.

Christian Identity

Christian Identity is an American religious movement which espouses white supremacy. This movement had its origins in nineteenth-century British Israelism, or Anglo-Israelism, which claimed that the population of Northern Europe, or Aryans, were the lost tribes of Israel. The original idea can be traced back to the eighteenth century when Richard Brothers, who lived from 1757 to 1824, claimed to have found biblical justification that Northern Europeans were in reality members of the lost tribes of Israel. John Wilson, a Scotsman, wrote the book *Lectures on Our Israelitish Origins* in 1840 which advanced this view. Among his arguments was that the British were the descendants of the tribe of Ephraim. He also traced the links between the last king of Judah, Zedekiah, and the British monarchy. Another British author, Edward Hine, published his book *Identification of the British Nation with Lost Israel* in 1871. His conversion to British Israelism began after hearing Wilson speak about it. He maintained that the Chosen People of the Bible were the people of the British Isles, not the Jews. Consequently, the Old Testament tells the story of the Aryans, not the Jews. In this version, Jesus was an Aryan, not a Jew. Subsequent interpretations continue that modern Jews are descendents of the Mongolian-Turkish Khazars.

The main outlines of British Israelism were brought to the United States and popularized in the 1880s. An early convert, Joseph Wild, the minister of the Union Congregational Church in Brooklyn, New York, was the first to suggest that the tribe of Manasseh had migrated to the American colonies and established the United States. Edward Hine visited America for four years between 1884 and 1888. Charles A. L. Totten, a U.S. Army officer, another convert to British Israelism, published a periodical, *Our Race: Its Origin and Destiny*. Totten served as the spokesperson for the movement during the rest of the nineteenth century. British Israelism also attracted various religious leaders in the United States, including Charles Fox Parham, a Kansas evangelical leader; J. H. Allen, the founder of the Church of God (Holiness); and Herbert W. Armstrong, the founder of the Worldwide Church of God. These prominent religious figures kept British Israelism alive in religious circles.

Howard B. Rand, an American lawyer from New England, and William J. Cameron, a Canadian anti-Semitic journalist, ensured that British Israelism stayed alive in American secular life in the early twentieth century. Rand traveled around the United States in the 1920s preaching the doctrine of British Israelism. He also published a British Israelism magazine, *Destiny*. Cameron was even more influential because he assumed the editorship of Henry Ford's newspaper, the *Dearborn Independent*. He provided much of the anti-Semitic material that appeared in that newspaper. Another impor-

tant figure was Reuben Sawyer, the pastor of the East Side Christian Church in Portland, Oregon. His activity in the **Ku Klux Klan** in the early 1920s brought the Klan's brand of **anti-Semitism** into British Israelism. In a series of conferences held in the late 1930s, leaders of British Israelism made contact with **Gerald Lyman Kenneth Smith** and his followers. Soon afterward, **Wesley Swift** started developing his interpretation, which led to the Christian Identity movement. His contribution was to add a more virulent brand of racism to British Israelism.

Modern Christian Identity has various ideological branches, but certain ideas are common to all of them. The theory of Christian Identity has no place for any other than the Aryans. In this doctrine, God commands that the white race dominate nonwhite people. The dark races, or "mud people," are products of whites mating with animals. Nonwhites are to be tolerated like animals, but they are not to be allowed to pollute the blood of white races. The Jews are the products of Satan's impregnation of Eve. Jews, as the products of the seed of Satan, deserve to be eradicated. Since the white race is God's chosen people, God directed his ordained representatives to come and gather in America. One of the lost tribes, the Manasseh tribe, settled in the American colonies. God gave the Manasseh tribe the message to compose the Declaration of Independence, the U.S. Constitution, and the Bill of Rights. Subsequent amendments to the Constitution are illegal and the products of Jewish interference. This social determinism is based on a crude Social Darwinism called Life Law by the movement. Society is in a perpetual war between the white race and the communist-Jewish forces. Unless society reverses its course, followers of Christian Identity believe that the white race will lose its struggle against the forces of darkness.

The Christian Identity movement has become a centralizing force among extremist groups. Before it gained acceptance by most of the right-wing groups, rivalries between the various factions was so intense that leaders spent almost as much energy and time fighting with each other over ideology and tactics as they did against the supposed enemy. This disunity has modified under the influence of **Richard Girnt Butler** and his efforts to unify the **white supremacist movement**. Now the Christian Identity movement allows its members to practice bigotry, hatred, and violence under the guise of religion. Other prominent Christian Identity leaders are **Peter Peters**, in Colorado; **Dan Gayman**, in Missouri; and Robert Millar, in Oklahoma. Although each of these leaders subscribes to his own interpretation of Christian Identity, they unite behind its basic tenet of white supremacy. **See also** Aryan Nations; Butler, Richard Girnt; Elohim City; Gayman, Dan; Peters, Peter; Swift, Wesley.

Suggested readings: James Coates, *Armed and Dangerous: The Rise of the Survivalist Right* (New York: Hill and Wang, 1987); Raphael S. Ezekiel, *The Racist Mind: Portraits of American Neo-Nazis and Klansmen* (New York: Penguin Books, 1995); Jeffrey Kaplan, *Radical Religion in America: Millenarian Movements from the Far Right to the Children of Noah* (Syracuse, N.Y.: Syracuse University Press, 1997); Timothy Miller, ed., *America's Alternative Religions* (New York: State University of New York Press, 1995); Scott Parks, "Outposts of Race-Based Theology," *Dallas Morning News* (August 5, 1995), p. 1G; Southern Poverty Law Center, "Identity Crisis: Expanding Race-Hate Faith Underlies Movement," *SPLC Intelligence Report* 89 (Winter 1998): 7–12; Jerome Walters, *One Aryan Nation Under God: Exposing the New Racial Extremists* (Cleveland: Pilgrim Press, 2000).

Christian Patriot Movement (See Common Law Courts Movement; Militia Movement)

Christian-Patriots Defense League (C-PDL)

The Christian-Patriots Defense League (C-PDL) once sponsored paramilitary survivalist training. John R. Harrell, the founder of this group, was a successful businessman who made a fortune selling mausoleums and agriculture real estate. After recovering from

cancer of the lymph glands in 1959, he decided to dedicate his life to fighting what he viewed as an international Jewish conspiracy. Harrell also established a tax-exempt church, the Christian Conservative Church, in Louisville, Illinois. In 1960 Harrell ran for the U.S. Senate in Illinois, but he was decisively defeated. He became a friend of **Robert Bolivar DePugh** and supported his anti-communist anti-government Minutemen organization. He spent four and a half years in prison in Terre Haute, Indiana, and Leavenworth, Kansas, for harboring a marine fugitive from military justice in the mid-1960s.

In 1969 he returned from prison to his hometown of Louisville, Illinois. In 1976 Harrell organized the Christian-Patriots Defense League as a paramilitary survivalist group. Headquarters for C-PDL was a 220-acre compound near Licking, Missouri. In 1984 Harrell opened another survivalist training site in West Virginia near Smithville. At both sites, trainers indoctrinated participants in survivalist ideology and conducted military training. Two of his key trainers were Colonel B. F. von Stahl and Colonel Gordon "Jack" Mohr. Harrell was a strict believer in the segregation of the races, and the ideology taught at these camps was that of the white supremacy of **Christian Identity**. The government estimates that more than a thousand participants passed through these camps. Each year Harrell held a Christian-Patriots Defense League Freedom Festival in Louisville, Illinois. At this festival, Harrell sponsored Christian Identity materials, paramilitary seminars, and survivalist gear and equipment. By the end of the 1980s, the C-PDL ceased to be a leader in the survivalist movement as other groups assumed much of its role. Many of its graduates, however, moved on to more activist organizations, and the training learned at these survivalist camps has been passed on to new extremists. Harrell also had close ties in the early 1980s with the **Covenant, the Sword, and the Arm of the Lord** (CSA). The C-PDL became defunct in the 1990s. By 1995 Harrell was broke and lived on his social security checks.

See also Christian Identity; DePugh, Robert Bolivar; Minutemen Movement.

Suggested readings: James Coates, *Armed and Dangerous: The Rise of the Survivalist Right* (New York: Hill and Wang, 1987); Vincent Coppola, *Dragons of God: A Journey Through Far-Right America* (Atlanta, Ga.: Longstreet Press, 1996); Phillip Finch, *God, Guts and Guns* (New York: Seaview/Putnam, 1983).

Christian Reconstruction (See Committee of the States and League of the South)

Church of the American Knights of the Ku Klux Klan

The Church of the American Knights of the Ku Klux Klan is the most active Klan organization in existence today, and it is a throwback to earlier violent Klan groups. Jeffery "Jeff" Berry started the American Knights of the Ku Klux Klan in Butler, Indiana, in 1995 and then in 1999 changed the name to the Church of the American Knights of the Ku Klux Klan. As the leader, he has assumed the title of imperial wizard. Berry operates his group out of his hometown of Butler, Indiana. Berry and his followers use hate language to attack opponents and recruit new members. To join the church, it takes $20 for an application fee and money to lease Klan robes. Leaders claim thousands of members in more than twenty states, but the exact number of Berry's followers is difficult to estimate. The best estimate made by the Southern Poverty Law Center in 1999 was 2,000, but the number of active members is much smaller. This group is attracting new members by targeting high school students at racially troubled schools.

Many members of the church have criminal records. Berry is no exception; he has a 1994 felony conviction involving a home improvement scam. He received a three-year suspended sentence along with a three-year term of probation. To win this reduced sentence, Berry had to become a drug informant for the local police. Berry had two other runins with the law in 1996, but efforts to revoke his probation proved unsuccessful. Five of Berry's close associates have been convicted of crimes ranging from rape to attempted murder. Jimmy Ray Shelton, Berry's former national security chief, was convicted in September 1999 of two counts of attempted capital murder of a police officer in Bastrop, Texas. In November 1999, Berry and his associates threatened two television reporters over videotapes of interviews and demanded the tapes. The Southern Poverty Law Center instituted a civil lawsuit over the incident.

Most of the modern Klan organizations have been trying to become more respectable by moderating their rhetoric and policies in an attempt to enter mainstream American politics. Berry and the members of the Church of the American Knights of the Ku Klux Klan have repudiated this more moderate approach, and they resort to the traditional hate messages of the old-fashioned Klan groups. Berry rails against the traditional Klan hate list of blacks, Jews, and the actions of the federal government. His confrontational tactics and frequent rallies have made life difficult for local law enforcement agencies. Other Klan organizations have downplayed the use of hoods and robes in public, but Berry and his group flaunt them. Berry has also looked for nontraditional ways to attract attention, including a 1996 appearance on Jerry Springer's television show. In March 1998, Berry blackmailed Cicero, Illinois, into giving him $10,000 to avoid a lawsuit over a parade permit. In 2000 Berry ran into legal problems stemming from the November 1999 unlawful false imprisonment of the two journalists and for the assault on a black man in Hazard, Kentucky, after a Klan rally. He tried to evade possible court judgments by transferring his financial assets to family members, but a state court order ended this attempt. See also Ku Klux Klan.

Suggested readings: Associated Press, "KKK Finds New Way to Spread Message," *Star Tribune* [Minneapolis] (April 17, 1998), p. 21A; William Claiborne, "Community vs. Klan in a

Context of Rights," *Washington Post* (January 19, 2001), p. A3; Southern Poverty Law Center, "Cornered Knight," *SPLC Intelligence Report* 100 (Fall 2000): 32–33; Southern Poverty Law Center, "Knights of Thuggery; Klan Group Builds Record of Aggressive Action," *SPLC Intelligence Report* 93 (Winter 1999): 33–37.

Church of the Creator (COTC)

The Church of the Creator, an anti-Christian, white supremacist, religious group, has been a leader in promoting extremism in the United States. **Ben Klassen** founded the church in 1973 in Lighthouse Point, Florida, before moving the church to Otto, North Carolina, in 1982. Klassen had long been active in extremist politics and had run for political office in Florida. He rejected the **John Birch Society** for being too liberal and repudiated George Wallace and his politics for being too soft. His rejection of American political institutions extended to an abhorrence of Christianity. He believed Christianity to be a religion for weaklings. In his two books, *Nature's Eternal Religion* and *The White Man's Bible*, Klassen reveals the white supremacy doctrinal underpinnings of his church. To reinforce his position within the Church of the Creator, Klassen proclaimed himself "pontifex maximus," or the supreme leader. He also claimed a federal tax exemption for the church as a religious organization. Later, state authorities overturned his tax-exempt designation. Despite the lack of members at his North Carolina church, the Church of the Creator expanded rapidly to the other parts of the country. By the middle 1980s, the Church of the Creator had become a leader in the anti-Christian **white supremacist movement**.

The Church of the Creator fell on hard times in the early 1990s because of legal problems. A minister in the Church of the Creator, George David Loeb, killed a black sailor in Florida in May 1991. Worried about the prospect of losing his property in the civil court case, Klassen sold his church property to **William Pierce** of the **National Alliance**. In ill health and depressed, he committed suicide in August 1993. The family of the sailor, Harold Mansfield, sued the Church of the Creator in March 1994 for contributing to their son's death. Despite Klassen's shift of property and other efforts to avoid payment, the Mansfields won a $1 million damage award against the Church of the Creator. Klassen's legacy was a series of Church of the Creator organizations around the United States and several spin-off churches. The most famous of the spin-offs is **Matthew Hale's World Church of the Creator**. Hale borrowed both the anti-Christian doctrine and the organization of Klassen's original church. **See also** Hale, Matthew; Klassen, Ben; World Church of the Creator.

Suggested readings: Quinton Elison, "Seeds of White Supremacist Group Sown in WNC, "*Asheville Citizen-Times* [North Carolina] (July 20, 1999), p. 1; Sarah Henry, Fariba Nawa, and Sunny Park, "Marketing Hate," *Los Angeles Times* (December 12, 1993), Magazine, p. 18; Robin Mitchell, "Hate Group Tied to Slayings Got Its Start in Florida," *St. Petersburg Times* (July 7, 1999), p. 1A; Ronald Smothers, "Supremacist Told to Pay Black Family," *New York Times* (May 20, 1996), p. A13; Southern Poverty Law Center, "Church of the Creator: A History," *SPLC Intelligence Report* 95 (Summer 1999): 21–25.

Church of the First Born of the Fullness of Times/Church of the Lamb of God

The Church of the First Born of the Fullness of Times and its offshoot, the Church of the Lamb of God, are dissident wings of the Church of Jesus Christ of Latter-Day Saints (LSD). Joel Franklin LeBaron and his brother **Ervil LeBaron** were raised as members of the Mormon Church, but they rejected the anti-polygamy stance of the church. In 1944 the leaders of the Mormon Church excommunicated the LeBaron family for practicing polygamy. The LeBarons affiliated themselves with other Mormon polygamists. Joel LeBaron had a vision in 1955 that he was the rightful successor of Joseph Smith, Jr., the founder of the LDS Church, and he needed to establish a new church. Joel LeBaron founded the Church of the First Born of the Fullness of Times on September 21, 1955. He preached that only by a strict adherence to the Ten Commandments would the Messiah return. Joel LeBaron appointed his brother, Ervil LeBaron, as patriarch of the new church in 1961. Soon it became apparent to the members that Ervil was too autocratic and unstable to continue as a leader in the church, and Joel removed Ervil as patriarch. This action infuriated Ervil and Joel responded by excommunicating him from the church. Ervil counterattacked by calling in public for Joel's removal as the head of the church and even for his death. Several of Ervil's followers killed Joel LeBaron on August 20, 1972. Ervil served one year of a twelve-year prison sentence for complicity in the murder of his brother before an appeals court overturned his sentence. In 1975 a close associate of Joel's was killed by some of Ervil's supporters. Again Ervil served prison time for complicity to the murder.

Since Ervil LeBaron no longer had a position in the Church of the First Born of the Fullness of Times, in 1975 he founded the Church of the Lamb of God. An older brother, Verlan LeBaron, became head of Joel's church shortly after Joel's death. Verlan retained control of the church until his death in an automobile accident in 1981. Ervil's new church was more authoritarian than his brother's church, but his new church had barely opened its doors before he was in legal trouble again. While a member of Joel's church, Ervil had developed the doctrine of civil law. In this doctrine, defectors from the faith, adulterers, and murderers were to suffer the death penalty. Following this doctrine, Ervil advocated that the enemies of his church must be destroyed. Anyone leaving his church had to be killed before believers could inherit God's kingdom on earth. He formed death squads to carry out his death sentences. For years, he plotted to have his followers assassinate Joel LeBaron's successor, Verlan LeBaron. In 1977 he ordered the murder of Rulon Allred, a staunch supporter of Joel LeBaron. Ervil may have ordered as many as two dozen other murders. He fled to Mexico to avoid prosecution for these murders. It was several years before authorities were able to arrest Ervil. In 1979 he was sentenced to life in prison for the Allred murder. Ervil continued to direct the affairs of his church from the Utah State Prison until he died of a heart attack in 1981. At his death, he left a 500-page book of names of people whom he had condemned to death for transgressions committed against him or his church.

Ervil's son, Aaron LeBaron, assumed control of the Church of the Lamb of God. Arthur LeBaron, the eldest son, was the natural successor, but he was unable to control the membership. Many members had defected during Ervil's last days, and dissension developed among the followers of Arthur LeBaron. A number of these dissidents disappeared and their bodies have never been found. Efforts were made by leaders of rival branches to reunite in 1982, but the hardliners refused to compromise on Ervil LeBaron's commandments. Arthur LeBaron and Leo Evoniuk started feuding, and Arthur was murdered in late December 1983. Later, Evoniuk and several of his key followers were killed in a series of murders beginning in 1983 and lasting to 1987. Heber LeBaron and Andre LeBaron assumed the leadership of the hard-line Mexican branch of the church, but Aaron LeBaron soon challenged them for leadership. They reached a compromise: Aaron became the spiritual teacher, and the others became chief ministers. After Aaron assumed the role of Ervil LeBaron, he continued the practice of polygamy and adherence to the civil law. In June 1988, three former members of the church, Duane Chynoweth, Mark Chynoweth, Edward Marston, and an eight-year-old girl were murdered in Houston and Dallas, Texas. The girl was killed because she had witnessed the other killings. Aaron LeBaron was arrested for the murders, and in June 1997 he received a forty-five-year prison sentence for murder and racketeering. He was also fined $134,000 in restitution to pay for the funerals of the victims. Both the Church of the First Born of the Fullness of Times and the Church of the Lamb of God are still in operation and the hostility remains, but their headquarters and services are centered in the Chihuahua region of Mexico. **See also** Cults; LeBaron, Ervil.

Suggested readings: Karina Bland, "Offspring Survive Polygamist Sect Horror," *Arizona Republic* (July 5, 1998), p. A1; Ben Bradlee and Dale Van Atta, *Prophet of Blood: The Untold Story of Ervil LeBaron and the Lambs of God* (New York: Putnams, 1981); Rena Chynoweth and Dean M. Shapiro, *The Blood Covenant* (Austin, Tex.: Diamond Books, 1990); James R. Lewis, *Peculiar Prophets: A Biographical Dictionary of New Religions* (St. Paul, Minn.: Paragon House, 1999); John Makeig, "Cultist LeBaron Is Convicted in Conspiracy to Kill," *Houston Chronicle* (March 1, 1997), p. 33; Sarah Moran, *The Secret World of Cults: From Ancient Druids to Heaven's Gate* (Godalming, U.K.: CLB International, 1999).

Church Universal and Triumphant

The Church Universal and Triumphant is a doomsday survivalist church. Mark L. Prophet founded the church in 1958 under the name Summit Lighthouse. A former salesperson, Prophet had been active in the I AM religious movement of Guy and Edna Ballard. From this group, he borrowed the concept of ascended masters. This theory maintains that great political and spiritual leaders have ascended to a place where they oversee human development and communicate with worthy living beings. Prophet also had contact with the Lighthouse of Freedom group of Francis K. Ekey. His new Summit Lighthouse was an offshoot of the latter group. In 1963 Prophet married Elizabeth Clare Wulf, and together they ran the new organization. The Prophets moved their headquarters from Beacons Head, Virginia, to Colorado Springs, Colorado, in 1966. Prophet believed that he was the intermediary between the ascended masters and the rest of humanity. During the next decade until his death in February 1973, Prophet pub-

lished his interpretations in a series of publications.

After his death, Prophet's wife, Elizabeth Clare Prophet, assumed control of the church. Under her leadership, the church concentrated on producing a blend of Eastern and New Age religious thought and practice with millennium overtones. In 1974 Elizabeth Prophet incorporated the church and renamed it the Church Universal and Triumphant. Following her late husband's lead, Elizabeth Prophet claims to be a messenger from God, speaking for a variety of ascended masters, including Jesus Christ, Buddha, Mohammed, Hercules, William Shakespeare, and several others. After moving the church from Colorado to Malibu, California, in 1978, Elizabeth Prophet transferred the church to a large ranch, Paradise Valley, in Montana near Yellowstone Park. In March 1990, Prophet, speaking as Guru Ma, warned of a coming nuclear attack on the United States by the Soviet Union. This prophecy caused a mad rush on the church's ranch which included underground bomb shelters. At this 30,000-acre property, the church sold survival condominiums at a premium price. Among the supplies gathered for the forthcoming Armageddon was a large stockpile of semiautomatic weapons and handguns. On May 11, 1990, nearly 3,000 members gathered at the compound to await the end of American society and possibly the world. When the expected event was not forthcoming, Prophet and the leaders of the Church Universal and Triumphant claimed that their prayers and faith had postponed the Apocalypse.

By the mid-1990s, the Church Universal and Triumphant had begun to experience financial difficulties. Although the leadership claimed credit for postponing the Apocalypse, many members found their faith in the church shaken. Defections started producing a cash-flow problem for the church. For a time the church was spending $120,000 a month more than the money it was earning. Even efforts to reduce expenses only lowered the deficit spending. To protect their investment in cattle from disease, church workers killed buffalo straying off Yellowstone National Park. These killings produced a backlash against the church when the press reported the incidents. Although Prophet had stepped down as church president in 1996, she was able to retain control of the church until she was diagnosed with Alzheimer's disease in November 1998. The church sold 12,000 acres of ranchland next to Yellowstone National Park's northern boundary in September 1999 to a coalition of federal and conservation groups who cooperated to buy the land for $13 million. These millions helped the church out of its financial debt, but the future of the Church Universal and Triumphant is in doubt because of the lack of a successor to Elizabeth Prophet. **See also** Cults.

Suggested readings: Sandi Dolbee and Philip J. Lavelle, "Her Own Prophet," *San Diego Union-Tribune* (June 27, 1997), p. E1; Sandi Dolbee and Philip J. Lavelle, "Troubled Karma; New Age Church Wants to Go Mainstream," *San Diego Union-Tribune* (November 12, 1997), p. A1; David Gelman, "From Prophets to Losses," *Newsweek* (March 15, 1993), p. 62; Holger Jensen, "Trouble in Paradise," *Macleans* (May 7, 1990), p. 33; James R. Lewis, *Peculiar Prophets: A Biographical Dictionary of New Religions* (St. Paul, Minn.: Paragon House, 1999); James R. Lewis and J. Gordon Melton, eds., *Church Universal and Triumphant in Scholarly Perspective* (Stanford, Calif.: Center for Academic Publishing, 1994); Harvey Shepherd, "Universal and Triumphant Rally Here, *Gazette* [Montreal] (August 22, 1998); Matthew L. Wald, "Federal Land Deal Protects Yellowstone Herd and Geysers," *New York Times* (August 22, 1999), p. 30.

Cleaver, Leroy Eldridge (1935–1998)

Eldridge Cleaver, one of the most militant leaders of the **Black Panther Party**, was born on August 31, 1935, in Wabbaseka, Arkansas. His father was a waiter and pianist and his mother was a schoolteacher. After his father obtained a job as a railroad waiter, the family moved first to Phoenix, Arizona, and then to Los Angeles, California, in the middle of World War II. Cleaver's parents divorced when he was twelve, and he had difficulty coping with the divorce. He began stealing and selling marijuana. His career at Belmont High School ended early with his arrest for distributing drugs. Cleaver finished high school at the Preston School of Industry before being sent to Soledad Prison in 1954. After his release from prison in 1957, Cleaver went on a crime spree and ended up back in jail with a two- to fourteen-year sentence at Folsom Prison. He educated himself in prison and became a Marxist. While in Folsom, Cleaver converted to the **Nation of Islam** following the example of **Malcolm X**. Malcolm X's assassination devastated him and made him want to follow in his footsteps. Beverly Axelrod, a white civil rights lawyer who was impressed with Cleaver's prison writings, lobbied for his early release from prison. During his eight years in Folsom, Cleaver wrote the book *Soul on Ice*. He was freed on parole in November 1966.

At a memorial to honor Malcolm X, Cleaver and **Huey P. Newton** renewed an earlier acquaintanceship. In February 1967, Cleaver joined the Black Panther Party as its minister of information. He helped start the party's newspaper, the *Black Panther*. Cleaver also wrote articles for the magazine *Ramparts*. In December 1967, he married Kathleen Neal. When Newton was arrested after a shoot-out with Oakland police, Cleaver organized a "Free Huey" campaign intended to classify Newton as a political prisoner. With Newton under arrest and **Bobby Seale** in prison, Cleaver became the de facto head of the Black Panthers. His parole board warned him that his political activities with the Black Panthers were endangering his parole and that he was in danger of going back to jail. On April 6, 1968, Cleaver found himself and other party members in a gunfight with the Oakland police. Bobby Hutton was killed and Cleaver was arrested. Financial aid and recruits flowed into the party, but Cleaver was charged with violating his parole. Freed from jail and facing a trial on three counts of attempted murder and three counts of assault with a deadly weapon on a police officer, Cleaver fled to Cuba in May 1969.

Cleaver was an international fugitive for nearly seven years. He left Cuba and moved to Algeria. In 1971 he broke with Newton over the direction of the party. Cleaver and his followers supported a revolutionary program in contrast to Newton's more moderate reformist approach. After a dispute with the Algerian government in 1973, Cleaver moved to Paris, France. Slowly Cleaver became disenchanted with Marxism. He decided to return to the United States in 1975 where he served eight months in jail and five years on probation. His next book, *Soul on Fire*, marked a complete change in his political orientation. He had repudiated Marxism and experienced a religious conversion. His advocacy of conservative Republicanism surprised and alienated many of his former colleagues in the Black Panther Party. In 1988 Cleaver found himself in legal trouble over charges of burglary and cocaine possession. Four years later, he was arrested again for cocaine possession. Cleaver died on May 1, 1998. **See also** Black Panther Party, Newton, Huey P.; Seale, Bobby.

Suggested readings: Bart Barnes, "Eldridge Cleaver, Author and Black Panther Leader, Dies," *Washington Post* (May 2, 1998), p. D6; Jim Haskins, *Power to the People: The Rise and Fall of the Black Panther Party* (New York: Simon and Schuster Books for Young Readers, 1997); John Hughes, "Former Panther Eldridge Cleaver: A Relic with a Cause," *Seattle Times* (May 3, 1998), p. L5; John Kifner, "Eldridge Cleaver, Black Panther Who Became G.O.P. Conservative, Is Dead at 62," *New York Times* (May 2, 1998), p. B8; Jennifer Warren, "Former Black Panther Eldridge Cleaver Dies at 62," *Los Angeles Times* (May 2, 1998), p. A1.

Committee of the States

The Committee of the States, an anti-government group, operated in California in the mid-1980s. William Potter Gale, a retired colonel in the U.S. Army and a World War II veteran, was the principal leader of the Committee of the States. Gale had been lobbying for its creation since 1982. His efforts were successful, and forty-four delegates from twelve states founded the organization on July 4, 1984. These delegates were a representative sampling of the leadership of the anti-government movement in the early 1980s. They signed a sixteen-page compact entitled, "Committee of the States in Congress, July 4, 1984." In this document, the delegates meeting at Gale's Manasseh Ranch near Mariposa, California, declared themselves an independent entity from the U.S. Congress and all other legislative bodies. They took the name Committee of the States and its legal precedent from the original Articles of Confederation of 1781, which had been instituted before the U.S. Constitution of 1787. The basis for their claim of independence was that the U.S. government was Satanic and illegal. The delegates wanted a theocracy, which is a society ruled by biblical law. This idea is based on the theory of Christian Reconstruction which is described in Rousas John Rushdoony's book *The Institutes of Biblical Law*, published in 1973. Consequently, members of the Committee of the States refused to recognize the authority of the federal government, including paying income taxes, abiding by state requirements for driver's licenses, and paying for license plates. A provision also existed in the compact that interference with the functions and activities of the Committee of the States or its delegates would result in the imposition of the death penalty. A paramilitary force, the Unorganized Militia, was entrusted to carry out its mandates. Richard Van Hazel, a Vietnam veteran and former Arizona law enforcement agent, was made commander in chief of the Unorganized Militia. Although Gale was the acknowledged leader of this movement, he did not sign the compact. His justification was that, as a retired military officer receiving a federal pension, he was ineligible to sign.

Federal agents became aware of the existence of the Committee of the States and took legal actions against it. The committee recorded its compact as a legal document in Mariposa less than a week after the delegates signed the document. A federal undercover operative infiltrated the organization shortly afterward. This agent reported threats against federal agents and judges. On October 23, 1986, federal officials arrested the seven principal leaders of the Committee of the States, including Gale and Fortunato "Slim" Parrino, a retired sheriff. In retaliation for Gale's being held in jail in Las Vegas, Nevada, Gale's supporters launched seven homemade pipe bombs at the Chet Holfield Federal Building in Laguna Niguel, California, on March 2, 1987. Although this attack did little actual damage, the government released Gale the next day.

After these arrests, David Moran, a member of the Committee of the States, went on a revenge crime spree. As protest, he robbed three liquor stores, a Seven-Eleven store, and an Arco minimart in the area around Winters, California, in early December 1986. Police determined that Moran was a suspect, and he went underground for almost a week. Two California highway patrolmen stopped Moran and a friend for a broken auto light on his car on December 8, 1986, and in the ensuing gunfight Moran was killed. He left a last will and testament in which he claimed that he was following in the footsteps of his hero, **Robert Jay Mathews.**

The principal leaders of the Committee of the States went on trial for conspiracy in 1987. In a trial held in Las Vegas, Nevada, beginning on September 15, 1987, William Potter Gale, Gary Dolphin, Mike McCray, Patrick McCray, Slim Parrino, and Richard Van Hazel, the defendants, were convicted of conspiracy to threaten government officials on October 2, 1987. Gale received a sentence of one year and one day in jail and a five-year probation. Parrino's sentence was identical to Gale's. The other sentences varied from Mike McCray's and Richard Van Hazel's seven years to one year in custody of the attorney general and a five-year probation. Terms of the probation prohibited their association with anti-government groups. Gale died within weeks of his sentence. Without Gale's leadership, the Com-

mittee of the States withered away. **See also** Gale, William Potter; League of the South.

Suggested readings: Robert A. Jones, "IRS Seizes Leader of Extremist Group in Death Threats," *Los Angeles Times* (October 30, 1986), part 1, p. 3; Metro Desk, "William P. Gale; Led Several Racist Groups," *Los Angeles Times* (May 4, 1988), part 1, p. 24; New York Times National Desk, "6 Face Trial on Charges They Threatened the I.R.S.," *New York Times* (September 15, 1987), p. A16; Cheri Seymour, *Committee of the States: Inside the Radical Right* (Mariposa, Calif.: Camden Place Communications, 1991).

Committee to Restore the Constitution (CRC)

The Committee to Restore the Constitution (CRC), a right-wing organization which fights those it believes intend to overthrow the U.S. Constitution, was founded by Archibald E. "Arch" Roberts in 1970 who serves as its director. Roberts, a retired U.S. Army lieutenant colonel, served in the 1960s under Major General Edwin A. Walker in the 24th Infantry Division in Europe. The military careers of both Walker and Roberts were shortened by their activities in support of right-wing causes while on active duty. The headquarters of the CRC is located in Fort Collins, Colorado, and Roberts, who is now in his mid-80s, remains the head of the organization. Others who have assumed importance in the CRC are John R. Rarick, a former U.S. representative from Louisiana; Lawrence T. Patterson, publisher of *Criminal Politics*; Eustace Mullins, a prominent anti-Semitic writer; and Ron Gostick, a Canadian anti-Semitic leader. The media organ for the CRC is the *Bulletin*. While anti-Semitic literature appears frequently in this publication, most of the space contains articles about purported domestic conspiracies to overthrow the U.S. government. Among the chief targets is the United Nations. Leaders of the CRC rail about the influence of the United Nations over the foreign policy of the United States. Another key target has been the Federal Reserve System. In Roberts's book *The Most Secret Science*, he charges that the Federal Reserve Act of 1913 is unconstitutional. The future of the CRC remains clouded because its fate is so closely tied to that of Roberts. The lack of an apparent successor and Roberts's age and health raise doubts about the CRC's future. **See also** Anti-Semitism: Common Law Courts Movement; Freemen Movement.

Suggested reading: Anti-Defamation League, *Danger: Extremism: The Major Vehicles and Voices on America's Far-Right Fringe* (New York: Anti-Defamation League, 1996).

Common Law Courts Movement

The Common Law Courts Movement unites a variety of anti-government groups that deny the legal authority of the federal and state governments and seek to create a new system to replace their legal institutions. Although the American legal system is based on English common law principles, political usage and court law have replaced many common law practices over the years. Common law extremists seek to return to an interpretation of common law that corresponds to their views, and in the process they reject federal and state legislation. Common law advocates believe that there are two types of law; political and common. They assert that political law is arbitrary because it changes with the political situation. Common law, in their view, is universal because it is a private legal system independent of politics. They further maintain that common law is made up of two parts: contract and criminal. Contract law is based on agreements between individuals, whereas criminal law is an encroachment on people and/or their property. Common law advocates believe that the American constitutional system is based on common law and reject criminal law outright. Outside of agreeing on these fundamental beliefs, common law advocates have widely different interpretations of history and politics.

Eugene Schroder, a farmer from Campo, Colorado, has been one of the most active leaders in the Common Law Courts Movement. Susan Hanson reported that, in a February 1996 interview at the headquarters of the American Agriculture Movement (AMM) in Colorado, Schroder made the statement that the federal government is now "an unconstitutional dictatorship." His view is that the national emergency laws passed in 1917 and the laws passed in 1933 to combat the Great Depression are unconstitutional, and legislation passed since these laws is illegal. Schroder has traveled the country expressing this interpretation and he has been able to attract those Americans who are embittered with the current legal system and those who oppose federal and state taxation systems.

Common law courts have been established in more than thirty states to transact official business. In cases of serious crimes, such as murder, robbery, and rape, these courts can mandate the death penalty, which is to be carried out the day after conviction. No lawyers or judges are allowed in the proceedings of common law courts, and the courts' judges are to be selected from the "most learned" in the group. In all cases, these courts return verdicts in favor of the plaintiff and against the federal, state, or local government. These courts produce pseudo-legal documents on foreclosures, taxes, and vehicle registration. Phony summonses and liens are also issued, which cause difficulties for real or perceived enemies. Traveling teams of instructors hold meetings around the country to educate followers in the ways in which to use the common law courts. A number of common law schools have been established since the mid-1980s to teach how to operate in a common law system.

Several political or protest groups have used common law courts to advance their anti-government agendas. An early convert was the **Posse Comitatus movement**. Although leaders of the Posse Comitatus movement used another legal pretext, which dates back to shortly after the Civil War, the intent is the same. After the demise of the Posse Comitatus movement, the Montana Freemen adopted the common law court system. Besides using false liens and summonses, the Freemen issued writs against local prosecutors and judges to intimidate them. These efforts led to a response by the federal and state governments which resulted in the Montana Freemen standoff in 1996. The next group to go this route was the Republic of Texas movement. The leaders of the Republic of Texas tried to use their common law court system against the state of Texas. The state reacted by arresting **Richard McLaren**'s faction of the Republic of Texas in Fort Davis and by passing a series of laws to ensure that the common law court system would be unable to intimidate Texas law enforcement agencies and the courts.

The refusal of common law advocates to obey laws has had tragic consequences. Early on the morning of June 28, 1995, Michael Hill, a former Canton, Ohio, policeman and a chaplain in the Ohio Militia, was killed after being stopped for displaying an illegal license plate. After declaring that the police lacked the authority to cite him for failure to have a legal license, he drove away. When he was forced to halt a second time, Hill brandished a 45-caliber handgun and was shot by a small-town policeman. Although a grand jury ruled that the shooting was justified, common law supporters have declared Hill a martyr to their cause. **See also** Freemen Movement; Posse Comitatus Movement; Republic of Texas.

Suggested readings: Stephen Braun, "Their Own Kind of Justice," *Los Angeles Times* (September 5, 1995), p. A1; T.C. Brown, "Justice for the Common Man?" *Plain Dealer* [Cleveland] (December 11, 1995), p. 1A; T. C. Brown, "Martyr for the Cause," *Plain Dealer* [Cleveland] (June 23, 1996), p. 6; T. C. Brown, "Uncommon Justice; Common-Law Courts," *Plain Dealer* [Cleveland] (March 2, 1997), p. 1A; Cara DeGette, "Waging Revolution with Rubber Checks," *Denver Post* (June 2, 1996), p. A1; Joel Dyer, *Harvest of Rage: Why Oklahoma City Is Only the Beginning* (Boulder, Colo.: Westview Press, 1997); Susan Hanson, "A True Patriot," *The American Lawyer* (May 1996), p. 59; Brad Knickerbocker, "New Tactics Run in Radicals; Law-Enforcement Agencies Are Prosecuting Militia, Tax Protesters More Successful," *Christian Science Monitor* (March 30, 1998), p. 1; Mike McIntire, "For Alienated Citizenry, Government Is the Enemy,"

Hartford Courant [Connecticut] (November 23, 1997), p. A1; Cheri Seymour, *Committee of the States: Inside the Radical Right* (Mariposa, Calif.: Camden Place Communications, 1991); Southern Poverty Law Center, "Crackdown: 'Common Law' Reels as 27 States Act," *SPLC Intelligence Report* 90 (Spring 1998): 12–13.

Communist Party USA/Provisional

The Communist Party USA/Provisional is a radical offshoot of the Communist Party USA, and its goal is to promote a revolution to overthrow the U.S. government and American society. Eugenio Parente-Ramos founded the party in 1972 on Long Island, New York, after leaving the more orthodox Marxist Progressive Labor Party (PLP). Parente-Ramos, whose real name was Gerald William Doeden, was a longtime supporter of left-wing revolutionary groups. At one time or another he had worked as a disc jockey and owned a left-wing bookstore in San Francisco, California. Parente-Ramos's death in March 1995 at the age of fifty-nine has left a leadership void in the party, but the party still functions and its members still consider it a revolutionary agent of change.

The Communist Party USA/Provisional has had a fluid membership history. At one time it had a membership as high as 800, but by the mid-1990s membership had slipped to the 150 to 400 range. While members reside in various states, including California, New Jersey, and Texas, most of the active members live in New York City. The organization recruits by offering young, idealistic individuals a variety of social services and then indoctrinates them into becoming antigovernment revolutionaries. Some former members describe the process as almost like belonging to a religious cult. A police raid in November 1996 in the Crown Heights section of Brooklyn, New York, demonstrates that the revolutionary orientation of the party remains in operation: thirty members of the party were arrested, and the authorities seized a large cache of rifles, shotguns, and submachine guns with ammunition and explosives. **See also** May 19th Communist Organization.

Suggested readings: Charisse Jones, "Grand Jury Seeks Reason Behind a Group's Arsenal," *New York Times* (November 14, 1996), p. B3; Fred Kaplan, "Raid Said to Expose Leftist Cult in NYC," *Boston Globe* (November 14, 1996), p. A3; Robert E. Kessler, "Shadowy Past/Gun Arrests Latest Event in Group's Secretive History," *Newsday* [New York] (November 17, 1996), p. A5; Steve Wick, "Effect of City Raid Being Felt on LI/Farm Group," *Newsday* [New York] (November 14, 1996), p. A6.

Coughlin, Charles (1891–1979)

Father Charles Coughlin, a Catholic priest, developed modern hate radio and turned his fascist views into a political weapon. He was born on October 25, 1891, in Hamilton, Ontario, Canada. His father held a variety of jobs as a coal stoker, baker, and salesman. His mother, who was a devout Catholic, wanted her only son to be a priest. Coughlin attended St. Michael's preparatory school in Toronto before entering the University of Toronto in 1907. Although his four years at the university showed him to be an indifferent student, he graduated in 1911. After a three-month tour in Europe, Coughlin began his studies for the priesthood at St. Basil's Seminary in Toronto. This institution was heavily influenced by the Basilian Order, whose members opposed modern economic development and wanted the world to return to a medieval, socially integrated society. After Coughlin was ordained a Catholic priest in June 1916, he left the order to become a diocesan priest in the Detroit area. His first job was teaching at Assumption College. Although he taught there for seven years, specializing in the dramatic arts, the school administrators were unhappy about his lack of cooperation with others and his unpopularity with other faculty members. After leaving the college, Coughlin's friendship with Bishop Michael Gallagher led the bishop to give Coughlin permission to establish the Shrine of the Little Flower in Royal Oak, Michigan.

Father Coughlin spent the rest of his life building this shrine. He worked closely with four other individuals to build his new church and further his career. These individuals were Fred and Lawrence Fisher, leading automobile suppliers; Eddie Rickenbacker, a World War I flying ace and president of Eastern Airlines; and George "Dick" Richards, the owner of the radio station WJR in Detroit and the owner of the Detroit Lions professional football team. His contacts with Richards allowed Coughlin to start his broadcasting career on October 17, 1926. Coughlin commenced these broadcasts to raise funds for his new church, but shortly after starting he turned to politics. Coughlin's magnificent voice and his mastery of mass psychology soon turned him into a national celebrity.

Father Coughlin was always an effective molder of public opinion, but the advent of the Great Depression after the 1929 Wall Street crash made him even more influential. He became a spokesperson for the victims of the depression who by now had become distrustful of the American financial and political establishment. His first target was communism, and he blamed it and atheism for the current state of affairs. His broadcasts were so popular that in the fall of 1930 the CBS national radio network picked up his broadcast. In a 1931 sermon he first introduced the theme that international financiers had caused the 1929 stock market crash and attributed the event to the inspiration of a Jew, Karl Marx. It was his increasingly hostile political attacks that led CBS not to renew his contract at the end of 1931; nevertheless, Coughlin was able to line up a chain of twenty-seven independent stations which covered the country from Bangor, Maine to Kansas City, Missouri for his broadcasts. He also started a series of brutal attacks against President Herbert Hoover. At this time, Coughlin met Franklin Delano Roosevelt for the first time and decided to support Roosevelt's presidential bid.

After Roosevelt was elected president, Coughlin had reservations about his policies, and in late 1934 he began to attack Roosevelt and his policies. The first attack came over the proposal for the United States to join the World Court. His help in defeating this bill in the U.S. Senate was the first blow in Coughlin's war on the New Deal. Earlier Coughlin had formed the National Union for Social Justice (NUSJ), a national grassroots lobbying organization of nearly 1.2 million supporters, to back his policies. Before the 1936 presidential election, Coughlin joined forces with **Gerald Lyman Kenneth Smith**, a former supporter of Huey Long and a notorious racist, and Dr. Francis E. Townsend, the head of the Townsend Clubs which lobbied for old age pensions, to form the Union Party to defeat President Roosevelt. This third party effort suffered an embarrassing defeat which further embittered Coughlin against Roosevelt and the New Deal.

After a brief respite from broadcasting to recover from the election, Coughlin returned to the airwaves with a vengeance. His hatred of Roosevelt increased, and Coughlin was drawn into the anti-Semitic camp. His close association with Henry Ford was an impetus. He came to share Ford's belief that an international Jewish conspiracy controlled the world's finances. Coughlin's acceptance of the authenticity of the *Protocols of the Elders of Zion* (1920) in 1938 marked his complete conversion into the fold of American **anti-Semitism**. From 1938 to 1940, Coughlin became increasingly shrill in his attacks on Jews and laudatory toward Adolf Hitler and Germany.

Father Coughlin's broadcasting career came to an end as a result of actions taken by the church hierarchy and America's entry into World War II. His mentor, Bishop Gallagher, died in January 1937, and his successor, Archbishop Mooney, attempted to control him. Mooney, however, had to act cautiously, and Coughlin used his national standing to thwart his efforts. In the end, Coughlin overstepped the boundaries of acceptability of the Catholic Church, and he was refused permission to continue to broadcast. The patriotism unleashed by

World War II made this action easier to justify. Coughlin retired to his church in Royal Oak and died in 1979. His legacy of hate radio, however, remains. **See also** American Fascism; Anti-Semitism.

Suggested readings: Sheldon Marcus, *Father Coughlin* (South Bend, Ind.: Notre Dame University Press, 1973); Charles J. Tull, *Father Coughlin and the New Deal* (Syracuse, N.Y.: Syracuse University Press, 1965); Donald Warren, *Radio Priest: Charles Coughlin the Father of Hate Radio* (New York: Free Press, 1996).

Council of Conservative Citizens (CCC)

The Council of Conservative Citizens (CCC) is the successor to the racist, anti-Semitic Citizens Councils of America (CCA) of the 1950s. Gordon Lee Baum founded the CCC on March 7, 1985, and its national headquarters is located in Saint Louis, Missouri. It publicizes itself as a grassroots organization fighting against the leftward bent of American government and society. By 1998 the CCC had formed chapters in twenty-two states with 15,000 dues-paying members. Baum remains the chief executive officer of the CCC. He was formerly a field director of the Citizens Councils of America and was instrumental in its merging into the CCC in 1989. Robert Patterson, the founder of Citizens Councils of America, is an active member of the CCC and speaks at its gatherings. The CCC publishes a newsletter, *Citizens Informer*, and has a Web site on the Internet. In the newsletter, on the Web site, and in its invitations to speakers, the CCC shows its orientation toward extremist views by sponsoring anti-black and anti-homosexual articles and speeches. Among the issues that this organization lobbies the U.S. Congress for are opposition to affirmative action, big government, gun control, and foreign immigration; behind these issues members of the CCC share a common anti-Semitic and white supremacy viewpoint. Members are opposed to the desegregation of public facilities, and they have been active in forming private white schools as alternatives to integrated school systems. Each issue of the

CCC's newsletter highlights minority crime statistics and editorializes against black crimes against whites. Among the most prominent speakers at its conventions have been **David Duke**, former leader of the **Ku Klux Klan** and an active white supremacist; Edward Butler, a **Christian Identity** preacher; Michael Collins Piper, a **Liberty Lobby** writer; and **James Wickstrom**, the former head of the **Posse Comitatus movement**. Recently the CCC has been leading the charge to retain the Confederate flag on the Mississippi state flag. **See also** Anti-Semitism.

Suggested readings: Allen G. Breed, "Council of Conservative Citizens; What Is This Group That Has Embroiled Senate Majority Leader Lott?" *Buffalo News* (February 7, 1999), p. 1H; Thomas B. Edsall, "Controversial Group Has Strong Ties to Both Parties in South," *Washington Post* (January 13, 1999), p. A3; Jo Mannies, "Gordon Baum Says He's Proud of His European Heritage; Critics Say He's a Racist," *St. Louis Post-Dispatch* (March 7, 1999), p. C1; Diane McWhorter, "Flag Vote Continues the Quest for Dixie's Soul," *USA Today* (April 17, 2001), p. 13A; Michael Powell, "White Wash: Suddenly, Gordon Baum, Small-Time Race Baiter, Is Big-Time News," *Washington Post* (January 17, 1999), p. F1; Southern Poverty Law Center, "Sharks in the Mainstream, Racism Underlies Influential 'Conservative' Group," *SPLC Intelligence Report* 93 (Winter 1999): 21–26.

Covenant, the Sword, and the Arm of the Lord (CSA)

The Covenant, the Sword, and the Arm of the Lord (CSA) was a paramilitary survivalist group with strong ties to the **Christian Identity** movement. Jim Ellison, a former fundamentalist minister from San Antonio, Texas, founded the CSA in 1971. Ellison had gone to college in Illinois before moving to San Antonio in 1962 to study at the School of the Ministry. He decided to form the CSA after surviving a serious accident while working as an iron worker. He moved the organization in 1976 to a mountain area on Bull Shoals Lake near Three Brothers, Arkansas. This 224-acre compound was given

the biblical name of Zarepath-Horeb. Leaders of the CSA built a complete society at this site with dormitories, factories, and electricity. Dozens of families lived in the compound and polygamy was practiced. At one time Jim Ellison had four wives.

The CSA made money in various ways. One of the factories was a firearms repair shop which converted semiautomatic weapons to illegal automatic weapons and constructed other weapons and explosives, including grenades. The factory made money by selling the altered weapons and explosives at gun shows. Weapons experts at the CSA also raised funds by holding weapons seminars. Another moneymaker was the running of military boot camps to train individuals in paramilitary tactics at the End-time Overcomer Survival Training School. Nonmembers of the CSA could attend this training session for a fee of $500. Randall Rader was the leader of the paramilitary wing of the CSA. The location of the CSA on the Arkansas-Missouri border allowed members to commit crimes in one jurisdiction and flee to safety in the other. Members of the CSA also collected welfare checks and stripped wrecked cars for additional funds.

The end of the CSA came in April 1985 after a series of criminal incidents made federal, state, and local police authorities suspicious about possible illegal activities at the compound. After the death of **Gordon Kahl**, a leader in the **Posse Comitatus movement**, at the hands of the police in 1983, members of the CSA established close ties with the **Aryan Nations** and launched a series of terrorist operations. Among the alleged crimes was the firebombing of a synagogue in Indiana, arson at a church in Missouri, and an effort to destroy a natural gas pipeline in Missouri. In 1983 Richard Wayne Snell, an active member of the CSA, killed a pawnbroker and a black Arkansas state trooper. Plans were made to assassinate a federal judge, but an automobile accident prevented the completion of this mission. David Tate, a member of **The Order**, murdered a Missouri state patrolman and wounded another on April 15, 1985, while heading for the CSA compound. Using information gathered about other fugitives from justice living in the CSA compound, an FBI SWAT team of nearly 200 agents raided the compound on April 18, 1985, where they found fugitives from justice, illegal firearms, and cyanide compounds for poisoning water supplies. All of the leaders of the CSA were arrested. In September 1985, six leaders were sentenced to prison terms on racketeering and illegal weapons charges. Ellison and Kerry Noble, second in command of the CSA, received five-year prison sentences and the others, two-year terms. Removal of its leadership caused the CSA to cease to exist as an organization. Members of the CSA, however, drifted to other Christian Identity communities. **See also** Christian Identity; Elohim City.

Suggested readings: James Coates, *Armed and Dangerous: The Rise of the Survivalist Right* (New York: Hill and Wang, 1987); Wayne King, "Anti-Semitism Links Violent Groups," *New York Times* (April 28, 1985), sec. 1, p. 22; Wayne King, "Survivalist and 4 Neo-Nazis Give Up," *New York Times* (April 23, 1985), p. A14; Kerry Nobel, *Tabernacle of Hate: Why They Bombed Oklahoma City* (Prescott, Ontario, Canada: Voyageur Publishing, 1998); Brent L. Smith, *Terrorism in America: Pipe Bombs and Pipe Dreams* (Albany: State University of New York Press, 1994).

Covington, Harold (1953–)

Harold Covington, the leader of the neo-Nazi National Socialist White People's Party (NSWPP), was born in 1953 in Burlington, North Carolina. His family moved to Chapel Hill, North Carolina, when he was quite young. Covington graduated from Chapel Hill High School in 1971. For a time, he had attended the Governor's School in Winston-Salem, North Carolina, where he studied drama. Shortly after graduation from high school, he joined the U.S. Army. By this time, he was a member of **George Lincoln Rockwell**'s **American Nazi Party**. He followed **Matt Koehl** into the NSWPP after Rockwell's death in 1967. His pro-Nazi activities in the army, including passing

out racist literature at Schofield Barracks in Hawaii, led to his discharge from the military in 1973. Unhappy with racial conditions in the United States, Covington moved to Johannesburg, South Africa, where he found a job as a payroll clerk. Intrigued by the war in Rhodesia, Covington traveled to Bulawayo, Rhodesia, where he formed the Rhodesian White People's Party. His racist agitation led to his expulsion from Rhodesia in 1976.

Covington returned to the United States and settled in Raleigh, North Carolina, where he joined Frank Collins's Chicago-based National Socialist Party of America (NSPA). Covington traveled to Chicago and marched with Collins at the plaza of the Federal Building in downtown Chicago on June 24, 1978. He remained in the party even after Collins's Jewish background was exposed by the federal government. While in Chicago, Covington found compromising films and pictures of Collins with little boys, and he turned the evidence over to the police. After Collins went to jail on a morals charge in 1980, Covington assumed leadership of the party. He also ran for public office as a Republican candidate for North Carolina Attorney General and won 43 percent of the vote in the primary. His position as the head of the NSPA lasted less than a year. **Gary Lex Lauck**, the deputy party leader, defeated him in a power struggle in August 1980. In April 1981 the new leadership suspended Covington from party membership. Within two years, the dissension in the party caused it to be disbanded.

Over the next decade, Covington spent time in and out of the United States working for white supremacist causes. From 1982 to 1987, he lived in South Africa, Great Britain, and Ireland. In 1987 Covington returned to the United States in time to have his book, *The March Upcountry*, published by Liberty Bell Publications. In this book, Covington articulates his white supremacy viewpoint and blames the decline of the white race on the failure of whites to act in their own best interests. He also started the Confederate National Congress (CNC) in Raleigh, North

Carolina. By 1992 Covington was again in Great Britain. By 1993 he had made contact with a British racist terrorist group, Combat 18, which has had a history of firebombings and assaults on racial minorities in England.

Covington returned to the United States in 1994. This time he formed a reorganized National Socialist White People's Party in Raleigh, North Carolina. Covington decided to move his party to Seattle, Washington, in October 1994. This move was intended to coincide with the efforts of various white supremacist groups to form a white homeland in the Pacific Northwest. Covington continues to publish a newsletter, *Resistance! The Revolutionary Voice of the NSWPP*. Besides this newsletter, his party runs an active Internet site. On this Web site, Covington praises Adolf Hitler, George Lincoln Rockwell, and the Nazis. **See also** American Nazi Party.

Suggested readings: Anti-Defamation League, *Danger: Extremism: The Major Vehicles and Voices of America's Far-Right Fringe* (New York: Anti-Defamation League, 1996); Harold Covington, *The March Upcountry* (Reading, Pa.: Liberty Bell, 1987); Leonard Doyle, "US Militias Show Way for British Fascists," *Independent* [London] (April 27, 1995), p. 7; Richard Norton-Taylor, "US Neo-Nazi Aids Violence in UK," *Guardian* [London] (April 19, 1993), p. 3.

Cuban American National Foundation (CANF)

The Cuban American National Foundation (CANF) is the largest, most radical Cuban exile group. Cuban exiles founded the organization in 1981 to liberate Cuba from Fidel Castro and communism. Until his death in 1997, Jorge Mas Canosa, one of the original founders of the CANF, was its autocratic head. Canosa was a self-made millionaire whose fortune came from laying cable for Southern Bell. The CANF's headquarters is located in Miami, but there are offices in New Jersey and in other areas where significant numbers of exiled Cubans live. The foundation has a $2 million operating budget and a 140-member board of directors. Each voting member of the board is

in business or has a professional career. Members of the board contribute at least $10,000 every year. Francisco "Pepe" Hernandez runs the CANF's day-to-day operations.

The leadership of the Cuban American National Foundation has learned to operate in and manipulate the American political system through extensive lobbying of politicians. Because Canosa had ambitions to succeed Castro as the head of Cuba, the CANF operates like a shadow government. The CANF has not only an active propaganda network, but also its own foreign policy and economic strategy. Cubans who oppose its policies find themselves retaliated against either in the political world or in their careers. More significant is the way in which the CANF uses its political and financial clout to lobby the U.S. Congress and the president of the United States. Because the majority of Cuban Americans are Republican voters, the CANF found itself in favor by producing Republican voters during the Reagan and Bush administrations in the 1980s. The CANF's leaders also made sure that campaign donations were made available to their friends in Congress. Successful ventures include the creation of the anti-Castro Radio Marti in 1985 and TV Marti in 1990. The tightening of the anti-Castro embargo in the 1992 Cuban Democracy Act was also sponsored by the CANF. Leaders of the CANF lobbied hard for the 1996 Helms-Burton Act which discourages foreign investment in Cuba. Lobbying of the state of Florida by the CANF produced the Endowment for Cuban American Studies to finance anti-Castro research and publications. Finally, the CANF obtained federal government approval for its short-wave radio station, Voice of the Foundation, which broadcasts anti-Castro propaganda to Cuba each day.

The CANF started losing it dominant position as the standard-bearer for the Cuban American community in the mid-1990s. After several years of policy and verbal support of the CANF, the Clinton administration began to pursue a more independent line beginning in 1995. In May 1995, the Clinton administration concluded an immigration accord with the Cuban government. Despite the CANF's success with the 1996 Helms-Burton Act, which tightened the embargo against Cuba, Cuban leaders continued to lose most of their political clout with the Clinton administration. Canosa's death on November 22, 1997, only intensified the downward spiral. The arrest of Cuban exiles aboard a ship filled with weapons in a 1997 assassination plot against Castro implicated the CANF's leadership. CANF supporters also clashed with the Clinton administration in 1999–2000 over the fate of six-year-old Elian Gonzalez. The return of Elian Gonzalez to Cuba was a blow to the Cuban American National Foundation, and it lost prestige in the Cuban community and in Congress. Cuban leaders of the foundation now pin their hopes on the new Bush administration to keep the pressure on Castro and Cuba. **See also** Omega 7.

Suggested readings: Ann Louise Bardach and Larry Rohter, "A Plot on Castro Spotlights a Powerful Group of Exiles," *New York Times* (May 5, 1998), p. A1; Susan Benesch and Rick Bragg, "Not Just a War of Words," *St. Petersburg Times* (March 29, 1992), p. 1A; Ricardo Chavira, "Capitalism's Hard-Liners; Critics Say Cuban Exiles Aim to Topple Castro to Install Own Tyranny," *Dallas Morning News* (November 28, 1992), p. 7; Guy Gugliotta, "Hard-Liners Dig In on the Issue of Embargo," *Washington Post* (January 21, 1998), p. A16; Christopher Marquis, "Cuban-American Lobby on the Defensive," *New York Times* (June 30, 2000), p. A12; Christopher Marquis, "Jorge Mas Canosa; From Refugee to Power Broker," *Miami Herald* (November 23, 1997), p. 1; Larry Rohter, "Jorge Mas Canosa, 58, Dies; Exile Who Led Movement Against Castro," *New York Times* (November 24, 1997), p. B7.

Cults

Many extreme religious and political groups have been classified as cults. Although scholars in the field of religious studies tend to reject the concept of a cult, the term is still in vogue to describe a variety of unorthodox religious and political groups. The groups of believers share certain characteristics. Foremost among these characteristics is the presence of a charismatic leader who defines the orientation of his or her followers. Almost always this charismatic leader is a dominant male figure, but a female leader may assume the mantle of a deceased or fallen founder. Often these successors are unable to continue to adhere to the policies of the original leader and start to deviate with mixed results. The charismatic leader determines orthodoxy for the group, and dissidents are humiliated and driven out of the group. Sometimes charismatic leaders believe that dissidents are so dangerous they need to be killed. On these occasions, members of the group sometimes band together to eliminate such dissidents.

Many cults have an apocalyptic message. Leaders of the cult study and find new meanings in the Bible's Book of Revelations. These leaders tell their supporters to expect an apocalyptic event which will either end the world as they know it or transform it profoundly. Members of apocalyptic cults also share a Golden Age Myth, when the world was a better place, a rejection of modern culture, a rigid adherence to scripture, an absolute right versus wrong worldview, and a conspiratorial view of history. Often the belief systems of cults reject mainstream Christianity or Judaism.

Both religious and political cults tend to change over time and with the rise and fall of their charismatic leaders. Because cults depend so heavily on a leader's charismatic personality, group members shift between groups and sometimes belong to more than one group in their cult experience. Cults are by nature unstable; new cults arise and disappear only to start again in another phase. Political cults tend to be more stable than religious ones, but in both cases members tend to be individuals of unstable nature who need the reassurance of the structure of a cult.

Suggested readings: Marilyn Haddrill, "Cults," *El Paso Herald-Post* (June 28, 1997), p. 1; Tim Madigan, "Chain Reaction: Mind-

Control Cults Become More Threatening as the Millennium Ends," *Fort Worth Star-Telegram* (April 2, 1995), p. 1; Timothy Miller, ed., *America's Alternative Religions* (New York: State University of New York Press, 1995); Margaret Thaler Singer, *Cults in Our Midst: The Hidden Menace in Our Everyday Lives* (San Francisco: Jossey-Bass, 1995).

D

Davis, Angela Yvonne (1944–)

Angela Davis, a leading left-wing radical intellectual, was born on January 26, 1944, in Birmingham, Alabama. Her schoolteacher parents represented the growing black middle-class in the South. They were also active members of the National Association for the Advancement of Colored People (NAACP). Her early childhood was spent in the Dynamite Hill area of Birmingham where **Ku Klux Klan** members raided on a regular basis. Davis was a precocious student and at an early age won a scholarship from the American Friends to attend school in New York City. While in New York City, she lived with the family of Reverend William Melish. Both in this home and at school Davis came into contact with socialist ideas. During high school, she was active in the Communist Party youth group. Davis attended Brandeis University and studied under Marxist scholar Herbert Marcuse. After graduate work at Frankfurt University in 1965 and 1967, under another Marxist scholar, Theodore Adorno, she returned to Brandeis University to work with Marcuse. She attended graduate school at the University of California at San Diego, earned a master's degree in philosophy in 1968, and began work on her doctorate in 1969.

During the course of her academic training, Davis became active in national politics. With the civil rights movement in full swing, she joined the Student Nonviolent Coordinating Committee (SNCC). She also participated in the Communist Party USA and the **Black Panther Party.** Her association with these last two organizations caused trouble for Davis when she took a job teaching philosophy at the University of California at Los Angeles (UCLA). She had joined the Communist Party in July 1968. Governor Ronald Reagan cited a California law that banned Communist Party members from teaching at a state university and had her fired. In the subsequent court case, the U.S. Supreme Court ruled that the state law was unconstitutional.

This court case proved to be less important then Davis's subsequent troubles over her association with the Black Panther Party. She had become friends with George Jackson, the prison leader of the group called the Soledad Brothers. Members of the Soledad Brothers had been accused of killing a prison guard at the Soledad Prison. Jonathan Jackson, the brother of George Jackson, tried to free his brother by kidnapping hostages at the Marin County Courthouse. The weapons used in the kidnapping were registered in Angela Davis's name. In a gunfight Jonathan Jackson and a judge were killed. Davis was accused of complicity and charged with conspiracy, kidnapping, and murder. A defense committee, the National United Committee to Free Angela Davis, was formed and a massive publicity campaign was launched. In 1972, after she had spent sixteen months in jail, her case went to trial. A jury acquitted her of all charges in June 1972. Shortly after the court case, Davis traveled to the Soviet Union to receive the Lenin Peace Prize. After the acquittal, the Davis committee transformed itself into the National Alliance Against Racist and Political Repression with Angela Davis as a co-chair. This committee undertook campaigns to free individuals accused of political crimes. These activities consumed most of Davis's energies for the next decade. She also served as the vice-presidential candidate on the Communist Party USA presidential ticket in 1980 and 1984, running with Gus Hall.

Davis maintained a lower political profile in the 1990s, but she has never relinquished her radical political views or been shy about expressing them. Most of her energy, however, has been devoted to advancing her academic career. Davis has written several books, including *If They Come in the Morning* (1971), *Angela Davis: An Autobiography* (1974), *Women, Race, and Class* (1983), and *Women, Culture, and Politics* (1989). She is a tenured professor of history of consciousness at the University of California at Santa Cruz. She broke with the Communist Party USA in 1991 and joined the Committee of Correspondence. This splinter group of former members of the Communist Party, Trotskyites, Maoists, and radicals attempted to combine the radical political left under one ideological umbrella. In 1995 Davis received the prestigious Presidential Chair at the University of California at Santa Cruz much to the displeasure of California's conservative legislators. She continues to travel around the United States speaking out against opponents of affirmative action, warning about the growing minority prison population, and advocating women's rights.

Suggested readings: Beverly Beyette, "Angela Davis Now; On a Quiet Street in Oakland," *Los Angeles Times* (March 8, 1989), part 5, p. 1; Angela Davis, *Angela Davis: An Autobiography* (New York: Random House, 1974); Gregory Freeman, "Prison Abolitionist's Angela Davis Seeks Overhaul of Penal System," *St. Louis Post-Dispatch* (November 15, 1998), p. B4; Natalie Pompilio, "Angela Davis Pushes for Social Change," *Times Picayune* [New Orleans] (October 22, 2000), p. 1; Mary Timothy, *Jury Woman: The Story of the Trial of Angela Y. Davis* (San Francisco: Glide Publications, 1975); Leroy Woodson, Jr., "So Says: Angela Davis" *Los Angeles Times* (March 2, 1986), Magazine, p. 28.

Decker, Bo (See American Nationalist Party)

DeFreeze, Donald David (1943–1974)

Donald DeFreeze, the leader of the radical leftist **Symbionese Liberation Army**, was born in 1943 in Cleveland, Ohio. DeFreeze was the eldest of eight children and never got along with his father. After dropping out of school at fourteen, he left the Cleveland black ghetto for Buffalo, New York, where he joined a street gang, the Crooked Skulls. In August 1960, DeFreeze had his first brush with the law and served two and a half years in the Elmira State Reformatory for stealing a car and a pistol. Out of prison at eighteen, DeFreeze moved to Newark, New Jersey, and married an older woman with three children. He worked at a number of jobs, but mostly for a painting contractor. Several times in the early 1960s, DeFreeze had troubles with the police over drinking, firearms, and bombs. In 1967 he and his family moved to Los Angeles, California. Again his drinking and weapons possession got him in trouble with the police. On one occasion, a judge gave him three years' probation. In December 1967, he robbed a prostitute, and after his arrest the police found more than 200 stolen guns at his home. He informed the police about his supplier. Because of this cooperation, DeFreeze received probation again after serving four months in jail. His marriage collapsed, and he violated the parole because of gun possession. Free on bond, DeFreeze fled to New Jersey. Over the next two years, during 1968 and 1969, he engaged in various petty crimes both in New Jersey and California. In November 1969, he was captured trying to cash a stolen cashier's check at a bank in Los Angeles. At his trial, the judge sentenced him to a three- to five-year sentence at Vacaville State Prison.

DeFreeze became a revolutionary in prison. The radical leftists in Northern California had splintered into several groups after the breakup of the **Students for a Democratic Society** (SDS). One of these new spin-offs was the Venceremos, a Maoist-oriented action group of mostly upper-middle class white activists and students. According to the Venceremos, the upcoming revolution in the United States had to be led by black and minority leadership. The group's revolutionary political ideas started spreading among the black prisoner population of California prisons. DeFreeze was thus exposed to the Venceremos ideology before he was transferred to Soledad State Prison in December 1972. On March 5, 1973, DeFreeze escaped from Soledad and got as far as Palo Alto where he contacted people in the Venceremos movement. Thero Wheeler, a staunch believer in the Venceremos movement, had vaguely known DeFreeze in prison, and after Wheeler escaped from prison in August 1973, the two met and discussed the formation of the Symbionese Liberation Army. By the fall of 1973, DeFreeze had assumed command of the SLA, but at this time it had only four active members: DeFreeze, Wheeler, Nancy Ling Perry, and Mizmoon Soltysik. DeFreeze, who had assumed the title and name of Field Marshal Cinque Mtume (Fifth Prophet), slowly was able to attract a small cadre of white left-wing militants, including Angela Atwood, Bill and Emily Harris, Russ Little, Joe Remiro, and Willie Wolfe. Other than this small band, most mainstream leftists ignored the SLA. After committing several burglaries to steal weapons, DeFreeze started training the SLA members for combat.

DeFreeze's career as the leader of the Symbionese Liberation Army was of short duration. His first tactical move was to plan and carry out the assassination of Marcus Foster, the Oakland superintendent of schools. Foster's murder was a political mistake, however, because it alienated Oakland's black community. The next operation was to kidnap Patricia Hearst, the daughter of millionaire William Randolph Hearst, the newspaper publisher. DeFreeze wanted her to bargain for the release of Little and Remiro, both of whom had been arrested after an armored car robbery. The strategy changed after DeFreeze and the others converted Hearst to their cause. DeFreeze decided that the San Francisco area had too big a police presence and he moved operations to the Los Angeles area. On May 17, 1974, DeFreeze and five other members of the SLA were identified in Los Angeles. In the subsequent gunfight, DeFreeze and his compatriots were killed in a bloody shootout. The Symbionese Liberation Army continued without DeFreeze, but it was never as effective without him. **See also** Symbionese Liberation Army.

Suggested readings: Miles Corwin, "The Shootout on East 54th Street; Violence: Twenty Years Ago, the LAPD and the Symbionese Liberation Army Exchanged Fire at a Home in South-Central," *Los Angeles Times* (May 18, 1994), p. B1; Chuck Haga, "Hearst Kidnapping Drew U.S. Attention to SLA in Berkeley," *Star Tribune* [Minneapolis] (June 17, 1999), p. 8A; Vin McLellan, and Paul Avery, *The Voices of Guns: The Definitive and Dramatic Story of the Twenty-Two-Month Career of the Symbionese Liberation Army—One of the Most Bizarre Chapters in the History of the American Left* (New York: Putnam's Sons, 1977).

DePugh, Robert Bolivar (1923–   )

Robert DePugh, the founder of the Minutemen militia movement, was born in April 1923 in Independence, Missouri, where his father was in local law enforcement. DePugh graduated from William Chrisman High School in 1941 with a reputation as a loner. After attending a semester at the University of Missouri-Columbia, he entered the U.S. Army in 1942. His military career as a radar specialist was undistinguished, and he was released from military duty in August 1944 for chronic nervousness and depression. While in the service, he met and married his wife and they had six children. In 1946 he attended Kansas State University but stayed for less than two years. After holding several jobs, mostly in sales, he ran for a seat in the U.S. House of Representatives in Missouri's Fourth Congressional District in the Democratic primary of 1952, but his bid was unsuccessful. Shortly afterward, in 1953, he started a dog food supplement business, Biolab Corporation, in Independence, Missouri. This business went bankrupt within three years. DePugh was briefly arrested for the practice of "check kiting," or issuing checks from various banks to keep them from bouncing. Charges were dropped after he made restitution to the banks. He then went to work for Hill Packing Company where he sold specialized animal foods to veterinarians. At the same time, he attended school at Washburn University in Topeka, Kansas. Again he left school without a degree, but this time he left to reorganize his animal drug business. DePugh reorganized the Biolab Corporation and moved it to Norborne, Missouri.

In the midst of his business activities, DePugh became disturbed over the direction of national politics. In the mid-1950s, he joined the **John Birch Society** because he shared the society's strong anti-communist viewpoint. DePugh was also active in opposing gun control legislation and was a loyal supporter of the National Rifle Association. When he decided that the John Birch Society was not militant enough, DePugh formed the Minutemen in 1960 to be an organization ready to fight those advancing communism in the United States. He envisaged the Minutemen as a paramilitary group armed and ready to wage warfare against communists and their sympathizers. His organization ran military camps to prepare his Minutemen for the coming struggle. Several Minutemen had trouble with federal authorities over firearm violations. In 1964 DePugh left the John Birch Society after its leadership accused him of trying to take over the soci-

ety. Lacking a political action group, DePugh started the Patriotic Party in 1966 to run candidates for public office. The Minutemen continued to build a stockpile of weapons and ammunition from 1960 to 1966. He also built an enemy file of over 65,000 and a list of 1,500 traitors to be eliminated in case of national emergency. DePugh published a handbook, *Blueprint for Victory* (1966), which outlined his ideas for ways in which the Minutemen could succeed. In 1966 DePugh was arrested on federal firearm charges and convicted of these offenses.

DePugh resigned as head of the Minutemen in 1967, but his influence on the group remained strong. In 1968, while he was free on appeal for the firearms conviction, the government indicted him for conspiracy to rob banks in Washington State. Apprehensive of a long prison sentence, DePugh fled federal jurisdiction. He was captured in Truth-or-Consequences, New Mexico, in July 1969. His prison sentence for firearms violations and bond jumping was for eleven years, but he only served four years before obtaining parole in May 1973. The Minutemen organization had almost collapsed by the early 1970s without his direction. While he was in prison, DePugh became a survivalist, and shortly after his release from prison he published *Can You Survive? Guidelines for Resistance to Tyranny for You and Your Family* (1973). Soon afterward, DePugh joined the **Christian Identity** movement. In 1981 he sold his pharmaceutical company and a printing business to devote himself to politics full time. He later became one of the leaders of the Committee of 10 Million, whose goal was to find 10 million voters to help change the American system of government. Although it cost only $10 to join the group, DePugh was able to attract only a fraction of his intended 10 million members. His brushes with the law continued in September 1991 with an arrest and conviction in Iowa on a morals charge involving pornographic pictures of a thirteen-year-old girl, and a federal firearms charge in 1992. The firearms offense resulted in a two-and-a-half-year prison sentence. Since then, DePugh has resigned from all political activity. His anti-government views, however, remain public. At the peak of his influence in the 1960s and early 1970s, he was the national spokesperson for the anti-government movement. **See also** Minutemen movement.

Suggested readings: Anti-Defamation League, *Danger: Extremism: The Major Vehicles and Voices on America's Far-Right Fringe* (New York: Anti-Defamation League, 1996); Philip Dine, "Ex-Survivalist Held in Child Sex Case; Police Seize Pornographic Photos from Founder of 'Minutemen,' " *St. Louis Post-Dispatch* (September 14, 1991), p. 6A; Phillip Finch, *God, Guts, and Guns* (New York: Seaview/Putnam, 1983); Neil A. Hamilton, *Militias in America: A Reference Handbook* (Santa Barbara, Calif.: ABC-CLIO, 1996).

Dominica Plot (See Black, Stephen Donald)

Droege, Wolfgang (1949–)

Wolfgang Droege, the current leader of the Canadian neo-Nazi **Heritage Front** and a former head of the Canadian **Ku Klux Klan**, was born in 1949 in Forchheim, Bavaria, Germany. His father was a veteran of the German Luftwaffe during World War II. His grandfather, a successful hotel owner, was a former friend of the notorious anti-Semitic Nazi leader Julius Streicher. His entire family remains unreconstructed Nazi supporters. In 1963 Droege followed his mother to Canada where she married a Canadian citizen. After returning to Germany for a lengthy stay as a teenager, Droege settled in Canada in 1967. During his visit to Germany, he attended meetings of Adolf von Thadden's neo-Nazi National Party.

In the early 1970s, Droege started looking for groups and individuals that shared his neo-Nazi views. In 1974 he made friends with **Donald Clarke Andrews** of the racist group **Western Guard** and joined his organization. In May 1975, Canadian police arrested Droege for painting racist slogans on buildings. He served fourteen days in jail and was placed on probation for two years. Ignoring the terms of his probation, Droege continued to get into trouble for his violent views and actions. He was able, however, to avoid participation in Andrew's plot to plant a bomb on the Israeli soccer team touring Canada. Andrews spent two years in prison for conspiracy in this plot. In Andrews's absence, Droege met James Alexander McQuirter, and together they traveled to New Orleans to a 1976 Ku Klux Klan rally. There they were introduced to the American Ku Klux Klan leader, **David Duke**, who impressed them with his political expertise and his views. They returned to Canada and formed a Canadian Ku Klux Klan organization. This body was soon named the Canadian Knights of the Ku Klux Klan. Several times Duke visited Canada on speaking tours to support the new Klan organization. Droege's day job at a printing company ended after adverse publicity about his connections with the Ku Klux Klan surfaced. From this time onward, Droege has devoted himself full time to organizing to support his political causes. McQuirter served as the spokesperson for the Klan and Droege as the organizer. In the late 1970s, the Canadian Klan grew at a rapid rate, especially among high school–age males.

In the middle of his success with organizing the Canadian Ku Klux Klan, Droege overreached himself and landed in an American prison. The American FBI arrested Droege in December 1979 in New Orleans for his involvement in an attempted mercenary takeover of the Caribbean island of Dominica. He had organized a band of mercenaries to restore former Dominican Prime Minister Patrick John to power and establish a white supremacist state. Droege was charged with violation of the U.S. Neutrality Act and was sentenced to three years in prison. Droege served his sentence at the medium-security facility in Sandstone, Minnesota. While Droege was in prison, the Canadian Knights of the Ku Klux Klan disintegrated after McQuirter left in 1982. After his release from prison in May 1983,

Droege tried to reestablish the Klan organization, but he soon decided to try another approach. He contacted the leaders of the **Aryan Nations** and **Robert Jay Mathews.** Finding himself in sympathy with their views, Droege was on the verge of forming a Canadian branch of the Aryan Nations when he was arrested again; this time the FBI arrested him in Huntsville, Alabama, for possession of a Teflon knife and four ounces of cocaine. Droege received a sentence of thirteen years for trafficking in drugs and a weapons offense. He served his sentence at the maximum-security prison in Lompoc, California. Shortly after he was released from prison in 1989, American authorities deported him to Canada.

Droege returned to Canada and immediately plunged back into Canadian right-wing politics. In September 1989, Droege and seventeen members of the National Party traveled to Libya as guests of Muammar Qaddafi. While he was in Libya consolidating financial support from Qaddafi, Droege discussed with his colleagues on the trip the formation of a larger, more influential white supremacist party in Canada. The result was the white supremacist group Heritage Front, which started operations in November 1989. Droege, the acknowledged leader of the Heritage Front, recruited the youthful **George Burdi** as his second in command. Together they have made the Heritage Front a powerful force in Canadian right-wing politics. **See also** Heritage Front; Ku Klux Klan; Neo-Nazis; Western Guard; White Supremacist Movement.

Suggested readings: Geoff Baker, "Secretive Skinheads Have Links to Militias, *Gazette* [Montreal] (May 5, 1995), p. A12; Rosie Di Manno, "Ex-Mercenary Aims for Country 'Uniquely' White," *Toronto Star* (June 19, 1991), p. A7; Peter Hum, "Recruiting for 'Holy Racial War,' " *Ottawa Citizen* (May 1, 1993), p. C3; Warren Kinsella, *Web of Hate: Inside Canada's Far Right Network* (Toronto, Ont., Canada: Harper-Collins, 1994); Jim Rankin, "Droege Wins Case on Alleged Hate Message," *Toronto Star* (March 28, 1996), p. A15; Don Sellar, "Neo-Nazi Given Free Publicity," *Toronto Star* (May 6, 1995), p. C2; Michael Tenszen, "Convicted Criminal Wolfgang Droege," *Toronto Star* (February 21, 1993), p. B5.

Duck Club

The Duck Club is a right-wing organization that operated as a lobbying group for extremist causes in the 1980s. Robert White, a Florida millionaire businessman, who had earned his millions by inventing an airport cleaning process, started a right-wing patriotic magazine, the *Duck Book*, in 1980 which featured a comical duck flying in a B-1 bomber. The duck became a symbol of opposition to federal government policies. White attacked what he perceived to be America's enemies, including the Council on Foreign Relations, the Federal Reserve Board, and the Trilateral Commission, because he believed that they were advancing one-world government. Readers could subscribe to issues by sending $10 to White. This publication lasted thirteen issues until December 1981. It had a circulation of around 100,000, but he lost money publishing it. To replace the periodical, White started publishing *Duck Book II* and then *Duck Book Digest*. His hardcore supporters numbered around 10,000.

White started organizing local chapters of the Duck Club to lobby for political causes. His intention in 1980 was for the clubs to raise funds for conservative politicians in 1982. By 1982 the club had more than 1,000 chapters nationwide and it served as a strong lobbying force for the next few years. However, the popularity of the clubs had diminished sharply by the mid-1980s. In 1986 only two chapters were still in operation: one in Yucca Valley, California, and one in Seattle, Washington. The organization would have faded away without further notice except for the action of David Lee Rice. The twenty-seven-year-old Rice was a frequent visitor to the Seattle chapter of the Duck Club. In one of the meetings, the head of the chapter charged that Charles Goldmark, a prominent Seattle lawyer, was the regional director of the American Communist Party. Rice, who had a history of mental

David Duke poses in his Klan robes in front of the House of Parliament in London in March 1978. Although he was banned from entering Britain, he arrived by way of a Skytrain flight from New York. (AP Photo)

instability, took this charge to heart. On December 24, 1985, Rice attacked and murdered Goldmark, his wife, and their two sons in their home. Rice was captured several days later. His lawyers argued that Rice had diminished capacity to distinguish between right and wrong. After the publicity of this case, the Duck Club ceased to exist except for one or two chapters in the Pacific Northwest. **See also** Common Law Courts; Minutemen Movement.

Suggested readings: Phillip Finch, *God, Guts, and Guns* (New York: Seaview/Putnam, 1983); National Desk, "The Duck Club: Anti-Communism and Investment Advice for Millionaires," *New York Times* (June 2, 1986), p. A10.

Duke, David (1950–)

David Duke is the leader of a white supremacist movement that combines **Ku Klux Klan** and other white supremacist groups in an effort to gain respectability in the American political process. He was born on July 1, 1950, in Tulsa, Oklahoma. His father, an engineer for Royal Dutch Shell Oil Company, had conservative leanings and favored segregation. In 1954 his family spent a year at the Royal Dutch Shell's headquarters in The Hague, the Netherlands. The next year the family moved to New Orleans, Louisiana. Duke, who had few friends at school, was well known for arguing about politics. Both Nazi and pro-segregationist literature attracted him. His father left Shell in 1966 and worked as a civil engineer in Vietnam for the U.S. Agency for International Development (AID) for the next nine years. His father sent him to a private military school, Riverside Military Academy in Gainesville, Georgia, for the eleventh grade, but his career there was undistinguished. After returning to New Orleans for his senior year, he graduated from John F. Kennedy High School. Duke attended Louisiana State University (LSU) beginning in 1968. While he majored in history, he spent almost as much time agitating for his neo-Nazi views as studying for his classes. Duke earned a reputation for his anti-black and anti-Semitic speeches at the public forum at LSU called Free Speech Alley. In November 1969, while still at school, he founded the National Socialist Liberation Front (NSLF), a student chapter of **Matt Koehl**'s National Socialist White People's Party (NSWPP). He soon renamed the group the White Youth Alliance (WYA) and then in 1971 recast it the National Party. After his junior year, Duke traveled to Laos in Southeast Asia where he worked as an English instructor in the Defense Department's American Language Institute before being fired for inappropriate teaching in July 1971. He married Chloe Hardin, a devoted follower of his National Party at LSU, in September 1972. In 1973 Duke returned to LSU and graduated in May 1974 with a degree in history.

Duke realized that Nazism was too inflammatory to appeal to the general public so he looked for alternatives and turned his attention to the Ku Klux Klan. Several times in 1972, Duke had been arrested for misconduct at demonstrations, but each time he had been rescued by a New Orleans real estate developer, James Lindsey. Lindsey, a veteran racist, soon became Duke's mentor. In 1973 Duke formed the Knights of the Ku Klux Klan. To legitimize it to other existing Klan groups, he declared that the Knights of the Ku Klux Klan was already in existence and that he was merely revitalizing it. Lindsey continued to help Duke until Lindsey was murdered in 1975 in an unsolved murder case involving his estranged wife. Since Duke's immediate goal was to make the Klan more respectable, he opened membership to Catholics and women. He also targeted the recruitment of college students. At the same time, Duke oriented his Klan group to attract **neo-Nazis** by becoming more vocal in his anti-Semitic attacks. Duke was con-

vinced that Jewish interests controlled the U.S. government. In September 1976, Duke was arrested for inciting a riot. In a trial in 1977 and a trial in 1979, he was found guilty. He was fined $500 and given a six-month suspended sentence.

Duke remained as head of the Knights of the Ku Klux Klan until he resigned in July 1980 to work with a new organization, the **National Association for the Advancement of White People** (NAAWP), and incorporated it as a nonprofit organization on December 20, 1979. **Elbert Claude Bill Wilkerson**, a rival in the Knights of the Ku Klux Klan and an FBI informer, maneuvered Duke into leaving the Knights of the Ku Klux Klan early to avoid a controversy over the selling of a members' mailing list. For the next five years, Duke used the NAAWP to unite various white supremacist bodies and work for common goals. In the early 1980s, Duke developed a friendship with **Willis Carto**, head of the **Liberty Lobby** and the **Institute for Historical Review**, and soon afterward became a proponent of the **Holocaust denial movement**.

In the late 1980s, Duke launched a political campaign to make his racist views more respectable to the general public. Earlier he had espoused strong anti-Semitic and white supremacist views. Now Duke started toning down his rhetoric without repudiating his basic position. His first efforts to win political office at the state level were unsuccessful. In January 1987, Duke was active in the Forsyth County, Georgia, anti–civil rights demonstration and gained national publicity for his actions. He was also arrested on a misdemeanor charge of obstructing a roadway, which garnered him a $55 fine and a one-year suspended sentence. Then, in 1988, Duke gathered 22,000 votes in the Louisiana primary as the Democratic candidate for president. Subsequently, he ran in the 1988 presidential election as the **Populist Party** candidate. By attacking affirmative action, the forced integration of schools, and the welfare system, Duke was able to repackage his message more successfully. He won a seat to the Louisiana state legislature in

1989 running as a Republican. In the campaign for the 1990 U.S. Senate seat in Louisiana, Duke lost, but he garnered more than 60 percent of the white vote in the state. Duke lost again in the 1991 Louisiana governor's race but only in a runoff election with former governor Edwin Edwards. The closeness of his campaign to winning scared the Louisiana power establishment, and this time he won 55 percent of the white vote.

Duke has continued to challenge the political establishment, but recently he has been less successful. In 1992 he attempted to garner the Republican nomination for president, but found himself outflanked by right-wing conservative Patrick Buchanan. Buchanan appropriated most of Duke's platform and neutralized him. Republican leaders also worked openly to keep him off of the national ballot in various states. Duke has been able to appeal to a disenfranchised part of the American electorate both in Lou-

isiana and in other parts of the country. He continues to receive political contributions from every state in the nation, although adverse publicity in newspaper articles about his gambling and womanizing has hurt him in the polls. The last of a long line of charges has been his misuse of campaign funds to finance his compulsive gambling. **See also** Black, Stephen Donald; Carto, Willis; Holocaust Denial Movement; Ku Klux Klan; White Supremacist Movement; Wilkerson, Elbert Claude.

Suggested readings: Tyler Bridges, *The Rise of David Duke* (Jackson: University Press of Mississippi, 1994); Tony Freemantle, "Duke Advances One-Issue Platform—the White Race," *Houston Chronicle* (January 19, 1992), p. 1; Douglas D. Rose, ed., *The Emergence of David Duke and the Politics of Race* (Chapel Hill: University of North Carolina Press, 1992); Michael Zatarain, *David Duke: Evolution of a Klansman* (Gretna, La.: Pelican, 1990).

E

Earth First!

Earth First!, an environmental group, has been a leader in developing tactics to fight against what its members consider the exploitation of the environment. Environmentalism became popular in the late 1960s, and by the 1970s the environmental movement comprised a series of national and grassroots organizations which lobbied on behalf of the environment. Foremost among these organizations were the Sierra Club and the Wilderness Society. Besides having large national memberships, they had an army of lobbyists in Washington, D.C., who were working to pass environmentalist legislation. They were successful in the passage of several important pieces of legislation protecting endangered species. By the mid-1970s, however, many environmental activists had come to believe that these organizations had become entrenched bureaucracies more interested in compromise with the resource industry than in fighting for the environment. It was a 1977 report, the *Roadless Area Review and Evaluation II*, which proposed only 15 million of the 62 million acres in the national forests be protected from resource development, that triggered a revolt by the activists in the environmentalist movement. Refusal of the national environmentalist groups to fight this review written by the Forestry Service infuriated many rank-and-file environmentalists. One of those disturbed by the growing cooperation between the environmental organizations and the resource industry was **David Foreman**, a Washington lobbyist for the Wilderness Society. He resigned his post as a lobbyist and moved to a new job in New Mexico.

Five political activists founded Earth First! on April 3, 1980, to fight what they deemed the exploitation of the environment. On a ten-day wilderness outing in the Pincacte Desert in Mexico, David Foreman, Ron Kezar, Bart Koehler, Mike Roselle, and Howie Wolke decided to launch a new organization to serve as a militant alternative to what they perceived to be the ineffectual policies of the Sierra Club and the Wilderness Society. They believed that these organizations had sold out to business interests. All of the founders were veterans of the environmentalist movement except Roselle, who had been active in several radical left-wing political organizations. Another shared experience was their admiration for the eco-rebels in Edward Abbey's novel *The Monkey Wrench Gang* (1975). These activists wanted a grassroots group that would take an uncompromising militant stance on the environment and be willing to use civil disobedience and guerrilla tactics. The motto for Earth First! was to be "No Compromise in the Defense of Mother Earth." They wanted to restore the wilderness to its natural state, not lobby for incremental change. Soon after its founding, Foreman started a newsletter, *Earth First!*, and leaders started making public appearances around the country spreading the new message of Earth First! By 1989 the organization had around 10,000 members and many more sympathizers.

A series of successful demonstrations initiated by Earth First! made it a force to be reckoned with in the development of wilderness areas. The first major action was a 1981 demonstration against the Glen Canyon Dam on the Colorado River. Leaders unfurled a three-hundred-foot black polyethylene banner which resembled a crack in the dam. This symbolic attack on the dam resulted in no arrests, but it was the first step in the organization's efforts to publicize its opposition to current environmental policies.

Another demonstration followed in July 1982 over oil exploration in the Gros Ventre Range of northwestern Wyoming. This action pitted Earth First! against the Getty Oil Company and the Reagan administration. Getty wanted to explore for oil in the Little Granite Creek area. A mass demonstration prevented the company from building a road to the Little Granite Creek. Earth First! supporters made their first use of sabotage of equipment as a tactic. Success on this occasion ensured that further resource development in this area would cease.

After these successful demonstrations, the leaders of Earth First! embarked on a long-range campaign of sabotage. "Ecotage" was the name given to the tactic of sabotaging road building or logging equipment. A more popular name was **monkeywrenching**, which tied sabotage to Abbey's novel *The Monkey Wrench Gang*. In the 1980s, ecotage was estimated to have caused between $20 million and $25 million a year to businesses engaged in road clearing or logging. Another popular tactic was tree spiking. A tree spike was no danger to the tree, but it destroyed tree saws and endangered loggers. Tree spiking became so widespread that Congress passed a law making it a felony. To avoid metal de-

tectors, some monkeywrenchers restored to tree pinning, or using hardened ceramic pins. Another tactic was tree sitting. Activists occupied a tree to prevent it from being cut.

Foreman and the rest of the original founders of Earth First! eventually found themselves displaced by new elements in the organization. As a mass movement mobilized around Earth First! it became less a group of direct action advocates to save the environment than a political organization with a social agenda. Foreman became disillusioned by the new direction of the organization, and he resigned in 1990. New leaders, such as **Judi Bari** and Darryl Cherney, replaced the older leadership and transformed the group's social agenda. These leaders concentrated in fighting big business logging of California redwoods. Bari's death in 1997 has allowed another generation of leaders to transform Earth First! into more of a mainstream environmentalist organization. **See also** Bari, Judi; Foreman, David; Monkeywrenching; Radical Environmentalism.

Suggested readings: Cheryl Downey, "Among Environmentalists It's in Earth First's Nature to Be a Little Salty," *Orange County Register* [Santa Ana, Calif.] (March 14, 1994), p. B1; Martha F. Lee, *Earth First!: Environmental Apocalypse* (Syracuse, N.Y.: Syracuse University Press, 1995); Christopher Manes, *Green Rage: Radical Environmentalism and the Unmaking of Civilization* (Boston: Little, Brown, 1990); Lance Robertson, "Earth First! Splinter Group Embraces Life of Sabotage," *Register-Guard* [Eugene Ore.] (October 27, 1998), p. 1; Rik Scarce, *Eco-Warriors: Understanding the Radical Environmental Movement* (Chicago: Noble Press, 1990).

Earth Liberation Front (ELF)

The Earth Liberation Front (ELF) is a left-wing, anti-government environmentalist group. Dissident members of Earth First! formed ELF in Great Britain in the early 1990s. An American version started operation in 1996 and allied with the **Animal Liberation Front** (ALF). These groups together were responsible for a series of arsons in

1997. The front first made the national news with the arson of five buildings and four ski lifts in Vail, Colorado, on October 17, 1998. Environmentalists had been fighting the Vail Resorts over an area that was wintering grounds for elk and a habitat for the endangered lynx. Since 1997 the Southern Poverty Law Center has attributed ELF with dozens of terrorist attacks and $30 million in damages. The latest arson attacks claimed by ELF were the May 21, 2001, arson at the Jefferson Popular Farms in Clatskanie, Oregon, and the University of Washington Center for Urban Horticulture in Seattle, Washington.

The Earth Liberation Front uses the **leaderless resistance** tactic developed by ALF and white supremacy groups to carry out operations. Craig Rosebraugh, a vegan baker from Portland, Oregon, is the primary spokesperson for ELF, but he claims not to be a member. He maintains that his job is to pass along anonymous communiqués from ELF leadership to the national media. ELF leaders have increasingly identified the U.S. government as the enemy because they believe that the government represents the interests of global capitalism. Targets of ELF have been logging companies, ski resorts, luxury homes, and other symbols of capitalism. Recent communications from ELF have threatened to bomb government buildings. So far, ELF has avoided animal and human casualties. **See also** Animal Liberation Front.

Suggested readings: Marego Athans, "ELF 'Eco-Terrorists' Target Those They See as Earth's Foes," *Baltimore Sun* (January 28, 2001), p. 1A; Dan Barry and Al Baker, "For 'Eco-Terrorism' Group, a Hidden Structure and Public Messages," *New York Times* (January 8, 2001), p. B1; Hal Bernton, "Radical Groups—Fiery Tactics," *Seattle Times* (May 24, 2001), p. A1; Tom Kenworthy, "A Green Crusade Erupts in Flames," *USA Today* (February 14, 2001), p. 3A; Kim Murphy, "Environmental Group Forms an Incendiary Core, FBI Says," *Los Angeles Times* (June 9, 2001), p. 12; Jack Reed, "Investigating Ecotage on Vail Mountain," *St. Petersburg Times* (March 4, 2001), p. 6D; Southern Poverty Law Center, "By Any Means Necessary," *SPLC Intelligence Report* 102 (Summer 2001): p. 65.

Eco-Feminism

Eco-feminism is a philosophy that combines the ideologies of feminism and ecology into a single movement. The term came into usage in 1974 to describe radical feminism's entry into the radical environmentalist movement. This philosophy equates all forms of oppression with male values and behavior. Male-centeredness brings about environmental destruction and the oppression of women. Male values of competitiveness, domination, individualism, and rationalism are the reasons for humanity's subjugation of nature and animals. In contrast, feminine values of connectedness, egalitarianism, nonaggression, and nurturing are more compatible with nature. It is this opposition to the male-oriented deep ecology doctrine that has caused feminists to attack the male leadership of the environmentalism movement. The theory of deep ecology came out of the writings of a Norwegian philosophy professor at the University of Oslo, Arne Naess, and it assigned "intrinsic value" to all forms of life, irrespective of their usefulness to humans. Each form of life, from mosquitoes to trees, has rights, and the environment should be left in peace. Eco-feminists accept the basic premise of deep ecology, but they object to the male monopoly of the issue. Leaders in the eco-feminism movement include feminist writers Carol Adams, Janet Biehl, Marti Kheel, and Ynestra King. These leaders have adopted a personal political stance that includes a vegan lifestyle and avoids dependence on animal products and animal testing. The eco-feminist orientation has become so strong in the radical wing of the environmentalist movement that feminism has become one of its basic tenets. Some eco-feminists have been attracted to the Wicca (witchcraft) movement and its Dianic goddess worship faction. **See also** Radical Environmentalism.

Suggested readings: David Nicholson-Lord, "Greenest of them All: Arne Naess," *Independent* [London] (May 31, 1992), p. 21; Rik Scarce, *Eco-Warriors: Understanding the Radical Environmental Movement* (Chicago: Noble Press, 1990); Noel Sturgeon, *Ecofeminist Natures:*

Race, Gender, Feminist Theory, and Political Action (New York: Routledge, 1997).

Elohim City (City of God)

Elohim City (City of God) is a **Christian Identity** community located in eastern Oklahoma where white supremacy is practiced as a way of life. Robert Millar founded Elohim City in the foothills of the Ozark Mountains in 1973. Millar, a Canadian-born Mennonite from Kitchener, Ontario, started his religious community in Maryland before moving it to Oklahoma. In 1997, 100 adults and children lived on the 1,100-acre ranch. The men work mostly on construction jobs, finding work when and where they can. Members of the community live in mobile homes or in crudely built stone and wood houses. Families are large and several men have more than one wife. Children receive schooling and religious instruction in a three-room schoolhouse. Religious activity is centered in a large stone church.

Religious beliefs in this community reflect Millar's brand of Christian Identity. Among these beliefs are that the new calendar year starts at the spring equinox in the middle of March. Christmas is celebrated between September 29 and October 3. Along with other Christian Identity sects, the members believe that God's chosen people are the white people of Northern Europe. This community, moreover, adheres to Old Testament dietary laws, avoiding pork and shellfish. Most Christian Identity churches are anti-Semitic and anti-minority, but this branch downplays its anti-Jewish feeling and racism.

While Millar claims that his community seeks no more members or supporters, white supremacists are aware that Elohim City is always available as a refuge from the outside world. Prominent white supremacists, including Jim Ellison, former head of the **Covenant, the Sword, and the Arm of the Lord**, have lived there. Ellison moved to Elohim City after marrying Millar's granddaughter. Richard Wayne Snell, a white supremacist leader, lived at Elohim City before he was convicted of murdering a pawnshop owner and an Arkansas black state patrol trooper. The state of Arkansas executed Snell for these crimes on April 19, 1995. Telephone records indicate that **Timothy James McVeigh** called Elohim City shortly before the Oklahoma City bombing on April 19, 1995. Members of the **Aryan Republican Army**, a group that conducted a series of bank robberies in the mid-1990s, used Elohim City as a meeting place to plan their operations. Despite these links to anti-government extremists, Millar claimed that terrorism is counterproductive and wants nothing to do with it.

Elohim City was able to avoid a succession crisis. Robert Millar died on May 28, 2001 several days after suffering a heart attack. His son John Millar assumed leadership of Elohim City and promised to continue his father's work. His assumption of leadership ended the speculation that his granddaughter's husband, Jim Ellison, would replace Robert Millar. **See also** Aryan Republican Army; Christian Identity; Covenant, the Sword, and the Arm of the Lord.

Suggested readings: Gustav Niebuhr, "A Vision of an Apocalypse: The Religion of the Far Right," *New York Times* (May 22, 1995), p. A8; Scott Parks, "Outposts of Race-Based Theology," *Dallas Morning News* (August 5, 1995), p. 1G; Andrew Phillips, "The City of God Mystery: Did a Canadian Ultra-Rightist in Oklahoma Have Links with McVeigh?," *Macleans* (April 7, 1997), p. 110; David Pugliese, "Meet the Keeper of the 'Holiday Inn of Hate,' " *Ottawa Citizen* (April 15, 2000), p. B1; Bill Schiller, "U.S. Sect Defies Dad's Fight to Get Back Kids," *Toronto Star* (June 30, 1986), p. A1; Judy L. Thomas, "We Are Not Dangerous, Leader of Separatists Says," *Kansas City Star* (March 17, 1996), p. A1; Sam Howe Verhovek, "Sect Leader Denies a Tie to McVeigh," *New York Times* (May 25, 1995), p. A26.

Estes Park Meeting

The Estes Park meeting, held between October 23 and 25, 1992, launched the anti-government **militia movement** in the United States. Peter J. Peters, a Colorado **Christian Identity** minister, hosted the closed-door meeting in Estes Park, Colorado. Approximately 160 of the most prominent right-wing extremist leaders attended this meeting. Held in the aftermath of the deaths in the **Ruby Ridge incident** of members of the **Randall Weaver** family and the siege and deaths of **Branch Davidians**, the participants were hostile toward the federal government. Other leaders were concerned about recent government efforts to control guns. After considerable discussion, two ideas emerged from the meeting: the need for militias and the tactic of **leaderless resistance**.

The first idea was the formation of a militia movement. Militias have always existed in American history, but this proposed militia movement had a distinct right-wing, anti-government orientation. These leaders proposed a grassroots militia movement directed against gun control. Some of these leaders also envisaged the movement furnishing a cadre of leaders to be recruited to engage in direct action campaigns.

A desire for direct action led to the second part of the initiative—leaderless resistance. Several of the leaders present at Estes Park had survived the federal government's attempt to jail them for a national white supremacist conspiracy at the **Fort Smith Sedition Trial**, but the proceedings had scared them. **Louis Beam** championed the concept of leaderless resistance, in which small cells of five or six activists carried out operations. This secret and independent action would prevent government agencies from tracing the cells back to the national leadership and prosecuting the leaders. Only after the fact would the national leadership learn of the operation; thus they would have built-in deniability. These leaders liked the deniability as well as the direct-action capability of this strategy.

Participants at the Estes Park Meeting adopted both strategies. Militia units were created all over the country and many of them started paramilitary training. The most prominent of these new militia units was **John Ernest Trochmann**'s **Militia of Montana** (MOM). Economic dislocation in rural areas and widespread fears of gun control attracted numerous supporters. Backers of

white supremacy never tried to take over these militia units, but they infiltrated them and formed small, direct-action cells. The strength of cell activity is also its major weakness. Lack of oversight means rogue cells can undertake an operation that discredits the movement. Although **Timothy James McVeigh** had only limited contact with the militia movement, his bombing in Oklahoma City has had a negative impact on it. See also Beam, Louis; Militia Movement; Militia of Montana; Peters, Peter J.; Trochmann, John Ernest.

Suggested readings: Morris Dees and James Corcoran, *Gathering Storm: America's Militia Threat* (New York: HarperCollins, 1996); Lou Kilzer and Kevin Flynn, "Militia Movement Had Roots in Estes," *Denver Rocky Mountain News* (May 14, 1997), p. 10A; Martin A. Lee, *The Beast Reawakens* (Boston: Little, Brown, 1997); Howard Pankratz, " '92 Meeting in Estes 'Kick-off' for Militias," *Denver Post* (September 19, 1996), p. A20; Kenneth S. Stern, *A Force upon the Plain: The American Militia Movement and the Politics of Hate* (Norman: University of Oklahoma Press, 1996).

Euro-American Alliance

The Euro-American Alliance is a white supremacist organization with strong neo-Nazi leanings. Donald V. Clerkin, a former high school history teacher in Illinois and Wisconsin, founded the Euro-American Alliance in 1976 and established its headquarters in Milwaukee, Wisconsin. Clerkin also publishes the official monthly publication of the Euro-American Alliance, *The Talon*, and a quarterly, *Euro-American Quarterly*. In these publications, Clerkin advances the cause of a whites-only country, which would exclude all Jews and minorities. He also claims to have the support of a paramilitary organization, the Euro-American Brigade, to defend the cause of white supremacy. Among the other tenets advanced by Clerkin and his Euro-American Alliance are Holocaust denial, Jewish responsibility for the Persian Gulf War, and Jewish blame for the Oklahoma City bombing. Clerkin and his organization sell copies of speeches made by the **American Nazi Party**'s **George Lincoln Rockwell** and pro-Nazi propaganda. The Euro-American Alliance cooperates with other white supremacist groups and has close ties to the **Liberty Lobby**. In 1999 Clerkin admitted that his group had not met for several years, but his publications still attract an audience. **See also** American Fascism; Holocaust Denial Movement; Neo-Nazis.

Suggested readings: Anti-Defamation League, *Danger: Extremism: The Major Vehicles and Voices on America's Far-Right Fringe* (New York: Anti-Defamation League, 1996); Katherine M. Skiba, "Report Cites Growing Number of Hate Groups; Lists 12 in Wisconsin," *Milwaukee Journal Sentinel* (March 10, 1999), p. 7.

Extremist Publications

Before the Internet became popular for the distribution of extremist literature, extremists used journals and newsletters to spread their viewpoints and recruit prospective members. Many of these publications have developed large subscription bases, and the funds gathered from them have supported the groups publishing them. Mainstream publication companies have in the past refused to publish them because of the controversial nature of these publications. Consequently, special printing businesses specialize in the publication of these serials.

The first important extremist journal was **Gerald Lyman Kenneth Smith**'s *The Cross and the Flag*. From 1942 until Smith's death in 1976, it spread his anti-Semitic and political views. The last issue appeared in December 1977. Smith started this journal because his radio talks were being censored during World War II, and he lacked other avenues to spread his isolationist and anti-Semitic views. Smith retained total editorial control over the journal and approved all of its articles. His biographer, Glen Jeansonne, estimated that 90 percent of all the writings in this publication came from the pen of Smith. While each issue of this monthly lost money, it was successful because of its large circulation, its influence among extremists, and its longevity. For nearly thirty-five years, this

publication was the most influential journal of opinion in extremist circles.

The successor to *The Cross and the Flag* was **Liberty Lobby**'s *Spotlight*. **Willis Carto**, the founder and head of the Liberty Lobby, founded this newsletter in August 1975 to provide a forum to publish his anti-government, anti–income tax, and anti-Semitic messages. It replaced the Liberty Lobby's earlier publication, *Liberty Letters*. *Spotlight* is published and distributed in Washington, D.C. At its peak of popularity in 1981, Frank P. Mintz reported that the newsletter had a circulation of more than 520,000. James Coates estimated its circulation at 150,000 in 1987. Circulation dropped in the mid-1990s to around 100,000. It is the acknowledged leading ultraconservative publication in the United States. Carto has always used this publication to promote his political agenda. Authors write articles for *Spotlight* that conform to Carto's viewpoint. Any author who breaks ranks with Carto over any issue will find himself or herself excluded from appearing in the newsletter again and will be savagely attacked by Carto in it. This happened to several writers who backed the **Institute for Historical Review** staff in its lawsuit against Carto. Carto has also used *Spotlight* to showcase other political causes, including the **Populist Party** in the 1980s.

The Jubilee is the leading national publication in the United States for **Christian Identity** members, **neo-Nazis**, racist **skinheads**, and anti-government militias. Paul Hall, Jr., started this bimonthly tabloid publication in 1988 and publishes it in Midpines, California. He remains both the publisher and the managing editor. Hall uses his newspaper to advance his political agenda, which includes accusing the federal government of carrying out the 1995 Oklahoma City bombing. Articles in *The Jubilee* routinely support anti-Semitism and promote the white supremacist ideology of Christian Identity. He sometimes sends special correspondents to cover controversial events. In 1993 he asked **Louis Beam**, a veteran white supremacist leader, to cover the **Branch Davidians** siege in Waco, Texas. Since 1988 Hall and his newspaper have sponsored and organized an annual Jubilation Celebration to promote unity among the white supremacist groups. These celebrations meet at various locations around the country and attract most of the leaders of the major extremist groups.

Another white supremacist publication is the *American Renaissance* founded in 1990. Jared Taylor, a white supremacist and a board member of the **Council of Conservative Citizens**, publishes this monthly journal in Oaktown, Virginia. Taylor, a graduate of Yale University and the Paris Institute of Political Studies, uses his writing skills to advance the thesis that blacks are genetically inferior to whites. His journal and its sponsor, Century Foundation, sponsor a series of conferences, the American Renaissance Conference, to be held every five years. In the latest conference, held in Reston, Virginia, in April 2000, participants decried the demographic decline of the white race and discussed ways to halt the decline. Taylor's latest cause in the *American Renaissance* is the defense of the Confederate battle flag.

The most racist of the extremist publications is *WAR*, the official journal of the **White Aryan Resistance** (WAR) and its leader, **Tom Metzger**. Metzger, who bills his publication as "the most racist newspaper on earth" is the editor, and he publishes it in Fallbrook, California. He started this newspaper in 1983 and has specialized in articles on white supremacist and neo-Nazi subjects. Besides revenue from subscribers, the journal advertises books, tapes, and videos which provide income to support WAR.

The magazine *Soldier of Fortune: The Journal of Professional Adventurers* represents the aspirations and worldview of the survivalist wing of extremism. Robert K. Brown, a Green Beret veteran, founded the magazine in 1975 in the aftermath of the Vietnam War. It is published monthly in Boulder, Colorado. Brown had a history of anti-communist activism while working with anti-Castro exiles in the late 1950s. His resentment against the policies of the U.S. government is contained in his phrase "good soldiers and gutless politicians." Since the 1980s, the *Soldier of Fortune* has become the most popular survivalist reading material on the mass market. The magazine has been described as the expression of the American warrior culture. It also provides a national forum for writers to vent their anger against the federal government. In the growing survivalist industry, the *Soldier of Fortune* steers a middle course in a movement thriving on discontent and unrest. Brown has avoided turning the magazine into a propaganda machine for the **white supremacist movement**, but the magazine does serve as an advertising source for right-wing publishers and booksellers. Brown also conducts an annual five-day conference which attracts a crowd of adventurers, gun enthusiasts, survivalists, and white supremacists. **See also** Christian Identity; Council of Conservative Citizens; Militia Movement; Smith, Gerald Lyman Kenneth; Survivalist Movement.

Suggested readings: John Berry, "Newspaper Focuses on Conspiracy Theories," *Atlanta Journal and Constitution* (June 11, 1995), p. 5B; James Coates, *Armed and Dangerous: The Rise of the Survivalist Right* (New York: Hill and Wang, 1987); Glen Jeansonne, *Gerald L. K. Smith: Minister of Hate* (New Haven, Conn.: Yale University Press, 1988); Jim Leusner and Ann Groer, "Patriot Press Features a Strong Point of View," *Orlando Sentinel* (April 27, 1995), p. A1; Frank P. Mintz, *The Liberty Lobby and the American Right: Race, Conspiracy, and Culture* (Westport, Conn.: Greenwood Press, 1985); Southern Poverty Law Center, "The Annals of Hate," *SPLC Intelligence Report* 93 (Winter 1999): 48–49; Jonathan Tilove, "White Nationalists Decry Caucasian America's Decline," *Times-Picayune* [New Orleans] (April 9, 2000), p. A22.

F

Farrakhan, Louis (1933–)

Louis Farrakhan, the charismatic leader of the militant Black Muslim movement of the Nation of Islam, was born on May 11, 1933, in New York City. His birth name was Louis Eugene Walcott. His mother, who was from Saint Kitts in the Caribbean, worked as a maid to raise her two sons. While Farrakhan was still an infant, his mother moved her family to Boston. Farrakhan excelled in academics, track, and music at Boston Latin High School. His musical talent showed on the violin and in voice. After high school, Farrakhan enrolled at the Winston-Salem Teachers College in North Carolina, but after two years he left school to pursue a music career as a calypso singer. His stage nickname was the "Charmer." His singing career was stagnating when he came into contact with **Malcolm X** and the **Nation of Islam.**

Malcolm X, the head of Boston Temple no. 11 of the Nation of Islam, recognized the abilities of Farrakhan. After his recruitment into the Nation of Islam and several years of grooming, Farrakhan replaced Malcolm X as head of the Boston temple when Malcolm moved to Harlem Temple no. 7. Following Black Muslim tradition, Farrakhan assumed the name of Louis X. Farrakhan showed his faith in **Elijah Muhammad** and supported him when Malcolm X broke with the Nation of Islam in 1964 over sexual scandals in the movement. Farrakhan's attacks on Malcolm X provided an atmosphere that led to Malcolm's assassination on February 21, 1965, by Nation of Islam members. Malcolm's family blamed Farrakhan for his death at the time and they still do. Elijah Muhammad rewarded Farrakhan for his loyalty by appointing him head minister of Harlem Temple no. 7 in May 1965. In 1968 Muhammad appointed Farrakhan as his radio spokesperson. Despite these favors, Elijah Muhammad always kept Farrakhan under tight control, despite the fact that two of Elijah Muhammad's family members married two of Farrakhan's daughters.

After the death of Elijah Muhammad in 1975, Farrakhan found himself faced with difficult choices. He flirted briefly with the idea of challenging for the leadership of the Nation of Islam. After discussions with selected members on his staff, he decided not to contest Muhammad's son, Wallace Deen Muhammad, for the top post. Wallace Deen Muhammad, nevertheless, distrusted Farrakhan and had him transferred to the Nation of Islam's Chicago headquarters. Over the next several years, Farrakhan found himself in direct opposition to Wallace Deen Muhammad's reorientation of the Nation of Islam toward orthodox Sunni Islam. In the fall of 1977, Farrakhan finally broke openly

Nation of Islam leader Louis Farrakhan addresses the Million Man March, on October 16, 1995, on Capitol Hill. Farrakhan proclaimed divine guidance in bringing to Washington the largest assemblage of black Americans since the 1963 March on Washington. Farrakhan's son, Mustafa, is at his left. (AP Photo/Doug Mills)

with Wallace Deen Muhammad and started a drive to re-create the Nation of Islam of Elijah Muhammad in New York City. His efforts resulted in an agreement with Wallace Deen Muhammad that Farrakhan would retain the name Nation of Islam and part of the old organization under his control. Farrakhan's new version of the Nation of Islam is much smaller than Wallace Deen Muhammad's American Muslim Mission, which follows a more traditionally Moslem orientation. In the mid-1990s, the Nation of Islam had about 20,000 regularly mosque-attending members in contrast to the 750,000 regular members of the American Muslim Mission.

Farrakhan's brand of leadership in the Nation of Islam has made him one of the most controversial leaders in the black community. He has never avoided political con-troversy and often picks fights. His statements calling whites "blue-eyed devils" and describing Judaism as a "gutter relig-ion," as well as his references to Hitler as a great man, have contributed to his reputa-tion as an extremist. In 1983 he endorsed Jesse Jackson's first presidential bid, but his negative comments on Jews forced Jackson to disassociate himself from Farrakhan. In 1990 his activities in the "Stop the Killing" tours to discourage black-on-black crime were interpreted as a positive act. Then in 1995 Farrakhan sponsored and participated in the Million Man March to uplift and re-new the social and political involvement of Afro-American men. Despite severe criticism from conservatives and women, this march was a success. Farrakhan followed these pos-itive activities by a 1996 tour of Arab coun-tries, including Saddam Hussein's Iraq and

Muammar Qaddafi's Libya, which increased his negative profile on the national scene. He continues to bewilder his enemies with his anti-Jewish comments, but in the last several years he has appeared to be more conciliatory and has toned down his attacks.

Farrakhan has had to deal with a variety of serious problems both inside and outside of the Nation of Islam in the last decade. Reports surfaced in the early 1990s that the Nation of Islam was experiencing financial problems. Charges have been made that the nation-affiliated businesses are riddled with debt, show incidents of fraud, and support the lavish lifestyles of Farrakhan, his relatives, and his top aides. More traditional Islamic organizations have attacked the Nation of Islam for heresy because of the belief that its founder, Fard Muhammad, was the embodiment of God and that Elijah Muhammad was a Messiah. This isolation from mainstream Islam has hurt the Nation of Islam's recruitment efforts. Finally, Farrakhan's illness with prostate cancer has curtailed many of his activities. He was first diagnosed with prostate cancer in 1991 and underwent hormone and radiation treatments. The cancer reappeared in 1999, and he underwent emergency surgery at Howard University Hospital in April 1999. On November 1, 2000, Farrakhan had prostate surgery to treat complications from radiation therapy. His illness highlights the lack of a designated successor to Farrakhan in the Nation of Islam. In the meantime, Farrakhan has been active in changing his anti-Jewish, anti-white stance to one of a political moderate willing to tolerate differences between the races. His appointment of Ava Muhammad to a leadership post in October 1999 and his acceptance of orthodox Islam in February 2000 are other signs that Farrakhan is receptive to making changes. **See also** Malcolm X; Muhammad, Elijah; Nation of Islam.

Suggested readings: Cathleen Falsani, "Nation of Islam Tones It Down," *Chicago Sun-Times* (February 25, 2001), p. 20; Mattias Gardell, *In the Name of Elijah Muhammad: Louis Farrakhan and the Nation of Islam* (Dur-

ham, N.C.: Duke University Press, 1996); Gregory Kane, "Critics Won't Let Farrakhan Be New Man He's Become," *Star Tribune* [Minneapolis] (October 22, 2000), p. 29A; Arthur J. Magida, *Prophet of Rage: A Life of Louis Farrakhan and His Nation* (New York: Basic Books, 1996); Michael Paulson, "Farrakhan's Nation of Islam Softening Stance," *Boston Globe* (March 4, 2000), p. B1; Robert Singh, *The Farrakhan Phenomenon: Race, Reaction, and the Paranoid Style in American Politics* (Washington, D.C.: Georgetown University Press, 1997).

Farrands, James W. (1935–)

James Farrands, the former head of the **Invisible Empire, Knights of the Ku Klux Klan** and the present head of the Unified Ku Klux Klan, was born in Shelton, Connecticut, in 1935. He earned his living as a tool and die maker in Shelton before engaging in political activity with the Klan. Unique among Klan leaders, Farrands is a practicing Catholic. He joined the Klan in Connecticut in the early 1950s. Among his other responsibilities, Farrands served as editor and later publisher of the official Klan publication, *The Klansman.* In 1981 he was appointed the grand dragon of the Connecticut branch of the Invisible Empire, Knights of the Ku Klux Klan. Late in 1985, he succeeded the founder of the Invisible Empire, **Elbert Claude "Bill" Wilkerson,** after Wilkerson was unmasked as an FBI informant. When Farrands assumed control, the Invisible Empire had approximately 2,000 members and was in a state of disarray.

Farrands began to rebuild the Invisible Empire by continuing Wilkerson's activism. In January 1987, Farrands led his Klan forces against civil rights demonstrators in Forsyth County, Georgia. Violence directed by members of the Klan against the civil rights marchers caused considerable publicity in the national media. Soon after this incident, Farrands moved the Invisible Empire organization to an eighty-five-acre farm in rural North Carolina. In 1988 Farrands and his organization lost a court case to the Southern Poverty Law Center for damages incurred during the Forsyth County Klan riot. A resulting court judgment in 1993 led to the Invisible Empire's dissolution, relinquishment of its mailing lists, and an agreement not to publish *The Klansman*. Because this settlement left Farrands without an organization to lead, he formed a new group, the Unified Ku Klux Klan. Despite his efforts to moderate the racist and white supremacist rhetoric of his new Klan group, Farrands' new Klan group is not as strong or as popular as the Invisible Empire. Most of his followers have migrated to other Klan or **Christian Identity** groups.

Suggested readings: Anti-Defamation League, *Danger: Extremism: The Major Vehicles and Voices on America's Far-Right Fringe* (New York: Anti-Defamation League, 1996); Lynne Duke, "Klan Unit Gives Up Assets in Rights Suit Settlement," *Washington Post* (May 20, 1993), p. A1; Bill Rankin, "Court Orders Klan Faction to Disband Settles Suit in Forsyth Attack," *Atlanta Journal and Constitution* (May 20, 1993), p. A1; Michael Winerip, "Catholic Connecticut Yankee Who Heads the Klan," *New York Times* (September 16, 1986), p. B2.

Fascism (See American Fascism)

Fields, Edward R. (1931–)

Edward Fields, a longtime leader in the **National State's Rights Party** (NSRP) and various **Ku Klux Klan** groups, was born in 1931 and raised in an affluent family in Marietta, Georgia. He attended school at the Marist Academy in Atlanta. After briefly attending law school, Fields transferred to the Palmer School of Chiropractic Medicine in Davenport, Iowa. Although he is a chiropractor by training, Fields has never established a practice. Fields and his friend **Jesse Benjamin Stoner** founded the NSRP in 1958. Fields, who has served as its national secretary and editor of its newsletter, the *Thunderbolt*, has devoted all of his energy to building extremist groups to advance the **white supremacist movement**. He was active in the 1981 founding of the New Order, Knights of the Ku Klux Klan and became its grand dragon. Always he has preached hatred of minorities

and has advocated the elimination of all Jews from positions of authority in the government and society. He led his Klan group in agitating against immigrant labor in Georgia. During Stoner's imprisonment for a 1958 church bombing, the executive committee of the NSRP voted him out of the party in August 1983. Grounds for the dismissal were charges of his personal immorality and alleged diversion of party funds to his Ku Klux Klan group. In May 1984, Fields was arrested for burglarizing and destroying files in the NSRP's office.

Fields responded to his ouster and legal troubles by becoming more engaged in extremist activities with other groups. Despite his break with the NSRP, he retained editorship of the *Thunderbolt*, but it ran into financial troubles in the late 1980s. Fields made appeals to save the paper and changed its name to the *Truth at Last* in an effort to attract more subscribers. Although his Klan group dissolved in the 1980s, he still maintained contact with most of the Klan leaders. In the mid-1990s, he co-founded the America First Party, which advocates **anti-Semitism** and white supremacy. He is also active in its short-wave radio program, America First Radio, which is aired on the World Wide Christian Radio (WWCR). Fields has become one of the elder statesmen of the American extremist movement. **See also** Ku Klux Klan; National State's Rights Party; Stoner, Jesse Benjamin; White Supremacist Movement.

Suggested readings: Anti-Defamation League, *Danger: Extremism: The Major Vehicles and Voices on America's Far-Right Fringe* (New York: Anti-Defamation League, 1996); Phillip Finch, *God, Guts, and Guns* (New York: Seaview/Putnam, 1983).

Forbes, Ralph Perry (1939–)

Ralph Forbes has long been a leader in white supremacist groups, but in the 1980s he became a convert to mainstreaming the **Ku Klux Klan** by running for state offices. He was born in London, Arkansas, in 1939. In 1960 Forbes joined **George Lincoln Rock-**

well's **American Nazi Party** (ANP). His early duty in the party was to serve as Rockwell's driver, but by 1961 he was one of the emerging leaders of the ANP. In April 1962 Forbes briefly resigned from the party over the reinstatement of John Patler, a former member who moved to New York City after a dispute with Rockwell, because he distrusted this future assassin. Forbes rejoined the party after Rockwell appointed him to head the California branch of the American Nazi Party. In 1965 Rockwell persuaded him to become the party's **Christian Identity** minister. Since leaving the ANP in 1967, he has been active in Arkansas state politics and in running in the Arkansas Republican primary for lieutenant governor in 1987. His strategy was to gain a platform for his white supremacist message. In 1988 Forbes became head of **David Duke**'s presidential campaign on the **Populist Party** ticket. Next, Forbes ran for Arkansas lieutenant governor in the Republican primary in 1990; this time, he lost in a runoff to a black businessman. During the race, a black politician assaulted Forbes, gaining him statewide publicity. In 1992 Forbes made the news again by being excluded from a political debate of the candidates in an Arkansas Educational Television debate. Forbes was running as an independent candidate for Arkansas' Third Congressional District. He sued and after a lower court refused to act, the Eighth Circuit Court of Appeals upheld his protest and required public broadcasters to offer a "viewpoint-neutral" reason for excluding candidates to debate on public stations. Forbes continues to advance the white supremacist cause by seeking public office and using political campaigns to advertise his views. **See also** American Nazi Party; Duke, David; Rockwell, George Lincoln.

Suggested readings: Anti-Defamation League, *Danger: Extremism: The Major Vehicles and Voices on America's Far-Right Fringe* (New York: Anti-Defamation League, 1996); Lee May, "Duke Victory Spurs 'Clone' Candidates," *Los Angeles Times* (June 27, 1991), p. A5; Jeffrey Kaplan ed., *Encyclopedia of White Power: A Sourcebook on the Radical Racist Right* (Walnut

Creek, Calif.: Altamira Press, 2000); Jim Nichols, "Arkansas GOP Race Pits Black, Neo-Nazi," *St. Louis Post-Dispatch* (June 8, 1990), p. 1C.

Foreman, David (1946–)

David Foreman, long a leader in the radical wing of the environmentalist movement, was born on October 18, 1946, and raised in various states because his father was an Air Force pilot. He was brought up in a staunchly conservative Republican family. He joined the Boy Scouts and became an Eagle Scout. Foreman graduated from Blythe High School in Blythe, California. At an early age, he was active in Republican Party politics and campaigned for Barry Goldwater in the 1964 presidential election. After high school, Foreman moved to San Antonio, Texas, where he attended a junior college. He decided to transfer in 1965 to the University of New Mexico, in Albuquerque. Here he became a convert to Ayn Rand's brand of libertarianism. After joining the Young Americans for Freedom, Foreman was selected its state chairperson in New Mexico in 1966. Attracted by service in the Vietnam War, Foreman joined the U.S. Marine Corps aspiring to be an officer. After finding himself opposed in principle to military life, Foreman ended up in the stockade after being absent without leave. After he received a dishonorable discharge from the marines, he returned to New Mexico. He decided to devote his full attention to environmentalism and married Debbie Sease. Foreman repudiated his youthful conservatism and became a Jimmy Carter supporter. In 1978 he moved to Washington, D.C., to work as a liaison between the Wilderness Society's field operations and its lobbying staff. His experience in the moderate wing of the environmental movement convinced him that unchecked capitalism would ruin the world's environment.

Foreman decided that a direct-action approach to environmentalism would be more effective in saving the environment. During a hiking expedition in the Pincacte Desert area of Mexico with four associates, Foreman and his companions agreed to form a new activist environmental group which would allow nothing to take precedence over the environment. They borrowed the ideas of a Norwegian philosopher, Arne Naess, and his emphasis on the primacy of life itself rather than on the dominance of human beings. This philosophy, called "deep ecology," removes humans from the center of life on earth to one of a number of species. It has had a revolutionary impact on **radical environmentalism**. Foreman adopted this philosophy, and in 1980 he helped form **Earth First!** Foreman, who distrusted intellectuals, wanted an organization of environmental activists willing to take risks. Under Foreman's leadership no tactic was too drastic to protect the environment. Destruction of mining equipment and the practice of driving metal spikes into trees, or "**monkeywrenching**" were acceptable to him. He drew the line, however, at violence directed toward individuals. In the aftermath of a successful demonstration against the Getty Oil Company in northwestern Wyoming, Foreman wrote a handbook of ecotage (ecological sabotage), *Ecodefense: A Field Guide to Monkeywrenching* (1982). This book serves as a practical guide to the use of sabotage against equipment being used by the resource industry.

As Earth First! attracted publicity and new members, Foreman lost control of the movement. Many former left-wing political activists migrated to the environmental movement in the mid-1980s. Among these were advocates of social justice and neo-Marxists eager to attack the existing political, social, and economic systems. **Judi Bari** represented the influx of socially active outsiders moving into the environmental movement. Foreman had little use for Bari and others of these new recruits. To Foreman the environment was the only issue of importance. Earth First! bogged down in the debate over population and population policy. Dissension developed between Foreman's supporters of deep ecology and those of the social justice wing. His disillusion was so

great that he resigned from a leadership position in Earth First! in 1989.

Foreman also ran into legal problems. The FBI started investigating him for his involvement with an ecoterrorist group, Evan Mechan Eco Terrorist International Conspiracy (EMETIC), and its anti-nuclear activities in the Prescott, Arizona, area. On May 13, 1989, FBI agents arrested him. Foreman pleaded guilty to a felony conspiracy charge in a 1991 trial, but he refused to turn state's evidence against his fellow defendants. He was sentenced to five years' probation after which the charge was to be reduced to a misdemeanor. He gave up his advocacy of monkeywrenching as part of the settlement. Despite this setback, he formed a new environment group, the North American Wilderness Recovery Strategy, to save ecosystems. During the last decade, he has continued to travel around the country advancing his views on ecology and the environment. **See also** Bari, Judi; Earth First!; Radical Environmentalism.

Suggested readings: Bill Dietrich, "Earth First Founder Reflects on Life as an 'Eco-Warrior,' " *Seattle Times* (March 12, 1991), p. B1; John Lancaster, "The Green Guerrilla; 'Redneck' Eco-Activist Dave Foreman, Throwing a Monkey Wrench into the System," *Washington Post* (March 20, 1991), p. B1; Christopher Manes, *Green Rage: Radical Environmentalism and the Unmaking of Civilization* (Boston: Little, Brown, 1990); Valier Richardson and Siobhan McDonough, "First Earth First!er Swings Different Ax," *Washington Times* (March 6, 1991), p. E1; Judd Slivka, "Earth First! Founder Hasn't Lost His Passion," *Arizona Republic* (February 8, 2001), p. B1; Susan Zakin, *Coyotes and Town Dogs: Earth First! and the Environmental Movement* (New York: Viking Press, 1993).

Fort Smith Sedition Trial

The Fort Smith Sedition Trial was an unsuccessful attempt made by the federal government to short-circuit the radical extremist movement by charging the national leaders of the **white supremacist movement** of conspiring to overthrow the U.S. government. The trial took place shortly after the militant wing of the **Aryan Nations**, **The Order**, had resorted to a violent campaign to destabilize the federal government by staging robberies, kidnappings, murders, and counterfeiting. Operation Clean-Sweep was a yearlong federal campaign to derail the growing antigovernment movement. The government indicted fourteen white supremacist leaders for sedition in 1987, and the trial was held in Fort Smith, Arkansas, in early 1988. The leaders were charged with planning a guerrilla war to be financed through robberies and counterfeiting. A planned terror campaign included bombings, pollution of municipal water supplies, and the assassination of federal officials and key politicians. The goal was the establishment of a white supremacist homeland in the Pacific Northwest. Those charged were Andrew Virgil Barnhill, **Louis Beam**, **Richard Girnt Butler**, Ardie McBreaty, **David Lane**, David Michael McGuire, **Robert Miles**, Lambert Miller, Bruce Carroll Pierce, Richard Scutari, Robert Neil Smalley, Richard Wayne Snell, Ivan Ray Wade, and William H. Wade. Two of the government witnesses against the defendants were Jim Ellison, former head of the **Covenant, the Sword, and the Army of the Lord,** and **Glen Miller**, a North Carolina **Ku Klux Klan** leader.

The trial was lengthy and full of recriminations between the defendants and the witnesses. Government prosecutors had a legal case that was difficult to prove, but evidence presented at the trial proved that The Order was part of the white supremacist strategy of violence. Despite this evidence and the testimony of witnesses, the defendants were acquitted of all charges in a case of jury nullification, which occurs when a jury ignores the evidence and instructions from the judge for political reasons. Ellison's testimony had inconsistencies, and the jurors believed that he testified to win a reduced prison sentence. Moreover, two of the women jurors fell in love with two of the defendants, and one of the romances resulted in marriage. Another male juror later confessed that he shared the views of the defendants. More important than the results of the trial was the poisoning

of the relationships among the leaders of the various groups and the outright hostility directed toward those who had turned state's evidence. It also proved to the leadership of the white supremacist movement how vulnerable they were to government retaliation. This trial cured them of taking chances. Soon afterward Beam and others developed the idea of **leaderless resistance**.

Suggested readings: Associated Press, "13 Supremacists Are Not Guilty of Conspiracies," *New York Times* (April 8, 1988), p. A14; Katherine Bishop, "14 on Trial; Judging the Danger on the Right Fringe," *New York Times* (March 6, 1988), sec. 4, p. 5; Wayne King, "10 Named in a Plot to Overthrow U.S.," *New York Times* (April 25, 1987), p. 1; Cheri Seymour, *Committee of the States: Inside the Radical Right* (Mariposa, Calif.: Camden Place Communications, 1991).

Fourth Reich Skinheads

The Fourth Reich Skinheads was a white supremacist group in California affiliated with the **White Aryan Resistance** (WAR). The membership of this group of skinheads ranged between eighteen and fifty young adults and teenagers from Southern California. The leader of the Fourth Reich Skinheads was Christopher David Fisher. His group had a loose affiliation with **Tom Metzger**'s WAR. Late in 1992, Fisher led his group and several other white supremacists in a bombing campaign in Southern California. They bombed two homes and an automobile. The same band then vandalized a Westminister, California, synagogue. Their next targets were Rodney G. King, who had become famous for being the subject of an illegal beating administered by Los Angeles Police Department officers, and the First African Methodist Episcopal Church, the oldest African American church in Los Angeles. They planned to kill King and blow up the church, to start a race war.

An undercover government agent penetrated the Fourth Reich Skinheads and forewarned the authorities about the plan. The agent had arrived in Southern California as a representative of **Matthew Hale's World Church of the Creator**. A team of federal agents and Los Angeles police officers arrested the leaders of the Fourth Reich Skinheads and their white supremacist allies on July 15, 1993. In a subsequent trial held in October 1993, Fisher pleaded guilty to one count of conspiracy and one count of bombing a residence. He received a ten-year prison sentence. Two other members of the Fourth Reich Skinheads were juveniles and received lesser sentences. Allies of the Fourth Reich Skinheads were convicted on illegal weapons charges and sentenced to long prison sentences. Metzger denied any ties with the Fourth Reich Skinheads or the white supremacists. **See also** Metzger, Tom; Skinheads; White Aryan Resistance.

Suggested readings: Gabe Martinez and Jim Newton, "FBI Infiltrator Was on Verge of Being Exposed," *Los Angeles Times* (July 19, 1993), p. A1; Jim Newton and Ann W. O'Neill, "Alleged White Supremacists Seized in Assassination Plots," *Los Angeles Times* (July 16, 1993), p. A1; Jim Newton, "4 Indicted in Hate Crimes, Illegal Guns," *Los Angeles Times* (July 30, 1993), p. B1; Jim Newton, "Hate Group Was Shadowed by Mysterious Informant," *Los Angeles Times* (July 18, 1993), p. A1; Jim Newton, "Skinhead Leader Pleads Guilty to Violence, Plot," *Los Angeles Times* (October 20, 1993), p. A1.

Frankhauser, Roy Everett, Jr. (1939–)

Roy Frankhauser, a longtime supporter of extremist causes, was born on November 4, 1939, in Reading, Pennsylvania. His parents divorced when he was still young and he became the subject of a lengthy custody battle. At the age of fourteen, he joined the **Ku Klux Klan**. After service in the U.S. Army, Frankhauser became a member of **George Lincoln Rockwell's American Nazi Party**. At about the same time, he joined **Jesse Benjamin Stoner's National State's Rights Party**. During the civil rights movement, Frankhauser, who attacked civil rights marchers on several occasions, was one of the more violent counterdemonstrators. By the early 1960s, he had become active in **Robert Shelton's United Klans of America** (UKA) and became the

grand dragon for the state of Pennsylvania. Frankhauser was also active in **Robert Bolivar De Pugh's Minutemen movement** for which he served as the coordinator for Pennsylvania. In 1965 he lost an eye in a barroom brawl in Reading over his Klan activities.

Frankhauser's role in the Ku Klux Klan movement and his reputation for violence soon attracted the attention of federal authorities. A congressional investigation of Klan activities led to an invitation for him to testify before the committee. In a February 1966 hearing, Frankhauser refused to answer all questions citing the Fifth Amendment to the Constitution. Many of the questions were about his role in the suicide of fellow Nazi and Klansman, **Daniel Burros**, in Frankhauser's house after Burros had been exposed by the media for being half-Jewish. Frankhauser was one of the few defendants at the hearings who was not sentenced to prison for contempt of Congress. Shortly afterward, he became an informant for the FBI. His exposure as an informant came after his arrest for stealing dynamite for the bodyguard of **Robert Miles**, a Michigan Ku Klux Klan leader, in 1971. Frankhauser pleaded guilty to this offense and in February 1974 received two five-year terms of probation. Shelton immediately had him dismissed as grand dragon and expelled from the United Klans of America.

After his banishment from the Klan movement, Frankhauser resurfaced in other extremist organizations. He was hired to be a security consultant to **Lyndon LaRouche's** neo-Nazi movement. His activities with LaRouche led to his being indicted in 1986 on federal fraud and conspiracy charges in a credit card scheme. In December 1987, Frankhauser was convicted and sentenced to three years in prison and fined $50,000. During the appeals process, he renewed his association with the Ku Klux Klan by working at rallies for **James Farrand's Invisible Empire, Knights of the Ku Klux Klan**. Frankhauser went to prison in 1989 and served his time at the federal prison in Duluth, Minnesota. After his release in the summer of 1990, he resumed his Klan activities. In April 1992, he was arrested for stabbing a Ku Klux Klan security guard at a Klan rally near Carlisle, Pennsylvania. He spent nearly a year in prison and at a mental institution before being acquitted of the charge by reason of self-defense.

Frankhauser continues to be an unreconstructed neo-Nazi racist. On most public occasions, he charges that the problem with the United States is its domination by Jews and racial minorities. Frankhauser is unable to stay out of legal trouble. He was indicted and convicted of obstruction of justice and destruction of evidence in a case involving a Massachusetts skinhead leader. In May 1995, he received a twenty-five-month prison sentence for this offense. Frankhauser's most recent activity has been in the harassment case of Bonnie Jouhari in Reading, Pennsylvania, in 1999. Jouhari had been active in ending housing discrimination in the Reading area by working as a representative of Housing and Urban Development (HUD). Frankhauser conducted a personal harassment campaign against Jouhari until authorities ordered him to stop. Although Frankhauser has never been a national leader in any of the extremist organizations that he has belonged to, his participation in most of the neo-Nazi and racist groups in the last forty-five years makes him an important case study of a life-long extremist. **See also** Burros, Daniel; Ku Klux Klan, LaRouche, Lyndon Hermyle; Neo-Nazis; United Klans of America.

Suggested readings: Anti-Defamation League, *Danger: Extremism: The Major Vehicles and Voices on America's Far-Right Fringe* (New York: Anti-Defamation League, 1996); Eric Lichtblau, "Klansman to Apologize for Harassment," *Los Angeles Times* (May 12, 2000), p. A19; Eric Lichtblau, "Neo-Nazi Must Pay $1.1 Million to Fair Housing Activist," *Los Angeles Times* (July 21, 2000), p. A19; Ronald J. Ostrow and Kevin Roderick, "Extremist's Ex-Aide Disclosed Alleged Statement; FBI Tells of Threat by LaRouche," *Los Angeles Times* (October 10, 1986), part 1, p. 19; Kevin Roderick, "Five LaRouche Groups, Aides Charged in Fraud," *Los Angeles Times* (October 7, 1986), part 1, p. 1.

Freemen Movement

The Freemen Movement, an anti-government protest movement, denies the political authority of federal, state, and local governments. **LeRoy Schweitzer**, a former crop-dusting pilot from Colfax, Washington, founded the Freemen in 1992 shortly after his exposure to the anti-government teachings of Roy Schwasinger. Schwasinger, an anti-government activist from Fort Collins, Colorado, taught a course during which he claimed that the federal government was unconstitutional and its currency was worthless. He advocated that citizens file claims against the federal government to get their share of $600 trillion in gold held by the government. Schweitzer seized on these ideas and incorporated them into other anti-government positions held by the **Posse Comitatus Movement** and the **Christian Identity** movement. He traveled around the Midwest and the West advocating a repudiation of all forms of government except those proposed by him.

Over the course of nearly five years, Schweitzer and his followers adopted an aggressive anti-government philosophy. They believed that the United States was an illegal political entity and that as white males they were no longer under federal or state political jurisdiction. All constitutional amendments after the Bill of Rights in the Constitution were unconstitutional and illegal because they were passed by Jewish-dominated legislatures. They subscribe to the common law doctrine that adheres only to the Bible, the Magna Carta, the Constitution and its first ten amendments, and the Uniform Commercial Code. The Uniform Commercial Code assumes great importance in their philosophy because they interpret it as a contract which they can break. Consequently, governmental requirements, such as social security cards, driver's licenses, marriage licenses, and income tax forms, are all illegal. Because the Federal Reserve System is also considered to be illegal, they are not reluctant to attack it and its policies.

Since the Freemen reject established insti-

Negotiators James "Bo" Gritz, left, and Jack McLamb, right, hold a news conference following their visit to the Freemen compound on April 27, 1996, west of Jordan, Montana. The Freemen holed up more than a month in their standoff with the FBI. McLamb is a former Phoenix policeman and Gritz was a Green Beret colonel. Gritz holds a statement issued by the Freemen. (AP Photo/Jim Mone)

tutions, leaders of the movement have set up shadow institutions. Followers bring their disputes to be settled in a series of common law courts, and these courts issue judgments. Often these judgments are liens filed against state and local government and elected public officials. Individuals have also issued bogus checks to pay off debts or to acquire merchandise. On occasion, check writers overpaid their debts with the expectation of getting large cash refunds. Sometimes Freemen have threatened judicial and police authorities. The situation became so severe in

the mid-1990s that the practices attracted the attention of both federal and state authorities.

The center for the Freemen Movement was in Justus Township in northeastern Montana. Several Montana farmers had experienced financial hardships in the mid-1980s. They blamed the federal government for their hard times and joined the Freemen Movement. Two of the farmers, Ralph Clark and William Stanton, joined with two Freemen leaders, LeRoy Schweitzer and Rodney Skurdal, to create their own local government in September 1995. They named their new political entity the Justus Township. In 1995 the Justus Township was a small community of a half dozen ranch homes about forty miles northeast of Jordan, Montana. People traveled from all over the country to attend classes at the Justus Township to learn how to issue fraudulent checks and liens. An estimate places the number of visitors for this training at between 500 and 800.

Several of the inhabitants of Justus Township had already had scraps with the law. In January 1994, Skurdal and Stanton were among a group that had seized the Garfield County Courthouse in Jordan for two hours. During those two hours, the Freemen proclaimed a common court in existence and videotaped the events. Stanton later stood trial for this offense and the writing of a $25,000 bogus check. Other participants in the courthouse incident became fugitives from the law.

Despite an overwhelming body of evidence implicating the leaders of the Freemen in Justus Township of criminal activities, federal and state officials were cautious about moving against them. Local residents fed up with the fraudulent business practices of the Freemen accused the government of suffering from **Weaver fever**, or a reluctance on the part of federal officials to use force to arrest political lawbreakers after the **Ruby Ridge incident** and the **Branch Davidians** affair. FBI agents initiated negotiations for the surrender of those charged with illegal offenses in the Justus Township. At the beginning of the siege, a federal grand jury had indicted eight persons in the Justus Township on charges ranging from armed robbery to threatening public officials. After an eighty-one-day standoff, the Freemen surrendered to federal authorities on June 13, 1996. Eleven Freemen were arrested and taken into custody.

In the legal proceedings held in March 1997, twenty-four Freemen stood trial. Earlier LeRoy Schweitzer and Daniel Peterson had been arrested and jailed for their Free-men activities. Each of the Freemen defendants rejected the right of the government to prosecute them. They refused to cooperate with their court appointed defense lawyers and were disruptive in the court. Government agents produced more than 300,000 documents scanned onto forty-three computer disks, 5,200 audiotapes of intercepted messages, and 9,674 pages of investigative reports. Before the Montana trial opened, two of the defendants, Russell Langers, of Four Oaks, North Carolina, and James Wells, of Zebulon, North Carolina, received thirty-year and twelve-year prison sentences, respectively, for domestic terrorism in a North Carolina trial in February 1997. **Also see** Common Law Courts movement; Militia Movement; Schweitzer, LeRoy.

Suggested readings: Dale Jakes and Connie Jakes, *False Prophets: The Firsthand Account of a Husband-Wife Team Working for the FBI and Living in Deepest Cover with the Montana Freemen* (Los Angeles: Dove Books, 1998); Clair Johnson, "Montana Freemen Scheme Was Spread Far and Wide," *Billings Gazette* (March 14, 1999), p. 1; Tom Kenworthy and Serge F. Kovaleski, " 'Freemen' Finally Taxed the Patience of the Federal Government," *Washington Post* (March 31, 1996), p. A1; David A. Neiwert, "Freedom's End: A Federal Court Sentences the Leaders of the Montana Freemen to Long Prison Terms," *SPLC Intelligence Report* 94 (Spring 1999): 23–25; David A. Neiwert, *In God's Country: The Patriot Movement and the Pacific Northwest* (Pullman: Washington State University Press, 1999); Kenneth S. Stern, *A Force upon the Plain: The American Militia Movement and the Politics of Hate* (Norman: University of Oklahoma Press, 1996); Leonard Zeskind, "Justice vs. Justus: Montana Freemen Trial May Mark End of an Era," *SPLC Intelligence Report* 90 (Spring 1998): 14–17.

Fuerzas Armadas de Liberación Nacional Puertorriqueña (FALN) (Armed Forces of the National Liberation of Puerto Rico)

The Fuerzas Armadas de Liberación Nacional Puertorriqueña (FALN), or the Armed Forces of the National Liberation of Puerto

Rico, was an insurrectionist movement for the independence of Puerto Rico from the colonial rule of the United States. Puerto Rican nationals in New York City formed the FALN in 1974 to carry out an armed struggle for Puerto Rico's independence. **William Morales** was the head of the FALN and planned most of its operations. This group never had more than 200 active members, but these activists carried out operations against targets in Chicago and New York City. The first major operation occurred on January 24, 1975, at the eighteenth-century Fraunces Tavern in New York City, located off Wall Street in the financial district. Members of the FALN exploded a bomb in the tavern while it was full of investment bankers and financial analysts; four died and fifty-five were wounded. Between 1974 and 1983, the FALN were responsible for 130 bombings and armed attacks, which killed five people and injured more than 100 others. Funds for these operations came from armed robberies carried out between the bombings. The last attacks occurred on December 31, 1983. A series of bombings on that day in New York City wounded three New York City police officers.

Federal authorities gave high priority to neutralizing the FALN. In a series of raids and arrests starting in 1980 the federal agents wiped out the leadership structure in the FALN. William Morales was arrested, tried, and sentenced to eighty-nine years in prison. Between 1980 and 1986, fifteen other FALN members were arrested and tried. Each of them received prison sentences ranging from thirty-five to more than a hundred years on charges ranging from seditious conspiracy to robbery. These stiff sentences were partly the result of the refusal of FALN members to recognize the legality of the trials. They declared that they were prisoners of war fighting for an independent Puerto Rico, and they refused to cooperate with the courts. Morales escaped to Mexico in 1979, but in 1983 he was arrested and sent to prison by the Mexican government. A spin-off group of the FALN, the **Macheteros**

(Machete Wielders), was formed in August 1978 under the leadership of Filiberto Ojeda Rios. Operations of the Macheteros were conducted primarily in Puerto Rico, but they engaged in bombings and a $7 million Wells Fargo robbery in September 1983 in the United States. By 1985 the FALN and the Macheteros no longer existed as viable extremist organizations.

The FALN hit the news in August 1999 when President Clinton offered conditional clemency to FALN members in American prisons. A Puerto Rican lobby group, Prolibertad, had formed in the early 1990s to campaign for commutation of the sentences of FALN members held in custody. On August 11, 1999, Clinton offered clemency to fourteen FALN inmates on the condition that they renounce terrorism. Eleven of the FALN members accepted the offer and left prison on September 10, 1999. Two other prisoners refused the offer, and a third prisoner was ineligible for release. This offer caused a political controversy with Republicans in Congress who accused Clinton of freeing the FALN prisoners to enhance his wife's campaign for a U.S. Senate seat in New York. Puerto Rican nationalists made the release a cause for celebration. **See also** Macheteros (Machete Wielders); Morales, William.

Suggested readings: Ralph Blumenthal, "New Blasts Show F.A.L.N. Resilience," *New York Times* (January 9, 1983), sec. 1, p. 29; William Claiborne, "Puerto Rican Group Claims Responsibility for N.Y. Blasts," *Washington Post* (March 22, 1977), p. A3; Dirk Johnson, "Puerto Ricans Clinton Freed Leave Prisons," *New York Times* (September 11, 1999), p. A1; Kevin McCoy, "FALN Prisoners; A Cause Celebre," *Daily News* [New York] (August 18, 1999), p. 26; E. R. Shipp, "Puerto Rican Nationalists Guilty of Plotting Bombings in Chicago," *New York Times* (August 6, 1985), p. A16; Brent L. Smith, *Terrorism in America: Pipe Bombs and Pipe Dreams* (Albany: State University of New York Press, 1994); Tom Squitieri, "FALN Brought Bloody Battle into American Streets; Puerto Rican Group Faded After Arrests," *USA Today* (September 21, 1999), p. 15A.

Furrow, Buford O'Neal (1961–)

Buford Furrow is a white supremacist who carried out a terrorist attack in California in 1999. He was born in 1961. His father was a career Air Force enlisted man who reached the rank of chief master sergeant. Most of Furrow's schooling took place in Olympia, Washington. He graduated from Timberline High School near Olympia in 1979. In 1980 Furrow enlisted in the U.S. Army and trained to repair helicopters at Fort McClellan in Anniston, Alabama, before a knee injury led to an honorable discharge. He attended several community colleges before entering Western Washington University in Bellingham, Washington. After almost six years of study, Furrow graduated from Western Washington University with a degree in engineering technology in 1981. After holding several jobs, he found work as a clerical employee in 1987 at the Puget Sound facility of Boeing Aircraft Company. This job lasted until May 1990. He then took a position as a mechanical engineer with the Northrop Grumman Corporation's B-2 Stealth Bomber facility in Palmdale, California.

Furrow had always been a loner, but in 1989 he became interested in a white supremacist group, the **Aryan Nations**. In 1989 he attended the Aryan World Congress held in **Hayden Lake**, Idaho. After leaving the Grumman job in 1993, he moved near the Hayden Lake compound of the Aryan Nations and volunteered for guard duty. While at the Aryan Nations compound, he met and wooed Debra Mathews, the widow of **Robert Jay Mathews**, the leader of **The Order**. After moving to Metaline Falls, Washington, Furrow married Debra Mathews in March 1996. His lack of a job and bad temper, however, caused the marriage to disintegrate. He left Metaline Falls in April 1997 and moved to Everett, Washington, and his wife divorced him. For almost a year, in 1998, he worked at Northwest Gears in Everett, Washington, as an engineer. Furrow began to experience symptoms of mental illness and underwent treatment at a psychiatric facility. After his release, he attempted to commit himself to a private psychiatric facility, and was arrested by police for assaulting personnel at the facility. In October 1998, he was sent first to a state psychiatric facility and then to jail to await trial for the assault. After receiving a six-month sentence, he was released from jail in May 1999. He moved back to Olympia, Washington. In early August 1999, Furrow traveled to Southern California with the mission to commit an act that, he told the FBI, would be "a wake-up call to America to kill Jews." On August 10, 1999, Furrow entered the North Valley Jewish Community Center in Granada Hills, California, and opened fire with an imitation Uzi, an Israeli submachine gun, spraying seventy rounds in less than thirty seconds. After wounding two adults and three children, he stole a woman's automobile. Furrow then traveled to Chatsworth, California, where he shot and killed a Philippine postal worker, Joseph Ileto, after firing nine times. He stayed the night at a Hollywood motel and the next morning rented a cab to take him to Las Vegas, Nevada, where he turned himself in to the local FBI office.

Furrow had little defense against the charge of murder and assault. He confessed to the shootings in a statement soon after his arrest. The government decided to ask for the death penalty for the killing of the postal officer, and the defense considered an insanity plea. Government prosecutors decided that Furrow's history of mental illness would make it almost impossible to secure a death sentence. They accepted Furrow's guilty plea on January 24, 2001. On March 26, 2001, the court sentenced Furrow to two life terms in federal prison. **See also** Aryan Nations; Hate Crime; White Supremacist Movement.

Suggested readings: Mike Carter and Kim Barker, "A 'Nobody' Driven by His Hatreds Furrow Was in State Hospital," *Seattle Times* (August 12, 1999), p. A1; Matt Krasnowski, "Suspect's Guilty Plea Relieves Families," *San Diego Union-Tribune* (January 25, 2001), p. A3; Josh Meyer, Nicholas Riccardi, and T. Christian Miller, "First a Loner, Then a Separatist" *Los*

Angeles Times (August 22, 1999), p. A1; Carol Morello and Patrick MacMahon, "Suspect Seen as a Seething Racist," *USA Today* (August 12, 1999), p. 1A; Jason Van Derbeken, Bill Wallace, and Stacy Finz, "L.A. Suspect Dreamed of Killing; History of Erratic Behavior, Ties to Neo-Nazi Group," *San Francisco Chronicle* (August 12, 1999), p. A1.

G

Gale, William Potter (1916–1988)

William Gale, a leader in the building of paramilitary organizations in the United States to support white supremacy groups, was born on November 20, 1916, in Saint Paul, Minnesota. His father was a policeman in Saint Paul who had, as a teenager, served in Theodore Roosevelt's Rough Riders in Cuba and then in the Philippines with the Fourth U.S. Cavalry. Gale's father reenlisted in the U.S. Army and Gale was raised in a military environment. Gale joined the U.S. Army Reserves in 1932 at the age of sixteen. The army sent him to San Pedro High School to graduate from high school. In 1941 Gale was commissioned as a second lieutenant in the regular army. He served as a staff aide to General Douglas MacArthur during World War II and participated in the liberation of the Philippines. During this campaign, Gale was promoted to lieutenant colonel, but he ruined his health permanently. After the war, he moved to Japan and worked on MacArthur's staff running the Japanese government. Gale retired from the military in 1950.

After leaving the army, Gale had a varied career. His first job was as a manager of government property control for Hughes Aircraft. He stayed with Hughes until 1953, living in Hollywood. Gale then studied for the ministry and became an ordained Episcopalian minister. Unhappy about various religious restrictions during his first church assignment, Gale formed his own church, the Ministry of Christ Church. After reading books written by Charles Totten, he was converted to Anglo-Israelism in 1946. He preached an early form of **Christian Identity** at his church. Two members of his church were **Richard Girnt Butler**, later head of the **Aryan Nations**, and **Tom Metzger**, later head of the **White Aryan Resistance** (WAR). In 1956 Gale started working in a securities brokerage business as a broker and salesperson. He was highly successful as a securities broker, but his prominent profile in rightwing causes led to his being fired. His marriage ended about the same time as his job. Using his extensive contacts in the military, Gale opened his own securities brokerage firm and soon became financially independent.

In the midst of his business and religious activities, Gale became active in politics. For a time, he worked for a conservative Republican politician and helped him win election in a California congressional race. One of his new business partners was active in the newly organized Constitution Party. This party's strong anti-communist orientation attracted Gale, and he joined the party in 1957. In 1958 he was a candidate for governor of California for the Constitution

Party, but he received little support from the California electorate. By now, Gale was convinced that the established political parties were ruining the country. He started attacking national leaders over civil rights and minority policies in the media. In 1960 he used his military expertise to form a paramilitary group, the California Rangers, to support the program of the Christian Identity movement. After the California attorney general attacked the rangers as a private army, Gale disbanded his paramilitary force. Still active in extremist politics, Gale joined with **Henry Lamont Beach** to form the **Posse Comitatus movement** in 1969. Gale's military experience was always in demand, and he was asked to form and train paramilitary organizations around the country. In 1984 he started another organization, the **Committee of the States**, which had an anti-government orientation. One of its main planks stated that the federal income tax law was unconstitutional.

Gale's anti-government activities finally caught the attention of the federal government. A federal undercover agent learned about threats directed toward government officials. Gale was arrested in October 1986. In a two-month trial held in September and October 1987, he was convicted of conspiracy to interfere with the Internal Revenue Service by a federal court. In consideration of his age and ill health, Gale was sentenced to a one-year and one-day prison term. He lived only a few weeks after the trial and died on April 28, 1988, in the Castle Air Force Base Hospital. He received a funeral with full military honors at the Riverside National Cemetery. His fellow Committee of the States colleagues were permitted to travel to California for the funeral. Gale is still revered in the Christian Identity and paramilitary circles for his anti-government activities. **See also** Christian Identity; Committee of the States; Minutemen Movement; Posse Comitatus Movement.

Suggested readings: Phillip Finch, *God, Guts, and Guns* (New York: Seaview/Putnam, 1983); Neil A. Hamilton, *Militias in America: A Reference Handbook* (Santa Barbara, Calif.: ABC-CLIO, 1996); Robert A. Jones, "IRS Seizes Leader of Extremist Group in Death Threats," *Los Angeles Times* (October 30, 1986), part 1, p. 3; Metro Desk, "William P. Gale; Led Several Racist Groups," *Los Angeles Times* (May 4, 1988), p. 24; Cheri Seymour, *Committee of the States: Inside the Radical Right* (Mariposa, Calif.: Camden Place Communications, 1991); Southern Poverty Law Center, "Roots of Common Law," *SPLC Intelligence Report* 90 (Spring 1998): 29–31.

Gay Bashing

The anti-gay orientation of many of the political and religious extremists has produced numerous cases of physical incidents directed against gays known as gay bashing. Gay bashing is defined as violence directed against gay males or lesbians for their sexual orientation. Studies of gay bashing by scholars indicate that the perpetrators are mostly male, in their late teens or early twenties, and strangers to the victims. They travel in groups. Religious extremists use quotes from the Bible as a source for their anti-gay stance. **Peter J. Peters**, a **Christian Identity** minister from Colorado, has gone so far as to demand the death penalty for committing homosexual acts. Other more mainstream Christian religions have also displayed an anti-gay bias that has promoted a hostile atmosphere for gays. Conservative Christian leaders interpret gay rights as part of the moral degeneration that will lead to the Apocalypse and the ultimate return of Christ. Gay rights have also threatened the macho image of political extremists. These extremists believe that they are the defenders of womanhood, and they promote large families to advance the white race. While religious leaders preach against the gay lifestyle; followers of political extremist groups resort to direct action. A series of beatings and killings of gays by **neo-Nazis** and **skinheads** shocked the nation in the 1990s. In 1996 alone, FBI statistics reported more than 1,000 attacks on individuals because of their sexual orientation. This figure is too low because many gays refuse to report attacks to the police.

The leading gay basher in the United States is **Fred Phelps**. Since June 1991, he has led an anti-gay crusade from his small church in Topeka, Kansas. He is a Bible-spouting fundamentalist who attacks gays and anyone who defends them. He and his large family travel around the country demonstrating against gay rights. They specialize in demonstrations at funerals of prominent people who have been supportive of gay rights. Their motto is "God hates fags." This campaign has garnered considerable national media attention and has encouraged others to take action against gays.

The most notorious case of gay bashing was the beating death of Matthew Shepard outside of Laramie, Wyoming, in 1998. Shepard was an openly gay, twenty-two-year-old student at the University of Wyoming. Two men, Russell Henderson and Aaron McKinney, approached him at a Laramie bar on the evening of October 6, 1998, with the intent of robbing him. The ensuing conversation led to Shepard's admitting to them that he was gay. They convinced the 5 foot, 2 inch, 105-pound Shepard to go with them. They beat him at least twenty times on the head causing six skull fractures. They then tied him to a fence on the morning of October 7. He died on October 12, 1998, in a Fort Collins, Colorado, hospital. His assailants and their accomplices went on trial for the murder. Henderson pleaded guilty and received two life sentences for first-degree felony murder and kidnapping. McKinney stood trial in October 1999 and received the same sentence. Their girlfriends were sentenced to short terms in jail for aiding and abetting the crime. Neither Henderson nor McKinney had any affiliation with extremist groups, but they shared anti-gay beliefs. **See also** Gay Liberation Front; Hate Crime; Peters, Peter J.; Phelps, Fred.

Suggested readings: Stephen Braun, "Pastor Who Takes Pride in Hate Traces the Emotion to Bible," *Los Angeles Times* (November 16, 1999), p. A5; Gregory M. Herek and Kevin T. Berrill, *Hate Crimes: Confronting Violence Against Lesbians and Gay Men* (Newbury Park, Calif.: Sage Publications, 1992); Didi Herman, *The Antigay Agenda: Orthodox Vision and the Christian Right* (Chicago: University of Chicago Press, 1997); Kevin McCoy, "Gay Revolutionaries; Standing Tall at Stonewall," *Newsday* [New York] (June 22, 1994), p. 15; Southern Poverty Law Center, "Anti-Homosexual Crime: The Severity of the Violence Shows the Hatred," *SPLC Intelligence Report* 88 (Fall 1997): 16–17; Southern Poverty Law Center, "Serious Violence Against Gays Said to Rise," *SPLC Intelligence Report* 94 (Spring 1999): 4–5.

Gay Liberation Front (GLF)

The Gay Liberation Front (GLF) was the first militant gay rights organization to form in the United States. Earlier gay organizations, such as the North American Conference of Homophile Organizations, the Daughters of Bilitis, the Mattachine Society of New York (City), and the Homophile Youth Movement, concentrated on local issues or on influencing politics from behind the scenes. Shortly after the rioting by New York City gays in protest of a police raid on a gay bar, Stonewall Inn, on June 27, 1969, members of the New York City gay community decided to form an organization to fight for gay rights. Members of two homosexual organizations, the Mattachine Society of New York and the Homophile Youth Movement, provided the leadership for a series of meetings held in July 1969 which led to the formation of the Gay Liberation Front. The first major debate in the GLF concerned how radical the organization would be. A number of its members had been active in the **Students for a Democratic Society** (SDS) and other radical political groups, and they advocated direct action. Despite this recommendation, the consensus in these meetings was that the GLF would be a radical political organization and that it would represent the interests of both male and female gays. One of the first GLF activities was to sponsor a series of gay dances. The first triumph for the new movement was pressuring a newspaper, the *Village Voice*, to accept advertisements with the word gay in them. It took a public demonstration by the

Gay Liberation Front before the newspaper gave in to their demands.

Soon news of the New York successes spread around the country, and other Gay Liberation Front organizations were established. One veteran gay activist, Harry Hay, one of the founders of the Mattachine Society, started a branch of the Gay Liberation Front in Los Angeles. The San Francisco GLF group started by agitating against the anti-gay orientation of the *San Francisco Examiner*. By the end of 1969, more than 100 organizations had formed primarily in major cities. Progress was slowed down because of resistance by state and local authorities to recognize gay rights. Earlier in the fall of 1969, the GLF in New York City experienced dissension in the ranks until another police raid on a gay bar, the Snake Pit, and a serious injury to a gay man revitalized it. One outcome of the dissension with the GLF was the formation, on December 21, 1969, of the Gay Activist Alliance (GAA) by about fifteen members who found the leaderless structure of the GLF frustrating. An organized gay community started using its political muscle on politicians in New York City, Chicago, Los Angeles, and San Francisco. Two New York City politicians, Bella Abzug and Edward Koch, were early supporters, but most politicians refused to respond to the political pressure. Several veteran politicians were voted out of office because of their anti-gay stances. After winning a few battles with politicians, GLF activists turned their attention to other professions. They demonstrated and attacked in the media professional organizations, psychologists, and psychiatrists at their GLF convention for their hostile positions on gays.

The AIDS epidemic has had a direct impact on the leadership and membership of the Gay Liberation Front. Much of the energy of the GLF has been directed toward political agitation at the national and local level to bring attention to gay issues. The fight over AIDS was a battle the leadership was willing to undertake, but its moderate approach alienated some of the more militant members of the GLF. These individuals migrated to more activist groups, such as **ACT UP** (AIDS Coalition to Unleash Power) and **Queer Nation**. This loss of activists has made the GLF more moderate, but it has also lessened its influence as a leader in the gay community. See also Gay Activist Alliance; Gay Liberation Movement; Hay, Harry; Stonewall Riots.

Suggested readings: Kevin McCoy, "Gay Revolutionaries; Standing Tall at Stonewall," *Newsday* [New York] (June 22, 1994), p. 15; Donn Teal, *The Gay Militants: How Gay Liberation Began in America, 1969–1971* (New York: St. Martin's Press, 1971); Stuart Timmons, *The Trouble with Harry Hay: Founder of the Modern Gay Movement* (Boston: Alyson, 1990).

Gay Liberation Movement

The Gay Liberation Movement was founded by gays and lesbians to remove barriers and eliminate discrimination toward their sexual orientation. Homosexuality was an accepted sexual practice during Greek and Roman times. This acceptance changed to hostility in the Christian era when homosexuality was considered a sin punishable by death. Homosexuality continued to exist but, until modern times, always underground. Sodomy laws existed in most European countries and in most states in the United States.

Only after World War II did homosexuality try to come out of the closet. In 1950 a number of homosexuals in Southern California, under the leadership of Harry Hay, formed the Mattachine Society to promote the acceptance of homosexuals. This society took the name Mattachine from medieval masked singers. Later in 1955, some lesbians established the Daughters of Bilitis. This name came from a contemporary of the Greek lesbian poet Sappho. Together these groups formed chapters around the country in major cities to work for a change in attitude toward homosexuals. They also lobbied the federal government and Congress to improve the lot of homosexuals. Their efforts led to the defeat of a legislative effort made in Congress to outlaw the Mattachine Society.

Gay men carry signs chanting "Human rights now" during the annual Gay Freedom Day March in San Francisco on June 26, 1977. The gay rights movement may have been born in June 1969, when drag queens at New York's Stonewall bar fought back against police harassment, but it came of age in the 1970s in San Francisco. (AP Photo)

Little progress was made in gaining public acceptance until the 1960s. Homosexuals began identifying themselves as gay to promote a more positive image. Many gays became politically active, first in the civil rights struggle and then in the anti–Vietnam War protests. By the end of the 1960s, a cadre of gay activists was in place. The catalyst for change was the New York City police raid on a gay bar, the Stonewall Inn, in Greenwich Village on June 27, 1969. Raids of gay bars had taken place routinely, but this time the gay population had had enough. After several nights of rioting, gay activists formed the **Gay Liberation Front** (GLF) and later the Gay Activist Alliance (GAA). Many of the gay leaders had left-wing backgrounds, but as the Gay Liberation Movement grew so did the number of political moderates in the movement. Gay rights became a battle cry among gay activists. Gays in the cities started mobilizing their supporters to target anti-gay politicians. This tactic was more successful in New York City and San Francisco than in other cities.

The successes of the Gay Liberation Movement produced a backlash. Anita Bryant, a conservative former beauty queen, organized an anti-gay crusade in Florida in 1977. The campaign, called "Save Our Children," promoted a fear of homosexuality and advocated the continuation of discrimination against gays. After Oklahoma passed a law against gay teachers teaching in public schools, the 1978 Briggs initiative in California threatened to fire gay public schoolteachers or any teacher who mentioned homosexuality positively in the classroom. Californians voted down this initiative overwhelmingly, but not before making gays feel vulnerable to anti-gay hysteria. The murder of gay activist Harvey Milk and Mayor

George Moscone on November 27, 1978 by city supervisor Dan White only pointed out how vulnerable high-profile gays were even in San Francisco. White, a conservative ex-policeman and ex-fireman, received only seven years for manslaughter in the famous "Twinkies defense." A prominent psychologist testified that a killer might not be responsible for his action because of additives in his junk food, or Twinkies. This verdict infuriated the gay community and violence broke out in San Francisco streets. Both militant gays and the police rioted causing heavy property damage and some severe injuries.

Just as the Gay Liberation Movement appeared to be making progress toward public acceptance of gays, the AIDS epidemic surfaced. Acquired immune deficiency syndrome (AIDS) had been diagnosed for several years, but it started making severe inroads in the gay community in the late 1970s. Some conservative politicians and religious leaders considered AIDS divine retribution for a sinful lifestyle and used this epidemic to preach against the gay lifestyle. The Reagan administration in the 1980s had little tolerance toward AIDS in the gay community. Resentment over this attitude resulted in the formation of a militant gay group, **ACT UP** (AIDS Coalition to Unleash Power). Members of this group believed that only confrontation and civil disobedience would force public officials to face up to the AIDS epidemic. They had some success with both the government and private businesses.

The Gay Liberation Movement has been unable to overcome the fear and hostility of many Americans. The 1986 Supreme Court decision that upheld the constitutionality of sodomy laws hurt the movement. Despite an estimated gay population in the United States of around 22 million, the gay community still suffers from discrimination in jobs, housing, and public accommodations. Anti-gay sentiment remains strong in the military. A 1984 survey of gays indicated that over 90 percent of American gays had suffered some form of discrimination at some time in their lives. At the end of the 1990s, twenty-eight states still have laws against sodomy. More significant to the gay movement has been the increase in gay bashing which has led to severe beatings and even deaths. The Gay Liberation Movement has advanced the rights of its gay members, but America remains a long way from full acceptance of gay rights. Certain states, however, are discussing gay rights issues, such as gay marriage and implementing legislation. **See also** Gay Liberation Front; Hay, Harry; Stonewall Riots.

Suggested readings: Dudley Clendinen and Adam Nagourney, *Out for Good: The Struggle to Build a Gay Rights Movement in America* (New York: Simon and Schuster, 1999); Margaret Cruikshank, *The Gay and Lesbian Liberation Movement* (New York: Routledge, 1992); Joseph Hanania, "The Debate over Gay Marriages," *Los Angeles Times* (June 13, 1996), p. E1; Harry Hay, *Radically Gay: Gay Liberation in the Words of Its Founder* (Boston: Beacon Press, 1996); Adam Nagourney, "Gay Politics and Anti-Politics," *New York Times* (October 25, 1998); sec. 4, p. 3 Lori Soderlind, "Rapid Growth of Gay Groups Is Sign of Change," *New York Times* (September 20, 1992), Stuart Timmons, *The Trouble with Harry Hay: Founder of the Modern Gay Movement* (Boston: Alyson, 1990); Urvashi Vaid, *Virtual Equality: The Mainstreaming of Gay and Lesbian Liberation* (New York: Anchor, 1995).

Gayman, Dan (1937–)

Dan Gayman, one of the leading **Christian Identity** apologists and theologians in the United States, was born in 1937 in Denver, Colorado. His family belonged to a dissident Mormon sect, the Church of Christ (Temple Lot). At an early age, the British Israelism doctrine of Herbert W. Armstrong attracted Gayman, but he soon realized that this interpretation of British Israelism was too moderate for him. He turned instead to the white racist wing of the movement. Gayman received much of his theological training at Kenneth Goff's Soldiers of the Cross Training Institute in Denver in 1964 and 1965. Goff's school produced right-wing fundamentalist ministers. Gayman was a high school principal in Missouri when the radical Christian Identity theology of **Wesley Swift** and **William Potter Gale** attracted him to the ministry. He joined his brother Duane's church in Denver, Colorado, and became a minister. His strong Christian Identity views led him to challenge his brother for control of that branch of the Church of Israel in the early 1970s. In the subsequent lawsuit in 1972, Gayman lost most of the assets of the Church of Israel to his brother.

After losing this lawsuit, Gayman decided to build a new church in a different locality. In 1973, he sent his followers to buy land around Schell City, Missouri, as a site for his new church, the Identity Church of Israel. Adherents of his church bought adjoining farms which enabled them to control the local grade school, high school, and other local institutions. By 1977 Gayman had his new church in place. He considered himself a bishop in the Christian Identity Church. Gayman's church has prospered by marketing videos of Gayman's views on Christian Identity. By the mid-1990s, the Identity Church of Israel had about 100 members, including men, women, and children. Gayman has encouraged the spread of his church by establishing an international ecclesiastical organization. Each diocese is named after one of the twelve tribes of Israel; the one in Missouri is the Diocese of Manasseh. This ecclesiastical structure encourages missionary work abroad. Some evidence exists of successful recruiting activities in Great Britain and in South Africa. His book, *The Two Seeds of Genesis* (1994), attempts to prove that Jews are the seed of Satan. Another work, entitled *For Fear of the Jews* (1996), continues his attacks on Jews. Gayman is a frequent speaker at **Aryan Nations** gatherings, and he often uses these occasions to argue in favor of a fundamentalist Christian education. He limits his effectiveness in the Aryan Nations organization by disagreeing with other Christian Identity leaders over strategy and tactics. Because Gayman was among those receiving funds from **Robert Jay Mathews's The Order**, he was peruaded

by the federal government to be a prosecution witness against white supremacist leaders at the **Fort Smith Sedition Trial** in 1988. Since that unsettling experience, Gayman has been less militant in his public speeches and continues to keep a low profile in the national **white supremacist movement. See also** Anti-Semitism; Christian Identity; Fort Smith Sedition Trial.

Suggested readings: Donald Bradley, "Afrikaners Find Kindred Souls," *Kansas City Star* (November 20, 1994), p. A1; Jeffrey Kaplan, *Radical Religion in America: Millenarian Movements from the Far Right to the Children of Noah* (Syracuse, N.Y.: Syracuse University Press, 1997); Marlon Manuel, "The Search for Eric Rudolph; Suspect May Be Linked to Extremist Church," *Atlanta Journal and Constitution* (March 6, 1998), p. 10A; Southern Poverty Law Center, "Coming Out," *SPLC Intelligence* 102 (Summer 2001): pp. 56–60.

Green Panthers

The Green Panthers organization, a pro-marijuana activist group, advocates armed resistance to the U.S. government as part of its agenda. Terry Mitchell, one of its founders, is the chief spokesperson for the Green Panthers. Mitchell came out of the radical leftist agitation of the 1960s, but he has also been affiliated with the Libertarian Party of Texas and worked in the Washington, D.C., office of the National Association to Reform Marijuana Laws (NORML). A group of marijuana use activists came together in Washington, D.C., in 1990 and started the Green Panthers. They wanted to end the harassment and criminalization of the nation's approximately 10,000 marijuana users. After studying other direct-action groups and their failures, the leaders of the Green Panthers decided to advocate arming their members to prepare for a future confrontation with the federal government along the lines of the **Black Panther Party**. Most members share the **militia movement's** anti-government viewpoint, but they differ with it on drug policy. The national headquarters is located in Cincinnati, Ohio, and the leaders publicize their views in their newsletter, *Revolu-*

Greenpeace activists hold a banner in front of the American Seafoods factory trawler *Ocean Rover* calling for the trawler to "Stop" overfishing for pollock, September 9, 1996, in the Bering Sea off Alaska. Greenpeace believes the factory trawlers are overfishing pollock stocks and destroying the North Pacific ecosystem. (AP Photo/Greenpeace, Robert Visser)

tionary Times. They also run a publishing house, Panther Press, which sells pro-marijuana and survivalist literature.

One of the most novel ideas of the Green Panthers is their demand for a separate homeland in the Pacific Northwest for marijuana users and their supporters. This homeland, Ganjastan, is to be a coastal strip of land twenty miles in width running from just north of San Francisco, California, to ten miles south of Portland, Oregon. This so-called Stoner Homeland would have a community-based libertarian society, and its economy would be based on the sale of high-quality marijuana. The method of acquisition of this homeland is uncertain, but the idea demonstrates the Green Panthers' fear and distrust of the federal government. This

scheme for a Pacific homeland resembles but is much smaller than the homeland proposed by the **Aryan Nations. See also** Aryan Nations: Black Panther Party.

Suggested readings: Terry Mitchell and Loey Glover, "About Green Panthers!" www. greenpanthers.org; Cletus Nelson, "The Bong and the Rifle," www.greenpanthers.org.

Greenpeace

Greenpeace is an environmental group that has served as a model for the radical wing of the environmental movement. A small number of Canadians and American expatriates from the anti–Vietnam War movement formed Greenpeace in 1969 in Vancouver, British Columbia. They wanted this organization, then called Don't Make a Wave Committee, to set up a protest against American nuclear testing at Amchitka Islands in the Aleutians. Members of the group used direct confrontation and publicity in the media to draw attention to their cause. Soon after the successful Amchitka protest, the group changed its name to Greenpeace Foundation. Then the group turned its attention to opposing French nuclear testing at Mururoa Atoll near Tahiti in the Pacific. For the next several years in the early 1970s, Greenpeace was virtually at war with French authorities. After a series of brief but violent confrontations with the French government, ending with the French taking their nuclear testing underground, Greenpeace turned to direct action against the whaling industries of several countries including the Soviet Union. Again in a series of ocean confrontations, Greenpeace activists turned world attention to the slaughter of whales which was instrumental in establishing the 1986 International Whaling Commission to ban commercial whaling. They also uncovered illegal whaling activities and reported guilty parties. With longtime activist **David Fraser McTaggart**, a former Canadian badminton champion, at its head, Greenpeace became an international organization with headquarters in London, Seattle, and Sydney. Greenpeace continued its anti–nuclear testing campaign against the French government in the 1980s. In July 1985 French commandos planted explosives on Greenpeace ship *Rainbow Warrior* in Auckland, New Zealand, killing a Greenpeace activist.

By the late 1980s, Greenpeace was the largest environmentalist organization in the world. At its international headquarters in Amsterdam, the Netherlands, Greenpeace has more than 400 full-time employees working for its nearly four million members. In 1987, Greenpeace USA, the American organization, formed Greenpeace Action to recruit members and lobby the U.S. Congress. Greenpeace organizations still specialize in direct action, but they have become less active in the field as other, more radical groups have replaced Greenpeace in taking direct action. An exception has been the antinuclear activities of David McTaggart near Mururoa Atoll in the South Pacific, where France conducted underground nuclear testing in the mid-1990s. The British group occupied an oil rig in the Cromarty Firth off Scotland in April and May 2001 in its latest direct-action campaign. Greenpeace's refusal to tolerate property destruction separates it from other radical environmentalist groups. While some of the leaders and supporters of the radical groups, such as **Paul Franklin Watson** of the **Sea Shepherd Conservation Society**, were former members of Greenpeace, relations between the Greenpeace leaders and the radical environmentalists remain hostile.

The death of McTaggart in a car crash on March 23, 2001, near his olive farm in Paciano, Italy, ended an era of direct action. Although he had retired from national leadership in 1991, he still led the radical wing of Greenpeace. His leadership in promoting direct action has been replaced by more bureaucratically oriented leaders. John Passacantando, the current leader of Greenpeace USA, is skilled in policy rather than action. The membership of Greenpeace USA has dropped from a high of one million in 1992 to about 300,000 in 2001. Other Greenpeace organizations have suffered similar declines. **See also** Radical Environmentalism; McTaggart, David Fraser; Sea Shepherd Conservation Society; Watson, Paul Franklin.

Suggested readings: Paul Brown, "David McTaggart; Campaigner Who Led from the Front in Making Greenpeace a Worldwide Organization," *Guardian* [London] (March 26, 2001), p. 22; Margarette Driscoll, "Green Pirates Deserted; Death of Co-Founder Signals Greenpeace's Gradual Shift Away from Its Radical Roots," *Gazette* [Montreal] (April 1, 2001), A5; Neal Hall, "Founding Father Tells How It All Got Started: Greenpeace," *Vancouver Sun* (July 18, 1995), p. B1; David Ross, "Protesters Vow to Continue Fight as Rig Demo Ends," *Herald* [Glasgow] (April 3, 2001), p. 7; Rik Scarce, *Eco-Warriors: Understanding the Radical Environmental Movement* (Chicago: Noble Press, 1990).

Greensboro Massacre

The Greensboro Massacre resulted from a clash between the supporters of the Communist Workers Party (CWP) and a coalition of **Ku Klux Klan** members and **neo-Nazis**. Members of the Communist Workers Party, then called the Worker's Viewpoint Organization (WVO), planned an anti-Klan rally to take place on November 3, 1979, in the black housing project of Morningside in Greensboro, North Carolina. This "Death to the Klan" demonstration was to protest recent incidents of Klan violence and to promote armed self-defense in the black community. For several years, activists in the CWP had been organizing unions in textile mills and hospitals in the North Carolina region. Klan leadership in the South considered union organizing almost as threatening as civil rights. An earlier clash between the CWP and the Klan in China Grove, North Carolina, in July 1979, had disrupted a Klan showing of the movie *Birth of a Nation*. This incident caused the Klan to lose face, and Klan and neo-Nazi leaders vowed revenge for this defeat.

Although the demonstration had been planned in advance and received the necessary march permits, some of the requirements for a safe demonstration were lacking. At the beginning of the rally on the evening of November 3, demonstrators moved into the housing project shouting anti-Klan slogans. Among these slogans was "Death to the Klan." Although several of the demonstrators carried weapons, most of them were unarmed following the requirement to obtain a march permit. Although the demonstration had a legal city permit and it required a police presence, no police were there when the demonstration started at the appointed time. Why the police were not there has never been explained; the place and time of the demonstration were written on the march permit. Moreover, the police had leaked information about the demonstration to the Klan several days earlier. A nine-car caravan of Ku Klux Klan members and neo-Nazis appeared and opened fire on the demonstrators. Five members of the CWP were killed outright; nine others were wounded, some seriously. Two of the dead were white medical doctors, two were white union organizers, and one, Sandi Smith, was a black female union organizer. All of the dead had been active in either the anti–Vietnam War movement or the black liberation movement. Only after the shootings occurred did the police arrive. Losses suffered at the demonstrations led the CWP to cease their pro-union organizing in North Carolina. One member of the Klan suffered a stray bullet wound from the gun of another member of the caravan.

Legal proceedings against the perpetrators of the shootings were prolonged, and the results were mixed. The prosecutors pressed for the death penalty, but their case was hampered by the distrust of the survivors of the march. They blamed the police and the authorities for allowing the massacre to take place. Two all-white juries acquitted the Klan and neo-Nazi defendants of all charges. In the course of the investigation, however, victims learned that one of the Klan leaders was a police informant and the police had prior knowledge of what was going to happen. This information was the basis for a civil suit against the city of Greensboro. In the civil suit, held in 1985, four Klan gunmen, two Greensboro police officers, and a Klan police informant were convicted of wrongful deaths. The city of Greensboro paid $351,000 to the survivors.

Both the event and the following legal proceedings have entered the mythology of the Klan and the radical left. Klan leaders take pride in this effort to repulse the communists from taking over a community and organizing businesses. The radical left uses the Greensboro Massacre as a lesson in how local police cooperate with right-wing extremists to turn away legitimate efforts to improve the lives of blacks and workers in the South. Both sides interpret the legal proceedings to reflect their viewpoints. **See also** Ku Klux Klan.

Suggested readings: Lorraine Ahearn, "Aftermath: Dark Day Haunts Greensboro; Shots Still Ringing in City's Ears," *Greensboro News*

& Record (October 30, 1994), p. A1; Elizabeth Wheaton, *Codename Greenkil: The 1979 Greensboro Killings* (Athens: University of Georgia Press, 1987).

Gritz, James "Bo" (1939–)

James "Bo" Gritz, long a major leader of the anti-government movement in the United States, was born on January 18, 1939, in Oklahoma and grew up in Enid, Oklahoma. His father was killed while serving in the military during World War II, and his mother worked as a ferry pilot during the war. His grandparents raised him in Enid. After attending local schools, he attended school at the Fort Union Military Academy. After his graduation, Gritz entered military service on the eve of the Vietnam War. He earned a commission as an officer and served in the Green Berets in South Vietnam, where he reached the rank of lieutenant colonel. In 1974 he obtained a master's degree in communications at American University. When Gritz retired from the army in 1979, he left as one of its most decorated soldiers. After retirement, he was active in the efforts to return American prisoners of war. He traveled to Southeast Asia several times to locate American prisoners of war. He maintains that he found evidence of the U.S. government's complicity in drug dealing operations in Southeast Asia, and he claims that he was the inspiration for the movie character Rambo.

Soon after leaving the military, Gritz began to gravitate toward the anti-government movement. In 1988 he flirted briefly with running as vice president on **David Duke's** **Populist Party** ticket. Instead, Gritz ran unsuccessfully for public office in Nevada as a Republican. He also became a close friend of **Peter J. Peters**, a **Christian Identity** minister in Colorado, and **Willis Carto**, head of the anti-Semitic **Liberty Lobby**. In 1992 he was the presidential candidate for the Populist Party. His platform included repeal of the federal income tax, the end of the Internal Revenue Service, abolishment of the Federal Reserve System, abolishing gay rights,

and repudiation of the United Nations. About this time, he severed his friendship with Pete Peters over Peters's advocacy of the death penalty for gays. In the midst of his campaign, Gritz was instrumental in persuading **Randall Weaver**, a former Green Beret veteran of the Vietnam War, to surrender to federal authorities at Ruby Ridge. Also in 1992, he wrote a book, *Called to Serve*, in which he attacks what he calls the New World Order and makes anti-Semitic references to the Federal Reserve System. After a poor showing in the 1992 presidential race, Gritz founded SPIKE (Specially Prepared Individuals for Key Events) in 1993 to train paramilitary groups for guerrilla and survivalist operations. In 1994 he started a planned community near Kamiah, in central Idaho, called Almost Heaven. Almost Heaven is a Christian covenant community whose citizens are heavily armed for protection against attacks by the federal government. Most of the inhabitants subscribe to Christian Identity beliefs. In 1995 Gritz formed the Center for Action in Mesa, Arizona. This organization distributes conspiracy literature for extremist groups.

Despite his high profile and status in anti-government circles, Gritz has experienced some recent setbacks. In April 1996, he attempted to play a role as a mediator between federal authorities and the Montana Freemen as he had done at Ruby Ridge, but this time the Freemen members rejected his intervention. In October 1996, Gritz and his son, James R. Gritz, were arrested in a custody kidnapping attempt of the children of Linda Wiegand in Suffield, Connecticut. After charges were reduced, Gritz and his son won acquittals in January 2000. His arrest and association with Wiegand caused a feud to develop between Gritz and other segments of the radical right, including **John Ernest Trochmann**, head of the **Militia of Montana**, and Clayton Douglas, editor of New Mexico pro-militia magazine *Free American*. His enemies have accused him of being more interested in gaining publicity than in being a dedicated white supremacist. His planned community has experienced difficulties as members have become unhappy about Gritz and what they perceive as his lack of leadership. Gritz moved to Almost Heaven in July 1996. When an associate lost nearly $1 million in revenue from land sales, it left Gritz in debt. Shortly after, his wife, Claudia Gritz, instituted divorce proceedings against him. Depression over these events led Gritz to attempt suicide in September 1998, but he recovered from his gunshot wound to the chest. Gritz has remarried and has returned to his anti-government activities. **See also** Freemen Movement; Militia Movement; Peters, Peter J.; Populist Party/American Nationalist Union; Ruby Ridge incident; Weaver, Randall.

Suggested readings: Richard Abanes, *American Militias: Rebellion, Racism, and Religion* (Downers Grove, Ill.: InterVarsity press, 1996); Neil A. Hamilton, *Militias in America: A Reference Handbook* (Santa Barbara, Calif.: ABC-CLIO, 1996); David Johnson, "Discontent Arises in Bo Gritz's Camp," *Lewiston Morning Tribune* [Idaho] (February 5, 1996), p. 1; David A. Neiwert, *In God's Country: The Patriot Movement and the Pacific Northwest* (Pullman: Washington State University Press, 1999); Kenneth S. Stern, *A Force upon the Plain: The American Militia Movement and the Politics of Hate* (Norman: University of Oklahoma Press, 1996); Steve Stuebner, "True Gritz; Will the Real Bo Gritz Please Stand Up?" *SPLC Intelligence Report* 92 (Fall 1998) 10–15; Mitchell Zuckoff, "Survivalist Gritz Fights for Freedom in a Conn. Court," *Boston Globe* (January 18, 2000), p. A1.

Guerrilla Girls

The Guerrilla Girls are a group of female artists and art world professionals who attack the white male domination of the world of art. This group of anonymous women who wear gorilla masks organized in 1985 and soon afterward started attacking art directors and heads of museums for their selection of artists. These women artists discovered that 95 percent of the work being shown in New York City was the work of white males. They also found that art dealers and critics paid attention only to artists whose art made it into the art galleries. It was the combination of an exhibit at the Museum of Modern Art in New York City in which women artists were underrepresented, and the comments of the curator, Kynaston McShine, that triggered the movement. McShine's assertion that "any artist who wasn't in the show should rethink 'his' career" infuriated the women artists. Besides disguising their appearance with gorilla masks, they adopted the names of dead women artists and writers to hide their identities. Since these artists and writers were attacking some of the most powerful figures in the art world, they wanted to avoid ruining their careers in art in the process.

The Guerrilla Girls decided to use splashy public demonstrations and Madison Avenue advertising to illustrate their points about discrimination against women artists. Most of the members of the Guerrilla Girls reside in New York City, but there are members and supporters in most of the major art centers in the world. Newspaper reporters estimate the number of Guerrilla Girls ranges from 25 to 100. Their campaign of direct action and publicity has made them more than an annoyance to the art world. They have challenged museum directors and art critics to justify the absence of women artists by confronting them and demanding reasons. Some art institutions have responded positively to their campaign for greater representation of women artists. Members of the Guerrilla Girls continue to participate on speaking tours and use their eye-catching posters to garner publicity and funds. In the early 1990s, the Guerrilla Girls started a journal, *Hot Flashes*, in which they document incidents of sexism and racism in the art world. Their latest cause is highlighting the lack of women movie producers and directors in Hollywood.

Suggested readings: Duncan Campbell, "Women Want Lights, Camera, Action," *Guardian* [London] (April 14, 2001), p. 18; Anita Chaudhuri, "Gorillas in a Twist," *Guardian* [London] (July 19, 1995), p. T10; Guerrilla Girls, *Confessions of the Guerrilla Girls* (New York: HarperPerennial, 1995); John Hancox, "Pride and Passion of a Guerrilla Girl; Jude Burkhauser," *Guardian* [London] (October 16, 1998), p. 22; Patti Hartigan, "A Guerrilla War on Male Dominion over the Art World," *Boston Globe* (January 23, 1993), p. 27; Christopher Hume, "The Art World's a Jungle; Guerrilla Girls Out to Undermine Male Dominance," *Toronto Star* (March 3, 1998), p. 55; Christopher Hume, "Guerrilla Girls Terrorize Male Art World," *Toronto Star* (October 15, 1992), p. 63; Nancy Kapitanoff, "The Bad Girls of the Art World," *Los Angeles Times* (January 19, 1992), p. 98.

H

Hale, Matthew "Matt" (1971–)

Matt Hale, the head of the white supremacist **World Church of the Creator**, was born on July 27, 1971, and raised in East Peoria, Illinois. His father is a former policeman in the East Peoria Police Department. Hale, the youngest of four brothers, was raised by his father after his parents divorced. From an early age, Nazism fascinated Hale, and he formed a **neo-Nazi** racist group, the New Reich club, in junior high school. After graduation from East Peoria High School, he attended Bradley University where he was almost expelled for distributing racist literature. Hale nearly went to jail in 1992 for obstruction of justice for lying about his brother's possession of a gun. The court imposed a six-month home confinement on Hale. In 1995 he ran for an East Peoria City Council seat, but his candidacy was overwhelmingly rejected. After this defeat, he studied law at Southern Illinois University in Carbondale, Illinois. During these years, he was briefly married.

Hale resurrected the ideas of **Ben Klassen** and his Church of the Creator by forming the World Church of the Creator in 1996 in East Peoria, Illinois. Hale assumed the title of "pontifex maximus" formerly held by Klassen. This church is unique because its doctrine is based on white supremacy and rejects traditional Christianity. Hale has expanded Klassen's teachings to a philosophy close to that of **Christian Identity** by classifying Blacks, Hispanics, Jews, Catholics, and Christians as subhuman. The minority races are "mud races." He believes that his church should be a leader in the Rahowa (racial holy war), in which the white race must conquer the other races or itself be destroyed. After graduating from law school, Hale passed the state bar examination only to have the Illinois regulatory panel turn down his application. On June 30, 1999, Hale's final appeal was denied. A member of his congregation, Benjamin Smith, went on a three-day rampage, starting on July 3, 1999, killing two individuals and wounding several others. Smith died after shooting himself at the end of a lengthy police chase. Hale has denied responsibility for Smith's actions, but he has never expressed remorse. Despite nationwide negative publicity, Hale continues to preach his brand of racial hatred at his church in East Peoria. **See also** Church of the Creator; Klassen, Ben; World Church of the Creator.

Suggested readings: Pam Belluck, "Avowed White Racist Is Denied Illinois Law License," *Times-Picayune* [New Orleans] (February 14, 1999), p. A6; Tom Cruze, Erin G. Bradley, and Ellen Domke, "Heat Turned Up on Supremacist Church," *Chicago Sun-Times* (July 11, 1999), p. 6; Amy Pagnozzi, "Matthew Hale's Comely

White supremacist Matt Hale of the World Church of the Creator, on February 6, 1999, in his East Peoria, Illinois, office, says he does not understand why his white supremacist views have prevented him from receiving a law license from the state. (AP Photo/Kari Shuda)

Brand of Racial Hate," *Hartford Courant* [Connecticut] (March 13, 2001), p. A3; Abdon M. Pallasch, "This Church Preaches Love, Loyalty—and Hate," *Chicago Sun-Times* (July 9, 1999), p. 6; Edward Walsh, "Midwest Gun Spree Suspect Is Dead; Man Shot Himself, Pursuing Police Say," *Washington Post* (July 5, 1999), p. A1.

Hate Crime

The term "hate crime" describes a violent act by a perpetrator or a group of perpetrators that is based on the victim's race, religion, ethnicity, and/or sexual orientation. Historically this type of crime has had no special designation because laws against arson, bombing, conspiracy, homicide, and rape covered it. In the 1980s, however, because of increased concern for civil rights and the growing number of hate-related crimes, this attitude started to change. In 1990 Congress passed the Hate Crime Reporting Act, which mandates that national statistics be compiled on crimes involving race, religion, ethnicity, and sexual orientation. Information on the number of these crimes led to new hate crime legislation at the state and local levels. By 2000 a majority of the states had adopted laws providing for longer prison sentences when hate crimes were involved. Some of this legislation has had First Amendment freedom of speech problems and federal courts have ruled against parts of the legislation. Nevertheless, hate crime legislation is now a permanent part of the legal landscape in the United States.

A series of hate crimes occurred around the country in the late 1980s and 1990s which made hate crime legislation popular. Among these crimes was the racially motivated dragging death of a black man, James Byrd Jr., in Jasper, Texas, in 1998. The beating death of a gay University of Wyoming student, Matthew Shepard, in 1998 was an example of gay bashing. Skinhead murders of immigrants Oumar Dia, in Denver, Colorado, in 1995, and Mulugeta Seraw, in Portland, Oregon, in 1988, are other examples of hate crimes. Benjamin Smith, a member of the **World Church of the Creator**, went on a four-day murder spree in Illinois and Indiana between July 2 and July 5 in 1999 during which he killed two minority people and wounded eight others. Finally, **Buford O'Neal Furrow**'s attack on a Jewish community center and his killing of a Philippine postal worker, Joseph Ileto, in California in 1999 are examples of a member of a white supremacist organization who commits hate crimes. All of these crimes were committed by individuals motivated by hate who belonged to groups that advocated violence against real or perceived enemies. All of the perpetrators of these crimes, except Smith who committed suicide, were caught by the police and sentenced to long prison terms. Despite the national program on reporting hate crimes, gay organizations report that 70 percent of assaults on gays are never reported to the police. Other types of hate crimes may be unreported for a variety of reasons including fear of the police, assailants, or publicity. See also Gay Bashing; Jasper Murder Case; Skinheads; Thill, Nathan; World Church of the Creator.

Suggested readings: Mandy Garner, "Fighting Hate Crime Armed with a Spreadsheet," *Times Higher Education Supplement* (March 2, 2001), no. 1476, p. 18; Bill Ghent, "What Happened to the Hate-Crimes Bill?" *National Journal* 31 (December 18, 1999) 51–52:3616; James B. Jacobs and Kimberly Potter, *Hate Crimes: Criminal Law and Identity Politics* (New York: Oxford University Press, 1998); Robert J. Kelly and Jess Maghan, *Hate Crime: The Global Politics of Polarization* (Carbondale, Ill.: Southern Illinois University Press, 1998).

Hawke, David Wolfgang (See American Nationalist Party)

Hawthorne, Eric (See Burdi, George)

Hay, Harry (1912–)

Harry Hay, a leading gay activist in the United States and the founder of the Mattachine Society, was born on April 7, 1912, in Worthing, England. His father, a mine executive, worked for the Anaconda Copper Company. After his father was injured in a mining accident in Chile, the family moved to Southern California in 1916, and then to Los Angeles in 1919. Hay attended school in Los Angeles, but he spent his summers in Nevada working on a ranch and becoming acquainted with American Indians. In 1929 he graduated from Los Angeles High School. The following year Hay went to college at Stanford University. By this time, he had recognized that he was a homosexual, and he embarked on several affairs. In 1932 he left Stanford for both health and financial reasons. He experimented with becoming an actor and performed in several plays. In 1934 Hay joined the Communist Party. Dividing his attention between the Communist Party and his acting career, Hay spent the late 1930s engaged in political action and working with left-wing musicians. His main musical interest was folk music, and he became friends with famous folksingers Woody Guthrie and later Pete Seeger. In 1938 he married a fellow communist, Anita Platky. In the early 1940s, he and his wife adopted two daughters. During World War II, he was active in Russian war relief and worked in the war industry. Hay found that he had talent as an industrial engineer, and he made a successful career as a production engineer. He also earned a reputation as one of the leading Marxist teachers in the United States.

In the early 1950s, Hay began to turn his energies away from his involvement in communist politics and toward gay politics. As early as 1948, Hay had begun discussing with other gay activists the possibility of forming a group to lobby for the reform of anti-gay laws. In November 1950, Hay and four other gays established the Mattachine Society. The name and idea come from the Italian Renaissance Mattachine dancers, or Dance of Fools: figures in masks hid their identities and paraded around in Italian society. Now totally committed to gay politics, he divorced his wife and resigned from the Communist Party in 1951. He directed his energies into building the Mattachine Society. His contribution to gay history was to define gays as an "oppressed cultural minority." Hay's solution was for gays to develop pride in themselves. In 1953 he helped start the gay magazine *One*. Also in 1953, he resigned from the Mattachine Society in disagreement over the future direction of the society.

From the mid-1950s to the present, Hay has been in the middle of the campaign for gay rights. Because of his communist background, he was called to testify before the House Un-American Activities Committee in July 1955. This incident did not prevent him from continuing to agitate for gay rights. Hay also spent part of the 1960s campaigning for Native American Indian rights. In July 1969, he participated in the formation of the **Gay Liberation Front** (GLF) in Los Angeles and was elected its first

chairperson. After spending nine years in New Mexico, from 1970 to 1979, Hay moved back to Los Angeles. With his health deteriorating, he has devoted most of his recent attention to writing about the historical origins of the gay movement. Among his most controversial stances has been his support for the North American Man/Boy Love Association (NAMBLA), which he has denied is a form of child molestation. Hay's writing and activities have led to his position as the grand old man of gay rights, and his views on gay rights still attract followers. **See also** Gay Bashing; Gay Liberation Front; Gay Liberation Movement.

Suggested readings: Harry Hay, *Radically Gay: Gay Liberation in the Words of Its Founder* (Boston: Beacon Press, 1996); Sylvia Rubin, "87-Year-Old Mattachine Society Founder Named Grand Marshal of Pride Parade," *San Francisco Chronicle* (June 13, 1999), p. 35; Stuart Timmons, *The Trouble with Harry Hay: Founder of the Modern Gay Movement* (Boston: Alyson, 1990).

Hayden Lake

Hayden Lake, Idaho, was the location of **Richard Girnt Butler**'s white supremacist group, the **Aryan Nations**. Butler purchased 19.6 acres of rural land just outside of Hayden Lake in April 1973. At the time, he was the minister of the Church of Jesus Christ Christian in Southern California, which was steadily losing members. Butler decided to revitalize the church by rededicating it at Hayden Lake in 1974. Over the years, a complex of a chapel and assembly hall (Aryan Hall), an office, a small school, and a number of cabins were built. In 1981 a bomb exploded in Aryan Hall and destroyed it. A caller claimed responsibility for the bombing, but he was never identified. At first Butler believed that the explosion was the work of the **Jewish Defense League** (JDL), but later he suspected a dissident former member. The hall was rebuilt and the security measures protecting the compound were intensified. Butler used this site as a center for planning his radical white supremacist operations. In his publications, he called it the "international headquarters of the white race." At one time or another all of the leaders and many of the rank-and-file supporters of white supremacist organizations attended functions at Hayden Lake. Butler also hosted youth gatherings each year at Hayden Lake, usually in April to coincide with Adolf Hitler's birthday.

The compound in Hayden Lake was a symbol of the Aryan Nations. Butler built it as a sanctuary for his movement. In July 1998, however, three security guards assaulted a woman, Victoria Keenan, and her son, Jason Keenan, after their vehicle backfired outside the Hayden Lake compound. The guards, Jess Warfield, John Yeager, and Shane Wright, had been drinking and thought the backfire was gunfire. They fired shots at the car before running it off the road and roughing up the Keenans. Lawyers from the Southern Poverty Law Center filed a civil suit on behalf of the Keenans and won a $6.33 million civil judgment on September 8, 2000, against the Aryan Nations and Butler. The sum of $330,000 was for actual damages, and the $6 million was for punitive damages. The share of Butler and the Aryan Nations in the judgment came to $5.1 million. On September 23, 2000, Butler deeded the Hayden Lake compound to the Keenans. The Keenans sold the compound to Greg Carr, the founder of the Internet service Prodigy, on March 8, 2001, for $250,000. Carr plans to turn the site into a museum and human rights center. He also expects to spend between $1.6 million and $2 million to build a memorial park to honor Anne Frank, a victim of the Holocaust. **See also** Aryan Nations, Butler, Richard Girnt.

Suggested readings: Associated Press, "Internet Millionaire Buys Aryan Nations' Former Compound," *St. Louis Post-Dispatch* (March 8, 2001), A12; William Claiborne, "Supremacy Group Faces Fateful Trial; Civil Verdict Could Bankrupt Aryan Nations," *Washington Post* (August 28, 2000), p. A3; Kevin Flynn and Gary Gerhardt, *The Silent Brotherhood: Inside America's Racist Underground* (New York: Free Press,

1989); Kim Murphy, "Jury Verdict Could Bankrupt Aryans," *Los Angeles Times* (September 8, 2000), p. 1; Tom Tugend, "In Idaho, Home of Supremacists, a Park will Honor Anne Frank," *Jerusalem Post* (July 22, 2001), p. 7.

Heaven's Gate

Heaven's Gate, an unidentified flying object (UFO) cult, ended in a mass suicide in California in 1997. The cult was founded in the early 1970s by **Marshall Herff Applewhite** and Bonnie Lu Nettles, who formed a number of UFO groups under various names, including Total Overcomers Anonymous, the UFO Society, the Christian Arts Center, and the Human Individual Metamorphosis (HIM) before deciding on the name Heaven's Gate. Even after the death of Nettles from cancer in 1985, Applewhite continued to recruit members to his cult. After a series of bad experiences with the media over a failed prophecy in 1975, Applewhite avoided publicity until 1993. He launched a public relations campaign featuring videos, but soon afterward discovered the Internet was a better way to contact potential converts. Membership in the Heaven's Gate was always small—never exceeding 200 at any one time—but the active members were always devoted to Applewhite and his mission.

The theology of the Heaven's Gate was based on Applewhite's and Nettles's interpretation of the scriptures with a belief in UFOs thrown into the mix. They believed they themselves were the witnesses referred to in the Bible's Book of Revelations. These witnesses had the task to select the 144,000 to be saved in the final judgment. As such, they were representatives of "the Level Above Human" to take believers to heaven on a UFO when one appeared. After Nettles's death in 1985, members venerated her as an intermediary in this process. To make themselves worthy of salvation, Applewhite insisted that the members of the cult give up drinking, drugs, and sex. Some of the male members, including Applewhite, had themselves castrated.

Applewhite moved Heaven's Gate from

New Mexico to California in 1996. Their former headquarters was located on a forty-acre compound in Manzano, New Mexico. After deciding that this site was too remote, the leadership of Heaven's Gate sold the compound for $60,000. Applewhite decided that San Diego, California, was the preferred new site for the cult. Members rented a $1.3 million mansion in Rancho Santa Fe and relocated. To pay the monthly rent of $6,792, the cult started a business, Higher Source Contract Enterprises, to design Web sites for local businesses. Enough computer expertise existed in the cult to make this business modestly successful. Profits from this business and individual paychecks from other jobs went into a communal pot shared by all.

Applewhite became convinced that the appearance of the Hale-Bopp comet masked a spacecraft that would enable the members of Heaven's Gate to ascend to heaven. He was able to convince the other members of the cult that this was the opportunity for them to shed their human bodies for the journey. At the time, Heaven's Gate had thirty-nine members living at the mansion in Rancho Santa Fe. Beginning on March 22, 1997, members packed suitcases, put on new Nike clothes, and prepared for the trip. Over a period of several days, three shifts mixed phenobarbital sleeping pills, in applesauce or pudding, with a shot of vodka, lay down on their bunk beds, and placed plastic bags over their heads. Members of later shifts cleaned up the area around the bodies and placed shrouds over the bodies. Only the last two helpers were not shrouded and still had plastic bags around their heads. In the front of their tunics, each member had a birth certificate, passport, or driver's license for identification; a $5 bill; and a handful of quarters. Applewhite left a videotaped message from the cult explaining that the suicides were timed to the appearance of the Hale-Bopp comet and the arrival of Easter. Of the thirty-nine bodies found by the authorities, twenty-one were women and eighteen were men. Among the dead was the estranged brother of television and movie ac-tress Nichelle Nichols of *Star Trek* fame. A medical examiner found that six of the men, including Applewhite, had undergone castration operations. On May 6, 1997, two more members of the cult attempted suicide in the Encinitas Holiday Inn Express not far from Rancho Santa Fe. One member died, but the other survived. **See also** Applewhite, Marshall Herff; Cults; Solar Temple Cult.

Suggested readings: William M. Alnor, *UFO Cults and the New Millennium* (Grand Rapids, Mich.: Baker Books, 1998); Barry Bearak, "Odyssey to Suicide—A Special Report; Eyes on Glory," *New York Times* (April 28, 1997), p. A1; James Brooke, "Death in a Cult; The History," *New York Times* (March 30, 1997), sec. 1, p. 1; Carey Goldbert, "Death in a Cult; The Compound," *New York Times* (March 31, 1997), p. A12; Gale Holland and Richard Price, "Earthly Woes Lead Many to Space Cult," *USA Today* (March 31, 1997), p. 1A; Gustav Niebuhr, "Death in a Cult; The Landscape," *New York Times* (March 30, 1997), sec. 1, p. 1; Rodney Perkins and Forrest Jackson, *Cosmic Suicide: The Tragedy and Transcendence of the Heaven's Gate* (Dallas, Tex.: Pentaradial Press, 1997); Todd S. Purdum, "Death in a Cult; The Scene," *New York Times* (March 30, 1997), sec. 1, p. 1.

Heritage Front

The Heritage Front has been one of the leading white supremacist organizations in Canada since its founding in 1989. A union of right-wing extremists, including **Wolfgang Droege**, Gerald Lincoln, James Dawson, and Grant Bristow, started Heritage Front to provide leadership for the racist right. The idea for the organization came out of a series of discussions held by Canadian right-wing participants on a tour of Libya in the summer of 1989. The first public appearance of the Heritage Front was in December 1990 when its leaders conducted a memorial for the deceased leader of The Order, **Robert Jay Mathews**. This organization developed close ties to other racist and white supremacist groups, including the **Aryan Nations**, **Ku Klux Klan**, and the **White Aryan Resistance**. Ties were especially close to the Canadian **Church of the Creator** and its leader,

George Burdi. Although the Heritage Front had relatively few members, they were able to stage street marches and music concerts to attract attention to their cause. Leaders tried to attract new recruits by having existing members join the Canadian armed forces to make contact with potential new members. This strategy also allowed members of the Heritage Front to receive military training. Key defections in the mid-1990s because of leadership disputes severely weakened the Heritage Front.

The Heritage Front reached the majority of its 2,000 members through various modes of communication. Foremost of these modes was its publication, *Up Front*, edited by Gerry Lincoln, which started publication in 1991. Another method of communications has been the Heritage Hot Line, operated by Gary Schipper, a member of the Heritage Front. This telephone hate line, however, soon caused legal difficulties for the Heritage Front. Complaints from Canadian citizens reached the Canadian Human Rights Commission and an injunction was issued to shut it down. For almost a year the leadership for the Heritage Front ignored the injunction, but ultimately it was enforced.

At the time when the Heritage Front was disintegrating as a force in Canadian politics, it became known that Grant Bristow was a Canadian government undercover agent. Bristow had been one of the Heritage Front's most violent leaders. The Canadian Security and Intelligence Service had employed him to infiltrate neo-Nazi groups for nearly five years. In June 1994, Brian McInnis, a communications adviser to former solicitor general Doug Lewis, leaked the news of the existence of an undercover agent to the *Toronto Star*. Writers for this newspaper published a series of articles identifying Bristow as the agent and he went underground. This affair caused a scandal in Canadian politics that lasted for several years. The final result was the collapse of the Heritage Front as an extremist organization. **See also** Droege, Wolfgang; Neo-Nazis.

Suggested readings: Aurel Braun and Stephen Scheinberg, eds., *The Extreme Right:* *Freedom and Security at Risk* (Boulder, Colo.: Westview Press, 1997); Dale Brazao, "Star Finds Grant Bristow," *Toronto Star* (April 20, 1995), p. A1; Rosie DiManno, "Ex-Mercenary Aims for Country 'Uniquely' White," *Toronto Star* (June 19, 1991), p. A7; Bill Dunphy, "Some Time Spent with Hatred," *Toronto Sun* (March 19, 1994), p. 12; Bill Dunphy, " 'Stir It Up'; Grant Bristow Didn't Just Spy on the Heritage Front—He Used Taxpayers' Money to Build Up the Racist Organization," *Toronto Sun* (August 14, 1994), p. 18; Marc Fisher and Steve Coll, "Hate Groups: an International Cooperative," *Washington Post* (May 11, 1995), p. A31.

Hill, Julia "Butterfly" (1974–   )

Julia "Butterfly" Hill, who achieved notoriety for spending two years in a redwood tree in northern California to protest the logging of old-growth redwoods, was born in 1974 in Arkansas. Her father was an itinerant preacher. Hill was working as a bartender in Fayetteville, Arkansas, when she was hurt in an August 1996 automobile accident, which caused a serious head injury that damaged her short-term memory and motor skills. In the course of her slow recovery, Hill decided to make her life count for something. She left Arkansas and traveled to California where, in the summer of 1997, she joined the radical environmentalist organization **Earth First!**, which was in the middle of a campaign against the logging practices of Pacific Lumber Company. Charles Hurwitz, who had acquired this logging company in 1986, announced his intention to triple the rate of logging of giant redwood trees in an effort to recoup the cost of acquisition. This announcement mobilized radical environmentalist groups to hinder the logging operations of his company. One tactic that had proven successful in the early 1980s was tree sitting. When a tree was occupied, loggers were unable to harvest it.

Soon after Hill arrived in California, she volunteered to occupy one of the giant redwoods to prevent it from being harvested by the logging company. She started her vigil on a tarp-covered wood platform on a tree she named Luna on December 10, 1997. The

600-year-old tree was located near Stafford, about 240 miles north of San Francisco. Hill remained on that redwood for just over two years. She negotiated a deal in the middle of December 1999 with representatives of Pacific Lumber Company that had as one of its conditions sparing Hill's tree and a surrounding 200-foot zone. In return, the supporters of Hill agreed to a $50,000 settlement with Pacific Lumber Company. This sum was to be donated by the company to Humboldt State University for forestry research. Hill's two-year media campaign made her one of the heroines of the environmentalist movement. She has undertaken publicity tours, talking about her adventures in Luna. A vandal attacked the giant redwood in November 2000, sawing through 60 percent of its trunk threatening to kill it. **See also** Earth First!; Radical Environmentalism.

Suggested readings: Barbara Brotman, "Out on a Limb; Julia Hill Took Fight to Save Redwoods to New Heights by Living in a Tree—For Two Years," *Gazette* [Montreal] (May 15, 2000), p. E5; Mary Curtius, "Tree-Sitter, Lumber Firm Reach an Agreement," *Los Angeles Times* (December 18, 1999), p. A27; Charles Lawrence, "How Julia Came to Live in a Tree," *Daily Telegraph* [London] (January 18, 2000), p. 17; Glen Martin, "Hitting the Ground Running," *San Francisco Chronicle* (May 30, 2000), p. D1; Stephanie Salter, "Attack on Luna Another Test for Hill," *San Francisco Chronicle* (December 3, 2000), p. A31; Carl Schoettler, "Lofty Principles," *Baltimore Sun* (March 23, 1999), p. 1E.

Hill, Paul Jennings (1954–   )

Paul Hill, a former minister active in the violent wing of the anti-abortion movement, was born in 1954. After a troubled youth experimenting with drugs in Coral Gables, Florida, in 1971 he underwent treatment for a drug dependency. While at the treatment center he started studying the Bible and became religious. He attended, and graduated with a B.A from, Belhaven College, a Bible institute in Jackson, Mississippi. The church of his choice was a conservative Presbyterian church. In the early 1980s, he attended the Reformed Theological Seminary in Jackson,

Mississippi, and graduated with a divinity degree in 1983. Hill then was ordained as a minister in the Presbyterian Church in America denomination in 1984. The anti-abortion stances of his church and of several of his professors in the seminary oriented him toward the anti-abortion movement. His authoritarian ministry style led to the loss of ministerial positions at Presbyterian churches in South Carolina and Florida. In 1988 Hill left the Presbyterian Church in America and joined the smaller Orthodox Presbyterian Church. This switch lasted only two years, and in 1990 Hill turned in his ministerial credentials. In 1992 he moved his family to Valparaiso, a town about fifty miles east of Pensacola, Florida, where he started an automotive paint touch-up business. He joined a local Presbyterian church, but he was soon excommunicated from the church because of his radical views on abortion.

Hill's opposition to abortion led him to condone violence against abortion providers. He started a loose-knit organization of only five supporters he called the Defensive Action. Hill formed a shadow organization with an address, a letterhead, and an activist philosophy. Members agreed that the killing of doctors who performed abortions was justifiable homicide. Hill publicly approved the assassination of an abortion doctor, Dr. David Gunn, in March 1993 in Pensacola, Florida, by Michael F. Griffin. Hill appeared on television shows and made public statements to justify his position. Among his most vocal supporters were **Michael Bray**, who had served time in prison for bombing abortion clinics, and Father **David Trosch**, a Catholic priest and anti-abortion activist. Griffin's inability to withstand police pressure and his blaming of the pro-life movement for his actions disturbed Hill. After several months of preaching about and debating the issue, Hill shot and killed Dr. John Bayard Britton, an abortion doctor, and James Barrett, a retired Army colonel, with a .12 gauge shotgun on July 29, 1994, outside the Ladies Center in Pensacola. He also wounded June Barrett, a retired nurse.

Police arrested Hill a short time after the shootings just a few blocks away.

During the subsequent trial, Hill made little effort to defend himself. He did not attempt to work with his defense lawyers before the trial, and he represented himself at trial. His only defense was his appeal that the homicide was justifiable because it prevented further abortions. When the judge rejected this defense, Hill refused to participate in the rest of the proceedings. In December 1994, Hill received two sentences of death for the murders and thirteen years in prison for wounding the third person. Earlier, in October, he had been the first person to be convicted of violating the Freedom of Access to Clinic Entrances (FACE) Act. Hill received two life sentences for the violation of FACE. Death sentences require mandatory reviews and take many years for appeals. In 1996 the Florida State Supreme Court upheld his double-murder convictions and the death sentences. During the lengthy appeals process, Hill is being held on Florida State Prison's death row. He is busy writing a book to justify his beliefs and actions. **See also** Anti-Abortion Movement; Army of God; Kopp, James; Salvi, John C. III

Suggested readings: Lynne Bumpus-Hooper, "Slaying Suspect Preached That Killing Was Justified to Halt Abortions," *Orlando Sentinel* (July 30, 1994), p. A7; Steve Goldstein, "Unrepentant Killer," *Buffalo News* (May 9, 1999), p. 13A; Mark Juergensmeyer, *Terror in the Mind of God: The Global Rise of Religious Violence* (Berkeley: University of California Press, 2000); Tom Kuntz, "Paul Hill; From Thought to Deed," *New York Times* (September 24, 1995), sec. 4, p. 7; Marlon Manuel, "True Believer Came to Hate Abortion, Bless Violence," *Atlanta Journal and Constitution* (October 2, 1994), p. A12; James Risen and Judy L. Thomas, *Wrath of Angels: The American Abortion War* (New York: Basic Books, 1998); Patty Ryan, "Some Think Hill Seen as Martyr," *Tampa Tribune* (December 7, 1994), p. 1.

Hoffman, Abbott Howard "Abbie" (1936–1989)

Abbie Hoffman, a leading left-wing radical in the United States from the 1960s to the 1980s, was born on November 30, 1936, in Worcester, Massachusetts, into a conservative Jewish family. His father ran a wholesale pharmacological business in Worcester. Hoffman was always a good student, but he displayed a rebellious streak as a teenager. While attending public high school, he was suspended for an altercation with a teacher. He enrolled in Worcester Academy, a private school, and graduated in 1955. Hoffman attended Brandeis University in Waltham, Massachusetts, as a pre-med student. He found the intellectual atmosphere at Brandeis stimulating and changed his major to psychology. After graduation in 1959, he was accepted in the master's degree program at the University of California at Berkeley. Political agitation on the Berkeley campus was just starting, and Hoffman was on the fringe of the activity. Hoffman married his college sweetheart and took a job as a staff psychologist at Worcester State Hospital before finishing his master's degree.

In the early 1960s, Hoffman became involved in left-wing causes. His first interest was the civil rights movement. In 1965 Hoffman and his wife visited the South to help in the civil rights struggle in Georgia and Mississippi. Later, he worked to help the Poor People's Corporation raise funds for Southern blacks fired from their jobs for participating in civil rights activities. When the civil rights movement started rejecting white supporters to empower blacks in the South, Hoffman disagreed with the strategy in a series of articles he wrote for the left-wing newspaper *Village Voice*.

Hoffman turned his attention to the anti–Vietnam War movement. After he and his wife divorced in 1966, Hoffman moved to New York City and became engaged in the bohemian lifestyle of the hippies and the anti–Vietnam War cause. Convinced that traditional politics could not be used to end the war, Hoffman and others organized a grassroots campaign to end it. This strategy meant conducting mass demonstrations. Hoffman used tactics designed to appeal to the national media and shock the public and

Antiwar activist Jerry Rubin, along with other defendants in the Chicago Seven conspiracy trial, speaks to the press in this February 1970 photo. Front row, from left: Rennie Davis, Jerry Rubin, Abbie Hoffman. Back row, from left: Lee Weiner, Bob Lamb, and Thomas Hayden. (Lamb was not one of the Chicago Seven.) (AP PHOTO)

turned away from nonviolence to direct confrontation. Among his theatrics was throwing money at the New York Stock Exchange in June 1967. With Jerry Rubin, a Berkeley antiwar activist, Hoffman staged a mass demonstration at the Pentagon in Washington, D.C. Hoffman next began to plan for a mass protest to be held at the 1968 Democratic National Convention in Chicago. About this time Hoffman and other leftists coined the term "Yippie" to describe politicized hippies.

The protests at the Democratic National Convention in Chicago in August 1968 ran into the determined opposition of Mayor Richard Daley. Hoffman's efforts to receive a permit for demonstrations were unsuccessful. Hoffman and Rubin began feuding over strategy and tactics. Daley's preconvention threats reduced the number of demonstra-

tors, and those who did show up stayed in Lincoln Park until Chicago police drove them out on August 27. In the middle of the convention, Hoffman was arrested. After posting bail, he returned to the demonstrations. Although Hoffman believed Chicago had been a triumph, American public opinion repudiated the actions of the demonstrators. Many activists became disillusioned and dropped out of the antiwar movement. Hoffman decided to write a book, *Revolution for the Hell of It* (1968), to explain his politics.

Hoffman's political activities gained him national exposure, but it also increased attention from federal agents and the police. He was arrested several times for minor infractions, and the police raided his office and home several times. On March 20, 1969, Hoffman was indicted in a Chicago federal court for conspiracy to cross state lines to promote a riot. Hoffman and his co-defendants, known as the Chicago Eight, stood trial starting in September 1969 for their role in the 1968 riots. Disruptions by Bobby Seale led to his case being separated from the others, who then became known as the Chicago Seven. Judge Julius Hoffman was a hostile judge, and the defendants turned the trial into political theater by attacking both the trial and the political system. A jury convicted Hoffman and the others of crossing state lines with intent to riot, but it acquitted them of conspiracy. Judge Hoffman sentenced each to five years in prison with a fine of $5,000 and revoked their bail. He also cited the defendants and their lawyers to 159 instances of contempt of court. Over the next three years, appeals courts reversed all of the convictions on the basis of judicial and prosecutorial errors. Hoffman spent less than two weeks in jail. During the appeals process, Hoffman made hundreds of speeches to raise money for court costs and encouraged students to commit themselves to changing the political system using any tactics available.

Hoffman continued to play an active role in the left-wing radical movement in the 1970s, but his role was changing. He found himself an outsider in two emerging movements: women's liberation and gay liberation. While he was sympathetic to both movements, he was never able to embrace them fully. In 1971 he wrote the book *Steal This Book*, a handbook on revolutionary activity which advocated bombing and violence. Hoffman's support for Democratic Senator George McGovern's 1972 campaign for president left him open to criticism from within the radical movement. In 1973 Hoffman was arrested in a cocaine deal that went bad. Hoffman went underground shortly before an April 1974 hearing on the cocaine delivery charges. He spent the next four years traveling in underground circles from Mexico to Canada. Hoffman made several attempts to join **Weather Underground,** but its leaders refused him admittance. His mental health started to deteriorate, and in 1980

a psychologist diagnosed him as suffering from bipolar mental disorder, sometimes called manic depression. He could control his mood swings only by taking the medicine lithium.

In the late 1970s, Hoffman became involved in environmental issues. By this time he was living in upper New York State under an assumed name. He formed the Save the River Committee to fight the plans of the U.S. Corps of Engineers to straighten and deepen the Saint Lawrence River channel for winter navigation. Hoffman, who operated behind the scenes as publicity director, defeated the attempt. Aware, however, that such political activity would eventually expose him to the authorities, Hoffman surrendered to New York City police on September 4, 1980, in exchange for a reduced sentence on the cocaine charge. On April 8, 1981, he was sentenced to three years in prison, but he served less than a year before being released on March 26, 1982.

After his release from prison, Hoffman spent the rest of his life fighting for radical and environmental causes. His opposition to a pumping station being built on the Delaware River helped delay the construction of the pumping station, but a court ruling resulted in its being built. Hoffman's next crusade was against the Reagan administration's policies in El Salvador and Nicaragua. He helped young activists form organizations and plan demonstrations against American policies in Central America. On June 16, 1988, he was seriously injured in an automobile accident. His physical health deteriorated and he became more depressed. On April 12, 1989, he was found dead in his apartment in Soleburg Township, Pennsylvania. He apparently had committed suicide. Of all the radical leftists from the 1960s and 1970s, Hoffman remained the most consistent in fighting for his ideas of a radical transformation of American society. **See also** Students for a Democratic Society; Radical Environmentalism; Weather Underground.

Suggested readings: Garry Abrams, "Abbie Hoffman; The Yippie Who Stayed in Tune with

'60s," *Los Angeles Times* (April 14, 1989), part 5, p. 1; Susan Campbell, "Abbie Hoffman's Dirty Linen," *Hartford Courant* [Connecticut] (August 22, 2000), p. D1; David Firestone and David Behren, "Radical Cheek; Abbie Hoffman's Brand of Agitation-Pop-Irreverent, Flamboyant, Obnoxious—Spanned Three Decades of Activism," *Newsday* [New York City] (April 14, 1989), part II, p. 2; Marty Jezer, *Abbie Hoffman: American Rebel* (New Brunswick, N.J.: Rutgers University Press, 1992); Bruce McCabe, "Why Did Abbie Hoffman Die?" *Boston Globe* (April 27, 1989), p. 77; Jonah Raskin, *For the Hell of It; The Life and Times of Abbie Hoffman* (Berkeley: University of California Press, 1997); Larry Sloman, *Abbie Hoffman and Hey, His Turbulent Times* (New York: Doubleday, 1998); Larry Sloman, *Steal This Dream: Abbie Hoffman and the Countercultural Revolution in America* (New York: Doubleday, 1998).

Holocaust Denial Movement

Supporters of the Holocaust denial movement argue that the Holocaust never occurred—that whatever happened to the Jews in Germany and Eastern Europe was part of the war and that no German plan to exterminate the Jews was ever in operation. They claim that the 6 million Jews killed by the Nazis escaped from Europe and made it safely to other lands. Moreover, they claim, the atrocities inflicted by the Allies on the Germans during the last stages of the war were more serious than the German treatment of the Jews. The most extreme adherents of this thesis declare furthermore that Adolf Hitler was a man of peace and was forced into conducting war with the Allies. Finally, adherents believe that the Jews have victimized Germany by perpetuating the myth of the Holocaust and in doing so received enough international sympathy to establish the State of Israel. Many of these Holocaust deniers are also admirers of German National Socialism and have used Holocaust denial as a way to rehabilitate Nazism.

A number of German and Nazi sympathizers initiated a Holocaust denial campaign shortly after the end of World War II. Early among these deniers were two French-men, Maurice Bardeche and Paul Rassinier. Soon American Nazi sympathizers Harry Elmer Barnes, a professor of history, and **George Lincoln Rockwell**, head of the **American Nazi Party**, were converted to Holocaust denial. Two other academics, Austin J. App, an English professor at LaSalle University, and Arthur Butz, an electrical engineering professor at Northwestern University, made significant contributions to the growth of Holocaust denial theory. In 1973 App published a book, *The Six Million Swindle*, which denies the Holocaust and claims that the Jews escaped into the Soviet Union. Butz's book, *The Hoax of the Twentieth Century* (1976), attempted to prove that the Holocaust was part of a Jewish conspiracy. More recent attempts have sought to prove the impossibility of the existence of gas chambers. One self-taught engineer, Fred Leuchter, analyzed the chemical composition of the walls at two of the concentration camps to prove that the gas chambers never existed. David Irving, a British historian, asserted that Anne Frank's *The Diary of a Young Girl* was a forgery and not written by a young Jewish girl. Irving suffered the indignity that his German publisher had to pay compensation to Anne Frank's father for a false claim in a German court. In a trial that made headlines around the world in 2000 Irving brought a civil suit against American historian Deborah Lipstadt and her publisher for libel. Lipstadt, in her book *Denying the Holocaust*, called Irving a Holocaust denier. He accused her of damaging his reputation as a historian. He lost the case, which hurt him financially, but it has not damaged him with his supporters in the **Institute for Historical Review** (IHR).

The most prominent Holocaust deniers have developed a close affiliation with the IHR. **Willis Carto** started the organization in 1979 to provide a forum for Holocaust denial research. Speakers and writers from the IHR travel around the country advancing the thesis that the Holocaust never happened. They repudiate both survivor accounts and written documents to advance their cause. An effort to extend Holocaust denial to college campuses has been made by the founding of IHR's affiliated Committee on the Open Debate on the Holocaust (CODOH). **Mark Weber,** the editor of the institute's *Journal of Historical Review,* and Bradley Smith, a co-worker, launched this campaign in 1987 and it has been moderately successful in bringing the Holocaust denial issue onto college campuses. **See also** Anti-Semitism; Carto, Willis; Institute for Historical Review; Irving Affair; Weber, Mark.

Suggested readings: David Cesarani, "The Denial Was Always There," *Sunday Times* [London] (April 16, 2000), p. 1; James D. Davis, "Erasing the Holocaust," *Sun-Sentinel* [Fort Lauderdale Fla.] (April 26, 1992), p. 1E; Richard J. Evans, *Living about Hitler: History, Holocaust and the David Irving Trial* (New York: Basic Books, 2001); Mitchell Jones, *The Leuchter Report: A Dissection* (Cedar Park, Tex.: 21st Century Logic, 1995); Deborah Lipstadt, *Denying the Holocaust: The Growing Assault on Truth and Memory* (New York: Plume, 1993); Frank Miele, "Giving the Devil His Due; Holocaust Revisionism as a Test Case for Free Speech and the Skeptical Ethic," 2 *Skeptic* 4:58–70; Southern Poverty Law Center, "Denying the Holocaust," *SPLC Intelligence Report* 97 (Winter 2000):61.

Hoskins, Richard Kelly (1928–   )

Richard Kelly Hoskins, one of the major white supremacist writers in the United States, was born in 1928 and raised in Lynchburg, Virginia. His family has lived in the Lynchburg area since early colonial times, and his father was a popular medical doctor. After attending local schools, he transferred to Fishburne Military School in Waynesboro, Virginia, and played football. Soon after graduation in 1947, Hoskins joined the U.S. Air Force as a small-arms instructor. After leaving the military in 1953, he returned to Lynchburg. He decided to go to college and attended Hampden-Sydney College for one year before finishing his degree in history at Lynchburg College. Hoskins worked as an investment advisor at several stock brokerages before settling at Anderson & Strudwick, a Lynchburg investment firm. He stayed at this firm until his white supremacy writing made him so notorious that he was fired. He started his own publishing business, Virginia Publishing Company, and now writes books advocating racial violence. His two most famous books are *War Cycles, Peace Cycles* (1985) and *Vigilantes of Christendom: The Story of the Phineas Priesthood* (1990). In these books, Hoskins rails against the evils of racial integration and glorifies the career of Adolf Hitler and the Nazis. More important, he offers a justification for vigilantism in the **Phineas Priesthood** story. He borrowed the story from the Bible's Old Testament Book of Numbers about the actions of an Israelite, Phineas, who kills another Israelite and his foreign wife and in the process saves the people of Israel from a plague. His descendants are then made hereditary priests. According to Hoskins, the Phineas Priests have the right to use violence to preserve white supremacy.

The story of Phineas Priesthood has become increasingly popular among white supremacists, anti-abortion activists, and anti-government extremists. After the FBI discovered that **Byron de la Beckwith,** the assassin of civil rights leader Medgar Evers, identified himself with the Phineas Priesthood, authorities have found other violent acts associated with Hoskins's philosophy. **Peter Kevin Langan** and Richard Lee Guthries, leaders of the **Aryan Republican Army,** robbed twenty-two banks and styled themselves as Phineas Priests. **Paul Jennings Hill,** an anti-abortionist activist, who was convicted of killing a doctor and his bodyguard outside an abortion clinic in Pensacola, Florida, has written about his support for the Phineas Priesthood. Although Hoskins has denied any responsibility for the violence, he continues to advance the vigilantism cause in his occasional newsletter, *Hoskins Report.* **See also** Aryan Republican Army; Beckwith, Byron de la; Hill, Paul Jennings; Langan, Peter Kevin; Neo-Nazis; Phineas Priesthood.

Suggested readings: Anti-Defamation League, *Danger: Extremism: The Major Vehicles and Voices on America's Far-Right Fringe* (New York: Anti-Defamation League, 1996); Associated Press, "Ideologue of Christian Identity Movement Denounces 'Unwarranted Killing,'" *St. Louis Post-Dispatch* (September 1, 1999), p. A4; Rex Bowman, "Delivering a World View in Shadows," *Richmond Times-Dispatch* (October 3, 1999), p. A1; Lori Lessner, "Hate Gospel Author Lives Quiet Life on Tree-Lined Va. Road," *Knight-Ridder Washington Bureau* (August 16, 1999), p. 1; Sally MacDonald and Carol M. Ostrom, "Hate Crimes in America—How White Supremacists See It," *Seattle Times* (August 12, 1999), p. A2; Loretta J. Ross, "Using the Bible to Justify Killing," *Baltimore Sun* (August 8, 1994), p. 7A.

Human Life International (HLI)

Human Life International, one of the most radical anti-abortion organizations in the United States, was founded by two Catholic priests, Father **Paul Marx**, a Benedictine priest, and Father Matthew Habiger, under the name of Human Life Center in 1972. The founders started this organization to wage war on abortion, contraception, radical feminism, and sex education in schools. In 1981 Marx renamed the organization Human Life International. HLI's headquarters was in Gaithersburg, Maryland, until 1996, when it was moved to Front Royal, Virginia. Marx claims that the organization has at least 30,000 members in at least thirty countries. The *Washington Post* (April 8, 2000) reported that in 2000 HLI had established eighty-eight overseas branches and had $12 million in assets.

In addition to its opposition to feminism and contraception, HLI has been most active in fighting abortion. Marx became the leader and the official spokesperson for the HLI. His most controversial stance has been his attack against Jews and Muslims who support abortion. Marx has gone so far as to accuse Jewish doctors of declaring war on Christian babies. Jewish leaders, in turn, accuse Marx and the HLI of **anti-Semitism**. Marx has denied this charge, but he continues to attack Jewish abortion providers. Leadership of the HLI developed extensive contacts with **Randall Terry**, the head of the

anti-abortion movement **Operation Rescue**, and other leaders of Operation Rescue during its heyday in the late 1980s. In public statements members of HLI have condoned the killing of abortion doctors. Although the HLI was started in the United States, it has been building its international contacts in Canada and Germany. Marx is also the author of *The Death Peddler: War on the Unborn* (1971), which advances his anti-abortion viewpoint.

Human Life International has been hurt most recently by a feud between the leaders and their followers. The current head of HLI, Reverend Richard Welch, who is a priest in the Catholic Redemptorist Order, deposed its founder, Reverend Paul Marx, in 1999. Marx now resides in a monastery in Minnesota. His followers have attacked Welch for his betrayal of Marx. Welch and his supporters claim that Marx retired because of ill health. They have had to clean up financial and administrative irregularities left by Marx. The change in leadership has marked a fundamental shift in tactics of Human Life International. Marx represented direct-action tactics with picketing abortion clinics and a hard-line approach to abortion. Welch wants to return the HLI to less direct action and more educational initiatives. This dispute has hampered HLI's operations and its fund-raising. **See also** Anti-Abortion Movement; Anti-Semitism; Marx, Paul.

Suggested readings: Janet Bagnell, "Rough Welcome Planned for Anti-Abortionists," *Gazette* [Montreal] (April 15, 1995), p. A1; Aurel Braun and Stephen Scheinberg, eds., *The Extreme Right: Freedom and Security at Risk* (Boulder, Colo.: Westview Press, 1997); Michael Cooper, "When Words Can Kill," *Montreal Gazette* (January 21, 1995), p. B2; Michele Mandel, "Fanning the Flames of Hatred," *Toronto Sun* (April 4, 1999), p. 5; Caryle Murphy, "Family Values Feud; Catholic Nonprofit Embroiled in Leadership Dispute," *Washington Post* (April 8, 2000), p. B1; Nolan Zavoral, "Human Life International Officials Reject Charges That Organization Is Anti-Semitic," *Star Tribune* [Minneapolis] (April 15, 1997), p. 2B.

Illuminati

The American extremist right claims that a secret international conspiracy exists to overthrow the American way of life and that the name of this elite group of conspirators is the Illuminati. A group of European intellectuals formed the Order of the Illuminati in May 1776, in Bavaria, Germany, under the leadership of Adam Weishaupt. Weishaupt's goal was to form a secret organization of European leaders to work for the Enlightenment version of revolutionary social change. Among its tenets were a rejection of organized Christianity, opposition to superstition, and an acceptance of free love. Bavarian authorities learned of the organization's existence after lightning killed a rider carrying documents of Illuminati leaders in 1785. Authorities outlawed the organization in 1786. During the French Revolution, the Jacobins adopted several ideas of the Illuminati. In 1797 French cleric historian Abbé Baruel made the interpretation that the Illuminati were the harbingers of the French Revolution. He considered the Illuminati as part of a general attack on Christianity started by the Order of Templars in the Middle Ages and continued to modern times by Freemasons. Also in 1797 John Robison, a professor of natural philosophy at Edinburgh University, wrote a book titled *Proofs of a Conspiracy*, in which he charged that the Illuminati had infiltrated Masonic lodges.

The American extremist interpretation of the Illuminati asserts that the members of the Illuminati merged into the radical Masonic movement in the nineteenth century to form a revolutionary movement. They claim that Jews assumed control of the new organization and have been behind most of the disasters of the twentieth century. In their interpretation, Karl Marx was a Mason and so were the communist leaders of the Russian Revolution of 1917. To them, forged evidence of an international Jewish conspiracy to rule the world in the *Protocols of the Elders of Zion* (1920) proves the existence of this conspiracy. They claim that members of this Jewish conspiracy have been conducting a holocaust against Christianity throughout the twentieth century and that part of this conspiracy is what they see as a Jewish domination of international banking and through it control of the world economy and manipulation of the Federal Reserve Bank. They claim that members of the Illuminati direct the policies of the U.S. Department of State and cater to the communists. This hatred by the extremists extends to the Trilateral Commission, a club of prominent businessmen from Europe, Japan, and the United States, and the Council on Foreign Affairs which they claim are controlled by a Jewish cabal and are part of the general conspiracy. Because prominent Democrats and Republicans belong to these groups, extremists believe both parties are active in the conspiracy. See also Anti-Semitism; Committee of the States; Survivalist Movement.

Suggested readings: James Coates, *Armed and Dangerous: The Rise of the Survivalist Right* (New York: Hill and Wang, 1987); Ted Daniels, ed., *A Doomsday Reader: Prophets, Predictors and Hucksters of Salvation* (New York: New York University Press, 1999); Paul Felman, "Conspiracy Talk a U.S. Tradition," *Los Angeles Times* (May 29, 1995), p. A3; Mark Fenster, *Conspiracy Theories: Secrecy and Power in American Culture* (Minneapolis: University of Minnesota Press, 1999); George Johnson, "A Web of Conspiracy Theories," *Ottawa Citizen* (November 28, 1996), p. A15; Cheri Seymour, *Committee of the States: Inside the Radical Right* (Mariposa, Calif.: Camden Place Communications, 1991).

Institute for Historical Review (IHR)

The Institute for Historical Review (IHR) is a pseudo-academic institute which attracts extremist political figures and authors who advance anti-Semitic viewpoints. **Willis Carto**, head of the **Liberty Lobby**, founded the IHR in 1979. Its primary purpose is to sponsor activities and publish books and pamphlets that deny the existence of the Holocaust and rehabilitate the reputations of Adolf Hitler and Nazi Germany. Another purpose is to gain academic respectability for Holocaust denial research. Perhaps its best propaganda was achieved in the *Journal of Historical Review*. For this publication, authors from around the world wrote articles attacking Jews and the existence of the Holocaust. This revival of **anti-Semitism** by the IHR led to the IHR's hosting a series of annual conferences, beginning in 1979. Among the participants were **David Duke**, then a leader in the **Ku Klux Klan**, and Frank Collins, head of the **American Nazi Party**. Among its publicity stunts was a proposed $50,000 award for anyone who could prove the Holocaust occurred. This publicity ploy was the brainchild of IHR's first director, William David McCalden, a British white supremacist. The IHR was to select the

judges for the award. One survivor of the Holocaust, Mel Mermelstein, sued the IHR after his submission of evidence was ignored. In a 1981 trial, a Los Angeles judge awarded Mermelstein damages of $90,000, and the IHR was ordered to apologize to him.

In 1987 **Mark Weber** and Bradley Smith launched the Committee on the Open Debate on the Holocaust (CODOH) to bring Holocaust denial to college campuses. Smith has devoted most of his energies in the past decade to accomplishing this task with some success and much publicity.

Bad publicity over the Mermelstein settlement and a dispute over a $10 million estate gift appropriated by Carto for his use alienated the staff of the IHR from Carto. In 1993 the staff of the IHR fired Carto over the money. Almost as important as the funds was the future direction of the IHR. Carto wanted to move the organization away from Holocaust denial and more toward advocacy of white supremacy. Mark Weber, the editor of the *Journal of Historical Review*, and his associates opposed this reorientation. In a court case tried in October and November 1996, the IHR won its independence from Carto and a judgment of $6.4 million. The cost was high, however, because Carto's allies pulled out their financial support. Carto, now an enemy of the IHR, has turned his attention to producing a rival publication, the *Barnes Review*. The IHR continues to be a leader in Holocaust denial research. Smith continues to conduct an outreach campaign on Holocaust denial on the campuses of American universities and colleges. The association with David Irving and his defeat in a British libel suit has had a negative impact on the IHR by discrediting a major Holocaust denier. See also Anti-Semitism; Carto, Willis; Holocaust Denial Movement; Irving Affair; Liberty Lobby; Weber, Mark.

Suggested readings: Doreen Carajal, "Extremist Institute Mired in Power Struggle," *Los Angeles Times* (May 15, 1994), p. A3; Richard J. Evans, *Lying About Hitler: History, Holocaust, and the David Irving Trial* (New York: Basic Books, 2001); Michael Granberry, "Judge Awards $6.4 Million to O.C. Revisionist Group"

Los Angeles Times (November 16, 1996), p. 1; Michael Granberry, "Revisionists' Founder Sued for $7.5 Million," *Los Angeles Times* (October 28, 1996), p. 1; Deborah E. Lipstadt, *Denying the Holocaust: The Growing Assault on Truth and Memory* (New York: Plume, 1993); Greg Moran, "Decision on Estate Fails to End Bitterness," *San Diego Union-Tribune* (November 16, 1996), p. B1; Kenneth S. Stern, *Holocaust Denial* (New York: American Jewish Committee, 1993); Leonard Zeskind, "Money Matters: Holocaust Denial Leaders Battle over Millions," *SPLC Intelligence Report* 87 (Summer 1997): 10–11.

Internet-Based Extremists

American extremists use the Internet to advance their agendas. The first to use the Internet for this purpose were Canadian right-wing extremists who were attempting to avoid Canada's stringent laws against hate literature. Some of the computer-literate members of extremist groups began experimenting with ways to use telecommunications and computers. Using the equipment available in the early 1980s, several computer bulletin boards were established. One of the first successful efforts was that of **Louis Beam**, a veteran white supremacist leader from Texas, who built the Aryan Nations Net. Both Beam and **Richard Girnt Butler**, the head of the **Aryan Nations**, were engineers by training, and they were intrigued by the potential of this new technology. Their bulletin board permitted them to spread Aryan Nations propaganda and at the same time provide a message center for communication among members.

Extremists have found the Internet an easy way to spread their messages. The Internet is inexpensive, and Web sites allow extremists to reach a national and international audience. A 1997 FBI report warned that the Internet allowed extremist groups to raise money, spread their propaganda, educate their supporters on weaponry and explosives, and recruit new members. It is also a way to distribute hate music and attract troubled teenagers. Two of the most prominent extremist Web sites are **Stephen Donald "Don" Black**'s Stormfront and **Ernst Christof Friedrich Zundel**'s Zundelsite. **Neo-Nazis** have been so successful in spreading their propaganda that the German government has launched a campaign against the neo-Nazi Web site in 2000 and has threatened to seek extradition of violators of German law against the spread of Nazi material.

The danger and effectiveness of Internet-based extremism were made evident in the Jouhari incident. Bonnie Jouhari worked as a fair housing specialist for the Reading–Berks County Human Relations Council in eastern Pennsylvania. She was also chairperson of the Hate Crimes Task Force for Berks County. In her research of the area's employment and housing patterns, she found a record of past discrimination against minorities in both Reading and the county, and she publicized her findings. Two extremists, **Roy Everett Frankhauser, Jr.**, a leader in the **United Klans of America** (UKA), and Ryan Wilson, of the neo-Nazi United States of America Nationalist Party, took exception to Jouhari's findings. Frankhauser organized a personal and physical harassment campaign; Wilson attacked Jouhari on his Web site, ALPHA HW. The combination of personal and Internet threats caused Jouhari, a single mother with a teenage daughter, to leave her job in November 1998. The family traveled to the Seattle, Washington, area and found new employment. Within months, however, the extremists had found her new home, and the threats started again. Wilson had posted Jouhari's picture on his Web site and classified her as a "race traitor." Jouhari moved again and started other jobs, but each time the harassment followed her. No matter to whom she complained—local police or the federal government—help was not forthcoming. Finally, in February 2000, the Department of Housing and Urban Development (HUD) filed suit against Wilson for violation of federal fair housing laws. This case was the first instance of the federal government's seeking civil rights sanctions against the operator of a hate-based Web site. Critics have attacked HUD's actions as a violation of Wilson's First

Amendment right to freedom of speech. Others fear the unfettered power of the Internet in the hands of extremists. See also Aryan Nations; Beam, Louis; Butler, Richard Girnt; Frankhauser, Roy.

Suggested readings: Anti-Defamation League, *Danger: Extremism: The Major Vehicles and Voices on America's Far-Right Fringe* (New York: Anti-Defamation League, 1996); Steve Dunne, "New Media; Where the Hate Is," *Guardian* [London] (June 25, 2001), p. 50 Peter Finn, "Neo-Nazis Sheltering Web Sites in the U.S.; German Courts Begin International Pursuit," *Washington Post* (December 21, 2000), p. A1; Wayne King, "Computer Network Links Rightist Groups and Offers 'Enemy List,' " *New York Times* (February 15, 1985), p. A17; Michael Marriot, "Rising Tide: Sites Born of Hate," *New York Times* (March 18, 1999), p. G1; Southern Poverty Law Center, "163 and Counting . . . ; Hate Groups Find Home on the Net," *SPLC Intelligence Report* 89 (Winter 1998): 24–28; Wayne Washington, "Skinheads, Others Find New Tool in Internet," *St. Petersburg Times* (March 13, 1999), p. 1B.

Invisible Empire, Knights of the Ku Klux Klan, The

The Invisible Empire, Knights of the Ku Klux Klan is a spin-off group from the Knights of the Ku Klux Klan. **Elbert Claude "Bill" Wilkerson** organized the Invisible Empire in 1980 shortly after leaving the Knights of the Ku Klux Klan. He had become dissatisfied with **David Duke's** style of leadership and with Duke's increasingly moderate stance on racism. His views were more rigid and confrontational. Wilkerson left the Invisible Empire after he attempted to blackmail Duke over Duke's alleged offer to sell the membership mailing lists of the Knights of the Ku Klux Klan. Wilkerson was successful in building the membership of the Invisible Empire by seeking out public controversies and exploiting them for the media exposure. He appeared to be the emerging national leader in the Klan movement until news leaked out that he was an FBI informant. Following this news and Wilkerson's resignation, mass resignations almost destroyed the Invisible Empire as a viable organization.

James W. Farrands assumed leadership of the Invisible Empire and rebuilt it after Wilkerson's sudden departure. He continued Wilkerson's policy of activism. In January 1987, he led the Klan in a violent confrontation against civil rights demonstrators in Forsyth County, Georgia. Although Farrands was a native of Connecticut, he moved the headquarters of the Invisible Empire to rural North Carolina later in 1987. His action against the civil rights demonstrators backfired, however, when the Southern Poverty Law Center sued the Invisible Empire over its actions. A 1993 court decision led to the demise of the Invisible Empire. This judgment caused Farrands to disband the organization, relinquish its mailing lists, and agree to cease publishing *The Klansman*. See also Duke, David; Ku Klux Klan; Farrands, James W.; Wilkerson, Elbert Claude "Bill."

Suggested readings: Peter Applebome, "To Settle Suit, Ex-Klansmen Agree to Study 'Lessons of Brotherhood,' " *New York Times* (July 25, 1989), p. A14; National Desk, "A Klan Imperial Wizard Says He Will Resign Post This Year," *New York Times* (September 2, 1984), sec. 1, p. 27; Bill Rankin, "Court Orders Klan Faction to Disband Settles Suit in Forsyth Attack," *Atlanta Journal and Constitution* (May 20, 1993), p. A1; Wendell Rawls, Jr., "Klan Group in Alabama Training for 'Race War,' " *New York Times* (September 28, 1980), sec. 1, p. 26; Ronald Smothers, "Suit Against the Klan Brings Verdict of Nearly $1 Million," *New York Times* (October 26, 1988), p. A20; Curtis Wilkie, "Lawsuits Prove to Be a Big Gun in Anti-Klan Arsenal," *Boston Globe* (June 17, 1993), p. 1.

Irving, David (See Irving Affair)

Irving Affair

The Irving affair refers to the conversion of a British historian to the **Holocaust denial movement** and the impact on his reputation as a historian. David Irving, a self-taught historian, specializes in modern German history. He has written several books on the

Nazi period and has tried to prove that Adolf Hitler and his policies have been misunderstood. In his 1977 book, *Hitler's War*, Irving claimed that Hitler had been unaware of a program for the mass extermination of European Jews until 1943. Irving's revisionist views were successful to a point, but in the early 1980s his interpretation began to include Holocaust denial as part of his rehabilitation of the Nazi regime. **Willis Carto** and the **Institute for Historical Review** made him their chief representative for the historical respectability of Holocaust denial. Irving testified for **Ernst Christof Friedrich Zundel**, a Canadian neo-Nazi, in his 1984 trial in Canada. Irving's conversion to Holocaust denial caused a number of American and British historians to question some of the research in his books. In the 1991 edition of *Hitler's War*, Irving repudiated his earlier version and did not mention the Holocaust at all. By this time, his reputation as a Holocaust denier had made publishers reluctant to publish his books, depriving him of income.

An American historian, Deborah Lipstadt, questioned Irving's misuse of history in her book *Denying the Holocaust: The Growing Assault on Truth and Memory* (1993). When a publisher refused to publish his book, *Goebbels: Mastermind of the Third Reich*, and Penguin Press issued Lipstadt's book in 1995 in Great Britain, Irving retaliated in 1998 by suing Penguin Press and Lipstadt in a British court for libel. Lipstadt, a professor of Jewish history at Emory University in Atlanta, found herself in the middle of a complex legal case. Because British libel cases make the defendants prove their case, Lipstadt had to prove her charges that Irving misrepresented historical facts. The possibility of a legal opinion over the existence of the Holocaust made the trial an international event. Both sides agreed to leave the final judgment in the hands of the judge, Mr. Justice Charles Gray. In a two-month London trial in the spring of 2000, Irving lost the case. The judgment cost him approximately $2.5 million pounds. Since Irving was on the verge of bankruptcy before the trial, the likelihood that Penguin Press or Lipstadt will ever receive any settlement remains uncertain. Irving has appealed the verdict and has traveled to the United States to raise funds. Irving's friends among the Holocaust denial crowd still consider him the centerpiece of their campaign to make their cause respectable. **See also** Carto, Willis; Holocaust Denial Movement; Institute for Historical Review; Weber, Mark.

Suggested readings: Richard J. Evans, *Lying About Hitler: History, Holocaust and the David Irving Trial* (New York: Basic Books, 2001); Jonathan Freedland, "Court 73 Where History Is on Trial," *Guardian* [London] (February 5, 2000), p. 3; Fiachra Gibbons, "Author with No Publisher and Few Funds Landed with Pounds 2.5m Bill," *Guardian* [London] (April 12, 2000), p. 5; D. D. Guttenplan, *The Holocaust on Trial* (New York: Norton, 2001); Deborah Lipstadt, *Denying the Holocaust: The Growing Assault on Truth and Memory* (New York: Plume, 1993); Cal Mccrystal, "Adolf Hitler? Innocent Until Proven Guilty," *Independent* [London] (January 16, 2000), p. 13; David Pallister, "Author Fights Holocaust Denier Judgment," *Guardian* [London] (June 21, 2001), p. 8; R. Reid, "U.S. Scholar Is Victorious in Holocaust Libel Trial; Historian's View on Hitler Rebuked in London Court," *Washington Post* (April 12, 2000), p. A18; Southern Poverty Law Center, "It's Official; David Irving is 'Pro-Nazi,' " *SPLC Intelligence Report* 98 (Spring 2000):3.

J

Jasper Murder Case

In a celebrated case of white supremacy run amok, three white men tortured and murdered James Byrd, Jr., in Jasper, Texas. In the early morning of June 7, 1998, Sean Berry, Russell Brewer, and Bill King offered Byrd a lift in their truck. Byrd, who was black, was returning from his sister's bridal shower. The three white men had been drinking before driving around Jasper looking for a party they had been invited to earlier in the evening. They took Byrd outside of town to a clearing along Huff Creek Road and beat him severely. They then chained him by his feet to Berry's truck and dragged him to death during a three-mile ride. They disposed of what was left of Byrd's body at the oldest black cemetery in Jasper, Rosewood Cemetery. A local farmer spotted the body and reported it to the police at around 8:00 A.M. The local sheriff and his men traced the trail of blood back to the Huff Creek Road site. There they found Byrd's wallet, keys, and dentures. At the clearing, the police found evidence that tied Sean Berry to the crime scene.

The Jasper police arrested Berry, and his arrest led to the arrests of Brewer and King. Berry had been in trouble with local police before, but he had never been known as a white supremacist. A local boy, he was popular and had held a variety of jobs in the Jasper area. Brewer and King, however, were both known criminals and white supremacists. They had only recently been released from prison and, while in prison, had been active in both the Confederate Knights of the Ku Klux Klan and the **Aryan Brotherhood**. Part of the initiation process in the Aryan Brotherhood was killing a black person, and Byrd was the chosen victim.

The news of the murder and the subsequent trials became national events. In a series of sensational trials held in 1999, Brewer and King received the death penalty for their roles in the murder. Berry was sentenced to life imprisonment after he blamed his companions for the crime. He claimed that he had been an unwilling witness. His case will come up for parole in forty years, but his life will be at risk in prison from white inmates because he turned on his friends and from black prisoners because of the nature of the crime. This senseless crime shocked the nation and proved the danger of white supremacy. **See also** Aryan Brotherhood; Hate Crime; Ku Klux Klan; White Supremacist Movement.

Suggested readings: Anne Barrowclough, "Chained to a Pick-Up Truck, James Byrd was Conscious for the First Two Miles His Body Was Dragged Along This Country Road," *Times* [London] (October 27, 1999), p. 1; Jim Henderson, "When James Byrd Was Dragged to Death in Jasper More Than Two Years Ago, the Town's Image Hit Rock Bottom," *Texas Magazine* (September 3, 2000), p. 8; Bob Hohler, "Texas Prison Is a School for Hatred," *Boston Globe* (June 27, 1998), p. A1; Patty Reinert and Richard Stewart, "Berry Was at Wheel in Jasper, Jury Told," *Houston Chronicle* (November 11, 1999), p. A1.

Jewish Defense League (JDL)

The Jewish Defense League (JDL) began as a Jewish self-protection group, but it developed into a Jewish extremist organization. The JDL was founded in June 1968—with the self-proclaimed mission of protecting Jews in New York City from their enemies—by Rabbi Meir Kahane; Morton Dolinsky, a public relations expert; and Bertam Zweibon, a probate lawyer. The three men shared an allegiance to right-wing Zionism and hostility toward blacks. The growing militancy of the African American community and the encroachment of blacks on Jewish neighborhoods frightened the Jewish inhabitants. Kahane used his position as a writer on the *Jewish Press* to publish stories about the mistreatment of Jews by minorities. When the first official meeting of the JDL was held on June 18, 1968, at the West Side Jewish Center in Manhattan, thirty-five potential members appeared. Kahane soon established himself as an expert on Jewish-minority relations. He was able to make contacts with the House Un-American Activities Committee (HUAC), and the JDL and the HUAC cooperated with each other for years. The JDL soon established a reputation as an extremist group that would attack any person or organization that the members believed was hostile to Jews or Israel. In 1969 the JDL started a summer camp to educate young Jews in self-defense. Its instructors emphasized firearms instruction and hand-to-hand combat.

Throughout the 1970s and 1980s, the JDL conducted disruption operations against its perceived enemies. Arabs, blacks, representatives of the Soviet Union, and other more moderate Jewish organizations fit this criterion. Robert I. Friedman traces how members of the JDL planted bombs and assaulted Palestinians, **neo-Nazis**, and American blacks. Most of the early demonstrations were over the control of the New York Public School System. J. Edgar Hoover directed the FBI to aid the JDL in neutralizing black extremism, especially the **Black Panther Party**, as part of the FBI's Counterintelligence Program (COINTELPRO) initiative. Kahane also made contacts with Israeli secret services and provided them with information about Arab Americans.

Israeli officials persuaded Kahane to redirect his anti-black campaign to agitate on behalf of Russian Jews. In November 1970, members of the JDL launched a terrorist campaign against Soviet officials in the United States, including at least four bombings and harassment of Soviet officials and their families. Other terrorist acts occurred in Europe. Membership in the JDL increased to almost 10,000 as the violence escalated. Suddenly the leadership of the JDL found that the organization was out of control; individuals or small groups were initiating actions without the knowledge of the leadership. In May 1971, Kahane and a dozen leaders of the JDL were arrested on charges of conspiring to manufacture explosives. Kahane pleaded guilty and received four years' probation. While he was receiving this sentence, he was also recruiting Alex Steinberg to build a Jewish terrorist underground to target Arabs, neo-Nazis, and Soviet officials. The first operation in this terrorist campaign was the January 26, 1972 bombing in Manhattan of the office of impresario Sol Hurok, who had scheduled Soviet entertainers to perform in the United States. The bombing killed Iris Kones, a Jewish secretary. Her death caused some of JDL's adherents to reconsider their support. Charges over Kahane's misuse of funds from the Israeli secret service caused the Israelis to sever their ties with him.

The activities of the JDL moderated slightly when Kahane immigrated to Israel in 1971 and turned his attention to Israeli politics. Although Kahane was still on probation, U.S. authorities allowed him to immigrate to Israel to get him out of the United States. Kahane soon faced charges that he was using American funds to finance his campaign to run for the Israeli Knesset. These charges produced a controversy among his JDL supporters in the United States because they wanted the funds to be used to help American Jews. Bert Zweibon, a lawyer and co-founder of the JDL, had become head of the JDL, but his relationship with Kahane became strained. In September 1974, Kahane removed Zweibon and most of the JDL executive board and replaced them with his supporters. Kahane's activities in directing violence in the United States led federal authorities in February 1975 to revoke his probation. He spent eight months in a Manhattan halfway house and four months in a minimum-security federal prison in Allenwood, Pennsylvania.

Shortly before going to jail, Kahane reorganized the radical wing of the JDL to form a new terrorist group, the Jewish Armed Resistance, to initiate an organized campaign against JDL's enemies. In June 1975, the forty-odd members of the Jewish Armed Resistance launched a bombing campaign against selected targets in 1975 and 1976. Most of the bombings were directed against Soviet officials living in the United States, but some were directed against American targets. Federal authorities had arrested most of the members of the Jewish Armed Resistance by late 1976. Five leaders were convicted and sentenced to prison terms, but Kahane escaped responsibility. Despite his recruitment of them, Kahane repudiated their actions and did little to help them at their trials or later.

In July 1977, the executive directors of the Jewish Defense League expelled Kahane. Kahane had been the heart and soul of the JDL, but he had been careless with JDL funds. When Kahane decided that he wanted a divorce from his wife, members of the executive board knew that the divorce would ruin the JDL with its Orthodox Jewish base. Orthodox Jewish leaders would never forgive Kahane for a divorce and then marriage to a former lover. On July 5, 1977, the board formally expelled Kahane from the JDL. Bonnie Pechter replaced him as head of the JDL, but she lasted only a short time after Kahane unleashed a campaign to discredit her. His supporters in the JDL made Pechter's life so miserable that she resigned after only a few months.

By 1980 Kahane had reestablished complete control over the Jewish Defense League. His efforts to discredit Bonnie Pechter and his other enemies in the JDL were complete. The price for this victory, however, was high as the JDL was only a shadow of its former self. Membership, which had been as high as 10,000 in 1970, was only about a third of that in 1980. In the summer of 1981, a Catskills paramilitary camp produced a new crop of fifty JDL terrorists. The result was a series of fifteen bombings in and around New York City in 1982. When news of a federal investigation of the bombings reached the JDL in 1983, these militants left for Israel.

Kahane's commitments in Israel hurt the JDL. He made five or six trips to the United States each year to raise funds. These trips garnered around $500,000 a year for Kahane, and he took all the money to Israel and left affairs in the JDL to his chosen representatives. By 1985 the JDL was broke and in disarray. Kahane's frequent feuds with American Jewish leaders also caused problems for the JDL. The JDL broke up into fiefdoms with East and West Coast operations headed by different leaders running separate organizations. Victor Vancier was head of the New York City branch of the JDL until he ran afoul of the law in November 1986. He received a ten-year sentence for a series of bombings in New York City between 1984 and 1986. Recognizing the dangers of lack of leadership, Kahane selected **Irv Rubin**, a member of the JDL recruited by Kahane out of college, to succeed him as national head of the JDL.

Kahane still maintained a relationship with the JDL for financial reasons until his assassination on November 5, 1990, in downtown New York City, while he was in the United States for one of his annual fund-raising trips. His alleged assassin was an Arab American, who was later acquitted of the murder but convicted of assault, coercion, and weapons charges. The acquittal led to widespread demonstrations by JDL members and their supporters who accused New York authorities of **anti-Semitism**. The Jewish extremist organization **Kahane Chai** (Kahane Lives), an offshoot of the JDL, still operates in the United States and in Israel. Rubin continues to head the JDL, but since the early 1990s he has oriented the organization away from direct confrontation and violence. His reasoning for a more moderate approach has been the loss of financial support from moderate Jews. **See also** Kahane, Meir; Kahane Chai (Kahane Lives); Rubin, Irv.

Suggested readings: Aurel Braun and Stephen Scheinberg, eds., *The Extreme Right: Freedom and Security at Risk* (Boulder, Colo.: Westview Press, 1997); Robert I. Friedman, *The False Prophet: Rabbi Meir Kahane—From FBI Informant to Knesset Member* (London: Faber and Faber, 1990); Joel Greenberg, "Soft Spoken Heir to Role of Anti-Arab Militant," *New York Times* (January 1, 2001), p. A6; David Haldane, "JDL's New Patrol: Leader of Militant Defense Group Wants to Change Its Approach, Image," *Los Angeles Times* (July 23, 1990), p. E1; Yossi Klein Halevi, *Memoirs of a Jewish Extremist: An American Story* (Boston: Little, Brown, 1995); Anthony Millican, "Armed-Patrol Plan Draws Fire," *Los Angeles Times* (February 7, 1991), p. B3; Julio Moran, "Jewish Leaders Reject JDL Role in South Bay," *Los Angeles Times* (September 12, 1985), part 9, p. 1.

John Birch Society

The John Birch Society has long been a leading organization on the American extreme right. **Robert Henry Winborne Welch, Jr.,** a candy-manufacturing executive, founded the John Birch Society in December 1958 with the assistance of eleven fellow businessmen. In a two-day meeting held in Indianapolis, Indiana, the businessmen agreed that big government and communism were the primary enemies of the United States. They also opposed the federal income tax because it

hurt individual initiative. Social security and welfare programs were targeted because they were hurting the welfare of the country by providing an unnecessary safety net. Another of their key points was the belief that the lack of religious practice was tearing apart the fabric of society. Finally, and most important, they believed that a communist conspiracy was in place to take over the federal government and enslave American citizens. These views were gathered together by Welch and published as the *Blue Book* (1961). This book continues to serve as the bible of the John Birch Society.

The John Birch Society was never envisioned as a mass movement but as one able to produce an elite to lobby and campaign for its causes. Welch named the organization in honor of Captain John Birch, who had been killed by the Chinese communists in 1945. Earlier Welch had written a book about him in which Welch claimed Birch was the first American victim of the international communist conspiracy. Because Welch believed in an authoritarian brand of leadership, he kept tight control over the society during his tenure as its head. He did allow an advisory council of between ten and twenty-five prominent members to provide him with counsel and advice. Reflecting Welch's staunchly anti-communist viewpoint, the society specialized in a hunt for communist agents and their influence on the federal government. Welch was a loyal supporter of Senator Joseph McCarthy and his pursuit of communists. He was also, in general, unsympathetic toward democratic institutions. Leaders of the society directed most of their energies toward manipulating public opinion by initiating massive letter-writing campaigns. These campaigns were managed through the society's *Bulletin*. Two major society efforts in the 1960s were to gain control of the Republican Party and to impeach the Chief Justice of the Supreme Court, Earl Warren. Members of the John Birch Society were delighted with the candidacy of Senator Barry Goldwater and worked hard for him in the 1964 presidential election. Membership of the John Birch Society peaked in 1964 at over 100,000.

After suffering through Goldwater's presidential election defeat, the leadership of the John Birch Society turned their attention to defeating the civil rights movement. Welch published a pamphlet, *Two Revolutions at Once*, in which he charged that the communists were behind and directing the civil rights movement. This anti–civil rights stance attracted an assortment of extremists and racists to the society. The idea that the John Birch Society was a radical organization ready to lead a counterrevolution, however, proved illusionary. Slowly John Birch members began to migrate to other, more extreme groups. In the mid-1970s, Welch turned the society over to younger leadership. One of these new leaders was Congressman Larry McDonald of Georgia, who was killed in September 1983 during the Soviet Air Force attack on Korean Airline Flight 007. This incident reinforced the belief among John Birch Society members of a worldwide communist conspiracy against them. By the early 1990s, only a hard core of around 25,000 remained in the society, but these members were still actively campaigning for a variety of right-wing causes. The society never recovered from the retirement and subsequent death of its founder, Robert Welch, and his leadership.

The John Birch Society has remained a viable political organization for over thirty years because it has provided an ideology that attracted a significant segment of the American populace. This ideology was a critique of American society that blamed all of its ills and weaknesses on the machinations of communists. Everything from civil rights agitation to public welfare was blamed on the communists. Other targets of control for the worldwide communist conspiracy were the United Nations, the Trilateral Commission, and the World Bank. The collapse of the Cold War led to a retrenchment of the John Birch Society and the transfer of its headquarters from Belmont, Massachusetts, to Appleton, Wisconsin. John McManus, a Brooklyn native and electronics engineer, is the society's current president and chief spokesman. Named president in 1991, he continues to advance the thesis that communist conspirators are running the U.S. government. Members of the John Birch Society attack both Republicans and Democrats with equal vigor. Although there was a resurgence in interest in the John Birch Society in the mid-1990s, today the John Birch Society has been relegated to a secondary status as an extremist organization. **See also** DePugh, Robert Bolivar; Minutemen Movement; Welch, Robert Henry Winborne, Jr.

Suggested readings: J. Allen Broyes, *The John Birch Society: Anatomy of a Protest* (Boston: Beacon Press, 1964); Benjamin R. Epstein, *The Radical Right: Report on the John Birch Society and Its Allies* (New York: Vintage Books, 1967); Edward Epstein, "John McManus; The President of the John Birch Society Expounds," *San Francisco Chronicle* (December 17, 1995), p. 3; Neil A. Hamilton, *Militias in America: A Reference Handbook* (Santa Barbara, Calif.: ABC-CLIO, 1996); Mack Reed, "Birch Society Is Not Dead," *Los Angeles Times* (September 27, 1993), p. B1; Jim Simon, "Nation's Move to Right Pulls Birchers Back from Brink," *Seattle Times* (August 7, 1995), p. A1; Jim Simon, "Ultraconservative Birch Society Apparently Making a Comeback," *Phoenix Gazette* (September 4, 1995), p. A19.

Jones, James Warren "Jim" (1931–1978)

Jim Jones, the leader of the **People's Temple** cult in the United States, was born on May 13, 1931, in Crete, Indiana. His father was a disabled veteran of World War I, and his mother worked in various factories. The Jones family moved to Lynn, Indiana, when Jones was quite young. His mother separated from his father when Jones was a teenager, and she moved to Richmond, Indiana. His sense of resentment about his background led him to display outrageous behavior and flirt with both communism and fascism before turning to religion. In 1949 Jones graduated with honors from Richmond High School. Shortly after starting college at Indiana University in Bloomington, he married his childhood sweetheart, Marceline Baldwin, a trained nurse. Jones and his wife moved to Indianapolis in 1951 where both of them held a variety of jobs.

Always an active churchgoer, Jones became dissatisfied with mainline religious churches and started a new church in Indianapolis in the mid-1950s. He preached a mixture of pleas for racial tolerance and vague communist beliefs within a framework of Pentecostalism. His first church was called the Community Unity Church. In 1956 Jones established a church which became known as the People's Temple. His advocacy of racial harmony and social justice was attractive to prospective members, and membership in the church increased dramatically. One of the unique features of his new church was its strong social outreach program, including a soup kitchen for the needy which handled 2,800 meals a month. In 1960 the Disciples of Christ denomination recognized the success of Jones and his church by accepting it as a member. Soon afterward, Jones was ordained as a minister. About this time, he also graduated from Butler University, and Jones's progressive social programs earned him an appointment as the first director of the Indianapolis Human Rights Commission.

By 1961 Jones had earned an enviable reputation as a socially progressive religious leader, but he soon began behaving erratically. He became obsessed about the possibility of a nuclear war which would destroy the United States. He moved his growing family to South America in 1962 to locate possible resettlement sites for his church to escape a possible nuclear holocaust. After returning to Indianapolis in December 1963, Jones decided to transfer his church to Redwood Valley near Ukiah, California. Despite this radical resettlement, about 140 church members uprooted their lives and followed him to California in 1965. The growth of his church in this locality was initially slow, and by 1969 the membership was about 300. Jones decided that he needed to adopt new tactics and he borrowed Madison Avenue techniques to spur recruitment. By using re-

ligious radio stations and bus trips, the People's Temple expanded its membership to 2,570 in 1973. Jones's erratic behavior intensified, and his church in Ukiah started resembling a military camp with guards and rigid security; however, he retained his political skills and maintained his contacts with the elite of the California Democratic Party in the San Francisco area. In 1972 Jones was named one of the top 100 most outstanding clergymen in the United States by *Religion in American Life*. Mayor George Moscone appointed him the chairperson of the San Francisco Housing Authority.

Jones had looked for a safe haven for his church for more than a decade before finding a suitable place in Guyana, South America. In 1974 Jones sent an advance party to a location in remote Guyana soon to be named Jonestown. In the mid-1970s, Jones and members of his church started having legal problems in California over their harsh discipline of minors and federal income tax charges. To avoid further legal difficulties over these possible charges, Jones began to transfer personnel and assets to Jonestown in 1977. By September 1977, 1,000 members had relocated there. Jones was one of the last to move to Jonestown. He had become convinced that his enemies—the CIA, the FBI, the media, and politicians—were plotting against him and his movement. To prepare for the forthcoming prosecution, Jones ordered his members to conduct suicide drills called "White Night."

Reports of harsh conditions and intimidation at Jonestown reached the families of the members of the People's Temple, and they began to lobby politicians for action. Leo Ryan, a Democratic U.S. representative from California, responded to their pleas and planned to conduct a fact-finding tour of Jonestown. On November 15, 1978, Ryan and a delegation of his advisors, relatives, and media representatives arrived at Jonestown. Ryan and his party expressed concern over conditions, and sixteen members of the People's Temple decided to defect and leave with Ryan's party on November 18. As Ryan and his group were in the process of leaving the airport at about 5:00 P.M., a truckload of People's Temple members opened fire with small arms. Congressman Ryan and four others were killed outright and several others were wounded. The murders called for mass suicide. Over the next few hours, 913 members of the People's Temple committed suicide or were murdered, including 276 children. Among the dead was Jim Jones. He died of a gunshot wound to the head. His body was recovered later and his ashes were scattered over the Atlantic Ocean.

In the postmortem of the Jonestown mass suicide, the American general public and the media wondered how such a tragedy could have happened. Reports surfaced about how Jones controlled church members by insisting on obedience, conformity, and belief in his absolute authority. Dissent or disobedience was not tolerated in any form. Recalcitrant members were placed in solitary confinement in "the box," an underground cubicle about the size of a coffin. Children were brutally punished by being dunked in the Jonestown well at night. By using informants, splitting families, separating children from parents, and conducting extramarital affairs with members of the temple, Jones left no rivals for loyalty. In the end, suicide was the final test of loyalty to Jim Jones. **See also** Cults; People's Temple.

Suggested readings: David Chidester, *Salvation and Suicide: An Interpretation of Jim Jones, the People's Temple, and Jonestown* (Bloomington: Indiana University Press, 1988); Ken Levi, ed., *Violence and Religious Commitment: Implications of Jim Jones' People's Temple Movement* (University Park: Pennsylvania State University Press, 1982); John Peer Nugent, *White Night* (New York: Rawson, Wade, 1979); James Reston, *Our Father Who Art in Hell* (New York: Time Books, 1981).

Kaczynski, Theodore John "Ted" (1942–)

Ted Kaczynski, the notorious anarchist Unabomber, was born on May 22, 1942, in Chicago, Illinois. His father worked in a sausage factory in Chicago. Showing early promise in mathematics, Kaczynski graduated from Evergreen Park Community High School in 1958 at the age of sixteen. As a National Merit Scholarship finalist, he obtained a scholarship to Harvard University were he earned a B.S. in mathematics in 1962. After Harvard, Kaczynski moved to the University of Michigan where he studied advanced mathematics receiving his M.A. in 1965 and his Ph.D. in 1967. While at Michigan University, he won a prize for writing the best dissertation. In 1967 Kaczynski was offered and he accepted the position of assistant professor of mathematics at the University of California at Berkeley. Apparently successful both as a teacher and a researcher, he was making steady progress toward tenure. In January 1969, he abruptly resigned his teaching position and announced that he wanted to leave the field of mathematics.

Kaczynski retired from organized society by moving to the wilds of western Montana. He and his brother, David Kaczynski, bought an acre and a half on Bald Mountain near Lincoln, Montana. By 1972 Kaczynski had built a 10-by-12-foot primitive wooden cabin with no toilet, no plumbing, no water well, no sewage, no telephone, and no electricity. He survived by hunting small game. With no visible means of support, Kaczynski lived on occasional checks from his mother and brother.

Kaczynski opened his campaign against modern society in 1978. He admitted later that he initiated his bombing campaign after a logging road was constructed near his cabin. On May 25, 1978, Kaczynski sent a bomb in a package that was found in a parking lot at the University of Illinois at Chicago. A security guard was injured at Northwestern University the next day while opening the package. Two more bombs were found in 1979, and one of them exploded in the cargo hold of an American Airlines passenger jet. In 1980 and 1982, two more bombs injured people who opened his packages. In 1985 four bombs were delivered, and one of them killed Hugh Scrutton in Sacramento, California, on December 11. By this time a national hunt was on by federal authorities to find the bomber who had been dubbed the Unabomber. On February 20, 1987, a witness in Salt Lake City, Utah, spotted Kaczynski planting a bomb. After this narrow escape, Kaczynski retired from bomb making for the next six years. When he returned to bomb making, his explosive devices were more powerful. His new mail

Theodore Kaczynski on June 21, 1996. Kaczynski kept a journal in which he admitted sixteen of the bombings attributed to the Unabomber. "I mailed that bomb. I sent that bomb," the journal entries said. (AP Photo/Elaine Thompson)

bombs injured two professors, one at the University of California at San Francisco and one at Yale University, in 1993. His last two bombs in 1994 and 1995 killed an advertising executive, Thomas Mosser, in New Jersey, and California Forestry Association president, Gilbert P. Murray, in Sacramento, California, respectively. His seventeen year-

bombing campaign left three dead and 23 injured.

Kaczynski's undoing was his change of tactics from anonymous package bombs to a publicity campaign to justify his actions. In June 1993, the Unabomber sent his first letter to the *New York Times* outlining his anarchist views. Soon afterward, a federal task force was formed to hunt him down. In June 1995, Kaczynski sent a 35,000-word manifesto to the *Washington Post* and the *New York Times*. He threatened more bombings if the manifesto were not published. On September 19, 1995, both the *Washington Post* and the *New York Times* published the manifesto in its entirety. In the manifesto, Kaczynski details his complaints against modern society and what he considers its overemphasis on technology. He concludes that modern society must be abolished. Hundreds of investigative agents worked on the Unabomber case. Their profile indicated that the author of the manifesto was a maladjusted individual with a scientific background. Despite this intensive investigation, it was a tip by his brother that led to the arrest of Ted Kaczynski on April 3, 1996.

The trial of Kaczynski was anticlimactic. It was held in Sacramento, California, beginning in the winter of 1998. On January 22, 1998, Kaczynski pleaded guilty to two of the bombing deaths to escape the death penalty. After a sentencing hearing, during which his victims and the victims' families testified against him, Kaczynski was sentenced on May 4, 1998 to four consecutive life sentences plus thirty years. The length of this sentence ensures that Kaczynski will never leave prison. Kaczynski showed no remorse at his sentencing and accused the government of misrepresenting his motives for the bombings. Prison authorities sent him to the maximum-security prison in Florence, Colorado. A fall 1999 ruling from the ninth U.S. Circuit Court of Appeals in San Francisco allowed him the right to demand a new trial based on the claim that he had been coerced into pleading guilty by his lawyers. Kaczynski made such a claim in May 2000. His seeking of a new trial means that Kaczynski could be subject to the death penalty in the event that he is found guilty a second time.

Suggested readings: Joel Achenbach and Serge F. Kovaleski, "The Profile of a Loner; Authorities Say Kaczynski Is Solution to Mysteries of Unabomber's Manifesto and His Trial of Terror," *Washington Post* (April 7, 1996), p. A1; Richard Cole, "Kaczynski Given Four Life Sentences," *Associated Press News Service* (May 5, 1991), p. 1; John E. Douglas, *Unabomber: On the Trail of America's Most-Wanted Serial Killer* (New York: Pocket Books, 1996); Stephen Dubner, "Brotherly Bond Blown Apart," *Sunday Telegraph* [London] (October 31, 1999), p. 4; Michael Mello, *The United States of America Versus Theodore John Kaczynski: Ethics. Power and the Invention of the Unabomber* (New York: Context Books, 1999); Howard Mintz, "Kaczynski's Claim Could Cost His Life," *Pittsburgh Post-Gazette* (May 28, 2000), p. A16; Chris Waits and Dave Shors, *Unabomber: The Secret Life of Ted Kaczynski* (Helena, Mont.: Helena Independent Record and Montana Magazine 1999).

Kahane, Meir (1932–1990)

Rabbi Meir Kahane, the leader of the most fanatical wing of the Zionist movement and the founder of the **Jewish Defense League** (JDL), was born on August 1, 1932, in Brooklyn, New York. His father was a rabbi and a staunch Zionist supporter of Ze'ev Jabotinsky, an early radical Zionist leader. At an early age, Kahane became a devout Zionist. When Kahane was six, Palestinian Arabs massacred members of his family in Palestine, and the event traumatized the family in the United States. He joined a right-wing Zionist youth organization, Betar, at the age of fourteen. His first political action, at the age of fifteen, occurred when Kahane physically attacked the British foreign minister, Ernest Bevin, who was visiting New York City for an address at the United Nations. He received a suspended sentence for this assault. In 1952 he joined the youth movement of the Orthodox Zionist Federation of Labor (B'nai Arkivah). Kahane attended the Brooklyn Talmudical Academy (BTA) beginning in 1945, but he was always an indifferent student. In 1949 he left the BTA and entered Brooklyn's Abraham Lincoln High School. Kahane returned to the BTA for the last semester of his senior year. He entered Brooklyn College and graduated with a degree in political science in 1954. Kahane then attended New York University where he obtained in 1957 a dual degree: a master's in international law and a law degree. At the same time, his studies at the Orthodox Yeshiva Mirrer led to his being ordained as a rabbi in 1957. In the midst of his studies, Kahane met and married Libby Blum.

After his schooling, Kahane combined his interests in religion and politics. For a time he served as a rabbi for a Howard Beach synagogue in Queens, New York. When his extreme orthodox views caused him trouble, he turned to journalism. Among his other jobs, Kahane worked as a writer for the *Brooklyn Daily* and the *Jewish Press*. He also served as a spy for the FBI monitoring left-wing radicals and the **John Birch Society**. He then worked for the CIA promoting support among orthodox Jews for the Vietnam War. He used his newspaper contacts to convince Jews to volunteer to fight in Vietnam. His viewpoint is best explained in a book written with his friend Joseph Churba, *The Jewish State* (1968).

Kahane became a national leader in the extremist wing of the Orthodox Zionist movement, in June 1968, when he founded the Jewish Defense League with Morton Dolinsky and Bertam Zweibon as a civilian protection group whose mission was to protect Jews from physical attacks by blacks on the streets of New York City. Soon, however, Kahane turned the JDL into an organization that attacked perceived enemies of Jews using all types of tactics including violence. Among these perceived enemies were Arabs, Palestinians, and Soviets. In May 1971, U.S government authorities imprisoned him briefly on charges of conspiracy to manufacture explosives. A Mafia boss, Joseph Columbo, bailed him out of jail. Kahane pleaded guilty and received four years' probation. Kahane's growing friendship with Columbo allowed the JDL to obtain weapons and money. Eager to carry his ideas to Israel and one step ahead of a federal indictment for his attacks on Soviet diplomats, Kahane immigrated to Israel in August 1971 along with a large number of his supporters.

Kahane earned a reputation in Israel as

the most radical exponent of extreme Zionism. Right-wing Israeli leaders, especially Menachem Begin, welcomed his arrival. Kahane was offered leadership positions in several conservative parties, but he rejected all of them to form a Jewish Defense League organization in Israel. He advocated the removal of Palestinians from all territories occupied by Israel and the settlement by Jewish settlers of these lands, including the West Bank. Kahane based his anti-Palestinian policy on the belief that violence is justified in the name of Jewish survival. To carry out this program, Kahane formed the Kach (Only Thus) Party in 1971. Kahane started an Israeli death squad, the Terror Against Terror (TAT), to assassinate Palestinian leaders and pro-peace Israelis. He also plotted to blow up the Dome of the Rock Mosque in Jerusalem. For these actions, Kahane spent six months in detention in 1980. While in detention, Kahane wrote the anti-Palestinian treatise *They Must Go*. After making several attempts to win a seat in the Knesset, Kahane was successful in 1984. Despite his status as a deputy, the Israeli government restricted his freedom of movement, and the minister of justice denied him access to public school students. The Israeli government banned Kahane's Kach Party from the 1988 election as being racist and undemocratic. Israeli authorities had been able to pass a racial incitement law in August 1986, and this law was used against Kahane in December 1989 for his actions in Jerusalem after a Palestinian attack on an Israeli bus. His provocative statements and violence-prone actions were an embarrassment to the Israeli government.

Kahane often traveled back to the United States to direct JDL activities there and to conduct fund-raising tours. He feuded with American JDL leaders, and in 1974 purged its leadership. Most of his dissatisfaction stemmed from his belief that the American JDL was not active or violent enough. His directives for more aggressive actions led federal authorities to revoke his probation in February 1975 and send him to jail for a year. The first eight months Kahane spent in a Manhattan halfway house, but his continued involvement in JDL activities infuriated the presiding judge. This judge had him transferred to a minimum-security facility in Allenwood, Pennsylvania, to serve out the last four months. Shortly before going to jail Kahane had formed a JDL terrorist group, the Jewish Armed Resistance, to carry out a terrorist campaign against selected American and Soviet targets. After a two-year campaign of bombings in 1975 and 1976, most of the members of this group were captured and sentenced to long prison terms. Kahane disavowed them and left them to their fates.

Kahane had always been able to control the American JDL, but in the summer of 1977 he came into open conflict with its executive board. Members of the board had always been loyal supporters, but they became increasingly concerned about his carelessness with JDL funds and rumors of a possible affair. In June, Kahane approached JDL supporters about divorcing his wife to marry his secretary, Gerri Alperin. They had been having an affair for months. News of this affair would have a devastating impact among JDL's Orthodox Jewish supporters. On July 5, 1977, the JDL executive board expelled Kahane from the JDL. Kahane never accepted this verdict but he did return to his wife. After initiating open hostilities against his successor, Bonnie Pechter, Kahane regained control of the JDL in 1980. This in-fighting seriously weakened the JDL. Kahane had to reestablish control over the JDL because fund-raising in the United States was contributing $500,000 a year to support his political career in Israel.

On one such fund-raising trip in 1990, a gunman assassinated Kahane on November 5 on a street in New York City. Kahane's funeral attracted most of the significant leaders of the Israeli radical right. An Egyptian-born Moslem, El Sayyid Nosair, was charged with murdering Kahane, but in a court trial was convicted and sentenced to a fifteen-year jail term only on assault, coercion, and weapons charges. Followers of Kahane protested vigorously against the murder acquittal and have campaigned for a

federal civil rights trial. Kahane was buried in Israel, and his grave is protected by his supporters. With his death, Kahane became a martyr to the extreme right and religious wings of the Zionist movement. **See also** Jewish Defense League; Kahane Chai (Kahane Lives; Rubin, Irv.

Suggested readings: Josh Friedman and David Firestone, "The Angry Rabbi," *Newsday* [New York] (November 7, 1990), part II, p. 4; Robert I. Friedman, *The False Prophet: Rabbi Meir Kahane—From FBI Informant to Knesset Member* (London: Faber and Faber, 1990); Laurie Goodstein, "Kahane Jurors Explain Acquittal on Main Counts," *Washington Post* (December 23, 1991), p. A4; Mark Juergensmeyer, *Terror in the Mind of God: The Global Rise of Religious Violence* (Berkeley: University of California Press, 2000); Tom Robbins, "No Immediate Links to the Assassination of Meir Kahane," *Daily News* [New York] (December 2, 1998), p. 69; Ehud Sprinzak, "Kahane; The Nightmare That Liberal Ideologues Could Not Imagine," *Los Angeles Times* (November 11, 1990), p. M1.

Kahane Chai (Kahane Lives)

Kahane Chai (Kahane Lives) is a small group of supporters of the late Rabbi **Meir Kahane** with members in both Israel and the United States. Binyamin Kahane, the son of Meir Kahane, founded this organization shortly after the assassination of his father in New York City on November 5, 1990. Binyamin Kahane was the group's leader in Israel. Mike Guzofshy, a longtime supporter of Meir Kahane, became the associate director and chief spokesperson for Kahane Chai in the United States. The exact size of the group in Israel is uncertain because the Israeli government banned it in March 1994 and arrested Binyamin Kahane. Although leaders of the American branch of Kahane Chai claim that thousands of American Jews support their group, actual membership ranges between 100 and 150. Kahane Chai has chapters in Baltimore, Chicago, Miami, New York City, and Philadelphia.

The Clinton administration supported the Israeli crackdown on Kahane Chai by designating it as a risk to peace in the Middle

East. In March 1994, the Israeli government outlawed the Kahane Chai in the aftermath of the February 25, 1994, massacre of thirty Palestinians in the West Bank city of Hebron by Dr. Baruch Goldstein, an American-born supporter of the **Jewish Defense League**. The U.S. Treasury Department used an executive order to block the use of a Kahane Chai bank account in New York City in November 1995. In March 1998, the Israeli Supreme Court cleared Binyamin Kahane of sedition charges for his protests against the Oslo Agreements, a series of agreements promoting peace between Israel and the Palestinians, but he continued to agitate against the Israeli government for being too soft on the Palestinians. The assassination of Israeli Prime Minister Yitzhak Rabin on November 4, 1995, by an Israeli student and follower of Meir Kahane's group Kach reinforced government attention to Kahane Chai. On January 1, 2001, the Palestinian Fatah faction assassinated Binyamin Kahane and his wife and wounded five of their six children in an ambush. The Kahane Chai is still active, but most of its influence is now in the United States. **See also** Kahane, Meir.

Suggested readings: Bill Bell, "The Boys from Brooklyn," *Daily News* [New York] (November 19, 1995), p. 26; Laurie Goodstein, "Rebirth of the 'Tough Jew,' " *Toronto Star* (March 11, 1994), p. A23; John M. Goshko, "Extremist Groups' Influences Examined; Some Israelis Suspect U.S. Links to Radicals," *Washington Post* (November 7, 1995), p. A17; Joel Greenberg, "Jewish Militants Hope to Block Israel–P.L.O. Plans," *New York Times* (February 21, 1994), p. A8; Charles W. Holmes, "Israeli Militants: Crackdown Forces Radicals Underground," *Atlanta Journal and Constitution* (March 28, 1994), p. A4; Etgar Lefkovits, "In the Footsteps of His Father, to the Very End," *Jerusalem Post* (January 1, 2001), p. 3; Dean E. Murphy, "F.B.I. Raids Brooklyn Office of Kahane Followers," *New York Times* (January 5, 2001), p. B3.

Kahl, Gordon (1920–1983)

Gordon Kahl, a tax resister and a recruiter for the anti-government Posse Comitatus, is more famous for his death in a gun battle with a law enforcement team than for his political activism. He was born on January 8, 1920, on a farm near Heaton, North Dakota. The oldest of five boys, he grew up on his father's farm. Although he was never a good student, Kahl graduated from the local high school in 1938. Shortly after graduation, he joined the New Deal's Civilian Conservation Corps and worked on construction projects for six months before traveling in the West picking up odd jobs. When World War II broke out, he joined the U.S. Army Air Corps in 1941 and served as a turret gunner on B-25 bombers. Kahl earned a Silver Star, Bronze Star, and a variety of other awards, including two Purple Hearts for wounds sustained in combat. The government awarded him a 30 percent disability pension for his injuries. After duty in both Europe and the Far East, he became a gunnery instructor in 1944. He married his childhood sweetheart, Joan Seil, in 1944. His tour of duty was in the South where he was exposed to anti-Semitic and anti-government views. After his military service, he returned to North Dakota and bought a 160-acre farm next to his father's farm near Heaton. Kahl enrolled in North Dakota State University to study electrical engineering. After a dispute with an English teacher, he left college. In the next few years, Kahl moved back and forth between mechanic jobs in California and working on the farm in North Dakota. His family continued to grow with six children.

Kahl's exposure to anti-Semitic and anti-government views led him into extremism. During his stays in California, he became attracted to the theology of **Christian Identity**. Although brought up a Protestant and later flirting with the Church of Jesus Christ of Latter-Day Saints, the white supremacy of Christian Identity fascinated him. He also briefly attended meetings of the **John Birch Society**, but he decided that this organization was not active enough. Next, Kahl joined Dr. Clarence Martin's Constitutional Party, which advanced the union of church and state, a strict fundamentalist interpretation of the Bible. At these meetings, Kahl heard speakers who advocated taxpayer resistance.

These speakers argued that the Sixteenth Amendment to the Constitution, the provision that instituted the federal income tax, was illegal and unenforceable. In April 1969, he notified the Internal Revenue Service that the income tax law was unconstitutional and that he would no longer pay taxes. This action started his difficulties with the federal government. Kahl no longer made working trips to California, but now worked part of the year in the oil fields of West Texas as a machine mechanic. In 1973 he joined the **Posse Comitatus movement** in protest against federal policies. In 1974 Kahl became the Posse Comitatus Texas coordinator. He started traveling the country spreading the anti-government views of the Posse Comitatus. He also worked on his survival skills at various Christian survivalist camps. His justification for his opposition to the federal government was that the government was Satanic and the income tax system was communistic.

As long as Kahl simply refused to pay taxes on a small income, federal authorities left him alone. When he began to recruit for the Posse Comitatus movement and encouraged these recruits to stop paying their taxes, the government intervened. His personal appearance on a 1976 television show during which he lobbied for others to cease paying taxes garnered him the attention of the government. Later in 1976, the government charged Kahl with income tax evasion. A federal court sentenced him in April 1977 to a one-year jail term and five years on probation. A requirement for his probation was to stay away from Posse Comitatus activities. He started his sentence on January 2, 1979, and spent eight months and four days of his sentence at the prison in Leavenworth, Kansas. After his release from prison, Kahl formed a Christian Identity church, the Gospel Divine Doctrine Church of Jesus Christ, to propagate his anti-government conspiratorial theories. In 1980 he broke probation by refusing to pay his 1980 taxes, ignoring his probation documents, and speaking at Posse Comitatus meetings. He challenged the federal authorities to do something about his breaking of probation. First, IRS agents seized eighty acres of his farm and sold it for back taxes. Next, a federal arrest warrant was issued on March 1, 1981 in Midland, Texas, revoking his probation and ordering his arrest.

On February 13, 1983, U.S. marshals attempted to serve an arrest warrant on Kahl for his probation violations on a road after a meeting of anti-government activists at Medina, North Dakota. A gunfight broke out between Kahl, his son Yorivon, and Scott Faul, and federal marshals during which two marshals were killed and four others were wounded. Evidence indicates that the first shot came from Kahl's group, but enough doubt exists that both sides could claim the other side fired first. Yorivon Kahl was wounded and captured. In a subsequent communication to the media, Kahl issued a document in which he declared war on the federal government. He blamed the Jewish conspiracy for his personal troubles and stated that he feared as its opponent that he would be killed. Kahl made his way to Arkansas where anti-government sympathizers hid him. Government agents lost track of Kahl until they received a tip from an informant. On June 3, 1983, government officials caught up with Kahl in a farmhouse of fellow survivalists Leonard and Norma Ginter, near the town of Smithville, Arkansas. In a gun battle Kahl and a county sheriff were killed. In the aftermath of his death, conflicting versions of the gun battle appeared from government and extremist sources. Anti-government activists claimed that Kahl was murdered and made him one of the heroes of the anti-government movement. His son, Yorivon Kahl, and Scott Faul received two concurrent life sentences plus fifteen years for their roles in the deaths of the two marshals. Two bomb attempts have been made on the life of the judge presiding over this case, and he has needed armed security guards to protect him. James Corcoran quotes Kahl's extremist colleagues, calling him the "first martyr of the Second American Revolution." **See also** Christian Identity; Posse Comitatus Movement.

Suggested readings: Howard L. Bushart, John R. Craig, and Myra Barnes, *Soldiers of God: White Supremacists and Their Holy War for America* (New York: Kensington Books, 1998); James Coates, *Armed and Dangerous: The Rise of the Survivalist Right* (New York: Hill and Wang, 1987); James Corcoran, *Bitter Harvest: Gordon Kahl and the Posse Comitatus: Murder in the Heartland* (New York: Viking Press, 1990); Art Harris, "Evader's End; Gordon Kahl, Sheriff Shot Each Other Before Blaze," *Washington Post* (June 5, 1983), p. A1; Dennis J. McGrath, "Lives Changed Forever When Gordon Kahl Took on the Law," *Star Tribune* [Minneapolis] (February 14, 1993), p. 1A.

Keegstra, James (1934–)

James Keegstra gained notoriety as the result of the trials that centered on his teaching of anti-Semitic ideas to high school students in Alberta, Canada. He was born in 1934 in Vulcan, Alberta. His parents, who were Dutch immigrants, lived on a farm in rural Alberta. His family had close ties to Protestant fundamentalism. Keegstra attended Premier Aberhart's Bible Institute in Calgary. At an early age, he joined the Social Credit Party and adhered to its emphasis on combining economic and religious principles. After high school, Keegstra worked for a period of time as an automobile mechanic. He went to college at the University of Alberta at Calgary where he majored in industrial arts. After receiving his degree, Keegstra found employment as a high school teacher. He moved around taking various teaching jobs until, in 1968, he located a position in Eckville, Alberta. Besides industrial arts, Keegstra began to teach social studies.

Keegstra soon found himself in trouble with school authorities for teaching his controversial views on Catholics and Jews. Parents of students complained to school authorities in 1981 about his teaching of anti-Jewish and anti-Catholic ideas. After an investigation and a warning to desist teaching about these subjects, Keegstra was fired from his teaching position. The Canadian government then tried him for teaching hatred against Jews in a 1985 trial in Red Deer,

Alberta. He was convicted of the charges and fined $5,000. On appeal, the Alberta Court of Appeals overturned the verdict in 1988 on the grounds that the sentence violated the freedom-of-speech guarantees in the new Canadian Charter of Rights and Freedoms. The Supreme Court of Canada overturned the lower court's ruling and sent the case back to the appeals court. This time the court ordered a new trial. Keegstra was retried in 1992 and convicted again with a fine of $3,000. In 1994 the Alberta Court of Appeals ruled that the second conviction should also be overturned. This decision provoked a firestorm of protest from Jewish groups. Final disposition of the case was made in the Supreme Court of Canada, which reinstated Keegstra's 1992 conviction for promoting hatred against Jewish people. During the various court trials and appeals, Keegstra worked as an auto mechanic.

American and Canadian right-wing extremists turned the Keegstra trials into a test case for their anti-Semitic cause. Keegstra had taught his high school students that Jews were the children of the devil and that an international Jewish conspiracy bent on world domination existed. He used materials to show that modern Jews were descendents of the Khazars and not descendents of the original Twelve Tribes of Israel. For this reason, he claimed that Zionism is a fraud. Keegstra also concluded that the Holocaust was a Jewish invention and the missing German and Polish Jews had simply migrated to other countries. Because so many of the leaders in the American and Canadian right-wing extremist movement shared these ideas, Keegstra gained their financial and moral support. His lawyer, Douglas Christie, was Canada's leading right-wing legal expert. Keegstra's supporters launched a money-raising campaign to pay for his legal defense. In February 1996, Keegstra lost his final appeal to the Supreme Court of Canada, ending nearly fifteen years of legal controversy. The court upheld his 1992 conviction for promoting hate propaganda and Keegstra received a two-year jail sentence. His final conviction only reinforced his belief that a Jewish conspiracy was at work. **See also** Anti-Semitism: Holocaust Denial Movement; Neo-Nazis.

Suggested readings: Arnold Ages, "How Absolute Is Right of Free Speech?" *Buffalo News* (February 6, 1994), p. 9; David Climenhaga, "Court Quashes Keegstra Conviction," *Ottawa Citizen* (September 8, 1994), p. A5; Alan Davies, ed., *Antisemitism in Canada: History and Interpretation* (Waterloo, Ont., Canada: Wilfrid Laurier University Press, 1992); Douglas Martin, "Canadian Wins Appeal on Anti-Jewish Book," *New York Times* (March 27, 1985), p. A14; Douglas Martin, "Hate-Mongering Teacher Tests Canada's Patience," *New York Times* (May 26, 1983), p. A2; Leonard Stern, "Keegstra a Hate-Monger, Top Court Rules," *Gazette* [Montreal] (February 29, 1996), p. A1.

Kehoe, Chevie O'Brien (1973–   )

Chevie Kehoe, the leader of a white supremacist attempt to establish an Aryan Peoples Republic in the Pacific Northwest, was born on January 29, 1973, in Orange Park, Florida, the eldest of eight children. His father, Kirby Kehoe, was a Vietnam veteran and worked as an automobile mechanic. The Kehoe family moved several times from Florida to Colville, Washington, with stops in Arkansas, Oklahoma, and Montana. Kehoe and his brother Cheyne were home schooled during junior high school. Chevie Kehoe married early and supported his growing family by working at various construction jobs. On occasion, Chevie Kehoe visited both the **Aryan Nations** compound in **Hayden Lake**, Idaho, and **Elohim City**, Oklahoma. After these visits, Chevie Kehoe adopted the **Christian Identity** worldview that the white race is in danger of extinction unless a white homeland is established.

Chevie Kehoe's conversion to white supremacy led him to launch a crime spree to obtain arms and funds to build an Aryan Peoples Republic. Soon after hearing about the bombing of the Murrah Federal Building in Oklahoma City on April 19, 1995, Kehoe started his new homeland campaign. With the help of his father, he burglarized the home of Arkansas gun dealer Bill Mueller at his Arkansas home in March 1995, stealing guns, silver coins, and military supplies. Although the Kehoes were old family friends, Mueller realized that they had committed the burglary and threatened Kirby Kehoe about it. Chevie Kehoe's next crime was more personal. He had come to accept polygamy because he believed it was sanctioned in the Old Testament. Chevie Kehoe recruited Faron Lovelace to murder his friend and former **skinhead**, Jeremy Scott, because Kehoe wanted his wife. She became his second wife. Kehoe then killed John Cox, a member of his team, because he had become a security liability. Cox had been bragging about Kehoe's plans to his girlfriend and others.

In need of funds and weapons, Chevie Kehoe implemented a plan based on **Robert Jay Mathews**'s scheme to destabilize the U.S. government. His campaign envisioned assassinating federal judges, holding up armored cars for funding, and setting off bombs at federal and state buildings. In June 1995, he kidnapped and robbed Colville business owners Malcolm and Jill Friedman. Remembering the guns and ready to settle a family feud, Kehoe and a friend, Danny Lewis Lee, disguised themselves as federal agents and, on January 5, 1996, murdered Mueller, his wife, and his eight-year-old stepdaughter. They stole $37,000 worth of guns and ammunition from Mueller's house. Some of the weapons wound up in the hands of the **Aryan Republican Army** and were used in robberies in seven Midwestern states. In April 1996, Kehoe and Lee planted a pipe bomb outside of the Spokane City Hall, which exploded at night without injuring anyone or causing much property damage.

Kehoe's crime spree ended not long after federal authorities initiated a national manhunt for him. Police arrested a neo-Nazi skinhead for possession of an assault rifle stolen from Bill Mueller's collection. He admitted Kehoe sold him the weapon. Aware of increasing police activity, Kehoe left the Spokane area with his brother Cheyne and their families. On February 15, 1997, Ohio state troopers stopped Kehoe and his brother in Wilmington, Ohio, for driving with expired Washington state license tabs, and a gun battle took place. Both Kehoes escaped, but a bystander was wounded in the shoulder. Another gunfight ensued later that same day. Again the brothers escaped. This time they traveled to a remote farm in Utah. Cheyne Kehoe became concerned about Chevie Kehoe's increasingly violent plans and left Utah to turn himself in to the Washington police on June 16, 1997. He also informed them of the whereabouts of his older brother. Kehoe was arrested on a small farm in southwestern Utah near Cedar City. In July 1997, Kehoe was served with a federal indictment listing fifty-seven separate crimes, including five murders, several robberies and kidnappings, and interstate transportation of stolen property. Kehoe also faced serious charges in Arkansas and Ohio. In April 1999, he went on trial in federal court in Little Rock, Arkansas, for the murder of Mueller and his family. A jury convicted Kehoe of murder and conspiracy on May 4, 1999, and sentenced him to life imprisonment without parole. His accomplice, Daniel Lee, received the death sentence. **See also** Mathews, Robert Jay; Order, The; White Supremacist Movement.

Suggested readings: Peggy Harris, "Race Killing Suspects Must Fight Strong Case," *Boston Globe* (April 19, 1999), p. A9; Kim Murphy, "Savage Saga of Radical Right Told in Trial," *Los Angeles Times* (April 18, 1999), p. A1; Southern Poverty Law Center, "Kehoe Republic: Trail of Death Follows White Supremacist Gang," *SPLC Intelligence Report* 92 (Fall 1998) 16–22; Jo Thomas, "How an Honor Student Became a White Warrior," *New York Times* (December 12, 1999), sec. 1, p. 38; Jim Woods, "Kehoe Brothers Lived off the Land While on the Lam," *Columbus Dispatch* (June 22, 1997), p. 3D.

Klassen, Ben (1918–1993)

Ben Klassen, the founder and leader of the anti-Semitic, racist **Church of the Creator** (COTC), was born on February 20, 1918, in Rudnerweide in the southern Ukraine. In 1924 his family moved first to Chihuahua, Mexico, and then two years later to rural Saskatchewan, Canada. He received a bachelor's degree in science from the University of Saskatchewan and a bachelor's degree in electrical engineering from the University of Manitoba. Among the many jobs that he held before turning to politics was teaching elementary school in Canada and working as an electrical engineer in California. Klassen moved to California in 1945 to take advantage of better job prospects there. Klassen, who became an American citizen in 1948, invented and patented one of the first electric can openers in 1954. In 1958 Klassen moved to Florida where he became a successful real estate agent. After a few years in Florida, Klassen ran for the Florida State Legislature as a Republican in 1965. After winning his election, he took a public stand against forced school busing and criticized the powers of the federal government over the states in the Florida legislature. He lost his seat to a court-ordered reapportionment and then ran for and lost a race for state senator in 1967. By this time, Klassen was an active member of the **John Birch Society** and opened the Birch-affiliated American Opinion Bookstore in Lighthouse Point, Florida. He left the John Birch Society in the late 1960s because he felt that it was not radical enough for him. In his next political activity, he was the Florida chairperson for George Wallace's 1968 presidential campaign.

After these political setbacks, Klassen became disillusioned by mainstream politics and turned his attention to the radical fringe. In 1973 he established the Church of the Creator in Lighthouse Point. In his first manifesto, *Nature's Eternal Religion* (1973), Klassen placed race at the core of the church and rejected Christianity outright. A second book, *The White Man's Bible* (1975), is one of the most anti-Semitic and racist books published in the United States since World War II. He also began to preach and write tracts against the Federal Reserve System, blaming Jewish interests for controlling it. In 1981 Klassen moved the headquarters of the Church of the Creator to Otto, North Carolina, where earlier he had purchased 160 acres. On this land Klassen built a two-story church headquarters, a thirty-person dormitory, a mail-order operation, and a school for gifted white boys. Despite his claims that the Church of the Creator was a functioning religious organization, the church lost its tax-exempt status in the county in 1991.

Klassen continued to attack minorities and Jews from his compound in North Carolina. By the early 1990s, he was calling himself the "pontifex maximus" (high priest), and his writings were published in a new monthly newsletter, *Racial Loyalty*. In his articles, Klassen preached RAHOWA (Racial Holy War) to preserve the white race. In 1991 he compiled his views into a small book, *The Little White Book*. Klassen started attracting **neo-Nazi skinheads** for weapons training at his compound firing range. Benefiting from adverse publicity about **Tom Metzger** and the **White Aryan Resistance** (WAR), the Church of the Creator's membership grew dramatically in the early 1990s. On May 17, 1991, a minister in the Church of the Creator, George David Loeb, killed a black sailor in Jacksonville, Florida. Loeb was convicted of murder, and the sailor's family initiated a lawsuit against Klassen and the Church of the Creator. Klassen, fearing a civil suit might cause his property to be seized, sold his compound at about 25 percent of its assessed value to **William Pierce** of the **National Alliance**. Despite this effort to disperse property and assets, the sailor's family won a $1 million judgment against the Church of the Creator. In 1996 a jury verdict made Pierce pay the black family the $85,000 profit he made when he, in turn, sold the land.

Over the years, Klassen had developed close ties to other white supremacist organizations. His closest relationships were with the **Liberty Lobby**, the National Alliance, and the White Aryan Resistance. He made an enemy of the Knights of the Ku Klux Klan because of his rejection of Christianity. His biggest detractor, however, was **Harold Covington**, a prominent neo-Nazi with ties to the British terrorist group Combat 18. On

August 6, 1993, Klassen's depression over the lawsuit and his failing health caused him to commit suicide by taking sleeping pills. Rich McCarty succeeded Klassen as the head of the Church of the Creator. The church is still in operation because its anti-Christian, anti-Semitic, and racist message is still attractive to the neo-Nazis and the skinheads.

Matthew Hale established his **World Church of the Creator** as a successor to Klassen's church. Hale established his church in East Peoria, Illinois, in the image of the Church of the Creator. Both the theology and titles are borrowed directly from Klassen. Klassen's writings serve as holy texts for Hale's church. **See also** Church of the Creator; Hale, Matthew; Liberty Lobby; National Alliance; Pierce, William; World Church of the Creator.

Suggested readings: Quintin Elison, "Seeds of White Supremacist Group Sown in WNC," *Asheville Citizen-Times* (July 20, 1999), p. 1; Bruce Henderson, "In Right-Wing Church's Creed, White Makes Right," *Atlanta Journal and Constitution* (September 15, 1991), p. M4; Sara Henry, Fariba Nawa, and Sunny Park, "Marketing Hate," *Los Angeles Times* (December 12, 1993), Magazine, p. 18; Sheryl James, " 'Loyalty' Rooted in a History of Hate," *St. Petersburg Times* (July 16, 1990), p. ID; Robin Mitchell, "Hate Group Tied to Slayings Got Its Start in Florida," *St. Petersburg Times* (July 7, 1999), p. 1A; Ronald Smothers, "Supremacist Told to Pay Black Family," *New York Times* (May 20, 1996), p. A13.

Knights of Freedom (See American Nationalist Party)

Knights of the Ku Klux Klan (See Duke, David)

Koehl, Matt (1935–)

Matt Koehl, who succeeded **George Lincoln Rockwell** as the leader of the American Nazi movement in 1967, was born in 1935 in Milwaukee, Wisconsin. He was a member of several right-wing groups before he turned to **neo-Nazi** groups. Koehl first met Rockwell in 1956. In 1958 he joined the **National State's Rights Party** and moved to Chicago where he took a job as an encyclopedia salesman. In November 1960, Koehl joined Rockwell's **American Nazi Party** (ANP). His rise in the party hierarchy was swift. By 1967 Koehl had been Rockwell's chief lieutenant in the ANP for several years. Although Koehl disagreed with the trend of the ANP away from Nazism toward white supremacy during the last few years of Rockwell's leadership, he never tried to challenge Rockwell for the leadership of the party. A special council appointed Koehl the head of the ANP in September 1967 upon Rockwell's death.

After he assumed leadership of the ANP, it became evident that he lacked the leadership skills necessary to keep the party viable. His opposition to Rockwell's recasting and renaming the party the National Socialist White People's Party (NSWPP) was vocal, but he retained the name after replacing Rockwell. In 1970 the NSWPP split into competing factions with Frank Collins, **William Pierce**, and Joseph Tommassi either leaving or forming competing groups. Tommassi formed the National Socialist Liberation Front (NSLF) and headed it until he was murdered in 1975. Koehl was able to reconstitute the NSWPP in 1973. By 1974, however, he lost control of the party again. Conditions in the United States had changed so much that Koehl decided to reorient the party again. On January 1, 1983, he adopted the name the New Order and restructured the party as a religious organization. This new religion is based on the "living faith of Adolf Hitler." In 1983 the Internal Revenue Service seized the party's headquarters in Arlington, Virginia. Koehl then moved the New Order from Arlington, Virginia, to New Berlin, Wisconsin. His party has about twenty-five activists and a core membership of around 100. Koehl replaced Rockwell also as head of the **World Union of National Socialists** (WUNS). **See also** American Nazi Party; Neo-Nazis; Pierce, William; Rockwell, George Lincoln.

Suggested readings: Mary Battiata, "IRS Moves to Seize Home of White People's Party," *Washington Post* (March 10, 1982), p. C5; Betty A. Dobratz and Stephanie L. Shanks-Meile, *"White Power, White Pride!": The White Separatist Movement in the United States* (New York: Twayne, 1997); Jeffrey Kaplan, ed., *Encyclopedia of White Power: A Sourcebook on the Radical Racist Right* (Walnut Creek, Calif.: Altamira Press, 2000); Leah Y. Latimer, "Arlington Takes Educational Tack on Nazi Session," *Washington Post* (October 13, 1983), p. A1.

Kopp, James C. (1954–)

James Kopp, a leader in the militant wing of the anti-abortion movement, was born in 1954 in Pasadena, California. His father was a lawyer; his mother, a registered nurse. His mother was active in the pro-life movement until her death in 1994. After high school, Kopp attended the University of California at Santa Cruz where he majored in marine biology. His graduate work in physics at the University of Texas at Austin earned him a master's degree. While he was in graduate school, his girlfriend had an abortion without consulting him. He became increasingly religious and joined the Catholic Church in 1988. His anti-abortion viewpoint caused Kopp to join the anti-abortion movement in the mid-1980s. He worked for **Operation Rescue** by serving as an advance person and scout for demonstrations. His nickname in the anti-abortion movement was "Atomic Dog."

Kopp moved to the extreme wing of the anti-abortion movement in the aftermath of Operation Rescue's 1988 Atlanta demonstrations. He was arrested at an abortion clinic and served a forty-day jail sentence with other anti-abortion activists, including John Arena, who later went to jail for using acid during clinic demonstrations; Andrew Cabot, who advocated the murder of abortion doctors; Shelley Shannon, who later shot an abortion doctor in Wichita, Kansas; and Father **Norman U. Weslin**, the leader of the **Lambs of Christ**. These activists, who had become dissatisfied with the moderate policies of Operation Rescue, influenced

Kopp to become more militant. After his release from jail, Kopp continued his association with Weslin and became active in **Army of God** circles. On October 23, 1998, a sniper killed Barnett A. Slepian, an abortion doctor in Amherst, New York, at his home. Using evidence from the rifle used in the murder, police were able to identify the sniper as Kopp. In May 1999, state authorities charged him with second-degree murder, and federal authorities charged him with violating the Freedom of Access to Clinic Entrances Act (FACE). Kopp, who lived as a fugitive hiding among anti-abortion activists, is a suspect in a number of sniper attacks in Canada and the United States. He was placed on the FBI's "10 Most Wanted" list, and Canadian authorities have posted a large reward for his apprehension. On March 29, 2001, French police arrested Kopp in Dinan, a small town 200 miles west of Paris. American authorities tried to extradite him, but the French will not send him to the United States as long as Kopp is subject to the death penalty. Attorney General John Ashcroft guaranteed the French that Kopp would not be subject to the death penalty as he sought Kopp's extradition in the summer of 2001. On October 15, 2001, Kopp lost his first appeal of an extradition order to the United States, but he remains in France in January 2002. **See also** Anti-Abortion Movement; Hill, Paul Jennings; Lambs of Christ; Operation Rescue; Weslin, Norman U.

Suggested readings: Dan Barry, "Tracing Anti-Abortion Network to a Slaying Suspect in France," *New York Times* (March 31, 2001), p. A1; Michael Beebe, "Details Revealed in Slepian Killing," *Buffalo News* (April 4, 2001), p. A1; Michael Beebe and Dan Herbeck, "Capturing Kopp; Dogged Work Led to Arrests," *Buffalo News* (March 30, 2001), p. A1; Phil Fairbanks, "Radical Fringe's Violent Bond Born in Confinement," *Buffalo News* (November 8, 1998), p. A1; Dan Herbeck, "Kopp Won't Face Death Penalty," *Buffalo News* (June 2, 2001), p. A1; James Risen and Judy L. Thomas, *Wrath of Angels: The American Abortion War* (New York: Basic Books, 1998); Southern Poverty Law Center, "Accused Assassin Arrested in France," *SPLC Intelligence Report* 102 (Summer 2001): 4.

Koresh, David (1959–1993)

David Koresh was the spiritual leader of the **Branch Davidian** cult, which confronted federal agents at Waco, Texas. Koresh was born Vernon Howell on August 17, 1959, in Houston, Texas, to an unwed fifteen-year-old girl. Bobby Howell, a carpenter, was his father. His mother married twice, but neither husband cared much for Koresh. A learning disability, dyslexia, hindered his schooling. Koresh always mentioned that he failed both the first and second grades. He dropped out of Garland High School in 1974 in Garland, Texas, before finishing the eleventh grade. His youthful interests were in playing the guitar and reading the Bible. In 1979 he started studying at a Seventh-day Adventist Church in Tyler, Texas. His preaching of his personal religious views and some other erratic behaviors caused him to be removed (disfellowshipped) from the church in April 1983. Koresh learned about the Branch Davidians from a friend and found a job at their Mount Carmel compound in Waco working as a handyman. In 1981 Koresh joined the Branch Davidian sect. Victor Houteff established the Mount Carmel compound in May 1935. After Houteff's death in 1955, his wife, Florence Houteff, succeeded him as its leader. She remained the spiritual head until a failed doomsday prophecy in 1959 discredited her. Benjamin Roden, an Adventist leader from Odessa, Texas, succeeded Florence Houteff and remained head of the sect until his death. His wife, Lois Roden, was the leading figure in the sect by the late 1970s. She recruited Koresh and allegedly had a sexual relationship with him.

Lois Roden used Koresh in her power struggle against her son, George Roden, to control the Branch Davidian movement. Her son had been threatening to supplant her as head of the Branch Davidians in the decade after his father's death. She realized that Koresh, as her consort, had the charisma to attract new converts. Lois Roden, however, was disappointed when Koresh married Rachael Jones, the fourteen-year-old daughter of the senior member of the Branch Davidian community. Lois Roden died in 1986. Koresh lost his power struggle to assume the leadership of the sect to George Roden, and he went into exile. Koresh and his supporters attempted to seize the compound in November 1987, and a gunfight resulted. Despite losing the gunfight, Koresh won control of the Branch Davidians after Roden received a six-year jail sentence for contempt of court for a previous offense.

As the acknowledged head of the Branch Davidians, Koresh proved his mentor, Lois Roden, right by his ability to attract new adherents. After several trips to Israel in the mid-1980s, Koresh became even more convinced of his divine mission. In 1990 he changed his name to the Biblical name of David Koresh. He also proclaimed himself the new Messiah based on his interpretation of the Seven Seals of Revelation in the Bible. After his assumption of the mantle of Messiah, Koresh claimed that as the Messiah he was the perfect mate for all the sect's female adherents. While this claim led some members to leave the Branch Davidians, those who remained were loyal to Koresh and his commandments. Koresh fathered seventeen children with several women, some of whom were underage. He enforced strict discipline and demanded complete obedience from his followers. His strict discipline in religious and dietary laws, however, was more for his followers than for himself.

Rumors spread of child abuse and possession of illegal weapons at the Branch Davidian compound. Federal agents of the Bureau of Alcohol, Tobacco and Firearms Agency (BATF) heard the reports and decided to stage a raid. News leaked out about the raid, and Koresh organized his followers to defend themselves. In a firefight on February 28, 1993, four federal agents and six Branch Davidians were killed. Koresh received abdominal and hand wounds which were slow to heal. He was in constant pain during the next few weeks as infection set in.

In the next seven weeks, federal negotiators attempted to persuade Koresh to surrender the compound. Federal agents expressed concern about the fate of the children in the compound and tried to talk Koresh into letting them leave. Negotiations were on the verge of success several times only to have Koresh back out citing a biblical interpretation against surrender. On the evening of March 1, Koresh finally promised to surrender. Survivors report that Koresh and other leaders considered a mass suicide scheme, but they decided against it. Finally, federal agents received orders from Attorney General Janet Reno to assault the compound. In the assault of April 19, 1993, the compound caught on fire destroying all of the buildings. A federal investigation concluded that the Branch Davidians started a series of fires. Over eighty members of the Branch Davidian sect died. Koresh also died in the assault. The controversy over government actions and the responsibility for the Branch Davidians' deaths has not died down even after a congressional inquiry, a government report, and a court ruling. Anti-government activists still blame the federal officials, and the incident is now part of what they believe is the federal government's conspiracy to take away American freedoms. See also Branch Davidians; Cults.

Suggested readings: Marc Breault and Martin King, *Inside the Cult: A Member's Chilling Exclusive Account of Madness and Depravity in David Koresh's Compound* (New York: Signet Books, 1993); William H. Freivogel and Terry Ganey, "Secrecy Led to Public Mistrust," *St. Louis Post-Dispatch* (July 23, 2000), p. A1; Terry Ganey, "Davidians' Wrongful Death Claims Against U.S. Are Denied," *St. Louis Post-Dispatch* (September 21, 2000), p. A1; David Leppard, *Fire and Blood: The True Story of David Koresh and the Waco Siege* (London: Fourth Estate, 1993); Dick J. Reavis, *The Ashes of Waco: An Investigation* (Syracuse, N.Y.: Syracuse University Press, 1995); Armando Villafranca, John C. Henry et al., "Investigation Clears Feds in Waco Tragedy," *Houston Chronicle* (July 22, 2000), p. A1; Stuart A. Wright, "What the Waco Jury Never Heard," *Houston Chronicle* (July 23, 2000), Outlook, p. 1.

Ku Klux Klan

The Ku Klux Klan, the oldest white supremacist organization in the United States, was

Ku Klux Klan members give the white power salute at the beginning of a rally on the steps of the statehouse in Columbus, Ohio, January 6, 1996. The rally was separated from a group of anti-Klan protesters by a double chain-link fence and a cordon of police officers. (AP Photo/Gary Gardiner)

founded on December 24, 1866, by five veterans of the Confederate Army in Pulaski, Tennessee. After an inauspicious start, the Klan has undergone peaks and valleys of popularity and influence. Its initial period of expansion was in the post–Civil War reconstruction era. The Klan developed its tactics of intimidation in 1867 under the leadership of a former Confederate general, Nathan Bedford Forrest. From the beginning, the Klan proclaimed itself a white Christian movement ready to preserve the Southern way of life. At first the Klan was determined to keep the Southern black population in its place; only later did the Klan become anti-Catholic and anti-Jewish. The Klan became so powerful and feared during Reconstruction that President Ulysses Grant initiated an army crackdown on its activities. After a series of incidents, General Forrest disbanded the Klan.

The Ku Klux Klan's influence waned after Reconstruction, but it revived in the 1920s as a result of the popularity and pro-Klan viewpoint presented in the movie *Birth of a Nation*. The Klan expanded outside the South by declaring Catholics and Jews its enemies. The Klan's mission was to purify America and restore the traditional white Protestant way of life. At the peak of its popularity, the Klan had four million members and was able to win elections for its supporters at both the national and state levels. Part of the secret of the Klan's success in the 1920s was its close association with Protestant fundamentalist ministers in attacking the evils of modern society. A series of scandals and excesses caused the Klan to lose popularity, but remnants of its former strength remained in the South.

The Ku Klux Klan has a special way of organizing and keeping its affairs secret. The organizational handbook of the Klan is titled the *Kloren*. A local cell is a klavern. Each klavern is headed by the exalted cyclops. Other ranks with specialized duties are the klaliff, klokard, kludd, kligrapp, kladd, kliabee, klexter, and klaroogo. A state director is called a grand dragon. The national head of the Ku Klux Klan is the imperial wizard. Klan members use secret identification codes including AKIA (A Klansman I Am) and other signals. Robert J. Kelly maintains that these secret codes and ceremonial rituals promote "a sense of camaraderie" among members of the Klan and "a mutual feeling of being victimized" by outsiders which permits members to use violence against others.

The end of segregation after a series of U.S. Supreme Court decisions beginning in 1954 revitalized the Ku Klux Klan. From a moribund group of three loosely organized Klan bodies with only a few thousand inactive members in the early 1950s, the Klan peaked at about 40,000 active members in 1965. Civil rights demonstrations in the 1960s intensified Klan activity. The Klan was so powerful in certain areas of the South that its supporters controlled the state courts and the local police. Various Klan groups met and formed the **United Klans of America** (UKA) in 1961 under the leadership of Imperial Wizard **Robert Shelton**. Shelton, a violently anti-communist Methodist Church member, led the Klan in its anti-black, anti-Jewish campaign against the civil rights movement. Much of the violence directed against civil rights demonstrators came from members of the UKA. Another violent Klan group was the **White Knights of the Ku Klux Klan** under **Samuel Holloway Bowers**. All of their violence against civil rights activists took place in Mississippi. For a time, open warfare broke out in the South with various Klan groups vying to outdo each other in violence against blacks, Jews, and civil rights workers.

A combination of FBI counterintelligence operations, congressional investigations, the diversion of Klan resources to George Wallace's presidential campaigns, and a growing sense of outrage over the violence in the South in other parts of the United States caused a sudden decline in Klan operations, Key leaders were arrested and sentenced for federal civil rights crimes. Shelton went to jail in 1969; Bowers, in 1970. Both organizations suffered from the loss of their leaders. By 1967 the testimony before the House Committee on Un-American Activities indicated that Klan membership had dropped to around 17,000. The FBI estimated the Klan had fallen to 1,500 active members. Some of the dislocation in the Klan movement was caused by a disinformation campaign run by the FBI under the code name COINTELPRO (Counterintelligence Program). In 1976 the FBI reported in a memo from declassified documents that the "bureau already had an adequate network of Klan informants" and further recruitment was unnecessary.

After the triumph of the civil rights movement and the introduction of a series of civil rights laws, the Klan broke up into various subgroups. At one time in 1970, twelve Klan groups were active with twelve imperial wizards. Further splintering took place after lawsuits targeted the Klan for damages. A new version of the Klan was introduced in the mid-1970s by **David Duke**. He reorganized the **Knights of the Ku Klux Klan** into a political power in the South. Duke's goal was to make the Klan respectable and achieve political power first in the states and then on the national level. After a scandal involving Klan membership lists, Duke left the Klan and moved to a white supremacist political organization, the **National Association for the Advancement of White People** (NAAWP), to further his political agenda. Klan leaders have scrambled to replace him, but none has achieved his success. Klan groups still emerge at regular intervals. Among the new groups are the Confederate Knights of the Ku Klux Klan, the **Church of the American Knights of the Ku Klux Klan**, the Southern White Knights of the Ku Klux Klan, the Unified Knights of the Ku Klux Klan, and the White Knights of the Ku Klux Klan. Most of the modern Klan groups have become linked with the Christian Identity movement because it gives a theological rationale for white supremacy. **See also** Bowers, Samuel Holloway; Church of the American Knights of the Ku Klux Klan; Duke, David; Klanwatch; Shelton, Robert; United Klans of America; White Knights of the Ku Klux Klan; White Supremacist Movement.

Suggested readings: Robert J. Kelly, "The Ku Klux Klan: Recurring Hate in America," in Robert J. Kelly and Jess Maghan, eds., *Hate Crimes: The Global Politics of Polarization* (Carbondale: Southern Illinois University Press, 1998); Wayne King, "The Violent Rebirth of the Klan," *New York Times* (December 7, 1980), sec. 6, p. 150; George Lardner Jr., "15 Years of Dirty Tricks Bared by FBI," *Washington Post* (November 22, 1977), p. A2; Chester L. Quarles, *The Ku Klux Klan and Related American Racist and Antisemitic Organizations: A History and Analysis* (Jefferson, N.C.: McFarland, 1999); Patsy Sims, *The Klan* (New York: Stein and Day, 1978); Wyn Craig Wade, *The Fiery Cross: The Ku Klux Klan in America* (New York: Simon and Schuster, 1987); Don Whitehead, *Attack on Terror: The FBI Against the Ku Klux Klan in Mississippi* (New York: Funk and Wagnalls, 1970); Craig Whitlock, "Little Left of Klan Except the Scary Name," *News & Observer* [Raleigh, N.C.] (March 30, 1997), p. 1.

L

Lambs of Christ

The Lambs of Christ is a radical anti-abortion group which specializes in conducting illegal and intimidating protests outside clinics and doctors' homes. Father **Norman U. Weslin**, the founder and the leader of this group, is a former paratrooper and Green Beret lieutenant colonel, who became a Catholic priest, Oblates of Wisdom order, after returning from military service. Weslin formed the Lambs of Christ in 1988 shortly after being jailed with other anti-abortion activists in Atlanta, Georgia. His jail term was for participating in violent demonstrations while a member of **Operation Rescue**. He organized the Lambs of Christ along paramilitary lines, and the members display discipline in their demonstrations.

Weslin has been arrested about seventy times for his anti-abortion activities. While Weslin claims that his organization has 4,000 supporters, including 600 activists, the government maintains that these figures are on the high side. On any occasion, however, he is able to mobilize thirty or forty highly motivated demonstrators. Most, but not all, members of the Lambs of Christ are Catholics. Some tension has been noted between the members of the Lambs of Christ and members of the fundamentalist Protestant organizations. Weslin denies that his organization has had anything to do with bombing clinics and murdering abortion providers, but members of his group have been implicated in violent activity. They have also been active in physical and psychological harassment of pro-abortionists. **James C. Kopp**, a fringe member of the Lambs of Christ, was charged in the sniper killing of Dr. Barnett A. Slepian, an abortion doctor. Despite legislation passed to prevent demonstrators from denying access to abortion clinics, Weslin still leads the Lambs of Christ in demonstrations. In May 2001, he had to stand before a judge in a non-jury trial on four criminal contempt charges for demonstrations held in the fall of 2000. **See also** Anti-Abortion Movement; Kopp, James C.; Weslin, Norman U.

Suggested readings: Dallas A. Blanchard, *The Anti-Abortion Movement and the Rise of the Religious Right: From Polite to Fiery Protest* (New York: Twayne, 1994); Kurt Chandler, "Protests Pressure Abortion Workers," *Star Tribune* [Minneapolis] (October 20, 1991), p. 1A; Phil Fairbanks, "Going to Extremes," *Buffalo News* (February 12, 2000), p. A1; Phil Fairbanks and Lou Michel, "Lambs Leader Denies Violence," *Buffalo News* (November 16, 1998), p. 1C; Gina Kolata, "Nomadic Group of Anti-Abortionists Uses New Tactics to Make Its Mark," *New York Times* (March 24, 1992), p. A12; Jodi Wilgoren, "Punching a Clock to Fight Abortion," *New York Times* (November 7, 1998), p. B1.

Anti-abortion protesters, including Father Norman Weslin, second from left, of the Lambs of Christ, link arms outside an entrance of the West Loop women's clinic in Houston on August 17, 1992. Police moved in to restore order and arrested more than three dozen abortion opponents who pushed through a line of abortion rights advocates. (AP Photo/Rick Bowmer)

Lane, David (1940–   )

David Lane, a former member of **Robert Jay Mathews**'s **The Order** and one of the leaders of the **white supremacist movement**, was born Vernon Eiden in 1940 in Iowa. He was adopted by the Lanes and raised in Aurora, Colorado, near Denver. His stepfather was a preacher. One of his sisters married a black man, and family members report that Lane never accepted them. He briefly attended a local community college in the Denver area, but he left after only one semester. Lane earned a living as a real estate agent until he lost his realtor's license over his refusal to sell homes to blacks in white neighborhoods. His next job was as a clerk in a Denver title insurance company. He married twice, but both marriages failed. His strong racial views led him to join the local **Ku Klux Klan** organization. Lane stayed in the Klan until he became involved in a leadership dispute with Fred Wilkins, the head of the Colorado branch of the Klan. Wilkins expelled him from the Klan in 1979. Later that year he volunteered to be an organizer in Denver for **David Duke**'s Knights of the Ku Klux Klan. He also wrote a pamphlet, *The Death of the White Race*, at this time. In 1981 he was appointed Colorado state organizer for the **Aryan Nations**. After a brief stay at **Richard Girnt Butler**'s Aryan Nations complex in **Hayden Lake**, Idaho, Lane returned to Colorado to work with **Tom Metzger**'s White American Political Association (WAPA). In 1983 Lane was head of the Colorado chapter of the WAPA. He also worked for Roderick Elliott's newsletter the *Primrose and Cattlemen's Gazetteer* in Denver as a security guard before it folded after being attacked by local radio talk show host Alan Berg for its racist viewpoints. In 1983 he joined Mathews's revolutionary group, The Order.

As a result of his participation in the crime spree committed by members of The Order in 1983 and 1984, Lane went to prison. His role as the driver of the getaway car in the murder of Alan Berg, on June 18, 1984, made Lane a wanted man. He also operated a message center in Boise, Idaho, to coordinate the activities of the group during the July 1984 Brink's armored car robbery near Ukiah, California. The FBI arrested Lane on a fugitive warrant on March 30, 1985, in North Carolina. In a Seattle trial held in December 1985, Lane was convicted of racketeering and received a forty-year sentence in a federal prison. In a November 1987 trial held in Denver, Colorado, Lane received a 190-year prison sentence for violating Alan Berg's civil rights. Lane was also tried in the 1988 **Fort Smith Sedition Trial**, but this time he was acquitted of all charges.

Lane has become the ideological leader of the white supremacist movement from his prison cell. His racist views and violent rhetoric, however, have caused prison authorities to transfer him periodically to different prisons. His initial sentence was to be served in the medium-security federal prison in Terre Haute, Indiana. While in this prison, Lane wrote the pamphlet *Identity: Under This Sign You Shall Conquer* and had it distributed outside of prison. Lane's political activities in prison led to his transfer in 1986 to the maximum-security penitentiary in Marion, Illinois. His next move was to the maximum-security federal prison in Leavenworth, Kansas. In January 1989, Lane and two compatriots in The Order, Bruce Pierce and Richard Scutari, tried to break out of prison, but prison authorities learned of the plot and foiled it. In 1994 prison authorities sent him to the brand new maximum-security federal prison in Florence, Colorado. Lane continues to write articles for the

extremist press, including the *Aryan Nations Newsletter, Racial Loyalty*, and the *Klansman*. He also spends his time recruiting prospects for the **Aryan Brotherhood** and the Aryan Nations. His wife, Katya Lane, has established a publishing company, 14 Word Press, in St. Maries, Idaho, to publish and distribute his prison writings. **See also** Aryan Brotherhood; Aryan Nations; Brink's Armored Car Robbery; Fort Smith Sedition Trial; Mathews, Robert Jay; Order, The.

Suggested readings: James Coates, *Armed and Dangerous: The Rise of the Survivalist Right* (New York: Hill and Wang, 1987); Kevin Flynn, "Alan Berg Raised Ire of Racists," *Denver Rocky Mountain News* (August 12, 1999), p. 43A; Julia Lieblich, "A Living Theology of Hate," *Plain Dealer* [Cleveland] (June 11, 1995), p. 11; National Desk, "Jury Told of Plan to Kill Radio Host," *New York Times* (November 8, 1987), sec. 1, p. 31; Stephen Singular, *Talked to Death: The Life and Murder of Alan Berg* (New York: Beech Tree Books, 1987).

Langan, Peter Kevin (1959–   )

Peter Langan, the operational leader of the white supremacist group the **Aryan Republican Army**, was born in 1959 in Saipan in the Marianas Islands in the Pacific. His father worked for the Central Intelligence Agency (CIA) as mid-level operative. Langan also lived for a while in South Vietnam. The family returned to the United States in 1965 and settled in Wheaton, Maryland. When Langan was nine years old, his father died. He began having trouble in school and ran away from home when he was sixteen. Langan later joined the U.S. Navy. He experienced difficulties in the military environment and was court-martialed in 1983. In the meantime, he had become friends with Richard Lee Guthrie. They had been friends during Langan's stay in Wheaton, and Langan renewed the friendship after his return there. Together they traveled around the United States but soon found themselves in legal trouble. In 1993 Langan served time in a Georgia jail for robbing a Pizza Hut. He was released from jail only because he agreed to work undercover with federal authorities to locate Guthrie. The FBI wanted Guthrie for threatening the life of President George H. W. Bush. After only minimal cooperation with federal agents, Langan disappeared into the white supremacist underground.

Langan and Guthrie became members of the Aryan Republican Army whose mission was to provide funds to establish a future white homeland in the Pacific Northwest. During their travels around the country, they fell under the influence of **Mark Thomas**, a veteran leader of the Pennsylvania **white supremacist movement** and the East Coast head of the **Aryan Nations**. He provided the inspiration and general planning; Langan and Guthrie, the tactical planning and the muscle. In a video entitled "The Armed Struggle Underground," recovered from the Aryan Republican Army, Langan explains that their goal was to eliminate federal and state governments above the county level, exterminate the Jews, repatriate minorities to their homeland, and return the country to the law of the Bible. Before starting their operations, Langan negotiated weapons from **Chevie O'Brien Kehoe**, a white supremacist who was later convicted of murder, and his father, Kirby Kehoe. Several members of the Aryan Republican Army traveled to **Elohim City**, the **Christian Identity** community in eastern Oklahoma, to acquire more weapons. Characterizing themselves as the Mid-Western bank bandits, Langan led a small team of four in a spree of twenty-two bank robberies. They modeled their operations on those advocated by **Robert Jay Mathews** and **The Order**. The robberies were scheduled about a month apart and conducted in smaller, out-of-the-way banks. Pipe bombs and explosives were left behind to hinder pursuit. Langan used the name of "Commando Pedro" as his operational code name. The team also engaged in bogus-refund scams at service stores. Most of the funds were sent to other white supremacist organizations. Thomas received about $80,000 for his planning efforts. Among the gifts was one to make a CD recording of **skinhead** music honoring Vicki and Sam Weaver, who

had been killed at Ruby Ridge, and Richard Wayne Snell, who was executed for killing a pawnbroker and state trooper.

Federal and state authorities undertook a national manhunt to find the bank robbers. After a brief gunfight, police arrested Langan on January 18, 1996, in Columbus, Ohio. Guthrie had been arrested earlier and had informed the authorities of Langan's whereabouts. Guthrie pleaded guilty to the robberies before committing suicide in July 1996. Langan stood trial in Columbus, Ohio, in the summer of 1996 and received a fifty-five-year prison sentence for assaulting federal agents. Other members of the gang were also convicted, but they were given lesser jail terms. **See also** Aryan Republican Army; Thomas, Mark.

Suggested readings: Richard Leiby, "The Saga of Pretty Boy Pedro; How a Wheaton Kid Became a Neo-Nazi Bank Robber," *Washington Post* (February 13, 1997), p. B1; Judy Pasternak, "A Bank-Robbing 'Army' of the Rights is Left in Tatters," *Los Angeles Times* (January 15, 1997), p. A1; Robert Ruth, "Interview Focused FBI on Langan," *Columbus Dispatch* (December 28, 1997), p. 1C; Robert Ruth, "Langan Speaks His Mind, Then Gets Life Term," *Columbus Dispatch* (December 19, 1998), p. 1C.

LaRouche, Lyndon Hermyle (1922–)

Lyndon LaRouche has built a political and financial empire based on his extremist views and, in the process, has become the leading neofascist politician in the United States. He was born on September 8, 1922, in Rochester, New Hampshire. His father was a United Shoe Machinery Corporation salesman. Both his father and mother were Quakers. Much of his childhood was spent in Lynn, Massachusetts. His contentious parents left the Quakers in 1941 over a financial dispute. LaRouche had a difficult childhood and was always an indifferent student. He entered Northeastern University in Boston in 1941 but continued to be a poor student. After a brief tour with the Civilian Public Service, LaRouche signed up with the U.S. Army as a noncombatant. He served in

Lyndon LaRouche talks with members of the news media in Harrisburg, Pennsylvania, on July 3, 1996, during his candidacy for the Democratic nomination for president in the Pennsylvania primary election. (AP Photo/Paul Vathis)

the China-Burma Theater as a private in medical and ordnance units. About this time, LaRouche experimented with communism before becoming a Trotskyite. After leaving the army in May 1946 and a brief stint at Northeastern University, LaRouche joined, in December 1948, the Socialist Workers Party, an affiliate of the Trotskyite Fourth International. For the next seventeen years, LaRouche worked in various jobs but remained a staunch Trotskyite. He became successful as a management consultant and displayed an active interest in early computers.

LaRouche concluded in the 1960s that he could become the leader of a national Marxist party. His first action was to establish a working relationship with the student-dominated Progressive Labor Party (PLP). His attempt to gain control of the **Students for a Democratic Society** (SDS) by operating behind the scenes with PLP leaders failed in 1968. LaRouche recovered by forming the National Caucus of Labor Committees (NCLC) and attacking other leftist groups. These actions led to his being expelled from the SDS. The NCLC under LaRouche's leadership launched a violent campaign against the Communist Party in Operation Mop-Up. In 1973 LaRouche directed the NCLC into a street war with black leaders in New York City. After this battle peaked, LaRouche turned his group to an attack on Jews and Zionism.

By the mid-1970s, LaRouche was ready for the transition from a left-wing agitator for a Marxist society to a leader in the American right wing promoting a neofascist regime. Some of his early actions as head of the NCLC demonstrated his orientation toward right-wing extremism, but it was his growing ties to **Willis Carto** and the **Liberty Lobby** that reinforced his commitment to neo-Nazism. Besides anti-minority agitation and **anti-Semitism**, LaRouche began preparing his followers for a possible military takeover by the right wing. His supporters started sounding out disgruntled military officers and invited them to join LaRouche's party. LaRouche believed that his chances for political power depended on a crisis in the international monetary system. He foresaw an impending international budget crisis caused by defaults by developing countries, and he began to plan to exploit this crisis. When the international budget crisis failed to materialize at the rate he had predicted, LaRouche turned to politics.

By the early 1980s, LaRouche had allied himself with the extremist wing of the **white supremacist movement**, and he decided to run for national office. His first race was for president in the 1982 national election running as a Democrat. Although his campaign raised over $33 million, LaRouche never had a chance to win the election. LaRouche returned to politics in 1984 and this time it was an unsuccessful campaign to win the Democratic nomination for president. In 1986 LaRouche moved his base of operations from New York City to a 171-acre compound in Leesburg, Virginia. This time he used a marketing campaign about AIDS to raise funds. LaRouche was able to maneuver two of his supporters onto the Democratic Party's governor's slate in Illinois. This tactic had little practical outcome, but it made LaRouche a more serious political force in the upcoming presidential election. Although LaRouche had no chance of beating Ronald Reagan for the presidency his fund-raising tactics attracted the attention of federal authorities. LaRouche and six members of his organization were convicted in Virginia in December 1988 for conspiracy, mail fraud, and tax evasion. Although LaRouche was sentenced to fifteen years in prison, he served only five years before being released in January 1994. During and after his jail stay, LaRouche's organization continued its close ties with right-wing extremists.

LaRouche still agitates against the U.S. government and looks for ways to remake it. His publications, the *New Federalist, 21st Century Science and Technology*, and *EIR— Executive Intelligence Review*, continue to express his conspiracy views that a secret society of Jewish bankers, British aristocrats, and fellow travelers seek to dominate the business world. LaRouche is particularly hostile toward the environmental movement because it is hindering the worldwide advance of technology. Since his legal troubles, LaRouche and his organization have maintained a low profile while waiting for the economic crisis foretold by LaRouche in the 1980s to take place.

Suggested readings: Don Davis, "LaRouche Indulges in Explosive Rhetoric," *San Diego Union-Tribune* (June 3, 1984), p. A1; David Gelman et al., "Lyndon LaRouche; Beyond the Fringe," *Newsweek* (April 7, 1986), p. 38; David Helvarg, *The War Against the Greens: The "Wise-Use" Movement, the New Right, and Anti-Environmental Violence* (San Francisco: Sierra Club Books, 1994); Dennis King, *Lyndon LaRouche and the New American Fascism* (New York: Doubleday, 1989); John Mintz, "Inside the Weird World of Lyndon LaRouche," *Washington Post* (September 20, 1987), Outlook, p. C1; John Mintz, "Loudoun Newcomer," *Washington Post* (January 13, 1985), p. A1; Megan Rosenfeld, "Lyndon LaRouche: A Most Unusual Candidate for President," *Washington Post* (February 22, 1980), D1.

Lauck, Gary Lex (1953–)

Gary Lauck, the chief propagandist for the American and European neo-Nazi move-

American neo-Nazi Gary Lauck, of Lincoln, Nebraska, leaves Denmark's Supreme Court in Copenhagen, on August 24, 1995. Lauck, 42, went on trial at Hamburg State Court, Germany, on May 9, 1996, on charges of inciting racial hatred and distributing illegal propaganda. (AP Photo/file, Bjarke Oersted)

ment, was born in 1953 in Milwaukee, Wisconsin, an American of German ancestry. His father was an engineering professor. When he was eleven, his family moved to Lincoln, Nebraska, when his father took a position at the University of Nebraska. He grew up in Lincoln, but much of his adult life has been spent in Chicago, Illinois. Lauck was briefly a member of Frank Collins's **American Nazi Party** before Collins was exposed as being half-Jewish and being

jailed as a pedophile. Lauck founded the National Socialist German Workers Party–Overseas Organization (NSDAP-AO) in 1974. He sells Nazi propaganda in Germany using his position as head of the NSDAP-AO. Besides providing nationalistic materials in ten languages for European right-wing movements, he publishes the bimonthly neo-Nazi newspaper *Nazi Battle Cry*. Lauck demands payment only in cash so the money can't be traced. He was arrested and jailed for a short time in Germany in 1976 for violating German laws concerning the distribution of Nazi materials. Lauck established connections with other neo-Nazis in the late 1970s, including the **Aryan Nations**. By the early 1990s, his association with the Aryan Nations was growing closer. His newsletter, *New Order*, had been made part of the Aryan Nations literature distribution system.

Lauck has continued to be a major distributor of neo-Nazi literature in the United States and in Germany. His propaganda efforts violate no American laws, but his literature is illegal in Germany. Moreover, most of Lauck's attention and interest have been in reviving Nazism in Germany. Lauck attended a neo-Nazi rally in Denmark in 1995, and Danish authorities arrested him for deportation to Germany. The international neo-Nazi movement mobilized its propaganda machine to prevent the deportation. American extremists were also caught up in the drive to free Lauck. These efforts were unsuccessful, and Lauck was deported to Hamburg, Germany. At a subsequent trial in Germany in 1996, he received a four-year prison sentence. In March 1999 Lauck was released from a German prison, and he returned to the United States. He settled in Chicago and is active in marketing pro-Nazi material. In 1999 he applied for a gun permit in Lincoln, Nebraska but failed to disclose his 1996 criminal conviction. His attempt to block prosecution failed in January 2001, and he now faces up to five years in prison and a $10,000 fine for failure to disclose his conviction. **See also** American Nazi Party; Neo-Nazis.

Suggested readings: Marc Fisher and Steve Coll, "Farm-Belt Hitler Sows Seed of Hate," *Guardian* [London] (May 13, 1995), p. 11; Maureen Harrington, "The Nazi of Lincoln; Nebraskan Feeds Europe's White Bias," *Denver Post* (April 24, 1994), p. C1; Toni Heinzl, "Germany Releases Lauck; the Neo-Nazi from Lincoln Has Ended His Prison Term and Will Live in Chicago," *Omaha World-Herald* (March 20, 1999), p. 11; Tamara Jones, "Hate from America's Heartland," *Los Angeles Times* (September 7, 1993), p. A1; Elizabeth Neuffer, "German Court Convicts US Nazi Publisher," *Boston Globe* (August 23, 1996), p. A2; Robynn Tysver, "High Court Turns Down Lauck Appeal," *Omaha World-Herald* (January 26, 2001), p. 12; Mary Williams Walsh, "Neo-Nazi Tests Denmark's Defense of Free Speech," *Los Angeles Times* (July 25, 1995), p. 4.

Leaderless Resistance

Leaderless resistance is a central concept of the war between right-wing extremists and the U.S. government. Various communist parties used the cell system to fight enemies, but the cells were controlled by strict party discipline. Leaderless resistance comes out of a different concern. In the 1988 **Fort Smith Sedition Trial**, the government tried the most prominent extremist leaders for conspiracy against the government. Federal authorities had become convinced, after the crime spree of **Robert Jay Mathews** and **The Order**, that a conspiracy existed among the major racist and white supremacist groups. Although the trial was a defeat for the government, the incident traumatized the defendants. They had received substantial funds from the robberies conducted by The Order, and these funds could be traced to the heads of the groups. The leaders wanted to isolate themselves from future government prosecution but, at the same time, advance the anti-government cause.

The leading exponent of leaderless resistance has been **Louis Beam**, who was one of the defendants at the Fort Smith sedition trial. In the last issue of his newsletter, *The Seditionist*, published in February 1992, Beam outlined his views on leaderless resistance. He asserted that Colonel Ulius Louis Amoss, the founder of International Service of Information Incorporated in Baltimore, Maryland, first advanced leaderless resistance in 1962 as a way to counter an eventual communist takeover of the United States. Beam transformed this tactic to fight what he considered was "federal tyranny." His view was that the pyramid system of organization did not work in opposition groups because infiltrators can destroy anything above or below their level of infiltration. He suggested a cell system in which each secret cell is totally independent of the other cells. These phantom cells operate independently and without contact with national leaders. Because these individuals share the same general outlook and philosophy and react to given situations in similar ways, they are reliable instruments against the government. Leaderless resistance leads to small or even one-man cells of resistance able to carry out the most difficult assignments.

Beam took his concept of leaderless resistance to the Estes Park, Colorado, meeting in October 1992. **Peter J. Peters** had called the meeting to plan a strategy against the federal government after the **Ruby Ridge incident**. The 160 extremist leaders who had gathered at the meeting broke into committees to study various questions. Beam made a presentation of his leaderless resistance tactic, and the leaders adopted it as part of their general strategy to build a **militia movement** to oppose the practices of the U.S. government. Since then, Beam has continued to advance this concept, and it has been adopted by most extremist groups. Its liability as a tactic, however, showed up in **Timothy James McVeigh**'s bombing of the Murrah Federal Building in Oklahoma City on April 19, 1995. McVeigh operated in a small cell of three members, and these members avoided any official contact with extremist groups. This bombing has rebounded to the detriment of the militia movement, and their efforts to avoid responsibility are in line with the theory of leaderless resistance. **See also** Beam, Louis; Estes Park Meeting; Fort Smith Sedition Trial; McVeigh, Timothy James.

Suggested readings: Betty A. Dobratz and Stephanie L. Shanks-Meile, *"White Power, White Pride!": The White Separatist Movement in the United States* (New York: Twayne, 1997); Matt Krasnowski, "Supremacists' 'Lone-Wolf' Tack Poses New Peril," *San Diego Union-Tribune* (August 29, 1999), p. A1; Bill Morlin, "The War Within," *Spokesman-Review* [Spokane, Wash.] (December 29, 1996), p. 1; Jim Nesbitt, "Hate Groups Keep Actions of Loners at Safe Distance,"

Plain Dealer [Cleveland] (July 8, 1999), p. 8A; Mark Potok, "Militant Militia Fringe Is Setting Off Alarms," *USA Today* (April 17, 1996), p. 4A.

League of the South (LOS)

The League of the South (LOS), a white supremacist group, works to preserve Southern culture and retain white domination of political and social life in the South. J. Michael Hill, a former college professor at Stillman College in Tuscaloosa, Alabama, and Reverend Steven J. Wilkins, pastor of the Auburn Avenue Presbyterian Church in Monroe, Louisiana, and thirty-nine others founded the League of the South in 1994, first known as the Southern League. The boards of directors of the LOS, dominated by academics, reflect a desire to return to the Confederacy. Preserving Southern culture and state's rights have attracted a growing membership that also fears an integrated society in which minority members have the same rights as they do. The growth of the LOS has been dramatic: from 4,000 members in 1998 to 9,000 members in 2000. Some of this rapid growth has been a result of the league's championing of the Confederate flag issue. The preservation of white supremacy is so important that the leadership of the LOS has threatened to launch a movement for Southern secession from the United States. Members lobbied for the defeat of the moderate Republican governor, David Beasley, in 1996 after he supported removing the Confederate flag from atop the state capitol. Close ties have been formed between the LOS and the **Council of Conservative Citizens** with a significant cross-membership. Another prominent member of the LOS is **Kirk Lyons**, a white supremacist lawyer and the head of the Southern Legal Resources Center. The LOS supports the Institute for the Study of Southern Culture and History. The League of the South has assumed a central role in the growing neo-Confederate movement in the South.

Recently the League of the South has made an effort to gain control of conservative churches in the South. Wilkins, the leader of this initiative, has been able to recruit ten other churches to join with his church in challenging for control of the Presbyterian Church in America (PCA), a conservative Southern denomination. Members of the LOS are converts to Christian Reconstruction, a modern form of theocracy in which church and state are united. This theory is based on Rousas John Rushdoony's book *The Institute of Biblical Law*, published in 1973. Christian Reconstructionists seek to impose their interpretation of Old Testament law on modern civil society. This interpretation includes execution for transgressors. The death penalty would be assessed for abandonment of faith (apostasy), adultery, astrology, blasphemy, heresy, homosexuality, incest, incorrigible juvenile delinquency, striking a parent, and lack of chastity before marriage. Other crimes would incur whipping, indentured servitude, or slavery. Because a theocratic society is one in which only one religious view predominates, the leaders of the LOS believe that the U.S. Constitution would have to be replaced by a theocratic one. In 2001 the Southern Poverty Law Center estimated that thirty churches in the South subscribe to Christian Reconstruction religious views. **See also** Council of Conservative Citizens; Lyons, Kirk.

Suggested readings: Saeed Ahmed, "Group Seeks Reparations for Civil War 'Atrocities,' " *Atlanta Journal and Constitution* (April 13, 2001), p. 6A; Duncan Campbell, "Neo-Confederates Want out of US," *Guardian* [London] (September 18, 2000), p. 15; James Langton, "Rebels March Again in the Deep South," *Sunday Telegraph* [London] (January 11, 1998), p. 26; Christopher Quinn, "Symbolism Is at Heart of Flag Flap," *Atlanta Journal and Constitution* (January 25, 2001), p. 1JQ; Dan Sewell, "For These Groups, Insults to South Are Fighting Words," *Milwaukee Journal Sentinel* (October 4, 1998), p. 3; Southern Poverty Law Center, "Confederates in the Pulpit," *SPLC Intelligence Report* 101 (Spring 2001): 51–55; Southern Poverty Law Center, "A League of Their Own," *SPLC Intelligence Report* 99 (Summer 2000): 13–17.

LeBaron, Ervil (1925–1981)

Ervil LeBaron, the religious leader of the Church of the Lamb of God and the architect of a blood-atonement cult, was born on February 22, 1925, in Colonia Juarez, Mexico. He was the ninth child of one of the leading polygamist families among the fundamentalist Mormons. Although the LeBarons lived in a Mormon polygamist community, other Mormon families ostracized them for their extreme beliefs and practices. His family moved to an area south of the Mormon colony and built the Colonia LeBaron. Ervil left formal schooling early to go with his brothers on a mission to central Mexico. He and his brothers, Alma and Joel, were formally excommunicated from the Mormon Church in June 1944. Two of his brothers, Ben and Sydney, and a sister, Lucinda, suffered from bouts of insanity and have been in and out of institutions most of their lives. On September 21, 1955, Joel LeBaron founded a new church in Salt Lake City, Utah, the Church of the First Born of the Fullness of Times, with the support of his brothers Ross and Floren. Joel claimed the mantle of leadership in the new church as the rightful heir of Joseph Smith, Jr. At first, Ervil was distressed at what Joel had done but, in 1956, Joel returned to Mexico and converted Ervil to the new church. By 1961 the church had attracted nearly 500 members in Mexico. By this time, Ervil was second in command of the church and fulfilling the role of theologian. His book *Priesthood Expounded* (1958) provided the doctrinal basis for the church. He was also a believer in militaristic discipline, and he imposed it on the membership of the church. Ervil married thirteen wives and attempted to recruit many others.

Ervil's troubles with his brother Joel came out of Ervil's challenge to assume the leadership of the Church of the First Born of the Fullness of Times. Ervil had embezzled church tithings to support himself and his growing family, and he had persuaded church members to give him their life savings on more than one occasion. In 1960 Ervil came to believe that he was the sole judge over people's lives. Ervil called this concept civil law, which prescribed the death penalty for traitors, adulterers, and murderers. Although the civil law concept came from Ervil, Joel allowed it to be added to the doctrine of the church. Ervil began to recruit a number of young church members to carry out the dictates of civil law. In 1967 Ervil challenged Joel for control of the church, but Joel withstood the challenge by enlisting the support of the elders of the church. In October 1970, Joel relieved Ervil of his position as patriarch of the church. Ervil plotted to kill Joel and Joel's key followers. On May 20, 1971 Ervil formed his own church, the Church of the Lamb of God. Joel excommunicated Ervil on August 8, 1972. On August 20, 1972, three followers of Ervil murdered Joel LeBaron in Ensenada, Mexico. Ervil's subsequent attempt to take over his brother's church failed, however, when a mob forced his followers to flee from Colonia LeBaron. Verlan LeBaron assumed control of the Church of the First Born of the Fullness of Times.

Ervil found himself in legal troubles over the activities of his church, but each time he escaped punishment. He was convicted in a Mexican court of complicity in Joel's murder and given a twelve-year prison sentence, but a Mexican supreme court in Mexicali overturned this verdict in suspicious circumstances. Ervil spent fourteen months in a Mexican jail before his release in February 1974. He launched open warfare with his death squads attacking members of the Church of the First Born of the Fullness of Times. Ervil's followers were convinced of his divine authority and never questioned his decisions. In a book, *Contest at Law*, Ervil threatened all of the members of his former church with death. On December 26, 1974, Ervil's death squad attacked the Los Molinos Colony of his brother Verlan's followers in Mexico, killing two and wounding thirteen others. Ervil decided to move his operations to Utah and began intimidating Mormon polygamists there. He tried to force the wealthy Kinston family, prominent polygamists, to accept him as their leader. At the same time, he plotted to murder the hierarchy of the Mormon Church. A Church of the Lamb of God member, Dean Vest, was killed by one of Ervil's wives on June 16, 1975, because he was planning to defect. On August 23, 1975, a death squad murdered Robert Simons, who had rejected Ervil's invitation to join his church. In February 1976, Ervil was in Mexico and was arrested for his role in the Los Molinos killings. While he was in a Mexican jail, he wrote a series of pamphlets threatening to kill a number of people, including President Jimmy Carter. Again Ervil avoided conviction because no hard evidence connected him to the raid although evidence appeared in court that he had ordered it. In April 1977, Ervil ordered his daughter, Rebecca Chynoweth, to be murdered because she was showing signs of rebellion against her father.

Ervil next schemed to rid himself of his two worst enemies. First, he ordered two of his women followers to kill the head of the most influential polygamist clan in the United States, Rulon Allred. Ervil selected Rena Chynoweth, one of his wives, and Ramona Marston, wife of one of his chief supporters, for the mission. On May 10, 1977, the two women killed Allred at his office in Murray, Utah. Ervil had made plans to assassinate his brother Verlan, the leader of the Church of the First Born of the Fullness of Times, at Allred's funeral. A team of three men made an appearance at the funeral, but the size of the crowd and the large police presence made them reconsider and leave. After these incidents, Ervil started losing control of his followers. Several key figures defected but Ervil remained in Mexico where he was immune from prosecution by Utah authorities. Throughout the period from 1977 to 1979, Ervil hid in the small Mexican town of Allixco about 130 miles southeast of Mexico City. The Mexican police caught him in late May 1979, and on June 1 he was turned over to U.S. authorities in Laredo, Texas.

Over the years Ervil had been able to escape his legal troubles by evasion and by issuing shadowy instructions to his subordinates, but this time the federal government had a strong case against him. His trial in federal court in Salt Lake City, Utah, started on May 12, 1980. A jury convicted Ervil of the first-degree murder of Rulon Allred and conspiracy to kill Verlan LeBaron. The judge imposed a life sentence for the murder and five years to life for the conspiracy count. He served his prison term in the maximum-security wing of the Utah State Prison until his death of a heart attack on August 16, 1981. His son Arthur LeBaron assumed Ervil's position in the Church of the Lamb of God. Ervil's legacy continues to the present with leaders and members of his church still believing in his interpretation of civil law and the blood-atonement doctrine. **See also** Cults; Church of the First Born of the Fullness of Times/Church of the Lamb of God.

Suggested readings: Garry Abrams, "A Family's Legacy of Death," *Los Angeles Times* (September 20, 1992), p. E1; Scott Anderson, *The 4 o'Clock Murders* (New York: Doubleday, 1993); Ben Bradlee and Dale Van Atta, *Prophet of Blood: The Untold Story of Ervil LeBaron and the Lambs of God* (New York: Putnams, 1981); Rena Chynoweth and Dean M. Shapiro, *The Blood Covenant* (Austin, Tex.: Diamond Books, 1990); Jan Kwiatkowsk, "The 'Mormon Manson' and His Never-Ending Cult of Murder," *Buffalo News* (March 7, 1993), Book Review, p. 7; Bella Stumbo, "No Tidy Stereotype; Polygamists: Tale of Two Families," *Los Angeles Times* (May 13, 1988), part 1, p. 1.

Leuchter Report

The Leuchter Report, written by Fred Leuchter, claims that there were no gas chambers at the Auschwitz Concentration Camp during World War II. This 1988 report is based on a chemical analysis made of the walls of the chambers to dispute the claim that cyanide gas was used by the Germans in the gas chambers. The full title of the report is *The Leuchter Report: The End of a Myth: A Report on the Alleged Execution Gas Chambers at Auschwitz, Birkenau and Majdanek, Poland*. Holocaust denial supporters have cited this report as proof of

their claim that the Holocaust never took place.

Leuchter was commissioned by Canada's leading **neo-Nazi, Ernst Christof Friedrich Zundel,** in January 1988 to study the concentration camps in Poland. After receiving $35,000 as an expert witness, Leuchter traveled to Poland where he collected samples of materials from the concentration camps of Auschwitz, Birkenau, and Majdanek. Zundel's intent was to discredit the existence of the gas chambers. Leuchter had made a reputation as a designer of electric chairs and other lethal devices, but he lacked the academic credentials or technical expertise to be an expert on gas chambers. His academic degree was in history. Despite his lack of a formal education in either engineering or science, he submitted the samples he collected to a chemist for chemical analysis. The chemist reported little trace of cyanide. Leuchter concluded in his report that, without significant evidence of cyanide residue, the gas chambers never existed.

Both Leuchter's scientific evidence and his conclusion produced a firestorm of criticism. His conclusion went against five decades of eyewitness testimony and confessions by German concentration camp officials and guards. After this debate subsided, the discussion moved into the field of science. Scientists disputed Leuchter's findings and questioned his scientific credentials. Several states investigated his credentials as an engineer and prohibited him from competing for state contracts. The more Leuchter and his report were attacked, the more intense was the defensive response from the Holocaust deniers associated with the **Institute for Historical Review** (IHR). Leuchter traveled to various conferences sponsored by the IHR to defend his report. Finally, in 1999, Errol Morris produced a documentary film, *Mr. Death: The Rise and Fall of Fred A. Leuchter Jr.*, in which Leuchter's evidence is challenged by the very chemist who performed the original chemical analysis. He was never told about the nature of the test for cyanide residue. In the documentary, this scientist reveals that cyanide adheres to a surface and does not penetrate much into a wall. Most of the Leuchter sample was taken from material found deep within the walls. Leuchter's evidence is flawed by this methodological error. Moreover, a subsequent French study did find evidence of cyanide on the surface of the gas chambers. This and other scientific evidence has led to the discrediting of the Leuchter Report. **See also** Carto, Willis; Holocaust Denial Movement; Institute for Historical Review; Zundel, Ernst Christof Friedrich.

Suggested readings: Paul Bilodeau, "The Zundel Trial: Expert Doubts Buildings Used as Gas Chambers," *Toronto Star* (April 21, 1988), p. A4; D. D. Guttenplan, *The Holocaust on Trial* (New York: Norton, 2001); Jordana Hart, "Death Machine Builder Under Scrutiny for Nazi Gas Report," *Boston Globe* (October 1, 1990), p. 17; Mitchell Jones, *The Leuchter Report: A Dissection* (Cedar Park, Tex.; 21st Century Logic, 1995); Michael H. Kleinschrodt, " 'Mr. Death' a Wry Portrait of Eccentric Engineer," *Times Picayune* [New Orleans] (February 25, 2000), p. L28; Deborah Lipstadt, *Denying the Holocaust: The Growing Assault on Truth and Memory* (New York: Plume, 1993); Nizkor Project, "The Leuchter Report; Holocaust Denial & the Big Lie," www.nizkor.org/faqs/leuchter/.

Libertarian Party

Members of the Libertarian Party espouse unregulated capitalism and individualism. Ayn Rand's novel *Atlas Shrugged* (1955) provides a unifying philosophy for the movement. Her anti-Christian brand of libertarianism attracted the anarchist wing of the American conservative body politic, but it also appealed to former New Left elements. At a conference of the conservative Young Americans for Freedom (YAF) held in 1969, the libertarian wing of the YAF broke away and joined with left-wing libertarian groups to establish a new group, the Society for Individual Liberty. Murray Rothbard, the society's most prominent intellectual and spokesperson, described its credo in his book *For a New Liberty*. Under his influence and that of another leader, Jerome Tuccille, the libertarians started distancing themselves from the militant leftists.

Unhappiness with political affairs and the direction of the Nixon administration led to the formation of the Libertarian Party in the summer of 1971. On August 15, 1971, five disgruntled Republicans formed the party in David Nolan's apartment in Denver, Colorado. Nolan was a writer for a small Denver advertising agency and a former member of the YAF. The co-founders were Hue Fritch, an anarchist; David Nelson, a college student; John James, a Denver architect; and Susan Nolan, wife of David Nolan. Nolan assumed the head of the new party on December 11, 1971.

The Libertarian Party positioned itself on the anarchist wing of the American political spectrum. Listed among its goals were the reduction of taxes, a decrease in government spending, the elimination of the Federal Reserve System, an end to all forms of censorship, the elimination of government intervention in labor relations, the abolition of the military draft, a repeal of the laws on the ownership of gold, a curtailment of laws on sexual conduct and drug use, and the end of all entangling foreign alliances. Leaders of the party attempted to win public office by promising to implement these goals, but their efforts had little success. They lacked corporate resources and an established party organization to win political power.

Suggested readings: Sara Diamond, *Roads to Dominion: Right-Wing Movements and Political Power in the United States* (New York: Guilford Press, 1995); Jane Ely, "At Very Least, Libertarians Excite Selves," *Houston Chronicle* (June 11, 2000), Outlook, p. 2; Adrianne Flynn, "Philosophy No Longer Burden to Libertarians," *Arizona Republic* (June 8, 1996), p. A1; Walter Goodman, "Libertarian Asking Less Government," *New York Times* (September 28, 1984), p. 2; Mike Patty, "Libertarians Celebrate Westminister Roots," *Rocky Mountain News* (August 15, 1996), p. 30A; Joe Sciacca, "The Naked Truth; Libertarians Have a Long Way to Go," *Boston Herald* (October 19, 1998), p. 6.

Liberty Lobby

Willis Carto founded the Liberty Lobby in August 1957 as a lobbying organization to advance his anti-communist and anti-Semite agenda. Curtis Dall served as the longtime chairperson, and a board of directors of prominent radical conservatives has provided support and advice. Carto has always been the dominant leader. He adopted as the official ideology of the Liberty Lobby the views of **Francis Parker Yockey** and his book *Imperium* (1949), in which the author proposes a society served by science where Jews would be controlled by an authoritarian government. **Anti-Semitism** and anti-black have long been the cornerstone of the Liberty Lobby. Members also supported segregation in the South, attacked the civil rights movement, and attempted to infiltrate the Republican Party to gain political control over it. Rampant anti-Semitism in the Liberty Lobby made it difficult for its supporters to interact with either the Republican Party or the **John Birch Society**. Despite these political failures, the Liberty Lobby found its niche in advancing its views through the lobby's numerous publications, including the *Liberty Letters, Liberty Lowdown, Washington Observer, Western Destiny*, and *American Mercury*. The first few of these publications were relatively moderate, but the latter ones appealed to racists and hard-line anti-Semites. The Liberty Lobby also published books and pamphlets from its Noontide Press in Los Angeles. By 1971 the Liberty Lobby's staff had grown to forty, and it had an annual budget of around $1 million.

The slowing of the expansion of the Liberty Lobby in the early 1970s caused its leadership to take a more radical orientation. A more sensationalist weekly newspaper, the *Spotlight*, replaced the old standby *Liberty Letters*. In the 1980s the new publication gained a circulation of more than 300,000. Then an effort was made to develop a radio program with the Mutual Broadcasting System. This contract was short-lived, but radio programming remained a part of the Liberty Lobby's publicity effort. The major shift in orientation, however, was the Liberty Lobby's strident advocacy of Holocaust revisionism. In 1979 Carto founded the **Institute for Historical Review** (IHR) to expose what he considered was the myth of the Nazi Holocaust. Besides sponsoring books denying the Holocaust, the IHR started the *Journal of Historical Review* to publish articles supporting this position. Soon most of the prominent anti-Semitic and anti-Zionist authors were writing for this journal. This emphasis on anti-Semitic literature over other issues was an indicator of a growing shift of Carto and the leaders of the Liberty Lobby away from traditional conservative right-wing issues to more extremist subjects.

As a representative of the extremist wing of the conservative movement, the Liberty Lobby began attacking moderate conservatives. Among its targets have been William F. Buckley and the *National Review*, for his establishment views and connections, and James J. Kilpatrick, for being a so-called conservative Quisling. Any person who did not follow the Liberty Lobby line became an enemy to be attacked. Unhappy about the direction of the country, leaders of the Liberty Lobby have toyed with the idea of establishing a paramilitary branch, the National Youth Alliance, but nothing concrete has come out of this initiative. **See also** Anti-Semitism; Carto, Willis; Institute for Historical Review; Holocaust Denial Movement.

Suggested readings: Lynn Darling, "Spotlight on Conspiracy with the Liberty Lobby," *Washington Post* (May 25, 1979), p. E7; Sara Diamond, *Roads to Dominion: Right-Wing Movements and Political Power in the United States* (New York: Guilford Press, 1995); Frank P. Mintz, *The Liberty Lobby and the American Right: Race, Conspiracy, and Culture* (Westport, Conn.: Greenwood Press, 1985); James Ridgeway, *Blood in the Face: The Ku Klux Klan, Aryan Nations, Nazi Skinheads, and the Rise of a New White Culture* (New York: Thunder's Mouth Press, 1990).

Long, Terry (1946–)

Terry Long, one of Canada's leading white supremacists and the former head of the Canadian **Aryan Nations**, was born in May 1946 in Red Deer, Alberta, Canada. His father was a combination truck driver, sawmill owner, and farmer. The family lived on a small farm west of Caroline, Alberta. In 1953 the Long family moved to Sacramento, California, because of better job prospects for the father. Long attended high school in Sacramento and spent two years in college there. Long returned to Caroline, Canada, in 1966. He enrolled at the University of Alberta at Edmonton in 1968 and graduated in 1972 with a degree in science with a specialization in electrical engineering. Shortly after graduation, he married a Canadian woman and they purchased a farm west of Bentley, Alberta.

Long was active in the Canadian Conservative Party before turning to more extremist groups. Because of his work in the Conservative Party, he was selected to be a director for an Edmonton area Progressive Conservative Party. Disillusioned by the moderate conservatism of the Conservative Party, Long shifted his allegiance in 1982 to the separatist party, Western Canada Concept, of Doug Christie. He ran for office representing the separatists in the provincial election. Although he lost the election, Long made a good showing and won over one of the other candidates. In the next year, Long completed his transition from a disillusioned conservative to a white supremacist. With two other neo-Nazis, Jim Green and Tom Erhart, he helped form, in September 1983, the Christian Defence League (CDL) to support the legal defense of white supremacist **James Keegstra**, who had been fired as a teacher for teaching Holocaust denial to students. By this time, Long's views were so extreme that he was asked to step down as the director of the CDL. He broke with both Green and Keegstra and joined the emerging **Christian Identity** movement and the Aryan Nations. When a Calgary bank foreclosed on his farm, Long blamed Jewish bankers for the loss of his farm and his being forced to move his family to his father's farm near Caroline. His father disagreed with his son's views on race and politics, and they had frequent arguments over these issues. After his father's accidental death in a sawmill accident in 1984, Long became even more violent in his views and actions. Long attended the fifth annual Aryan Nations World Congress in July 1984 in **Hayden Lake**, Idaho. At this meeting, Long made a good impression on **Richard Girnt Butler**, the head of the Aryan Nations, and Butler appointed him in November 1985 as the head of the Canadian branch of the Aryan Nations.

Long expected followers to flock to the Canadian Aryan Nations movement, and he was disappointed when only a few joined. Later in 1985, Long decided to stimulate recruitment in Canada by building a Hayden Lake–like compound on his farm near Caroline. News of this plan caused a media uproar in Canada and promoted a confrontation between him and representatives of the **Jewish Defense League** (JDL). This controversy stimulated publicity, but over the next several years Long was able to build the Aryan Nations in Canada into an organization of 200 members. These gains earned him considerable respect within the American Aryan Nations for his organizational abilities. Long's involvement with several racist **skinheads** and their physical attack on Keith Rutherford in April 1990 led to a lawsuit being instituted against him. An Aryan Nations rally held in Provost, Alberta, in September 1990 also caused a controversy. The Alberta Human Rights Commission forced Long to testify before it over human rights violation charges. In the middle of the hearing and after he was instructed to bring a list of members of the Canadian Aryan Nations, Long fled Canada for sanctuary in the United States. A warrant for his arrest was issued, but it expired in 1992. After expiration of the warrant, Long returned to Canada and lived in south central British Columbia. His lengthy absence as the head of the Canadian Aryan Nations led Butler to replace him with another leader. In April 1995, Long returned to his farm in Caroline. By this time, he was active in forming a breakaway faction of the Aryan Nations. In the last five years, Long has kept a lower profile in white supremacist circles than before, but he is still an influential figure in the Canadian extremist movement. **See also** Aryan Nations; Butler, Richard Girnt.

Suggested readings: Stanley R. Barrett, *Is God a Racist? The Right Wing in Canada* (Toronto: University of Toronto Press, 1987); Marcus Gee and John Howse, "Campaigning Against Hate," *Maclean's* (September 1, 1986), p. 12; Tim Harper, "Canadian Forces Ignored Racism Edict," *Toronto Star* (September 2, 1993), p. A18; Warren Kinsella, *Web of Hate: Inside Canada's Far Right Network* (Toronto: HarperCollins, 1994); Bill Walker, "The Chilling Chant of Racism Echoes from the Idaho Woods," *Toronto Star* (August 10, 1986), p. H5.

Lundgren, Jeffrey Don (1950–   )

Jeffrey Lundgren, the charismatic leader of a Mormon blood-atonement cult, was born in 1950 in Independence, Missouri. Both parents were active in the Slover Park Reorganized Church of Jesus Christ of Latter Day Saints (RLDS). His father was a U.S. Navy veteran and a successful businessman in the Independence area. Lundgren attended William Chrisman High School where he excelled in sports. Despite his success in sports, however, he had few friends. After graduation in 1968, he decided to go to college at Central Missouri State University in Warrensburg, Missouri. At college, Lundgren met and married Alice Keehler and shortly thereafter flunked out of college. To avoid the draft, he enlisted in the U.S. Navy, serving as an electrician. On his second assignment aboard the destroyer *U.S.S. Shelton*, Lundgren found his ship in several engagements with North Vietnamese shore batteries between October and December 1972. After leaving the Navy, Lundgren returned to school at Central Missouri State University. His grades improved and he soon became a leader for the conservative RLDS faction on campus. When Lundgren and his wife lost control of their personal finances, he was forced to leave school. Several times over the next few years he lost jobs because of misappropriation of funds. He also started writing bad checks.

Lundgren had always been interested in religion and, in the midst of his personal financial troubles, he turned to his church for achievement. In October 1983, he was ordained in the RLDS priesthood. Lundgren soon found himself in opposition to the liberalization policies of the head of the RLDS Church, Wallace B. Smith. His unhappiness with the church's approval of ordaining of women into the priesthood drove him into outright rebellion. After losing a Sunday School class assignment in Independence because of his increasingly strident fundamentalist views, Lundgren decided to move to Kirtland, Ohio, in August 1984, where he worked at the Kirtland Temple as an unpaid guide. He continued to attack the liberal policies of the church and started attracting a following among the conservative members of the Kirtland church. His target was the liberal RLDS state president, Dale Luffman. In the fall of 1986, Lundgren decided that he was a "prophet of God." His path to revealed truth in the Bible and the Book of Mormon came through chiastic analysis (secret truths in the scriptures by diagraming poems). By finding these hidden meanings in the texts, he could interpret God's will. Because only he could find these passages and interpret them, his followers had to submit to his will. Followers were required to give all their cash and future earnings to Lundgren. In the spring of 1987, Lundgren started preparing for Armageddon by acquiring weapons and supplies. Later in that summer, Lundgren lost his tour guide position. An audit proved that he had been stealing from church funds. Because his resignation was kept secret by church authorities to avoid scandal, Lundgren claimed that his removal as a guide came as a result of his teachings.

Lundgren established a commune on a fifteen-acre farm on the southern edge of Kirtland for his family and followers in September 1987. Nearly all of his close followers moved there with him. These commune members were disenchanted with the liberalization movement in the RLDS church and were looking for spiritual guidance. Besides the Lundgren family of five, thirteen adults belonged to the commune. Lundgren controlled them by holding lengthy religious classes interpreting biblical and Mormon passages. He also dictated to them his standards of personal behavior. Everyone worked at the farm producing foodstuffs except Lundgren and his wife. All salaries went into a common pot, but Lundgren made the final decision on all expenditures.

After a few weeks on the commune, Lundgren plotted to take over the Kirtland Temple and depose Luffman. He began preaching on the necessity and biblical justification for violence. Everyone in a one-block radius of the temple would be killed. Luffman and his family would be sacrificed in the temple as a blood atonement. This action, scheduled for May 3, 1988, would start the process culminating in Armageddon. A former member of the commune, Kevin Currie, warned the FBI and the local Kirtland police about the plot. An investigation by local police convinced Lundgren to postpone and then abandon the temple takeover. Lundgren decided, instead, to replace that plot with another type of blood atonement. By killing the "wicked," Lundgren would receive the "power" to take members of his commune before the presence of God. In the midst of these events, Luffman instituted proceedings to excommunicate Lundgren from the RLDS church. Lundgren interpreted this excommunication effort to the first step toward the Apocalypse. The second step would be the sacrifice of the Avery family—husband, wife, and three daughters—as a blood atonement. The Averys were members of the commune and Lundgren made the five of them sacrificial victims. Every member of the commune participated in the preparations for the sacrifice.

During these preparations, local police and the FBI initiated a full investigation of Lundgren's commune. Another former commune member confirmed the existence of a plot to take over the temple. The scheme to murder the Avery family, however, remained secret. On April 17, 1989, Lundgren executed the five members of the Avery family, and members of the commune buried their bodies in the barn. The next day, the police conducted a probing operation at the farm, but without a search warrant nothing was

learned about the murders. Plans had already been made by Lundgren to leave Kirtland, and the commune moved quietly to Yellow Creek Hollow in Tucker County, West Virginia. Lundgren's sexual fantasies and his attentions to the wives of other members began to cause dissension. After several weeks at the West Virginia location, police attention led the members of the commune to break up and go their separate ways. Keith Johnson's wife had left him for Lundgren, and, in revenge, he informed police authorities about the Avery murders. After the bodies were found, Lundgren and his family were arrested on January 4, 1990, in San Diego, California.

Lundgren maintained his claim of being a prophet from God at his Ohio trial. His wife, Alice, was tried first. She was charged with fifteen counts from complicity to murder to kidnapping. She received a prison sentence of 150 years. Lundgren's trial was held later in September 1990, and he was convicted of five aggravated murders and five counts of kidnapping. He was sentenced to die in the Ohio state electric chair. Other members of the cult received lesser sentences, except for his son, Damon Lundgren, who received a life sentence. Lundgren still resides on death row and maintains that God will release him from prison. **See also** Cults.

Suggested readings: James Bradshaw, "Death Term Ok'd for Cult Leader," *Columbus Dispatch* (August 31, 1995), p. 9D; Pete Earley, *Prophet of Death: The Mormon Blood-Atonement Killings* (New York: William Morrow, 1991); Amand Garrett and Maggi Martin, "Ten Years Later, Kirtland Cult Members Break Their Silence," *Plain Dealer* [Cleveland] (April 11, 1999), p. 1A; Dirk Johnson, "Police Wanted to Arrest Commune Leader Before Killings of 5," *New York Times* (January 13, 1990), sec. 1, p. 10; Amy Wallace, "Cultist Linked to Deaths Seized Near San Diego," *Los Angeles Times* (January 8, 1990), p. A1.

Lyons, Kirk (1957–   )

Kirk Lyons is the chief legal representative for white supremacist groups in the United

States. He attended college at the University of Texas at Austin where he majored in social and behavioral sciences. After graduation, Lyons obtained his law degree from Bates College of Law at the University of Houston. His first legal involvement with extremists came in the 1988 **Fort Smith Sedition Trial** in which he represented a fellow Texan, **Louis Beam**. His role in defeating the charges made him a celebrity in extremist circles. Lyons decided to expand his area of operations after the trial. Although a native Texan, Lyons transferred his legal offices from Dallas, Texas, to North Carolina in 1991. He also changed the name of his legal office from Patriots' Defense Foundation to CAUSE Foundation (CAUSE is an abbreviation for Canada, Australia, South Africa, and Europe, areas in which Lyons believes the white inhabitants are in danger of losing their supremacy.) The CAUSE Foundation is intended to be a clearinghouse for information and legal assistance for extremists. Lyons has been active making contacts with his legal counterparts in extremist groups both in Canada and in Germany.

Lyons's relationship with **neo-Nazis** and white supremacist groups is close because he shares their viewpoints. In September 1990, he married Brenda Tate at the **Aryan Nations Hayden Lake** compound. **Richard Girnt Butler** officiated at the wedding. His wife's brother, David Tate, a former member of **Robert Jay Mathews**'s **The Order**, is in prison for killing a Missouri state highway trooper. Beam was the best man at the wedding.

Lyons has been active in most of the controversial cases involving extremists arrested for criminal offenses. After the sedition trial, he became active in the **Randall Weaver** case. Lyons tried to intervene on the side of the **Branch Davidians** during the siege in Waco. Shortly after the end of the Branch Davidian siege, Lyons filed a $520 million lawsuit against the U.S. government on behalf of relatives of those killed there. He was in charge of the legal appeal for **Tom Metzger**, head of the **White Aryan Resistance** (WAR), after Metzger was found liable for the actions of WAR-recruited skinheads in the killing of an Ethiopian immigrant in Portland, Oregon. He decided in the late 1990s to disband the CAUSE Foundation and replace it with the Southern Legal Resources Center. He has been providing legal counsel to various neo-Confederate groups, including the **League of the South**, in fighting attacks on the Confederate flag. **See also** Aryan Nations; CAUSE Foundation; Fort Smith Sedition Trial; League of the South.

Suggested readings: Susan Ladd and Stan Swofford, "Defender on the Right," *Greensboro News & Record* [N.C.] (June 26, 1995), p. B1; Southern Poverty Law Center, "In the Lyons Den," *Intelligence Report* 99 (Summer 2000): 18–23; David Ward, "Families' U.S. Lawyer Denies 'White Supremacist' Claims," *Guardian* [London] (January 26, 1995), p. 3.

M

Macheteros (Machete Wielders)

The Macheteros, or Machete Wielders, organization was a Puerto Rican independence terrorist group affiliated with the Fuerzas Armadas de Liberación Nacional Puertorriqueña (FALN). Filiberto Ojeda Rios founded the Macheteros in August 1978 to agitate for independence for Puerto Rico from the United States. Ojeda, who was born in 1933 in Barrio Rio de Naguabo, Puerto Rico, was a professional trombone player in Puerto Rico and New York City. In 1961 he joined the Cuban intelligence service, and his mission was to lead the Puerto Rican independence movement. His second in command was Juan Segarra Palmer, a Harvard University graduate and Puerto Rican nationalist. Ojeda and Segarra intended for the Macheteros to conduct operations in Puerto Rico and let the FALN operate in the United States. In their first operation the Macheteros randomly killed a policeman, Julio Rodriguez Rivera, on the beach at Naguabo, Puerto Rico, on August 24, 1978. American military installations in Puerto Rico were the main targets of bombings in 1979. An attack on a U.S. Navy bus on December 3, 1979, caused the death of two American sailors and the wounding of ten others. On January 12, 1981, members of the Macheteros destroyed eleven fighter planes at Muniz Air National Guard Base with a series of bombings.

The terrorist attacks conducted by the Macheteros were destructive and brought the group considerable public attention, but it was a Wells Fargo robbery that earned the group notoriety. On September 12, 1983, Victor Manuel Gerena, a guard for Wells Fargo in West Hartford, Connecticut, stole $7 million from a Wells Fargo depot. Gerena fled the United States with most of the money and was last reported living in Cuba. Segarra had recruited Gerena and planned the operation in detail. The funds allowed the Macheteros to buy protection and supplies. American authorities recovered only about $80,000 of the lost money.

The U.S. government used this robbery as an opportunity to destroy the Macheteros. In 1985 the government arrested nineteen members of the Macheteros. These individuals were charged with robbery of federally insured bank funds, theft from interstate shipment, and obstruction of commerce by robbery. In a series of trials lasting more than six years, fifteen members of the Macheteros were convicted of complicity in the robbery, including Ojeda and Segarra. Ojeda jumped bond in the late 1980s and disappeared underground. Segarra received a sentence of sixty-five years in prison and is still in a federal prison in Florida. He was not eligible for amnesty under President Clinton's guidelines for amnesty in 1999 because he refused to renounce the use of violence to bring about independence for Puerto Rico. Many Puerto Rican nationalists consider the Macheteros still in prison as heroes. **See also** Fuerzas Armadas de Liberación Nacional Puertorriqueña.

Suggested readings: Richard L. Madden, "Wells Fargo Robbery Case Takes a Long Route to Trial," *New York Times* (December 28, 1987), p. B1; Edmund Mahony, "Secret Tapings, Bickering Revolutionaries," *Hartford Courant* (November 13, 1999), p. A1; Edmund Mahony, "The Untold Tale of Victor Gerena," *Hartford Courant* (November 7, 1999), p. A1; Marisa Osorio Colon, "Motives Still Debated, 10 Years After Heist," *Hartford Courant* (September 12, 1993), p. A1; Jo Thomas, "Armed Puerto Rican Groups Focus Attacks on Military," *New York Times* (January 16, 1981), p. A13.

Malcolm X (1925–1965)

Malcolm X was the second most powerful leader after **Elijah Muhammad** in the **Nation of Islam** until his defection and assassination in 1965. He was born on May 19, 1925, with the name Malcolm Little in Omaha, Nebraska. Malcolm X's father was a Baptist minister and businessman. He was also a sympathizer of the political ideals of Marcus Garvey. After the family moved to Lansing, Michigan, local **Ku Klux Klan** members burned the family home. Not long after this incident, unknown white assailants murdered his father. After a period of living in abject poverty, the family of the mother and eleven children was separated, and Malcolm X was placed in an institution for boys. He attended a local public school until the eighth grade and then made his way to Harlem in New York City where he soon learned to operate in the Harlem underworld. Despite some financial success as a criminal, he found himself in prison on several occasions. During his last prison stay in 1947 at a maximum-security prison in Concord, Massachusetts, a fellow convict converted him to the Nation of Islam.

Malcolm X rose quickly within the hierarchy of the Nation of Islam. Despite having only an eighth-grade education, Malcolm X was intelligent, and he had educated himself by reading extensively while serving time in prison. He proved to be an exceptional speaker. By the mid-1950s, Malcolm X was one of the Nation of Islam's most important figures. He was made the head of the Boston Temple no. 11 where he recruited **Louis Farrakhan.** Elijah Muhammad later appointed Malcolm X to lead the important Harlem Temple no. 7 and to serve as the national spokesperson for the Nation of Islam. In return, Malcolm X was loyal to him and the Nation of Islam. Malcolm X was in total agreement with Elijah Muhammad's emphasis on uplifting the black community and his anti-white message.

In the early 1960s Malcolm X began to have reservations about the leadership of Elijah Muhammad. Malcolm X heard rumors of moral lapses of Elijah Muhammad with young women and a lifestyle that was out of character for the Nation of Islam. On his part Elijah Muhammad was receiving anti–Malcolm X advice from members of his inner circle who were jealous of Malcolm's high profile in the Nation of Islam. The first concrete evidence of these tensions was Malcolm X's ninety-day suspension over his caustic remark about "chickens coming to roost" regarding the assassination of President John F. Kennedy. In March 1964, Malcolm X seceded from the Nation of Islam and formed his own organization. He named the new organization the Muslim Mosque, and he also formed a secular wing, the Organization of Afro-American Unity. Malcolm X knew that the break with the Nation of Islam was a dangerous act. Whether with or without Elijah Muhammad's complicity, followers of the Nation of Islam assassinated Malcolm X on February 21, 1965. Neither at this time or later did Elijah Muhammad show remorse over Malcolm X's death.

Soon after Malcolm X's death, his reputation in the black community and on the national scene began to grow. Alex Haley published his autobiography, and soon a cult developed around Malcolm X and his ideas. Despite efforts of the leaders of the Nation of Islam to discredit him, Malcolm X's ideas to convert blacks to an orthodox version of Islam gained strength in the black community. **See also** Farrakhan, Louis; Muhammad, Elijah; Nation of Islam.

Suggested readings: Michael Eric Dyson, *Making Malcolm: The Myth and Meaning of Malcolm X* (New York: Oxford University Press, 1995); Peter Goldman, *The Death and Life of Malcolm X (New York*: Harper and Row, 1973); C. Eric Lincoln, *The Black Muslims in America*, 3d ed. (Grand Rapids, Mich.: William B. Eerdmans, 1995); Malcolm X and Alex Haley, *The Autobiography of Malcolm X* (Harmondsworth, U.K.: Penguin Books, 1968); Halasa Malu, *Elijah Muhammad: Religious Leader* (Los Angeles: Melrose Square Publishing, 1990); Bruce Perry, *Malcolm: The Life of a Man Who Changed Black America* (Barrytown, N.Y.: Station Hill Press, 1991).

Manson, Charles Milles (1934–   )

Charles Manson was the leader of a personality cult, the Family, which committed a series of ghastly murders. He was born on either November 11 or 12, 1934, in Cincinnati, Ohio. His father was unknown, but his mother, Kathleen Maddox, filed a bastardy suit in 1936 against a Colonel Scott and won compensation. She was only sixteen when Manson was born. During part of his youth, she served three years of a five-year term in prison for a 1939 armed robbery. Outside of prison, she was an alcoholic prostitute with little regard for her son. Manson was shifted from home to home before he was placed in the Gibault School for Boys, in Indiana, in 1942. He ran away from the school and supported himself by burglarizing businesses. After he was captured by the police when he was thirteen, he was sent to Father Flanagan's Boys Town, but he escaped after only four days. He resumed his crime spree but was caught again. This time he spent three years at the Indiana School for Boys at Plainfeld. At sixteen years of age, in 1951, Manson broke out of juvenile detention and, after stealing a car, robbed fifteen gas stations on his way to California. Captured

again in Utah, he was sent to the National Training School for Boys in Washington, D.C. Manson was transferred to several institutions over the next few years as a troublemaker until he modified his behavior and won parole in May 1954. During his terms in jail, he became an accomplished musician on both the violin and guitar. In 1955 he was married briefly and had a son. Manson found himself in legal trouble again after stealing automobiles, but he was given five years' probation. In 1956 he violated his parole and was sent to the Terminal Island Penitentiary in San Pedro, California, for three years. In September 1958, Manson was released from prison and placed on probation. His next legal problems were over pimping and check cashing incidents, but again authorities placed him on probation. Still unable to adjust, his probation was finally revoked, and he was sent to the U.S. penitentiary at McNeil Island, Washington. Manson was finally released from prison in March 1967.

After his release, Manson moved to San Francisco, California. He dabbled in several Satanic groups without becoming a member. He merged into the hippie lifestyle and started his own personality cult. Manson was able to attract a number of followers, mostly young women. Drugs and sex were the staples of life with Manson's Family. In 1969 he obtained access to the abandoned Spahn Movie Ranch outside of the Bay area. About fifty of his followers lived at the ranch at any one time. Manson tried to break into the pop music world as a singer guitarist, but he had little success. This failure appears to have embittered him against those individuals who had become successful. Manson was an admirer of Adolf Hitler, sharing with him the belief that the white race is superior to other races. Manson hated blacks and he had shot and wounded a black drug dealer, Bernard Crow, over a bad drug deal. He believed and expressed fear about the possibility of a race war breaking out. His greatest fear was that blacks would start and win the race war before whites had a chance to oppose them. Only by hiding from the race war

Convicted murderer Charles Manson stares at the parole board in San Quentin, California, on February 4, 1986. (AP Photo/Eric Risberg)

in Death Valley, California, could Manson and his followers survive this battle and benefit from it.

Using the term "Helter Skelter" from a Beatles song, Manson decided to initiate a race war. His first victim was Gary Hinman, a rich musician. Members of his team tortured him hoping to extort money from him before killing him. Next, Manson sent a four-person team of his followers to the home of film director Roman Polanski and his wife actress Sharon Tate on Friday, August 8, 1969, to murder them. Their instructions were to make the murders look like they were race related. Polanski was out of the country, but the team killed the five people who were at his home early on the morning of August 9. The victims were Sharon Tate, Abigail Folger, Voytek Frykowski, Jay Sebring, and Steven Earl Parent. Manson was upset over the gore at the murder scene and, on the next night, August 10, he went along with six other members to the residence of Leno La Bianca, a supermarket president. He and his wife, Rosemary, were stabbed to death. The last murder committed was that of a ranch hand, Donald "Shorty" Shea, who knew too much about the other killings.

Despite the publicity surrounding the murders, it took the police nearly a year to solve the cases. The confused natures of the crime scenes and misleading clues complicated the cases. Several days after the killings, members of the Manson gang were arrested for suspicion of auto theft, but the police were unaware of their connection with the murders. Manson and his cult were finally implicated in the crimes by Susan Atkins and arrested. Atkins, one of those arrested by the police on arson and auto theft charges, confessed to the murders to two cellmates, Ronnie Howard and Virginia Graham. Other tips came to the police, but the investigators were slow to believe the informers. The trial was a circus: Manson refused to cooperate with his lawyers and disrupted court proceedings. Key evidence came from one of his followers, Linda Kasabian, who turned state's evidence for a reduced sentence. At the end of the trial, which lasted nine and a half months and cost over a million dollars, Manson and his associates received the death penalty for seven murders. Manson also received a life sentence for the murders of Gary Hinman and Donald Shea in a subsequent trial. The 1972 abolishment of the death penalty in California caused these sentences to be reduced to life imprisonment. Manson is now serving seven life sentences with no possibility of parole. Despite serving life sentences, most of his women followers still swear allegiance to Manson and the Family.

Manson still manages to be a pest to prison authorities. In the mid-1990s, he was busy building a personal Web site. In the summer of 1997 he was caught dealing drugs. This transgression led to his transfer from Corcoran State Prison to the tougher, more austere Pelican Bay State Prison, where he was housed in a segregated security hous-ing unit. This punishment lasted for about a year before Manson was returned to the more relaxed Corcoran State Prison. **See also** Cults.

Suggested readings: Susan Atkins and Bob Slosser, *Children of Satan, Child of God* (Plainfield, N.J.: Logos International, 1977); Vincent Bugliosi and Curt Gentry, *Helter Skelter: The True Story of the Manson Murders* (New York: Norton, 1974); Charles Manson and Nuel Emmons, *Manson in His Own Words* (New York: Grove Press, 1986); Sara Moran, *The Secret World of Cults: From Ancient Druids to Heaven's Gate* (Godalming, U.K.: CLB International, 1999).

Martell, Clark Reid (1960–)

Clark Martell, an early leader of the American neo-Nazi skinhead movement, was born in 1960 and raised in Blue Island, Illinois. He dropped out of high school after failing. In 1979 he received a four-year prison sentence for an arson attack against a Hispanic family in Chicago. While in prison, Martell read Adolf Hitler's *Mein Kampf* and became a devoted fan of Hitler's ideas. After his release from prison in 1983, he joined the Chicago-based **American Nazi Party**. His job was drawing cartoons for the party's newsletter, *Public Voice*. He was arrested in September 1984 for defacing public property by painting swastikas. About this time, he started listening to the white power "Oi" music from Great Britain. After becoming a devotee of Skrewdriver, a British skinhead band, Martell formed his own racist skinhead group, Romantic Violence, in late 1984. Romantic Violence was the first organized group of **skinheads** in the United States. His group raised funds by selling Skrewdriver records and cassettes in the Chicago area. Martell also tried several times to interest Skrewdriver in an American tour. His skinhead group formed its own white power band, the Final Solution, in the spring of 1985. Martell began to align his small group with the American Nazi Party and with other national white supremacist groups. He held several meetings with **Rob-**

ert **Miles**, a former **Ku Klux Klan** and **Aryan Nations** leader, at Miles's home in Michigan.

Over the next three years, Martell led his Romantic Violence skinhead group in a campaign of violence in the Chicago area. His group assaulted six Hispanic women in 1987 alone. To celebrate the anniversary of Nazi Germany's *Kristallnacht* on November 9, 1987, Martell led Romantic Violence in trashing three Chicago-area synagogues. Other Jewish businesses were also attacked and vandalized. In December 1987, Martell assaulted his girlfriend in her apartment because she had talked with several African Americans on the street. Martell was arrested for these crimes in January 1988 and sentenced to a long prison term. Without his leadership, the Romantic Violence group disbanded. Most of his followers moved on to other skinhead groups in the Midwest. While Martell languishes in prison, other racist skinhead groups have formed and are even more violent than Romantic Violence. **See also** American Nazi Party; Miles, Robert; Neo-Nazis; Skinheads.

Suggested readings: Mark S. Hamm, *American Skinheads: The Criminology and Control of Hate Crime* (Westport, Conn: Praeger, 1993); Imre Karacs, "Skinhead Group Is Outlawed in Neo-Nazi Crackdown," *Independent* [London] (September 15, 2000), p. 16; National Desk, "6 Indicted in Attack with Racial Overtone," *New York Times* (February 21, 1988), sec. 1, p. 31.

Martinez, Thomas (1955–)

Thomas Martinez, a key figure in the radical white supremacist group **The Order**, was born in 1955 in Philadelphia, Pennsylvania. His father, of Spanish and Swedish heritage, worked as a routeman for a bakery. Martinez was the youngest of three boys. When his Philadelphia junior high school was integrated in 1967, the school became a racial battleground. Martinez attended Thomas Edison High School, but he left in the tenth grade after being threatened by members of a black gang. In 1973 he joined the U.S. Army to learn to be a baker, but instead the army assigned him to building bridges. He left the army after less than a year. Martinez found a job baking donuts and married his childhood sweetheart. This job lasted until he quit over the issue of insurance coverage.

Martinez's hatred of blacks led him to join extremist groups. In 1976 **David Duke**'s brand of **Ku Klux Klan** ideology attracted Martinez, and he joined the Knights of the Ku Klux Klan. He found a better job in a dye factory, but his Klan activities consumed a large portion of his time outside of work. Slowly, however, Martinez became disillusioned with the Klan and began to look for a group promising more action. In 1980 he turned to **William Pierce's National Alliance**. Martinez first met **Robert Jay Mathews** at the 1981 National Alliance Convention in Arlington, Virginia. He found the **anti-Semitism** at the conference disquieting because he was more anti-black than anti-Jewish. The refusal of Pierce to give him any financial help in the aftermath of his run-in with the law over ethnic slurs led him to leave the National Alliance in 1983.

Martinez was at loose ends until Mathews recruited him for The Order. Martinez has confessed that he was never a dedicated member of this group, but he considered himself a follower of Mathews. One of Martinez's first acts as a member of The Order was to pass some dye-damaged money from Mathews's Seattle bank robbery on December 20, 1983, in the Philadelphia area. Next, Mathews persuaded him to pass counterfeit money. Martinez had become uncomfortable with Mathews and his group after the assassination of Alan Berg, a Denver Jewish radio–talk show host, but he was involved too deeply to get out. On June 28, 1984, the police arrested Martinez for passing counterfeit money. Martinez then learned that Walter West, a member of the group, had been killed because members of The Order suspected that West might be talking to the wrong people. West's murder scared Martinez. Just before his scheduled trial in October 1984 for counterfeiting, Martinez decided to inform to the authorities about the activities of The Order. His information was a complete surprise to the FBI. Even with information gathered from Martinez, FBI agents had trouble locating Mathews and his followers. Martinez traveled to Idaho to help the FBI capture Mathews, but Mathews escaped. By this time, members of The Order suspected that Martinez had turned on them. After government agents killed Mathews in December 1984, word was put out in extremist circles that Martinez was to be killed. Martinez entered the Government Witness Protection Program, but he has continued to speak out against white supremacists. **See also** Mathews, Robert Jay; National Alliance; Order, The; Pierce, William.

Suggested readings: Associated Press, "Court Upholds Conviction of Neo-Nazi," *Los Angeles Times* (December 20, 1986), part 1, p. 36; Kevin Flynn and Gary Gerhardt, *The Silent Brotherhood: Inside America's Racist Underground* (New York: Free Press, 1989); Thomas Martinez and John Guinther, *Brotherhood of Murder: How One Man's Journey of Fear Brought The Order—The Most Dangerous Racist Gang in America—to Justice* (New York: McGraw-Hill, 1988).

Marx, Paul (1920–   )

Paul Marx, the former head and spiritual leader of the Catholic anti-abortion group **Human Life International**, was born on May 8, 1920, in Saint Michael, Minnesota. Marx is the fifteenth of seventeen children of a staunchly Catholic dairy farming family. He joined the Benedictine Order as a teenager in 1937. For years, he was a monk at St. John's Abbey in Collegeville, Minnesota. In 1957 Marx earned a doctorate in family sociology from the Catholic University of Washington, D.C.

Marx's concern over the evils of abortion and contraception led him to join a colleague, Father Matthew Habiger, in forming the Human Life Center in 1972. This organization has as its goal educating the public about the dangers of abortion, contraception, radical feminism, and sex education. Marx, who has a charismatic personality,

soon became the leader and principal spokesperson for the organization whose headquarters was in Gaithersburg, Maryland. In 1981 Marx renamed the group Human Life and redirected it to a more confrontational style of operations. At the same time, he established a good working relationship with **Randall Terry's Operation Rescue**. This affiliation and successful fundraising among Catholics soon made Human Life the most significant Catholic anti-abortion organization in the United States. In 1981 Marx renamed the group again—Human Life International (HLI)—to reflect his efforts to make opposition to abortion an international issue. By the mid-1990s, HLI had about 30,000 supporters and nearly $12 million in assets. In 1996 Marx moved the headquarters of HLI to Front Royal in the Shenandoah Valley of Virginia.

In his drive to build Human Life International, Marx earned a reputation as an anti-Semitic extremist because he has accused Jews and Muslims of supporting abortion as part of a war against Christian babies. These attacks have led Jewish leaders in the United States to accuse Marx and the HLI of leading an anti-Semitic crusade. While Marx has denied the anti-Semitic label, he has continued to attack Jewish abortion providers.

Marx lost control of the HLI in a power struggle in the late 1990s. Reverend Richard Welch, a priest in the Catholic Redemptorist Order, led a coup against Marx and replaced him as head of the organization. Welch has claimed that Marx retired because of ill health in 1999, but Marx's supporters have repudiated this explanation. They maintain that Marx's emphasis on direct action and his hard-line approach to abortion threatened Welch and his supporters. Marx now resides in retirement at a monastery in Minnesota. **See also** Anti-Abortion Movement; Human Life International.

Suggested readings: Peggy Curran, "You Can't Argue with Dogma," *Gazette* [Montreal] (April 20, 1995), p. A3; Bob Harvey, "They Love Him or Hate Him," *Ottawa Citizen* (February 22, 1992), p. J4; Caryle Murphy, "Family Values Feud; Catholic Nonprofit Embroiled in Leadership Dispute," *Washington Post* (April 8, 2000), B1; James Risen and Judy L. Thomas, *Wrath of Angels: The American Abortion War* (New York: Basic Books, 1998); Nolan Zavoral, "As Conference Opens, HLI Leader Returns to His Native State," *Star Tribune* [Minneapolis] (April 17, 1997), p. 9B.

Mathews, Robert Jay (1953–1984)

Robert Mathews, the founder and leader of the militant white supremacist group **The Order**, was born on January 16, 1953, in Marfa, Texas. His father served in the U.S. Air Force and then ran an appliance store in Marfa before the family moved to Arizona. In Arizona, his father worked for the Graham Paper Company and served in the U.S. Air Force Reserves. Mathews, who attended McClintock High School in Phoenix, was an average student in all subjects except history. He took up wrestling and weight lifting to control a juvenile weight problem. At an early age he found the ideas espoused by the **John Birch Society** and the Minutemen intriguing. Although he was raised in a Protestant church, Mathews joined the Church of Jesus Christ of Latter-Day Saints in his late teens. About the same time, he also became a member of an anti-tax group. Mathews failed to graduate from high school on schedule because he refused to complete an economics course that taught Keynesian economics. An application to attend West Point Military Academy was rejected after a background check indicated his membership in a tax-protest group in Arizona. Instead of attending a military school, Mathews, at age twenty-one, formed a small anti-communist group he named the Sons of Liberty. According to this group of young Mormons and survivalists, the federal income tax was a part of the hidden agenda of a Jewish international conspiracy to rule the world as outlined in the anti-Semitic *Protocols of the Elders of Zion* (1920). To support himself, he worked in a variety of low-paying jobs in the Phoenix area. He was arrested in July 1973 for tax evasion, but he received a six-month probation. By now Mathews was disillusioned by the lack of support from his fellow right-wingers and decided to leave Arizona.

Mathews moved to Metaline Falls, Washington, in July 1974, because he loved the countryside there. His parents moved with him after he promised to avoid further extremist political activity. During the day he worked at the Bunker Hill Mine and then at a cement plant, and in the evening he worked on his sixty-acre ranch. He married Debbie McGarity, and they adopted a son. He tried to make a living off his ranch, but he never found a way to make it profitable.

Mathews was unable to keep his promise to stay out of extremist politics, and he started experimenting with various groups. In 1980 he became intrigued with the ideas and program of **William Pierce**'s white supremacist **National Alliance**. This organization attracted Mathews because it seemed to have a stronger intellectual base than the other groups. Mathews was also fascinated with the anti-government story in Pierce's novel *The Turner Diaries* (1977) The idea in the novel that the federal government was under the control of the **ZOG** (**Zionist Occupied Government**) reinforced his anti-government beliefs. To make money and spread his beliefs, Mathews started distributing National Alliance literature. Soon he came under the influence of **Richard Girnt Butler**, the leader of the **Christian Identity** movement and the **Aryan Nations**. Although Mathews soon realized that Butler was not a man of action, Mathews adopted Butler's idea of a white homeland in the Pacific Northwest as his goal. While aspects of the Christian Identity doctrine attracted Mathews, he was more interested in the warrior ethos of **Odinism**, a modern derivative of the pagan beliefs of the Vikings, than in any form of Christianity. In 1983 his father died and Mathews devoted more time to his political causes. One of his first tasks was to build a barracks to house friends and supporters.

Mathews decided that he needed to mold his own unit to be able to undertake a campaign to destabilize the U.S. government. Using the resistance to the government scenario in *The Turner Diaries* as a blueprint, Mathews formed The Order in 1983 to conduct a full-scale military operation against the federal government. He also called his group the Silent Brotherhood, to reflect the unity within the group. While this group never had more than twelve active members at any one time, these members were willing to do whatever was necessary to carry out Mathews's plans, including bombings, murders, counterfeiting, and robberies. Their first operation was the robbery of a pornographic bookstore, the Worldwide Video Adult Bookstore, in Spokane, Washington, on October 28, 1983, which netted them $369. Another operation was printing counterfeit $50 bills at the Aryan Nations compound at **Hayden Lake**. When Butler found out about the counterfeiting, he banished Mathews from the compound. On December 20, 1983, Mathews robbed a bank in Seattle, the Innis Aden Branch of City Bank, and took away $25,000. Some of the money was damaged by an exploding package of red dye, but most was recoverable. **Thomas Martinez** passed the money in the Philadelphia area. Later, Mathews engineered the assassination of a Jewish Denver radio–talk show host, Alan Berg, on June 18, 1984, and a **Brink's armored car robbery** on July 15, 1984, which netted the group $3.6 million. Mathews made the mistake of leaving a weapon at the scene of the robbery, and federal authorities were able to trace it to him. Shortly after this armed robbery, Mathews was cornered on Whidbey Island, Washington, and in a shootout with federal law enforcement agents was killed on December 7, 1984. His barricaded house was incinerated after a magnesium-illuminated flare started a chain reaction of ammunition and grenades. His death in action against the federal government made him a martyr to the **white supremacist movement**. See also Brink's Armored Car Robbery; Lane, David; Martinez, Thomas; Order, The.

Suggested readings: James Coates, *Armed and Dangerous: The Rise of the Survivalist Right* (New York: Hill and Wang, 1987); Kevin Flynn and Gary Gerhardt, *The Silent Brotherhood: Inside America's Racist Underground* (New York: Free Press, 1989); Thomas Martinez and John Guinther, *Brotherhood of Murder: How One Man's Journey of Fear Brought The Order—The Most Dangerous Racist Gang in America—to Justice* (New York: McGraw-Hill, 1998).

May 19th Communist Organization (M19CO)

The May 19th Communist Organization (M19CO) succeeded the radical leftist **Weather Underground** of the early 1970s. This group was formed in 1978 out of an amalgamation of former supporters of Weather Underground. It was a unique organization inasmuch as nearly all of its members were white women. The leaders of the M19CO were **Marilyn Jean Buck**, a veteran of the **Students for a Democratic Society** (SDS) and Weather Underground; Judith A. Clark, a former Weather Underground activist; and **Kathy Boudin**, a former member of the Weather Underground. Leadership of the M19CO concluded an alliance with the **Black Liberation Army** (BLA) and the Puerto Rican national liberation group **Fuerzas Armadas de Liberación Nacional Puertorriqueña** (FALN). The first product of the alliance between the M19CO and the Black Liberation Army was the planning and execution of the prison escape of the BLA's Assata Shakur on November 2, 1978. These alliances were always informal, and M19CO members only rarely participated in BLA operations and never with the FALN.

The most spectacular and deadly operation of the M19CO was its participation with the BLA in the 1981 Brink's armored car robbery in Nyack, New York. Although the robbery netted them $1.6 million, the killing of a Brink's security guard and two state patrolmen unleashed the full power of the state against them. Several of its most active members were arrested, and the rest went underground. Like so many other radical leftist groups, the M19CO lost its appeal and faded away in the early 1980s. **See also** Black Liberation Army; Boudin, Kathy;

Buck, Marilyn Jean; Students for a Democratic Society; Weather Underground.

Suggested readings: John Castellucci, *The Big Dance: The Untold Story of Kathy Boudin and the Terrorist Family That Committed the Brink's Robbery Murders* (New York: Dodd, Mead, 1986); Arnold H. Lubasch, "Race Struggle Cited in Brink's Trial," *New York Times* (August 30, 1983), p. B3; Robert D. McFadden, "Brink's Holdup Spurs U.S. Inquiry on Links Among Terrorist Groups," *New York Times* (October 25, 1981), part 1, p. 1; Robert D. McFadden, "Fugitive in $1.6 Million Brink's Holdup Captured," *New York Times* (May 12, 1985), sec. 1, p. 1; Robert D. McFadden, "Issue of Conspiracy," *New York Times* (October 26, 1981), sec. B, p. 8; Brent L. Smith, *Terrorism in America: Pipe Bombs and Pipe Dreams* (Albany: State University of New York Press, 1994).

McDonald, Andrew (See Pierce, William)

McLamb, Gerald "Jack" (1944–)

Jack McLamb is a former Phoenix police officer who has become one of the leading exponents of the American militia movement. He was born in 1944. His involvement with the anti-government paramilitary group the **Arizona Patriots** in the early 1980s led to his retirement from the Phoenix Police Department in 1986. He then founded the organization Police Against the New World Order (PATNWO). His intent was to convince law enforcement officers of a world conspiracy to overturn American liberties. McLamb uses short-wave radio and a militia newsletter, *Aid and Abet Police Newsletter*, to spread his views. He also wrote a book *Operation Vampire Killer 2000; American Police Action, Plan for Stopping World Government Rule* in 1995. This book is his exposé of the purported **New World Order** and how it operates in the United States.

McLamb was active in the 1990s negotiating between extremists and the federal government. He is a close friend of **James B. "Bo" Gritz**, the former Green Beret officer and anti-government activist, and they worked together to negotiate the surrender

of **Randall Weaver** to end the **Ruby Ridge incident** in August 1992. In January 1994, McLamb again collaborated with Gritz in supporting Martin "Red" Beckman in his dispute with local law enforcement agents and the Internal Revenue Service in Billings, Montana. They were less successful with their negotiations with the Freemen in Montana in 1996. The Freemen rejected both McLamb and Gritz as spokespersons.

In the late 1990s, McLamb was a real estate developer near Kamiah, Idaho. The subdivision he developed, Doves of the Valley, is located near Bo Gritz's Almost Heaven subdivision. Both subdivisions appeal to individuals who are uncomfortable around federal government institutions. McLamb and Gritz continue to collaborate in anti-government activities. **See also** Gritz, James B. "Bo"; Freemen Movement; Militia Movement.

Suggested readings: Bill Hart, "How Can Folks So Wrong Have the Right Instincts?" *Phoenix Gazette* (July 18, 1996), p. B1; Russ Hemphill, "Former Officer Beats Police Again in Court," *Phoenix Gazette* (August 25, 1994), p. B1; Kevin McDermott, "Militia Negotiator Defends Police Actions in Standoff," *St. Louis Post-Dispatch* (October 15, 1997), p. 1B; Kim Murphy, "Year 2000; Survivalists Chaos 'Still Coming,' " *Los Angeles Times* (January 2, 2000), p. 28; Dee Norton, "Forged Letter Helps Open Door to Weaver's Surrender," *Seattle Times* (September 1, 1992), p. A1; David Pugliese, "Waiting for Armageddon," *Ottawa Citizen* (January 3, 1999), p. C3; Kenneth S. Stern, *A Force upon the Plain: The American Militia Movement and the Politics of Hate* (Norman: University of Oklahoma Press, 1996).

McLaren, Richard (1953–)

Richard McLaren was the leader of the most radical wing of the **Republic of Texas** movement which declared that Texas was an independent state since it had been illegally annexed to the United States. He was born on August 18, 1953, in Saint Louis, Missouri, but his mother and grandmother raised him in Wilmington, Ohio. While in the third grade, he wrote a book report on

Richard McLaren stands with an 1845 map of the Republic of Texas inside his home near Fort Davis, Texas, on March 6, 1997. McLaren sought to reestablish Texas as a sovereign nation based on the contention that Congress never legally annexed the Lone Star State in 1845. (AP Photo/Ron Heflin)

the Alamo that stimulated his interest in history. In 1972 he graduated from high school in Wilmington. In 1975 he married his high school sweetheart, and, in 1977, they moved to Fort Worth, Texas, where McLaren worked in a variety of jobs from carpentry to selling insurance. After deciding to go into

the wine-making business, McLaren and his wife moved to Fort Davis, Texas, in October 1979. Making wine in Fort Davis, however, was not a money-making proposition. McLaren bought some land, but in 1984 he informed the owner of the land that he no longer had to pay for the land because of a faulty claim to title. In a lawsuit, which took more than ten years to settle, McLaren won an out-of-court settlement in 1994. In the settlement, McLaren received twenty lots, two buildings, and $87,900 from the sale of other land. Near the end of the lawsuit in 1994, McLaren started the Fort Davis Mountain Land Commission. He claimed that, in his research of land claims, Texas had been illegally annexed to the United States. McLaren also started feuding with local government over its policies and restrictions.

McLaren used the claim of illegal annexation of Texas to launch the Republic of Texas movement in 1995. He wrote a letter to Texas Governor George W. Bush on September 18, 1995, informing him of the existence of the Republic of Texas and the steps it was taking to gain international recognition. At a convention of the Republic of Texas, John C. Van Kirk was selected president and McLaren was named ambassador-at-large. This arrangement lasted only a few months before a McLaren-backed faction ousted Van Kirk in March 1996. McLaren and his followers were more militant than Van Kirk, and they wanted to force the issue of independence. On March 6, 1996, McLaren drafted an order issued by the Republic of Texas common law court in Tarrant County, Texas, for Governor Bush to relinquish the governor's office. Republic of Texas followers started bombarding Texas courts with phony legal documents demanding the recognition of the Republic of Texas. On May 4, 1996, McLaren was arrested for contempt of court for refusing to obey federal laws. Efforts made by the Texas state government to restrain McLaren's financial dealings by court orders were ignored by McLaren. In the midst of his fight with the state of Texas, the executive board of the Republic of Texas removed McLaren from his post as ambassador-at-large on November 19, 1996. In December, both the federal government and the state of Texas made efforts to cite him for criminal acts.

Despite the growing list of charges against him, McLaren initiated the events of the Fort Davis standoff. He became infuriated when two of his supporters, Robert Jonathan Scheidt and Jo Anne Turner, were arrested in the first week of April 1997. Three Republic of Texas supporters, Gregg Paulson, Karen Paulson, and Franklin Keyes, seized Joe Rowe and his wife, Margaret Ann, on April 27 and held them hostage in their Fort Davis home to pressure Texas authorities to release Scheidt and Turner. McLaren started bargaining over the hostages, demanding the release of Scheidt and Turner and a referendum on Texas independence. Texas authorities traded Scheidt and Turner for the Rowes, because Joe Rowe had been injured and had a heart condition. Negotiations then opened for the surrender of McLaren and his supporters. Several times armed Republic of Texas followers were prevented from joining the McLaren group. Republic of Texas leaders, however, tried to persuade McLaren and his supporters to surrender. After a full week of the siege, McLaren surrendered to state of Texas and federal authorities on May 3. Only two members, Keyes and Mike Matson, another follower of McLaren, refused to surrender, and they attempted to retreat into the Davis Mountains. Several days later Matson was killed in a gunfight after killing one dog and wounding two others. Keyes was captured months later in east Texas.

McLaren's trial for his crimes started in October 1997. His trial was shifted to Brewster County, Texas, to ensure a fair verdict. McLaren refused to recognize the jurisdiction of the court and ignored his court-appointed lawyers. A jury convicted him of engaging in criminal activity. The judge sentenced him to ninety-nine years in prison and a $10,000 fine. This sentence was later overturned on appeal and the sentence vacated. McLaren is serving a fifteen-year sentence in the Huntsville State Prison on a fraud charge for phony liens. On August 8, 2001, McLaren pleaded guilty to one count of possessing explosives and faces an additional ten-year prison sentence. His conditional pleas leave an appeal of the sentence open, and McLaren has indicated that he will appeal this new sentence. **See also** Common Law Courts Movement, Freemen Movement; Republic of Texas.

Suggested readings: Mike Cox, *Stand-off in Texas: "Just Call Me a Spokesman for the DPS"* (Austin, Tex.: Eakin Press, 1998); Marla Dial, "Republic of Texas: McLaren's Defense, Demeanor Full of Contradictions," *San Angelo Standard-Times* (November 2, 1997), p. 1; Thaddeus Herrick, "Ranger's 'Tough Decision' Ended Standoff," *Houston Chronicle* (May 11, 1997), p. A1; Eduardo Montes, "Republic of Texas, Associates Are Sentenced," *Houston Chronicle* (November 5, 1997), p. A31; Evan Moore, "Portrait of Separatist: McLaren Is a Study in Contrasts/Midwestern Native Began His Obsession with Texas in 1970s," *Houston Chronicle* (May 4, 1997), p. 1; Richard Stewart, "Republic Movement Splintered," *Houston Chronicle* (March 9, 1997), p. A1; Robert G. Wieland, "Texas Separatist Leader Convicted," *Associated Press News Service* (April 15, 1998), p. 1.

McTaggart, David Fraser (1932–2001)

David McTaggart, the founder of the international environmental organization **Greenpeace** International, was born on June 23, 1932, in Vancouver, British Columbia. As a teenager in Vancouver, he played a variety of sports and was the Canadian national badminton champion three times. He left school when he was seventeen and became a forestry worker before forming a construction business. His construction firm was financially successful until a 1969 ski lodge accident in Bear Mountain, east of San Francisco. This uninsured accident forced his company into bankruptcy. McTaggart escaped his financial problems by sailing in the South Pacific on a thirty-eight-foot ketch for three years.

In 1979 McTaggart formed the Greenpeace organization. He had seen an advertisement for volunteers for the Don't Make a Wave committee in 1972. Renaming his ketch, Greenpeace III, McTaggart joined others in a protest against French nuclear testing at the Polynesian atoll of Muroroa. During several confrontations with the

French navy, McTaggart was beaten up and his right eye was damaged permanently. In 1979 McTaggart and a colleague, Patrick Moore, formed the alliance of Greenpeace International. McTaggart became its first chairperson.

McTaggart was an activist leader. Besides leading demonstrations against French nuclear testing, he launched campaigns to save the whales, end the dumping of nuclear waste in the ocean, and protect the Antarctic continent from oil and mineral exploitation. McTaggart remained head of Greenpeace International until 1991. He retired to an olive-producing estate in Paciano, Italy. His interest in Greenpeace remained constant, and, on occasion, he participated in demonstrations. One of his last protests was against French underground nuclear tests on Muroroa in the South Pacific in the mid-1990s. McTaggart remained the head of the activist wing of Greenpeace International until his death in an automobile crash near Castiglione del Lago, Italy, on March 23, 2001. **See also** Greenpeace; Radical Environmentalism.

Suggested readings: Paul Brown, "David McTaggart: Campaigner Who Led from the Front in Making Greenpeace a Worldwide Organization," *Guardian* [London] (March 26, 2001), p. 22; Margarette Driscoll, "Green Pirates Deserted; Death of Co-Founder Signals Greenpeace's Gradual Shift Away from Its Radical Roots," *Gazette* [Montreal] (April 1, 2001), p. A5; Lynda Hurst, "The Rainbow Returns," *Toronto Star* (July 23, 1995), p. F1; Geoffrey Lean, "Greenpeace 'Fatcat' Leaders Condemned by Founders," *Independent* [London] (November 3, 1996), p. 1; Tony Samstag, "The Greening of the World," *Times* [London] (September 26, 1985), p. 1; Nicolaas van Rijin, "Greenpeace Visionary 'Shook World,'" *Toronto Star* (March 24, 2001), p. 1.

McVeigh, Timothy James (1968–2001)

Timothy McVeigh achieved infamy for his role in the bombing of the Alfred P. Murrah Federal Building in Oklahoma City, Oklahoma. He was born on April 23, 1968, in Pendleton, New York. His father worked

Timothy James McVeigh is escorted from the Noble County Courthouse in Perry, Oklahoma, on April 21, 1995. (AP Photo/David Longstreath)

in a radiator assembly plant in Lockport, New York, and his mother was a travel agent. His family was Catholic. When McVeigh was in high school, his mother left his father and moved to Florida. She returned later to New York, but they divorced in 1985. The separation was very hard for McVeigh, and he was never close to his mother. While he was attending Starpoint High School in Pendleton, where he was a good student, he showed an interest in guns and in survival training. After working at a local fast food restaurant, he left home to go to Bryant and Stratton College, a two-year business school in Williamsville, New York, to study computer programming, but he left school after only a semester. It was at this time that McVeigh started reading white supremacist **William Pierce's** *The Turner Diaries*, (1978). After obtaining a gun permit, McVeigh found a job in 1987 at the Burke Armored Car Service in Buffalo, New York. Still unable to settle down, McVeigh joined the U.S. Army on May 24, 1988.

McVeigh was an instant success in the military. He was in his element in the army, and he enjoyed the training, especially the weapons exercises. His military duty was serving as a gunner on a Bradley fighting vehicle. In the periodic weapons tests, he proved himself by far the best gunner in the unit. In September 1990, McVeigh reenlisted for another four-year tour of duty. McVeigh was so outstanding as a soldier that he was rapidly promoted in rank. In January 1991, McVeigh was sent to serve in the Persian Gulf War as part of Task Force Ranger, Charlie Company, 2nd Battalion, 16th Infantry, 1st Infantry Division. While in Saudi Arabia, McVeigh was promoted to sergeant. McVeigh performed admirably under fire and won several decorations for his role in heavy fighting, but he also found out that killing others was a distasteful business.

After his return from the Gulf War, McVeigh entered Special Forces training. He had always dreamed of becoming a Green Beret. No longer in peak physical and mental condition because of the war, he had an option to delay his entry into the program, but his eagerness caused him to turn down this delay. McVeigh was unable to handle the physical demands of the program and dropped out after the second day. This reverse was so devastating that McVeigh decided to leave the army. During his tour of duty in the army, he had been exposed to anti-government propaganda. He had become a devoted fan of the right-wing magazine *Soldier of Fortune*. His favorite reading material continued to be *The Turner Diaries*, and he began selling copies of it to others. He briefly joined the **Ku Klux Klan**. Earlier he had become friends with two soldiers, **Terry Lynn Nichols** and Michael Fortier, both of whom disliked the army and were hostile toward the federal government. In 1991 McVeigh left the army.

McVeigh returned to civilian life disillusioned and looking for a purpose in life. After failing to find a computer-related job, he was forced to take the same job that he had had before joining the army as a private security guard in Buffalo, New York, with the Burke Armored Car Service. McVeigh remained resentful about how he was treated in the army, but he joined the National Guard's 174th Infantry to earn extra money. Soon he became upset about gun control legislation under consideration in the U.S. Congress. Unhappy with what he considered the liberal attitudes of his co-workers, he quit his security job and started making the rounds of the gun shows talking with other anti-government activists. Over the next two years, he attended about eighty gun shows. Two incidents, the Brady Gun Control Bill and the **Ruby Ridge incident**, proved to McVeigh that the federal government was conspiring against its citizens.

The culminating event that turned McVeigh to anti-government violence was the **Branch Davidian** siege. McVeigh traveled to Waco in March 1993 to witness the standoff between federal agents and **David Koresh**'s Branch Davidians. He sympathized with the Branch Davidians in their struggle against the federal government and made public statements supporting them. By the end of the siege on April 19, 1993, McVeigh was staying at the Nichols farm in northern Michigan. After the final confrontation, McVeigh started collecting anti-government propaganda about the Branch Davidians, including Linda Thompson's video, *Waco, the Big Lie*. He became obsessed with Waco and the adults and children killed there.

McVeigh's obsession turned to a desire for revenge against the federal government and its agents. He started talking to Nichols and Fortier about blowing up a federal building on the second anniversary of the Branch Davidian tragedy. In the meantime, McVeigh lived in Kingman, Arizona, working at small jobs and traveling to gun shows. He decided to start collecting explosives to build a large bomb. He traveled to Kansas and Texas to collect a large supply of ammonium nitrate fertilizer and three barrels of nitromethane racing fuel.

McVeigh selected the Alfred P. Murrah Federal Building in Oklahoma City because he believed that the orders for the attack on the Branch Davidians came from officials in this building. To him, no federal employee was guiltless. On April 15, 1995, McVeigh rented a twenty-foot Ryder truck in Junction City, Kansas. On April 18, McVeigh met Terry Nichols, and they mixed the fertilizer and racing fuel to make a huge bomb, which was to be detonated by blasting caps and dynamite. Later that evening, McVeigh started on his trip to Oklahoma City.

On the morning of April 19, 1995, the Alfred P. Murrah Federal Building exploded. McVeigh had parked the truck in front of the building near a circle drive. Several people noticed the truck, but nothing about it was suspicious. The bomb exploded at 9:02 A.M. and killed 168 persons: 149 adults and 19 children. Hundreds more were injured and maimed. For the next several days, efforts were made to find survivors, but none were found in the wreckage of the building. The devastation was so complete that the building had to be bulldozed and the area cleared.

During his escape from Oklahoma City, McVeigh made a stupid mistake. An Oklahoma State Highway Patrol trooper, Charlie Hanger, noticed that McVeigh's 1977 Mercury Marquis lacked a license plate. When he stopped McVeigh for this infraction, Hanger noticed that the car contained a weapon: a Glock handgun. He arrested McVeigh and booked him into the Perry County Jail. At first, it was rumored that the explosion was the work of international terrorists, and attention was focused on a Palestinian American living in Oklahoma City. It was only after the investigators found a truck axle that attention turned toward a white American male. Within two days, the FBI had identified McVeigh as the bomber and located him in the Oklahoma jail.

McVeigh spent the next year in a federal penitentiary in El Reno, Oklahoma, while federal agents prepared their case against him. On April 17, 1995, a preliminary hearing was held in El Reno and government witnesses produced enough evidence to connect McVeigh with the crime. Two federal public defenders excused themselves from

defending McVeigh because they knew many of the victims of the bombing. Stephen Jones, a prominent Republican politician and lawyer from Enid, Oklahoma, assumed the task of defending McVeigh. In the meantime, an army of FBI agents combed the country gathering evidence for the forthcoming trial. They questioned Nichols, Fortier, McVeigh's father, James and sister, Jennifer, and slowly they built their case. On August 10, 1995, a federal grand jury indicted McVeigh and Nichols in an eleven-count conspiracy case for the bombing. Fortier pleaded guilty for the offense of prior knowledge of the planning of the crime and received a twenty-three-year prison sentence.

McVeigh's trial took place in Denver, Colorado, in 1997. Judge Richard P. Matsch presided over the trial. One of his first rulings was to grant McVeigh and Nichols separate trials. In the months preceding the trial, McVeigh's lawyer tried to tie the bombing to a mysterious unknown person, John Doe, or a conspiracy among other right-wing extremists. The trial started on May 27 and lasted for nine weeks. Despite attempts to blame others, the jury issued a guilty verdict against McVeigh on August 30. In the penalty phase of the trial, the jury gave McVeigh the death penalty. McVeigh was held in prison pending mandatory appeals of the death sentence. The state of Oklahoma also contemplated holding a state murder trial for McVeigh. McVeigh was scheduled for execution on May 16, 2001, but news about the failure of the FBI to disclose interview material caused Attorney General John Ashcroft to postpone the execution until June 2001. He was executed by lethal injection at the federal prison in Terre Haute, Indiana, on June 11, 2001. His execution was a relief to many of the families of the victims of the Oklahoma bombing, but it was controversial in other circles from anti–capital punishment advocates to anti-government sympathizers. **See also** Militia Movement; Oklahoma City Bombing; Nichols, Terry Lynn.

Suggested readings: Kim Bobb, "McVeigh

Russell Means, of the American Indian Movement, testified before a special investigative committee of the Senate Select Committee on Capitol Hill. (AP Photo/Marcy Nighswander)

Without Remorse As Execution Carried Out," *Houston Chronicle* (June 12, 2001), p. A1; Ann Hull, "McVeigh's Road to Oklahoma City," *St. Petersburg Times* (March 30, 1997), p. 1A. Lou Michel and Dan Herbeck, *American Terrorist: Timothy McVeigh and the Oklahoma City Bombing* (New York: ReganBooks, 2001); Richard A. Serrano, *One of Ours: Timothy McVeigh and the Oklahoma Bombing* (New York: Norton, 1998); Richard A. Serrano, "What Created Timothy McVeigh?" *Newsday* [New York City] (June 11, 2001), p. A5; Crocker Stephenson, "Death of a Terrorist, Legacies of the Victims," *Milwaukee Journal Sentinel* (June 11, 2001), p. 1A.

Means, Russell (1939–)

Russell Means, one of the principal leaders of the militant **American Indian Movement** (AIM), was born on November 10, 1939, at Porcupine on the Sioux Pine Ridge Reservation in South Dakota. His father was an Oglala Sioux and his mother a Yankton Sioux, but in the Sioux culture he was raised as a Yankton. Shortly after his birth, his family moved to northern California where his father worked at the Mare Island Naval Shipyard. After the war, his family moved briefly back to Huron, South Dakota, before returning to California. Means and his brothers attended schools in both Vallejo and San Leandro. He was always in trouble, often for dealing drugs, but he graduated from San Leandro High School in 1958. After leaving school, he traveled around California working at odd jobs and married a Hopi woman. Although Means went to several business schools and colleges and acquired some computer expertise, he never earned a degree. He also earned a reputation for engaging in barroom brawls. In 1967 he obtained a job as director of the management information systems office in the Community Action Program office at the Sioux

Rosebud Reservation. In 1968 he left Rosebud for a position as director of the American Indian Center in Cleveland, Ohio.

The leadership of the new American Indian Movement recruited Means for their growing organization. Means embraced AIM and its policies enthusiastically and was soon appointed national field coordinator for AIM. His being a member of the Sioux tribe helped make AIM more than a local Indian movement. Means seized on the chance to advance both the Indian cause and his own ambitions. In February 1972, he became embroiled in the aftermath of the killing of Raymond Yellow Thunder in Gordon, Nebraska. Means led a caravan throughout Nebraska protesting the lack of punishment of the killers. The police chief was fired in the aftermath of the protests. Next, Means became one of the chief leaders of the Wounded Knee standoff in February 1973. Means and AIM challenged both the FBI and tribal leaders for sovereignty of the Rosebud Reservation. He proclaimed the establishment of a sovereign nation for the Sioux and demanded recognition of its sovereignty by the federal government. Casualties of the standoff were two dead Indians and a paralyzed federal marshal. Means was tried in a federal court for his participation in the Wounded Knee standoff, but the judge dismissed the case because of federal prosecutor misconduct.

Means tried the political approach in the Indian movement, but he was unsuccessful. He ran for tribal chief of the Sioux against the government-sponsored Richard Wilson and lost in a close election. Although there were charges of voter fraud, the Bureau of Indian Affairs (BIA) accepted the election. Wilson retaliated against the dissidents, and a BIA official shot Means. Means recovered from his gunshot wound and for the next seven years agitated against both the federal and tribal governments. His reward was a one-year jail sentence for assault. Means sued the federal government in 1981 over lost Sioux lands in the Black Hills. In 1988 he left his leadership post in AIM and moved to California. In his subsequent career in the movies he has had several good roles, including Chingachook in the movie *Last of the Mohicans*. Means's career as an extremist for Indian causes slowed down in the 1990s, but during the turbulent 1970s he was one of AIM's most effective leaders. **See also** American Indian Movement; Banks, Dennis.

Suggested readings: Russell Means and Marvin J. Wolf, *Where White Men Fear to Tread: The Autobiography of Russell Means* (New York: St. Martin's Griffin, 1995); Paul Chaat Smith and Robert Allen Warrior, *Like a Hurricane: The Indian Movement from Alcatraz to Wounded Knee* (New York: New Press, 1996); Kate Zernike, "Champion of the American Indian Threatens Hard-Won Autonomy," *Boston Globe* (February 6, 1999), p. A1.

Metzger, Tom (1938–)

Tom Metzger, the leader of the American white supremacist group the **White Aryan Resistance** (WAR), was born in April 1938 and raised in Warsaw, Indiana. After his parents divorced, Metzger lived with his mother and stepfather in northern Indiana; his father, an engineer, lived on the West Coast. After graduating from high school, Metzger served in the U.S. Army until 1961. Before turning to politics, Metzger made a living as a television repairman running a small electronics firm. After starting out as a conservative Republican, he moved first to the **John Birch Society** and then to the **Ku Klux Klan**. In the mid-1950s, Metzger attended **William Potter Gale**'s church where he learned about the **Christian Identity** dogma of white supremacy. He became the head of **David Duke**'s Knights of the Ku Klux Klan in California. In 1981 he started his own Ku Klux Klan group. In the midst of this organizing activity, Metzger ran for public office beginning with the race for San Diego County Supervisor in 1978 and culminating in a race for the Democratic nomination for the U.S. Senate in 1982. His first confrontation with the federal government was with the Internal Revenue Service (IRS) over his withholding of income taxes. His dispute with the IRS lasted over a decade before it was finally resolved in favor of the federal government.

Metzger decided in 1982 to form a revolutionary white supremacist party. His first name for the party was the White American Political Association (WAPA), but he soon renamed it the White Aryan Resistance (WAR). He intended this group to serve as the spearhead of a national **white supremacist movement**. While most of his organizing activities have been conducted in Southern California, Metzger has been active establishing branches elsewhere. His organization publishes a newsletter, *War!*, which provides a forum for its propaganda. Metzger has been effective in publicizing his party through television appearances and educational videos. He was able to gain access to a public access channel, Channel 38, in Southern California and produced a video program titled *Race and Reason*. His followers then pressured other public-access channels around the county to air the program. Critics have described him as being the most cynical and most dangerous of the white supremacist leaders. Metzger differs from other white supremacists in rejecting the basic tenets of the Christian Identity church. Instead, he considers himself the champion of the Third Force, which is racism oriented toward attracting the white working class and is anti-capitalist in orientation. Metzger believes in racial separation within designated areas for different racial groups, except for the Asian Americans who would be expelled.

Metzger has tried to make WAR into a mass movement, and he decided to recruit racial **skinheads** for their combination of energy and propensity for violence. This propensity for violence, however, has led Metzger into legal problems. Three skinhead members of WAR assaulted and killed an Ethiopian man, Mulugeta Seraw, in Portland, Oregon, in November 1988. Lawyers from the Southern Poverty Law Center's **Klanwatch** sued Metzger and his son for $10 million in 1989. Using the testimony from members of WAR, the lawyers proved that

Metzger was liable for the assault. In October 1990, a jury awarded Seraw's family $12 million in damages. Tom Metzger found himself owing $3 million, his son John $4 million, and WAR the rest of the judgment. This judgment has hurt Metzger and WAR, but he still is actively promoting his white supremacist views. In August 1991, Metzger and several co-defendants were convicted of participating in an illegal cross burning in Los Angeles in December 1989. While Metzger received only a six-month jail term, his efforts to disassociate himself from his fellow defendants hurt his stature in the white supremacist movement. After losing an appeal in 1993, his home and other assets were seized to pay the 1990 judgment. He continues to be a significant leader in the neo-Nazi movement, but most of his influence remains in Southern California. **See also** Klanwatch; Ku Klux Klan; Skinheads; White Aryan Resistance; White Supremacist Movement.

Suggested readings: Vincent Coppola, *Dragons of God: A Journey Through Far-Right America* (Atlanta: Longstreet Press, 1996); Morris Dees and Steve Fiffer, *Hate on Trial: The Case Against America's Most Dangerous Neo-Nazi* (New York: Villard Books, 1993); Raphael S. Ezekiel, *The Racist Mind: Portraits of American Neo-Nazis and Klansmen* (New York: Penguin Books, 1995); John M. Glionna, "Unfavorite Son," *Los Angeles Times* (October 30, 1990), p. E1; Michael Granberry, "Film Spurs Review of Metzger's Probation," *Los Angeles Times* (June 5, 1992), p. B1; Richard A. Serrano, "Anti-Racists View Metzger as a Top White Supremacist," *Los Angeles Times* (February 27, 1988), part 2, p. 1; Richard A. Serrano, "Metzger Must Pay $5 Million in Rights Death," *Los Angeles Times* (October 23, 1990), p. A1; Mary William Walsh and Lee Romney, "Canada Deports Metzgers Back to U.S.," *Los Angeles Times* (July 3, 1992), p. B1.

Michigan Militia

The Michigan Militia, one of the largest, most active anti-government militia groups, was founded in April 1994 by Ray Southwell, a Michigan real estate agent, and the Reverend Norman Olson, a Baptist minister and gun store owner. They first consulted with **John Ernest Trochmann**, the head of the **Militia of Montana**, about organizational structure. Olson was the early commander general and spokesperson for the Michigan Militia. His outspoken anti-government views caused so much controversy that, in 1995, he was asked to resign from his post. Lynn Van Hizen replaced Olson as the commander general. Van Hizen expresses more moderate views, but members of the Michigan Militia still campaign for complete freedom to own and use guns, an end to immigration, and a more conservative orientation for society. At its peak in the mid-1990s, the Michigan Militia had between 6,000 and 7,000 members. Members train twice monthly and conduct live-fire exercises. Nearly all of Michigan's counties have militia units in them. The nickname of the Michigan Militia is the Wolverine.

The Michigan Militia has received considerable negative publicity. Olson's outspokenness and his violent anti-government rhetoric have brought him to the attention of the national news and have alienated national and state government officials. The militia has also suffered from its association with **Timothy James McVeigh** and **Terry Lynn Nichols**. Although the leadership of the Michigan Militia claims that McVeigh was never a member, his attendance at Michigan Militia meetings has proved to be an embarrassment.

Another instance of negative publicity has been the militancy of Michigan Militia member Mark Koernke. Koernke, a janitor at the University of Michigan, has used short-wave radio broadcasts as "Mark from Michigan" to promote his anti-government views. His charges against the U.S. government, his conspiracy theory about the United Nations, and his attacks on One World Government have attracted the attention of federal authorities. In response to this attention, Koernke has gone into hiding. Since then, Koernke has broken with the Michigan Militia and has formed his Michigan Militia at Large. He now travels around the country speaking at militia gatherings and has been busy avoiding legal problems.

Suggested readings: Morris Dees and James Corcoran, *Gathering Storm: America's Militia Threat* (New York: HarperCollins, 1996); Neil A. Hamilton, *Militias in America: A Reference Handbook* (Santa Barbara, Calif.: ABC-CLIO, 1996); Kathy Marks, *Faces of Right Wing Extremism* (Boston: Branden Publishing, 1966); Tom Rhodes, "Michigan Militia Joins Up with FBI to Fight Anarchy," *Sunday Times* [London] (August 15, 1999), p. 1; Kenneth S. Stern, *A Force upon the Plain: The American Militia Movement and the Politics of Hate* (Norman: University of Oklahoma Press, 1996); Maryann Struman, "He's 'Mark from Michigan'; Janitor, Far-Right's Point Man," *Detroit News* (August 20, 1995), p. A1.

Mid-Western Bank Bandits (See Aryan Republican Army)

Miles, Robert (1925–1992)

Robert Miles, a national leader in the **white supremacist movement** in the United States, was born in 1925 in Bridgeport, Connecticut. His father was an autoworker. Miles served as a radioman on small planes operating with the Free French Resistance during World War II. After the United States entered the war, Miles joined the U.S. Navy and participated as a radio operator in the Pacific Theater. In the immediate postwar period, he trained Ukranian anti-communists in radio procedures for the Ukranian resistance movement. Miles worked as an engineer before becoming an insurance executive. He left his job as an insurance company branch manager in 1970 to devote all of his energies to racist politics. At first, he was a member of the Michigan Republican Party, but he resigned from the party after the Detroit race riots of 1967. Miles served as a campaign manager for George Wallace in Michigan before becoming the grand dragon of the **Ku Klux Klan** for Michigan in 1969.

Miles found traditional party politics unsatisfactory and moved deeper into extremist politics. Soon he joined the ranks of the white supremacists and turned to violence. Miles served six years of a nine-year prison sentence in a Marion, Indiana prison for burning several school buses in 1971 and for tarring and feathering a school principal to express his hatred of busing for racial equality in the Pontiac School District in Pontiac, Michigan. While in prison, he recruited prisoners to the white supremacist movement. After his release from prison in 1979, Miles continued his efforts to attract adherents to the white supremacy cause. Terms of his probation were for him to end his association with the Ku Klux Klan, but this prohibition let him associate with other extremist groups. He started a newsletter, *Behind the Bar . . . the Star!*, for prisoners and mailed thousands of newsletters to inmates monthly.

After the end of his prison term and probation, Miles settled in the small rural community of Cahoctah outside of Flint, Michigan. On his seventy-acre farm he avoided any direct association with violence, but he advised other extremists on policies to pursue. He continued to develop ties among the various white racist groups. Because he was always an effective speaker and writer, his influence increased in the white supremacist movement. Among his contributions was the adoption of the strategy that national leaders eschew violence but promote others to take action. In the mid-1980s, Miles converted to the **Christian Identity** church and started a branch, the Identity Mountain Church, in Cahoctah. He devoted most of his activities in the white supremacy movement to unifying it around certain principles. Miles died in 1992. See also Aryan Brotherhood; Aryan Nations; Christian Identity; Ku Klux Klan.

Suggested readings: Wayne King, "Racist Aryan Nations Group Inducts New Disciples," *New York Times* (October 20, 1985), part 1, p. 31; Wayne King, "White Supremacists Voice Support of Farrakhan," *New York Times* (October 12, 1985), sec. 1, p. 12; James Ridgeway, *Blood in the Face: The Ku Klux Klan, Aryan Nations, Nazi Skinheads, and the Rise of a New*

White Culture (New York: Thunder's Mouth Press, 1990); Brent L. Smith, *Terrorism in America: Pipe Bombs and Pipe Dreams* (Albany: State University of New York Press, 1994); Sam Walker, "Michigan Town Battles Image of Racism," *Christian Science Monitor* (October 3, 1994), p. 7.

Militia Movement

The modern militia movement is a protest movement against the U.S. government. Militias have existed in America since colonial days. These early militias were armed, local, self-protection forces called into service to defend against local threats, primarily Indian attacks. Later, militia units were formed to defend the colonists against the British. In most respects, the original Continental Army during the American Revolution was an amalgamation of militia units turned into a regular army by General George Washington and his staff. During the Civil War, local militias were turned into regular army forces on both the Confederate and Union sides. This tradition of armed volunteers ready to defend against real or perceived tyranny has been a mainstay of American history.

The framers of the Constitution recognized the importance of maintaining a regulated, armed militia in the Second Amendment of the Constitution's Bill of Rights. This right to bear arms and the right for a militia force to exist have passed down to the present day. Most of the debate has been over whether militias fall under state and local control, or reside as a right of private citizens to form private militias. Constitutional scholars have opted for governmental control, but others have insisted on the right of private militias to be established to guard against real or perceived tyranny by federal, state, or local governments. In 1960 **Robert Bolivar DePugh** organized a militia organization, the Minutemen, to fight first against a communist invasion of the United States and then against a potential communist takeover of the U.S. government. His militia group became so radical and violence prone that fed-

Norman Olson, right, Michigan Militia leader, carrying a stuffed animal and a Bible, walks with Ray Southwell, as they approach an FBI roadblock to the restricted area around the Montana Freemen's compound outside Jordan, Montana, on April 17, 1996. Olson and Southwell were denied entrance to the restricted area. (AP Photo/Jack Smith)

eral authorities suppressed it. In the end, the leaders of the **Minutemen movement** came to consider the federal government the main enemy.

The militia movement reemerged in the early 1990s in the guise of an anti-government instrument. Extremist leaders had long been hostile to the U.S. government, but it took two incidents—the death of Posse Comitatus leader **Gordon Kahl** in Arkansas in 1983 and deaths in the **Randall Weaver** family at Ruby Ridge in Montana in 1992—to overlook their differences and unite against the government. In a meeting of 160 extremist leaders held in Estes Park, Colorado, in October 1992, a decision was made to form militia organizations in all of the states. These paramilitary organizations would have separate identities, but the aim of all was to prepare to defend their liberties against a hostile federal government. The most important of the new militias was the **Militia of Montana** (MOM) under **John Ernest Trochmann**. Besides being one of the first, MOM has been one of the more militant of the militia groups. Trochmann has used it to spread pro-militia literature around the country. By 1997 the Southern Poverty Law Center, an anti-Klan and anti-extremist watchdog organization, estimated that there were 858 militia groups active in the United States. These militias are private armies run by self-appointed generals. Opposition to federal gun control, taxes, regulations, and environmental policies ties these groups together. All of these beliefs combine into perceived federal attacks on constitutional issues. Militia members share anger over the economic hardships in rural America imposed by the new global economy and hostility toward societal gains made by minority groups. The peak of the militia movement was in 1996; the total number of groups had dropped to 435 in 1998. The Southern Poverty Law Center reported that the number of militia groups has continued to fall in 2001, but other reports indicate that the militia movement is consolidating its most hard-core followers. **See also** Estes Park Meeting; DePugh, Robert Bolivar; Militia of Montana; Minutemen Movement; Trochmann, John Ernest.

Suggested readings: Paul Brinkley and Rich Robertson, "Militia Movement Carries Weapons and Deep Grudges," *Arizona Republic* (April 23, 1995), p. A1; Charles P. Cozic, *The Militia Movement* (San Diego: Greenhaven Press, 1997); Morris Dees and James Corcoran, *Gathering Storm: America's Militia Threat* (New York: HarperCollins, 1996); John M. Goshko and Anne Swardson, "Militias, an Angry Mix Hostile to Government, Waco, Idaho Confrontations Aid Recruiting," *Washington Post* (April 23, 1995), p. A1; Robert L. Snow, *The Militia Threat: Terrorists Among Us* (New York: Plenum Trade,

1999); Southern Poverty Law Center, "The World of Patriots," *SPLC Intelligence Report* 94 (Spring 1999): 10–11; Catherine McNicol Stock, *Rural Radicals: Righteous Rage in the American Grain* (Ithaca, N.Y.: Cornell University Press, 1996).

Militia of Montana (MOM)

The largest and most prominent of the modern American militia organizations is the Militia of Montana (MOM). **John Ernest Trochmann**; his brother, David Trochmann; his nephew, Randy Trochmann; and John's wife, Carolyn Trochmann, formed the Militia of Montana on January 1, 1994 in the aftermath of the **Ruby Ridge incident**. Both Trochmann and his wife were friends of **Randall Weaver** and supported him and his family during the government siege. John Trochmann had initiated ties earlier with **Richard Girnt Butler**'s **Aryan Nations**, but he decided that MOM needed to be more in the mainstream of American politics. He followed the militia model recommended at the 1992 **Estes Park meeting** calling for a mass movement with small direct-action cells. The leadership of MOM proposed that the organization be composed of semiautonomous cells of no more than seven members. Cells that recruited more than seven members were to split off and form new cells. Organizational structure is explained in the organization's manual, the *Blue Book*.

Almost from its beginnings, MOM has been the leading militia organization and it has helped others form militia groups. The Trochmanns operated MOM out of Noxon, Montana, about fifty miles from Ruby Ridge. Recognizing the need for publicity, the leadership started publishing a newsletter, *Taking Aim*. A mail-order operation distributes books, videotapes, and manuals. Much of its influence comes from its *MOM Manual*, which has been distributed across the United States. This manual gives a biblical justification for the militia movement along with instructions on how to carry out anti-government activities from bomb construction to blowing up facilities. MOM members have developed sophisticated techniques to distribute their anti-government message using the Internet, short-wave radio, videos, and other electronic methods. The Trochmanns have also developed close ties with **Willis Carto**'s **Liberty Lobby**'s *Spotlight*. Much of their propaganda effort is devoted to outlining purported conspiracy plots by the federal government against the American people. **See also** Estes Park Meeting; Michigan Militia; Trochmann, John Ernest.

Suggested readings: Morris Dees and James Corcoran, *Gathering Storm: America's Militia Threat* (New York: HarperCollins, 1996); Serge F. Kovaleski, " 'One World' Conspiracies Prompt Montana Militia's Call to Arms," *Washington Post* (April 29, 1995), p. A1; Patrick May, "Militia Movement Alive and Extreme as Ever," *Denver Post* (August 9, 1998), p. A8; Josh Meyer, Paul Feldman, and Eric Lichtblau, "Militia Members' Threats; Attacks on Officials Escalate Violence," *Los Angeles Times* (April 27, 1995), p. A1; Kim Murphy, "Militia Leaders Urge Calm in 'Freemen' Standoff," *Los Angeles Times* (March 28, 1996), p. A8.

Miller, Glen (1941?–)

Glen Miller is the head of the **White Patriots Party** in North Carolina. Factual evidence is lacking, but he was probably born in 1941. A twenty-year veteran of the U.S. Army, he served two tours of duty in South Vietnam as a Green Beret. His career in the Army ended after an undercover military agent caught him distributing Nazi literature. After a brief stay in the **American Nazi Party**, he joined the **Ku Klux Klan**. In 1980 he formed a new Klan group under the name Carolina Knights of the Ku Klux Klan. Miller was the head of this Klan organization when members of his group killed five anti-Klan demonstrators during the 1979 **Greensboro massacre**. Reacting to negative publicity over this incident, Miller changed the name of his group to the White Patriots Party. Miller received about $300,000 from **Robert Jay Mathews** out of the loot gathered from the July 1984 robbery of a Brink's armored car by members of **The Order**. In

1984 Miller ran for the governorship of North Carolina, but collected only 5,000 votes. In 1985 he made himself a candidate for the U.S. Senate for North Carolina. Again Miller was unsuccessful in his quest for a political office, but this failure did not discourage him.

Miller and the White Patriots Party ran into legal problems over its association with the U.S. Army. In 1984 his Klan group lost a lawsuit to Morris Dees and the Southern Poverty Law Center after his group had harassed a black prison guard. In the consent decree Miller agreed to stop harassing blacks and was prohibited from taking any steps to operate a paramilitary group. Miller ignored the latter restriction, turned his organization into a paramilitary unit, and attracted over 300 adherents. Miller was also able to recruit active duty military personnel to conduct paramilitary training. This use of military personnel sympathetic to the White People's Party led to a lawsuit instituted by Morris Dees and the Southern Poverty Law Center. A federal court order was issued prohibiting Miller from any further paramilitary training. In the spring of 1986, Miller and another leader, Robert Jones, were caught violating this court order. They went underground and issued a declaration of war against the United States. Miller was arrested in the Ozark Mountains of Missouri in the following year. To avoid a long prison term, Miller agreed to testify against other extremist leaders in the 1988 **Fort Smith Sedition Trial** in return for participation in the Federal Witness Protection Program. His evidence was unable to obtain convictions for the government in the trial, and his testimony ruined his reputation in extremist circles. Miller served three years in a federal prison in New York and then was placed in the witness program. His new home is in Springfield, Missouri, where he earns a living as a long-distance truck driver. His whereabouts is known because Miller publicized it in a number of interviews with the press. **See also** Ku Klux Klan: White Patriots Party.

Suggested readings: Morris Dees and James

Corcoran, *Gathering Storm: America's Militia Threat* (New York: HarperCollins, 1996); James Ridgeway, *Blood in the Face: The Ku Klux Klan, Aryan Nations, Nazi Skinheads, and the Rise of a New White Culture* (New York: Thunder's Mouth Press, 1990); Brent L. Smith, *Terrorism in America: Pipe Bombs and Pipe Dreams* (Albany: State University of New York Press, 1994).

Minutemen Movement

The Minutemen was an organization that consisted of armed, right-wing extremists active in the 1960s and 1970s. **Robert Bolivar DePugh,** an owner of a small veterinary drug business in Norborne, Missouri, founded the Minutemen in 1960. His intent was to organize an underground paramilitary force to fight against the imminent communist takeover of the United States. At first, the emphasis was to prevent a communist invasion of the United States, but then the emphasis shifted to countering the internal threat of communists taking control of the federal government. DePugh and his followers considered American liberals as allies of the takeover. The leaders of the Minutemen considered all liberals as traitors, and their policy was to target them for destruction. Finally, the Minutemen leaders came to consider the federal government as the main enemy. Because they considered themselves in a state of war, the Minutemen practiced extreme secrecy.

The Minutemen organization was never as large as its public image indicated. At the height of its popularity in the mid-1960s, the Minutemen movement attracted between 1,000 and 2,000 active members, mostly in the Midwest and the West. A number of policemen and individuals serving in the armed forces became active members. By 1968 the FBI estimated membership at less than 500. These figures contrast sharply with DePugh's unofficial estimate of 25,000 members. Members could join for as little as $2 a month, but the organization requested a higher figure of $10. Regardless of the amount, Minutemen members had a poor record of paying their dues. Dues were to be paid in cash so bank records could not be

used to trace membership. Members were also expected to provide their own weapons and ammunition. The biggest expense for the organization was paying attorney fees and bail bondsmen's fees for DePugh's legal troubles. Another expense was publishing the newsletter, *On Target*. DePugh used this newsletter as a forum to spread his ideas and recruit new members.

DePugh guided the Minutemen into the political arena. Because he believed that the Kennedy administration was full of communist agents, DePugh directed attacks against it. After Kennedy's assassination, the Minutemen organization backed Barry Goldwater in the 1964 presidential race and threatened to sabotage the Lyndon Johnson campaign. DePugh published his political agenda in his book *Blueprint for Victory* in 1966. Soon after the publication of this book, in July 1966, DePugh started the Patriotic Party. His goal for the Patriotic Party was for it to run a candidate for the 1972 presidential election. This candidate was to call for the complete reorganization of the federal government and the courts, as well as the purging of communists and communist sympathizers from them. Other initiatives would be the abolition of the federal tax system and unleashing of the military establishment to fight wars against the communists. While the Patriotic Party never became a force in American politics and died a natural death during DePugh's subsequent legal troubles, the platform of the party attracted attention, and other extremist parties in the 1980s and 1990s have adopted most of it.

In the decade following its founding, elements within the Minutemen movement started plans to carry out operations, including bombings and shootings, against those it considered enemies. Members acquired automatic and semiautomatic weapons and ammunition and hid them for the day when they would be needed. These weapons caches were hidden all over the country. News of the weapons caches and plans to use the weapons attracted the attention of the federal authorities. On October 30,

1967, New York City Police raided a Queens Minutemen group and arrested nineteen men. They also seized bombs, guns, and rockets. These individuals had intended to bomb and destroy three camps which, they thought, were being run by communists. An undercover agent unearthed another plot in January 1968 to bomb a Redmond, Washington, police station and rob four banks.

News of plans for Minutemen operations caught the interest of federal and state authorities in DePugh's comings and goings. Government agents had arrested DePugh on kidnapping two young women in early 1966, but lack of reliable evidence led the charges to be dismissed. In August 1966, he was arrested again, this time for conspiracy and weapons charges. In November 1966, a federal jury convicted DePugh and two other Minutemen leaders, Troy Houghton and Walter Peyson, for conspiracy and weapons offenses. DePugh received a four-year sentence with another five years of probation. Houghton and Peyson received lesser sentences but both sentences included probation. Terms of the probation were that none of them could associate with any extremist group. DePugh fled federal jurisdiction in February 1968 to prevent imprisonment and the introduction of new charges for Minutemen activities around the country. By 1970 the Minutemen movement had suffered enough setbacks that it was no longer classified as a threat to security by federal agencies. More violent elements of the Minutemen split off in 1970 and formed the **Secret Army Organization** (SAO) to continue the armed struggle.

The Minutemen proved to be a failure as an organization, but it provided an example for successive movements on what to do and what not to do. DePugh was erratic as a leader, but his anti-government rhetoric and orientation caused many of his ex-followers to look for other anti-government groups. Many of them joined the **Posse Comitatus movement**. Several of the leaders of the **militia movement** in the 1990s had experience with or were familiar with the Minutemen movement. **See also** DePugh, Robert Bolivar; John Birch Society.

Suggested readings: Phillip Finch, *God, Guts, and Guns* (New York: Seaview/Putnam, 1983); J. Harry Jones, *The Minutemen* (Garden City, N.Y.: Doubleday, 1968).

Monkeywrenching

Monkeywrenching is a radical environmentalist tactic designed to sabotage logging operations. The name and concept came from a 1976 novel written by Edward Abbey, titled *The Monkey Wrench Gang*. In this novel, the author describes the adventures of four environmental saboteurs who carry out a campaign of random ecosabotage. Radical environmentalists adopted this tactic and named it monkeywrenching. **David Foreman,** one of the founders of **Earth First!**, collected and expounded on the various approaches to sabotage in an underground handbook, *Ecodefense: A Field Guide to Monkeywrenching* (1985). This handbook details ways to sabotage earth-moving and logging equipment by pouring sand into gas tanks, flattening tires with knives, making combustion agents, and using glues and concrete to immobilize equipment. The intent of monkeywrenching is to damage equipment, not hurt people. One exception is tree spiking. By driving nails or spikes into trees the danger exists that a logger could suffer an injury by hitting one of them. Only one logger has been injured this way, but the possibility exists. Monkeywrenching is normally carried out in secret, but **Paul Franklin Watson** of the **Sea Shepherd Conservation Society** seeks publicity for his actions in planting spikes in the forests of British Columbia, Canada.

Monkeywrenching became less prevalent in the 1990s. Federal legislation aimed at preventing sabotage discouraged it, but more important was the negative publicity in the national media. One of the conditions for Foreman's probation for environmental offenses was his repudiation of monkeywrenching. Other tactics, such as tree sitting, proved more successful in garnering positive public attention. Partisans of monkey-wrenching still retain faith in it as a tactic, but they have been maintaining a low profile since logging in public forests has lessened. **See also** Earth First!; Foreman, David; Radical Environmentalism; Watson, Paul Franklin.

Suggested readings: Dave Foreman, "Anarchist with an Attitude," *Los Angeles Times* (July 17, 1994), Book Review, p. 1; Martha F. Lee, *Earth First!: Environmental Apocalypse* (Syracuse, N.Y.: Syracuse University Press, 1995); Anita Manning, "Ecology; An Eco-Warrior Tones Down His Tactics," *USA Today* (March 12, 1991), p. 6D; Jim Okerblom, "Rednecks' Fight to Save Land," *San Diego Union-Tribune* (November 24, 1985), p. B1; Walter Schwarz, "Faith, Heresy and the Fight for Eden," *Guardian* [London] (December 27, 1991), p. 1; Howie Wolke, "The Earth's Own Day," *Newsday* [New York City] (April, 15, 1990), p. 5; Susan Zakin, *Coyotes and Town Dogs: Earth First! and the Environmental Movement* (New York: Viking Press, 1993).

Morales, William (1950–)

William Morales, one of the founders and leaders of a Puerto Rican liberation group, the **Fuerzas Armadas de Liberación Nacional Puertorriqueña** (FALN), was born on February 7, 1950, and raised in New York City. After studying the history of Puerto Rico, Morales became a Puerto Rican nationalist and was instrumental in the founding of the FALN in 1974. Several Puerto Rican liberation groups were in existence at that time, but only the FALN operated in the continental United States. Members specialized in bombings, and in the period between 1974 and 1983 the FALN committed more than 130 bombings, primarily in Chicago and New York City. The most famous bombing occurred at the Fraunces Tavern in New York City on January 24, 1975, which caused four deaths and wounded fifty-five. Morales planned operations until he was seriously wounded in 1977 at a bomb-making factory accident. He lost most of his teeth, his jaw, one hand, and most of the fingers of the other hand. This accident temporarily put him out of action. His subsequent arrest and imprisonment on a sentence of from twenty-nine to eighty-nine years in state prison and ten years in a federal prison for bombings curtailed his activities further.

Morales's escape from prison, in 1979 while he was receiving medical treatment at Bellevue Hospital prison ward for his injuries, allowed him to regain his position in the FALN. Bolt cutters were smuggled into Morales and he used them to escape. Members of the radical leftist **May 19th Communist Organization** assisted him in his flight from the hospital and his trip to Mexico. Morales continued to direct FALN operations from Mexico until Mexican police in Puebla arrested him in May 1983. His gunfight and the death of one of the policemen landed him in a Mexican jail until he was released in June 1988. The refusal of the Mexican government to extradite Morales to the United States after his release caused an international incident with the Reagan administration. Morales's stay in jail and the arrest by American law enforcement authorities of the remainder of FALN's leadership in the early 1980s ended the group's activities. Morales found political asylum in Cuba where he remains to this day. **See also** Fuerzas Armadas de Liberación Nacional Puertorriqueña.

Suggested readings: Jorge G. Castaneda, "Terrorist—A Case Lost in Translation; Mexico Let Morales Go on Principle," *Los Angeles Times* (July 1, 1988), part 2, p. 7; Bill McAllister, "U.S. Denounces Mexico's Release of Convicted Terrorist," *Washington Post* (June 29, 1988), p. A18; Robert D. McFadden, "Fugitive Puerto Rican Terrorist Arrested in Mexico," *New York Times* (May 28, 1983), sec. 1, p. 1; Roberto Santiago, "Conversation with Terrorist," *Plain Dealer* [Cleveland] (August 1, 1993), p. 17; Robert Santiago, "Terrorism American Style; the Guillermo Morales Story," *Plain Dealer* [Cleveland] (August 1, 1993), p. 8.

MOVE

MOVE, a black back-to-nature communal group in Philadelphia, was almost wiped out by the Philadelphia police in 1985. Vincent

Leapheart founded MOVE in 1973 in Philadelphia, Pennsylvania. He assumed the name John Africa, and other members also took the surname Africa in recognition that all human life originated in Africa. The headquarters of MOVE was located in a house on Osage Street in West Philadelphia.

Soon after its founding, MOVE found itself in an adversarial relationship with the Philadelphia police. MOVE first made headlines in 1973 by protesting the caged exploitation of animals in the Philadelphia Zoo. Members of MOVE came into conflict with the police and accused the police of brutality. MOVE headquarters was barricaded and turned into an armed compound. In 1978 a confrontation with the police resulted in the death of a policeman. Mumia Abu-Jamal, a journalist and former member of the **Black Panther Party**, was given the death penalty in July 1983 for the policeman's death. Nine other members of MOVE were sentenced to between thirty and a hundred years for the same crime.

An armed truce existed between MOVE and the Philadelphia authorities until 1985. Complaints about noise and the unconventional lifestyle of MOVE members caused the police to stage a raid on May 13, 1985. In a day-long siege, the police fired around 10,000 rounds of ammunition at the MOVE house before bombing it. A helicopter dropped one-half pound of plastique on the roof, which started a fire that consumed the house and sixty-one neighboring houses. Eleven members of MOVE were killed, including five children. The fire also left 250 people homeless. Ramona Africa, the only adult MOVE member to survive, was badly burned. Later she was convicted of conspiracy of rioting and served a six-year prison term. She was released from prison in May 1992. MOVE still has a presence in West Philadelphia, but Philadelphia officials now tolerate MOVE's presence and ignore it.

The political fallout from the MOVE bombing ruined the careers of a number of Philadelphia politicians. The promising political career of Mayor W. Wilson Goode ended, and both the police chief and fire commissioner resigned. A commission investigated the incident and blamed the mayor and his administration for "unjustifiable homicide." It took $8.27 million to rebuild thirty-nine of the sixty-one houses destroyed. In June 1996, a jury in a civil suit ordered the city and former officials to pay $1.5 million to Ramona Africa and relatives of two MOVE members for violations of their constitutional rights.

Suggested readings: Retha Hill, "1 of 2 Survivors of '85 Police Attack on MOVE House Walks out of Prison," *Washington Post* (May 14, 1992), p. A3; Victoria Irwin, "A Year After MOVE, Residents Still Displaced, Mayor on Shaky Ground," *Christian Science Monitor* (May 13, 1986), p. 3; Gaylford Shaw, "Experts Question Use of Explosives in Siege Situation," *Los Angeles Times* (May 15, 1985), p. 1; Jim Fletcher, Tanaquil Jones, and Sylvere Lotringer, eds., *Still Black, Still Strong: Survivors of the U.S. War Against Black Revolutionaries; Dhoruba Bin Wahad, Mumia Abu-Jamal, and Assata Shakur* (Brooklyn, N.Y.: Semiotext (e), 1993).

Muhammad, Abdul Khalid (1948–2001)

Khalid Muhammad, the head of the militant **New Black Panther Party** (NBPP), was born Harold Moore Vann in January 1948 in Houston, Texas. In 1966 he graduated from the all-black Wheatley High School in Houston where he was a class leader and star football quarterback. His scholastic achievement won him a scholarship to Dillard University in New Orleans, Louisiana. He also spent several semesters at Harvard University. While at Dillard University, he met **Louis Farrakhan** in 1967 and became a disciple of **Elijah Muhammad**'s **Nation of Islam**. Khalid Muhammad dropped out of college in 1970 without graduating and joined Farrakhan's staff. By 1981 he had become one of Farrakhan's top assistants. His job was raising money for the Nation of Islam. Later, he was appointed minister of mosques in Atlanta, Los Angeles, and New York. Khalid Muhammad was such an effective speaker that he was used as a recruiter. In 1989 he became the supreme captain of the Fruit of Islam, the Nation of

Islam's security force. The following year, he assumed the post of the Nation of Islam's chief spokesperson. His fiery anti-gay, anti-Semitic, anti-white rhetoric caused him trouble with Farrakhan. His rebelliousness and outspokenness caused Farrakhan to dismiss him in 1994 from the Nation of Islam. Later that year, former members of the Nation of Islam shot him in the leg while he was making a speech at the University of California in Riverside.

Khalid Muhammad joined the New Black Panther Party in 1994. Michael McGee, a Milwaukee politician, had founded this group in 1990 as an urban guerilla group. Khalid Muhammad had become acquainted with the leadership of the NBPP in 1993, and its militant anti-Semitic and anti-white stances attracted him. The NBPP lacked a leader of national stature, and Khalid Muhammad had the national reputation needed by this group. He also realized the potential of the NBPP. After an apprenticeship of nearly four years, Khalid Muhammad became the NBPP's national commander in 1998. Although the NBPP had a decentralized administrative structure, it still allowed him a national platform to advance his views and perform as, what he called, a "truth terrorist." In a series of demonstrations and protests, Khalid Muhammad brought the NBPP onto the national scene, as did his sponsorship of the Million Youth Marches in Harlem, New York, in 1998, 1999, and 2000. At the height of his influence over the NBPP, Khalid Muhammad suffered a brain aneurysm on February 13, 2001, and drifted into a coma. He died at the Wellstar Kennestone Hospital in Marietta, Georgia, on February 17, 2001. **See also** Black Panther Party; Farrakhan, Louis; New Black Panther Party.

Suggested readings: Solomon Moore, "Khalid Abdul Muhammad; Formed New Black Panthers," *Los Angeles Times* (February 18, 2001), p. B7; Southern Poverty Law Center, "Snarling at the White Man," *SPLC Intelligence Report* 100 (Fall 2000): 16–23; Ernie Suggs and S. A. Reid, "Hard-Line Black Activist Dies at 53; Muslim Leader Khalid Muhammad Was Best Known for Riling Whites," *Atlanta Journal and Constitution* (February 18, 2001), p. 1G.

Muhammad, Elijah (1897–1975)

Elijah Muhammad, the longtime leader of the **Nation of Islam** (NOI), was born Elijah Poole on October 7, 1897, at Bolds Springs near Sandersville, Georgia. His father was a poor sharecropper and a Baptist preacher. Muhammad was the sixth of thirteen children. At an early age, Muhammad witnessed the lynching of a black man, and he never forgot the incident. His family moved to Weona, Georgia, when he was six years old. Muhammad had to quit school after the fourth grade to help his father in the fields. He left home at age sixteen and married Clara Evans in 1917. After holding several jobs in Georgia, Muhammad and his wife and son moved to Detroit, Michigan, in April 1923. His first job was with the American Can Factory. Almost as soon as he arrived in Detroit, he joined the Universal Negro Improvement Association (UNIA). He worked at various industrial plants in the mid- and late 1920s but the advent of the Great Depression cost him his job. His family had to resort to local welfare and soup kitchens for survival since no work was available.

Muhammad joined the new Islamic movement of Farad Muhammad in 1931. This new movement was the creation of Farad Muhammad, who proclaimed that Islam was the natural religion of African Americans Farad Muhammad was later identified as Wallace Dodd Ford, who had only recently been released from San Quentin prison. He had arrived in Detroit in 1930, and his preaching soon attracted adherents. Elijah Muhammad became a devoted disciple of this new leader and was made one of the top officials in the new Nation of Islam. As supreme minister, Muhammad proved to be a skillful organizer. When Farad Muhammad disappeared in 1934, probably at the instigation of the Detroit police, Muhammad replaced him as the leader. Serious opposition from other leaders in the Detroit

Nation of Islam prevented Muhammad from a peaceful assumption of power. Tensions between Detroit education authorities over Black Muslim schools also disturbed Elijah Muhammad. He moved to Chicago and established the national headquarters there. Again internal dissension broke out and Elijah Muhammad decided to leave Chicago. For the next seven years, Muhammad traveled around the country building up the Nation of Islam. Pro-Japanese statements and his advice to members to avoid the draft landed him in jail in 1942. Although he was nearly past draft age, Muhammad refused to sign up for the draft. He was convicted of failing to take part in the draft and encouraging others to evade it and was sentenced to five years in prison. Muhammad spent the next four years in the federal prison in Milan, Michigan. During his absence, he retained control of the affairs of the Nation of Islam.

After his release from prison in 1946, Elijah Muhammad spent the remainder of his life building the Nation of Islam. He never deviated from a policy of maintaining strict separation from white society and lobbying for a black homeland. Elijah Muhammad preached that Christianity was a black-slave-making religion and that Allah was a god of peace, righteousness, and dignity. His views were apocalyptic and he claimed that at the end of the world 144,000 blacks would be spared. The mission of the righteous was to follow the teachings of Allah and prepare himself or herself for that day sometime in the near future. His position as the leader of the Nation of Islam was never seriously challenged. Muhammad based his leadership upon the premise that Farad Muhammad was Allah and that Elijah Muhammad was the messenger of Allah. Orthodox Moslems regarded this belief as heresy, and it prevented the Nation of Islam from joining the mainstream Islamic movement. Nevertheless, Muhammad's emphasis on self-improvement and self-reliance in the black community made the Nation of Islam popular. After leaving prison, Elijah Muhammad started recruiting among the lower classes, and he built a self-sustaining economic empire. Growth was particularly strong in the 1950s and 1960s. Because Elijah Muhammad was a black separatist, he never accepted the civil rights movement and placed himself in opposition to other black leaders who were fighting for the integration of blacks into white society. This stance came to both help and hurt the Nation of Islam in the turmoil of the 1960s.

Muhammad's greatest challenge as a leader was the defection of **Malcolm X** in 1964. Malcolm X had served as his spokesperson for the Nation of Islam and had a good reputation with the rank-and-file members. Two factors led to Malcolm X's defection: rumors of moral lapses of Elijah Muhammad with young women and the failure of the Nation of Islam to conform to orthodox Islam. Elijah Muhammad never showed any remorse over Malcolm X's assassination in 1965. More embarrassing was the participation of Nation of Islam members in the murder. This association caused the Nation of Islam to lose face in the black community.

In the last few years of his life, the Nation of Islam experienced the problems of an organization with an aging leader. Muhammad replaced Malcolm X with **Louis Farrakhan**, but he never allowed Farrakhan the freedom that he had allowed Malcolm X. Muhammad had six sons and a daughter. Two of his sons married two of Farrakhan's daughters. Criticism of Muhammad's lifestyle and that of his family hurt the image of the Nation of Islam. He lived a comfortable lifestyle with a villa in the Hyde Park area near the University of Chicago. His winters were spent on a ranch in Phoenix, Arizona. On February 25, 1975, Elijah Muhammad died of congestive heart failure at Mercy Hospital in Chicago. His estate had $5.7 million in assets, and his nineteen legitimate and illegitimate children fought over the estate for almost twenty years. His eldest son, Wallace Deen Muhammad, succeeded him. Relations between father and son had been strained over the years. Wallace Muhammad decided to reorient the Nation of

Islam toward more orthodox Islam. This reorientation proved controversial within the Nation of Islam. In the end, Wallace Muhammad abandoned the name and the mission of the Nation of Islam to Louis Farrakhan. Farrakhan moved the Nation of Islam back to Elijah Muhammad's original vision. **See also** Farrakhan, Louis; Malcolm X; Nation of Islam.

Suggested readings: Mattias Gardell, *In the Name of Elijah Muhammad: Louis Farrakhan and the Nation of Islam* (Durham, N.C.: Duke University Press, 1996); Nalu Halasa, *Elijah Muhammad: Religious Leader* (Los Angeles: Melrose Square Publishing, 1990); C. Eric Lincoln, *The Black Muslims in America*, 3d ed. (Grand Rapids, Mich.: William B. Eerdmans, 1995).

N

Nation of Islam (NOI)

The Nation of Islam (NOI), the most extreme black religious movement in the United States, was founded in Detroit, Michigan, in 1930. The founder, Farad Muhammad, had a criminal record, but he was able to convince members of the black community that Islam was its natural religion. Christianity, in contrast, was the religion of their white oppressors. Many of the early followers of Farad Muhammad had been affiliated with the black nationalism movements of Marcus Garvey and Noble Drew Ali. Farad Muhammad taught his followers that they were not Americans and that they owed no allegiance to the American flag. After his disappearance in 1934, probably under Detroit police pressure, **Elijah Muhammad** assumed the leadership of the Nation of Islam. At the time of Farad Muhammad's disappearance, the movement had about 8,000 adherents. Elijah Muhammad's assumption of power, however, was not without serious challengers. Driven out of Detroit by his enemies, he moved to Chicago where he established the national headquarters of the Nation of Islam. Elijah Muhammad achieved recognition from his followers as the messenger of Allah in the late 1940s. By 1974 the Nation of Islam had mosques or study groups in every state and in the District of Columbia.

Muhammad's views on racial separation and his anti-white philosophy became influential in segments of the African American community. According to the Nation of Islam, God is a black man. All progress in the arts and sciences throughout the ages came from early black civilizations. Among these black civilizations was the tribe of Shabazz. Blacks were the chosen people who would soon be freed from the bondage of white culture. The white race is evil, and white world supremacy would soon be replaced by a new black culture of Islam. For these theological reasons, Elijah Muhammad argued that blacks in America should be given their independence and allowed a separate homeland in either North America or Africa. To help in the struggle against the whites and to encourage the proper behavior of members, the Nation of Islam formed a paramilitary organization, the Fruit of Islam.

Members of the Nation of Islam adhered to a rigid moral code. Black Muslims were forbidden to gamble, smoke, drink liquor, or overeat, and they were discouraged from using credit. All members were expected to give a fixed percentage of their income to the local mosque. Women had a special role as companions and mothers, and the leaders insisted that they be respected. The Fruit of Islam enforced discipline and the rules of the mosque. Elijah Muhammad determined how members were to vote in elections, but in most cases he discouraged voting.

Recognizing economic realities in the black community, the Nation of Islam established an economic empire. Taking donations and using the labor of members to make money, the leaders of the NOI looked for ways to make the organization self-sufficient. These leaders gave special emphasis to starting businesses in the black community. Businesses from bakeries to a bank were launched. Agents from the NOI acquired commercial and residential real estate in several major cities. The NOI also started a transportation system that included all modes of transportation from trucks to aircraft. Other agents purchased tens of thousands of acres of land in Alabama, Georgia, and Michigan. The goal of self-sufficiency for the Nation of Islam was achieved in the early 1970s.

The Nation of Islam spread its message by a combination of missionary work and the use of mass media. Initial recruitment in the 1930s was among low-income groups with minimal education. Later, recruitment drives approached the more prosperous and more educated segments of the black community. To attract members, most of the temples and mosques were built in the black ghettos. Open meetings, mass rallies, and street-corner talks were effective ways to approach prospective recruits. In 1960 **Malcolm X** started a newspaper, *Mr. Muhammad Speaks*. This newspaper soon became the most influential newspaper in black America with a circulation of around 600,000 copies a week. Despite these efforts of recruitment, the Nation of Islam had a poor record in attracting black intellectuals. Elijah Muhammad distrusted intellectuals and felt uncomfortable with them in the Nation of Islam.

For all of its apparent successes, the Nation of Islam underwent a period of turmoil from the early 1960s to the late 1970s. Malcolm X served as the spokesperson for the Nation of Islam in the early 1960s. Because the Nation of Islam was a separatist movement, Elijah Muhammad and its leadership opposed the civil rights movement and in-tegration. This stance alienated many of the moderate leaders in the black community. Concerned about scandals involving several young pregnant women in the personal life of Elijah Muhammad, Malcolm X left the Nation of Islam. After establishing his own version of the Nation of Islam and seeking a reorientation to more traditional Islam, Malcolm X was assassinated on February 21, 1965. His murder by gunmen affiliated with the Nation of Islam provided the first instance of the intensity of conflict within the Nation of Islam. Malcolm X's successor as the spokesperson for the NOI was **Louis Farrakhan**. Elijah Muhammad, however, was careful not to allow Farrakhan as much authority in the Nation of Islam as Malcolm X formerly had. The major problem within the Nation of Islam in the mid-1970s was the issue of naming a successor to the aging Elijah Muhammad. On February 25, 1975, Elijah Muhammad died of heart failure.

Internal divisions in the Nation of Islam showed themselves during the struggle for succession. Farrakhan flirted with the idea of challenging the designated successor, Wallace Deen Muhammad, the son of Elijah Muhammad, before deciding against it. Wallace Deen Muhammad had been trained in orthodox Sunni Islam and he wanted to bring the Nation of Islam into the mainstream of Moslem thought. Such a reorientation, however, would require changes in the unique theology of Elijah Muhammad and its anti-white emphasis. Farrakhan resisted this change and used his influence within the organization to fight it. In 1977 Farrakhan finally broke with Wallace Deen Muhammad. He formed the Nation of Islam into a separatist organization. Wallace Deen Muhammad took the majority of the members of the old Nation of Islam and started a new organization under the name of the American Muslim Mission.

Besides retaining the name of the Nation of Islam, Farrakhan reestablished the theology of Elijah Muhammad and its anti-white message. Farrakhan was a controversial figure, and soon his negative comments on Jews attracted national attention. Some critics have suggested that his attacks on the Jews were a calculated effort to appeal to frustrations in the black community. Many of these attacks on Jews have been made in the newspaper of the Nation of Islam, *The Final Call.* By the mid-1990s, Farrakhan had maneuvered the Nation of Islam into a position of leadership in the black community, and he has been able to command a presence on the national scene. Since his illness of cancer of the prostate in the late 1990s, Farrakhan has become less strident in his anti-Semitic remarks, but he still retains control of the Nation of Islam and maintains it on a steady course. Farrakhan has experienced a series of health crises, and a recent prostate operation raises the issue of succession once again for the Nation of Islam. In the last several years, Farrakhan has become more open to reforms, and women are taking a more important role in the Nation of Islam. He has also improved relations with other Muslim groups in the United States and has considered the possibility of bringing NOI's theology closer to that of orthodox Islam. **See also** Farrakhan, Louis; Malcolm X; Muhammad, Elijah.

Suggested readings: Aurel Braun and Stephen Scheinberg, eds., *The Extreme Right: Freedom and Security at Risk* (Boulder, Colo.: Westview Press, 1997); Brian Cathcart, "A Family Affair; the Nation of Islam Is Usually Associated with Confrontational Racial Politics and Intimidating-Looking Men in Suits," *Independent* [London] (October 3, 1999), p. 11; Mattias Gardell, *In the Name of Elijah Muhammad: Louis Farrakhan and the Nation of Islam* (Durham, N.C.: Duke University Press, 1996); C. Eric Lincoln, *The Black Muslims in America*, 3d ed. (Grand Rapids, Mich.: William B. Eerdmans, 1955).

Nation of Yahweh

The Nation of Yahweh is a black religious cult whose leaders have been jailed for their use of violence. Julon Mitchell, Jr., founded the Nation of Yahweh in 1979 soon after moving to Miami, Florida. After launching the Nation of Yahweh, Mitchell changed his name to Yahweh ben Yahweh (God, son of God). He is a former instructor in the U.S. Air Force and a former law school student. At one time, Yahweh had been a Black Muslim. Yahweh ben Yahweh was considered by the membership of the cult to be God's representative on earth to lead his followers to a new Promised Land. It is his belief that black people are the original Jews and God and Jesus are black. Members took new names with Israel always being the surname.

The group developed strong support in the black community in Miami for its anti-drug and pro-family programs. These programs were so popular that the mayor of Miami, Xavier Suarez, proclaimed a Yahweh day in the mid-1980s. Leadership of the Nation of Yahweh also invested heavily in real estate in South Florida. While in 1992 the cult claimed a financial empire of $100 million, authorities believed that their property was worth in the range of $8 million and most of it was heavily mortgaged. At its peak, the Nation of Yahweh had a membership of around 10,000 in forty-five urban localities around the country. Yahweh promoted his brand of religion by making videotapes and using paid cable access on Black Entertainment Television and Sable Communications. These efforts reached a potential audience of 3 million listeners.

The Nation of Yahweh began to suffer from internal dissension and aberrations in its practices beginning in 1981. Yahweh ben Yahweh had absolute control over the Nation of Yahweh, and he began demanding sexual favors from his female disciples. He began calling his group the "Temple of Love." Any opposition was ruthlessly dealt with by force, and dissidents started disappearing. Yahweh ben Yahweh became more fanatical and started preaching a race war. In 1990 Yahweh and fifteen of his followers were indicted by federal authorities on racketeering charges and the murders of fourteen people. Eight of the victims were dissident members of the Nation of Yahweh; the others were randomly chosen whites. These murders, which took place between 1981 and 1987, began shortly after Yahweh started preaching that anyone who blasphemed the name of Yahweh should be put to death. Yahweh was also accused of telling his followers that they should kill "white devils" to repay them for past wrongs. Several of his close supporters in the "Circle of Ten" had participated in the random killings of whites. Supporters of the Nation of Yahweh attacked these murder charges as evidence of a government-sponsored vendetta against a new religion. In a trial held in 1992, Yahweh and six of his closest disciples were convicted on racketeering and conspiracy charges. Yahweh received an eighteen-year prison sentence and a $20,000 fine. He served his sentence in the Lewisburg Federal Penitentiary. These convictions and subsequent prosecutions of other members of the Nation of Yahweh for murder have slowed the growth of the Nation of Yahweh, but it still has retained a significant following in the black community in Miami and other cities.

The Nation of Yahweh reappeared in the news in 1999 with the arrest of Robert Rozier for murder. Rozier, a former National Football League player, had joined the cult and adopted the name of Neariah Israel (Child of God). He was arrested in 1986 and convicted for participating in seven murders. After testifying against Yahweh, he was released from prison in 1996 and placed in a federal witness protection program. Rozier moved to California, but he was unable to stay out of trouble and wrote bad checks. New Jersey authorities arrested him in March 1999 for the sacrificial murder of a homeless white man in Newark. At the time, Rozier was the head of the Nation of Yahweh's Newark Temple. Rozier and John Armstrong, a member of the Nation of Yahweh, have been charged with murder.

Authorities released Yahweh ben Yahweh from prison on August 17, 2001, after he served eleven years of his sentence. He has expressed his intention to reclaim his leadership role in the Nation of Yahweh, but conditions of his parole bar him from contacting followers. His lawyers are trying to find ways to end this restriction. The Nation of Yahweh is a much smaller group in 2001 with around 1,000 adherents, but its members remain devoted to the teachings and sayings of Yahweh ben Yahweh. **See also** Cults; Nation of Islam.

Suggested readings: Sydney P. Freedberg, *Brother Love: Murder, Money and a Messiah* (New York: Pantheon, 1994); Jonathan Kirsch, "The Demonic Leadership of a Self-Proclaimed Messiah," *Los Angeles Times* (December 21, 1994), p. E5; Sarah Moran, *The Secret World of Cults: From Ancient Druids to Heaven's Gate* (Godalming, U.K.: CLB International, 1999); Lisa Ocker, "Yahweh, 6 Others Guilty, 7 Acquitted," *Sun-Sentinel* [Fort Lauderdale, Fla.] (May 28, 1992), p. 1A; Warren Richey, "Star Witness's Explosive Testimony Rejected in Yahweh Case, Juror Says," *Sun-Sentinel* [Fort Lauderdale, Fla.] (May 29, 1992), p. 1B.

National Alliance

The National Alliance has been characterized as the single most dangerous organized **neo-Nazi** organization in the United States. **William Pierce** founded the National Alliance in 1970. Pierce has a doctorate in physics from the University of Colorado. He worked as a research scientist at a government laboratory in New Mexico and had been a professor of physics at Oregon State University before turning to racial politics. In 1966 he abandoned a research job and joined **George Lincoln Rockwell's American Nazi Party**. Pierce soon became the ideological leader of the party, but after Rockwell's assassination in 1967 he became restless with the leadership of **Matt Koehl**. In 1970 he formed the National Youth Alliance to attract young people to the neo-Nazi message. This group had originally been established as Youth for Wallace in the 1968 presidential campaign with **Willis Carto** as the chief sponsor. Pierce realized the potential for this group, seized control of it, and recast the group as the National Youth Alliance (NYA).

Pierce, who renamed the group the National Alliance in 1974, has used this organization to advance his national agenda of preparing the United States for a race war. He believes that the Aryan race is endowed by nature with superior qualities and that these qualities are to be used to fight for the survival of the white race. His most vicious attacks, however, are directed against Jews. Pierce also attacks the federal government for its enfranchisement of women and minorities. His reputation grew after the publication of his anti-government novel, *The Turner Diaries*, in 1977. In this novel, he casts a band of white supremacists in a war with the U.S. government and characterizes the government as under the control of the **ZOG** (**Zionist Occupied Government**).

Pierce moved the headquarters of the National Alliance from Arlington, Virginia, near Washington, D.C., to a 265-acre rural compound in Pocahontas County, West Virginia. Membership in the National Alliance is small, but in recent years membership has expanded to around 5,000. The Southern Poverty Law Center estimates that the National Alliance has sixteen active cells and is active in twenty-six states. Members receive the National Alliance's *Bulletin*, the forum for the most virulent of Pierce's attacks on his enemies inside and outside the **white supremacist movement**. Pierce also publishes a glossy magazine, *National Vanguard*. He uses the *Bulletin*, the *National Vanguard*, novels, and other writings to advance the cause of white supremacy. Pierce also reaches potential members in his weekly radio program, *American Dissident Voices*, and an Internet Web site. The National Alliance plays a leading role in the neo-Nazi movement and serves as the key outlet for Pierce's views. He ensures that the quality of the message of the National Alliance remains constant by his dictatorial control over it. Pierce's recent acquisition of **Resistance Records** has increased the National Alliance's appeal to **skinheads**, neo-Nazis, and teenagers. Sale of racist music has increased the financial viability of the National Alliance. The Southern Poverty Law Center reports that the National Alliance remains "the richest and most influential neo-Nazi organization in the United States and in Europe" at the turn of the century. **See also** American Nazi Party; Carto, Willis; Pierce, William.

Suggested readings: Anti-Defamation League, *Explosion of Hate: The Growing Danger of the National Alliance* (New York: Anti-Defamation League, 1998); Southern Poverty Law Center, "The Alliance and Its Allies," *SPLC Intelligence Report* 93 (Winter 1999) 10–16; Southern Poverty Law Center, "Inside the Alliance; A Former National Alliance Insider Speaks," *SPLC Intelligence Report* 93 (Winter 1999): 17–20; Southern Poverty Law Center, "The Rise of the National Alliance," www.splcenter.org/intelligenceproject/alliance.html.

National Association for the Advancement of White People (NAAWP)

The National Association for the Advancement of White People (NAAWP) was formed by **David Duke** in 1979 to advance his white supremacist agenda. Duke achieved fame in the 1970s as the head of the Knights of the Ku Klux Klan, but he became discouraged over the Klan's inability to recruit members outside of the South. President Ronald Reagan's brand of conservatism also attracted moderate racists to look to alternatives to the Klan. On December 20, 1979, Duke founded the NAAWP to appeal to a broader public, and this effort has been modestly successful. In July 1980, Duke left the Knights of the Ku Klux Klan to devote all of his energies to the new NAAWP. Using this organization to appear more politically respectable, Duke soon was a political force in his home state of Louisiana. The headquarters of the NAAWP was located in the basement of Duke's home in Metaire, Louisiana. Duke ran impressive campaigns for public office and won a seat in the Louisiana legislature. In 1982 the NAAWP started a publication, the *Newspaper of the National Association for the Advancement of White People*. This publication is more restrained and more sophisticated than most white supremacist publications, but it consistently charges that there is a Jewish-federal government plot to discriminate against the white race. A special target of this publication has been the black civil rights leadership and, in particular, the reputation of Martin Luther King, Jr. Duke held the presidency of the NAAWP until the late 1990s when Paul Allen succeeded him. By 1996 the NAAWP had eighteen chapters in a number of states. **See also** Duke, David; Ku Klux Klan; White Supremacist Movement.

Suggested readings: Tyler Bridges, *The Rise of David Duke* (Jackson: University Press of Mississippi, 1994); Betty A. Dobratz and Stephanie L. Shanks-Meile, *"White Power, White Pride!": The White Separatist Movement in the United States* (New York: Twayne, 1997).

National Socialist German Workers Party/Overseas Organization (See Lauck, Gary Lex)

National Socialist Party of America (See American Nazi Party; Skokie March Controversy)

National State's Rights Party (NSRP)

The National State's Rights Party (NSRP) is an extremist group that has been active fighting the civil rights movement in the South and pursuing an anti-Semitic campaign. **Edward R. Fields** founded the party in Knoxville, Tennessee, in 1958. Fields, a chiropractor by training, gave up his profession to build up the National State's Rights Party. His close friend, **Jesse Benjamin Stoner**, joined the party in 1959 as its legal counsel. Together they worked to make the party a political force in the South. Party headquarters was moved several times before it was located in 1971 in Marietta, Georgia, just outside of Atlanta. Several times leaders of the National State's Rights Party have attempted to win public office on a racial program but without much success. Stoner ran a campaign in 1972 for the Georgia Democratic primary for the U.S. Senate on a platform calling for making Judaism a crime punishable by death. He received about 6 percent of the vote. The party publishes a widely read newsletter, *The Thun-*

derbolt, which takes an anti-Semitic and anti-minority line.

The National State's Rights Party was in the forefront of the anti–civil rights movement. Stoner and Charles Conley "Connie" Lynch worked together to stir up violent confrontations with civil rights marchers. Lynch would incite violence against the demonstrators, and Stoner would provide legal representation in the subsequent legal proceedings. Stoner was convicted in 1980 for planting the bomb in 1958 that destroyed the Bethel Baptist Church in Birmingham, Alabama. Fields retained control of the party during Stoner's term in prison until the executive board of the party rebelled against him in 1984. The board ousted Fields, and the party terminated its activities shortly afterward. This ending after twenty-five years of existence was anticlimactic for a party that had trained a generation of extremists. **See also** Anti-Semitism; Fields, Edward R.; Stoner, Jesse Benjamin "J.B"; White Supremacist Movement.

Suggested readings: Glenn Frankel, "Guerrilla-Style Training of KKK Alleged in 7 States," *Washington Post* (October 24, 1980), p. A29; Kathy Marks, *Faces of Right Wing Extremism* (Boston: Branden Publishing, 1996); Peggy Peterman, "Don't Forget the Lessons of the Past," *St. Petersburg Times* (January 24, 1987), p. 5B; Bill Richards, "Gun-Toting Klansman Denies Bombing Black Birmingham Church in 1958," *Washington Post* (September 29, 1977), p. A5.

Nationalist Party (See Barrett, Richard)

Nazi Low Riders

The Nazi Low Riders, a California **skinhead** group that specializes in assaulting minorities, is headquartered in Lancaster, California, in the racially divided Antelope Valley. Members win status symbols for beating and killing minority people. Although the group is small, with never more than a dozen followers and associates, it has a growing reputation for violence. Members have been in and out of trouble with local authorities for various assaults. Skinhead groups exist all over the United States, but the Nazi Low Riders have received more publicity than most of the others.

The Nazi Low Riders received national publicity after three members beat and killed a homeless black man in November 1995. Randall Lee Rojas, Rich Briant, and Jessica Anne Colwell attacked Milton Walker, Jr., on November 25, 1995, in Lancaster, California, after he allegedly struck a white woman. Rojas and Briant were members of the Nazi Low Riders and Colwell was a close associate. They beat Walker on two separate occasions an hour apart. Walker died after receiving from six to nine severe blows to the head. Both Rojas and Briant were already in legal trouble for earlier assaults on minorities. Trial records indicate that Rojas and Briant became excited about winning the right to wear two lighting bolt tattoos for the killing of a minority. In a November 1999 trial, Rojas and Briant received life in prison and an additional five years for circumstances of the crime. Colwell received a lesser sentence of nine years for involuntary manslaughter. These sentences have been unable to deter the operations of skinhead groups similar to the Nazi Low Riders. See also Skinheads.

Suggested readings: Scott Harris, "Skinhead Life: Consider It a Warning Sign," *Los Angeles Times* (June 7, 1998), p. 1; Dade Hayes, "Man Pleads Guilty to Racial Assaults," *Los Angeles Times* (October 28, 1997), p. 1; Evelyn Larrubia, "Hate Crime Issue Will Be Focus of Trial," *Los Angeles Times* (October 10, 1999), p. 1; Evelyn Larrubia, "Supremacist Convicted of Racial Killing," *Los Angeles Times* (November 5, 1999), p. B1; Evelyn Larrubia, "White Supremacist Gets Life in Prison Without Parole," *Los Angeles Times* (November 23, 1999), p. 1; Southern Poverty Law Center, "Youth at the Edge," *SPLC Intelligence Report* 96 (Fall 1999):6–15.

Neo-Confederates (See League of the South)

Neo-Nazis

Neo-Nazis are extremists who identify closely with the ideas and goals of the German National Socialist Workers Party (NSDAP) of Adolf Hitler. Numerous groups have formed since World War II to claim the neo-Nazi mantle. These groups and individuals use Nazi symbols, revere the life of Hitler, and classify themselves as Nazis or National Socialists. They believe that the white race is the master race, and they show no tolerance or acceptance of other races. While these groups are always small in number, they make up for their lack of size in agitation. They generally subscribe to an idealized vision of Nazi Germany. Neo-Nazi leaders develop rituals using Nazi symbols and plan holidays to show their reverence for the memory of Hitler. Many early neo-Nazis were former members of William Pelley's **Silver Shirts**, but others, such as **George Lincoln Rockwell**, came to Nazism from the study of the writings of Hitler and **Francis Parker Yockey**. Yockey has become an important figure among the neo-Nazis, almost rivaling Hitler. Yockey was an admirer of Hitler, and his book *Imperium* (1949) has had almost as much impact on neo-Nazi admirers as Hitler's *Mein Kampf*.

Neo-Nazism has been repackaged in the 1990s for American youth culture. Modern neo-Nazis have become attuned to the youth culture. This culture has a religion that is either racist Christianity or **Odinism**, and it has a white power, black metal music. All segments of the neo-Nazi movement subscribe to the thesis that the Holocaust never happened; it is a hoax perpetrated by Jews. Nationalism is no longer considered important, and most neo-Nazis are advocates of an international white super-commonwealth that would include Europe and the United States. See also Holocaust Denial Movement; Odinism; Rockwell, George Lincoln; Yockey, Francis Parker.

Suggested readings: Betty A. Dobratz and Stephanie L. Shanks-Meile, *"White Power, White Pride!": The White Separatist Movement in the United States* (New York: Twayne, 1997); Kim Murphy, "Lawsuits Threaten to Drain the Life out of Hate Groups," *Los Angeles Times* (August 22, 2000); p. A1; Greg Sandoval, "Agencies Target Hate Crimes in Antelope Valley," *Los Angeles Times* (February 16, 1997), p. B1; Southern Poverty Law Center, "Reconstructing Nazism," *SPLC Intelligence Report* 96 (Fall 1999):20–21; Eric K. Ward, Jonn Lunsford, and Justin Massa, "Sounds of Violence," *SPLC Intelligence Report* 96 (Fall 1999):28–32.

New American Movement (NAM)

The New American Movement (NAM) was the successor organization to the radical left-wing **Students for a Democratic Society** (SDS). Many of the radical leftists of the new left had become dissatisfied with the policies and the direction of the SDS. Two veteran leftists, James Wernstein and Staughton Lynd, investigated the possibility of forming a new radical leftist organization, but they soon became discouraged and withdrew. A group of radical leftists organized a convention in Davenport, Iowa, in November 1971, to launch an alternative to the SDS in the New American Movement. Leaders of the NAM attempted to avoid the organization mistakes of SDS and concentrated on organizing a national office with strong ties to local chapters. These local chapters were to determine the activities and priorities of the NAM. Two basic principles had to be acknowledged and accepted by all members of the NAM: the necessity for the triumph of socialism, and the centrality of feminism in the movement. Michael Lerner, a former member of the new left, wrote a book, *The New Socialist Revolution*, in 1973 arguing for a new revolutionary socialist party. His appeal began to attract leftists looking for a cause. Membership in the NAM never exceeded 1,500, and most of its membership strength was concentrated in the major cities and on large university campuses.

Although the NAM played a central role in the discussions among the American left in the late 1970s and early 1980s, the loss of influence of left-wing radicalism among the American public after this period caused a general decline in its fortunes. The NAM's greatest weakness was that it never expanded beyond academic discussions and failed because of little support and no growth. Michael Harrington's Democratic Socialist Organizing Committee (DSOC) was NAM's main rival among the remnants of the American left. Harrington, who had been a member of Norman Thomas's old Socialist Party, was resolutely anti-communist but intent on promoting socialism in the United States. The DSOC had been founded in October 1973. Harrington's emphasis on national politics and alliances with liberals made his organization more successful in lobbying and recruiting than the NAM. In 1982 the New American Movement merged with the DSOC. Several of the more militant members of the NAM refused to accept this merger and resigned. The failure of a new left organization showed how much the American public had repudiated left-wing radicalism. By the mid-1980s, the new left, which had been so active in the 1960s, had so few adherents that they were no longer visible on the American political scene. **See also** Students for a Democratic Society.

Suggested readings: Stanley Aronowitz, *The Death and Rebirth of American Radicalism* (New York: Routledge, 1996); Marie Jo Buhl and Dan Georgakas, *Encyclopedia of the American Left* (New York: Garland, 1990); Ronald Radosh, *Commies: A Journey Through the Old Left, the New Left and the Leftover Left* (San Francisco: Encounter Books, 2001); Michael White, "Left Moves Towards the American Dream," *Guardian* [London] (April 22, 1987), p. 1.

New Black Panther Party (NBPP)

The New Black Panther Party (NBPP) is the successor to the **Black Panther Party** (BPP) of the 1960s and 1970s. Although this group has been in existence since 1990, the NBPP made its appearance on the national scene in June 1998 in Jasper, Texas. Leaders of the NBPP announced that their purpose was to defend blacks in Jasper, Texas in the aftermath of James Byrd, Jr.'s, murder by white supremacists. Michael McGee, a Milwaukee alderman, organized the Black Panther Militia in Milwaukee, Wisconsin, in 1990. Soon afterward, he changed the name of the group to the New Black Panther Party. McGee organized chapters in other cities and became its national commander. Other black leaders joined McGee and the NBPP, including Aaron Michaels from Dallas, Texas, and Mmoja Agabu from Indianapolis, Indiana. Their goal was to form a party to lobby for the separation of the races and the overthrow of the U.S. government. This program attracted Black Muslim leader **Khalid Abdul Muhammad**, who had been expelled from **Louis Farrakhan**'s **Nation of Islam** after Farrakhan had disciplined him for making intemperate anti-white remarks. Muhammad joined the NBBP in 1994, and by 1998 he had replaced McGee as its national commander. Malik Zulu Shabazz, a Washington, D.C., lawyer, serves as the group's chief spokesperson. In the beginning of 2000, the Southern Poverty Law Center estimated that the NBPP had chapters in at least thirteen cities, including Atlanta, Dallas, Detroit, Houston, New York City, and Washington, D.C. Although the national commander administers the national program, chapters operate independently with locals conducting operations and demonstrations.

The New Black Panther Party has an aggressive anti-white agenda. Khalid Muhammad carried his anti-Semitic and anti-white rhetoric with him to the NBPP. Among his more controversial stands has been his blaming of the Jews for both black slavery and the Holocaust. He has also accused whites for the ills of modern society. In a September 2000 speech, reported verbatim by the Southern Poverty Law Center, given at the First Holy Temple of God in Christ in Detroit, Michigan, Muhammad stated, "There's only two kinds of white folks, there's only two kinds, bad white folks and worse white folks." Former leaders of the original Black Panther Party, David Hilliard and **Bobby Seale**, have repudiated both the rhetoric and philosophy of the NBPP. Seale characterized it in a newspaper article in March 1997 as "a black racist hate group."

This hostile reaction did not fáze Muhammad and other NBPP leaders. The leaders have specialized in intervening in racial controversies with heavily armed protesters. The Southern Poverty Law Center reports that such tactics have backfired and alienated large segments of the black community. The death of Khalid Muhammad of a brain aneurysm on February 18, 2001, left a leadership void in the NBBP, which was filled when Malik Zulu Shabazz, a lawyer and former chief aide to Khalid Muhammad, assumed control of the organization in March 2001. **See also** Black Panther Party; Farrakhan, Louis; Jasper Murder Case; Muhammad, Abdul Khalid; Shabazz, Malik Zulu.

Suggested readings: Jay Apperson, "The New Voice of Black Power," *Baltimore Sun* (April 22, 2001), p. 1C; Tony Freemantle, "Vitriolic Visionary; Quanell X Wages a Rhetorical War on the White Man," *Houston Chronicle* (March 4, 2001), p. A33; Christopher Goodwin, "Old Panthers Pounce on New Black Radicals," *Sunday Times* [London] (March 16, 1997), p. 1; Alex Kershaw, "The Return of the Black Panthers," *Guardian* [London] (August 22, 1992), p. 10; Ray Sanchez, "End of His March," *Newsday* [New York City] (February 18, 2001), p. A5; Southern Poverty Law Center, "Snarling at the White Man," *SPLC Intelligence Report* 100 (Fall 2000): 16–23; Ernie Suggs and S. A. Reid, "Hard-Line Black Activist Dies at 53; Muslim Leader Khallid Muhammad Was Best Known for Riling Whites," *Atlanta Journal and Constitution* (February 18, 2001), p. 1G.

New World Order

The establishment of a New World Order is the worst fear of many American extremists. A catchall term, the New World Order describes a worldwide conspiracy aimed at destroying American freedoms and liberties. Pat Robertson, the evangelical Christian leader and founder of the Christian Broadcasting Network (CBN), helped make the conspiratorial theories about the New World Order respectable by the publication of his book, *The New World Order*, in 1991. This book, which sold more than 500,000 copies, synthesizes all the conspiracy theories into one source. When President

George H. W. Bush made reference to a New World Order in a speech at the conclusion of the Persian Gulf War, it only confirmed to American extremists that a group of international elitists had constituted a secret conspiracy against the United States. They trace the origins of the conspiracy back to Adam Weishaupt and the **Illuminati**. According to these extremists, modern representatives of the Illuminati are such international organizations as the Trilateral Commission, the Council on Foreign Relations, and the Bilderberg Group; American, European, and Japanese businessmen and academics who made recommendations on foreign and economic policy. Antigovernment forces believe that the members of these groups are plotting against American citizens. **Willis Carto**'s newsletter, *Spotlight*, has taken the lead in tracing this purported international conspiracy without finding proof of its existence. Nevertheless, the secrecy of the international organization's proceedings and the elite memberships of these organizations lend themselves to conspiracy theories. The goal of international organizations of bringing global understanding and peace only reinforces the distrust of American extremists that America's sovereignty is threatened. Reference to the United Nation only compounds this fear. Intertwined in this fear of the New World Order is a belief by most extremists that Jews are behind this conspiracy. Any global initiative from a multinational corporation or from Israel becomes part of this conspiracy. **See also** Carto, Willis; Illuminati; Liberty Lobby; Militia Movement.

Suggested readings: Peter Carlson, "Vast Winged Conspiracies," *Washington Post* (March 16, 1999), p. C1; Ted Daniels, ed., *A Doomsday Reader: Prophets, Predictors, and Hucksters of Salvation* (New York: New York University Press, 1999); Paul Feldman, "Conspiracy Talk a U.S. Tradition," *Los Angeles Times* (May 29, 1995), p. A3; David Fritze, "Patriots Vow to Fight Off 'One-World Government,'" *Arizona Republic* (February 5, 1995), p. A1; James A. Fussell, "The New World Order?" *Kansas City Star* (January 8, 1995), p. G1; Robert L. Snow, *The Militia Threat: Terrorists Among Us* (New York: Plenum Trade, 1999); Richard White, "The Government as Grand Conspirator," *Star Tribune* [Minneapolis] (July 3, 1997), p. 27A.

Newkirk, Ingrid (1949–)

Ingrid Newkirk, one of the founders of the radical animal rights organization **People for the Ethical Treatment of Animals** (PETA), was born in 1949 in Surrey, England. Her father was an engineer and her mother worked in Mother Teresa charities. Much of her girlhood was spent in New Delhi, India. At the age of eighteen, she moved with her family to Florida. She met and married Steve Newkirk, a racecar driver, in Florida. They moved to Poolesville, Maryland, and Newkirk planned on a career as a stockbroker. A chance encounter with a neighbor's desertion of nineteen cats made her reconsider her career choice. She started working at dog pounds. She moved to the sheriff's department in Montgomery County, Maryland, and became director of animal cruelty investigations for the Washington Humane Society. In 1974 Newkirk was appointed poundmaster for the District of Columbia. Her experiences with mistreated animals led her to adopt a vegetarian lifestyle.

Newkirk met **Alex Pacheco** in 1980, and they formed an animal rights organization PETA. The original staff of PETA consisted of Newkirk, Pacheco, and five volunteers who operated out of her apartment in Takoma Park, Maryland. PETA's first target was an investigation of animal abuse at the Institute for Behavioral Research in Silver Springs, Maryland. This operation gained PETA national media attention. Next, the members of PETA staged a demonstration at the National Institutes of Health in Bethesda, Maryland, protesting the use of baboons in football helmet safety tests. Her aggressive tactics have included sending undercover operatives to film cruelty to animals, throwing a pie at a CEO, and lying down nude to protest the manufacturing of fur coats. She has been arrested several times; sixteen days was her longest jail stay. Newkirk is a revolutionary for animal rights, and her direct-action approach has made her many enemies. One of the most important of these enemies is the medical research community.

Newkirk has helped make PETA the largest animal rights organization in the world. In 1999 PETA had a worldwide membership of more than 650,000, and a budget in the neighborhood of $13 million. Most of the budget is spent on animal rights campaigns, cruelty investigations, animal rescues, and basic education about animals. In 1996 PETA moved to Norfolk, Virginia, to larger quarters. Newkirk lives a simple life. She does not own a car and walks to her Norfolk office. Her annual salary is about $25,000. She has written several books on animal rights. Newkirk continues to advance the cause of PETA by adhering to its goal that "animals are not ours to eat, wear, experiment on or use for entertainment." **See also** Animal Rights Movement; Pacheco, Alex; People for the Ethical Treatment of Animals.

Suggested readings: Mary Braid, "Catwalks and Dog Pounds," *Independent* [London] (November 28, 1998), p. 31; Ranny Green, "To PETA's Newkirk, All Mammals Are Family," *Seattle Times* (October 24, 1993), p. 18; Lydia Martin, "No Chicken-Hearted: PETA Founder Boldly Fights for Animals," *Arizona Republic* (April 24, 1999), p. D2; Nick Rosen, "Animal Passion; Is Activist Ingrid Newkirk a Beloved Leader or an Antichrist? *Guardian* [London] (October 12, 1993), p. 7; Howard Rosenberg, "Fighting Tooth & Claw; Ingrid Newkirk's Combative Style and Headline-Grabbing Stunts Have Shaken Up the Animal-Rights Movement," *Los Angeles Times* (March 22, 1992), Magazine, p. 18.

Newton, Huey P. (1941–1989)

Huey Newton, the founder and leader of the **Black Panther Party** (BPP), was born on February 17, 1941, in Louisiana. His father was a handyman and longshoreman. In 1944 his family moved to Oakland, California, so his father could find work. Newton, the youngest of seven children, grew up in a tough neighborhood in Oakland. Although he preferred the streets to school, Newton gradu-

ated from Berkeley High School. He then pursued a college degree at Merritt College (then named Oakland City College). Despite a poor high school academic record, his grades in college were excellent. While taking political science courses, Newton decided that socialism offered more opportunity for blacks than did capitalism. He soon earned a reputation as a campus radical. Newton also got into trouble with the Oakland police over the knifing of a fellow student in an argument. After a conviction of felonious assault with a deadly weapon, Newton spent six months in prison and served a lengthy probation period.

The civil rights movement was in full swing in the South, but Newton rejected Martin Luther King, Jr.'s, philosophy of nonviolence in favor of black nationalism. He admired **Malcolm X**, but he found the theology and the practices of the **Nation of Islam** unacceptable. During his stay at Merritt College, he met **Bobby Seale**. They were only casual acquaintances until they got together in February 1965 to commiserate over the death of Malcolm X. After several conversations, they decided that the revolutionary ideas of Frantz Fanon's *The Wretched of the Earth* (1963) were worth fighting for. They combined their talents to form the Soul Students Advisory Council (SSAC) to develop black leadership on campus. After a dispute with other members of the SSAC over tactics, Newton and Seale left it and moved into the Oakland community. In the summer of 1966, Newton worked as a community organizer canvassing the Oakland black community about its needs. In the fall, Newton and Seale decided that a new type of self-defense organization was needed. They founded the Black Panther Party for Self-Defense on October 15, 1966, and they drafted a ten-point program for black liberation. Among these ten points was a demand for education for blacks, the exemption of black men from military service, and a United Nations–supervised plebiscite of only black citizens.

Almost from its beginnings, the Black Panther Party was controversial and con-

Black Panther Party Minister of Defense Huey Newton speaks at a press conference in New York City on August 22, 1970. (AP Photo)

frontational. Newton and Seale began to attract adherents eager to follow the two leaders. They started patrols to monitor the activities of the Oakland police and started purchasing guns to protect themselves. In a series of confrontations with the police, the party soon gained a reputation for militancy. On the morning of October 28, 1967, Newton and a friend, Gene McKinney, were out driving and were stopped by Oakland policemen. A gunfight broke out in which one policeman was killed and another was wounded. Newton was also wounded in the exchange of gunfire and was arrested in a hospital. Authorities charged him with first-degree murder, assault with a deadly weapon, and kidnapping. While in jail, **Leroy Eldridge Cleaver** started a "Free Huey" campaign charging that Newton was on trial for his political beliefs. Newton spent two years in prison on a manslaughter conviction, but the conviction was overturned on appeal. Charges were dropped after two retrials resulted in hung juries.

Newton regained control of the Black Panther Party after leaving jail, but dissension within the ranks and his increasingly erratic personal behavior had doomed the Black Panthers by the mid-1970s. He had a dispute with Eldridge Cleaver over tactics, and other members turned to revolutionary activity. Newton and David Hilliard tried to retain control of the radicals in New York City, but they ended up expelling most of them, the so-called New York 21, from the party. The FBI's COINTELPRO campaign also helped to discredit Black Panther leadership by spreading false rumors and staging incidents to stir up dissension. After the collapse of the Black Panthers, Newton went back to school at the University of California at Santa Cruz and earned a Ph.D. with a dissertation titled "War Against the Panthers: A Study of Repression in America." Newton still had legal problems with a 1974 accusation of his murdering a prostitute. This trial also ended in a hung jury. Later in 1974, he was accused of pistol-whipping a tailor, but this charge never went to trial. Newton fled to Cuba for three years to escape his legal troubles. After returning to the United States, Newton found himself in trouble over several weapons charges and an allegation that he had embezzled funds from a Panther-run elementary school. He had developed a drug addiction to cocaine, heroin, and alcohol. His friend comedian Richard Pryor paid for him to attend a drug abuse program in 1984, but his addiction continued. In 1989 he was sentenced to ninety days in San Quentin Prison for possessing drug paraphernalia and violating parole for an earlier offense. A drug dealer killed him on the street in West Oakland, California, on August 22, 1989. **See also** Black Panther Party; Seale, Bobby; Cleaver, Leroy Eldridge.

Suggested readings: Jim Haskins, *Power to the People: The Rise and Fall of the Black Panther Party* (New York: Simon and Schuster Books for Young Readers, 1997); Dennis Hevesi, "Huey Newton Symbolized the Rising Black Anger of a Generation," *New York Times* (August 23,

1989), p. B7; Jonathan Kaufman, "Huey Newton Died Violently—As Did the Black Panthers," *Boston Globe* (August 27, 1989), p. A25; Hugh Pearson, *The Shadow of the Panther: Huey Newton and the Price of Black Power in America* (Reading, Mass.: Addison-Wesley, 1994); Mark A. Stein and Valarie Basheda, "Black Panther Founder Huey Newton Is Killed," *Los Angeles Times* (August 23, 1989), part 1, p. 1.

Nichols, Terry Lynn (1955–)

Terry Nichols, the accomplice of **Timothy James McVeigh** in the bombing of the Alfred P. Murrah Federal Building in Oklahoma City, Oklahoma, was born on April 1, 1955, and raised on a farm in Lapeer County in Upper Michigan. His parents were prosperous farmers who had fallen on hard times in the late 1970s. Stress of these hard times led his parents to divorce in 1974. After graduating from Lapeer West High School in 1973, Nichols attended Central Michigan University as a pre-med student. He quit school after only one semester. In 1976 he moved to Colorado and obtained a real estate license. In 1977 Nichols returned to Michigan to help his older brother on the family farm. He married a twice-divorced local realtor. Together they formed a real estate firm and sold insurance. They also had a son. Nichols became disillusioned by business and the sad state of the farming community. Trying to keep him from becoming too depressed, his wife encouraged him to join the army.

Nichols followed his wife's advice and joined the U.S. Army in 1988, but he proved to be an enthusiastic but indifferent soldier. Most of his military career was spent serving as a chauffeur for officers. At Fort Benning, Georgia, Nichols developed a friendship with Timothy McVeigh and Michael Fortier. After a transfer to Fort Riley, Nichols and McVeigh became inseparable friends. Before his term of enlistment was up, his wife left him and moved to Las Vegas, Nevada. Nichols received a hardship discharge in May 1989 to look after his young son.

After his discharge from the army, Nichols

lacked a purpose until he discovered right-wing causes. He worked at a variety of jobs on farms. In 1989 Nichols and his brother James renounced their U.S. citizenship over disgust with the policies of the U.S. government. He had become converted to the **common law movement** which asserts that banking is illegal. In 1992 the Chase Manhattan Bank sued Nichols to recover a credit card debt of over $18,000. He also had other difficulties with the authorities over his refusal to pay child support for his first child. In the meantime, he had married a Philippine mail-order bride with a young son. McVeigh was visiting on the Nichols farm on April 19, 1993, when news came about the end of the **Branch Davidian** siege and the heavy casualties. Nichols agreed with McVeigh that something needed to be done about the federal government.

Nichols's role in the Oklahoma bombing was planning and gathering the materials required to make the bomb. He had returned from visiting the Philippines with his wife and had bought a small house in Herington, Kansas. Nichols helped McVeigh gather the ingredients for the bomb, including twenty-two gallons of diesel fuel. FBI agents found the detonator cord, blasting caps, and ammonium nitrate at Nichols's home after the explosion on April 19, 1995. Testimony from Michael Fortier, a friend of both Nichols and McVeigh, incriminated Nichols in the planning of the bombing. This evidence was used against Nichols in his 1997 trial on the charge of involuntary manslaughter for the deaths of eight federal agents. He was acquitted of first-degree murder on these charges but received a life sentence for his participation in the Oklahoma City bombing.

New developments in the spring of 2001 increased the chance of a new federal trial for Nichols. Lawyers for Nichols have been active in trying to reopen Nichols's case based on the FBI's failure to disclose all documents at his 1997 trial. On April 16, 2001, the U.S. Supreme Court asked the U.S. Justice Department to explain why the Nichols case should not be reopened. This is an unusual request from the highest court and a new trial was possible. At the same time the State of Oklahoma decided to retry Nichols on state murder charges, in an attempt to secure a death penalty conviction. On October 1, 2001, the U.S. Supreme Court refused to reconsider Nichols's appeal for a new federal trial. Nichols requested a two-year delay in the Oklahoma court proceedings in late October 2001 because his attorneys didn't have enough money to continue defending him. See also McVeigh, Timothy James; Militia Movement.

Suggested readings: Sylvia Adcock, "Mysterious Moves; a Quiet Family Man, But Nichols Led Double Life," *Newsday* [New York City] (May 12, 1995), p. A25; Stephen Braun and Judy Pasternak, "Nichols Brothers Swept Up in Dark Maelstrom of Fury," *Los Angeles Times* (May 28, 1995), p. A1; Kim Cobb, "Oklahoma Battling for Bomb Evidence," *Houston Chronicle* (May 27, 2001), p. A8; Todd J. Gillman and Bruce Nichols, "Bombing Suspect Nichols' Rocky Life," *Phoenix Gazette* (May 11, 1995), p. A1; Gaylord Shaw, "Court Questions Fate of Nichols," *Newsday* [New York City] (June 5, 2001), p. A28; Joe Swickard, "Oklahoma Bombing: The Aftermath; Nichols," *Atlanta Journal and Constitution* (May 12, 1995), p. 10A.

Northpoint Tactical Teams

The Northpoint Tactical Teams is a group of political and religious extremists who live in a well-armed compound in North Carolina. Nord W. Davis, Jr., founded this group in the mid-1970s. He had been an executive at International Business Machines (IBM) in Massachusetts before retiring at age thirty-six and moving to North Carolina in the early 1970s. He established a compound near the town of Andrews in northeastern Cherokee County. Members describe themselves as "patriots" who are fighting against a government out of control. Davis, a prolific writer, sent monthly newsletters around the country. At one time, he spent $30,000 on a mailing shipment. Although Davis claimed that the Northpoint Teams did not constitute a militia, his adherents kept a well-equipped arsenal of weapons to fend off possible attacks by federal agents.

Davis had close connections with others in the anti-government movement. He was a close friend of **James B. "Bo" Gritz**, who ran for president in 1992 with **David Duke** as his running mate. The accused Atlanta bomber, **Eric Robert Rudolph**, lived in Cherokee County, and he had contact with the Northpoint Tactical Teams at one time or another. Despite his anti-government activities, an assault charge, and evidence that he had failed to pay federal taxes for twenty-five years, federal, state, and local authorities left him alone in his compound of three buildings and an underground bunker. Davis died in September 1997 of prostate cancer, but his group is still functioning without interference from government officials. **See also** Gritz, James B. "Bo"; Militia Movement; Rudolph, Eric Robert.

Suggested readings: Southern Poverty Law Center, "Hills of Rebellion," *SPLC Intelligence Report* 95 (Summer 1999): pp. 23–28; Bob Williams, "Hate Groups Active in N.C.," *News and Observer* [Raleigh, N.C.] (May 16, 1999), p. 1.

O

Odinism

Odinism is the white supremacist wing of the neo-pagan **Asatru** religious movement. Although both Asatru and Odinism share a belief in the pre-Christian Nordic gods, Odinism has roots back to pre-Nazi Germany. Alexander Rud Mills, an Australian Nazi supporter, decided to launch a movement in the 1930s to return to a purified pre-Christian past. In his book, *The Odinist Religion: Overcoming Jewish Christianity*, Mills charged that Jews had transformed Christianity from its original purity. Moreover, Europe was the true birthplace of civilization, not the Middle East. In an effort to return to a purified religion, he established the Anglican Church of Odin, but it languished in obscurity. His ideas gathered dust until a husband and wife team, Else and Alex Christensen, rediscovered them and founded the Odinist Fellowship in 1971. They started a journal, the *Odinist*, to spread the Odinist cause. At first the newly emerging Asatru movement and the Odinist movement shared common beliefs, but the racist orientation of Odinism soon caused them to take divergent paths.

Odinism attracts white supremacists because it has a strong racist theme and a warrior ethic. Soon after the Odinist Fellowship was formed, various extremist groups became interested in its potential. A leading neo-Nazi, George Dietz, realized that a Nazi revival was unlikely in Germany, but the United States was a more amenable market if Nazism was repackaged around Odinism. He created the Odinist Study Group (OSG) to infiltrate the Odinist movement with neo-Nazis. Odinism with its pre-Christian pagan rituals and the aspiration of members to join the Norse god Odin in Valhalla after perishing in battle appealed to the **neo-Nazis**. Adherence to the nine noble virtues of courage, discipline, fidelity, honor, hospitality, industriousness, perseverance, self-reliance, and truth was another attraction. Odinist groups have been formed under various names, but the most powerful one is the White Order of Thule. It is an offshoot of another group called Black Metal.

Odinism has become a popular religion for those incarcerated in prisons. It attracts members because of Odinism's reliance on personal virtues and its association with Northern Europeans. Many of the adherents of Odinism learn of its existence for the first time in prison. While several states have banned the practice of Odinism in their prison systems because of its association with white supremacy, other states allow it. At least two violent incidents have been linked to individuals with ties to Odinism. One of the suspects in the **Jasper murder case** had been a member of an Odinist group of the **Aryan Brotherhood** in prison. An initiation rite of this group was the killing of a black man. James Byrd, Jr., was the victim in such a killing in Jasper, Texas, in June 1998. In another case, an Odinist **skinhead** murdered a black man in Denver, Colorado, in November 1995. At present, the membership of Odinism is small, but it remains attractive to biker gangs, skinheads, and white supremacists. See also Asatru; Aryan Brotherhood; Jasper Murder Case.

Suggested readings: Jeffrey Kaplan, *Radical Religion in America: Millenarian Movements from the Far Right to the Children of Noah* (Syracuse, N.Y.: Syracuse University Press, 1997); Southern Poverty Law Center, "The New Barbarians: New Brand of Odinist Religion on the March," *SPLC Intelligence Report* 89 (Winter 1998): 15–16; Southern Poverty Law Center, "The New Romantics," *SPLC Intelligence Report* 101 (Spring 2001): 56–59; Southern Poverty Law Center, "Pagans and Prison," *SPLC Intelligence Report* 98 (Spring 2000): 25–29; Jack Sullivan, "Suspect May Have Joined Racist Group in Prison," *Boston Herald* (June 21, 2001), p. 5.

Oliphant, Jack (1924–1995)

Jack Oliphant, one of the godfathers of the Arizona militia movement, was born on November 3, 1924. Not much is known about his past except that he served in the military during World War II and once lived in Florida. He broke his back during the war and drew a lifelong military disability pension. He later suffered a shotgun wound in an accident that blew off his right arm in a dispute over a gold mine. He claimed that he was a former Central Intelligence Agency agent and an explosives expert. Oliphant moved from Florida to Arizona in 1976. At one time, he ran a Christian-oriented youth camp near Wickenburg, Arizona, known as Ranch Challenge for teenagers with drug and behavioral problems. The camp was closed after charges were made public that Oliphant was exploiting the youths for free labor.

Oliphant preached his brand of white supremacy from his 320-acre ranch in rural Arizona. This ranch, named Hephzibah, is located at the headwaters of the Knight Creek near Kingman, Arizona. For years, Oliphant traveled around the country preaching that Americans should prepare themselves to fight the federal government to protect their liberties. He also predicted a future race war. Oliphant was a close friend of the anti-government activist Colonel Gordon "Jack" Mohr, who was active in the Christian-Patriots Defense League.

Oliphant joined Ty Hardin's **Arizona Patriots** group in the early 1980s, and he allowed members of the Arizona Patriots to train for operations on his ranch. Members of this group plotted to bomb federal installations, but federal authorities, using undercover operatives, broke up the gang before any such action could be taken. The group's intent was to destabilize the federal government by blowing up the federal building in Phoenix, IRS offices, and a synagogue. In 1986 Oliphant was sent to prison for four years for his participation in a plot to hijack a Brink's armored truck money shipment from Nevada casinos. Funds from this robbery were intended to finance further white supremacist operations. He was also videotaped talking about making bombs and blowing up federal office buildings.

After serving prison time, Oliphant curtailed many of his anti-government activities. He continued to publish an anti-government, white supremacist newsletter, *Hephzibah Newsletter* and maintained contact with leaders in the **Aryan Nations** and other white supremacist organizations. Although he defended **Timothy James McVeigh**'s right to attack the government, he publicly stated in a newspaper article in the *Arizona Republic* that McVeigh's daytime bombing "has put the patriot movement back 30 years by blowing up a building with people inside." Oliphant and his wife survived on their ranch by collecting Social Security checks and disability payments for his military service until his death on November 15, 1995. See also Arizona Patriots; Militia Movement.

Suggested readings: Tony Perry, "Godfather of Arizona's Militiamen," *Los Angeles Times*

(May 21, 1995), p. A3; Mark Shaffer, "Did Arizona Militia Leader Aid Bomber?" *Arizona Republic* (June 10, 2001), p. A12; Mark Shaffer, "Supremacist Sees 'Blood in Streets' Says War in U.S. Is Coming," *Arizona Republic* (May 16, 1995), p. A1; Dennis Wagner, "FBI Keeping Tabs on Kingman Man," *Phoenix Gazette* (April 27, 1995), p. A1.

Omega 7

Omega 7, a Cuban American extremist group, carried out terrorist operations against Cuban targets and Cuban sympathizers in the late 1970s and early 1980s. Eduardo Arocena founded Omega 7 on September 11, 1974. He established two cells—one in Miami and the other in New Jersey—where there were large concentrations of Cuban émigrés. Arocena, who had been born in Caibarien, Cuba, had been a Cuban wrestling champion before fleeing Cuba to the United States in 1965. He settled in Elizabeth, New Jersey, and worked for a large food warehouse. Becoming more frustrated with Castro's Cuba, he recruited six other Cuban Americans—Pedro Remon, Andres Garcia, Jose Julio Garcia, Eduardo Losada-Fernandez, Eduardo Ochoa, and Alberto Perez—to form the New Jersey branch of Omega 7.

During the next decade, the Omega 7 organization carried out an assassination and bombing campaign against Cuban targets in the United States. Federal authorities first noticed Omega 7 after three bombings took place at New York's Kennedy Airport in March 1979. One of the group's primary targets was Cuban leader Fidel Castro, but the members were unable to reach him. The leadership decided instead to attack Cuban nationals in the United States. In November 1979, the leadership of Omega 7 claimed responsibility for the assassination of Cuban émigré Eulalio José Negrin in Union City, New Jersey, because the leaders considered him a communist. Next, the organization bombed Cuba's United Nations mission in New York City and injured two U.S. police officers. On March 25, 1980, members of the group attempted but failed in a bomb attempt on the life of Cuban UN Ambassador Raul Roa Kouri. Omega 7 members assassinated Felix Garcia Rodriguez, an attaché with the Cuban Mission to the United Nations, on September 11, 1980. Federal authorities attempted to solve these crimes, but they received little cooperation from the Cuban community. Federal officials arrested five of the key leaders of Omega 7 in October 1982 for the 1980 bombing. These arrests led to the indictment of Omega 7's leader Eduardo Arocena in December 1983. In February 1984, three Omega 7 members pleaded guilty to conspiracy in making and exploding bombs in Florida between 1980 and 1983. A federal court found Arocena guilty of the assassination of Felix Garcia Rodriguez and the attempted assassination of Raul Roa Kouri along with assorted bombings and involvement with a drug trafficker in September 1984. His sentence was life plus thirty-five years. In another trial held in Miami, Florida, Arocena received a twenty-year sentence. The loss of Arocena and other leaders to long terms in prison ended Omega 7's anti-Cuba campaign. The American Cuban community considers these individuals heroes in the struggle against Castro's Cuba. **See also** Cuban American National Foundation.

Suggested readings: Arnold H. Lubasch, "Exile Is Convicted as Omega 7 Leader," *New York Times* (September 23, 1984), sec. 1, p. 1; Arnold H. Lubasch, "Judge Sentences Omega 7 Leader to Life in Prison," *New York Times* (November 10, 1984), sec. 1, p. 28; Selwyn Raab, "F.B.I. Says Cuban Aide's Murder May Mark Shift by Terrorist Group," *New York Times* (September 13, 1980), sec. 1, p. 1; Brent L. Smith, *Terrorism in America: Pipe Bombs and Pipe Dreams* (Albany: State University of New York Press, 1994); Joseph B. Treaster, "Suspected Head of Omega 7 Terrorist Group Seized," *New York Times* (July 23, 1983), sec. 1, p. 1.

Operation Rescue

Operation Rescue, the leading **anti-abortion movement** in the United States in the late 1980s, was founded by **Randall Terry** in

Members of the anti-abortion protest group Operation Rescue march in front of the Gentilly Women's Clinic on April 11, 1995, in New Orleans. (AP Photo/Bill Haber)

1986. Terry had used a local group, Project Life, to fight against abortions in Binghamton, New York, but he believed that a national organization was needed to conduct a massive national campaign. He convinced the Evangelical community that Operation Rescue was atonement for ignoring the bloodguilt of abortion. Terry used this argument to recruit fundamentalist ministers,

but at first he had only limited success. At a rally in Pensacola, Florida, in November 1986, he was able to convince anti-abortion activists to back his new organization. Despite this support, it took almost two years before Operation Rescue was ready to launch its demonstrations. Operation Rescue's first major operation was scheduled for Philadelphia, but a massive police presence caused Terry to move the protest to Cherry Hill, New Jersey. A peaceful and successful conclusion at this demonstration made Terry a national figure, and Operation Rescue started attracting nationwide ministerial support. Operation Rescue's success in the Philadelphia area was followed by massive demonstrations in New York City in May 1988. By now Operation Rescue had attracted nationwide media attention, and strong financial and volunteer support soon followed.

Operation Rescue's next big test was staging anti-abortion protests at the July 1988 Democratic National Convention in Atlanta, Georgia. These demonstrations lacked the prior planning of previous operations, and the local leadership of Operation Rescue managed to alienate the Atlanta police by their arrogance. Most of the demonstrators were arrested and served forty-day jail sentences. Terry decided to increase the pressure and make Atlanta the test case for his movement. Consequently, he recruited more volunteers to clog and disrupt the local legal and political system. To make it more difficult for the Atlanta authorities, Terry told his followers to refuse to give their names and addresses when arrested. Hundreds of arrests followed in the next six weeks. Soon the leadership of Operation Rescue decided that this tactic was counterproductive since their most dedicated demonstrators were always in jail. Terry regrouped and called for a mass attack on Atlanta's abortion clinics in October. Atlanta police had become frustrated and responded to these renewed demonstrations by overreacting with unnecessary force garnering Operation Rescue even more publicity.

After Atlanta, Operation Rescue engaged in anti-abortion demonstrations and protests around the country. In retrospect, the high water mark for the movement came in 1989. Money and recruits flooded into the national headquarters allowing Operation Rescue to increase staffing and fund recruiting trips for its leaders. In the midst of this success, the U.S. Supreme Court made a ruling on *Webster v. Reproductive Health Services* over

when life begins, which went against Operation Rescue's position. This decision by the Reagan Supreme Court was a minor setback. Operation Rescue appeared to be on the verge of even greater successes against abortion rights. Terry and the other leaders of Operation Rescue believed that it was only a matter of time before abortions would become illegal again.

Two factors hurt Operation Rescue. First, the enemies of Operation Rescue finally recognized the seriousness of the threat of Operation Rescue and started mobilizing their political resources. Both the National Organization of Women (NOW) and Planned Parenthood mustered their legal and political staffs to attack the criminal side of Operation Rescue. Leaders of Operation Rescue had long ignored legal restrictions directed against their demonstrations at abortion clinics. This refusal to heed legal injunctions began to hurt the organization when judges started to fine and jail supporters of Operation Rescue. Second, the autocratic leadership style of Randall Terry alienated some leaders and they drifted away from Operation Rescue in increasing numbers. Terry's open anti-feminism caused difficulties with some of his female supporters.

The end for Operation Rescue came out of a combination of internal dissension and a shift of key members toward a more violent approach to the abortion issue. Terry had received a six-month jail term in Atlanta for his role in earlier demonstrations there. While he was in jail, other leaders worked to reform Operation Rescue and make its decision making more decentralized. Meanwhile, Terry began to have reservations about serving time in jail, and, contrary to the wishes of the other leaders, he wanted an early release. When Terry obtained his early release, he learned about the attempts at reform and fired the architects of the changes. Because Terry was still suffering from psychological burnout from his time in jail, he turned Operation Rescue over to his loyal subordinate, Keith Tucci. Tucci renamed the movement Operation Rescue National, and by the fall of 1990 the anti-abortion movement had become more militant, and the mass demonstrations of the old Operation Rescue were no longer making news. In an effort to regain lost glory, Tucci with Terry's support turned to a national campaign against a Wichita, Kansas, abortion provider. While the Wichita demonstrations lasted several months into the summer of 1991, it proved to be Operation Rescue National's last major success. After Wichita, the organization slowly drifted without leadership. Former members and fellow travelers turned increasingly toward more violent tactics. Assassinations of abortion providers turned public opinion away from violence.

Operation Rescue has undergone another leadership change. In February 1994, Reverend Flip Benham, a Methodist minister and head of the Operation Rescue Dallas–Fort Worth, became the leader of Operation Rescue succeeding Tucci. Passage of the Freedom of Access to Clinic Entrances Act (FACE) in June 1994 has made it more difficult for Operation Rescue's tactics to work. This legislation and growing public disapproval of violence have weakened the effectiveness of Operation Rescue. Operation Rescue has been renamed Operation Save America to broaden its political base. In the middle of July 2001, Operation Save America demonstrated in Wichita, Kansas, at Dr. George Tiller's clinic, hoping to revitalize the anti-abortion movement. **See also** Anti-Abortion Movement; Terry, Randall.

Suggested readings: Dallas A. Blanchard, *The Anti-Abortion Movement and the Rise of the Religious Right: From Polite to Fiery Protest* (New York: Twayne, 1994); Kurt Chandler, "Abortion Opponents Forced Onto the Defensive," *Star-Tribune: Newspaper of the Twin Cities* (May 29, 1993), p. 1B; William Claiborne, "A Decade Later, Abortion Foes Again Gather in Wichita," *Washington Post* (July 16, 2001), p. A3; Gayle Reaves, "Operation Rescue Names Benham National Director," *Dallas Morning News* (February 9, 1994), p. 1A; James Risen and Judy L. Thomas, *Wrath of Angels: The American Abortion War* (New York: Basic Books, 1998); Sarah Tippit, "Inside the Anti-Abortion Bootcamp," *Sun-Sentinel* [Fort Lauderdale, Fla.] (July

11, 1993), p. 6; Jeffrey Weiss, "Wichita a Test Case for Abortion Foes," *Dallas Morning News* (August 11, 1991), p. 1A.

Order, The (The Silent Brotherhood)

The Order, or the Silent Brotherhood, was an American domestic terrorist group with close ties to the white supremacist **Aryan Nations. Robert Jay Mathews** founded The Order in 1983 with the goal of fomenting a right-wing revolution and establishing a white homeland in the Pacific Northwest. With close contacts in both the neo-Nazi **National Alliance** and the Aryan Nations, he was able to recruit a small body of supporters to launch a campaign of bank robberies, murders, counterfeiting, and bombings. His blueprint for operations was **William Pierce's** *The Turner Diaries* (1977). To ensure loyalty and to tie members closely to the group, members were required to earn points by committing violent acts, including robberies, bombings, and assassinations. Randall Rader, a member of the **Covenant, the Sword, and the Arm of the Lord (CSA)**, trained members of the group in marksmanship and commando tactics. He also arranged for them to acquire automatic weapons.

The Order's crime spree started in April 1983 with small operations, but soon larger, more profitable operations were undertaken. A raid on a Spokane, Washington, adult bookstore garnered only $369. Initial attempts at counterfeiting were unsuccessful, and two members, Bruce Pierce and **David Lane**, were arrested for trying to pass fake money. A Seattle, Washington, branch bank robbery on December 20, 1983, netted them more money, but a dye bomb ruined some of the $25,900. In a March 1984 armored car robbery at a Fred Myers Store in Seattle, they obtained $43,000 in cash. Another armored car robbery at the Northgate Mall in Seattle on April 23, 1984, resulted in their first big stake, $500,000. On June 18, 1984, a hit team of members of The Order assassinated a Jewish talk-show host, Alan Berg, in his own driveway in a Denver, Colorado, suburb. Bruce Pierce did the shooting with support from Robert Jay Mathews and Richard Scutari. David Lane drove the getaway car. These crimes attracted the attention of the police, but it was the robbery of $3.6 million from a Brink's armored truck in Ukiah, California, that alerted federal authorities. Mathews had been able to make contacts with employees of Brink's, which enabled him to plan and execute the robbery.

Federal agencies initiated a national manhunt for the robbers. A weapon left at the scene of the robbery was traced to Mathews. Federal officials learned about the extent of the activities of the group when one of the members, **Thomas Martinez**, informed on the others. Martinez had been arrested for passing counterfeit money in the Philadelphia area and made a deal with the federal government. Law enforcement agents tracked down Mathews and most of his followers to the state of Washington. Mathews was killed in a gun battle with the FBI on Whidbey Island, Washington, on December 7, 1984. Most of the gang was captured later. Survivors of The Order were convicted for a variety of crimes including counterfeiting, robbery, bombing, and murder. All of them received sentences of from 40 to 100 years. Despite the failure of his movement, Mathews's fight and death have made him a hero in the **white supremacist movement**. None of the money stolen was ever recovered, and federal officials believe that Mathews had distributed it to other white supremacist leaders and organizations. **See also** Brink's Armored Car Robbery; Lane, David; Mathews, Robert Jay.

Suggested readings: Kevin Flynn and Gary Gerhardt, "Alan Berg; Neo Nazis Failed to Realize the Mad Goals That Spurred Them to Kill Radio Host a Decade Ago," *Denver Rocky Mountain News* (June 19, 1994), p. 36A; Kevin Flynn and Gary Gerhardt, *The Silent Brotherhood: Inside America's Racist Underground* (New York: Free Press, 1989); Stephen Singular, *Talked to Death: The Life and Murder of Alan Berg* (New York: Beech Tree Books, 1987).

Order II

The Order II was a successor group to **The Order**. Several members of the **Aryan Nations** had been sympathetic to the goals and tactics of **Robert Jay Mathews**. They were upset by his death and the imprisonment of his followers. David Dorr, a former member of the Aryan Nations security force, and his wife, Deborah, were the principal leaders of this new group. They recruited another couple, Edward and Olive Hawley, as well as Robert Pires and Kenneth Shray and officially formed the group in November 1985. In December 1985, Dorr started making preparations for a bombing and counterfeiting campaign. By February 1986, the group was passing counterfeit $20 bills. Their first effort at bombing—the store of a Jewish businessman near **Hayden Lake**, Idaho—was unsuccessful on March 6, 1986. Another more successful bombing attempt was made on August 7, 1986, at a classic automobile restoration business also near Hayden Lake. Later in August, Dorr and Pires killed Shray because they thought he might be an informer. The two couples, the Dorrs and the Hawleys, appeared on the *Oprah Winfrey Show* in Chicago to defend their extremist views.

Encouraged by their successes, Order II intensified their campaign to destabilize the government. On September 16, 1986, they bombed a Catholic priest's home near Hayden Lake. Next, they raided the Aryan Nations compound and stole computers and photographic equipment. Dorr and Pires planned a major operation to rob two local Idaho banks for funds and an Idaho Army National Guard armory for weapons. To accomplish this ambitious plan, the plotters set off four time bombs in Coeur d'Alene, Idaho, on September 29, 1986, to provide a diversion for the robberies. This plan proved too complex, and all five members of Order II were captured during the robbery attempt. They were tried on Racketeering Influenced and Corrupt Organizations (RICO) charges. Pires testified against the others to avoid a first-degree murder charge for the killing of

Shray. Dorr and Pires each received twenty-year sentences, but Deborah Dorr and Edward Hawley were given eight-year sentences. Olive Hawley's six-year sentence was suspended, and she was placed on five years of probation.

Order II proved to be a poor imitation of The Order. None of the participants had the knowledge or expertise to make their plans work. Moreover, neither Dorr nor Pires had the leadership qualities of Mathews. Perhaps their biggest mistake was conducting all of their operations in the same area, alerting law enforcement authorities to their presence. **See also** Aryan Nations; Mathews, Robert Jay; Order, The.

Suggested readings: Associated Press, "Man Tied to White Supremacists Faces Charges in Idaho Bombings," *New York Times* (October 7, 1986), p. A22; Associated Press, "3 Linked to Racist Group Arrested in Idaho Probe," *San Diego Union-Tribune* (October 3, 1986), p. 1; Vincent Coppola, *Dragons of God: A Journey Through Far-Right America* (Atlanta: Longstreet Press, 1996); Brent L. Smith, *Terrorism in America: Pipe Bombs and Pipe Dreams* (Albany: State University of New York Press, 1994); Wallace Turner, "3 in Racist Group Held on Counterfeiting Charges," *New York Times* (October 4, 1986), sec. 1, p. 28.

Order of the Solar Temple (See Solar Temple Cult)

P

Pacheco, Alex (1958?–)

Alex Pacheco, one of the co-founders and chairperson of the animal rights organization **People for the Ethical Treatment of Animals** (PETA), was born around 1958 in Mexico. His father was a doctor. Pacheco grew up in Mexico and then in Ohio. After graduating from high school in Ohio, he entered Ohio State University planning to enter the priesthood after graduation. While at Ohio State, he founded a campus animal rights group after a visit to a slaughterhouse. During the summer of 1979, he worked with the **Sea Shepherd Conservation Society** and **Paul Franklin Watson**, the head of the Sea Shepherds. Portuguese authorities briefly jailed Pacheco after the ship *Sea Shepherd* rammed the *Sierra*, a Portuguese whaling vessel. Later he traveled to England and joined the Hunt Saboteurs Association, an anti-hunting animal rights group devoted to disrupting foxhunts. He decided to transfer from Ohio State University to George Washington University and study political science.

In 1980 Pacheco joined with **Ingrid Newkirk** to found PETA. Pacheco was working at a local dog pound where he met Newkirk. They shared a common interest in protecting animals from scientific experimentation. One of Pacheco's first actions in PETA was a four-month undercover assignment at the Silver Springs laboratory of Maryland researcher Edward Taub. Neurological research at this facility involved surgical operations on monkeys to study sensory communication between the brain and limbs. At the end of the experiment, the monkeys were killed and their spinal cords were examined for evidence of neuron regeneration. Pacheco recorded evidence of animal abuse and removed the monkeys from the laboratory. His 1981 exposé of the mistreatment of the Silver Spring monkeys was a milestone in the **animal rights movement**. Not only did the laboratory face adverse publicity about animal abuse, it lost its federal grants. Taub received a citation for animal abuse although authorities later dropped the charges. Under Pacheco's leadership, PETA has become the largest animal rights organization in the United States. In 2000, PETA had over a half million members in three countries—Canada, Great Britain, and the United States. **See also** Animal Rights Movement; Newkirk, Ingrid; People for the Ethical Treatment of Animals.

Suggested readings: Peter Carlson, "The Great Silver Springs Monkey Debate," *Washington Post* (February 24, 1991), Magazine, p. W15; Howard LaFranchi, "Animal Research Debate Heats Up," *Christian Science Monitor* (March 10, 1989), p. 8; Gary Libman, "On the Cutting Edge of Animal Rights Activism," *Los Angeles Times* (April 28, 1989), part 5, p. 1; David

Treadwell, "PETA Sues Writer of Magazine Story It Calls 'False . . . Malicious,' " *Los Angeles Times* (April 12, 1990), p. E13.

Patriot Movement

The patriot movement is a term that encompasses the various American organizations and groups that oppose the U.S. government. Earlier groups, such as the **John Birch Society** and the **Liberty Lobby**, initiated the patriot movement, but other groups, such as the Minutemen and Posse Comitatus, continued the tradition. **Christian Identity** groups form the right wing of this movement. Survivalist and militia groups joined it in the 1980s and 1990s. A common theme among these groups is opposition to the internationalism of the **New World Order**. By the mid-1990s, it was estimated that around 5 million Americans subscribe to some group that belongs to the patriot movement. Liberty Lobby's *Spotlight* serves as the chief propaganda arm for the movement.

The patriot movement is an umbrella for a variety of groups which espouse competing ideas and ideologies. One topic that unites these groups is opposition to gun control. Many of these groups are overtly anti-Semitic and racist, but others are not. Members of some of the groups want to withdraw from American society, but others want to destroy all remnants of it. Anti-government groups reject the current political system from the political parties to the federal economic system. Because the patriot movement is such a broad-based movement, no national leader or leadership has come to mobilize it. The closest occasion came in October 1992 with the **Estes Park meeting** where extremist leaders from numerous groups met to plan strategy and promote the start of the **militia movement**. A total of 160 individuals from thirty states participated in this gathering. Since then, however, little progress has been made because the national leaders of the various groups neither trust nor admire each other. The only other possibility is for a national leader, such as **David Duke** or Patrick Buchanan, to mobilize and energize the various elements of the patriot movement, but at present this is not likely.
See also Estes Park Meeting; Militia Movement; New World Order; Survivalist Movement.

Suggested readings: Paul Brinkley-Rogers and Dennis Wagner, "Patriot Movement Gains Momentum, Desperation," *Arizona Republic* (April 14, 1996), p. A1; Kim Cobb, "Terror on the Right," *Houston Chronicle* (April 20, 1997), p. 33; Morris Dees and James Corcoran, *Gathering Storm: America's Militia Threat* (New York: HarperCollins, 1996); David Fritze, "Patriots Vow to Fight-Off 'One-World Government,' " *Arizona Republic* (February 5, 1995), p. A1; Carol McGraw, "Growing 'Patriot' Movement Spews Hard-Core Hate," *Buffalo News* (June 30, 1996), p. 9F; Mike McIntire, "For Alienated Citizenry, Government Is the Enemy," *Hartford Courant* (November 23, 1997), p. A1; Nicholas Riccardi, "Easy Money . . . Hard Reality," *Los Angeles Times* (April 22, 1996), p. 1.

Patterson, Lawrence T. (1937–)

Lawrence Patterson, one of the leading anti-government and anti-Semitic writers in the United States, was born in 1937. Patterson is a graduate of Miami University in Ohio with an undergraduate degree in science. He obtained a master's degree in business administration from the University of Michigan. Most of his professional life has been spent in sales and marketing. He now lives in Cincinnati, Ohio, and operates a financial planning service for those interested in international investments.

Patterson started his career in publishing extremist literature in 1975. He launched the *L. T. Patterson Strategy Letter* to provide a forum for his right-wing political and economic views. Later, Patterson changed its title to *A Monthly Lesson in Criminal Politics*. Finally, in 1989, the periodical was renamed *Criminal Politics*. Patterson uses this periodical to advance his thesis of an international Jewish conspiracy. According to Patterson, Zionists control the economic and political policies of the United States, Russia, and the United Nations. Among those making his "villains list" are George H. W. Bush, William Clinton, Robert Dole, Alan Greenspan, Saddam Hussein, Henry Kissinger, and the Rockefeller family. The Federal Reserve System and the Trilateral Commission are also special targets for Patterson's attacks.

Patterson has been associated with or affiliated with several other prominent extremist organizations. For a time, he was an official of Redeem Our Country (ROC) and active in the **Committee to Restore the Constitution** (CRC). Both of these groups were grassroots anti-government organizations. He was a frequent contributor to **Liberty Lobby**'s *Spotlight* until he backed the staff of the **Institute for Historical Review** (IHR) in its power struggle with IHR's founder **Willis Carto**. Since this incident, writers in *Spotlight* have castigated Patterson and his views. Despite these attacks, Patterson still ranks as one of the leaders in the propaganda war being waged against the federal government by extremist writers. **See also** Anti-Semitism; Carto, Willis; Liberty Lobby.

Suggested readings: Anti-Defamation League, *Danger: Extremism: The Major Vehicles and Voices on America's Far-Right Fringe* (New York: Anti-Defamation League, 1996); Bill Sloat, "Conservative Publisher Sues to Prevent Use of Mailing List," *Plain Dealer* [Cleveland] (May 6, 1995), p. 5B.

People for the Ethical Treatment of Animals (PETA)

The largest, most influential organization in the **animal rights movement** is the People for the Ethical Treatment of Animals (PETA), founded by **Ingrid Newkirk** and **Alex Pacheco** in 1980. The headquarters was located in Rockville, Maryland, until 1996 when a move was made to Norfolk, Virginia. Revenue comes from small donations, and PETA spends less than 25 percent of its budget for administrative purposes. Employees have low salaries and the turnover rate is high. Reports from former employees suggest that there is little tolerance for differences of opinion. Membership and sup-

porters account for nearly 300,000 people in the United States. Since PETA became an international organization in the 1990s, worldwide support may be as high as 500,000.

PETA members share a commitment to end animal testing for scientific or commercial reasons, discourage the wearing of furs and encourage an end to the fur business, and promote general humane policies for animals. This organization's tactics include the use of public demonstrations, rallies, guerrilla operations to free animals, media blitzes, publicity campaigns, and documentary files, slides, and pictures. Their tactics include shock, insult, and sometimes nudity to gain publicity. Undercover operatives infiltrate businesses, institutes, or organizations under investigation, and instances of animal abuse are reported by PETA to the national media. An undefined relationship exists between the leadership of PETA and the **Animal Liberation Front** (ALF). PETA representatives have served as the news outlet for the more violent actions of the ALF, but none of PETA's members have been found to participate in ALF activities. Despite this separation from ALF, PETA is one of the most feared animal rights organizations. PETA leaders do not hesitate to investigate and demonstrate against any individual or business that it deems to be an enemy to animal rights. **See also** Animal Liberation Front; Animal Rights Movement; Newkirk, Ingrid; Pacheco, Alex.

Suggested readings: Lorraine Adams, "What's PETA's Beef?" *Washington Post* (May 28, 1995), p. F1; Peter Carlson, "Spy in the Henhouse; Michele Rokke's Undercover Life for Animal Rights," *Washington Post* (January 3, 1998), p. C1; Harold D. Guither, *Animal Rights: History and Scope of a Radical Social Movement* (Carbondale: Southern Illinois University Press, 1998); Gina Kolata, "Tough Tactics in One Battle over Animals in the Lab," *New York Times* (March 24, 1998), p. E1; Scot Lehigh, "Doing Right by Animals," *Boston Globe* (October 22, 1995), p. 73; Bill Sizemore, "Former Members Criticize Animal Rights Group PETA," *San Francisco Chronicle* (December 24, 2000), p. B4.

Bodies are strewn around the Jonestown Commune in Jonestown, Guyana, where more than 900 members of the People's Temple committed suicide in November 1978. (AP Photo/file)

People's Temple

The People's Temple, a religious cult, ceased to exist after the mass suicide of its members at Jonestown, in Guyana, South America, in November 1978. **James Warren "Jim" Jones** founded this religious cult in Indianapolis, Indiana, in 1956. Jones made it into a socially progressive church by promoting racial unity and operating a variety of social outreach programs, including soup kitchens. In 1960 the Disciples of Christ accepted the church for membership and soon afterward Jones was ordained as a minister. The church had a slow but steady growth in Indianapolis until Jones became concerned about the possibility of a nuclear war. He visited South America for a year and a half leaving his church in the hands of others. On his return, Jones decided to move the church and its membership to Ukiah, California, in 1965.

The People's Temple prospered in California; the church grew from 300 members in 1969 to 2,570 in 1973. Most of this growth was a result of high-powered recruitment programs using religious radio stations and bus trips. The more the church prospered, however, the more erratic became the behavior of Jim Jones. Rumors reached California authorities about irregularities in the church ranging from child abuse to financial improprieties. Jones started to look for other places to locate the church, and he soon found an area in Guyana, South America. The church's board of directors approved a branch church and an agricultural mission to be established in Guyana in 1973. An advance party arrived in Guyana in 1974, and plans for a new community to be named Jonestown were made. By September 1977, Jones had moved nearly 1,000 members of the People's Temple to Jonestown. Newspaper articles exposing Jones and recommending that authorities investigate the activities of the People's Temple prompted the final move.

Conditions at Jonestown were primitive, and control of the members of the People's Temple by Jones was complete. Jones had become so paranoid that he expected his enemies to attack him and his church. He included the CIA, the FBI, the media, and politicians among his enemies. Beginning early in 1978, Jones started conducting mass suicide drills called "White Nights." These drills took on the urgency of emergency fire drills and were often called by Jones in the middle of the night. No dissent or opposition to Jones was tolerated. Those who were recalcitrant in any manner were punished by time in solitary confinement in a coffin-like structure called "the box." Discipline was especially harsh toward wayward children. Children deemed to deserve punishment were dunked in the Jonestown well at night. Only complete obedience to the will of Jones was acceptable.

Tales of child abuse and cult-like behavior had tarnished the image of the People's Temple. Relatives of members of the Temple complained to politicians and asked them to investigate conditions at Jonestown. U.S. Representative Leo Ryan, a Democrat from California, organized a fact-finding tour in November 1978 to investigate these complaints. Ryan and his entourage of concerned relatives, political aides, and media representatives arrived in Guyana on November 15, 1978. During the next few days, Ryan talked to leaders and individual members of the People's Temple. He found sixteen Temple members ready to return to the United States with him. These imminent defections signaled to Jones that the end of his church was near. Tensions became so high that a member of the Temple attacked Ryan with a knife, but he only injured himself. Ryan decided to leave Jonestown with the dissidents. On November 18, 1978, a band of loyal members of the Temple followed the Ryan group to the Port Kaituma airstrip. At about 5:00 P.M. they opened fire with small arms killing Ryan and four others in the initial volley. Three of the dead were news media representatives, and one was a defector. Twelve others suffered wounds of varying degrees of seriousness. Once news reached Jones of the killings, he ordered a White Night mass suicide operation. Throughout the night members of the People's Temple either committed suicide or were killed. In all, 913 individuals died; 276 of them were children. Among the dead were Jim Jones, his wife, his children, and his grandchildren. Jones died of a gunshot wound to the head.

The mass suicide and the resulting publicity ended the story of the People's Temple. A few survivors remained to tell the story, but without a charismatic leader the cult ceased to exist. Several of the survivors committed suicide within a few months of leaving Jonestown. In 1979 the Mills family, Al and Jeanne Mills and their daughter, Linda, were found murdered in Berkeley, California. They had been outspoken critics of their experiences with the People's Temple. Larry Layton, a key advisor to Jim Jones, was the only survivor to be prosecuted for his role in the events of November 18. After two trials, he was convicted in 1986 of conspiring to murder Leo Ryan. He is now serving a life sentence in the federal prison at Lompoc, California. Every year on November 18, a memorial service for the victims is held at Evergreen Cemetery in Oakland, California, where 260 of the children are buried. **See also** Cults; Jones, James Warren "Jim".

Suggested readings: David Chidester, *Salvation and Suicide: An Interpretation of Jim Jones, the People's Temple, and Jonestown* (Bloomington: Indiana University Press, 1988); Deborah Layton, *Seductive Poison: A Jonestown Survivor's Story of Life and Death in the Peoples Temple* (New York: Anchor Books, 1998); Shiva Naipaul, *Black and White* (London: H. Hamilton, 1980); John Peer Nugent, *White Night* (New York: Rawson, Wade, 1979); Ken Levi, ed., *Violence and Religious Commitment: Implication of Jim Jones' People's Temple Movement* (University Park: Pennsylvania State University Press, 1982).

Peters, Peter J. "Pete" (1947–)

Pete Peters, a **Christian Identity** minister famous for his radical political positions, was born in 1947 on a ranch in western Nebraska. Peters attended both the University of Nebraska and Colorado State University. With degrees in agrobusiness and economics, he worked for years for the U.S. Department of Agriculture. Peters studied religion at the Church of Christ Bible Training School in Gering, Nebraska, and then served as a minister in a Christian Identity church in Laporte, Colorado. His first exposure to the glare of media attention occurred when Colorado police officials learned that the assassins of the Denver talk-show host, Alan Berg, had attended his church. Peters is the author of a booklet, *Death Penalty for Homosexuals*, in which he advocates the death penalty as a way to curb homosexuality. In another book, *Handbook for Survivalists, Racists, Tax Protesters, Militants and Right-Wing Extremists*, Peters glorifies the concept of the **Phineas Priesthood** to fight what he terms "race polluters."

In the late 1980s and early 1990s, Peters increased his influence in the Christian Identity movement by taking confrontational stances on the **Ruby Ridge incident** and the **Branch Davidians**. Peters persuaded **James B. "Bo" Gritz**, an anti-government activist, to go to Idaho to negotiate the surrender of **Randall Weaver** at Ruby Ridge. He took the initiative and a leadership role in the October 1992 **Estes Park meeting**, which laid the groundwork for the beginning of the modern American **militia movement**. His militant anti-government activities increased his profile for the authorities in the state of Colorado. These officials used a fine over an election law violation and Peters's stubborn refusal to pay it as justification to seize Peters's church and to freeze his bank accounts. Despite the loss of these assets, Peters continues to teach Christian Identity doctrine, but now primarily through an Internet Web site. Peters continues to deny his lofty status in the Christian Identity movement, but he is accepted by Christian Identity leaders as one of its most articulate spokespersons. **See also** Christian Identity; Estes Park Meeting; Gritz, James B. "Bo; Militia Movement; Order, The (The Silent Brotherhood); Weaver, Randall.

Suggested readings: Richard Abanes, *American Militias: Rebellion, Racism, and Religion* (Downers Grove, Ill.: InterVarsity Press, 1996); Jeffrey Kaplan, ed., *Encyclopedia of White Power: A Sourcebook on the Radical Racist Right* (Walnut Creek, Calif.: Altamira Press, 2000); Lou Kilzer and Kevin Flynn, "Militia Movement Had Roots in Estes," *Denver Rocky Mountain News* (May 14, 1997), p. 10A; Kenneth S. Stern, *A Force upon the Plain: The American Militia Movement and the Politics of Hate* (Norman: University of Oklahoma Press, 1996); Leonard Zeskind, "And Now, the Hate Show," *New York Times* (November 16, 1993), p. A27.

Phelps, Fred (1929–)

Fred Phelps, the leading anti-gay extremist in the United States, was born on November 13, 1929, in Meridian, Mississippi. His father was a detective on the Southern Railroad, and his mother died of cancer when Phelps was five years of age. After schooling in Meridian, he was ordained as a Baptist minister at age seventeen in Utah. Phelps enrolled but never graduated from Bob Jones University. He moved to Topeka, Kansas, in 1954 where he formed the unaffiliated Westboro Baptist Church in 1956. Phelps earned a law degree in 1961 at Washburn University in Topeka, Kansas, and worked for several years as a civil rights lawyer. He was disbarred by the state of Kansas in 1979 for improper conduct and lack of legal ethics. Phelps also had political ambitions and twice has run for governor and was a candidate for the U.S. Senate in Kansas in 1992.

Phelps is aggressive in his **gay-bashing** activities and uses the Bible as the basis for his opposition to homosexuality. Most of his time is spent in leading demonstrations at parks, funerals, government buildings, schools, churches, and newspaper offices protesting against gay rights. He started his anti-gay campaign in June 1991. His protests at the funerals of AIDS victims led the Kansas legislature to ban such demonstrations in 1992. In 1994 Phelps earned national attention for his violent verbal confrontation with poet Maya Angelou, forcing her to cancel a speaking engagement at Emporia State University. He attacked her because she had spoken at a public function with President Bill Clinton. Phelps believed in retaliating against anyone associated with President Bill Clinton because he believed Clinton was pro-gays. Several times Phelps has been arrested for assault, but he has never served time in jail. Phelps has spent the last decade traveling around the country promoting anti-gay demonstrations, including those at the funerals of former U.S. Senator Barry Goldwater, Frank Sinatra, and President Clinton's mother. Anyone that Phelps interpreted as soft on gays was a target. Phelps's most high-profile protest came at the 1998 funeral of Matthew Shepard, a University of Wyoming student who was killed because he was gay. His financial support comes from members of his church, most of whom are members of his family. Three of his thirteen children have repudiated him and have accused him of being an abusive parent, but the others strongly support him with funds gathered from their law practices. Eleven of his children are lawyers.

Phelps intimidates his opponents by threatening and instituting lawsuits. Politicians in the state of Kansas have been reluctant to confront him. His insistence that the only true Jews are Christians and his attacks on gays horrify mainstream religious leaders. Phelps spends around $250,000 annually traveling around the country fighting gay rights. Phelps also operates a Web site that advances his anti-gay program. **See also** Gay Bashing; Gay Liberation Movement.

Suggested readings: Stephen Braun, "Pastor Who Takes Pride in Hate Traces the Emotion to Bible," *Los Angeles Times* (November 16, 1999), p. A5; Sandi Dolbee, "Witness for the Persecution," *San Diego Union-Tribune* (June 2, 2000), p. E1; Annie Gowen, "Holy Hell; Fred Phelps, Clergyman, Is on a Crusade," *Washington Post* (November 12, 1995), p. F1; Jim Henderson, "Preaching Hate," *Houston Chronicle* (August 2, 1998), p. 1; Southern Poverty Law Center, "A City Held Hostage," *SPLC Intelligence Report* 101 (Spring 2001): 19–27; Southern Poverty Law Center, "Halting Abusive Lawyers," *SPLC Intelligence Reports* 101 (Spring 2001): 60.

Phineas Priesthood

The Phineas Priesthood, part of the terrorist wing of the **white supremacist movement**, takes its name from biblical references in the Bible's Book of Numbers. A priest named Phineas killed an Israelite man and his foreign wife to prevent a plague brought by this woman from infecting the Israelites. For this action, Phineas was honored when his family members were declared hereditary priests. White supremacists interpret this story as a justification for the use of force to prevent interracial contact between whites and minorities. **Richard Kelly Hoskins** first advanced the theory of the Phineas priesthood in his book, *Vigilantes of Christendom: The Story of the Phineas Priesthood* (1990). He describes the cells of modern priests who will carry out God's will by killing mixed-race couples, civil rights leaders, abortion providers, or any other perceived enemies of the **Christian Identity** movement.

The Phineas Priesthood was formed to carry out Hoskins's ideas after publication of his book in 1990. There is no formal membership, and there are no meetings and no headquarters. Phineas Priests form small independent cells of males from which individuals can carry out operations. Because these cells consist of a small number of activists, or even a single member, and act alone, the leaders of the white supremacist movement can never be convicted of conspiracy or complicity in the priests' actions. This deniability is part of the philosophy of **leaderless resistance** first proposed by veteran white supremacist **Louis Beam**.

Several violent acts have been attributed to Phineas Priesthood operations. In 1984 three masked men robbed a gay bookstore in Shelby, North Carolina, and executed the three people in the store. They then set fire to the store, killing a fourth man. Two white supremacists, Robert "Jack" Jackson and Doug Sheets, were implicated in these murders, but the charges were never proven. Later information came to the police that these murders were part of a Phineas Priesthood operation. Another confirmation of the Phineas Priesthood's existence came in the aftermath of the 1991 arrest of **Byron de la Beckwith** for the murder of civil rights leader Medgar Evers. Beckwith had earlier become a member of the Christian Identity movement, and the FBI found proof that he considered himself a Phineas Priest. Two convicted bank robbers in Muskogee, Oklahoma, in 1992, claimed that the money stolen was taken to support Phineas Priesthood activities. **Paul Jennings Hill**, who was convicted of killing an abortion doctor, Dr. John Britton, considered himself a Phineas Priest. The next action linked to the Phineas Priesthood involved three individuals, Charles Barbee, Robert Berry, and Verne Jay Merrell, who robbed a bank in Spokane, Washington, on July 12, 1996. They escaped, but after another robbery attempt on October 8, 1996 in Portland, Oregon, federal agents arrested them. These self-proclaimed Phineas Priests were convicted of eight counts of robbery and bomb making. Another Phineas Priesthood incident was the murder, by self-proclaimed Phineas Priest Larry Ashbrook, of four teenagers and three adults on September 15, 1999, in the Wedgwood Baptist Church in Fort Worth, Texas. Seven other church members were wounded before Ashbrook committed suicide. Ashbrook was unhappy that Baptists were supposedly trying to convert Jews to the Baptist Church. **See also** Hill, Paul Jennings; Hoskins, Richard Kelly.

Suggested readings: Joseph Mallia, "Act of Hatred; Violent Group Inspired by Biblical Figure," *Boston Herald* (August 12, 1999), p. 4; David A. Neiwert, *In God's Country: The Patriot Movement and the Pacific Northwest* (Pullman: Washington State University Press, 1999); Jim

Nesbitt, "Mixing the Bible with Bullets,"*Denver Post* (August 22, 1999), p. H6; Tom Rhodes, "Race-Hate Link to Church Slaughter," *Sunday Times* [London] (September 19, 1999), p. 1; Loretta J. Ross, "Using the Bible to Justify Killing," *Baltimore Sun* (August 8, 1994), p. 7A.

Pierce, William (1935–)

William Pierce is the head of the **National Alliance**, but he is most famous for his authorship of the bible of the **white supremacist movement**, *The Turner Diaries* (1978). He was born in 1935 in Atlanta, Georgia, but much of his youth was spent in Texas where he attended a military high school. In 1958 he received a doctorate in physics from the University of Colorado at Boulder. He interned at the Los Alamos National Laboratory. After working at the University of Colorado as a science laboratory researcher, he became an assistant professor of physics at Oregon State University. Pierce claims that the civil rights movement and anti–Vietnam War protests made him believe that racial equality was not possible. Leaving Oregon State University after only three years, Pierce worked at a private science laboratory in Connecticut for a number of years. He joined the **John Birch Society** but left because he considered the society too passive. In 1966 he left the field of physics research to enter politics as a member of the **American Nazi Party**. Serving as the party's in-house intellectual, Pierce created and edited the publication *National Socialist World*. He directed this publication toward intellectuals hoping to attract academic support. After becoming one of its top leaders under **George Lincoln Rockwell**, he remained a member after Rockwell's death in 1967. Pierce became increasingly dissatisfied with **Matt Koehl** as Rockwell's successor and left the National Socialist White People's Party in 1970. He took over the former **Willis Carto** organization Youth for Wallace and renamed it the National Youth Alliance.

Pierce recast the National Youth Alliance into a new organization, the National Alliance, in 1974. His intent was to make it serve as the major organization in the United States to preserve white supremacy. He also founded the Cosmotheist Church in the late 1970s in an unsuccessful attempt to gain a tax-exempt status. The church won tax-exempt status in 1978 but lost it in 1983. Under the auspices of the National Alliance, Pierce produced a flood of racist and anti-Semitic literature which culminated in his writing and publishing *The Turner Diaries* under the pen name of William MacDonald in 1977. In this novel, the hero fights (**ZOG**) **the Zionist Occupied Government** to save the white race from Jews and other minorities. Although it was unknown in most of the publishing world, this book was a best-seller in extremist circles with over 200,000 copies. Pierce moved the National Alliance from Washington, D.C., to a 265-acre farm near Mill Point, West Virginia, in 1985. He continues to write tracts attacking what he perceives to be enemies of the white race. After watching the unsuccessful attempt at revolutionary violence by **Robert Jay Mathews**'s group **The Order**, Pierce wrote another novel in 1989, *Hunter*, in which he advocates single-action violence rather than large-scale revolutionary operations. Despite his remoteness at his West Virginia compound, Pierce retains an influence within the white supremacist movement through his novels and other writings. He puts out two national publications, *National Vanguard* and the *Bulletin of the National Alliance*. His propaganda efforts also include a radio program and an Internet Web site.

Pierce has extended his attention to building the **militia movement**. Much of the material in his publications began to appeal to the growing militia movement in the early 1990s. He also started directing his recruiting to military personnel. The murder of a black couple in Fayetteville, North Carolina, on December 7, 1995, by three active duty soldiers incriminated the National Alliance. The soldiers had National Alliance materials in their possession at the time of the murders. Evidence exists that **Timothy James McVeigh** used the bombing of a federal building in Pierce's novel *The Turner Diaries*

as a model for the bombing of the Alfred P. Murrah Federal Building in Oklahoma City, Oklahoma, on April 19, 1995. Pierce has tried to distance himself from the Oklahoma City bombing, but his efforts have been unsuccessful.

Pierce was able to retain a high profile in the white supremacist movement in the late 1990s by his writings and by his acquisition of **Resistance Records**. In 1999 he bought the white supremacist black rock music company from Willis Carto. Pierce moved the distribution part of the company to his Hillsboro compound in West Virginia. Erich Gliebe, a National Alliance leader from Cleveland, Ohio, and a former professional fighter, manages the company for him. His acquisition of Resistance Records is an effort by Pierce to attract more youthful members to his National Alliance. This company is also highly profitable, and newspaper sources report that he can make almost $300,000 annually from selling records and CDs. Pierce has been able to use these funds to increase the budget for the National Alliance. **See also** American Nazi Party; Militia Movement; National Alliance; Resistance Records.

Suggested readings: Betty A. Dobratz and Stephanie L. Shanks-Meile, *"White Power, White Pride!": The White Separatist Movement in the United States* (New York: Twayne, 1997); Eric Harrison, " 'Diaries'; Racist Fantasy, or Primer for War of Hate?" *Los Angeles Times* (February 18, 1990), p. A1; David Segal, "Music to Hate By," *Newsday* [New York City] (January 24, 2000), p. B6; David Segal, "The Pied Piper of Racism," *Washington Post* (January 12, 2000), p. C1; Southern Poverty Law Center, "The Alliance and Its Allies," *SPLC Intelligence Report* 93 (Winter 1999): 10–16; Michael Tierney, "America's Fuehrer; Timothy McVeigh Planted the Oklahoma Bomb, William Pierce Inspired Him," *Herald* [Glasgow] (May 12, 2001), p. 8.

Pioneer Fund

The Pioneer Fund is a **neo-Nazi** foundation that has been a leader in the funding of scientific racism projects and in lobbying against liberalizing immigration legislation.

Wickkliffe Draper, a wealthy textile manufacturer from Hopedale, Massachusetts, founded the Pioneer Fund in 1937. Earlier his company had lost a labor battle with the International Workers of the World, and Draper expressed a desire to return to a period of control by an industrial and social elite. The fund's initial goal was to back projects that promoted the improvement of the white race through selective breeding. Draper and the fund's first president, Harry Laughlin, were firm believers in Adolf Hitler's eugenics and race programs. They lobbied the U.S. Congress to curb Jewish immigration on the eve of World War II.

Despite the worldwide repudiation of Nazi racial research, the Pioneer Fund continued sponsoring racial research activities after World War II. Since 1945 the fund has spent millions of dollars sponsoring research projects on the relationship among race, heredity, and IQ with the intent of proving the intellectual inferiority of minority people. Among the academics receiving Pioneer Fund grants have been leaders in race science studies, including William Shockley, a Stanford University Nobel Prize–winning physics professor and advocate of voluntary sterilization because he considers blacks inferior; Arthur Jensen, an educational psychologist and critic of black low IQ scores as an indicator of racial inferiority; and J. Philip Rushton, a psychology professor at the University of Western Ontario who argues that blacks are lower on the evolutionary scale than whites.

This tax-exempt foundation has turned much of its attention in the 1990s to fighting against immigration. Funding has been directed to the Federation for American Immigration Reform (FAIR) to lobby for stricter immigration controls. Funds from the Pioneer Fund helped in the 1994 introduction of Proposition 187 to deny illegal immigrants education, non-emergency health care, and other government benefits in California. News of the ties between the Pioneer Fund and Proposition 187 was instrumental in its defeat by California voters. The Pioneer Fund's efforts to perpetuate white su-

premacy continue by using funding of grants to promote favorable research, and by its lobbying in Congress against current immigration laws and efforts to liberalize immigration laws.

Suggested readings: Arthur Brice and Don Melvin, " 'Bell Curve' Research Tied to Supremacist Group," *Atlanta Journal and Constitution* (November 23, 1994), p. A1; Paul Feldman, "Group's Funding of Immigration Measure Assailed," *Los Angeles Times* (September 10, 1994), p. B3; Tim Kelsey and Trevor Rowe, "Academics Were Funded by Racist American Trust," *Independent* [London] (March 4, 1990), p. 4; Martin A. Lee, *The Beast Reawakens* (Boston: Little, Brown, 1997); Peter Lennon, "Mind Games: IQ-1," *Guardian* [London] (July 18, 1992), p. 4; Ben MacIntyre, "The Dubious Search for a Super Race," *Sunday Telegraph* [London] (March 12, 1989), p. 23; Barry Mehler, "Race and 'Reason': Academic Ideas a Pillar of Racist Thought," *SPLC Intelligence Report* 93 (Winter 1999): 27–32.

Poole, Elijah (See Muhammad, Elijah)

Populist Party/American Nationalist Union

The Populist Party is a political movement formed by a variety of extremist groups to influence the direction of American politics. **Willis Carto** started the party in 1982 to unite the anti-government, anti-Semitic, and racist groups into a monolithic party. Robert Weems, a veteran member of the Mississippi Ku Klux Klan, was its first chairperson. Supporters of the Populist Party came from a number of splinter groups: the American Independence Party, the American Party of Indiana, the Constitution Party, various **Ku Klux Klan** groups, and **Christian Identity** groups. Using the doctrine of "constitutional fundamentalism," the party attracted supporters by rejecting all government institutions not mandated in the original U.S. Constitution. A popular target was the Federal Reserve System. Strategy for the Populist Party came from its national executive committee of which Carto was the most prominent member. The **Liberty Lobby's** *Spotlight* provided much of the news and a forum for the recruitment of members to the Populist Party.

Almost from its start the Populist Party experienced dissension. Bob Richards, the party's presidential nominee in 1984 and a former Olympic champion, withdrew from the campaign after a political fight with Carto over Carto's **anti-Semitism**. Bill Shearer, head of the American Independence Party and an early supporter of the Populist Party, was the next to start feuding with Carto. This time the dispute was over money and Carto's role in raising funds. Shearer had Carto voted off the national executive committee. Soon afterward, both Carto and Shearer headed rival populist groups. Carto's group ran **David Duke** as its candidate for the 1988 presidential election. Slowly these divisions and the constant infighting discredited all versions of the Populist Party. By 2000, the Populist Party had been replaced by other political organizations seeking to appeal to its constituencies. See also Carto, Willis; Liberty Lobby.

Suggested readings: Edward Nichols, "Populism? Why, It's the Rage," *San Diego Union-Tribune* (June 2, 1985), p. C4; James Ridgeway, *Blood in the Face: The Ku Klux Klan, Aryan Nations, Nazi Skinheads, and the Rise of a New White Culture* (New York: Thunder's Mouth Press, 1990); Scripps-Howard News Service, "Populists Aim at Banks, Taxes," *San Diego Union-Tribune* (August 20, 1984), p. 1; Vicki Torres, "Olympic Champion Seeks Presidential Gold," *San Diego Union-Tribune* (June 12, 1984), p. 1.

Posse Comitatus Movement

The Posse Comitatus, Latin for "power of the county," movement became the leading anti-government force in the United States in the 1970s. **Henry Lamont Beach**, a retired dry cleaning executive, founded the movement in 1969 in Portland, Oregon. **William Potter Gale**, a retired military officer, helped Beach organize the movement. Their policy was to establish local chapters for a modest fee (initially $21 in dues) and signatures of seven men. Once a chapter was established it was on its own except for nominal support from the national office. This decentralization allowed freedom of action for the individual chapter; it also allowed the national office to avoid a conspiracy charge. The national leadership published a newspaper, *National Chronicle*, and distributed anti-government literature around the country. Tigerton Dells, Wisconsin, was the leading center of the Posse Comitatus movement until the inhabitants ran afoul of federal and state laws. Members of this community had established a sovereign township and refused to obey federal and state laws and regulations. The leader of the Tigerton Dells community, **James Wickstrom**, went to jail for impersonating a municipal officer after the government raid on the community.

Members of this movement subscribed to the view that the local sheriff is the supreme governmental figure and all governmental authority flows from this office. Posse Comitatus theorists traced its authority back to Old English common law in which all authority resided in the locality and in the hands of the county sheriff. They pointed to the Posse Comitatus Act in the post–Civil War era during the Ulysses Grant administration. In this act, the U.S. Congress forbade the federal military from intervening in local police matters. Consequently, leaders of the Posse Comitatus have claimed that all institutions above this office are unconstitutional and therefore have no authority. They believe that the federal income tax is illegal as is the Federal Reserve System. All law comes from God's laws, and the power to interpret these laws comes from common law courts and Christian grand juries. The only individuals allowed to participate in this system were white, Christian males. All others, Jews, minorities, non-Christian white males, and women were excluded from this process. The Posse Comitatus leaders believed that the U.S. Constitution was divinely inspired, but all amendments after the Bill of Rights were unconstitutional and void. Some members became so alienated from the federal government that they renounced their citizenship in a process called asseveration (severing their contractual relationship with the state).

The Posse Comitatus movement was successful in attracting adherents in the 1970s in the farm belt and in the West. Bankruptcies and foreclosures among farmers and ranchers and the threats of further such actions made the Posse Comitatus movement attractive to them. Posse Comitatus leaders also directed attacks on Jewish control of banking and the Federal Reserve Board. To avoid both the Federal Reserve System and banks, members formed the National Commodities and Barter Association to convert money into bullion and store it. All transactions were paperless and untraceable. When federal agents raided five of these bank/warehouses, they found ten tons of silver bullion. They also found evidence of nearly 20,000 participants in the scheme. This idea had been the brainchild of a Denver Posse Comitatus leader, John Grandbouche. A federal judge returned the bullion to Grandbouche because a programmer had designed a virus to destroy all the records making it impossible for the government to prove fraud. In another example of the use of the National Commodities and Barter Association, many of the subscribers lost their money after a Denver coin dealer committed suicide after irregularities in his handling of funds appeared. Evidence of fraud also appeared in Roderick Elliott's idea of securing loans from farmers to be used to help other farmers in financial difficulties. Elliott went to jail after he was convicted on fourteen counts of theft. He had long been teaching resistance to the Federal Reserve System both at seminars and in his publication *Primrose and Cattlemen's Gazette*.

Despite these fiscal and fraud problems, the Posse Comitatus showed growth in the 1970s. As the farm crisis of the late 1970s and early 1980s intensified so did the number of members joining the Posse Comitatus. The national leadership claimed at one time that the Posse Comitatus had 400,000 members. An FBI estimate in 1976 suggested that Posse Comitatus chapters had a total membership of between 12,000 and 50,000. In the late 1970s and early 1980s, several incidents caused by Posse Comitatus members led federal and state authorities to direct their attention to the group's activities, but it was **Gordon Kahl**'s killing of two federal marshals and his subsequent manhunt and death that brought the activities of the Posse Comitatus movement to the national stage. In the resulting crackdown staged by federal and state authorities, many of the supporters of the Posse Comitatus migrated to more extreme groups, including militia, survivalist, and white supremacist groups.

The most extreme wing of the Posse Comitatus movement produced a group willing to declare open warfare on the Internal Revenue Service (IRS) and the federal government. Wilhelm Ernst Schmidt, a former award-winning engineer at Lockheed Missile and Space Company, formed a small group to carry out terrorist operations against the government. Schmidt had been the leader of the anti-tax movement in Minnesota and had served time in jail for threatening an IRS agent in 1969. After his release from prison, he settled in Bemidji, Minnesota, living off income from the patents for his earlier inventions. Schmidt became head of the local Posse Comitatus and with three fellow members initiated a campaign to overthrow the federal government. In October 1984, federal agents raided the homes of the conspirators and found machine guns, grenade launchers, and bomb-making equipment. They also found instructions on using the weapons against judges and IRS agents. Schmidt was convicted of conspiracy and sentenced to twenty-six years in a federal penitentiary. His compatriots received less stringent sentences of seven years in prison.

In another high-profile case, a Posse Comitatus supporter, Arthur Kirk, challenged law enforcement officers after defaulting on a loan. Kirk was a Nebraska farmer going through hard times in 1984. He sold fifty head of cattle to repay a loan, but the sold cattle had been held as collateral for the loan. The bank initiated legal proceedings against Kirk to foreclose on his farm and claim the rest of his cattle. When state authorities attempted to seize the cattle, Kirk responded by opening fire on the SWAT team sent against him. He was killed in the resulting firefight. **See also** Beach, Henry Lamont; Kahl, Gordon.

Suggested readings: James Coates, *Armed and Dangerous: The Rise of the Survivalist Right* (New York: Hill and Wang, 1987); James Corcoran, *Bitter Harvest: Gordon Kahl and the Posse Comitatus: Murder in the Heartland* (New York: Viking Press, 1990); Bill Prochnau, "For the Posse, Ready Arms Hold Hostile World at Bay," *Washington Post* (June 21, 1983), p. A1; Brent L. Smith, *Terrorism in America: Pipe Bombs and Pipe Dreams* (Albany: State University of New York Press, 1994); Southern Poverty Law Center, "Roots of Common Law" *SPLC Intelligence Report* 90 (Spring 1998): 29–31.

Pratt, Larry (1943–)

Larry Pratt is an American politician whose leadership role in several extremist organizations allows him to lobby for extremist causes. He was born in 1943 in Virginia. Pratt is a former Virginia legislator from Fairfax, Virginia, with extensive contacts in the Republican Party. After losing a race for a second term in 1981, Pratt became one of the principal lobbyists against gun control. In 1975 he founded Gun Owners of America (GOA), with headquarters in Springfield, Virginia. Pratt is the executive director. He opposes all gun control efforts and claims that his organization is a no-compromise alternative to the National Rifle Association (NRA). In the late 1990s, the GOA had between 150,000 and 200,000 members. While this organization is much smaller than the NRA, it serves the right wing of the pro-gun movement. Pratt has accused the NRA of being too moderate and ineffectual. In 1990 Pratt authored a book, *Armed People Victorious*, which glorifies vigilante movements.

Pratt is also active in other extremist groups. He is the head of the Committee to Protect the Family Foundation. This organization has supported the public disobedience tactics of **Operation Rescue** and lobbies

Congress to oppose abortion. He is also active in English First, which lobbies to end bilingual education. In the mid-1990s, Morris Dees of the Southern Poverty Law Center estimated that this organization had more than 250,000 members. Pratt has also made contacts with the **white supremacist movement**. In October 1992, he was a participant in the **Estes Park meeting** in Colorado to plan anti-government activities and establish the **militia movement**. His involvement in this meeting came back to haunt him in 1996 while he was serving as an administrative aid to Patrick Buchanan's presidential campaign. A public policy group in Washington, D.C., Center for Public Integrity, publicized his Estes Park role and his donation of money to extremist lawyer **Kirk Lyons's CAUSE Foundation**. Negative publicity about these incidents led to his resignation as an aide to Pat Buchanan on February 15, 1996. Pratt's role continues to be as a conduit between extremist groups and conservative politicians. **See also** Anti-Abortion Movement; CAUSE Foundation; Estes Park Meeting; Lyons, Kirk.

Suggested readings: Morris Dees and James Corcoran, *Gathering Storm: America's Militia Threat* (New York: HarperCollins, 1996); David Goldstein, "Buchanan Loses Chairman," *Kansas City Star* (February 16, 1996), p. A1; Martin Kasindorf, "Linked to Militias," *Newsday* [New York City] (February 16, 1996), p. A5; Dennis B. Roddy, "Pratt Is Linked to Anti-Semitic Group," *Pittsburgh Post-Gazette* (February 17, 1996), p. A1; Kenneth S. Stern, *A Force upon the Plain: The American Militia Movement and the Politics of Hate* (Norman: University of Oklahoma Press, 1996).

Protocols of the Elders of Zion

The *Protocols of the Elders of Zion* was the most dangerous political hoax perpetrated in the twentieth century. The inspiration for the *Protocols of the Elders of Zion* came from a novel, *Biarritz*, authored by a former official of the Prussian postal service, Hermann Goedsche, in 1868, under the pseudonym of Sir John Retcliffe. He described a conspiracy of Jewish leaders who, representing the twelve tribes of Israel, met in the Jewish Cemetery in Prague to make their plan to rule the world. Russian anti-Semites seized on this fabrication and by the early 1870s proclaimed this conspiracy as fact. By the early 1880s, the so-called Rabbi's Speech in the Prague cemetery had been accepted in European anti-Semitic circles as proof of an international Jewish conspiracy.

The main text of the *Protocols of the Elders of Zion* came into the hands of Russian anti-Semitic writers in the period between 1903 and 1907. Some evidence exists that the *Protocols* were written in France in 1897 or 1898 in the middle of the anti-Jewish agitation of the Dreyfus Affair. Alfred Dreyfus had been convicted by a military court of treason for providing Germany with secret documents, but many advocated his innocence. G. P. Butmi, a retired Russian officer, and Sergey Nilus, a Russian landowner and writer in favor with the Court of Nicholas II, seized upon the *Protocols* to justify a series of pogroms against Russian Jews. German anti-Semitic writers were responsible for the appearance of the *Protocols* in its final form in 1920. The Jewish conspiracy theory was in the open.

Almost immediately after the appearance of the *Protocols of the Elders of Zion*, English writers discovered that the text had been plagiarized from a French writer, Maurice Joly. Joly had written a pamphlet in 1864 attacking the Second Empire of Napoleon III. This work, *Dialogue au enfers entre Montesqui et Machiavel*, had been published in Belgium and smuggled into France. Joly had intended the pamphlet to be a defense of political liberalism. He was tried in a French court in April 1865 and imprisoned for fifteen months. His pamphlet was banned. Russian officials obtained the pamphlet and transformed it into proof of a Jewish world conspiracy. Approximately three-fifths of the pamphlet was borrowed verbatim.

Regardless of its bogus origins, anti-Semitic writers have long cited the *Protocols* as evidence of an international Jewish conspiracy. The *Protocols of the Elders of Zion* gained acceptance among White Russian forces during the Russian Civil War in 1918–1919. They identified the Bolshevik Revolution of 1917 with the Jews and used the *Protocols* as evidence of a Judeo-communist conspiracy. In America, Henry Ford had the *Protocols* printed in his weekly Michigan newspaper, *Dearborn Independent*, as proof of a Jewish conspiracy. Before and during World War II, the Nazis used the *Protocols* as partial justification for their persecution of the Jews. In the postwar era, the protocols have reappeared in both the Moslem world and among white supremacist groups. Copies of the *Protocols of the Elders of Zion* appear routinely at gatherings of white supremacists and sales are steady. Despite proof that the pamphlet is a forgery, the *Protocols* continue to serve as a pretext for attacks on Jews around the world. **See also** Anti-Semitism; Neo-Nazis.

Suggested readings: Norman Cohn, *Warrant for Genocide: The Myth of the Jewish World Conspiracy and the Protocols of the Elders of Zion* (London: Serif, 1996); James Ridgeway, *Blood in the Face: The Ku Klux Klan, Aryan Nations, Nazi Skinheads, and the Rise of a New White Culture* (New York: Thunder's Mouth Press, 1990); Benjamin W. Segel, *A Lie and a Libel: The History of the Protocols of the Elders of Zion* (Lincoln: University of Nebraska Press, 1995).

Q

Queer Nation

The Queer Nation was the most militant of the gay activist groups in the United States in the 1990s. A loose coalition of gays and lesbians formed this group in 1990 to confront anti-gay activities. Each major city has a local chapter, but total membership remains low. Local chapters combine to conduct large national protests; demonstrations often involve between 1,000 and 2,000 participants. Almost from the beginning, the Queer Nation has specialized in direct-action confrontations with their tactics often verging on violence. Leadership in the Queer Nation is difficult to determine since local leaders assume the spotlight in local demonstrations. The most prominent national leaders, however, have been Steven Reichert and Michael Petralis. A common theme of all the leaders is to seek maximum publicity at all times. The organizational rallying cry is, "We're here, and we're queer."

Among their more notable confrontations in their drive for national publicity was their fight to march in Boston's St. Patrick's Day Parade in March 1992. After several demonstrations, a court case decided that the Queer Nation could march in the parade. Other demonstrations have been held at the 1992 Houston GOP National Convention and at a Houston grocery store. One of the Queer Nation's biggest defeats has been their vocal campaign to gain the military's acceptance of gays in the armed forces. Although the groups have different orientations, the leadership of Queer Nation has in the past worked closely with the AIDS activist group, **ACT UP** (AIDS Coalition to Unleash Power). Members often cross over and participate in the activities of both organizations. In the late 1990s, the Queer Nation became less active and less confrontational. **See also** ACT UP (AIDS Coalition to Unleash Power); Gay Liberation Movement.

Suggested readings: Don Aucoin, "Queer Nation at Center of Parade Debate," *Boston Globe* (March 11, 1992), p. 1; Margaret Cruikshank, *The Gay and Lesbian Liberation Movement* (New York: Routledge, 1992).

R

Radical Environmentalism

The radical environmentalism movement uses direct action and sometimes violent tactics to protect the wilderness and the environment. Two events helped radicalize the environmental movement before 1980. The first was the debate over the Glen Canyon Dam and the creation of Lake Powell in 1956. More significant was the Forest Service's Roadless Area Review and Evaluation (RARR) surveys in the early and late 1970s. These events were perceived by some in the environmental movement as defeats of moderate lobbying efforts at the national level. Radicals in the environmental movement interpreted these decisions as promoting corporate wealth at the expense of the wilderness with the federal government siding with commercial interests and denying the public good.

The anti-environment program of the Reagan administration was a call to action for radical environmentalists. An alliance of business interests, ranchers, and right-wing politicians instigated the federal government's transferring of public lands to the states for final disposition to private interests; it was the last straw for the environmentalists. This anti-environmental alliance became known as the Sagebrush Rebellion. Several veterans of the environmental movement formed a radical environmentalist group, **Earth First!**, to oppose the anti-environmentalists. Among the tactics of radical environmentalists in this group have been civil disobedience and sabotage. These eco-warriors consider themselves at war against the despoilers of the environment. They have adopted the philosophy of deep ecology, which challenges the primacy of human beings in nature. In their view, all creatures are worth saving and need a place in the environment. Destruction of the technology threatening the ecology is known as ecological sabotage, or **monkeywrenching**.

The most recent radical environmentalist organization is **Earth Liberation Front** (ELF). This organization made its first appearance in Great Britain in the early 1990s, but it was active in the United States by 1996; by 1998, it was the leading radical environmentalist group in the United States. The ELF, modeled on the **Animal Liberation Front** (ALF), specializes in arson attacks. Members of the ELF are responsible for more than a dozen arson operations causing more than $30 million in damages. Law enforcement has found it difficult to make arrests for these incidents because of the secret nature of the ELF. **See also** Bari, Judi; Earth First!; Foreman, David; Hill, Julia "Butterfly"; Monkeywrenching.

Suggested readings: Marego Athans, "ELF 'Eco-terrorists' Target Those They See as Earth's

Foes," *Baltimore Sun* (January 28, 2001), p. 1A. Martha F. Lee, *Earth First! Environmental Apocalypse* (Syracuse, N.Y.: Syracuse University Press, 1995); David Nicholson-Lord, "Greenest of Them All; Arne Naess," *Independent* [London] (May 31, 1992), p. 21; Rik Scarce, *Eco-Warriors: Understanding the Radical Environmental Movement* (Chicago: Noble Press, 1990); Walter Schwarz, "Faith, Heresy and the Fight for Eden," *Guardian* [London] (December 27, 1991), p. 1; Southern Poverty Law Center, "By Any Means Necessary," 102 (Summer 2001), p. 65; Susan Zakin, *Coyotes and Town Dogs: Earth First! and the Environmental Movement* (New York: Viking Press, 1993).

Republic of Texas

The Republic of Texas is a **common law courts movement** that asserts that Texas joined the United States illegally in 1945 and is now a sovereign republic. **Richard McLaren** founded the Republic of Texas movement in 1994 in the aftermath of a dispute over land titles involving his vineyard near Fort Davis, Texas. McLaren maintains that during his historical research he discovered that Texas had been illegally annexed to the United States. News of this claim soon made the rounds of right-wing talk shows. In the meantime, McLaren started the Fort Davis Mountain Land Commission and began filing liens against banks, businesses, and private individuals in West Texas courts. He became unpopular with his Fort Davis neighbors because of his constant agitation over his rights. At a convention held in 1996, representatives of the new Republic of Texas movement formed a cabinet, adopted a flag, and proclaimed the independence of Texas. The original cabinet included John C. VanKirk, president; Archie Huel Lowe, secretary of defense; and Richard McLaren, ambassador-at-large. The unhappiness of some leaders with several of Van Kirk's actions led to his replacement as president by Archie Huel Lowe. Members of the Republic of Texas called on Governor George W. Bush to relinquish the governorship and recognize the provisional government of the Republic of Texas. Governor Bush ignored this suggestion.

The original intent of the Republic of Texas movement was to restructure the state government. McLaren envisaged the new state government as a common law minimalist one. Because citizens would have only a few specific laws to worry about, there would be no need for professional politicians or lawyers. In fact, lawyers would be barred from practicing law in the republic. Driver's licenses would not be required, and there would be no speed limits on Texas highways. All financial transactions would be based solely on gold and silver. A new financial system with new banks would wipe out all farm and homeowner debt. Once every ten years a jubilee would be proclaimed canceling all debts. All taxes would be abolished, except import and export taxes, because administrative and regulatory offices would be abolished. All schools would be local, and no state tax funds would be used to support them. State universities would be privatized. Because there would be so few laws to break, only a few peace officers would be required. Finally, a state militia would provide a military force loosely based on the Swiss model.

Almost from the start, the supporters of the Republic of Texas experienced legal problems from the state of Texas. At first, the movement seemed to be no more than a curiosity to state authorities and the public. After the leaders of the Republic of Texas set up district courts in Lubbock and Arlington, Texas, and started issuing indictments and liens against property, authorities started taking notice. Complaints began to surface in Austin about suits against public officials and property liens harassing citizens. A federal judge jailed McLaren for thirty-five days in 1996 to stop him from filing bogus liens. Dan Morales, the Texas attorney general, filed a civil suit against the Republic of Texas in June 1996 for filing bogus liens. On October 28, 1996, members of the Republic of Texas were found in contempt of court because of their efforts to seize assets in state bank accounts.

In the middle of the campaign of the Republic of Texas to overturn the Texas government, a schism developed within the movement. The issuance of warrants and bank charters provided the catalyst for the schism. Lowe and McLaren opposed the sale of bank charters to members of the Republic of Texas's ruling council charging that this practice constituted a conflict of interest. Instead, Lowe and McLaren created a trust to hold the assets seized from the state of Texas. David Johnson, the leader of the dissidents, maintained that this action was unconstitutional. He was able to persuade the Arlington Common Law Court of Pleas to nullify the trust. Johnson then charged Lowe and McLaren with conspiracy and treason. In retaliation, Lowe's supporters accused Johnson of sedition and removed his backers from the ruling council. The result of these charges and countercharges was the formation of a second Republic of Texas group complete with Johnson as its president and a new ruling council. This second group repudiated the confrontational tactics of McLaren and has been working on a more peaceful approach to the reestablishment of the Republic of Texas.

McLaren brought national attention to the Republic of Texas movement during a standoff against federal and Texas law enforcement agents at Fort Davis in April and May 1997. In December 1996, McLaren and a small, armed group of supporters holed up in his Fort Davis compound to avoid arrest on a federal contempt of court charge resulting from his filing of false liens against federal and state officials. Federal and state officials had been reluctant to force the issue over a contempt citation; however, when three of McLaren's backers, Richard Keys, Greg Paulson, and Karen Paulson, seized two hostages on April 27, 1997, the stakes became high enough for police intervention. McLaren had been angered by the recent arrest of two of his followers, Jo Ann Turner, on contempt charges over a bogus lien, and Robert Jonathan Scheidt, on a weapons charge. The hostages were taken to provide leverage in bargaining with Texas officials for the release of his two followers. Some 300 federal and state law enforcement officers blockaded the compound and initiated negotiations. After only a week of negotiations, McLaren, his wife, and four others surrendered to the authorities. Two others, Mike Matson and Richard Keyes, escaped. Matson was later killed in a gunfight with police, and Keys was captured in September 1997. McLaren received two trials and was given a ninety-nine-year sentence for the hostage kidnapping and a twelve-year sentence for filing false liens. In 1999 an El Paso appeals court overturned McLaren's ninety-nine-year sentence. On August 8, 2001, five members of the Republic of Texas, including Richard McLaren, pleaded guilty in Midland, Texas, to one count of possessing explosives. McLaren faces a maximum ten-year prison term; the others, five-year prison terms.

The notoriety over the Fort Davis siege severely hurt the Republic of Texas movement. Even before the incident, the Republic of Texas had split into three factions: Johnson, Lowe, and McLaren. Both the Lowe and Johnson factions have tried to distance themselves from the McLaren faction but without much success. Lowe and several of his key followers were charged with federal fraud, and they have served time in jail. Members of the Johnson faction have also been indicted for fraud. The passage of an emergency law in the Texas legislature, making it a criminal offense to file fraudulent liens, simulate the legal process, or impersonate public officials, has made the tactics of the Republic of Texas easy to prosecute. This legislation and the determination of Texas prosecutors to enforce the law have ended the efforts of the Republic of Texas to subvert the Texas legal and political processes. All that is left now is for the leaders of the Republic of Texas movement to convince Texans on the merits of their campaign for an independent Republic of Texas. In September 2000, Daniel Miller replaced Lowe as the head of the Lowe faction of the Republic of Texas. Later in October, Republic of Texas leaders announced the purchase of forty-two acres in Dewitt County to build a provisional capital for the Republic of Texas. See also Common Law Courts Movement; McLaren, Richard.

Suggested readings: Mike Cox, *Stand-off in Texas: "Just Call Me a Spokesperson for the DPS"* (Austin, Tex.: Eakin Press, 1998); Marla Dial, "Republic of Texas; McLaren's Defense, Demeanor Full of Contradictions," *San Angelo Standard-Times* (November 2, 1997), p. 1; Eduardo Montes, "Republic of Texas Leaders, Associate Are Sentenced," *Houston Chronicle* (November 5, 1997), p. 31; Scott Parks, "Court Overturns Convictions of Two Separatists; Republic of Texas Kidnapping Charges Weren't Proved," *Dallas Morning News* (August 28, 1999), p. 35A; Southern Poverty Law Center, "Texas Promised (Second) Capitol," *SPLC Intelligence Report* 100 (Fall 2000): 5; Richard Stewart, "To Many, the State of Things Is No State at All," *Houston Chronicle* (October 6, 1996), p. 1; Thomas G. Watts, "Republic of Texas Schism Creates Confusion," *Dallas Morning News* (February 2, 1997), p. 47A.

Resistance Records

Resistance Records is the recording label for a record company which produces and distributes white supremacist hate music. None of the major record distributors carry this label in their inventories; even alternative and punk stores deny handling this label. **George Burdi**, who also goes by the name of Reverend Erick Hawthorne of the **Church of the Creator**, founded Resistance Records in April 1994 in Detroit, Michigan. He moved his band to Detroit in 1993 to escape the harsh penalties of the Canadian laws against hate crimes. Burdi is also the lead singer of the group RAHOWA (Racial Holy War). This white power rock resembles standard heavy metal or punk music except the lyrics express violence and racial hatred. This type of music has come to be known as black metal music. Resistance Records claimed that it sold in the neighborhood of 20,000 recordings in 1996. The figures and the income of around $300,000 made Resistance Records a minor factor in the recording industry, but the income helped finance a part

of the extremist right. Resistance Records also published a quarterly magazine, *Resistance Magazine*, for the fans of pro-white music. In the mid-1990s, this magazine had a circulation of about 15,000. This magazine still exists but under new management.

Resistance Records went through several changes of ownership in the late 1990s. Burdi ran into legal troubles in Canada and had to sell the record company. Poor management practices had allowed the company to run into financial difficulties. **Willis Carto**, head of the **Liberty Lobby**, bought the company in 1998 and transferred it to California. Todd Blodgett was Carto's partner in Resistance Records, but they soon had a falling out. Carto also had financial problems dating back to his lawsuit with the **Institute for Historical Review**. Resistance Records was put on the market, and **William Pierce** of the **National Alliance** purchased it by acquiring two-thirds ownership in March 1999 and the final third in August 1999. Pierce then transferred distribution operations to his headquarters in rural Hillsboro, West Virginia. His intention was to increase the appeal of the National Alliance with youth by distributing music appealing to them. He appointed Erich Gliebe, a resident of the Cleveland, Ohio, area and a staunch supporter of the National Alliance, to manage Resistance Records. Gliebe, a former professional boxer and trainer, is one of the National Alliance's rising young leaders. His job is to recruit musical talent for Resistance Records. Pierce also acquired a Swedish Record Company, Nordland, to expand Resistance Records' holdings. Patrons order the music through the Resistance Web site or by mail order. Most of the music is classified as **skinhead**, racist, or hate music. Pierce believes that the money and contacts made by Resistance Records can reinvigorate the National Alliance. By June 2000, Resistance Records had an inventory of 80,000 compact discs, and orders were being placed at a rate of fifty a day. See also Burdi, George; National Alliance; Pierce, William.

Suggested readings: Kim Murphy, "Behind

Tiffaeny Lanigan gives a clenched fist salute to Ku Klux Klan members as Klan national director Thomas Robb responds with a Nazi salute at a Ku Klux Klan rally in Tulsa, Oklahoma, on May 4, 1996. (AP Photo/David Crenshaw)

All the Noise of Hate Music," *Los Angeles Times* (March 30, 2000), p. 1; Clint O'Connor, "Sounds of Hate; Resistance Records," *Plain Dealer* [Cleveland] (March 5, 2000), p. 11; Southern Poverty Law Center, "Money, Music, and the Doctor," *SPLC Intelligence Report* 96 (Fall 1999):33–36; Southern Poverty Law Center, "Resisting Arrest; Racist Resistance Records Isn't Slowing Down," *SPLC Intelligence Report* 89 (Winter 1998):17–18; Southern Poverty Law Center, "Sounds of Violence," *SPLC Intelligence Report* 96 (Fall 1999):28–32; Gail Swainson, "Toronto Boasts North America's First Record Label Trading Exclusively in Hate Rock," *Toronto Star* (August 14, 1993), p. B1.

Revolutionary Anti-Capitalist Bloc (See Black Bloc)

Robb, Thomas Arthur "Thom" (1948–   )

Thom Robb, a prominent leader in the American **Ku Klux Klan**, was born in 1948 in Detroit, Michigan, but his family moved to Tucson, Arizona, when he was a teenager. His father was in construction and sometimes worked as an insurance salesman, and his mother worked in the retail trade. His mother was an avid supporter of the **John Birch Society** and conservative causes. As a teenager, Robb joined the John Birch Society. Robb attended Kenneth Goff's **Christian Identity** seminary Soldiers of the Cross Bible Institute in Evergreen, Colorado, and was ordained as a Christian Identity minister. He moved to Missouri and worked in a poultry operation before moving to Harrison, Arkansas. Using his experience as a printer, Robb started publishing anti-Semitic and racist literature in the 1970s. Among his publications have been *The Message of Old Monthly*, *The Torch*, and *Robb's Editorial Report*. In 1982 he was active in Stanley McCollum's faction of the Knights of the Ku Klux Klan. Robb's role was planning and leading Klan demonstrations. He became the national director of the Knights of the Ku Klux Klan in 1989.

Robb also served as a minister in the Christian Identity, Church of Jesus Christ. In 1991 Robb acquired forty acres of land in the Ozark Mountains of Arkansas. His plans to build a compound there into a center for white supremacists modeled on the **Aryan Nations Hayden Lake** compound. Robb has political ambitions and ran for political office in 1992 as a Republican. This bid came to nothing because the Republican Party refused to certify his candidacy.

Although Robb has always been a militant who loudly expresses his racist views, some members of the Knights of the Ku Klux Klan have found him and his policies too moderate. His association and friendship with **David Duke** helped convince him of the need to make the Klan more moderate to appeal to a broader constituency. His views have made him a controversial figure within the Klan. His protégé, Shawn Slater, a Denver chef, broke with him over the change in tactics. Nearly half of the membership of Robb's Knights of the Ku Klux Klan seceded in 1994 with Slater and formed the more

militant Federated Knights of the Ku Klux Klan. Robb remains an important leader in the Ku Klux Klan movement, but his power support base has eroded in the last decade. His most recent activity was winning a lawsuit in Missouri in 1999 permitting the Knights of the Ku Klux Klan to sponsor cleaning a section of the Missouri highway. **See also** Christian Identity; Duke, David; Ku Klux Klan.

Suggested readings: Anti-Defamation League, *Danger: Extremism: The Major Vehicles and Voices on America's Far-Right Fringe* (New York: Anti-Defamation League, 1996); Oscar Avila, "Klan Drive Sparks Opposition," *Kansas City Star* (June 6, 1999), p. B1; Vincent Coppola, *Dragons of God: A Journey Through Far-Right America* (Atlanta: Longstreet Press, 1996); Mary George, "Klan's Influence Fading; Group Wracked by Internal Strife," *Denver Post* (January 8, 1995), p. B1; Eric Johnson, "In Strife, Klan Sees Fertile Ground," *Newsday* [New York City] (December 21, 1992), p. 17; Suzanne P. Kelly, "Klan Watchers Say New Image Doesn't Hide the Old Message," *Star Tribune* [Minneapolis] (May 30, 1992), p. 1A.

Roberts, Archibald E. "Arch" (1916–)

Arch Roberts, the founder and longtime head of the **Committee to Restore the Constitution** (CRC), was born in 1916. A career military officer in the U.S. Army, he reached the rank of lieutenant colonel. His military specialty was psychological warfare. Roberts served under Major General Edwin A. Walker, the controversial right-wing commander of the 24th Division in Europe. In 1962 Major Roberts accused Los Angeles Mayor Samuel Yorty and G. Mennen Williams, former governor of Michigan and the assistant secretary of state in the Eisenhower administration, of being communist- and/or holding leftist leanings. The army relieved him from active duty over his remarks. A U.S. court of appeals ruling reinstated him to active duty in 1964, but Roberts's military career was at an end and he retired as a lieutenant colonel in 1965.

On his return to civilian life, Roberts launched a political campaign against communists and leftists. Roberts used his first organization, the Council of 1776, to advance the thesis that left-wing conspirators were running the U.S. government. In 1970 he founded the Committee to Restore the Constitution and established its headquarters in Fort Collins, Colorado. Two of his special targets were the United Nations and the growth of specialized government institutions, such as the Council on Foreign Affairs and the Federal Reserve System. He blamed President Richard Nixon for encouraging the dictatorship of the federal government. Roberts has written four books: *Victory Denied* (1966), an anti–United Nations treatise; *Peace: By the Wonderful People Who Brought You Korea and Vietnam* (1992), an anti-regionalism book; *The Most Secret Science* (1998), an anti–Federal Reserve System publication; and *Emerging Struggle for State Sovereignty* (1979), which attacks American federalism. Roberts continues to travel around the United States publicizing his brand of anti-government propaganda. He became the president of a tax-exempt organization, Foundation for Education, Scholarship, Patriotism and Americanism (FESPA), which intends to reestablish the American values embodied in the Constitution. In recent years, Roberts's writings in his *Bulletin of the Committee to Restore the Constitution* have become more extremist, blaming the Jews for the disintegration of American culture. He has published Holocaust denial material in his newsletter. **See also** Committee to Restore the Constitution; Holocaust Denial Movement.

Suggested reading: Anti-Defamation League, *Danger: Extremism: The Major Vehicles and Voices on America's Far-Right Fringe* (New York: Anti-Defamation League, 1996).

Rockwell, George Lincoln (1918–1967)

George Lincoln Rockwell, the founder and leader of the **American Nazi Party** and the chief figure in the revival of neo-Nazism in the United States, was born on March 9, 1918, in Bloomington, Illinois. His father was a noted vaudeville and radio comedian,

"Doc" Rockwell, and his mother was a former vaudeville dancer. His parents were divorced when Rockwell was young, and he had a lonely and difficult childhood and moved frequently. He attended schools in four localities before he graduated from a Rhode Island school, Providence's Central High School, in 1936. After attending another high school and the Hebron Academy in Maine, he entered Brown University in 1938. In March 1941, Rockwell joined the U.S. Navy and received training as a naval aviator. He was commissioned as an ensign on December 9, 1941. His duty assignment was with aerial anti-submarine warfare, and he served in both the South Atlantic and the Pacific. Rockwell left the Navy with the rank of lieutenant commander in the Naval Reserves. After the war, he went to the Pratt Institute of Commercial Art in Brooklyn to study for a career in commercial art. Although he was a successful student at Pratt, Rockwell left school early to work on a business venture in Maine. Rockwell was called up for duty in the Korean War and received a promotion to commander. After separation from the service, he founded a magazine, *US Lady Magazine*, in 1954. After a successful start, Rockwell left the magazine after a falling out with the other owners.

Rockwell's fascination with Nazism and **anti-Semitism** led him to found the American Nazi Party. He began his study of Nazism in the early 1950s in the midst of a divorce. His attendance at a speech given by **Gerald Lyman Kenneth Smith** in San Diego, California, increased his fascination with Nazism. He thought briefly of starting a conservative newspaper, but funding was unavailable. Rockwell decided that conservative movements were too weak and his biographer William H. Schmaltz reports that he believed that there existed a need for an organization able to use "force, terror, and power." Rockwell was able to start the American Nazi Party because of the political backing of De West Hooker, a wealthy and influential New Yorker, and financial support from Harold V. Arrowsmith, a wealthy businessman from Baltimore, Maryland. Arrowsmith

George Lincoln Rockwell of the American Nazi Party. (AP Photo)

bought a house in Arlington, Virginia, and a printing press for Rockwell's use. Rockwell's party started on July 27, 1958, as the National Committee to Free America from Jewish Domination (NCFAJD). Within months, however, Rockwell had alienated both sponsors and they abandoned him. In 1959 he renamed the party the American Nazi Party.

Under Rockwell's leadership, the American Nazi Party began to conduct a violent and provocative campaign against American Jews and the U.S. government. His advocacy of the sterilization of Jews, the confiscation of Jewish property, the deportation of Amer-

ican blacks to Africa, and a purge of American political leaders scared his opponents. These positions were part of Rockwell's strategy to agitate Jews and blacks enough to give him publicity to make his movement grow. Rockwell also became an early leader in the Holocaust denial movement because he believed that the Holocaust was an impediment to a revival of Nazism. The first American Nazi Party rally took place on April 3, 1960, in Washington, D.C. Rockwell had the party publish the *National Socialist Bulletin* to attract attention and possible recruits. Later, the bulletin was replaced by *Stormtrooper*. Rockwell also published an autobiography, *This Time the World*, in 1961.

Rockwell soon found himself in trouble with the authorities over his violent confrontational tactics. Aggressive tactics of confronting Jews had some success in the beginning, but by 1961 Jewish leaders had decided that the best approach was to ignore Rockwell and the American Nazi Party. Rockwell had more success in attempting to establish relations with the **Nation of Islam**. In an attempt to extend his influence, Rockwell ran for Virginia governor's office in 1965. This effort gave him public exposure, but he garnered less than 1 percent of the vote. Despite increasing police attention, Rockwell entertained serious hopes of being elected president of the United States in 1972. This idea drove him despite the fact that the American Nazi Party never had more than 100 active members at any one time, and at its peak could attract only about 500 supporters. Moreover, his organization was always on the verge of bankruptcy. In 1966 the Internal Revenue Service seized all of the party's possessions, including the headquarters building in Arlington, Virginia, and auctioned everything off to pay a lien for delinquent taxes.

Despite his legal and organizational problems, Rockwell was instrumental in the first attempt to unify the Nazi movement into an international movement in 1962. The British government denied Rockwell a visa, but he slipped into Great Britain in disguise. In a meeting held in England in the summer of 1962, Rockwell and a body of international leaders of Nazi movements in various countries vowed in the Cotswold Agreement to destroy the international Jewish conspiracy and Zionism. They formed the **World Union of National Socialists** (WUNS); Rockwell was the acknowledged leader.

In the middle of his growing political agendas, a gunman assassinated Rockwell on August 25, 1967. The assassin was John Patler, who had been expelled from the party by Rockwell in May 1967. A feud had developed between Rockwell and Patler. Rockwell had just finished his book, *White Power*, and was starting to direct the party away from Nazism and toward white supremacy. Other members of the party suspected that **Matt Koehl** and a clique unhappy with Rockwell's change of party direction had Rockwell removed. He was to have been buried in the Culpepper Cemetery in Virginia in a Nazi uniform, but the government refused this request. Rockwell was cremated and Koehl has retained his ashes for his new neo-Nazi party, the New Order. Rockwell's legacy has been as an unrelenting white racist and anti-Semite. Despite unsubstantiated rumors that he had been an undercover government agent, the **white supremacist movement** reveres him. Patler was found guilty of his murder on December 15, 1967, and sentenced to twenty years in prison. **See also** American Nazi party; Neo-Nazis.

Suggested readings: Chris Patsilelis, "The View from Hatemonger Hill; George Lincoln Rockwell's Life," *Houston Chronicle* (September 12, 1999), Zest, p. 21; William H. Schmaltz, *Hate: George Lincoln Rockwell and the American Nazi Party* (Washington, D.C.: Brassey's, 1999); Frederick J. Simonelli, *American Fuehrer: George Lincoln Rockwell and the American Nazi Party* (Urbana: University of Illinois Press, 1999).

Ross, Malcolm (1946–)

Malcolm Ross, one of the leading anti-Semitic writers in Canada, was born in May 1946 in Winnipeg, Canada. His father was a Presbyterian minister who traveled widely over Canada preaching. His family finally settled in the Miramichi region of New Brunswick, near Newcastle. All of Ross's education was in schools in the North Shore and Miramichi region. He attended the University of New Brunswick and graduated in 1968 with a degree in education. Ross found a job in a school district in rural New Brunswick teaching math and English. His last teaching position was as a remedial instructor in Moncton, New Brunswick, in the junior high school.

Ross's notoriety stems from a series of books he wrote outlining a Jewish world conspiracy to destroy Christianity. In 1978 he wrote the book *Web of Deceit*, in which he proposes that both Anne Frank's diary and the Holocaust were hoaxes and proof of a Jewish international conspiracy. Furthermore, international communism, international financiers, and international Zionists have united to destroy the Christian religion. He accepts the authenticity of the *Protocols of the Elders of Zion* (1920). Members of the racist right embraced the ideas in this book, but other reviewers found it objectionable. His right to teach children was challenged first by parents and then by school administrators. The New Brunswick Human Rights Commission issued a report claiming that it had insufficient evidence to prosecute Ross for promoting hate literature. In 1983 Ross wrote another book, *The Real Holocaust: The Attack on Unborn Children and on Life Itself*, in which he contrasts the alleged Holocaust with the evil of abortion. This time Ross charges that Jews are guilty of genocide against whites by operating abortion clinics. Again criticisms and complaints against Ross were directed to New Brunswick authorities. Several investigations were conducted without any action being taken against Ross. In 1988 he published a third book, *Spectre of Power*, which rehashes his conspiracy theories about international Zionism and includes information about his legal troubles over his earlier writings.

By the late 1980s, Ross and his writings were well known by American and Canadian white supremacists. They launched a movement to protect Ross from reprisals for his writings. In another hearing, the local school board was instructed to find him a nonteaching position or fire him. Doug Christie, Ross's attorney and a supporter of white supremacist causes, appealed the decision and an appeals court overturned the school board's ruling. Ross returned to the classroom. He remained a schoolteacher and continued to advance his anti-Jewish theories in his writings and presentations until the Supreme Court of Canada upheld Ross's removal from the classroom in 1996. In 1998 Ross won a lawsuit against the editorial cartoonist of the *Saint John Telegraph-Journal*, Josh Beutel, for portraying him at the New Brunswick Teachers' Association as a Nazi. A judge ordered Beutel to pay Ross $7,500 in damages and the association $2,200 in court costs. This judgment has been appealed, and in January 2000 the appeals court accepted the appeal. This case has attracted national attention in Canada with its focus on free speech and the rights of extremists to express their views. See also Anti-Semitism; Holocaust Denial Movement.

Suggested readings: Stephen Bindman, "Judges Rule for Racists in Libel Trials," *Gazette* [Montreal] (July 6, 1998), p. A7; Warren Kinsella, *Web of Hate: Inside Canada's Far Right Network* (Toronto, Canada: HarperCollins, 1994); Alan Story, "CBC Show Sparks Investigation of N.B. Racist," *Toronto Star* (February 13, 1987), p. A20; David Vienneau, "Holocaust Denier Barred from Teaching," *Toronto Star* (April 4, 1996), p. A10.

Rubin, Irv (1946–)

Irv Rubin, the leader of the **Jewish Defense League** (JDL), was born in 1946 and raised in Montreal, Canada. His family moved to the United States in 1961 when Rubin was fifteen years old. They settled in the Los Angeles, California, area where he attended high school at Granada Hills High School. He graduated from high school in 1963. As a high school student, he was active in the California Republican Party. Rubin became a citizen of the United States in 1966 after enlisting in the U.S. Air Force. After serving his four-year tour of duty reaching the rank of sergeant, Rubin entered California State University at Northridge. Rubin's first exposure to the Jewish Defense League was when JDL founder Rabbi **Meir Kahane** made a speech at his school in 1971. Soon after a personal interview with Kahane, Rubin joined the JDL. Rubin makes a living as a free-lance private investigator in Monrovia, California.

Rubin found himself at home in the Jewish Defense League and was promoted into a leadership position. In 1973 he left for Israel after the outbreak of the 1973 Yom Kippur War and served in the civil defense corps. After returning to the United States, Rubin continued to enhance his reputation in the JDL by demonstrating against **neo-Nazis** and Arab activists. He has been arrested more than thirty times for violent activities ranging from malicious mischief to conspiracy to commit murder, but the authorities have never been able to convict him of any serious charges. In 1978 he offered a $500 reward to anyone killing, maiming, or seriously wounding a member of the **American Nazi Party**. This offer landed Rubin in jail briefly, but he was acquitted of solicitation of murder in a court trial.

Rubin replaced Meir Kahane as head of the JDL in August 1985. Kahane made Rubin his personal choice as his successor. Shortly after his assumption of the leadership of the JDL, the western director of the American-Arab Anti-Discrimination Committee, Alex Odeh, was killed when a booby trap exploded at his Santa Ana, California, office on October 11, 1985. Several JDL activists were implicated in the bombing, but they escaped to Israel. In 1989 Rubin was sentenced to one year of probation and fines and court penalties totaling $772 for his role in a demonstration against a white supremacist leader, **Jesse Benjamin Stoner**, which turned violent. Unfavorable publicity and the cut off of funding from Jewish organizations made Rubin try to moderate the policies of the JDL in the 1990s. This more moderate approach did not prevent Rubin from participating in a September 1999 anti–**Aryan Nations** demonstration at **Hayden Lake**, Idaho. **See also** Jewish Defense League; Kahane, Meir.

Suggested readings: Laurie Becklund and Paul Lieberman, "JDL's Rubin, Held in Murder Plot, Is Freed," *Los Angeles Times* (March 11, 1992), p. B1; Marcia Chambers, "Jewish Defense League's New Leader to Press Weapons Training," *New York Times* (November 11, 1985), p. A17; David Haldane, "JDL's New Patrol; Leader of Militant Defense Group Wants to Change Its Approach, Image," *Los Angeles Times* (July 23, 1990), p. E1; Paul Lieberman and Laurie Becklund, "Arrest Cast Spotlight on Private Life of JDL's Rubin,"*Los Angeles Times* (March 8, 1992), p. A1; Eric Malnic, "Irv Rubin; West Coast Coordinator for Jewish Defense League Chosen to Succeed Rabbi Kahane as National Chief," *Los Angeles Times* (August 9, 1985), part 2, p. 1; Anthony Millican, "Armed-Patrol Plan Draws Fire," *Los Angeles Times* (February 7, 1991), p. 1 Esther Schrader, "JDL Leader Pleads No Contest," *Los Angeles Times* (July 20, 1989), p. B3.

Ruby Ridge Incident

The Ruby Ridge incident has entered into the mythology of the extremist movement of the United States as an example of a federal conspiracy to destroy the **white supremacist movement**. A Bureau of Alcohol, Tobacco and Firearms (BATF) undercover agent persuaded **Randall Weaver**, a member of the **Christian Identity** movement and a separatist, to sell him sawed-off shotguns on October 24, 1989. Federal agents then attempted to enlist Weaver as an informant against fellow white supremacists, in particular, **John Ernest Trochmann** of the Militia of Montana (MOM), to avoid a federal weapons charge. Weaver, a former Green Beret in the U.S. Army, refused to work for the government as an informer. A warrant was issued for Weaver's arrest. After BATF agents arrested Weaver, a local magistrate released him with no cash bond. Weaver failed to respond to a court appearance in February 1991 and later claimed that he had been given the wrong court date. In August 1992, a Federal Bureau of Investigation (FBI) Hostage Rescue Team initiated an operation to arrest Weaver. Since the Weaver home on Ruby Ridge was well protected and the Weaver family was heavily armed, a reconnaissance team of U.S. marshals was sent to investigate the layout on August 21, 1992. Striker, the Weaver family dog, spotted the marshals and sounded the alarm. A gunfight ensued during which a deputy U.S. marshal, William F. Degan, fourteen-year-old Sammy Weaver, and the dog were killed.

In the following siege, a government sniper, Lon Horiuchi, killed Weaver's wife, Vicki, on August 22. Gunshots also wounded Randy Weaver and Kevin Harris. After the intervention of two white supremacist negotiators, **James B. "Bo" Gritz** and **Gerald "Jack" McLamb**, the Weavers surrendered to federal authorities on August 31.

The aftermath of the Ruby Ridge gunfight found the federal government more on trial than the Weavers. Randy Weaver was convicted for failure to appear in court, but the judge dismissed the original weapons charge as entrapment. During the trial, the Southern Poverty Law Center reported that members of the jury received the book *Citizen's Rule Book* from supporters of the Weavers. This book tells jurors that they do not have to listen to judges instruct them on the law; instead, they have the right and obligation to veto wrongful prosecutions. This action is called jury nullification. After several politically inspired investigations were undertaken in Congress, the federal government made a no-fault settlement of $3.1 million to the Weaver family. Members of the FBI started making charges and countercharges against each other. Michael Kahoe, the FBI official in charge of an internal review, destroyed documents reflecting badly on the FBI's actions at Ruby Ridge. In December 1996, Kahoe pleaded guilty to a charge of obstruction of justice and received an eighteen-month prison term. The outcome of this incident has become staple fare for extremist groups in the United States to attack the actions of the federal government in any confrontation with extremists. They consider Ruby Ridge as part of a long stream of events revealing a government conspiracy against them. Events at Ruby Ridge were instrumental in extremists' plans for the **militia movement** at the **Estes Park meeting** later in 1992. See also Christian Identity; Weaver, Randall.

Suggested readings: Howard L. Bushart, John R. Craig, and Myra Barnes, *Soldiers of God: White Supremacists and Their Holy War for America* (New York: Kensington Books, 1998); George Lardner Jr., "Justice Dept. Closes Probe of Ruby Ridge," *Washington Post* (August 16, 1997), p. A8; Bill Morlin, "Agent Sentenced in Cover-Up," *Spokesman-Review* [Spokane, Wash.] (October 11, 1997), p. 1; Kim Murphy, "Both Sides Still Wrestling with Horrors of Ruby Ridge," *Los Angeles Times* (August 20, 1995), p. A1; Jess Walter, *Every Knee Shall Bow: The Truth and Tragedy of Ruby Ridge and the Randy Weaver Family* (New York: Regan Books, 1995).

Rudolph, Eric Robert (1967–   )

Eric Robert Rudolph has been the object of one of the biggest manhunts ever conducted in American history for his involvement in abortion clinic bombings and the 1996 Atlanta Olympic Park bombing. Rudolph was born on September 16, 1967, in Homestead, Florida. His father was an airline pilot, and his mother always displayed anti-government feelings. Shortly after his father died of cancer, his mother moved him and two brothers and a sister to the Nantahala community in northwestern Macon County, North Carolina, in 1981. Rudolph went to school at Nantahala and played football. He was fascinated by the mountain countryside and soon became an accomplished outdoorsman. Although extremely intelligent, he dropped out of high school. Later, he earned his GED. Rudolph attended Western Carolina University in Cullowhee, North Carolina, but, after two semesters of college, he left school and joined the U.S. Army. From August 1987 until January 1989, he served in the military but never rose above the rank of private. Whether from discipline problems or drug use, Rudolph was released from the military before his term of enlistment was up. He returned to North Carolina and worked as a self-employed carpenter. In 1996 he sold the property in Nantahala for $65,000 and moved to Cherokee County, North Carolina.

Rudolph had long been exposed to extremist views, but after his return from military service he became more active in anti-government activities. He was raised in the Church of Israel, which espoused the white supremacy doctrine of **Christian Iden-**

tity. Rudolph shared his mother's distrust of the federal government. Nord Davis and his **Northpoint Tactical Teams** were active in Rudolph's neighborhood. Davis had been preaching from his compound near the town of Andrews in northeastern Cherokee County for years against the New World Order Dictatorship. Before his death from prostate cancer in September 1997, Davis had been leader of the anti-government forces in North Carolina. Rudolph moved to Cherokee County within a year of Davis's death. They shared the same strong anti-government views.

Rudolph has been charged with starting a series of bombing attacks in 1996. The first bombing occurred at the Centennial Olympic Park in Atlanta, Georgia, on July 27, 1996, which killed a woman and injured more than 100 others. The bomb's explosive was smokeless gunpowder with shrapnel of masonry nails. Police authorities were baffled for months over the means of delivery and the motivation of the bomber. A claim of responsibility by the shadowy **Army of God** only complicated the issue. Rudolph's next target was an abortion clinic in the Atlanta area. This January 16, 1997, attack killed a policeman and severely wounded a female office worker. This time the bomb was dynamite and masonry nails. A gay nightclub in the Atlanta area was the next to be bombed on February 21, 1997; the same type of bomb was used. Federal authorities still had no serious leads directing them toward Rudolph until the January 29, 1998, bombing at a Birmingham, Alabama, abortion clinic. This bomb was a hand-detonated one, and an eyewitness identified his pickup truck in the vicinity of the bombing. Police confirmed that he was the bomber when flooring nails in a storage shed rented by Rudolph in Cherokee County were found to match those at one of the bombings.

By the time Rudolph had been identified as the key suspect in the bombings, he had disappeared into the 530,000 acres of the Nantahala National Forest. This country is filled with an underground complex of caves with which Rudolph has been familiar since exploring them as a teenager. Federal authorities organized a massive manhunt to locate Rudolph, but hindering this effort has been the strong anti-government sentiment of the local inhabitants. Most consider Rudolph to be more a hero than a villain, and he is one of their own. Various individuals have given him supplies and he has raided for supplies. Federal and state authorities appear to be no closer to finding him than before. Rudolph remains on the FBI's Ten Most Wanted list, and a $1 million reward for information leading to his arrest remains unclaimed. See also Anti-Abortion Movement; Army of God; Christian Identity; Northpoint Tactical Teams.

Suggested readings: Barbara Blake, "Rudolph Called Follower of Extremist Religion," *Asheville Citizen-Times* [EN.C.] (February 15, 1998), p. 1; Lewis Kamb, "Witness Raised Near Davis Estate," *Birmingham Post Herald* (February 3, 1998), p. 1; Jeff Klinkenberg, "Deep Caves; Black Bears; Venomous Snakes; Mountain Gorges; Murky Forest; the Unknown; the Hunt for Eric Rudolph," *St. Petersburg Times* [Fla.] (July 18, 1999), p. 1F; Kathy Scruggs and John Harmon, "The Rudolph Family: Talented, Tragic, Mysterious," *Atlanta Journal and Constitution* (March 22, 1998), p. 6C; Nick Paton Walsh, "America's Most Wanted," *Observer* [London] (October 8, 2000), Observer Life, p. 26.

Ryan Survivalist Commune

The Ryan Survivalist Commune, a **Christian Identity** survivalist community, earned nationwide notoriety for its crimes. Michael Ryan founded the commune in Rulo, Nebraska, in 1983. Ryan was born in Anthony, Kansas, and left high school early with an undistinguished academic record. After serving a tour of duty in the U.S. Army in South Vietnam, he returned to Whiting, Kansas, and married. He held a variety of menial jobs until he started driving an eighteen-wheel truck hauling meat. In 1982 Ryan became fascinated with Posse Comitatus literature. Later that year, he met the Wisconsin Posse Comitatus leader, **James Wick-**

strom, and soon was a devoted follower. In his conversations with Ryan, Wickstrom showed him an arm test that was supposed to demonstrate the will of Yahweh. The arms are held out straight and the arms rise and fall as the person is questioned about the will of Yahweh. Wickstrom was using the technique known as applied kinesiology; the effect is entirely due to the expectations of the operator. Ryan learned this technique and used it to acquire a number of disciples.

Ryan formed a commune in Nebraska with his newfound disciples. He had been able to attract around twenty-five followers, many of them women and children. In April 1983, Ryan and his group acquired access to an eighty-acre farm near Rulo, Nebraska. A compound was built to house the members of the commune. Ryan maintained complete authority over the compound by making the women his wives and humiliating the men. He preached that Armageddon was approaching and forming the commune was enabling his followers to survive. To prepare for doomsday, members of the compound were sent out to steal cattle, farm equipment, and weapons. When Ryan decided he needed to punish a dissident, James Thimm, he tortured him. Ryans's fourteen-year-old son, Dennis Ryan, then shot Thimm. Next Ryan killed a one-year-old boy, Luke Stice, for being the spawn of the Satan. Rumors of thefts and murders led police officials to raid the Rulo compound. They arrested Michael Ryan and his followers on charges of murder, torture, theft, and weapons charges. In a 1985 trial, Michael Ryan was sentenced to death for the murders, and his son, Dennis, was found guilty of second-degree murder and sentenced to life in prison. Michael Ryan remains on death row in a Nebraska prison, but Dennis Ryan received a new trial in 1995 after the Nebraska Supreme Court mandated a new trial over a procedural issue. On April 15, 1997, Nebraska authorities released Dennis Ryan from prison for time served. **See also** Cults; Survivalist Movement; Wickstrom, James.

Suggested readings: James Coates, *Armed and Dangerous: The Rise of the Survivalist Right* (New York: Hill and Wang, 1987); Rod Colvin, *Evil Harvest: A True Story of Cult Murder in the American Heartland* (New York: Bantam Books, 1992); Butch Mabin, "Dennis Ryan Is Released," *Lincoln-Journal Star* (April 16, 1997), p. 1; James Ridgeway, *Blood in the Face: The Ku Klux Klan, Aryan Nations, Nazi Skinheads, and the Rise of a New White Culture* (New York: Thunder's Mouth Press, 1990).

S

Sahara Club

The Sahara Club is an anti-environmentalist organization which uses violence against environmentalists. Louis McKey and Rick Sieman, both avid motorcycle bikers, founded the Sahara Club in Southern California in the fall of 1987 to protest the cancellation of the Barstow-to-Vegas Motorcycle Race in the early 1980s. They blamed environmentalists for cancellation of the event and vowed revenge. In 1987, when members of **Earth First!** sabotaged a motorcycle race, the leadership of the Sahara Club renewed their pledge to get even. In 1988 they founded a newsletter and attacked both Earth First! and the Sierra Club. Although this group has remained small, with only about a dozen activists and nearly a hundred supporters, Sahara Club members believe in direct action. Using their biker contacts, members of the Sahara Club have targeted the Bureau of Land Management, Sierra Club, **Greenpeace**, and Earth First! for special harassment by means of protests, disruptions, hate phone calls, and death threats. They specialize in dirty tricks such as forging licenses with wrong year stickers and then informing the police to stop and ticket the victims who are environmentalists. The Sahara Club's newsletter has offered a $100 bounty to any member who can get an environmental activist arrested by any means.

Whereas there is no direct evidence that the Sahara Club receives more than moral support from other anti-environmentalist organizations, it serves as the direct-action element of the anti-environmentalist movement. **See also** Earth First!; Radical Environmentalism.

Suggested readings: Michael Connelly, "The Greens Have Them Seeing Red," *Los Angeles Times* (December 12, 1990), p. B1; Michael Connelly, "Sahara Club Revving Up to Claim Ecology Groups' Turf," *Los Angeles Times* (December 10, 1990), p. B3; Russ Nichols, "Here's the Dirt on Sahara Club," *San Diego Union-Tribune* (September 2, 1991) p. A3; Susan Zakin, *Coyotes and Town Dogs: Earth First! and the Environmental Movement* (New York: Viking Press, 1993).

Salvi, John C. III (1973–1996)

John Salvi, an anti-abortion activist, was responsible for one of the worst massacres of abortion providers in history. Born in 1973, he was raised in Ipswich, Massachusetts. His father made and marketed dentures, and his mother taught piano. Family members were staunch Catholics, and his early education took place in parochial schools. At age eleven, in 1983, the Salvi family relocated to Naples, Florida. Salvi attended Naples High School where he was an indifferent student, interested mostly in wrestling. Most of his classmates characterized him as a loner. After high school, he briefly attended Edison Community College in Fort Myers, Florida. He worked in maintenance for a friend of the family's business before enrolling and finally completing the Fort Myers Fire Department's training program. In February 1993, Salvi returned to Ipswich. He found a succession of jobs as an unarmed security guard, a roofer, and, finally, a hairdresser.

By the time Salvi moved back to Massachusetts he had become preoccupied with religion. Besides studying the Bible and memorizing appropriate passages, Salvi started preaching against abortion. He attended protests being staged at various Massachusetts abortion clinics. In 1994 Salvi visited several meetings of the local Massachusetts Citizens for Life, but he never formally joined the group. By this time, Salvi had completed his training as a hairdresser and had moved to Hampton Beach, New Hampshire, where he worked as a part-time hairdresser. Shortly afterward, he made contact with **Human Life International** and acquired photographs of fetuses and anti-abortion literature. Salvi also purchased two handguns and practiced shooting them for several months. His behavior became bizarre. He believed that a secret Masonic conspiracy was in place to discriminate against Catholics. He reasoned that by opposing abortion he was upholding the influence and power of the Catholic Church. To display his opposition to abortion, he posted pictures of aborted fetuses on his 1987 pickup truck.

Salvi decided to take direct action against abortion. On December 30, 1994, he entered the Planned Parenthood Clinic in Boston, Massachusetts, and opened fire with small arms in the reception area. His gunfire killed the receptionist, Shannon Lowney, 25, and wounded three other people. Salvi drove away to the Preterm Health Services Clinic about two miles down Beacon Street where he opened fire again. At this clinic, Salvi killed another receptionist, Leanne Nichols, 38, and wounded two other persons. In an exchange with a security guard Salvi dropped a duffel bag with incriminating in-

formation in it. Again Salvi drove away. Salvi managed to escape before being arrested the next day in Norfolk, Virginia, shortly after firing nearly two dozen gunshots at the Hillcrest Clinic.

After his extradition to Massachusetts, Salvi stood trial for the murders of the two clinic employees. The trial was held in Dedham, Massachusetts, in the winter of 1996. While the facts in the killings were never in doubt, Salvi's mental condition was a key issue. Salvi's lawyer tried to have him declared mentally incompetent, but Salvi refused to plead diminished capacity. A psychiatrist testified that Salvi suffered from schizophrenia and was delusional about conspiracies against Catholics. Despite these arguments, Salvi was convicted of the murders in March 1996 and received two consecutive life terms. Prison authorities sent him to the state prison in Walpole. On November 29, 1996, Salvi committed suicide in his prison cell. Because the appeal process was never completed, Salvi's murder convictions were dismissed on January 21, 1997.

Because Salvi was a loner and had only a tenuous tie to the anti-abortion movement, his legacy has been less significant than other martyrs in the movement. Anti-abortion leaders excused his actions by declaring that abortion providers committed murder themselves when they performed abortions. Salvi's actions helped discredit the violent wing of the anti-abortion movement, however, because his victims were receptionists, not abortion doctors. **See also** Anti-Abortion Movement; Lambs of Christ; Hill, Paul Jennings.

Suggested readings: Richard Chacon, "Suicide Finding Upheld; Salvi Acted Alone," *Boston Globe* (December 1, 1996), p. B1; Kevin Cullen and Brian McGrory, "Abortion Violence Hits Home," *Boston Globe* (December 31, 1994), p. 1; Kevin Golden and Brian McGrory, "Clinic Shooting Suspect Captured," *Boston Globe* (January 1, 1995), p. 1; Michael Matza, "Salvi Found Guilty in Abortion Clinic Killings," *Philadelphia Inquirer* (March 18, 1996), p. 1; Charles M. Sennott and Matthew Brelis, "Religious Fervor Fueled John Salvi's Rising Rage," *Boston Globe* (January 8, 1995), p. 1.

Scheidler, Joseph (1939?–)

Joseph Scheidler developed many of the tactics adopted by the militant wing of the **anti-abortion movement** to attack abortion providers. Family details are lacking, but he was probably born around 1939. Twice he attempted to join Catholic religious orders, but each time he was unable to make the final commitment. In the anti-abortion movement, however, he found a substitute for religious orders. Scheidler was working at a public relations firm in Chicago when the U.S. Supreme Court announced in 1973 the *Roe v. Wade* abortion rights decision. He was so upset by this ruling that he quit his job in June 1973, and, by January 1974, he was the director of the Illinois Right to Life Committee. Although he was a successful recruiter for this organization, he soon believed that peaceful dissent was not effective enough to stop abortions. Scheidler organized and sponsored some demonstrations in 1978 which led to his being fired as director. Scheidler joined a new group, Friends for Life, in April 1978 and began to organize another series of confrontations. Even the more militant types in this group soon found Scheidler difficult to restrain, and in 1980 he was removed from a leadership role in the Friends for Life. This time he formed his own group, the Pro-Life Action League. Scheidler used his public relations and marketing skills to build this new organization. He employed a variety of tactics, from harassing abortion providers to hassling women entering abortion clinics. In 1985 he wrote a book on his tactics, *Closed: 99 Ways to Stop Abortion.*

By the mid-1980s, Scheidler was recognized as a national leader in the anti-abortion movement. Scheidler was the instigator of the first national anti-abortion activist organization, the Pro-Life Action Network (PLAN), an attempt to bypass the more moderate National Right to Life organization. Militants from all over the country came together to plan strategy at a 1985 national convention of PLAN. Among those attending was **Randall Terry**, soon to be

head of **Operation Rescue.** Terry was selected as one of the five regional directors of PLAN. PLAN was under way at the peak of anti-abortion violence in 1985, and Scheidler openly supported the violence. He kept in contact with jailed anti-abortion activists **Michael Bray** and Don Benny Anderson. Scheidler became so prominent in the anti-abortion movement by his traveling and advocacy of violent tactics that the leadership of the National Organization for Women (NOW) filed a class action suit against him. He was charged with racketeering and conspiracy under the Racketeering Influenced and Corrupt Organizations (RICO) Act.

Scheidler was at the height of his influence in the anti-abortion movement in 1988 when he had a falling out with Randall Terry. Terry, who had founded Operation Rescue in 1986, was about to launch major protests in New York City and Chicago. Scheidler was to manage the Chicago operation. Terry's tactics depended on massive civil disobedience, which would lead to mass arrests. Scheidler had always avoided being arrested, if possible, because of fears of imprisonment. This tactic of using mass arrests to break down the legal system frightened him. He walked out of a meeting with Terry after a disagreement over tactics. Terry banished him from Operation Rescue. Terry then replaced Scheidler as the anti-abortion movement's most prominent leader. Scheidler still found time to start a litigation project that helped activists file lawsuits against abortion clinics. This tactic backfired, however, when Scheidler lost a class action suit for his anti-abortion activities. On May 2, 1998 Scheidler and two associates were fined $85,926.92 by a Chicago court for damages to abortion provider clinics in Milwaukee, Wisconsin and Wilmington, Delaware. Since it was a RICO Act conviction, the amount awarded was tripled. Scheidler made a public statement that the clinics would never collect from him, because he lacked the money. In the last several years, Scheidler has maintained a high profile in the anti-abortion movement by traveling and speaking on abortion topics in Ireland and the United States. **See also** Anti-Abortion Movement; Operation Rescue; Terry, Randall.

Suggested readings: Patricia Baird-Windle and Eleanor J. Bader, *Targets of Hatred: Anti-Abortion Terrorism* (New York: Palgrave, 2001); Dallas A. Blanchard, *The Anti-Abortion Movement and the Rise of the Religious Right: From Polite to Fiery Protest* (New York: Twayne, 1994); Jennifer Coburn, "A Violent Agenda; When Abortion Protests Go Too Far," *San Diego Union-Tribune* (May 6, 1998), p. B9; Judy Pasternak and John Beckham, "Jury Rules Against Abortion Protesters," *Los Angeles Times* (April 21, 1998), p. 1; James Risen and Judy L. Thomas, *Wrath of Angels: The American Abortion War* (New York: Basic Books, 1998); David G. Savage, "Court Allows Abortion Suits Under RICO," *Los Angeles Times* (January 25, 1994), p. A1.

Schweitzer, LeRoy (1939?–)

LeRoy Schweitzer, the leading figure in the **Freemen movement**, was born in 1939 and raised near Bozeman, Montana. Schweitzer was brought up in the Catholic Church and attended a local Catholic school. He graduated in 1957. After marriage, he and his wife moved to Moscow, Idaho, where Schweitzer found a job as a crop-duster pilot with Fountain Flying before starting his own crop-dusting business, Farm-Air, in Colfax, Washington.

Schweitzer joined the tax-protest movement after a dispute over taxes with the Internal Revenue Service (IRS). In 1977 the IRS claimed that he owed the government $700 in unpaid taxes. Schweitzer disputed this claim and the IRS froze his bank account. He joined the anti-government Posse Comitatus with another tax protester and local rancher, Ray Smith. Schweitzer decided to stop paying taxes altogether, and he sold his crop-dusting business in the mid-1980s. After moving to Belgrade, Montana, he opened a fireworks business. Finding support from other local tax protesters, he refused to obey federal and state regulations. His refusal to hold a driver's license or ob-

tain vehicle registration got him in trouble with local authorities. Schweitzer started issuing false documents and liens against property. In 1992 federal agents seized his home and airplane.

Unhappy about losing his property to the federal government, Schweitzer decided to retaliate. He attended a November 1992 seminar held by Roy Schwasinger, a Colorado anti-government activist and head of the We the People group. Schwasinger claimed that citizens could reclaim a share of the $600 trillion held illegally by the U.S. government since the gold standard had been abandoned in 1933. Schweitzer and his friends formed a new sovereign legal entity, The Freemens, in March 1995 with a functioning common law court and government. They used this new governing system to bombard federal and state governments with judgments and liens. The phony documents had the effect of clouding the target's title to property and credit. It also allowed them to create bogus money orders that paid off debts and even garnered them funds. Between 1992 and 1995, Schweitzer and his followers flooded the court system with their phony documents. In April 1995, an arrest warrant was issued for Schweitzer for his leadership role in the seizure of the Garfield County Courthouse and the demand for $500 million in minted silver from the federal government. In March 1995, a "criminal syndicalism" charge was issued against Schweitzer. Schweitzer also publicly threatened federal judges that intervened. On October 23, 1997, Schweitzer was convicted on failure to pay income taxes and refusing to appear for trial. He was sentenced to twenty-seven months in prison, fined $200,000, and instructed to pay $112,683 in back taxes. In his next trial for banking conspiracy and threatening to kill a federal judge in 1996, Schweitzer received, on March 16, 1999, a prison sentence of twenty-two and a half years. He is now serving these prison sentences. **See also** Common Law Courts Movement; Freemen Movement; Posse Comitatus Movement.

Suggested readings: Tom Kenworthy, "Incarceration Fails to Change 'Freemen,' " *Washington Post* (December 26, 1996), p. A4; Bill Morlin, "Bogus Checks and Balances Run Amok," *Spokesman-Review* [Spokane, Wash.] (March 26, 1996), p. 1; Bill Morlin, "Tax Woes Launched Freemen Leader's Militancy," *Spokesman-Review* [Spokane, Wash.] (March 26, 1996), p. 1; David A. Neiwert, *In God's Country: The Patriot Movement and the Pacific Northwest* (Pullman: Washington State University Press, 1999).

Sea Shepherd Conservation Society

The Sea Shepherd Conservation Society is a radical environmental organization devoted to the protection of whales, dolphins, and marine mammals. **Paul Franklin Watson**, a Canadian and former member of **Greenpeace**, founded the Sea Shepherd Conservation Society, or Sea Shepherds, in June 1977. At first the organization was named Earthforce, but later the name was changed to the Sea Shepherd Conservation Society. Watson left Greenpeace in 1977 after violating the Greenpeace nonviolence policy. This expulsion started his lifelong feud with the chairperson of Greenpeace, **David Fraser McTaggart**. Watson formed the Sea Shepherds to confront by direct action those harvesting whales and other marine mammals. The Sea Shepherds bought their first ship, the *Sea Shepherd*, in 1979 after receiving a $120,000 grant from Cleveland Amory's Fund for Animals and a $50,000 grant from Great Britain's Royal Society for Prevention of Cruelty to Animals. Watson used this ship in his confrontation with illegal whaler, the *Sierra*, ramming and severely damaging the *Sierra* in Portuguese waters on July 16, 1979. Watson sank the *Sea Shepherd* rather than turn it over to Portuguese authorities. Since then, the Sea Shepherd Conservation Society has used a variety of ships to combat illegal or immoral whaling or hunting.

The most spectacular action of the Sea Shepherd was a raid on the Icelandic whaling fleet on November 9 and 10, 1986. Although an international moratorium had been established on whaling, the Icelandic government continued whaling under the guise of conducting research on whales. Two members of the Sea Shepherds, Rod Coranado and David Howith, infiltrated the Icelandic whaling fleet and sank two of the whaling ships. They also sabotaged a whale-processing plant causing over $2 million in damage to equipment and a computer system. The incident caused an international controversy, but it also ended Iceland's efforts to circumvent the whaling ban.

In the early 1980s, Watson moved the headquarters of the Sea Shepherds from Vancouver, British Columbia, to Santa Monica, California. By the mid-1990s, the society had a membership of around 25,000, and an annual budget of nearly $700,000. Watson's record of fighting for animal rights has attracted a variety of supporters from Edward Abbey, the environmental novelist, to Buckminster Fuller, an architect and lecturer. Cleveland Amory, the newspaper columnist and animal rights activist, was always a key backer. Financial contributions have allowed the organization to build a substantial fleet to carry out its direct-action campaigns. In 1999 the fleet had three ships: the *Ocean Warrior*, a former Norwegian research ship; *Sirenian*, a former U.S. Coast Guard patrol boat; and *Mirage*, a former Norwegian Navy two-person submarine.

The Sea Shepherds' latest controversy was its campaign to prevent the Makah Indians of Washington State from hunting gray whales. The Makah had claimed that hunting whales was a tribal tradition and had received permission from the U.S. government to conduct a whale hunt in the fall of 1998. Watson and the Sea Shepherds tried to prevent the hunt. They were unsuccessful, and the Makah killed a gray whale on May 17, 1999. This defeat, however, has not deterred Watson from continuing his activities as head of the Sea Shepherd Conservation Society. Attention has now been directed toward fighting efforts of countries to start whale hunting again. **See also** Animal Rights Movement; Greenpeace; McTaggart, David Fraser; Watson, Paul Franklin.

Suggested readings: Owen Bowcott, "Buc-

Sea Shepherd Conversation Society leader Paul Watson, top right, stands aboard his ship *Sirenian* as Makah Whaling Commission vice president Arnie Hunter turns away after handing him a letter asking the anti-whaling group to take its two boats elsewhere, on October 15, 1998, in Neah Bay, Washington. The letter, signed by council president Ben Johnson, Jr., was a response to an anti-whaling publicity campaign that has intensified with the approach of the tribe's first whale hunt in more than seventy years. (AP Photo/Elaine Thompson)

caneer Spirit of a Sea Wolf," *Guardian* [London] (September 21, 1994), p. T2; Matthew Grant, "Truly, Madly, Deeply; Sea Shepherds Make Greenpeace Look Wimpy," *Scotland on Sunday* [Edinburgh] (February 16, 1997), Spectrum, p. 2; Christopher Manes, *Green Rage: Radical Environmentalism and the Unmaking of Civilization* (Boston: Little, Brown, 1990); David B. Morris, *Earth Warrior: Overboard with Paul Watson and the Sea Shepherd Conservation Society* (Golden, Colo.: Fulcrum Publishing, 1995); Christy Scattarella, "Sea Shepherd Society Chases Its Flock on High Seas of North Pacific Ocean," *Seattle Times* (July 31, 1992), p. B1; Robert W. Stewart, "Militants Damage Iceland Whale Processing Plants," *Los Angeles Times* (November 11, 1986), part 1, p. 8; Bella Stumbo, "Sea Shepherd Society; Modern-Day Pirates Fight the Whalers," *Los Angeles Times* (June 13, 1987), part 1, p. 1; Emmett Watson, "Maverick Group Acts as Ecological Po-

lice on Open Seas," *Seattle Times* (May 22, 1990), p. B1; Paul Watson and Warren Rogers, *Sea Shepherd: My Fight for Whales and Seals* (New York: Norton, 1982).

Sea Shepherds (See Sea Shepherd Conservation Society)

Seale, Bobby (1936–   )

Bobby Seale, one of the principal leaders of the **Black Panther Party**, was born on October 22, 1936, in Dallas, Texas. His father was a master carpenter. During World War II, the family moved to Berkeley, California. After high school, Seale joined the U.S. Air Force. He spent three years in the service, but he was court-martialed and received a bad conduct discharge. After returning to civilian life, he worked at a variety of jobs in California aircraft plants. On one such job, he worked the night shift and attended Merritt College (then named Oakland City College) during the day. At Merritt College Seale met **Huey P. Newton** in September 1962. Seale belonged to a black cultural nationalist group on campus, the Revolutionary Action Movement (RAM), but he was uncomfortable with its anti-white racism. Newton refused to join RAM for the same reason, and the two became friends. Both Seale and Newton joined the Soul Students Advisory Council (SSAC) at Merritt College. After a brush with the law and charges of misusing money, both of them left the SSAC. They decided to leave school and go into the black community in Oakland to organize it. In June 1966, Seale found a job at the North Oakland Neighborhood Anti-Poverty Center working as a foreman in the summer youth work program. He also married and within a year was a father.

Seale and Newton formed the Black Panther Party (BPP) in October 1966 in Oakland, California. Their first action was to draft a ten-point program explaining the goals of the party. Seale became the chairman of the Black Panther Party; Newton, the minister of defense. Together they went into the black community and recruited members. Newton was always the ideological leader of the BPP, but Seale was its action leader. Seale led an armed demonstration at the state capitol in Sacramento, California, to oppose anti–Black Panther legislation banning arms-carrying groups and was arrested. While Seale was serving a six-month jail sentence in the fall of 1967, Newton was seriously wounded in a confrontation with Oakland police. Seale started coordinating the "Free Huey" campaign as soon as he was released from jail in December 1967. He was active in the February 17, 1968, rally at the Oakland Auditorium which raised $30,000 for Newton's defense. Seale also missed **Leroy Eldridge Cleaver** and Bobby Hutton's gunfight with Oakland police.

Seale's next adventure was as one of the defendants in the trial of the Chicago Eight in March 1969. Seale had been active in the student demonstrations during the Democratic National Convention in Chicago during the summer of 1968. His activities there led to his arrest and trial. The other defendants were the white leaders of the demonstrations in Chicago. Seale refused to cooperate with the judge in the 1969 trial and accused the judge of misconduct. His refusal to cooperate and his courtroom disruptions led to his being tried separately. Although he was declared innocent of the charges of inciting riots, Seale spent two years in jail for contempt of court. Seale spent most of his time waiting for his trial by writing an autobiography, *Seize the Time* (1970). By the time he was released from jail, the Black Panther Party was in a state of disarray. FBI's Counter-Intelligence Program (COINTELPRO) efforts had been successful in encouraging dissension between Black Panther leaders and among the rank-and-file members. Seale became discouraged and left the party in 1974.

Seale is now an unofficial spokesperson for the Black Panther Party. He lives in Philadelphia and works as a community activist. Seale directs Project REACH, which teaches young people construction skills. He travels around the country speaking about the Black Panther Party and the 1960s. He has been outspoken in his condemnation of **Abdul Khalid Muhammad**'s **New Black Panther Party** because of its anti-Semitic and anti-white platform. **See also** Black Panther Party; New Black Panther Party; Newton, Huey P.

Suggested readings: Glenn Giffin, "Still an Idealist," *Denver Post* (May 7, 1998), p. E5; Paul Hendrickson, "Revolutionary at Rest," *Washington Post* (March 10, 1978), p. A4; Bobby Seale, *Seize the Time: The Story of the Black Panther Party and Huey P. Newton* (New York: Random House, 1970); Jay Ellen Spiegel, "Former Black Panther Still Taking the Heat," *Pittsburgh Post-Gazette* (April 6, 1994), p. B3; Jack J. Woehr, "From Black Panther to Youth Motivator," *Denver Rocky Mountain News* (May 1, 2000), p. 42A.

Secret Army Organization (SAO)

The Secret Army Organization (SAO) was the militant wing of the **Minutemen movement**. **Robert Bolivar DePugh**, a businessman from the Kansas City, Missouri, area, had founded the Minutemen in 1960 to fight against what he considered was the imminent takeover of the United States by communists. From a high of between 1,000 and 2,000 in the mid-1960s, the Minutemen had dropped to only about 500 active members by 1968. Unhappy with the loss of membership and with the moderate stance of the leadership of the Minutemen, the most militant faction formed the SAO in 1970. They wanted to intensify the fight against the communist conspiracy to take over the U.S. government. Members initiated a series of bombings and shootings. Leaders of the SAO became so disenchanted with President Richard Nixon and his initiatives with the Soviet Union and China that he was targeted for elimination as a traitor. After an SAO unit blew up a theater in 1972 in downtown San Diego, California, almost killing several city officials, federal agencies moved against the SAO. By the end of 1972, the SAO was no longer operational. Government authorities arrested several key officials and they received long terms in prison. Many of the former adherents of the SAO moved on to the next extremist groups being formed. The most popular of the new groups was the Posse Comitatus. See also DePugh, Robert Bolivar; Minutemen Movement; Posse Comitatus Movement.

Suggested reading: J. Harry Jones, *The Minutemen* (Garden City, N.Y.: Doubleday, 1968).

Shabazz, Malik Zulu (1966–)

Malik Zulu Shabazz is the head of the **New Black Panther Party**. He was born in 1966 in Los Angeles, California, with the name Paris Lewis. His father, who was an early follower of the **Nation of Islam**, died when Shabazz was young, and his mother was a successful businesswoman in Los Angeles. After high school, Shabazz attended and graduated from Howard University, in Washington, D.C. He then earned a law degree from Howard University Law School. At Howard, he founded a group called Unity Nation, which brought controversial black speakers to campus. After passing the bar examination, he practiced personal injury and criminal law in the Washington, D.C. area. Shabazz showed an early interest in politics by serving as a spokesperson and sometime body guard for Washington Mayor Marion Barry. In the early 1990s he twice made unsuccessful runs for Washington's City Council.

Shabazz had a long association with the Nation of Islam before joining the New Black Panther Party. His grandfather was also a member of the Nation of Islam and introduced him to the brand of Islam preached by **Elijah Muhammad**. Shabazz became a follower of Louis Farrakhan before leaving the Nation of Islam to support **Abdul Khalid Muhammad** after he assumed control of the New Black Panther Party. He served as attorney and chief lieutenant to Abdul Khalid Muhammad until Muhammad died on February 13, 2001. Shabazz was instrumental in organizing the Million Youth March in Harlem, New York in September 1998, and gained the reputation as a champion of black nationalism. He also earned notoriety for his public attacks on Jews and whites. Shabazz became the party chairperson in March 2001. Most of his activities since taking over control of the New Black Panther Party have been carrying out the policies of Abdul Khalid Muhammad. He has traveled from New York City, where he protested former President Bill Clinton moving his office into Harlem, to Cincinnati, Ohio, where he led the NBPP in demonstrations against the shooting of an unarmed nineteen-year-old black man. **See also:** Muhammad, Khalid Abdul; New Black Panther Party.

Suggested readings: Jay Apperson, "The New Voice of Black Power," *Baltimore Sun* (April 22, 2001), p. 1C; Austin Fenner, "Afrocentric Lawyer Force Behind the Youth March," *Daily News* [New York] (September 5, 1998); Jonathan Tilove, "Rally Organizers March Down

Very Different Paths," *Times-Picayune* [New Orleans] (August 23, 1998), p. A10.

Shakur, Mutulu (1950–)

Mutulu Shakur, the principal leader of the **Black Liberation Army** (BLA), was born Jeral Wayne Williams on August 8, 1950, in Baltimore, Maryland. His father was a painter. In 1968 Shakur joined the Republic of New Afrika (RNA), a black separatist movement founded on March 31, 1968, in Detroit, Michigan. Leaders of the RNA tried to form a black homeland in the South in the early 1970s, but the attempt failed. Also in 1968 Shakur became a Sunni Muslim. In 1970 he helped start an anti-drug program in the South Bronx, New York City. This program was called the Lincoln Detox, and Shakur became the assistant addiction counselor, specializing in acupuncture. Shakur spent 1977 in Montreal, Canada, studying advanced acupuncture and was awarded the doctor of acupuncture degree by the Acupuncture Association of Quebec. Besides being a practitioner of acupuncture, Shakur taught acupuncture at the Lincoln Hospital in the South Bronx.

Shakur organized and recruited members for the revolutionary Black Liberation Army. The Black Liberation Army had been founded in 1971 by Geronimo Pratt, a former Black Panther, but his murder conviction in 1972 led the way for Shakur to become its leader. In the mid-1970s, he began to plan robberies as a way to raise money for a black revolution. Several dissidents from **Leroy Eldridge Cleaver**'s wing of the Black Panther Party, the New York 21, had been expelled from the BPP and they were available for revolutionary activities. Shakur gathered together a small group of activists and attempted an armored-car robbery in downtown Pittsburgh, Pennsylvania, on December 6, 1976. The attempt was bungled. Of the three participants, Shakur was the only one to escape capture. Between May 1977 and May 1978, Shakur led three robberies which netted the group slightly less than $30,000. In November 1978, the

mayor of New York City, Edward Koch, closed the Lincoln Detox program and transferred its assets to the Lincoln Hospital under the name Lincoln Substance Abuse Program. Shakur, realizing that he would have no role in the reorganized program, resigned. He turned all of his attention to his revolutionary group. A robbery of an armored car on December 19, 1978, garnered the BLA $200,000. The next robbery, another armored-car robbery on September 11, 1979, at the Garden City Plaza Mall in New Jersey, raised $105,000. On June 2, 1980 the BLA conducted its last successful robbery when it came away with $292,000 from a Brink's armored car at the Chase Manhattan Bank branch in the Bronx.

These robberies provided the Black Liberation Army with large sums of money, but Shakur needed all the funds he could obtain. He had started a new acupuncture clinic in Harlem, New York, but it lost money. Shakur and his associates had developed an expensive cocaine habit. He was so short of funds that he recruited an associate to rob small-time cocaine dealers for drugs and cash. Moreover, his addiction to cocaine was causing him to lose influence in the Black Liberation Army. Two of his key supporters, Sekou Odinga and Tyrone Rison, had become disaffected, and Odinga was becoming a rival for group leadership. Odinga believed drug use was counterrevolutionary.

Shakur was in such desperate straits for money that he planned a risky armored-car robbery in Nanuet near Nyack, New York. After surveying plans for the operation, Odinga and Rison refused to participate because they considered the job suicidal. Their absence meant that Shakur had to recruit inexperienced manpower for the job. His ally, the **May 19th Communist Organization** (M19CO) under the leadership of **Marilyn Jean Buck** and **Kathy Boudin**, provided support in finding vehicles and getaway cars. The robbery, on October 20, 1981, turned into a bloody shootout: one guard was killed at the scene of the robbery, and two Nyack policemen were killed and one wounded later. Shakur and several of his key associates escaped with most of the $1.6 million. Several members of the M19CO and key operatives were captured and received lengthy prison terms. For the next few months, Shakur hid out in Washington, D.C., before moving back to New York City. Eventually he moved to Los Angeles, California, where he was captured in March 1986. He is now serving a life sentence. See also Black Liberation Army; Boudin, Kathy; Buck, Marilyn Jean; May 19th Communist Organization.

Suggested readings: John Castellucci, *The Big Dance: The Untold Story of Kathy Boudin and the Terrorist Family That Committed the Brink's Robbery Murders* (New York: Dodd, Mead, 1986); Ellen Frankfort, *Kathy Boudin and the Dance of Death* (New York: Stein and Day, 1983); John Kendall, "Killing Suspect Ordered Returned to N.Y.," *Los Angeles Times* (February 19, 1986), part 2, p. 3.

Shelton, Robert (1929–   )

Robert Shelton, the leader of the most violent, long-lasting modern **Ku Klux Klan** organization, the **United Klans of America** (UKA), was born in 1929 and has been a lifelong resident of Tuscaloosa, Alabama. Shelton attended the University of Alabama for two years, but he dropped out of school because of low grades. After military service in the U.S. Air Force, he returned to Tuscaloosa and worked for the B.F. Goodrich Company. His first job was in the tire plant and later he was promoted to salesperson. Upon returning to Tuscaloosa, he joined the U.S. Klans of Eldon Lee Edwards. Despite differences of opinion and tactics with Edwards, Shelton was soon appointed the grand dragon of Alabama. His support and the resulting backing of the Klan for the candidacy of John Patterson for Alabama governor culminated in Goodrich's receiving a lucrative state contract of $1.6 million. Increasing unhappiness with Edwards's leadership led Shelton to bolt from his organization. Shelton's Alabama Klan group merged with a large Georgia Klan group to form the United Klans of America (UKA) in July 1961. UKA membership appointed

Shelton as imperial wizard. At thirty-two years of age, Shelton was the youngest head of a major Klan organization in Klan history.

Under Shelton's leadership, the United Klans of America was the largest, most violent Klan group in the 1960s. Shelton had always been an active member of the Methodist Church, and he wanted the UKA to have a strong Christian foundation. His religious beliefs, however, did not interfere with Shelton's hatred for blacks, Jews, and communists. He also included on his personal hate list labor unions and foreign imports. Part of the violent reputation of the UKA came from Shelton's approval of training seminars on the making and handling of explosives. Not long after this training ended, a series of bombings took place in Alabama directed against civil rights leaders and black churches. Shelton approved of this violence and supported the three UKA members who killed Viola Liuzzo, a white civil rights worker from Detroit, Michigan. Liuzzo was shot while driving participants in the Alabama Freedom March between Selma and Montgomery on March 25, 1965.

In the middle of the UKA's campaign of terror, Shelton found himself in trouble with the federal government. State and local police tolerated and sometimes backed the UKA and Shelton, but federal authorities were less supportive. In 1965 the House Un-American Activities Committee (HUAC) called on Shelton to testify about Ku Klux Klan activities in the South. Although he appeared, he refused to answer questions citing the 5th Amendment to the Constitution as his protection. He received a contempt of Congress citation and a jail sentence of one year. After losing an appeal in a federal court, Shelton served nine months of a one-year sentence in a federal prison in Texarkana, Texas, in the late 1960s.

During his absence, the UKA suffered from organizational disarray. Shelton had always held tight administrative control over the UKA, and no leader could replace him during his absence. In the meantime, the civil rights movement had changed forever the old power structure in the South. Shelton's first concern after being released from prison was reestablishing his control over the UKA. Because the UKA was no longer prosperous enough to support a full-time leader, Shelton worked part-time selling used cars. By a skillful use of white resentment against affirmative action and school busing, Shelton was able to attract new members to the UKA. This resurgence, however, came to a premature end with the emergence of a new crop of young Ku Klux Klan leaders. By the late 1970s, Shelton had become increasingly jealous of the media attention received by the younger Klan leaders, especially **David Duke** and **Elbert Claude "Bill" Wilkerson**. Shelton retained his influence over the UKA until two members of a local chapter killed a black teenager, Michael Donald, in Mobile, Alabama, March 20, 1981. Klanwatch lawyers from the Southern Poverty Law Center saw an opportunity to destroy the last vestiges of power in the UKA. In a lengthy court case that lasted from June 1984 to February 12, 1987, the jury awarded $7 million in damages to the mother of the dead teenager, causing the UKA to go into bankruptcy. Shelton no longer has an organization to lead, and his influence in Klan circles has diminished. **See also** Klanwatch; Ku Klux Klan, United Klans of America.

Suggested readings: Anti-Defamation League, *Danger: Extremism: The Major Vehicles and Voices on America's Far-Right Fringe* (New York: Anti-Defamation League, 1996); Michael Corman, "KKK; A Postmortem; Ex-Klan Leader Concedes It's Now Defunct," *Newsday* [New York City] (July 4, 1995), p. A13; Jules Loh, "Ku Klux Klan Is Dead," *Ottawa Citizen* (December 27, 1994), p. D11; Wyn Craig Wade, *The Fiery Cross: The Ku Klux Klan in America* (New York: Simon and Schuster, 1987).

Sheriff's Posse Comitatus (See Posse Comitatus Movement)

Silent Brotherhood (See Mathews, Robert Jay; Order, The)

Silver Legion (See Silver Shirts)

Silver Shirts

The Silver Shirts movement was the pre–World War II American fascist organization which proved to be the breeding ground for postwar **neo-Nazi** groups. William Dudley Pelley, a journalist and novelist, formed the Silver Shirts, or the Silver Legion, January 31, 1933. He had been born in 1890 in Lynn, Massachusetts, and his father was a toilet paper manufacturer. Pelley had published two country newspapers before they went bankrupt around World War I. After these failures, he turned to creative writing. In 1927 he underwent a spiritual conversion which turned him into an anti-Semite and an occultist. Among his more bizarre claims was one that he had spent seven minutes in heaven during which he talked with God. In his occultist journal, *Liberation*, Pelley prophesized a time of troubles and the reappearance of the Messiah. He watched the growth of the German National Socialist Workers Party and its leader, Adolf Hitler. The platform of the rejuvenation of Germany and anti-Semitism, as well as organization around a single leader, impressed him. The success of Hitler's peaceful assumption of power in Germany in 1933 encouraged Pelley to imitate him in the United States.

Pelley modeled the Silver Shirts after Hitler's Brown Shirts. The American right wing's initial response was positive. Pelley made his headquarters in Asheville, North Carolina. At the peak of the group's popularity in 1934, the Silver Shirts had a membership somewhere between 15,000 and 50,000. Even on the eve of World War II, the organization still retained about 5,000 active members. Most of its strength was in the South, Pacific Northwest, and California. The Silver Shirts' close affiliation with the German Nazis and the German-American Bund was both its strength and ultimately its weakness. The Silver Shirts had access to a cadre of true believers, but, after the entry of the United States into the war, their affiliation with fascism killed the movement. Pelley was charged in 1942 with violation of the Espionage Act and sentenced in August 1942 to a fifteen-year jail term. During his absence in prison, the Silver Shirts withered away. The failure of the Silver Shirts is less important, however, than the role it played informing the American anti-Semitic right. Among those attracted to the Silver Shirts was white supremacist leader **Gerald Lyman Kenneth Smith**. At the time of Pelley's incarceration, Smith assumed the leadership of the American anti-Semitic movement. **See also** American Fascism; Anti-Semitism.

Suggested readings: Cecilia Rasmussen, "Self-Styled Prophet Hoped to Be Another Hitler," *Los Angeles Times* (July 4, 1999), p. B3; James Ridgeway, *Blood in the Face: The Ku Klux Klan, Aryan Nations, Nazi Skinheads, and the Rise of a New White Culture* (New York: Thunder's Mouth Press, 1990).

Silver Spring Monkeys

The first major animal liberation cause was the case of the Silver Spring monkeys. The Institute for Behavioral Research (IBR) in Silver Spring, Maryland, had been conducting federal medical research using monkeys for tests. In May 1981, **Alex Pacheco**, one of the founders of the **People for the Ethical Treatment of Animals** (PETA) undertook an undercover job at IBR to expose animal abuse. He found that the monkeys were neglected and that injuries caused by the experiments and accidents were left untreated. Moreover, the results of the research were inconclusive and directed more toward gaining further research grants then making scientific breakthroughs. Pacheco gathered evidence of animal cruelty and gave the photographs and affidavits from other researchers to the Silver Spring police. The police confiscated both the monkeys and the research files, and charges were brought against Dr. Edward Taub, the head researcher. Taub was convicted of six counts of animal cruelty, but the Maryland Court of Appeals reversed his conviction citing that

researchers who receive federal funding are immune from state anti-cruelty laws.

The fate of the seventeen monkeys was the second part of the controversy. During the original court trial, a PETA member had housed the monkeys. The judge ordered the monkeys returned to the Institute for Behavioral Research, but PETA members hid the monkeys to prevent their return. Three members of PETA were briefly arrested before PETA leadership and the police concluded an agreement not to turn the monkeys over to the IBR. Ignoring this agreement, the judge ordered the monkeys returned to IBR. A few days later, one of the monkeys died in mysterious circumstances. Police seized the body and sent it away for an autopsy. The judge then ordered the surviving monkeys to be housed at the National Institute of Health's (NIH) Primate Quarantine Center in Poolesville, Maryland. PETA leaders tried for several years to gain control of the monkeys and place them in a primate sanctuary in Texas, but they were unsuccessful.

The battle over the Silver Spring monkeys was the opening salvo in the campaign for animal liberation. PETA gained favorable publicity for its role in exposing animal cruelty at a federal medical research facility and attracted recruits. It was the first instance in which the local police supported a major animal cruelty complaint against a federal installation. Evidence accumulated by Pacheco showed that the federal government could not be counted upon to enforce its own regulations protecting research animals. PETA leaders also learned that direct action produces more results than relying on uncertain legal remedies. **See also** Animal Liberation Movement; Newkirk, Ingrid; Pacheco, Alex; People for the Ethical Treatment of Animals.

Suggested readings: Neal D. Barnard, "Animal Experimentation; The Case of the 'Silver Spring Monkeys,'" *Washington Post* (February 25, 1990), p. B3; Peter Carlson, "The Great Silver Spring Monkey Debate," *Washington Post* (February 24, 1991), Magazine, p. W15; Lawrence Finsen and Susan Finsen, *The Animal Rights Movement in America: From Compassion* *to Respect* (New York: Twayne, 1994); Kay Snow Guillermo, *Monkey Business: The Disturbing Case That Launched the Animal Rights Movement* (Washington, D.C.: National Press Books, 1993); Howard LaFranchi, "Animal Research Debate Heats Up," *Christian Science Monitor* (March 10, 1989), p. 8; Janny Scott, "For Simians, It's out of Limelight to Isolated Lives," *Los Angeles Times* (November 15, 1987), part 1, p. 3.

Skinheads

Skinheads are the latest extremist movement to become a significant political factor in the United States. The Skinhead movement originated in England in the early 1970s among the young working-class elements, who were reacting against the hippie movement, English class society, and the lack of job and social opportunities. In compensation, the skinheads formed their own society and value structures. Members shaved their heads, hung suspenders or braces on their blue jeans, and wore Doc Martens boots. Music united the skinheads. Their white power or "Oi" (Hey) music glorified white supremacy and violence. Racism is another unifying theme among skinheads, and skinheads gained an early reputation for assaulting minorities and gays. There are two other identifying traits of English skinheads: their devotion to heavy drinking and their love of soccer. Their territoriality can be witness in their allegiance to the local soccer team, and they are willing to fight supporters of other teams.

The most important figure in the British skinhead movement was Ian Stuart Donaldson. After shortening his name to Ian Stuart, he formed a punk rock band, Skrewdriver, in 1977 and developed with the assistance of other bands the "Oi" white power sound. By the early 1980s, he had helped form a subculture of racist skinheads. Stuart also started in 1979 an alliance with the neo-Fascist British National Front (BNF). This new white power rock soon started attracting followers from outside Great Britain. Stuart started a magazine called *Blood and Honour* which publicized his and Skrewdriver's activities. His death in an automobile accident in 1987 only made him a bigger international hero in the skinhead movement. The skinhead movement had become an international phenomenon by the mid-1970s.

Most skinheads are racist or **neo-Nazis**, but one branch of the movement is antiracist: the Skinheads Against Racial Prejudice, or SHARP. They enjoy some of the same music and lifestyle, but the two sides differ decidedly over politics. Open hostilities exist between the racist and nonracist skinheads, and violence breaks out between them on occasion. Each side has about the same number of adherents so the battles are normally even, but the casualties are heavy.

By the early 1980s, the skinhead movement had reached the United States. **Clark Reid Martell** started one of the first neo-Nazi skinhead groups in the United States, Romantic Violence, in 1984. Operating in Chicago, Martell recruited twelve members and began making unprovoked attacks on Jews and minorities. Martell went to jail for these crimes in 1988, and members of Romantic Violence joined other skinhead groups. By the early 1990s a variety of skinhead groups had formed around the country. In 1993 the Anti-Defamation League identified 160 gangs with a membership of between 3,300 and 3,500 in forty states. They operated under a variety of names, including American Front, Aryan National Front, Aryan Resistance League, Confederate Hammerskins, Fourth Reich Skinheads, Northern Hammerskins, SS Action Group, and SS of America. The most elite skinhead group is perhaps the Hammerskin Nation, which includes groups with various names from Confederate Hammerskins to Eastern Hammerskins. The Hammerskin Nation has no national leader, but each chapter subscribes to common racial beliefs and a commitment to violence.

Efforts made by other white supremacist groups to recruit skinheads have been moderately successful. **Tom Metzger** and his **White Aryan Resistance** (WAR) has been the most active. Metzger learned, however, the cost of depending on such volatile young people. A civil suit against Metzger in Portland, Oregon, for the beating death of an Ethiopian immigrant by several of his skinhead recruits cost him a $12.5 million judgment. Other groups have had less success in recruiting skinheads. Some, such as the **Ku Klux Klan** groups, have avoided contact with skinheads because of the skinhead reputation for violence. **See also** Klanwatch; Metzger, Tom; Neo-Nazis; White Aryan Resistance.

Suggested readings: Anti-Defamation League, *The Skinhead International: A Worldwide Survey of Neo-Nazi Skinheads* (New York: Anti-Defamation League, 1995); Anti-Defamation League, *Young Nazi Killers: The Rising Skinhead Danger* (New York: Anti-Defamation League, 1993); Mark S. Hamm, *American Skinheads: The Criminology and Control of Hate Crime* (Westport, Conn.: Praeger, 1994); Kim Murphy, "Behind All the Noise of Hate Music," *Los Angeles Times* (March 30, 2000), p. A1; Southern Poverty Law Center, "Chaos to Conspiracy: Racist Skinhead Violence Growing More Organized," *SPLC Intelligence Report* 92 (Fall 1998): 23–24; Southern Poverty Law Center, "Youth at the Edge," *SPLC Intelligence Report* 96 (Fall 1999): 6–15.

Skokie March Controversy

The Skokie march controversy centered over First Amendment rights of a neo-Nazi group and a community that opposed the presence of **neo-Nazis**. Frank Collins, the head of his version of the **American Nazi Party**, was the architect of the Skokie march controversy. In one of those ironies of history, Frank Collins had been born Frank Cohn. His family was Jewish, and his parents were both Holocaust survivors. Despite or maybe because of his Jewish background, Collins had joined **George Lincoln Rockwell**'s American Nazi Party. He was expelled from that group after the FBI exposed his Jewish background. Collins immediately moved to Chicago and formed another version of the American Nazi Party under the name National Socialist Party of America. The goal of this party

was to deport forcibly all blacks, Jews, and Hispanics. Although his party never consisted of more than two dozen active supporters, Collins always looked for ways to publicize his group. His headquarters was located in the Marquette Park area of southwestern Chicago. Collins used resentment against blacks in the heavily Lithuanian neighborhood to publicize his movement. In 1976 the city of Chicago ended all political demonstrations in Chicago by requiring an insurance bond of $150,000 for demonstrations. This action ended Collins's activities in Chicago until his lawsuit against this requirement was settled, which he knew would take many months.

Collins decided to move his neo-Nazi demonstrations to one of the most prominent suburbs of Chicago, Skokie. Skokie, just north of the city of Chicago, has a large Jewish population with many survivors of the Holocaust. In February 1977 Collins requested permission from Skokie officials to hold a demonstration on May 1, 1977. In replying to Collins's request for a march permit, the city of Skokie insisted on an insurance bond of $350,000. Collins decided to make Skokie a target and challenged the bond requirement. It looked as though a compromise would be worked out, and outraged Jewish citizens blocked the compromise. In a series of court cases, the American Civil Liberties Union won Collins the right to demonstrate in Skokie despite the objections of its inhabitants. In the end, Collins and his followers never did march in Skokie; instead, they conducted a fifteen-minute demonstration on federal property in downtown Chicago.

Collins only had a brief time in the spotlight before running into legal problems. In the early 1980s, the Chicago police arrested Collins for possession of pornographic pictures of underaged boys. A rival for party leadership, **Harold Covington**, had reported these pictures to the police. Collins received a prison term of seven years in the Illinois penal system. Shortly after his prison sentence, the members of his party expelled Collins. He served his prison sentence and then disappeared from public view. **See also** American Nazi Party; Covington, Harold.

Suggested readings: Jerry Gladman, "Don't Ignore the Purveyors of Hate," *Toronto Sun* (May 15, 1995), p. A19; David Hamlin, *The Nazi/Skokie Conflict: A Civil Liberties Battle* (Boston: Beacon Press, 1980); Myra MacPherson, "The Nazis and Skokie," *Washington Post* (November 17, 1981), p. B1; Myra MacPherson and Rob Warden, "The Survivors and the Neo-Nazis," *Washington Post* (April 20, 1978), p. B1; Morton Mintz, "Court Won't Review Ruling Upholding Nazis' Civil Rights," *Washington Post* (October 17, 1978), p. A8.

Smith, Gerald Lyman Kenneth (1898–1976)

Gerald L. K. Smith, the godfather of the modern American anti-Semitic, **white supremacist movement**, was born on February 27, 1898, in Pardeeville, Wisconsin. His father was a combination small farmer and minister in the local First Christian Church. After local schooling in the small towns of Viola and Viroque, Wisconsin, Smith went to college at Valparaiso University. He worked his way through college at various jobs and obtained a bachelor degree in oratory in 1918. At the age of eighteen, Smith had become a minister in the First Christian Church in Deep River, Indiana, and the money he earned from his preaching helped pay his way through school. During the next decade, Smith proved to be a successful minister and preached in a number of churches in Wisconsin, Illinois, and Indiana. When his wife developed tuberculosis, they moved to the warmer climate, for his wife's health, of Shreveport, Louisiana, in 1929, where Smith assumed the post of minister at the King's Highway Christian Church. Soon after taking this position, Smith came under the influence of Louisiana politician Huey Long and his populist movement. His close association with Huey Long caused elements in his church to demand his resignation, and, in August 1934, Smith resigned. Later, in 1934, he briefly joined William Dudley Pelley's fascist **Silver Shirt** movement, but the political charisma of Huey Long appealed

more to him than fascism. He went to work for Long's Share Our Wealth clubs as an administrator. His abilities as an orator made him an important figure in the Long political machine. As a firm supporter of Huey Long and his program, Smith became a determined foe of Franklin Delano Roosevelt and his policies. After Long's assassination in 1935, he was fired by Long's successors. Smith then joined Dr. Francis Townsend, **Charles Coughlin,** and William Lemke in the Union Party's abortive attempt to win the presidency away from Roosevelt. Undeterred by this setback, Smith made his next effort to expand his political influence by starting the Committee of One Million in 1937. This effort to launch an anti-Roosevelt grassroots campaign also failed.

Despite his flirtations with the Silver Shirts and Huey Long's Democratic Party, Smith remained a conservative Republican until the late 1930s. His concentration on the issues of anti-communism, racism, **anti-Semitism,** and anti-Catholicism marked his transition from conservative Republican to fascism. Smith was a personal acquaintance of Henry Ford and admired him as a great man. Although he frequently denounced Nazism, Smith's program resembled an American brand of fascism with a Southern twist. Consequently, he was active in the isolationism movement to keep the United States out of World War II. He ran for the 1942 nomination for the U.S. Senate seat in Michigan, but he was easily defeated. In March 1942, he started a magazine, *The Cross and the Flag,* to express his extremist viewpoints. Smith never lost his hatred for President Roosevelt and always retained an admiration for Adolf Hitler. He was the founder of the America First Party, which ran him as a candidate for the presidency in 1944.

Smith became more of an extremist in the postwar era. He never believed in the Holocaust and maintained that all the missing Jews had migrated to the United States and voted for Roosevelt. His hatred of communists and Jews led him to oppose the founding of the United Nations. After the war, Smith moved to Los Angeles, California. In

1947 he established a successor to the America First Party in the Christian National Crusade. He ran for president again in 1948 on the Christian National Crusade ticket and lost badly again. In his view, communism and Jews were linked together in an international conspiracy against Christian America. Smith used his organization as a forum to charge various national political leaders, including President Dwight David Eisenhower, as being Jews or pawns of Jews. Most of Smith's followers were white, Protestant, and female. In 1952 he wanted to draft General Douglas McArthur for the Republican presidential candidate mainly to forestall Eisenhower's candidacy. He claimed that Eisenhower was a "Swiss Jew." After this ploy was unsuccessful, Smith revived his presidential campaign and ran against Eisenhower and Adlai Stevenson with no more success than before. In 1964 he supported the candidacy of Arizona Senator Barry Goldwater and campaigned for him. After Goldwater's defeat, Smith shifted his allegiance to the governor of Alabama, George Wallace. Smith had always had ties with **Ku Klux Klan** organizations and had little trouble working against the civil rights campaign. Smith hated blacks and Martin Luther King, Jr., in particular. Smith's continuous attacks on communists, Jews, and racial minorities attracted to him a number of disciples. The most prominent of his early disciples was **Wesley Swift**, who later founded the **Christian Identity** movement.

After living in California for a number of years, Smith moved to Eureka Springs, Arkansas, where he served as the elder statesman of the white supremacist movement. Smith lived off the contributions of supporters and in his later years was financially independent. These contributions allowed him to buy a home in Eureka Springs, and construct a statue, *Christ of the Ozarks*. During the last decade of his life, he became increasingly bitter about his failure to gain political power. Smith continued to preach and publish his views to a multitude of followers until his death on April 15, 1976, in Glendale, California. His newsletter *The Cross and the Flag* ceased publication in 1977. **See also** American Fascism; Anti-Semitism; Swift, Wesley.

Suggested readings: Glen Jeansonne, *Gerald L. K. Smith: Minister of Hate* (New Haven, Conn.: Yale University Press, 1988); Philip Rees, *Biographical Dictionary of the Extreme Right Since 1890* (New York: Simon and Schuster, 1990); James Ridgeway, *Blood in the Face: The Ku Klux Klan, Aryan Nations, Nazi Skinheads, and the Rise of a New White Culture* (New York: Thunder's Mouth Press, 1990).

Solar Temple Cult

The Solar Temple Cult was a European UFO (unidentified flying object) cult whose members have been involved in a series of mass suicides in Canada and Switzerland. In the early 1980s, Luc Jouret, a Belgian homeopathic doctor started a homeopathic practice in Annemasse, France. In 1984, Jouret joined the Order of the Solar Temple in Switzerland. Jouret, a former medical student at the Free University in Brussels and a former Belgian paratrooper, had a history of belief in faith healing and had been a member in other cults. The Order of the Solar Temple was a doomsday cult that had three purifying stages beginning with the first, the physical, and ascending to the final, higher spiritual plane. Jouret considered himself the Messiah, but not all of the members agreed with his self-assessment.

The Solar Temple started stockpiling weapons for the coming Apocalypse. Jouret and Joseph Di Mambro, a financial partner and co-founder of the Order of the Solar Temple, bought a farm in 1987 near Quebec, Canada, and property in a suburb of Quebec. The new cult attracted middle-class adherents who like the specialized ceremonies. In July 1993, Jouret and several of his followers pleaded guilty in a Canadian court to conspiracy charges for stockpiling weapons. The courts sentenced them to six months of unsupervised probation. After some members questioned Jouret's use of the cult's funds, Jouret returned to Switzerland in late 1993.

The violent nature of the cult first became apparent in the autumn of 1994. Canadian police discovered the bodies of two members of the cult on October 4, 1994, at the scene of a house fire in a Morin Heights Chalet. A day later, Swiss police found in a suburb of Quebec, Canada, forty-eight bodies, including eleven Canadians, at a farmhouse and two chalets in the small Swiss villages of Cheiry and Granges-sur-Salvan. Most of the bodies were laid out in a ritualistic fashion. Among the dead were Jouret and Di Mambro. Canadian police then discovered three more bodies in the chalet fire in Morin Heights. A couple and their three-month-old son, Christopher Emmanual Dutoir, had been stabbed to death. Police later learned that the leaders of the cult believed the baby was the antichrist.

Authorities in both Canada and Switzerland believed that, with the leaders of the Order of the Solar Temple dead, there was no longer a threat of further mass suicides. This assumption proved to be wrong. On December 23, 1995, another sixteen bodies were found around a campfire in a star formation on a plateau in Switzerland. The bodies had been burned after sedatives or toxic drugs had been consumed by the members. Bullets were also found in the bodies. On March 22, 1997, five more bodies were found in Saint-Casimir, sixty-five miles west of Quebec, in another suicide pact. There has been no further activity from the Solar Temple cult since the last of these mass suicides, but Canadian and Swiss authorities remain cautious about predicting its end. **See also** Cults.

Suggested readings: Geoff Baker, "Cult Leader Ordered Killing of 3-Month-Old 'Antichrist' Child," *Montreal Gazette* (November 19, 1994), p. A1; James R. Lewis, *Cults in America: A Reference Handbook* (Santa Barbara, Calif.: ABC-CLIO, 1998); James R. Lewis, *Peculiar Prophets: A Biographical Dictionary of New Religions* (St. Paul, Minn.: Paragon House, 1999); William Marsden, "Luc Jouret and His Temple of Doom," *Montreal Gazette* (October 15, 1994), p. B3; William Marsden, "Mythology Occult Inspired Cult's Bizarre Beliefs," *Montreal Gazette* (October 29, 1994), p. B3; Katherine

Witton, "Police Fear Cult Plans New Mass Suicide," *Ottawa Citizen* (April 4, 1996), p. A1.

Stoner, Jesse Benjamin, "J. B.," Jr. (1924–)

J. B. Stoner, an active leader in various **white supremacist movements** in the United States for over fifty years, was born in 1924 in Walker County, Georgia. One of three children, his father died when he was five years of age, and his mother passed away when he was sixteen. As a child Stoner contracted polio, which left him with a permanent limp. His schooling took place in public schools in Atlanta, Georgia, and Chattanooga, Tennessee. Shortly before his mother's death, Stoner joined the **Ku Klux Klan**. He was only eighteen years old when Imperial Wizard James Colescott named him kleagle for Tennessee. Stoner soon became dissatisfied with the Klan, because it was too moderate and hesitated to resort to violence.

His unhappiness with the Klan led Stoner to start his own neo-Nazi party. In 1945 he formed an anti-Semitic party, the National Anti-Jewish Party. The mission of this party was to expel Jews from the United States by whatever means possible, including threatening the reluctant with the death penalty. Among his anti-Semitic statements was that Adolf Hitler had been too easy on the Jews. In 1952 Stoner renamed his party the Christian Anti-Jewish Party. The same year he transferred his organization to Atlanta, Georgia, where he made the acquaintance of **Edward R. Fields**. The two men became lifelong friends.

The close working relationship between Stoner and Fields produced the **National State's Rights Party**. Soon after Stoner moved to Atlanta, he enrolled in law school and earned a law degree. At the same time, Fields obtained a chiropractic degree. In 1958 Fields founded the National State's Rights Party, and the next year, Stoner abandoned his Christian Anti-Jewish Party to work for the National State's Rights Party as its legal counsel. For the next thirty years, they worked to make the National State's Rights Party a political force in the South.

The first challenge facing the National State's Rights Party was the civil rights movement. Stoner and a colleague, Charles Conley "Connie" Lynch, worked together to provoke violence against civil rights marchers. Stoner used his legal expertise for party members in the court cases that followed the violence. Stoner, a specialist in the handling of high explosives, was a prime suspect in several major bombing incidents, including the June 19, 1958 bombing of the Bethel Baptist Church in Birmingham, Alabama, and the September 16, 1963 bombing of the Sixteenth Street Baptist Church in Birmingham. His advocacy and use of violence against civil rights demonstrators made his reputation in the **Ku Klux Klan** and white supremacist groups.

Unable to stem the progress of the civil rights movement, Stoner turned to running for public office to publicize his racist views. In the 1960s and 1970s, he was a candidate on the National State's Rights Party ticket in six elections. His first race was for the National State's Rights Party's vice presidential candidate in 1964; his last major race was for the Georgia U.S. Senate post in 1972. In 1974, 1978, and 1980 he was a candidate for high office in Georgia. Each campaign served as an occasion for Stoner to express his hatred of blacks and Jews. Always running as the candidate for white people's rights, he spent little money expecting political support from Ku Klux Klan members. Despite never winning an election, his voting support remained consistent and even increased in each subsequent race.

Stoner's record of violence caught up with him in the late 1970s. In September 1977, he was indicted by an Alabama grand jury for the 1958 bombing of the Bethel Baptist Church in Birmingham. After a lengthy extradition battle, Stoner was finally tried for the bombing in 1980. Stoner was convicted of the offense on May 15, 1980 and sentenced to ten years in an Alabama prison. After losing all of his appeals, Stoner refused to surrender to Alabama authorities in 1983.

In an effort to delay proceedings, Stoner was a fugitive for nearly four months. He turned himself in and served three and one-half years in prison. After his release from prison on November 6, 1986, Stoner was disbarred as a lawyer.

Stoner continued his activities in the white supremacist movement. In 1987 he formed a new organization, Crusade Against Corruption. This organization, located in Marietta, Georgia, provides a new forum for Stoner's attacks on blacks and Jews. Among his pronouncements is praise for the AIDS epidemic because it is killing blacks and gays. He travels around the white supremacist lecture circuit making speeches advancing his views. Although he is advancing in age, Stoner continues to devote all of his energies to his campaign of hate. **See also** Fields, Edward R.; Ku Klux Klan; National State's Rights Party.

Suggested readings: Anti-Defamation League, *Danger: Extremism: The Major Vehicles and Voices on America's Far-Right Fringe* (New York: Anti-Defamation League, 1996); Bill Richards, "Gun-Toting Klansman Denies Bombing Black Birmingham Church in 1958," *Washington Post* (September 29, 1977), p. A5; Patsy Sims, *The Klan* (New York: Stein and Day, 1978).

Stonewall Riots

The Stonewall riots marked the beginning of the gay rights movement in the United States. Before these riots occurred, the gay movement had been unfocused and underground. The Stonewall Inn was a gay bar on Christopher Street in New York City's Greenwich Village. This bar was most popular with Puerto Rican drag queens and lesbians, but its clientele included other gays. Although the New York City police had frequently raided gay bars, the crackdown in June 1969 was especially harsh. On the evening of June 27, 1969, the police raided the Stonewall Inn and made widespread arrests. A crowd formed outside the bar and started throwing things at the police and setting small fires. When the police realized that the situation was getting out of control, they called for reinforcements to quell the disturbances. These reinforcements rescued the police trapped in the Stonewall Inn, but a free-for-all continued well into the night. The police estimated the initial crowd at about 400, but others have maintained that it was as high as 2,000.

As news of the raid spread around the city's gay community, tension escalated between the police and the gays. Police showed up in riot gear, and a full-scale battle ensued and continued into the early morning. Over the next three nights, riots continued in Greenwich Village. The gay population had had enough of persecution by police and others. Many had been active in both the civil rights and the anti–Vietnam War movements, and these veterans of demonstrations decided that a gay rights organization to fight for civil rights for gays was necessary. Within weeks, the **Gay Liberation Front** was formed. The Stonewall riots have entered the mythology of the gay movement, and the June 27 anniversary is commemorated at gay pride marches around the country. See also Gay Liberation Front; Gay Liberation Movement.

Suggested readings: Margaret Cruikshank, *The Gay and Lesbian Liberation Movement* (New York: Routledge, 1992); Edward Guthmann, "Return to 'Stonewall,' " *San Francisco Chronicle* (July 21, 1996), p. 32; Dan Levy, "Stonewall Riots' Legacy of Freedom to Come Out," *San Francisco Chronicle* (June 27, 1994), p. A6; Jim Marks, "The Road from Stonewall," *Washington Post* (June 13, 1999), Book World, p. X5; Karen Matthews and Greg Morago, "It was 30 Years Ago Today That Gays Truly Came Out," *Gazette* [Montreal] (June 27, 1999), p. A1.

Stream of Knowledge

The Stream of Knowledge, a black supremacist group based in Albuquerque, New Mexico, is preparing for a race war. John McGee III, a commissary worker at Kirkland Air Force Base in Albuquerque, and Carl Anthony Bennett, a Veterans Administrations Medical Center clerk in Albuquerque, founded the Stream of Knowledge in 1992. This group subscribes to the Black Hebrew

Israelite ideology: God is black, and whites are the products of Satan. They believe that blacks are the true Israelites and are the chosen people of the Bible. Although no direct ties exist between the Stream of Knowledge and the now defunct **Nation of Yahweh**, they subscribe to many of the same views.

In 1997 the Stream of Knowledge was a small, all-male group with less than 100 members. Its leaders have been recruiting among blacks in the military and in prisons. Small groups of the Stream of Knowledge exist in other states, including Arizona, Colorado, Florida, Oklahoma, and Texas. Women cannot be members and must assume a subservient role in relationships with members. The group has been gathering weapons and supplies for the eventual war with whites. Although leaders predicted a race war in 2000 in which blacks would be victorious, the year passed uneventfully. See also Nation of Yahweh.

Suggested readings: Southern Poverty Law Center, "Born on the Bayou:," *SPLC Intelligence Report* 94 (Spring 1999): 14–18; Southern Poverty Law Center, "Rough Waters: 'Stream of Knowledge' Probed by Officials," *SPLC Intelligence Report* 88 (Fall 1997): 9–10.

Students for a Democratic Society (SDS)

The Students for a Democratic Society (SDS) was a radical leftist organization in the 1960s and early 1970s. The SDS was an outgrowth of the Student League for Industrial Democracy (SLID), which was the student branch of the social democratic League for Industrial Democracy (LID). The SLID was undergoing a decline in membership and financial support until it was revitalized by a young University of Michigan student, Robert Allan "Al" Haber. Haber was elected president in 1960 of the renamed Students for a Democratic Society, and the organization's magazine, *Venture*, began to publish newsworthy features on civil rights and student movements. Despite opposition from the old guard, Haber isolated his opposition and turned the SDS into a student action group. Haber recruited Tom Hayden and made him a field organizer in the South. Hayden was also given the task of formulating the initial draft of the manifesto for the June 11–15, 1962, convention.

At the June 1962 convention, held in Port Huron, Michigan, members decided to take the SDS in a new direction. Fifty-nine student activists from a variety of elite American universities, including Columbia University, Harvard University, Swarthmore College, the University of California at Berkeley, and the University of Michigan, issued the Port Huron Statement, which created the "new left." In this statement, the SDS called for the creation of a new society based on "a democracy of individual participation." It also called for an activist student movement to ensure the transition toward a new society. The call was a repudiation of the old American left. Major concentration was on the issues of civil rights and Third World revolutions rather than on the traditional ideological battles among the left. Members picked Tom Hayden as the president of a new national executive committee. Soon Hayden's vision of a radical student activist movement won out over Haber's more pragmatic position. In the beginning, the major issues were racial equality, integration, disarmament, and an end to poverty. Slowly the leaders and then the rank and file of the SDS became more radical. One of the reasons for the radical shift was SDS decentralization with local chapters being able to take independent action. Two other factors were the free speech movement at the University of California at Berkeley campus and the Vietnam War. In the early 1960s, members of the SDS were active in anti-nuclear protests and in the civil rights movement. From the mid-1960s onward, the main preoccupation was with ending the Vietnam War.

As the SDS became a larger organization, internal division within it began to cause dissension among the leadership. At its peak in 1969, the SDS had as many as 100,000 members. This influx of new members was both a success and the cause for its downfall.

In 1967 the Progressive Labor Party (PLP), a Maoist spin-off from the American Communist Party, joined the SDS and undertook an ideological battle to control the SDS. Leaders of the SDS were not able to respond to this challenge. Frustrations with the inability to end the Vietnam War and differences of opinion on the need for a revolutionary struggle caused the SDS to split into competing factions. The moderate wing turned to working for social change within the system. The radical wing became revolutionary and formed **Weather Underground**. A third segment of the growing feminist element within the SDS opposed what they interpreted as the sexism of the male leadership of the SDS and turned to radical feminism. By the early 1970s, the SDS no longer existed because all of its leaders and members had migrated to other organizations or had withdrawn from politics altogether. **See also** Weather Underground.

Suggested readings: Garry Abrams, "Former Student Radicals Reclaim the Past," *Los Angeles Times* (April 7, 1986), part 5, p. 1; Stanley Aronowitz, *Death and Rebirth of American Radicalism* (New York: Routledge, 1996); Frederick D. Miller, "The End of SDS and the Emergence of Weatherman: Demise Through Success," in Jo Freeman, ed., *Social Movements of the Sixties and Seventies* (New York: Longman, 1983); Mark Muro, " '60s Radicals: What's Left," *Boston Globe* (June 11, 1991), Living, p. 97; George R. Vickers, *The Formation of the New Left: The Early Years* (Lexington, Mass.: Lexington Books, 1975).

Survivalist Movement

The survivalist movement differs from the other extremist movements in one way: instead of promoting anti-government activity or white supremacy, the members are preparing for a forthcoming disaster. At first, survivalists feared the outbreak of a nuclear war, and they prepared for it by stockpiling foodstuffs and weapons. Some of the survivalists even welcomed the idea of a nuclear war as a way to cleanse the United States of its enemies and allow the building of a new society. Later, survivalists turned their attention to other societal disasters, including a possible communist takeover of the U.S. government, racial discord, and any other natural, man-made, or supernatural disasters. The two organizations that have attracted the most survivalists are the Minutemen, in the 1970s, and the Posse Comitatus, in the 1980s. Many of these survivalists identify with the doomsday prophecy in the Book of Revelations in the Bible and the coming of the millennium. Consequently, survivalists are not interested in making efforts to reform the system, but only in surviving the collapse of the current system. For many of them, a primary concern is the building of a new society. The primary media source for the survivalists is the periodical *Soldier of Fortune: The Journal of Professional Adventurers*. This magazine, which has over 100,000 subscribers, appeals primarily to mercenaries, militia supporters, and paramilitary types. What all of these individuals have in common is a distrust and sometimes hatred of authority— the U.S. government; the Internal Revenue Service; the Federal Bureau of Investigation; the Bureau of Alcohol, Tobacco, and Firearms; Jews, minorities, and immigrants; and the **New World Order**. Many survivalists have found the militia or the patriot movements a place where they can find others who share their worldview. Predictions of the end of the world or at least social dislocation because of the Y2K computer problem mobilized survivalists in the late 1990s. The lack of any serious repercussions after January 1, 2000, caused some of the survivalists to question earlier predictions, but it has not shaken their faith in the final outcome. **See also** Militia Movement; Minutemen Movement; Posse Comitatus Movement.

Suggested readings: James Coates, *Armed and Dangerous: The Rise of the Survivalist Right* (New York: Hill and Wang, 1987); Wendy Grossman, "A Diet of Worms for When It All Falls Apart Millennium," *Daily Telegraph* [London] (August 20, 1998), p. 8; Jean Marabella, "No Use for 'Gubmint' in Republica," *Sun* [Baltimore] (July 19, 1998), p. 2A; Kim Murphy,

"Survivalists Certain: Chaos 'Still Coming,' " *Los Angeles Times* (January 2, 2000), p. A28; David Pugliese, "Waiting for Armageddon," *Ottawa Citizen* (January 3, 1999), p. C3.

Swift, Wesley (1913–1970)

Wesley Swift, the founder of the modern **Christian Identity** movement, was born on September 6, 1913, in New Jersey. His father was a fundamentalist Methodist minister, who spent most of his life at a small church in Collinswood, New Jersey. Swift also became an ordained Methodist minister. He joined the **Ku Klux Klan** and later the anti-Jewish Christian Nationalist Crusade of **Gerald Lyman Kenneth Smith**. In the late 1930s, he moved to the Los Angeles area and attended the British Israel's Kingdom Bible College. He replaced Smith as the publisher of the racist newsletter *The Cross and the Flag*. By 1946 Swift had developed the basic outlines of his Christian Identity theology. He moved, in 1946, to Lancaster, California, where he became a preacher at Amy Semple McPherson's Foursquare Church in the Los Angeles area. Later, he started a new church, the Church of Jesus Christ Christian, with the assistance of Smith's former lawyer, Bertrand Comparet. Swift also became the West Coast contact for Smith.

Swift built the theology of the Christian Identity church out of the beliefs of Anglo-Israelism. Anglo-Israelism theology claims that the northern Europeans are the chosen people of the Bible, not the Jews. Swift extended this doctrine to include the idea of racial purity and exclusiveness. His teachings soon spread to churches in California and the southeastern states. Swift had learned the benefits of paramilitary training and, with **William Potter Gale**, an antigovernment activist, started the California Rangers. Among Swift's early recruits was the future head of the **Aryan Nations, Richard Girnt Butler**. Swift died in a Mexican hospital in 1970 of complications from diabetes. He had refused to take treatments from American doctors because so many doctors were Jewish. Butler succeeded Swift as the head of his California church. **See also** Gale, William Potter; Butler, Richard Girnt; Christian Identity; Smith, Gerald Lyman Kenneth.

Suggested readings: Michael Barkun, *Religion and the Racist Right: The Origins of the Christian Identity Movement* (Chapel Hill: University of North Carolina Press, 1997); Editorial Writers Desk, "Rage, Rage Against Hate," *Los Angeles Times* (August 12, 1999), p. 8; Peter Y. Hong and Ken Ellingwood, "A Trip to the Birthplace of Racist Ideologies," *Los Angeles Times* (August 12, 1999), p. A1; Jeffrey Kaplan, ed. *Encyclopedia of White Power: A Sourcebook on the Radical Racist Right* (Walnut Creek, Calif.:, Altamira Press, 2000).

Symbionese Liberation Army (SLA)

The Symbionese Liberation Army (SLA), a radical leftist group, engaged in a campaign of terror in the mid-1970s. **Donald David DeFreeze**, who escaped from Soledad Prison on March 5, 1973, while serving time in prison for bank robbery, formed the Symbionese Liberation Army on March 26, 1973. His goal was to overthrow what he called the white bourgeois capitalist system. Thero Wheeler, who had also escaped from prison in August 1973, provided much of the inspiration for the development of the SLA. With the support of several early followers, DeFreeze was able to recruit new members for the SLA by May 1973. DeFreeze was by now using the name Cinque Mtume (Fifth Prophet). His recruits were white, upper-middle-class, university-educated radical leftists from California. Most of them were veterans of other left-wing groups affiliated with the **Students for a Democratic Society** (SDS).

Once the SLA had been organized, the next step was to launch operations. Their first operation was the assassination of the Oakland superintendent of schools, Marcus Foster, on November 6, 1973. Foster was selected because the SLA considered him a puppet of the white power structure. DeFreeze, Mizmoon Soltysik, and Nancy Ling Perry carried out the assassination. The mur-

der, however, isolated the SLA from the black community. Foster had been popular in the black community. Other leftists condemned the act as adventuristic and counterproductive. Potential recruits still in prison also reacted negatively. Wheeler, who already had doubts about the success of the SLA, left for Houston, Texas, after a clash with DeFreeze. The next operation occurred on January 7, 1974. This armored-car robbery in Berkeley, California, by Russell Little and Joe Remiro, garnered them $4,000 in cash. Three days later, on January 10, 1974, Little and Remiro were arrested after a shootout with the police. During a raid on the Oakland headquarters of the SLA, police captured weapons and gathered intelligence information on the group. A list of over twenty-five names of possible kidnap victims was found including the name of Susan Ford, daughter of Vice President Gerald Ford, and Patricia "Patty" Hearst, daughter of millionaire publisher Randolph Hearst.

The SLA's next major operation was kidnapping Patty Hearst. After scouting out Hearst's location and her living arrangements with her boyfriend, three members of the SLA kidnapped Hearst from her apartment on the evening of February 4, 1974. Originally, the kidnapping was supposed to be used in a trade of her for Little and Remiro, but the plan changed to demanding food for the poor. SLA communications informed her family that Patty Hearst was being held as a prisoner of war. After going underground, the SLA members found themselves in financial difficulties and internal dissension broke out. In the meantime, Randolph Hearst, Patty's father, delivered $2 million to a tax-exempt charitable organization to distribute foodstuffs to the poor and needy. SLA's leaders decided that this effort was not enough and demanded an additional $4 million be added. The Hearst family trust offered to fulfill the ransom demand in return for Patty Hearst's release.

During the course of her confinement, Patty Hearst became converted to the SLA cause. Psychologists have noted the attachment of victims to their captors in terrorist situations and named this attachment the Stockholm syndrome after a kidnapping incident that occurred in Stockholm, Sweden. Patty Hearst displayed signs of this syndrome. Members of the SLA used extensive coercive persuasion to reorient her political and social ideas and convert her into Tania, the revolutionary fighter. On April 3, 1974, Patty Hearst declared herself a member of the SLA in a public communiqué using a San Francisco radio station. It was her participation in an April 15, 1974, bank robbery at the Sunset Branch of the Hibernia Bank in San Francisco, however, that proved her conversion was valid. This robbery produced $10,692.51 for the SLA.

The San Francisco area was becoming too hot for the SLA and operations were shifted to the Los Angeles area. Three members of the SLA, William Harris, Emily Harris, and Patty Hearst, had to shoot their way out of a shoplifting incident at a sporting goods store in the Los Angeles suburb of Inglewood on May 16, 1974. This incident alerted the Los Angeles police to the presence of the SLA, and a manhunt ensued. In the meantime, DeFreeze and five others fled to a small stucco house in a black area of Los Angeles. Word leaked out of their presence, and a Los Angeles SWAT team assaulted the house on May 17. During the hour-long gunfight, the house caught on fire and all six members of the SLA—Donald DeFreeze, Nancy Ling Perry, Camilla Hall, Mizmoon Soltysik, Angela Atwood, and Willie Wolfe—died of gunshot wounds or burns.

The SLA was always a small organization, and the losses sustained in May 1974 made it even smaller and less revolutionary. William and Emily Harris and Patty Hearst were the only survivors of the original group. William Harris assumed command of the SLA and adopted the code name General Teko. The next step was to recruit Kathleen Soliah and James Kilgore. Soliah then persuaded her brother, Steve Soliah, and her sister, Josephine Soliah, to join the SLA. Shortly thereafter, Michael Bortin and Wendy Yoshimura were recruited. The group left California, and the members spent the summer of 1974 in rural Pennsylvania and New York. In September 1974, the SLA moved operations to Sacramento, California. Plans were made to break Little and Remiro out of jail, but the leadership decided first to rob a bank to raise funds. On February 25, 1975, the SLA robbed a savings and loan bank in suburban North Sacramento. Plans for the prison break fell through, and the group decided instead to conduct a bombing campaign in the San Francisco area. In August 1975, three San Francisco police cars blew up from bombs planted by the SLA. Further attempts were made in Los Angeles, but all attempts were unsuccessful. Federal and state authorities engaged in a massive effort to locate and destroy the SLA. In September 1975, the FBI arrested William and Emily Harris and Patricia Hearst.

The Hearst trial was a sensation that attracted national attention. Patty was the granddaughter of the publishing magnate William Randolph Hearst and her wealthy family could afford the best lawyers, including the famous trial attorney F. Lee Bailey. Her conversion from kidnap victim to a revolutionary made the trial a natural media story. The trial was held in federal district court in San Francisco, California, in March 1976. Hearst was convicted for her participation in the April 15, 1975 Hibernia Bank robbery and for the use of a firearm in the commission of a crime. She was sentenced to seven years in prison. President Jimmy Carter commuted her sentence on humanitarian reasons on February 1, 1979, after she had served two years. Hearst received a presidential pardon from President Bill Clinton on January 20, 2001.

Several of the other members of the SLA escaped arrest. James Kilgore and Kathy Soliah escaped arrest in 1975. They went into the revolutionary underground and after a while began new lives. Kilgore is still at large, but Soliah was arrested in Minnesota in 1999 living under the name of Sarah Jane Olson with her husband and three children. Her arrest reintroduced the controversy over the Symbionese Liberation Army and the difficulty of conducting legal proceedings long after the dates of the crimes. After a number of legal delays over the next two years, Olson pleaded guilty on October 30, 2001 to the crimes of attempting to blow up Los Angeles Police Department (LAPD) cars in 1975 and the murder of police officers. She defended the guilty plea by maintaining that "she could not receive a fair trial because of the September 11, 2001 terrorist attacks" in New York City and Washington, D.C. Olson received a sentence of 20 years to life, but she can be released after five years. Part of her guilty plea allows that she can serve her sentence in a Minnesota prison.

The investigation into the background of the Soliah case caused California authorities to reexamine an old SLA bank robbery and murder case. Members of the SLA robbed a Crocker National Bank in the Sacramento suburb of Carmichael on April 21, 1975, and, during the course of the robbery, Myrna Lee Opsahl, a 42-year-old mother of four, was killed by a shotgun blast. This case had never been prosecuted, because of lack of evidence. Mrs. Opsahl's son had been actively lobbying prosecutors for several years for the case to be reopened. During the preparation for the Soliah trial, police authorities used new forensic testing procedures to discover new evidence linking the SLA with the robbery and murder. Interviews with Patri-

cia Hearst also provided backup information. On January 16, 2002 authorities arrested Michael Bortin, Emily Harris, and William Harris and charged them with first-degree murder. James Kilgore was also charged for this crime, but he remains a fugitive.

Suggested readings: Marilyn Baker and Sally Brompton, *Exclusive! The Inside Story of Patricia Hearst and the SLA* (New York: Macmillan, 1974); Duncan Campbell, "It Has Turned into My Trial," *Guardian* [London] (May 2, 2001), p. 6; William Carlson, "The Kidnapping That Gripped the Nation," *San Francisco Chronicle* (February 4, 1999), p. A1; James Glazov, "The Terrorist Next Door," *Ottawa Citizen* (February 19, 2001), p. A13; Anna Gorman and Steve Berry, "Olson Enters Surprise Guilty Plea in SLA Case," *Los Angeles Times* (November 1, 2001), p. A1; Anna Gorman and Nancy Vogel, "Bomb Plot Gets Olson 20 to Life," *Los Angeles Times* (January 19, 2001), p. A1; Patricia Campbell Hearst and Alvin Moscow, *Every Secret Thing* (Garden City, NY: Doubleday, 1982); Vin McLellan and Paul Avery, *The Voices of Guns: The Definitive and Dramatic Story of the Twenty-Two-Month Career of the Symbionese Liberation Army—One of the Most Bizarre Chapters in the History of the American Left* (New York: Putnam's Sons, 1977); Michael Taylor, "New Focus on Old SLA Killing," *San Francisco Chronicle* (January 23, 2001), p. A1; Michael Taylor, "27 Years Later, 4 SLA Figures Arrested," *San Francisco Chronicle* (January 17, 2002), p. A1; Maryanne Vollers, "Was This Soccer Mom a Terrorist?" *New York Times* (May 20, 2001), sec. 6, p. 38.

T

Tarrants, Thomas Albert (1947–   )

Thomas Tarrants, the bomb expert for the **White Knights of the Ku Klux Klan** during its bombing campaign in 1967 and 1968, was born on December 20, 1947, in Mobile, Alabama. His father, a used-car salesman, was a staunch segregationist. Tarrants attended Murphy High School in Mobile when the school was in the middle of desegregation. One of the students arrested for violently demonstrating against the federal court order, he was charged by police with disorderly conduct. In his junior year, Tarrants dropped out of school and began working with several local segregationist leaders. With several young, right-wing radicals, he formed the Christian Military Defense League. Several times Mobile police stopped him and found weapons on his person. Each time he was let off with probation or without charges. In August 1967, he started a job as a maintenance worker at the Masonite plant in Laurel, Mississippi.

Tarrants approached the head of the White Knights of the Ku Klux Klan, **Samuel Holloway Bowers**, with a plan to launch a bombing campaign against prominent Jews and key civil rights leaders in Mississippi. At first, Bowers was reluctant to trust Tarrants because of the fear that he might be a federal undercover agent. To prove his dedication, Tarrants, and his accomplice **Kathryn Madlyn Ainsworth**, planted a bomb in Jackson's Temple Beth Israel Synagogue on September 18, 1967. This bombing convinced Bowers that Tarrants was sincere in his commitment to the White Knights. Because Tarrants was unknown to the rank-and-file members of the White Knights, federal agents had no clues to his identity. Tarrants conducted three more bombings in the autumn of 1967. State police had a lucky break when a policeman in Collins, Mississippi, stopped a car with Bowers and Tarrants in it in December 1967. Tarrants was arrested for possession of a 45-caliber machine gun. Federal agents looking for the bomber, however, were still unaware of the significance of this arrest.

Tarrants's career as a bomber ended when federal authorities learned about his next target. Still unaware of his existence, federal agents started looking for ways to break the case. They interrogated the Roberts brothers, Allon Wayne and Raymond, and bribed them into providing information about Tarrants. The Roberts brothers, veteran members of the White Knights, were in serious trouble with the law over their Klan activities. They were also close enough to Bowers to know about Tarrants. Tarrants's next assignment was to bomb the home of Meyer Davidson, a prominent member of the Jewish community, in Meridian, Mississippi. On the night of June 28, 1968, Tarrants picked up Kathy Ainsworth to carry out the bombing. As Tarrants approached the house early in the morning of June 29, state and local police opened fire wounding him. Tarrants ran back to the car just in time to hear Kathy say that she was hit. She died of a gunshot wound to the throat. Tarrants tried to escape, but the police wounded him several more times before they captured him. His wounds were so severe that the doctors informed the police that he had no more than forty-five minutes to live. Somehow he survived, and, in the subsequent trial, Tarrants received a thirty-year prison sentence to be served in Parchman State Prison.

Tarrants's life changed in prison. At first, he was unrepentant. In July 1969, Tarrants and two companions broke out of prison with the help of White Knights sympathizers. He was free only a few days before he was recaptured but not before a gunfight during which one of his companions was killed. After his return to the maximum-security prison, Tarrants decided to educate himself. His studies of philosophy and religion led him to question both his racial beliefs and his political activism. Tarrants decided that his racist and anti-Semitic ideas had been wrong. When rumors of his conversion reached outside the prison, some of his former police adversaries came to visit him and were impressed by his change of attitude. These law enforcement agents worked to win him an early release from prison. Tarrants won an early release after ten years in prison. His repudiation of the Ku Klux Klan and his former life has been genuine. He was married and is no longer active in politics. **See also** Ainsworth, Kathryn Madlyn "Kathy"; Bowers, Samuel Holloway; Ku Klux Klan; White Knights of the Ku Klux Klan.

Suggested readings: Lance Hill, "Justice for None," *Times-Picayune* [New Orleans] (February 21, 1993), p. E6; Herbert Mitgang, "The Klan's War Against Jews in the Deep South," *New York Times* (February 24, 1993), p. C19; Jack Nelson, *Terror in the Night: The Klan's Campaign Against the Jews* (New York: Simon and Schuster, 1993); Jean Torkelson, "Ex-Racist Found God in a Mississippi Jail Cell," *Denver Rocky Mountain News* (July 10, 2000), p. 5A.

Terry, Randall (1958–)

Randall Terry, the most prominent anti-abortion activist in the United States and the founder of **Operation Rescue**, was born in April 1958 in Rochester, New York. His father was a public schoolteacher, and later his mother became a teacher also. The Terry family moved to Henrietta, a suburb of Rochester, when Terry was young. Terry's early interest was in music, and he played both the piano and the guitar. He showed exceptional ability in school and advanced quickly through grades until his junior year at Charles Roth High School. By this time, both he and his best friend were heavily into the local drug scene. A few months before graduation, Terry left school over his parents' objections to start a music career on the West Coast. He was finally living on a beach in Galveston, Texas, before he returned home. Back at home, he worked at an ice cream stand until September 1976 when he underwent a religious conversion through the intervention of a friend. Terry abandoned his drug-using friends and earned a high school degree from a three-year unaccredited school that provided a strict fundamentalist interpretation of the Bible. Terry was such a successful student that in the third year he was elected student body president. By this time, he had been converted to Christian Reconstructionism. Behind this theology is a movement that wants to reestablish a biblical society and deny religious liberty to the enemies of God. Their list of enemies included any type of social deviants and any opposed to their theocratic society. These enemies needed to be eliminated. In the midst of his studies, Terry met and married Cindy Dean. After graduation, Terry worked as a tire salesperson for Montgomery Ward and started participating in 1983 in anti-abortion protests in Binghamton, New York.

Soon after his participation in these anti-abortion protests, Terry decided that fighting abortion was his mission in life. He

Randall Terry, founder of Operation Rescue, in 1992. (AP Photo/ Michael Okoniewski)

began by working in the ranks of the abortion movement, but he soon displayed a drive to assume a leadership role. He had also become a follower of **Joseph Scheidler** and his brand of activism. Scheidler made him one of the regional directors of his Pro-Life Action Network (PLAN) in 1985. Terry was not satisfied with just being one of the leaders and formed Operation Rescue in January 1986. At the Pensacola meeting of anti-abortion leaders held in November 1986 to protest Joan Andrews's lengthy jail term for an abortion clinic raid, Terry proposed a national campaign of civil disobedience to coincide with the 1988 presidential election. His Operation Rescue would replace Scheidler's PLAN as the agenda for the anti-abortion movement. This new plan envisaged storming abortion clinics in a nationwide wholesale destruction of equipment and intimidation of abortion providers. This proposal for an escalation of violence scared other anti-abortion leaders, and they persuaded him to tone down some of his plans. This ambitious plan ultimately caused the breakdown of the alliance between Terry and Scheidler.

In the period from 1987 to 1991, Terry led Operation Rescue into a campaign of massive civil disobedience against abortion clinics and abortion providers. Terry had an autocratic administrative style, and no plans or organizational decisions could be made without his approval. At first, his leadership seemed to work as he targeted facilities in certain areas. Terry was also able to attract a cadre of devoted followers ready to undertake any tactic he could devise. Friendly politicians and a mild police response helped his campaign at key points. As his demonstrations turned more violent and confrontational, some of his support started drifting away. Federal authorities had a benign neglect strategy toward Operation Rescue until public opinion started turning against the violence. Terry had counseled his followers to ignore court injunctions counting on enough arrests to overwhelm any legal system. Slowly, violated court rulings and injunctions caught up with Operation Rescue. Terry had to serve a jail term in Atlanta for a violent demonstration staged in 1988, and he found his six-month sentence difficult to serve. While he was in jail, other leaders undertook some administrative reforms hoping to moderate Terry's autocratic style. After Terry arranged an early release, he turned on the reformers and banished them from Operation Rescue.

Dissension at the high ranks in Operation Rescue had a negative impact. Rank-and-file activists began to question decisions and tactics. After an interval of reestablishing his authority, Terry decided to resign from the leadership of Operation Rescue in 1990 and devote himself to other issues. His relationship with subsequent leaders of Operation Rescue has deteriorated since the mid-1990s, Terry and Flip Benham have engaged in a lengthy feud over Benham's leadership and less confrontational tactics. In 1998 Terry ran for Congress in New York but received

little support. Several abortion clinics won civil judgments against Terry causing him to file for bankruptcy to avoid $1.7 million in debts. Terry has continued to campaign for abortion issues, but he has run into personal difficulties. A controversy over his divorce from his wife alienated many of his followers. His church in Binghamton, New York, censured him in 2000 for abandoning his wife. Leaders in the renamed Operation Save America have been ostracizing Terry because of his divorce and his habits of cursing, smoking, and consuming alcohol. Terry has remarried, and his new wife is a former assistant in Operation Rescue. His income depends heavily on donations from followers and his feud with Flip Benham and Operation Save America has hurt him financially. Terry is still trying to reestablish himself as a political force by campaigning against gay marriages and stem-cell research. **See also** Anti-Abortion Movement; Army of God; Operation Rescue; Scheidler, Joseph.

Suggested readings: Dan Barry, "Icon for Abortion Protesters Is Looking for a Second Act," *New York Times* (July 20, 2001), p. A1; Dallas A. Blanchard, *The Anti-Abortion Movement and the Rise of the Religious Right: From Polite to Fiery Protest* (New York: Twayne, 1994); Diane Derby, "Terry, Church at Odds," *Rutland Herald* [Vt.] (February 10, 2000), p. 1; Diane Derby, "Terry's Crusade; Abortion Foe Is Back in Town, This Time Fighting Gay Marriage," *Times Argus* [Montpelier, Vt.] (February 6, 2000), p. 1; Mark McDonald, "Randall Terry," *Dallas Morning News* (July 5, 1992), p. 1F.

Thill, Nathan (1978–)

Nathan Thill, a **neo-Nazi skinhead** with ties to the **Aryan Nations**, declared war on minorities in Denver, Colorado. He was born in 1978. After his family moved to the Denver area, his childhood was marred by juvenile delinquent behavior. By the age of nine, Thill had been sent to a residential youth-crisis center. After that, he moved to the Colorado Mental Health Institute at Fort Logan, Colorado, and then the Lookout Mountain Juvenile Detention Center. At the detention center, Thill was exposed to the white supremacist theories of the Aryan Nations. Soon afterward, Thill announced himself a neo-Nazi skinhead warrior in the coming race war. In March 1995, Thill robbed a man in an adult bookstore using a knife as a weapon. He pleaded guilty to a third-degree assault but served only a minimum sentence as a juvenile offender.

Thill made headlines in November 1995 for his murder of an African immigrant man from Senegal. On November 18, 1995, Thill and a companion, Jeremiah Barnum, killed Oumar Dia, who had been working at a hotel in downtown Denver. Before shooting him, Thill taunted him about his willingness to die for being black. After killing Dia, Thill shot and seriously wounded a nurse, Jeannie Van Velkinburgh, paralyzing her for life. Thill tried to kill her because she was a witness to Dia's murder. The police arrested Thill shortly after the shootings. Thill confessed to the police about killing Dia and wounding Van Velkinburgh, but his confession was thrown out of court because of an inadequate Miranda warning—the required statement informing suspects that they have the right to see a lawyer before talking to the police. Thill's confession to a television reporter, however, stood up in court. His lawyers used his prior commitments to psychiatric institutions as a defense against the imposition of the death penalty after the trial was moved from Denver to Pueblo, Colorado. Even in Pueblo, the jurors confessed after the trial that they had been concerned about the prospect of judging a racist skinhead. After a hung jury over the death penalty, a new trial was scheduled until Thill pleaded guilty to the murder and the assault in exchange for a life sentence. The judge sentenced him in December 1999 to life in prison plus thirty-two years. Thill remained unrepentant at his sentencing and contended that he had won by escaping the death penalty. See also Neo-Nazis; Skinheads.

Suggested readings: Diane Carman, "Revenge Won't Be Justice for Thill," *Denver Post* (November 30, 1999), p. B1; Sue Lindsay, "Penalty on Trial in Murder of Dia," *Denver Rocky Mountain News* (September 6, 1999), p. 4A; Howard Pankratz, "Judge Locks Up Thill for Life; Skinhead Boastful, Laughing at Sentencing for Dia Murder," *Denver Post* (December 21, 1999), p. A1; Howard Pankratz, "Thill Pleas to Avert Painful Retrial," *Denver Post* (December 20, 1999), p. B7; Howard Pankratz, "Witness: Thill Drawn to Skinheads; Psychologist Testifies He Found 'Sense of Worth,' " *Denver Post* (November 24, 1999), p. B6.

Thomas, Mark (1951?–)

Mark Thomas, the leader of the **white supremacist movement** in Pennsylvania and the sponsor of the **Aryan Republican Army**, was born in 1951 in Pennsylvania. He left school after the eighth grade. His home since 1980 has been a farm in Longswamp Township, near Allentown, Pennsylvania. Besides small-time farming, Thomas has worked as a part-time truck driver. Thomas was a member of the **Invisible Empire, Knights of the Ku Klux Klan** until its demise in the early 1990s. He was also an early convert to the **Christian Identity** movement. Richard Girnt Butler, the head of the **Aryan Nations**, appointed him to head the Pennsylvania Aryan Nations. He replaced **James Wickstrom** as its head after Wickstrom was sent to jail in 1990. After Wickstrom's early release in 1991, they became rivals. Thomas sponsored and organized weekend rallies for Klansmen, **neo-Nazis**, and racist **skinheads** on his farm from 1992 to 1995. He also published a neo-Nazi monthly newsletter, *The Watchman*. In March 1995, Thomas's role with training neo-Nazis received negative publicity with the murder of a family by two neo-Nazi skinhead brothers, Bryan and David Freeman, who had spent considerable time at the Thomas compound. The Freemans killed their parents, Dennis and Brenda, and their brother, Eric, by beating and stabbing them.

In the mid-1990s, Thomas helped form the Aryan Republican Army (ARA). He organized a small band of white supremacists to carry out a series of bank robberies to raise funds to finance an overthrow of the U.S. government and establish a white homeland. Operational leaders were **Peter Kevin Langan** and Richard Lee Guthrie. Between November 1992 and December 1996, the ARA carried out a series of bank robberies in seven Midwestern states. At least twenty-two banks were robbed of more than $250,000. None of the money was recovered after the arrest of the robbers. Federal authorities suspect that it had been dispersed to various white supremacist groups. Thomas received around $80,000 of it. Federal authorities arrested Thomas in 1996. At first he denied any affiliation with the ARA, but after several weeks of questioning he finally confessed his leadership role in it. Soon after his confession was made public, Butler removed him as head of the Pennsylvania Aryan Nations. Thomas pleaded guilty in February 1997 to plotting a series of bank robberies and was sentenced to eight years in federal prison. He is now serving this sentence. **See also** Aryan Liberation Army; Aryan Nations; Ku Klux Klan; Langan, Peter Kevin.

Suggested readings: Anti-Defamation League. *Danger: Extremism: The Major Vehicles and Voices on America's Far-Right Fringe* (New York: Anti-Defamation League, 1996); Julia Lieblich, "A Living Theology of Hate; White Supremacists Believe in Violence," *Plain Dealer* [Cleveland] (June 11, 1995), p. 11; Robert Ruth, "Neo-Nazi Says He Had No Part in Bank Gang," *Columbus Dispatch* (January 16, 1997), p. 4C; Robert Ruth, "White Supremacist Is Subpoenaed as Witness," *Columbus Dispatch* (January 31, 1997), p. 1C; Keith Schneider, "Triple Murder Highlights Growth of Hate Groups," *Ottawa Citizen* (March 30, 1995), p. E11; Joseph A. Slobodzian and Mark Fazlollah, "White Supremacist Pleads Guilty to Conspiring to Rob Banks," *Philadelphia Inquirer* (February 18, 1997), p. 1.

Thompson, Linda (1953?–)

Linda Thompson is one of the most militant advocates for the American **militia movement**. Little is known about her early life except that she was probably born in 1953. She enlisted in the U.S. Army in the mid-1970s and worked as a clerk-typist reaching the rank of sergeant first class. During part of her tour of duty, she served in the Netherlands as an assistant to the U.S. Army Commanding General of NATO (North Atlantic Treaty Organization). After her military service, Thompson studied at the University of Maryland where she obtained an undergraduate degree. During this period she married and had three children. In 1988 she earned a law degree from Indiana University. Although she is a lawyer, Thompson has never belonged to a law firm or practiced law. Most of her legal affairs take place out of her office at the American Justice Federation (AJF) in Indianapolis, Indiana, where she specializes in militia issues. Her second husband is Al Thompson, a computer technician who works as a computer systems operator at the American Justice Federation.

Thompson has become the most vocal representative of the radical wing of the militia movement. She has christened herself the "acting adjutant general of the unorganized militia of the U.S.A." Acquaintances claim that she has always been eager to sue people or institutions for what she perceives as wrongs. She has also been active in ascribing opponents of hers as part of a conspiracy against her. Radicalizing events in her life have been the **Ruby Ridge incident** and the **Branch Davidians** incident. In both cases, she maintains that the federal government's use of force was illegitimate and part of a conspiracy in favor of the **New World Order**. To make her point, she has produced a series of videos, including *Waco: The Big Lie*, *Waco II: The Big Lie Continues*, and *America Under Siege*. These videos, popular in extremist circles, earned her upwards of $300,000 by the mid-1990s. In 1994 she founded the American Justice Federation as a support institution for the militia movement. Thompson has been active spreading her conspiracy theories over the Internet through the AJF's computer bulletin board.

Thompson remains an important figure in the militia movement, but her flamboyant and erratic statements have hurt her effectiveness. In 1994 she began agitating for militia groups to unite and march on Washington, D.C., to "hang the bastards."

Among her demands were for Congress to repeal the Fourteenth Amendment (equal protection of the law), the Sixteenth Amendment (federal income tax), and the Seventeenth Amendment (popular election of senators) to the U.S. Constitution. The Brady Bill, which provides for a waiting period for handgun purchases, and the North American Free Trade Agreement have also been targeted by her as unacceptable. She has also accused the federal government of complicity in the bombing of the Alfred P. Murrah Federal Building in Oklahoma City on April 19, 1995. Other leaders of the militia movement have ignored her appeals for revolutionary action, and the leaders of the **John Birch Society** have classified her as unstable. The leadership of the **Militia of Montana** (MOM) has criticized her statements and recommendations. Thompson's radical positions and other erratic statements have made other members of the militia movement question her motives. Thompson has responded by classifying her critics as traitors or government agents. **See also** Branch Davidians; Militia Movement; Militia of Montana.

Suggested readings: Richard Abanes, *American Militias: Rebellion, Racism and Religion* (Downers Grove, Ill.: InterVarsity Press, 1996); David Armstrong, "Rightists Assisting Barricaded Couple," *Boston Globe* (August 25, 1997), p. B1; Elinor Burkett, *The Right Women: A Journey Through the Heart of Conservative America* (New York: Touchstone Books, 1998); Neil A. Hamilton, *Militias in America: A Reference Handbook* (Santa Barbara, Calif.: ABC-CLIO, 1996); Mark Sauer and Jim Okerblom, "Patriotism or Paranoia?" *San Diego Union-Tribune* (May 4, 1995), p. E1; Kenneth S. Stern, *A Force upon the Plain: The American Militia Movement and the Politics of Hate* (Norman: University of Oklahoma Press, 1996); Jason Vest, "The Spooky World of Linda Thompson," *Washington Post* (May 11, 1995), p. D1.

Trochmann, John Ernest (1943–)

John Trochmann, one of the founders of the most militant American militia group—the **Militia of Montana** (MOM)—was born on August 23, 1943, on a farm near Newfolden, Pennington County, in northwestern Minnesota. His parents were farmers, but his father also doubled as a preacher. After dropping out of Newfolden Community High School, he joined the U.S. Navy's aviation branch. Trochmann began his naval service career as an engine mechanic, but he was promoted to flight engineer. After leaving the navy, Trochmann used his service skills to build an auto repair and race-car business in Delano, Minnesota. Later, his business also sold snowmobiles. Trochmann has been married five times and has three children. His younger brother, David Trochmann, moved to Montana in 1984, and John Trochmann followed him in 1988.

Trochmann had always been interested in politics, but the move to Montana stimulated his further involvement. In 1990 he attended the annual National Aryan Nations Congress meeting at **Hayden Lake**, Idaho. While there, he expressed his support for the **Aryan Nations'** white supremacist views and its **anti-Semitism**. At this meeting, he met and became friends with **Randall Weaver**. On January 26, 1992, Trochmann declared his personal sovereignty and repudiated his American citizenship. His anti-government views intensified after the **Ruby Ridge incident** and the **Branch Davidians** incidents. After a brief sojourn in Alaska to get away from civilization, Trochmann returned to Noxon, Montana, to play a more active political role. The Brady Bill and other efforts toward gun control disturbed him. Together with his brother, David; his nephew, Randy; and his wife, Carolyn, John Trochmann founded the Militia of Montana on January 1, 1994.

Almost from the beginning, the Militia of Montana has been one of the most influential of the militia organizations. Trochmann had long advised the Aryan Nations to drop their **neo-Nazi** paraphernalia and mainstream into the Christian right. By downplaying his neo-Nazi and racist views, he wanted to extend his anti-government views to a wider audience. This effort earned him a rebuke from **Richard Girnt Butler**, the head of the Aryan Nations. Trochmann's ef-

John Trochmann of the Militia of Montana (MOM), left, calls on a reporter during a Capitol Hill news conference on May 25, 1995. Bob Fletcher of MOM, center, and Leroy Crenshaw of the Massachusetts Militia, look on. (AP Photo/Mark Wilson)

forts to form a mass **militia movement** have only been partially successful. He has used MOM's manuals, newsletter, and Web sites to advise militia members to arm themselves for guerrilla warfare. In 1994 Trochmann and six associates were arrested in Roundtop, Montana, and the police found two dozen handguns and rifles. Charges against them were dropped when the Montana attorney general's office decided that the weapons case was too weak to prosecute. Trochmann played a low-profile role in the Freemen standoff in Montana in the mid-

1990s. His refusal to intervene on the side of the Freemen hurt him among elements of the militia movement, but he believed that supporting them would weaken the militia cause. Trochmann remains suspicious of the federal government and watches for any indication of government misconduct. **See also** Freemen Movement; Militia Movement; Militia of Montana.

Suggested readings: Richard Abanes, *American Militias: Rebellion, Racism and Religion* (Downers Grove, Ill.: InterVarsity Press, 1996); Serge F. Kovaleski, " 'One World' Conspiracies

Prompt Montana Militia's Call to Arms," *Washington Post* (April 29, 1995), p. A1; Patrick May, "Militias Retrench with Hard-Core Followers," *Times-Picayune* [New Orleans] (August 9, 1998), p. A32; David A. Neiwert, *In God's Country: The Patriot Movement and the Pacific Northwest* (Pullman: Washington State University Press, 1999); Katherine Seligman, "Hate Groups See Conspiracy in Withheld Evidence," *San Francisco Chronicle* (May 13, 2001), p. A19; Kenneth S. Stern, *A Force upon the Plain: The American Militia Movement and the Politics of Hate* (Norman: University of Oklahoma Press, 1996).

Trosch, David (1936?–   )

David Trosch is a leader of the most violent wing of the anti-abortion movement. Family details are lacking, but he was probably born around 1936. In 1982 he was ordained as a Roman Catholic priest, and most of his career has been spent at Magnolia Springs Parish near Mobile, Alabama. In 1993 he tried to place an ad in a newspaper justifying the killing of abortion providers. Shortly thereafter, Catholic Archbishop Oscar Lipscomb suspended Trosch from his parish for his public advocacy of violence. He is quoted as saying in the August 17, 1993, *Times-Picayune*, "If 100 doctors need to die to save over 1 million babies a year, I see it as a fair trade." In 1994 he attempted to place a drawing labeled "Justifiable Homicide" in the Mobile, Alabama, and Pensacola, Florida, newspapers after Michael Griffin, an anti-abortion activist, shot and killed Dr. David Gunn in Pensacola on March 10, 1993. Neither newspaper would publish the drawing. Trosch was a member of **Paul Jennings Hill's** Defensive Action group which called for violence against abortion providers. In July 1995, Trosch called for an insurrection against abortion doctors. Shortly after this call, a number of abortion doctors were shot and several killed. Trosch, a supporter of Paul Hill, considered Hill's assassination of an abortion doctor, John Bayard Britton, and his bodyguard, James Barrett, in Pensacola, Florida, on July 29, 1994, justifiable homicide. Despite a circle of colleagues who share his views, Trosch denies

that there is a conspiracy to use violence against abortion providers. **See also** Anti-Abortion Movement; Hill, Paul Jennings.

Suggested readings: Sandi Dolbee, "God's Will or Terrorism?" *San Diego Union-Tribune* (January 13, 1995), p. E1; Mimi Hall, "Priest Removed After Condoning Doctor's Slaying," *USA Today* (August 24, 1993), p. 68; Parker Holmes, "Priest of 'Kill-Doctors' Ad Is on a Crusade," *Times-Picayune* [New Orleans] (August 17, 1993), p. A8; Debbie Howlett, " 'Courage' or Crime,' " *USA Today* (January 10, 1995), p. 1A; Marlon Manuel, "Duty in Name of God to Kill Abortionists?" *Atlanta Journal and Constitution* (August 28, 1994), p. A3; Gerald Renner and Frank Spencer-Molloy, "Clinic Killer's Morality Unsettles Anti-Abortion Drive," *Hartford Courant* (January 7, 1995), p. A1.

Turner Diaries, The

The Turner Diaries, a novel written by white supremacist author **William Pierce**, serves as the bible for extremist groups in the United States and abroad. Pierce received a doctorate in physics and was a professor of physics at Oregon State University and a researcher before turning to extremist politics. He joined **George Lincoln Rockwell's American Nazi Party** and served as its ideological advisor until after the death of Rockwell in 1967. In 1970 Pierce formed a white supremacist organization, the **National Alliance**, to serve as an outlet for his racist propaganda. When he had been a member of the **John Birch Society**, Pierce had read the book *The John Franklin Letters*, which related the story of a struggle by American patriots against a communist takeover of the United States. Pierce found the diary approach suggestive. Using this book as a model, Pierce wrote *The Turner Diaries* in 1978 and published it under the name of Andrew McDonald to raise funds for his new party and to recruit new members. In the book, he tells the tale of Earl Turner and his band of white rebels in their struggle to defeat an oppressive U.S. government, or what they called the ZOG (**Zionist Occupied Government**). Their intent is to turn America into a purified white racist state. In carrying out this mission, the author describes how to form terrorist undergrounds, how to construct bombs, and how to explode them.

This novel has been the most successful of Pierce's propaganda efforts. Although mainstream publishing ignored its existence, *The Turner Diaries* has sold over 200,000 copies. Among its contributions to the growth of extremism has been that it has solidified thinking in white supremacist circles about the idea of the ZOG. This book served as the inspiration for **Robert Jay Mathews**'s The Order and its campaign of bombings, counterfeiting, murders, and robberies. **Timothy McVeigh** read the book and the Oklahoma City bombing on April 19, 1995, resembles a bombing portrayed in the novel. The decision by a commercial publisher, Lyle Stuart, to publish *The Turner Diaries* for Barricade Books in April 1996 provoked significant controversy but did not persuade the publisher to change his mind. **See also** Mathews, Robert Jay; McVeigh, Timothy; National Alliance; Order, The; Pierce, William.

Suggested readings: Scott Canon, "Book Labeled as Bomb Blueprint," *Kansas City Star* (May 18, 1997), p. A1; James Coates, *Armed and Dangerous: The Rise of the Survivalist Right* (New York: Hill and Wang, 1987); Ted Daniels, ed., *A Doomsday Reader: Prophets, Predictors, and Hucksters of Salvation* (New York: New York University Press, 1999); Charles Enman, "Customs Bans Turner Diaries," *Ottawa Citizen* (July 29, 1997), p. A1; Marc Fisher and Phil McCombs, "The Book of Hate," *Washington Post* (April 25, 1995), p. D1; Eric Harrison, " 'Diaries': Racist Fantasy or Primer for War of Hate?" *Los Angeles Times* (February 18, 1990), p. A1; Linton Weeks, "Publisher to Market Racist 'Turner Diaries,' " *Washington Post* (April 24, 1996), p. C1.

U

Unabomber (See Kaczynski, Theodore John "Ted")

United Freedom Front (UFF)

The United Freedom Front (UFF) was the most active left-wing radical extremist group in the decade from 1975 to 1985. Raymond Luc Levasseur was the leader of this small Marxist group, which was formed by former members of the **Students for a Democratic Society** (SDS). Levasseur was a Vietnam veteran, who had spent two years in a Tennessee prison for drug dealing. After his release from prison, he attended the University of Maine and majored in political science. While in school, he joined the Maine chapter of the Vietnam Veterans Against the War. By the early 1970s, he and his wife, Patricia Gros, and Thomas and Carole Manning had formed a prison reform group, the Sam Melville–Jonathan Jackson Unit, named after two prisoners who had been killed in prison. This small group started engaging in direct action against selected targets to destabilize the government.

The United Freedom Front was formed in 1975 to carry out an urban guerrilla campaign against the U.S. government. Seven members of the UFF committed nineteen bombings, ten bank robberies, and one murder over the next decade. Another husband and wife team, Karl Jaan Laaman and Barbara Curzi, and Richard Williams joined Levasseur, Gros, and Thomas and Carole Manning. Members directed the bombings against corporations, courthouses, and selected military targets in Connecticut, Maine, Massachusetts, New York, and Vermont. Despite the sensational aspects of the bombings and robberies, law enforcement agencies had difficulty locating the perpetrators. The three couples lived within thirty miles of each other in northern Ohio. They took extreme precautions to ensure that they resembled normal families. Two of the couples were busy raising three children each during the decade of their operations.

Law enforcement finally broke up the United Freedom Front on November 4, 1984. At the time of the arrest of Levasseur, Laaman and their wives, and Williams the FBI had conducted one of the longest, most intense manhunts in FBI history. The Mannings escaped the November dragnet and went underground, but they were arrested a year later in Virginia. In a series of trials held on a variety of charges in 1985 and 1986, all of the defendants received prison terms from fifteen to fifty-three years. Thomas Manning stood trial for killing a state trooper and was sentenced to life imprisonment. Williams pleaded guilty and received a seven-year prison sentence. In 1987 six de-

301

fendants were indicted on federal seditious conspiracy and Racketeering Influenced and Corrupt Organizations (RICO) charges. In a raucous ten-month political trial held in Massachusetts starting in January 1989, the jury returned not guilty verdicts on most counts and was deadlocked on the remaining counts. After the judge declared a mistrial, the six members of the UFF returned to prison to serve out their sentences. **See also** Students for a Democratic Society.

Suggested readings: Leonard Buder, "Jurors Return Final Verdicts in Bomb Trial," *New York Times* (March 8, 1986), sec. 1, p. 31; Robert Hanley, "Fugitives Were Aloof, Neighbors Say," *New York Times* (April 26, 1985), p. B2; Robert Hanley, "Ohio Suspects Tied to 10 Bomb Blasts," *New York Times* (November 9, 1984), p. A1; Robert Hanley, "Suspect in Jersey Trooper's Slaying Seized by F.B.I. at Norfolk Home," *New York Times* (April 25, 1985), p. B2; John H. Kennedy, "US Drops Charges vs. Two of Seven Radicals," *Boston Globe* (September 1, 1988), p. 1; Brent L. Smith, *Terrorism in America: Pipe Bombs and Pipe Dreams* (Albany: State University of New York Press, 1994).

United Klans of America (UKA)

The United Klans of America (UKA) is the oldest and one of the most violent of the modern **Ku Klux Klan** organizations. **Robert Shelton**, a rubber plant worker and salesperson from Tuscaloosa, Alabama, founded the UKA on July 8, 1961. Shelton negotiated an amalgamation of two splinter Klan groups—one from Alabama and the other from Georgia. His reward was an appointment as imperial wizard of the new group. Besides being the oldest Klan group, it has been one of the most secretive and suspicious of outsiders. Members of the UKA come from all segments of Southern society, but most of the activists have been blue-collar workers and high school dropouts. Because of its extreme secrecy, estimates of the size of the UKA's membership have always been suspect. FBI estimates place active membership in the UKA at around 26,000 in the mid-1960s. Shelton's one-year jail term starting

in February 1969 for contempt of Congress in the late 1960s had a negative impact on its membership and recruiting.

Almost from its beginnings in the middle of the civil rights movement, members of the UKA resorted to violence. This violence erupted not long after members of the UKA received training seminars on the making and handling of explosives. UKA members have been convicted of murders and bombings across the South. Among its victims have been four young black girls in the Sixteenth Street Baptist Church bombing in 1963; Lieutenant Colonel Lemuel Penn in 1964; Viola Liuzzo in 1965, a Detroit civil rights worker; and teenager Michael Donald in 1981. These crimes drew the attention of federal authorities and resulted in a campaign to end the UKA's reign of terror. The FBI launched its counterintelligence program (COINTELPRO) campaign to discredit the leaders by planting false rumors and other types of disinformation. These efforts were partially successful in curtailing major crimes, but less successful in the courtroom. It was always difficult to convict Klan members with all-white Southern juries.

In the mid-1970s, the UKA had a resurgence in popularity in the South. Shelton was able to construct alliances with other right-wing extremist groups. His leadership of the Committee of Ten Million (COTM) allowed him access to a new crop of recruits. He was able to exploit resentment among whites about affirmative action and school busing through his writings in the Klan's newsletter, the *Fiery Cross*. This resurgence, however, proved to be short lived. An influx of younger leaders in rival Ku Klux Klan groups started making inroads among traditional UKA supporters in the late 1970s. By the early 1980s, the ranks of the UKA had diminished to around 900 activists.

The United Klans of America suffered its biggest defeat in the courtroom. Two members of the Mobile, Alabama, branch of the UKA murdered a black teenager, Michael Donald, in 1981. Both members were convicted of murder in 1983, and one of them received the death sentence for the brutal killing. Evidence of the complicity of the leaders of the Mobile UKA in the murder persuaded the **Klanwatch** lawyers of the Southern Poverty Law Center to initiate a lawsuit against the UKA. Michael Donald's mother was the plaintiff. Lawyers from Klanwatch built such a convincing case that an all-white jury returned judgments of liability against the UKA and implicated each of the individual Klan leaders. The award was $7 million in damages. In the weeks following the conclusion of the case in 1987 the UKA turned over its national headquarters building and its assets to the plaintiff. This headquarters building was later sold for almost $80,000. This legal case ended the existence of the United Klans of America as a viable organization. With no apparent assets and discredited leadership, members of the UKA migrated to other Klan and white supremacist groups. **See also** Klanwatch; Ku Klux Klan; Shelton, Robert.

Suggested readings: Associated Press, "U.S. Jurors Award $7 Million Damages in Slaying by Klan," *New York Times* (February 13, 1987), p. A1; Frank Judge, "Slaying the Dragon," *American Lawyer* (September 1987), p. 83; George Lardner, Jr., "15 Years of Dirty Tricks Bared by FBI," *Washington Post* (November 22, 1977), p. A2; Gita M. Smith, "Alabama Case Showed How Father's Sins Were Visited on Son," *Atlanta Journal and Constitution* (June 8, 1997), p. 4A; Bill Stanton, *Klanwatch: Bringing the Ku Klux Klan to Justice* (New York: Grove Weidenfeld, 1991).

V

Vann, Henry Moore (See Muhammad, Abdul Khalid)

Viper Militia

The Viper Militia, an Arizona militia group, planned several major anti-government operations in the mid-1990s. This group, which had only twelve members, operated out of the Phoenix, Arizona, area. Members were anti-government activists who resembled the **Arizona Patriots** of a decade earlier in size and ideology. They planned to bomb at least seven government buildings and the KPNX television station. Using a videotape demonstrating how to blow up a building, the leaders acquired the same type of explosives that were used in Oklahoma City to destroy the Alfred P. Murrah Federal Building on April 19, 1995. Members conducted tests of the explosives in the Tonto National Forest.

The Viper Militia was unknown to federal authorities before a hunter in the national forest tipped them off about the tests of explosives. An undercover agent infiltrated the group and exposed its plans. Federal agents raided the Viper Militia on July 1, 1996, and arrested all the members. Only one of the twelve charged escaped without prison time. Charles Knight stood trial and received a sentence of fifty-seven months for conspiracy to make and possess explosives. The others pleaded guilty to making and possessing explosives and were sentenced to prison terms ranging from one to nine years. Critics of the government's case have charged that members of the Viper Militia were upholding their First and Second Amendment rights and the government overreacted. **See also** Arizona Patriots; Militia Movement.

Suggested readings: James Brooke, "Agents Seize Arsenal of Rifles and Bomb-Making Material in Arizona Militia Inquiry," *New York Times* (July 3, 1996), p. A18; Carol Morello and Gwen Florio, "The Evolution of an Uprising," *Toronto Star* (July 7, 1996), p. F7; Louis Sahagun, "Case Closed, Informant Abandoned," *Los Angeles Times* (November 29, 1997), p. 2B; Louis Sahagun and Tina Daunt, "Agents Link Bombs, Arms to Arizona Militia," *Los Angeles Times* (July 3, 1996), p. A1; Mark Shaffer, "State Game and Fish Employee Infiltrated Viper Militia," *Arizona Republic* (July 4, 1996), p. A1; Robert L. Snow, *The Militia Threat: Terrorists Among Us* (New York: Plenum Trade, 1999).

Agents with the Federal Bureau of Alcohol, Tobacco and Firearms load one of several drums containing explosive material onto a truck following the search of a north Phoenix home on July 2, 1996. The residence housed one of the main caches of weapons and explosives for the Arizona Viper Militia group. Twelve militia members were charged with plotting to blow up government buildings in the Phoenix area. (AP Photo/Scott Troyanos)

W

Waco Siege (See Branch Davidians; Koresh, David)

Walcotte, Louis Eugene (See Farrakhan, Louis)

Warner, James K. (1947?–)
James K. Warner is a leading **Christian Identity** minister in the South. His birthdate is unavailable, but he was probably born in 1947. He served in the U.S. Air Force before being discharged for neo-Nazi agitation. Warner joined **George Lincoln Rockwell's American Nazi Party** (ANP) in the summer of 1959. He became dissatisfied with Rockwell's leadership and left in late 1960 after Rockwell had denounced him as dishonest and disloyal. Warner left the ANP with an exposé of the party titled *Swastika Smearbund* (1961). In 1961 he was ordained as a minister in the Church of God. Next, Warner joined the National State's Rights Party (NSRP), but his stay there was short; NSRP's leaders accused him of trying to steal its mailing list. Warner was convicted of conspiracy to interfere with the integration of schools in Alabama in 1963. Warner became a follower of **Wesley Swift** and a convert to Christian Identity. After being ordained in the Identity church in 1970, he started his New Christian Crusade Church in Los Angeles, California, in 1971. **Tom Metzger** was a disciple of Warner, and Warner ordained him as a minister in the church before Metzger broke away from religion. Warner became affiliated with **David Duke** and was appointed the grand dragon of the Knights of the Ku Klux Klan and its director of information in 1975.

In 1976 Warner moved the New Christian Crusade Church to Louisiana. Then in 1977 Warner founded the Christian Defense League (CDL) and became its first director. His church is now located in Metairie, Louisiana, a suburb of New Orleans. Another of his organizations is the Sons of Liberty. Besides his preaching and speaking engagements, Warner publishes a newsletter, *Christian Vanguard*. In this publication Warner advances the ideas of Christian Identity and attacks racial minorities. In 1978 Warner protested over and attempted to disrupt a CBS television docudrama on the Holocaust. According to Warner, the Holocaust never happened but was an invention of an international Jewish conspiracy. Warner left politics in the 1990s, but his wife Debra Coleman Warner ran for political office in the mid-1990s, losing in 1993 and 1995. **See also** American Nazi Party; Christian Identity; Duke, David; Holocaust Denial Movement, Metzger, Tom.

Suggested readings: Tyler Bridges, *The Rise of David Duke* (Jackson: University Press of Mississippi, 1994); Betty A. Dobratz and Stephanie L. Shanks-Meile, *"White Power, White Pride!" The White Separatist Movement in the United States* (New York: Twayne, 1997); Jeffrey Kaplan ed., *Encyclopedia of White Power: A Sourcebook on the Radical Racist Right* (Walnut Creek, Calif.: Altamira Press, 2000).

Washington State Militia (WSM)

The Washington State Militia initiated plans to attack the U.S. government before federal authorities closed it down. John Pitner, a painter by trade from the Bellingham, Washington, area; Fred Fisher, a Bellingham contractor; Gary Kuenoehl, an unemployed gunsmith; and Ben Hinkle, former head of the Citizens for Liberty, met on a farm near Deeming, Washington, in May 1993, and formed the Washington State Militia. They were disturbed at what they considered the government's misconduct during the **Ruby Ridge Incident** and decided to build a militia group to prepare for a war with the U.S. government and the **New World Order**. Another stated goal was to prevent a United Nations takeover of the United States. In a series of secret meetings held throughout late 1993 and 1994, the leaders of WSM recruited members. At no time did the WSM have more than 100 members, and the number of active members was around 60. Members started stockpiling weapons and bomb-making materials. Up until November 1995, the WSM was an underground organization, but on November 11, 1995, Pitner announced its existence at a public meeting just outside of Bellingham.

Soon after this public announcement, federal authorities began to show interest in WSM's activities. Reports from an informant in the WSM mentioned the group's ownership of bomb-making paraphernalia. Government officials were also concerned about the growing ties between the WSM and **John Ernest Trochmann**'s **Militia of Montana**. At one of the meetings held in his Deeming home in February 1996, Pitner in-structed his followers in ways to construct homemade bombs. About this time Pitner's wife and sole financial support left him causing him to start withdrawing from WSM activities. Some of the more violent elements within the WSM started taking over leadership and made plans to launch a bombing campaign. They planned to blow up a radio tower and a Bellingham train tunnel. At a bomb-making class on July 27, 1996, FBI agents arrested the eight participants. Pitner and other leaders were arrested later on the same day. Four of the seven defendants received jail sentences after a court in a January 1997 trial declared them guilty of possessing illegal weapons and bomb-making equipment, but the major charge of conspiracy was never levied because one juror held out against conviction. The other defendant pleaded guilty to illegal gun possession. **See also** Militia Movement; Militia of Montana; Trochmann, John Ernest.

Suggested readings: Susan Byrnes, Lily Eng, and Jennifer Bjorhus, "8 from Area Arrested in Bomb-Making," *Seattle Times* (July 29, 1996), p. A1; Timothy Egan, "Terrorism Now Going Homespun as Bombings in the U.S. Spread," *New York Times* (August 25, 1996), sec. 1, p. 1; Lily Eng, "Alleged Plot Key to Militia Case," *Seattle Times* (January 17, 1997); p. B1; Lily Eng, "Militia Conspiracy Trial Nearly Ready for Jury—Defendants Called Dumb and Dumber," *Seattle Times* (February 19, 1997), p. B3; David A. Neiwert, *In God's Country: The Patriot Movement and the Pacific Northwest* (Pullman: Washington State University Press, 1999); Carol M. Ostrom and Danny Westneat, "Militia Leader Sought 'Peaceful' Image for Group," *Seattle Times* (July 30, 1996), p. A1.

Washitaw Nation

The Washitaw Nation is a Louisiana common law separatist group. Verdiacee Turner, a black woman born in 1927, is the leader of the Washitaw Nation. Her position is that the United States illegally bought the lands of the Louisiana Purchase from France in 1803. These lands had been settled by what she calls the "Ancient Ones"—an African tribe which was one of the twelve tribes of

Israel. Consequently, she claims that the land belongs to the original inhabitants, and the rights of ownership have been passed down to her through the matriarchal line. She claims to be the empress over the 30 million acres of the original Louisiana Purchase with the title Empress Verdiacee "Tiari" Washitaw-Turner Goston El-Bey. The Washitaw Nation falls into the Black Judaism tradition. Since the leaders consider the Washitaw Nation a sovereign state, its leaders signed, in November 1996, a treaty of friendship with the leaders of the **Republic of Texas**.

Turner has had a checkered legal past. She arrived in Richwood, Louisiana, in the mid-1970s and helped it incorporate as a town. Turner twice served as mayor from 1975 to 1976 and again from 1979 to 1984. During both terms, she was a controversial mayor. In 1984 she was accused of stealing $150,000 in federal government money, but the charges were later dropped for lack of evidence. In operating a common law movement operation out of her home near Richwood, she has been investigated by the states of Colorado and Louisiana for banking fraud, selling illegal license plates, and providing phony documents. The Southern Poverty Law Center estimated that in 1999 the Washitaw Nation had around 200 members. Many of her closest followers have had legal problems for fraud and several are serving prison terms. Individuals claiming membership in the Washitaw Nation have run afoul of the law in Missouri and Kansas. On March 21, 1999, federal agents raided Turner's home and seized documents for evidence of tax evasion and mail fraud. Turner remains free during the investigation, but federal and state authorities are closely monitoring her activities. **See also** Common Law Courts Movement; Republic of Texas.

Suggested readings: Southern Poverty Law Center, "Born on the Bayou," *SPLC Intelligence Report* 94 (Spring 1999): 14–18; Southern Poverty Law Center, "A Louisiana 'Empress' Faces the Law," *SPLC Intelligence Report* 98 (Spring 2000): 2; Southern Poverty Law Center, "Starting Small," *SPLC Intelligence Report* 94 (Spring

1999): 16–17; Judy L. Thomas, "Hard-Line Approach Used on Extremists Common-Law Lien," *Kansas City Star* (August 18, 1997), p. A1.

Watson, Paul Franklin (1950–)

Paul Watson, the founder and leader of the radical environmentalist organization the **Sea Shepherd Conservation Society**, was born in 1950 in Toronto, Canada, the eldest of seven children. His father joined the Canadian military forces and served in the Korean War. When he was six, the family moved to Saint Andrews, New Brunswick. One of his early childhood experiences was witnessing a seal hunt, an experience that sickened him. His mother died in childbirth when Watson was thirteen. When he was fifteen he ran away from home, went to sea and worked on Norwegian and Swedish freighters; later he served in the Canadian Coast Guard. After leaving the Coast Guard, he studied communications and media for a semester at Simon Fraser University in British Columbia. Watson also did some freelance writing for Vancouver's radical weekly, *Georgia Strait*.

In the early 1970s, Watson became interested in political activism. He was one of the initial members of the **Greenpeace** Foundation in 1971 and participated in several of its anti-nuclear demonstrations. In 1973 he traveled to Wounded Knee, South Dakota, and participated in the American Indian Movement (AIM) as a medic. The Oglala Sioux named him Grey Wolf Clear Water. Following the Wounded Knee siege, Watson rejoined the Greenpeace movement. He was a leader in the 1975 Greenpeace campaign against seal hunting. During one protest against the seal slaughter, Watson was almost killed when the seal hunters dragged him over the ice and dunked him in the Arctic Sea. Watson was expelled from Greenpeace after resorting to violence against a seal hunter in 1977.

Watson formed the Sea Shepherd Conservation Society, or Sea Shepherds, in June 1977. He first named the group the Earth Force Environmental Society, but soon changed it. His first action was to acquire a ship, the *Sea Shepherd*, which he used to harass and almost sink a Portuguese whaling ship, the *Sierra*, off the Portuguese coast. After the Portuguese government seized his ship, Watson retaliated by having it scuttled in December 1979 to keep the ship from being confiscated by the Portuguese government. Later in January 1980, a team of divers attached a limpet mine to the *Sierra* and sank it. In 1981 he documented illegal whaling being conducted by a Soviet whaling fleet. Canadian authorities arrested Watson in 1983 for violation of the Seal Protection Act and sentenced him to a twenty-one-month prison term for interfering with a harp seal hunt. In April 1985, he was out of jail and appealing his sentence when the Canadian Supreme Court decreed the Seal Protection Act unconstitutional. His ship, *Sea Shepherd II*, had been impounded for two years during the appeal. Without a ship, Watson became active in demonstrations against the Canadian government's campaign to exterminate the gray wolf.

In subsequent years, Watson has been actively interfering in whaling hunts, seal hunts, and logging. Watson was the first to initiate a widespread **monkeywrenching** campaign by spiking trees in British Columbia forests. During the course of his operations, he has sabotaged at least seven more ships from a variety of countries. In 1994 the Norwegian Navy attacked Watson's vessel, *Whales Forever*, to prevent it from interfering with a Norwegian whaling fleet. Besides these direct-action activities, Watson teaches courses on environmental philosophy and the history of environmental action at the Arts College of Design in Pasadena, California. Watson draws no salary from the Sea Shepherds and supports himself from lectures, writing, and teaching. He was a close friend of another animal activist, the late Cleveland Amory. Watson has published his autobiography, *Sea Shepherd: My Fight for Whales and Seals*, in 1982, and two other books, *Cry Wolf* (1985) and *Ocean Warrior* (1994).

By the 1990s, Watson had become the leading figure in the ongoing fight against whaling and seal hunting. Rik Scarce places Watson in the school of "ecocentrism" where "everything in nature possesses inherent or intrinsic worth or value." His acceptance of violence to support his ecocentric views has made him an enemy of the more moderate Greenpeace organization. His rivalry with **David Fraser McTaggart**, the founder of Greenpeace, is legendary. In 1998 Watson led the Sea Shepherds against the reintroduction of whaling by the Makah Indians in the state of Washington. Watson remains a controversial figure in the environmental movement. His enemies describe him as headstrong, combative, and arrogant. To his supporters, however, he remains the Robin Hood of the environmentalist movement. **See also** Radical Environmentalism; Sea Shepherd Conservation Society.

Suggested readings: Stewart Bell, "Grey Wolf Clear Water," *Vancouver Sun* (May 29, 1993), p. T2; Owen Bowcott, "Buccaneer Spirit of a Sea Wolf," *Guardian* [London] (September 21, 1994), p 25; Paul Dean, "20,000 Leagues Under the Sea," *Los Angeles Times* (November 9, 1993), p. E1; Charles Laurence, " 'A Pirate? Of Course I am,' " *Daily Telegraph* [London] (April 19, 2001), p. 25; David B. Morris, *Earth Warrior: Overboard with Paul Watson and the Sea Shepherd Conservation Society* (Golden, Colo.: Fulcrum Publishing, 1995); Rik Scarce, *Eco-Warriors: Understanding the Radical Environment Movement* (Chicago: Noble Press, 1990); Bella Stumbo, "Sea Shepherd Society; Modern-Day Pirates Fight the Whalers," *Los Angeles Times* (June 13, 1987), part 1, p. 1.

Weather Underground (WU)

The Weather Underground was the most radical left-wing group that evolved from the **Students for a Democratic Society** (SDS) and the student unrest of the 1960s. A number of leftist extremists had become disenchanted with what they considered the moderate approach of the SDS and turned to violence. The original name of the group was the Weathermen from the lyrics of a song by Bob Dylan. In a meeting held in

Flint, Michigan, from December 27 to 31, 1969, the organizers of the Weathermen decided to launch open warfare against the American power structure. Because many of the key operatives in the group were women, the name was soon changed to Weather Underground. Between 1971 and 1981, members of Weather Underground participated in twenty-five bombings of government and state buildings. Loss of life was low in these bombings, but property damage was high. Several Weather Underground members died while constructing the bombs. Federal and state authorities launched a massive manhunt to locate the hundred or so members of Weather Underground, but the members had a strong support system, and most of them remained secure in safe houses under assumed names.

The more these radical leftists resorted to violence, the less popular support they received. Weather Underground's last major action was the participation of several of its members with the **Black Liberation Army** and the **May 19th Communist Organization** in the robbery of a Brink's armored car in October 1981 during which two policemen and a security guard were killed. Although this crime netted the robbers $1.6 million, it also ended the group's viability as a force in American politics. Federal and state authorities' efforts to crack down on the organization were thinning out the leadership ranks of Weather Underground. As the political climate became hostile, several of the leaders of the movement abandoned direct action and went so far underground that they ceased operations. Slowly over the years, some of these figures have surfaced and have faced legal proceedings for crimes committed twenty or thirty years ago. Bernadine Dohrn and William Ayers are the most notable examples and they received fines and probation. Statute of limitations has allowed some to escape prosecution altogether. Susan L. Rosenberg, a leader in the Weather Underground, received a presidential pardon from President Bill Clinton in January 2001. **See also** Black Liberation

Army; May 19th Communist Organization; Students for a Democratic Society.

Suggested readings: M. A. Farber, "Behind the Brink's Case: Return of the Radical Left," *New York Times* (February 16, 1982), p. A1; Anthony Lewis, "Dohrn Got Probation, but What of Others," *New York Times* (January 18, 1981), sec. 4, p. 6; Robert D. McFadden " 'Weather' Fugitive Is Seized in Killings," *New York Times* (October 22, 1981), p. B4; Frederick D. Miller, "The End of SDS and the Emergence of Weatherman: Demise Through Success," in Jo Freeman, ed., *Social Movements of the Sixties and Seventies* (New York: Longman, 1983); Abe Peck, *Uncovering the Sixties: The Life and Times of the Underground Press* (New York: Citadel Press, 1991); Edward Wong and Sherri Day, "Former Terrorist Is Among Those Pardoned or Freed in Clinton's Final Acts in Office," *New York Times* (January 21, 2001), sec. 1, p. 32.

Weathermen (See Weather Underground)

Weaver, Randall "Randy" (1948?–)

Randy Weaver, the key participant in the **Ruby Ridge incident** in 1992, was born in Grant, Iowa, probably in 1948. His father was an agricultural supply salesman. The family moved to Jefferson, Iowa, near Fort Dodge in 1962. Weaver graduated from Jefferson High School in 1966. After a brief sojourn at Iowa Central Community College, he joined the U.S. Army. His training in the army was as a combat engineer. Weaver was successful as a soldier and received airborne and Special Forces training and reached the rank of sergeant. He was stationed at Fort Bragg, North Carolina, and never served in Vietnam. After leaving the army, he returned to Iowa and married Vicki Jordison in November 1971. They moved to Cedar Falls, Iowa, so he could go to Northern Iowa University to study to become a federal law enforcement agent. After several semesters, Weaver left school in 1972 to work at the John Deere Tractor Factory in Waterloo, Iowa.

In about 1978, the Weavers started par-

Randy Weaver leaves the Boundary County Courthouse in Bonners Ferry, Idaho, on December 16, 1997, with his friend Linda Thompson, right, after Weaver testified in the probable cause hearing of FBI sharpshooter Lon Horiuchi. (AP Photo/Jeff T. Green)

ticipating in Bible studies and came to the conclusion that modern society was corrupt and the Day of Judgment was coming. In March 1983, they sold their house and left Cedar Falls for Idaho, partly because Idaho law made it easier to home school their children than Iowa law. They bought twenty acres for $5,000 and a moving truck. The Weavers spent 1984 building a cabin. Vicki educated the three children in reading, writing, and the Bible. Kevin Harris, a homeless teenager, joined the family in 1984 and soon shared their lifestyle. In the meantime, Weaver was feuding with his neighbors. One neighbor complained to the FBI about Weaver and his anti-government talk but, after a brief interview, Weaver was left alone.

Northern Idaho is known as a hotbed of anti-government and white supremacist activities, and Weaver soon found himself in the middle of it. White supremacists wanted to make Idaho part of a white homeland. Weaver soon attended **Aryan Nations** meetings held in **Hayden Lake**, Idaho, and he shared the **Christian Identity** views with his wife. It was at one of these meetings that the Weavers became friends with **John Ernest Trochmann** and his wife. The Weaver home at Ruby Ridge was located in Boundary County, Idaho, and, in 1988, Weaver ran for sheriff of Boundary County on a program of allowing Idaho citizens to escape the burdens of unpopular laws. He garnered the votes of nearly 25 percent of the county electorate.

Weaver's strident anti-government activities finally attracted the attention of federal authorities. Agents of the Bureau of Alcohol, Tobacco and Firearms (BATF) set up a sting operation in 1989 to uncover illegal weapons transactions among Idaho's white supremacists. The agents wanted Weaver to inform on the activities of John Trochmann, the leader of the **Militia of Montana**. Weaver was indicted on a weapons charge in December 1990 after selling two illegally sawed-off shotguns to one of the undercover agents of the BATF on October 24, 1989. BATF agents tried to use the indictment as leverage to convince Weaver to work as an undercover operative among the white supremacists, but he refused. A warrant was issued for his arrest. After BATF officials arrested Weaver, a local magistrate released him on personal recognizance with no cash bond. Weaver failed to respond to a court appearance in February 1991 and later claimed that he had been given the wrong court date. At the same time, he had made it plain that he would resist any efforts to arrest him again. Weaver, his family, and Harris were known to be heavily armed. Federal authorities were reluctant to force the issue because of the danger that Weaver's children might be hurt in a confrontation. The local press started a media campaign for Weaver's arrest citing a double standard for right-wing wrongdoers.

The confrontation at Ruby Ridge was the result of a combination of miscalculations. Six U.S. marshals conducted a surveillance patrol, on August 21, 1992, to estimate what it would take to arrest Weaver at his home. The marshals were not wearing bulletproof vests because they were not expecting a confrontation. In the course of the patrol, Striker, the family dog spotted the marshals and dashed toward one of them followed by fourteen-year-old Sam Weaver. The marshal shot and killed the dog, and Sam Weaver retaliated by shooting at Marshal William F. Degan. More gunfire resulted in the deaths of Sam Weaver and Degan. It took nine hours before two of the deputies could be rescued and Degan's body removed. Faced with an assault of an armed

household, the authorities changed the rules of engagement on the use of deadly force. On August 22, a government sniper, Lon Horiuchi, shot at Harris in the house but killed Vicki Weaver. After the initial gun battle was over, the government strategy was to wait out Weaver and negotiate; however, Weaver refused to talk to federal negotiators. Finally, **James B. "Bo" Gritz**, a former Green Beret lieutenant colonel and a leader in the anti-government movement, and Gerald "Jack" McLamb, a former Phoenix, Arizona police officer, persuaded him to surrender on August 31.

Weaver and the confrontation at Ruby Ridge became a national event and a source of controversy. Anti-government forces interpreted the attempt to arrest Weaver as part of a government conspiracy to undermine American liberties. Because the affair had been so badly bungled by the federal authorities, the government soon found itself on the defensive. In a subsequent court case, in September 1995 Weaver's defense attorney, Gerry Spence, put the government on trial. During the trial, the Southern Poverty Law Center reported that jury members received the *Citizen's Rule Book*. This book informed the jurors that they did not have to listen to judges instruct them on the law; instead, they have the right and obligation to veto wrongful prosecutions. This action is called jury nullification. Weaver escaped his legal proceedings with a fine for failure to appear in court. In return, the government gave Weaver $3.1 million to settle claims for the wrongful deaths of Sam and Vicki Weaver. In the aftermath of the court defeat and amidst criticism of the government's role in the affair, members of the FBI made charges and counter charges against each other. Weaver has moved back to Jefferson, Iowa, and remarried. He has become a folk hero of the anti-government and white supremacist crowds. In 1998 he wrote a book, *The Federal Siege at Ruby Ridge*. He is unrepentant about his belief that the federal government is the real enemy of the American people. **See also** Aryan Nations; Ruby Ridge

Incident; Trochmann, John Ernest, Weaver Fever.

Suggested readings: Anne Hull, "Randy Weaver's Return from Ruby Ridge," *Washington Post* (April 30, 2001), p. A1; George Lardner, Jr., "Justice Dept. Closes Probe of Ruby Ridge," *Washington Post* (August 16, 1997), p. A8; Dee Norton, "Forged Letter Keeps Open Door to Weaver's Surrender," *Seattle Times* (September 1, 1992), p. A1; Kenneth S. Stern, *A Force upon the Plain: The American Militia Movement and the Politics of Hate* (Norman: University of Oklahoma Press, 1996); Jess Walter, *Every Knee Shall Bow: The Truth and Tragedy of Ruby Ridge and the Randy Weaver Family* (New York: Regan Books, 1995).

Weaver Fever

Weaver fever is a term that describes the reluctance of federal officials to enforce the laws against anti-government activists. Mistakes in judgment committed by federal agents during the **Ruby Ridge incident** and against the **Branch Davidians**, as well as the adverse publicity and punishments handed out to agents, have made federal officials reluctant to enforce the laws on the books. Both the damage settlement of $3.1 million for wrongful death given to the Weaver family and severe criticism from the Senate Subcommittee on Terrorism have made federal law enforcement leaders hesitant to take direct action. Consequently, anti-government activists have flourished in the Pacific Northwest and parts of the South. The situation became so obvious during the Freemen stalemate from March 25 to June 13, 1996 that local inhabitants in Montana wrote letters to their local newspapers complaining about federal and state inaction. Citizens in areas where extremism is strong have found themselves intimidated and sometimes have become victims of financial or physical threats. Resentment has also built up over the cost to local government of dealing with extremists. Because local law enforcement officials have found themselves heavily outnumbered and outgunned, they have either been inactive or have stepped aside for federal agents. Only in extreme cases, such as the Oklahoma City bombing, have federal agents responded and escaped Weaver fever. **See also** Branch Davidians; Freemen Movement; Ruby Ridge Incident; Weaver, Randall.

Suggested readings: Tom Kenworthy and Serge F. Kovaleski, " 'Freemen' Finally Taxed the Patience of Federal Government," *Washington Post* (March 31, 1996), p. A1; David A. Neiwert, *In God's Country: The Patriot Movement and the Pacific Northwest* (Pullman: Washington State University Press, 1999); Kenneth S. Stern, *A Force upon the Plain: The American Militia Movement and the Politics of Hate* (Norman: University of Oklahoma Press, 1996).

Weber, Mark (1951–)

Mark Weber, the director of the **Institute for Historical Review** (IHR) and a veteran anti-Semite, was born in 1951 in Portland, Oregon. His high school education took place at a Jesuit high school in Portland. He later earned a master's degree in history from Indiana University. In the mid-1970s, Weber joined **William Pierce's National Alliance**. He worked himself up the organizational ladder until May 1978 when he became the news editor of the *National Vanguard*. Using this publication as a forum for his **anti-Semitism**, he wrote anti-Jewish articles and highlighted Holocaust denial literature. By 1984 he had established close contacts with the Institute for Historical Review in Costa Mesa, California. Weber joined the IHR's editorial advisory committee in 1985. He was soon established as an IHR regular, and he traveled to Canada in March 1988 to defend **Ernst Christof Friedrich Zundel**, the Canadian neo-Nazi, against spreading false news denying the Holocaust. He was also active with Bradley Smith in founding the Committee on Open Debate on the Holocaust (CODOH) in 1987 to spread the **Holocaust denial movement** on college campuses. In 1992 Weber was promoted to the editorship of IHR's flagship journal, *Journal of Historical Review*.

Weber found himself, in 1993, in the middle of a power struggle between the staff of the IHR and the IHR's founder, **Willis Carto**. The issue was the control of a large inheritance Carto had appropriated for his own personal use. In reality, however, the bigger issue was the political direction of the IHR. Carto wanted to start downplaying Holocaust denial and move toward a white supremacist orientation. Weber and the staff of the IHR were more comfortable in retaining Holocaust denial and anti-Semitism. The IHR staff won their suit against Carto on November 15, 1996. They received $6.4 million in a court judgment and control of the IHR. The win, however, earned Weber and the IHR staff Carto's undying enmity, and since 1993, he has attacked Weber and the IHR through his **Liberty Lobby** and its newsletter, the *Spotlight*. The suits and countersuits that have been directed toward both sides of the dispute have taken a toll on the staff and the operations of the IHR. Weber has had to reduce staff numbers and limit the number of articles for the journal. Weber continues to be the director of the Institute for Historical Review, but his role had been reduced to almost a one-person operation. **See also** Carto, Willis; Holocaust Denial Movement; Institute for Historical Review; Liberty Lobby; National Alliance.

Suggested readings: Paul Bilodeau, "The Zundel Trial Testimony of Survivors' 'Unreliable,' Court Told," *Toronto Star* (March 24, 1988), p. A2; Michael Granberry, "Judge Awards $6.4 Million to O.C. Revisionist Group," *Los Angeles Times* (November 16, 1996), p. B1; Deborah Lipstadt, *Denying the Holocaust: The Growing Assault on Truth and Memory* (New York: Plume, 1993).

Welch, Robert Henry Winborne, Jr. (1899–1985)

Robert Welch founded and became the head of the anti-communist, right-wing **John Birch Society**. He was born on December 1, 1899, on a cotton farm in Chowan County, North Carolina. His father was a cotton farmer, but both parents had college educations. His mother home taught him except for his last two years in high school. He entered the University of North Carolina at the age of twelve and graduated from there at the age of seventeen. After college, Welch spent two years at the U.S. Naval Academy in Annapolis, Maryland, but he left before graduation. A two-year stay at Harvard Law School followed, but again Welch left before graduation in 1921. This time Welch left because he had started a candy business in Boston that consumed all of his time and energy. After going bankrupt in the candy business, Welch moved to New York City where he started another candy-manufacturing business. This and another business venture failed. In 1932 he started work for the nation's largest candy maker, E. J. Brach and Sons. Welch returned to Boston in 1934 to work for his brother's candy-making business, James O. Welch Company. Welch was made one of the vice presidents of the company and for the next twelve years devoted himself exclusively to business affairs. By the mid-1950s, he was a multimillionaire.

Welch became interested in politics beginning in 1946. His first venture was working for the election of Republican Governor Bradford in the Massachusetts gubernatorial election of 1946. Attracted by the lure of political office, Welch ran in the Republican primary for lieutenant governor of Massachusetts and finished second in a field of four. In 1952 he supported the candidacy of Senator Robert Taft and never forgave Dwight David Eisenhower for defeating Taft. In the early 1950s, he started a conservative magazine, *One Man's Opinion*. Throughout his career, Welch remained a supporter of Wisconsin Senator Joseph McCarthy and his hunt for communists in the U.S. government.

When Welch decided that the traditional parties were unable to contain the communist threat, he formed the John Birch Society in December 1958. He invited eleven prominent businessmen to attend a conference held in Indianapolis, Indiana, to investigate the formation of a new anti-communist group. Welch provided the inspiration and the ideas that appeared in the philosophical and organizational manual *Blue Book of the John Birch Society* (1961). In this manual,

Welch outlines the anti-communist and pro-capitalist agenda of the Society. Welch named the group the John Birch Society in honor of Captain John Birch, an intelligence officer killed by the Chinese Communists in 1945.

Welch spent the rest of his life building the John Birch Society. He established its headquarters in Belmont, Massachusetts. Among the issues Welch fought against were civil rights, desegregation, federal aid to education, foreign aid, income tax, the North Atlantic Treaty Organization (NATO), the social security system, Supreme Court Chief Justice Earl Warren, unions, and the United Nations. In a privately published book, *The Politician* (1960), he accused President Eisenhower and his secretary of state, John Foster Dulles, of being agents of a communist conspiracy. By the mid-1960s, the John Birch Society had nearly 100,000 members, and its members campaigned for Arizona Senator Barry Goldwater for president in 1964. After the 1960s, the John Birch Society slowly lost members to other conservative organizations and its influence diminished. Welch remained the head of the John Birch Society until a stroke caused him to resign in October 1983. During the last few years of his life, his health was poor. He died in Winchester, Massachusetts, on January 7, 1985. **See also** DePugh, Robert Bolivar; John Birch Society; Minutemen Movement.

Suggested readings: J. Allen Broyes, *The John Birch Society: Anatomy of a Protest* (Boston: Beacon Press, 1964); Benjamin R. Epstein, *The Radical Right: Report on the John Birch Society and Its Allies* (New York: Vintage Books, 1967); Robert D. McFadden, "Robert Welch Jr. Dead at 85; John Birch Society's Founder," *New York Times* (January 8, 1985), p. B6; Michael Seiler, "Robert Welch, Founder of Birch Society, Dies at 85," *Los Angeles Times* (January 8, 1985), part 1, p. 1.

Weslin, Norman U. (1931?–)

Father Weslin, a Catholic priest who has been active in the violent wing of the **anti-abortion movement**, was born in 1931. Weslin is a military veteran with service as a paratrooper, a Green Beret, and an artillery commander. He retired as a lieutenant colonel after twenty years of military service. Weslin was married with two adopted children. His wife died in an automobile accident in 1980. While his wife was alive, they had been active in the pro-life movement in various organizations. After her death, he became a missionary priest of the Oblates of Wisdom. His experience in various anti-abortion groups convinced him that only direct action could prevent abortions.

Weslin has used his military expertise to plan his anti-abortion operations. In July 1988 Weslin founded the Lambs of Christ, a group of radical anti-abortion protesters. He organized the Lambs of Christ into a guerrilla strike force moving from city to city to attack abortion clinics. When arrested, members of the group refuse to cooperate with authorities citing a higher law as justification for their actions. Weslin claims that he has been arrested more than seventy times, and he has served short terms in jail. His most recent jail term, for four months, was in a federal prison for violation of the Federal Access to Clinic Entrances (FACE) Law in October 2000.

Weslin has developed ties with other anti-abortion activists, including **James C. Kopp**, the suspected assassin of Dr. Barnett A. Slepian. Weslin and Kopp served time together in an Atlanta jail in 1988 in the aftermath of an anti-abortion demonstration staged with **Randall Terry's Operation Rescue**. Weslin has denied involvement in the death of Slepian and has pursued lawsuits against newspapers over reports tying him to any murders. **See also** Anti-Abortion Movement; Lambs of Christ.

Suggested readings: Dallas A. Blanchard, *The Anti-Abortion Movement and the Rise of the Religious Right From Polite to Fiery Protest* (New York: Twayne, 1994); Phil Fairbanks, "Going to Extremes," *Buffalo News* (February 12, 2000), p. 1A; Phil Fairbanks and Lou Michel, "Lambs Leader Denies Violence, Assails Media," *Buffalo News* (November 16, 1998), p. 1C; Gina

Kolata, "Nomadic Group of Anti-Abortionists Uses New Tactics to Make Its Mark," *New York Times* (March 24, 1992), p. A12; James Risen and Judy L. Thomas, *Wrath of Angels: The American Abortion War* (New York: Basic Books, 1998).

Western Guard

The Western Guard was one of Canada's leading white supremacist organizations in the 1970s and early 1980s. Elements of the militant wing of the Edmund Burke Society founded the Western Guard on February 23, 1972. These members believed that the fiercely anti-communist Edmund Burke Society was too moderate on racial matters. **Donald Clarke Andrews**, one of the founders of the Edmund Burke Society, assumed the leadership of the Western Guard. Besides Andrews, the new organization had an executive council, which included a secretary, a treasurer, a publicity chief, and a chief of security. The primary effort of the Western Guard was to spread its white supremacy racial message, and the main vehicle for doing so was its newsletter, *Straight Talk*. During the next four years, articles in the newsletter became more stridently racial in tone. Attacks on blacks and immigrants from Third World countries were common, and slowly, over time, more anti-Semitic literature was published. Members of the Western Guard also resorted to direct action against selected targets, and several members were arrested for committing violent acts. Andrews participated in some of these incidents. He was arrested several times, but he was always released because of the lack of evidence. His involvement in an arson plot against an Israeli soccer team in 1976, however, resulted in a two-year jail term and another eighteen months in a provincial reformatory. His absence led to his replacement as head of the Western Guard.

In Andrews's absence, John Ross Taylor assumed the leadership post in the Western Guard. He had been a member of a pre–World War II fascist party and had joined the Western Guard in 1972. By 1973 he had been selected to its executive board. Taylor's specialty was propaganda. Almost as soon as Taylor took over the leadership of the Western Guard, he launched a campaign to discredit Andrews and his policies. His principal argument against Andrews was that he had been too moderate. Taylor moved the Western Guard away from Andrews's anti-black orientation to an anti-Jewish one. He equated communism with Judaism. Taylor also stopped publishing *Straight Talk* and replaced it with a new publication, *Aryan*. His next project was to start a series of white-power recorded telephone messages. These hate messages soon attracted the attention of Canadian legal authorities and a cease-and-desist order was issued in August 1979. After ignoring this order, Taylor was sentenced by a Canadian court to a one-year jail term and a fine of $5,000. This sentence was suspended on the condition that the recorded messages cease. Again Taylor disregarded the warning and the sentence was imposed. He spent almost a year in prison and was released in 1982. By the time of his release, Taylor's hold over the Western Guard had been lost and the organization had withered away. Membership had never been large, probably never more than 100 activists. These activists drifted to other organizations during this leadership vacuum. The Western Guard's significance was that it served as a training ground for a generation of Canadian extremists, most of whom moved on to other, more violent extremist groups. **See also** Andrews, Donald Clarke.

Suggested readings: Stanley R. Barrett, *Is God a Racist? The Right Wing in Canada* (Toronto, Ont., Canada: University of Toronto Press, 1987); Robert Mason Lee, "John Ross Taylor: A Hate-Monger Set Free by Faint Hearts," *Ottawa Citizen* (October 13, 1991), p. B1; Tracey Tyler, "Rights Body Action Riles Jewish Groups," *Toronto Star* (February 16, 1989), p. A5.

White Aryan Resistance (WAR)

The White Aryan Resistance (WAR) is the white supremacist organization founded by

Tom Metzger, who had been the leader of a California **Ku Klux Klan** group until 1980. After Metzger lost a California Congressional race in that year, he decided to leave the Klan and form a political action group. Metzger formed the White Aryan Political Association (WAPA) in 1982 and made its mission to recruit white supremacist supporters to back candidates for public office. After limited success in attracting either viable candidates to run or backers to vote for them, Metzger transformed the WAPA into the White Aryan Resistance in 1983. The headquarters of the WAR is in Fallbrook, California. Metzger and his son, John Metzger, provide the leadership for the WAR. John Metzger is the leader of WAR's youth movement. They publish a newsletter, *WAR*, which promotes its white supremacy message and attempts to recruit new members. Metzger was an early adherent of reaching possible new recruits by using computer bulletin boards. In October 1984, he started using his bulletin board for WAR propaganda. The WAR now has an active Web site broadcasting its viewpoint. Besides advancing the cause of white supremacy, Metzger has conducted a violent anti-Semitic campaign through print and computer media.

Despite Metzger's efforts to attract a mass of white supremacist activists, the WAR has had only modest success in California and nationwide. It was this lack of recruiting success that encouraged Metzger to recruit **skinhead** members. Because Metzger rejects organized religion, including **Christian Identity**, the nihilism of skinheads attracts him. His success in recruiting skinheads for the WAR has cost both Metzger and his organization dearly. His home, personal income, and profits from the WAR have had to be sold to satisfy a $12 million lawsuit to the family of an Ethiopian immigrant killed by skinhead members of the WAR in November 1988 in Portland, Oregon. Metzger continues to use the WAR to advance his white supremacist platform, but the organization is nowhere as successful as Metzger envisaged when he founded it in 1983. **See also** Metzger, Tom; White Supremacist Movement.

Suggested readings: Anti-Defamation League, *Danger: Extremism: The Major Vehicles and Voices on America's Far Right Fringe* (New York: Anti-Defamation League, 1996); John M. Glionna, "Unfavorite Son," *Los Angeles Times* (October 30, 1990), p. E1; Darlene Himmelspach, "Metzger Says His Defeat Was Only Financial," *San Diego Union-Tribune* (October 20, 1991), p. B1; Serge F. Kovaleski, "American Skinheads; Fighting Minorities and Each Other," *Washington Post* (January 16, 1996), p. A1; Josh Meyer, "Flyers Spread Message of Hate in the Valley," *Los Angeles Times* (January 2, 1994), p. A1; Tracy Wilkinson, "Metzger to Go on Trial in Cross-Burning Case," *Los Angeles Times* (July 22, 1991).

White Knights of the Ku Klux Klan

The White Knights of the Ku Klux Klan was one of the most violent Klan groups in the 1960s and 1970s and now is one of the best examples of a well-organized terrorist organization. **Samuel Holloway Bowers**, a businessman from Laurel, Mississippi, was one of the founders of the White Knights on February 15, 1964. After drafting the constitution and establishing the organizational structure, Bowers assumed the leadership post and the title of imperial wizard. Agitation against the civil rights movement and desegregation in Mississippi had been under the direction of the White Citizens' Councils since the mid-1950s, but Bowers and his associates wanted a more militant approach. Unlike most Klan organizations, membership in the White Knights was restricted to white citizens of Mississippi, and the organization had no auxiliary groups attached to it. Bowers built a lean organization focused on direct action, and he recruited those who were ready to commit violent actions. Because of its militancy, the White Knights operated in secrecy and avoided publicity. Bowers, by nature a loner, retained complete control of all operations. The White Knights followed Bowers's brand of militant Christianity. He rejected any role in society for blacks, Catholics, and Jews. Anti-Semitic feeling was especially strong in the White Knights. Because Bowers believed that a race war was imminent, the White Knights purchased arms and ammunition for the forthcoming battle. They studied ways to build bombs and conduct guerrilla operations. Bowers advocated using social, economic, and physical intimidation against real or perceived enemies. A newsletter, the *Klan-Ledger* was one of the several means used to identify the targets for intimidation.

Soon after he became imperial wizard, Bowers initiated a recruitment drive for the White Knights, and the response was overwhelming. Many of the recruits came from among the 2,500 employees of the Masonite Corporation in Laurel, Mississippi, a company which was trying to comply with the federal government's efforts to provide equal job opportunities for blacks. The White employees resented these efforts and were fearful of losing their jobs. Others joined for a multitude of reasons from racism to the excitement about fighting the civil rights movement. An early recruit was the accused assassin of civil rights leader Medgar Evers, **Byron de la Beckwith**. Although still in jail awaiting trial for the murder, Beckwith worked as a recruiter. Most of the members were blue-collar workers eager to fight to preserve segregation. Klan leaders gave special attention to recruiting local law enforcement officials and highway patrolmen, because they could protect Klan members from the law. These efforts were successful, and these recruits proved their usefulness many times. Because of its extreme secrecy, no accurate accounting of the membership is possible, but membership may have been as high as 6,000 in 1965. Any attempt by a member to betray the oath of secrecy to the White Knights would result in a sentence of death. On at least one occasion, a breach of secrecy led to the execution of the guilty party.

Members of the White Knights perpetrated two of the worst crimes committed in the civil rights era. With the cooperation and participation of local police in Philadelphia, Mississippi, three civil rights leaders, Jim

Chaney, Andy Goodman, and Michael Schwerner, were murdered on June 21, 1964. Evidence exists that Bowers initiated the plot for the murders. Next, on January 10, 1966, members of the White Knights firebombed and killed Vernon Dahmer, an official of the National Association for the Advancement of Colored People (NAACP). Again Bowers was implicated in the planning of the attack. In the middle of these events, the leadership of the White Knights traveled to Washington, D.C., to testify about Klan activity in the South before the House Un-American Activities Committee (HUAC). All of them refused to answer questions citing their Fifth Amendment protection rights. The controversies following the violence and the congressional appearances hurt the image of the White Knights. The increased attention paid to their activities by federal agents caused members to migrate to other less visible Klan groups.

Bowers responded to this threat to the future of the White Knights by unleashing in the fall of 1967 a bombing campaign against Jewish targets. He sponsored **Thomas Albert Tarrants**'s plans to bomb a synagogue in Jackson, Mississippi, and the homes of several civil rights and Jewish leaders. After these bombings, Bowers directed Tarrants to bomb the Meridian, Mississippi, home of Meyer Davidson, a prominent Jewish civil rights leader. Unbeknownst to them, however, the FBI and the Meridian police had persuaded two Klansmen, the Roberts brothers, to inform on Tarrants's next operation. Tarrants and **Kathryn Madlyn Ainsworth** were caught in the act, and in the subsequent gunfight Ainsworth was killed and Tarrants was captured after being seriously wounded. Materials on both Tarrants and Ainsworth implicated Bowers in the bombing attack, but Tarrants never implicated Bowers in any of the bombings.

The imprisonment of Bowers and several of the leading members of the White Knights in 1970 caused its supporters to go underground. Bowers was convicted for his role in the deaths of the three civil rights workers in 1964. He was sent to the Mississippi State

Penitentiary at Parchman. During his absence, the White Knights suffered from organizational disarray and within a few years were no longer functional. After his release from prison, law enforcement tried Bowers for the death of Vernon Dahmer. On August 21, 1998, a Hattiesburg, Mississippi, court sentenced Bowers to life imprisonment for the murder of Dahmer. **See also** Ainsworth, Kathryn Madlyn "Kathy"; Beckwith, Byron de la; Bowers, Samuel Holloway; Ku Klux Klan; Tarrants, Thomas Albert.

Suggested readings: Rich Bragg, "Ex-Klansman Implicates Chief in Killing," *New York Times* (August 20, 1998), p. A12; Rich Bragg, "Justice Catches Up with KKK Killer 32 Years On," *Observer* [London] (August 23, 1998), p. 19; Reed Massengill, *Portrait of a Racist: The Real Life of Byron de la Beckwith* (New York: St. Martin's Griffin, 1996); David Templeton, "Police Expect Increase in Hate Crimes," *Pittsburgh Post-Gazette* (October 8, 1995), p. W1; Curtis Wilkie, "In Klan Verdict, a Reckoning with Mississippi's Past," *Boston Globe* (August 23, 1998), p. 31.

White Patriots Party (WPP)

The White Patriots Party was a white supremacist paramilitary organization. **Glen Miller** formed the White Patriots Party in 1979 shortly after his North Carolina Knights of the Ku Klux Klan had participated in the **Greensboro massacre** of American communists on November 3, 1979. Miller established his group as a paramilitary body with military uniforms, training, and units. Headquarters for the party was in Angier, North Carolina. The party was growing under Miller's leadership until his contacts with soldiers at Fort Bragg resulted in legal proceedings. Soldiers from Fort Bragg had been providing training at White Patriots Party field exercises and stealing equipment from the army for the group. Morris Dees of the Southern Poverty Law Center initiated a lawsuit against the WPP in 1986. His suit led the U.S. Army to end the collaboration between soldiers on active duty and the WPP, and the court ruled that Miller should cease paramilitary training.

Miller was placed on probation, but he ignored the judge's ruling. After the judge revoked Miller's probation, he went into hiding. He was later arrested in Missouri and entered the government's witness protection program after testifying against other extremist leaders at the **Fort Smith sedition trial** in 1988.

Miller's legal difficulties and absence had a chilling effect on the White Patriots Party. Membership dropped after Miller went into hiding. Loss of the military expertise from off-duty soldiers in the army also damaged the group. Cecil Cox attempted to revitalize the party in 1987 by renaming it the Southern National Front, but the effort failed, and in 1987 Cox led the group into an alliance with Gary Gallo's National Democratic Front. **See also** Greensboro Massacre; Fort Smith Sedition Trial; Ku Klux Klan; Miller, Glen.

Suggested readings: Dudley Clendinen, "North Carolina Jury Getting Case Against Klan Paramilitary Group," *New York Times* (July 25, 1986), p. A8; Marshall Ingwerson, "Klan More Active in Pockets," *Christian Science Monitor* (January 27, 1986), p. 3; Robert L. Jackson, "5 Klansmen Accused of Plot to Steal Military Weapons," *Los Angeles Times* (January 9, 1987), part 1, p. 35; Jonathan S. Landay, "Army Brass Rattled by Ties of Soldiers to White Supremacists," *Christian Science Monitor* (December 19, 1995), p. 3; Kathy Marks, *Faces of Right Wing Extremism* (Boston: Branden Publishing, 1996).

White Supremacist Movement

The white supremacist movement is an umbrella term which includes a number of groups and organizations that advocate the supremacy of the white race. Earliest among these groups was the **Ku Klux Klan**. Klan efforts to maintain the superior status of Southern whites started soon after the foundation of the Klan in 1866. This effort continued during the revival of the Klan in the 1920s. The civil rights movement of the 1960s reinforced the Klan's efforts to preserve white supremacy in the South. Militant action undertaken by the Klan and other allied groups backfired, however, and the civil rights movement changed society in the

South. Political figures, such as **David Duke**, have tried to change the Klan into a more proactive, pro-white political agenda. Success of a white supremacist party has limited appeal except in certain states and regions.

Modern white supremacy lives off resentment against the progress of other segments of the population. Affirmative action, crime, diversity, education, and immigration are white supremacist issues. They maintain that whites suffer discrimination in employment, promotion, and educational opportunities. Disillusioned white males believe that their interests are no longer being represented by the federal government or by the states. The greatest fear among white supremacists, however, is interracial sexuality. They believe that race mixing is a threat to the racial purity of the white race. White supremacist groups consider that the civil rights movement, gay rights, and feminism are all enemies of the social order and contribute to the degeneracy of the white race.

The **Christian Identity** church has been able to give a theology to white superiority, but many white supremacists are not religious. Both the **Church of the Creator** of **Ben Klassen** and the **World Church of the Creator** of **Matthew Hale** are resoundingly anti-Christian but are also white supremacist. Most of the white supremacist groups advance ideas for a white homeland, usually in the Pacific Northwest, where the white race would prosper without contact from non-whites. While these plans have little chance of implementation in the current political scene, the desire for a white homeland springs eternal among these groups.

White supremacist leaders have been active in the recruitment of new members. The **neo-Nazi skinheads** have attracted their attention because of their white supremacist views and acceptance of the use of violence. This alliance of older white supremacists and the youthful skinheads has not been without its problems. Skinheads are difficult to control, and their violence has brought legal problems to their sponsors. **Tom Metzger**, for example, had to declare personal bankruptcy after losing a lawsuit over three skinheads' beating an immigrant to death in Portland, Oregon. **See also** Christian Identity; Metzger, Tom.

Suggested readings: Abbey L. Ferber, *White Man Falling: Race, Gender, and White Supremacy* (Lanham, Md.: Rowman and Littlefield, 1999); John Kifner, "Finding a Common Foe; Fringe Groups Join Forces," *New York Times* (December 6, 1998), sec. 4, p. 3; Brad Knickerbocker, "White Separatists Plot 'Pure' Society," *Christian Science Monitor* (April 20, 1995), p. 1; Michael Lind, "The Beige and the Black," *New York Times* (August 16, 1998), sec. 6, p. 38; Sally MacDonald and Carol M. Ostrom, "Hate Crimes in America—How White Supremacists See It," *Seattle Times* (August 12, 1999), p. A2; Jim Nesbitt, "White Supremacists: New Generation Prepares for the Millennium Ahead," *Seattle Times* (October 31, 1999), p. A2; Ellen Uzelac, "White Supremacists Find Eager Recruits Among 'Skinheads,' " *St. Louis Post-Dispatch* (January 8, 1999), p. 5B.

Wickstrom, James (1943–)

James Wickstrom, a longtime leader in extremist politics and an active follower of the **Christian Identity** creed, was born in 1943. Wickstrom joined the U.S. Army in the 1960s and served a tour of duty in South Vietnam. After leaving the military, he ran a small tool business in central Wisconsin. Unhappy with the direction of national politics, he sold his business and became a minister in a Christian Identity church, the Life Science Church. Shortly thereafter he became a convert to the **Posse Comitatus movement** with its belief that all political power resides at the local level. **William Potter Gale** served as his mentor. Wickstrom traveled around the country advocating his political and religious views. He made speeches charging that Jews controlled the U.S. government and stating that he was taking steps to fight the situation. His pamphlet *The American Farmer: 20th Century Slave* blamed Jewish bankers and politicians for the farm crisis of the 1970s and 1980s. He ran for public office on the Constitution ticket in Wisconsin for the Senate in 1980 and for governor in 1982, but the returns in both elections were disappointing.

After making attempts to influence national and state politics through traditional means, Wickstrom turned to indirect means. He was active in setting up a Posse Comitatus community in Tigerton Dells, Wisconsin. He assumed a leadership role and the role of a public official. His activities soon caught the attention of federal and state authorities. In 1983 he was convicted of impersonating a government officer at Tigerton Dells and served a prison term of thirteen months. After leaving prison, Wickstrom moved to Homer City, Pennsylvania, where he opened a Christian Identity church. He also became the head of the **Aryan Nations** in Pennsylvania. In 1988 Wickstrom was again in trouble with the police; this time, facing charges in a counterfeiting scheme. His conviction on the counterfeiting charge on August 7, 1990, resulted in a sentence of thirty-eight months in prison and three years of probation. **Mark Thomas** replaced him as head of the Aryan Nations in Pennsylvania during his absence. After his early release from federal prison in 1991, Wickstrom was again active in a Christian Identity church in Ulysses, Pennsylvania. He challenged Thomas for leadership in the Aryan Nations in Pennsylvania, but his challenge was unsuccessful. Wickstrom moved in 1995 to Munising, Michigan, where he operates another Christian Identity church, the Life Science Church, and an anti-government law school, the Christian Liberty Academy. Wickstrom continues to earn publicity for his preaching of anti-government, anti-tax, and anti–loan repayment messages. **See also** Aryan Nations; Christian Identity; Posse Comitatus Movement; White Supremacist Movement.

Suggested readings: Wayne King, "Panel Considering Currency Charges," *New York Times* (July 3, 1988), sec. 1, p. 10; Bill Prochnau, "For the Posse, Ready Arms Hold Hostile World at Bay," *Washington Post* (June 21, 1983), p. A1; Megan Rosenfeld, "Dodge City Showdown Racist, Anti-Semitic Radio Broadcast Alleged," *Washington Post* (May 7, 1983), p. C1.

Wilkerson, Elbert Claude "Bill" (1943–)

Bill Wilkerson, the founder and one time leader of the **Invisible Empire, Knights of the Ku Klux Klan,** was born in 1943 in Galvez, Louisiana. A precocious student, he graduated from high school at the age of sixteen. Soon afterward, he joined the U.S. Navy and served on a nuclear submarine, the *Simon Bolivar*. After leaving the service, Wilkerson worked for a concrete manufacturer in Denham Springs, Louisiana. On the side, he owned and operated a small electrical contracting firm.

Wilkerson joined **David Duke**'s Knights of the Ku Klux Klan in 1974. After a short stay as a member, Wilkerson broke away to form his own Klan group in 1975: the Invisible Empire, Knights of the Ku Klux Klan. The official reason given for his defection was a quarrel with Duke over financial proceeds from a Klan rally, but Wilkerson was also tired of the personality cult developing around Duke. Wilkerson proclaimed himself the imperial wizard of the Invisible Empire in 1975 and started recruiting members. His negotiations over the mailing lists of the Knights of the Ku Klux Klan with David Duke and his charges of Duke's malfeasance over the lists made Wilkerson enemies in other Klan organizations. In the late 1970s, Wilkerson was able to mine the white backlash over affirmative action, school busing, and several high-profile criminal cases to increase the membership in his group. He also directed his recruiting toward active duty soldiers in the military services.

After deciding that Duke's moderate strategy for the Klan was too slow, Wilkerson started a calculated policy of exploiting racial hotspots around the country. He traveled around the nation finding controversial cases to intervene in to raise funds and find new members. To dramatize his cause, Wilkerson led a Klan march in August 1979 to reenact the 1965 Selma to Montgomery voting rights march as a segregationist protest. This tactic backfired when he and 200 of his followers were arrested for violating the

Montgomery parade permit law. Wilkerson escaped this charge easily, but rumors began surfacing that he had been an FBI informant during his tenure as a member of Duke's Knights of the Ku Klux Klan, and the charges were published in the *Christian Science Monitor* (August 31, 1981) and the *New York Times* (December 7, 1980). These rumors and hostile newspaper stories hurt the recruiting efforts of the Invisible Empire. In 1982 **Klanwatch**, of the Southern Poverty Law Center, initiated a lawsuit over Wilkerson's Invisible Empire's attack on civil rights demonstrators on May 26, 1979 in Decatur, Alabama. Legal costs of this trial and an IRS settlement caused Wilkerson to declare bankruptcy for his organization in 1983. Another adverse court judgment in 1984 and the bankruptcy ended Wilkerson's effectiveness in the Klan. Wilkerson resigned as head of the Invisible Empire in 1984. Wilkerson had been the most visible and effective leader in the Ku Klux Klan movement with the possible exception of his rival David Duke. Discredited by his association as an FBI informant, Wilkerson is no longer a force in the **white supremacist movement** in the United States. **See also** Duke, David; Invisible Empire, Knights of the Ku Klux Klan, The; Ku Klux Klan.

Suggested readings: Clara Germani, "KKK Leader Has Given FBI Data 7 Years," *Christian Science Monitor* (August 31, 1981), p. 2; Wayne King, "The Violent Rebirth of the Klan," *New York Times* (December 7, 1980), sec. 6, p. 150; Bill Richards, "Bill Wilkerson: In Forefront of Newly Active Klan," *Washington Post* (August 17, 1979), p. A4; Wyn Craig Wade, *The Fiery Cross: The Ku Klux Klan in America* (New York: Simon and Schuster, 1987).

Winrod, Gerald Burton (1900–1957)

Gerald Winrod, a Protestant fundamentalist minister, became infamous for his Nazi ties and his advocacy of the existence of a Jewish world conspiracy. He was born on March 7, 1900, in Wichita, Kansas. His father was a bartender with strong evangelical Christian beliefs. Winrod started preaching in churches at the age of twelve. Almost from the beginning, Winrod reacted against the realities of modern life of the 1920s. In 1925 he joined with other fundamentalist leaders in Salina, Kansas, to form the organization Defenders of the Christian Faith. In the next year, Winrod was one of the founders of a monthly magazine, the *Defender*, which advanced his fundamentalist Christian beliefs. By 1934 his magazine had attracted around 100,000 subscribers.

In the early 1930s, Winrod became convinced that the Bible proved the existence of a Jewish plot to rule the world. He also believed that the ***Protocols of the Elders of Zion*** (1920) was an accurate depiction of the Jewish world conspiracy even if the publication itself might be a forgery. Soon afterward, Winrod began to express his public approval of the Nazi attitude toward German Jews. On a trip to Germany in 1934, he visited with Nazi leaders and church officials before returning to the United States full of praise for the Nazi regime. In 1938 he ran for a U.S. Senate seat from Kansas, but he finished a distant third even with support from the Kansas **Ku Klux Klan**. He joined the isolationist movement to keep the United States out of World War II. His support of the Nazis won him the nickname the "Jayhawk Nazi." After the entry of the United States into the war, Winrod blamed the Jews for America's participation. Winrod was indicted by the federal government in *United States v. McWilliam* in July 1942 for conspiracy to cause insubordination in the armed forces. After a mistrial in this case, Winrod returned to Wichita where he continued to be active in writing anti-Jewish tracts for his magazine, which attracted a new generation of believers in the 1950s. Winrod died on November 11, 1957, in Wichita, Kansas. Although he was a leading anti-Semite speaker and writer in prewar and postwar United States, his most enduring legacy was his son, **Gordon Winrod**, who succeeded him as one of America's leading anti-Semites. **See also** Anti-Semitism; Neo-Nazis.

Suggested readings: Philip Rees, *Biographical Dictionary of the Extreme Right Since 1890*

(New York: Simon and Schuster, 1990); James Ridgeway, *Blood in the Face: The Ku Klux Klan, Aryan Nations, Nazi Skinheads, and the Rise of a New White Culture* (New York: Thunder's Mouth Press, 1990).

Winrod, Gordon (1928–)

Gordon Winrod is the successor to the mantle of his father, **Gerald Burton Winrod**, a leading anti-Jewish activist in the United States. He was born in 1928 in Wichita, Kansas. His ministerial training took place at the Concordia Seminary in Illinois. After graduation, Winrod was ordained a minister in the Missouri Synod of the Lutheran Church. Winrod was a minister at several Lutheran churches before his anti-Jewish views led to his suspension in 1960 as a Lutheran minister. Shortly before his ouster, Winrod had started publishing an anti-Semitic monthly, the *Winrod Letter*. His next position was as national chaplain of the white supremacist **National State's Rights Party** (NSRP). After only a short stay as NSRP chaplain, Winrod used a radio program and his publications to attack what he perceived as the international Jewish conspiracy. Over the last forty years, Winrod and now his son, David Winrod, have repeatedly blamed Jews for the ills of the world and of society. Winrod is now a minister at Our Savior's Church and Latin School, a Christian Identity church, in Gainesville, Missouri. His son has a church, Our Savior's Church of the Wilderness, near the town of Hydaburg, in Alaska.

In May 2000, Missouri police arrested Winrod for kidnapping his six grandchildren. Tim and Joel Leppert had received joint custody of the children after their divorces from Winrod's daughters, Quinta and Sharon. Winrod and several of his children removed the grandchildren from their homes near Dickey, North Dakota, in 1994 and 1995. The grandchildren had been taken to Gainesville, Missouri, where Winrod had control of their education and behavior. In 1998 one of the grandchildren, Erika Leppert, who was by then eighteen, escaped and complained about mistreatment, including beatings and solitary confinement. In May 2000, police raided Winrod's farm and, after a four-day standoff, arrested him and two of his children. In a trial held in January 2001, Winrod represented himself in court and accused the judge, prosecutor, and police of participating in a Jewish plot to destroy him. On March 19, 2001, the judge sentenced him to a maximum of thirty years in prison for abducting his six grandchildren and indoctrinating them in his Christian Identity beliefs. The children have been returned to the custody of their fathers. Winrod's case is now under appeal. **See also** Anti-Semitism; Christian Identity; National State's Rights Party; Winrod, Gerald Burton.

Suggested readings: Richard Meryhew, "Anti-Semitic Cleric Targets Minnesota," *Star Tribune* [Minneapolis] (February 11, 1994), p. 1A; Southern Poverty Law Center, "Racist Preacher Gets 30 Years in Kidnapping," *SPLC Intelligence Report* 102 (Summer 2001): 3; Matt Stearns, "Angry Supremacist Leaves Jury Selection," *Kansas City Star* (January 30, 2001), p. B3; Matt Stearns, "Anti-Semite Convicted; Faces 30 Years in Prison," *Kansas City Star* (February 2, 2001), p. B1; Carolyn Tuft, "Couple Say Christian Identity Church Destroyed Their Family," *St. Louis Post-Dispatch* (August 19, 1999), p. A1.

World Church of the Creator (WCOTC)

The World Church of the Creator (WCOTC), founded by **Matthew Hale** in 1996, is the leading hate church in the United States. Hale founded the WCOTC in East Peoria, Illinois, to teach the ideas of **Ben Klassen**'s **Church of the Creator**. Hale considers himself the natural successor of Klassen as "pontiflex maximus." The church is distinctively anti-Christian, and members worship the white race rather than a religious ideal. Members pay dues of $35 a year and must buy literature passed out by Hale. Hale spends all of his time working for the WCOTC and lives on the proceeds of donations given to him by members of the church. Despite the church's anti-Christian viewpoint, Hale uses many of the rituals and practices of mainstream religions—commandments, baptism, confirmation, marriage, and funeral services. Hale claimed in 2000 that the World Church of the Creator had nearly 4,000 adherents scattered around the country. Hale ordains new ministers after they complete a 200-point ministerial examination. This test is compiled and graded by Hale. Several branches of the WCOTC have been established in Sacramento, California, and Milwaukee, Wisconsin.

The World Church of the Creator has received considerable adverse publicity about the violent actions of its members. Four members of the WCOTC pistol-whipped a Jewish video-store owner and stole his money in Hollywood, Florida, in 1997. They were convicted of federal civil rights violations and sentenced to up to eight years in prison. In August 1997, other members, Raymond Leone and some friends, were arrested for brutally beating a black man and his son outside a musical theater in Fort Lauderdale, Florida. These incidents were overshadowed, however, by the two-state murder spree of church member Benjamin Smith between July 2 and July 5, 1999. Smith killed two minorities, including ex–Northwestern University basketball coach Ricky Byrdsong, and wounded eight others in Illinois and Indiana before he committed suicide at the end of a police chase. Hale has tried to downplay the church's role in these incidents. His press secretary, Stephen Daniels of Ormond Beach, Florida, who uses the press name of Kelly O'Reilly, issued statements absolving the World Church of the Creator from any responsibility for them. Nevertheless, Hale has continued to preach his message of hate toward minorities. **See also** Hale, Matthew; Klassen, Ben; Church of the Creator.

Suggested readings: Tom Cruze, Erin G. Bradley, and Ellen Domke, "Heat Turned Up on Supremacist Church," *Chicago Sun-Times* (July 11, 1999), p. 6; Quintin Elison, "Seeds of White Supremacist Group Sown in WNC," *Asheville Citizen-Times* [N.C.] (July 20, 1999), p. 1; Michael Greenwood, "The Unvarnished Face of Racism" *Hartford Courant* (August 28, 2000), p. A1; Joe Holland, "World Church Aims Its Venom at Race," *Sun-Sentinel* [Fort Lauderdale, Fla.] (July 7, 1999), p. A1: Abdon M. Pallasch, "This Church Preaches Love, Loyalty—and Hate," *Chicago Sun-Times* (July 9, 1999), p. 6; Southern Poverty Law Center, "The Great Creator," *SPLC Intelligence Report* 95 (Summer 1999):1; Edward Walsh, "Midwest Gun Spree Suspect Is Dead; Man Shot Himself," *Washington Post* (July 5, 1999), p. A1.

World Union of National Socialists (WUNS)

Some neo-Nazi leaders founded the World Union of National Socialists (WUNS) to form a network of Nazi parties to encourage an international Nazi revival. This idea was **George Lincoln Rockwell**'s whose first name for this potential alliance was the World Union of Free Enterprise National Socialists (WUFENS). Rockwell began contacting other neo-Nazi leaders in 1959. His first major contact was the leader of the British National Socialist Movement, Colin Jordan. Jordan who agreed in principle, introduced Rockwell to other leading European **neo-Nazis**. Two other significant neo-Nazis, Savitri Devi and Bruno Ludtke, lent their support. Ludtke was especially influential and supported Rockwell's claim to leadership in the new organization. In July 1962, a convention of neo-Nazi leaders from seven countries—Austria, Belgium, France, Great Britain, Ireland, United States, and West Germany—met at a site in the Cotswold Hills of Gloucestershire in Great Britain. During the course of the six-day conference, the representatives formed the World Union of National Socialists with Rockwell and Jordan as co-leaders of the movement. Participants drafted the Cotswold Agreements, which served as the constitution for the WUNS. In this agreement, all members acknowledged the spiritual leadership of Adolf Hitler and pledged to destroy the international Jewish conspiracy and Zionism. By 1965 WUNS had operating chapters in nineteen countries. Jordan, in Great Britain, handled most of the organizational details even after he was jailed in Aylesbury Prison for his pro-Nazi activities. While Rockwell was the acknowledged leader of WUNS, travel restrictions prevented him from visiting various chapters. Rockwell's premature death in 1967 ended the chances of the WUNS to be more than a passing footnote in history. Rockwell's successor, **Matt Koehl**, succeeded him as head of the WUNS, but he lacked the charisma and international stature of Rockwell and was unable to make the WUNS an international force. A succession of leaders attempted to keep the WUNS active, but it had disappeared by the mid-1990s. **See also** American Nazi party; Neo-Nazis; Rockwell, George Lincoln.

Suggested readings: Jeffrey Kaplan, ed., *The Encyclopedia of White Power: A Sourcebook on the Radical Racist Right* (Walnut Creek, Calif.: Altamira Press, 2000); William H. Schmaltz, *Hate: George Lincoln Rockwell and the American Nazi Party* (Washington, D.C.: Brassey's, 1999); Frederick J. Simonelli, *American Fuehrer: George Lincoln Rockwell and the American Nazi Party* (Urbana: University of Illinois Press, 1999); Frederick J. Simonelli, "The World Union of National Socialists and Postwar Transatlantic Nazi Revival," in Jeffrey Kaplan and Tore Bjorgo, eds., *Nation and Race: The Developing Euro-American Racist Subculture* (Boston: Northeastern University Press, 1998).

Y

Yockey, Francis Parker (1917–1960)

Francis Parker Yockey, the intellectual god-father of the American white supremacist and neo-Nazi movements, was born in 1917 near Chicago, Illinois. Extremely intelligent, with an IQ of 170, he was also a trained classical pianist. After graduating from high school, he attended Georgetown University where he received a B.A. degree. Later, he obtained a law degree from Notre Dame University. Yockey also spent some time studying at Michigan State University. Although he was intelligent and articulate, his outspokenness and dictatorial manners alienated those around him. Despite his early sympathies toward Nazi Germany, he enlisted in the U.S. Army and served at a G-2 intelligence unit in Georgia. In July 1943, Yockey received an honorable discharge from the military after suffering a nervous breakdown. By then, his name appeared on a government list of Americans suspected of being pro-Nazi. Yockey became an assistant prosecuting attorney for Wayne County, Michigan. Despite his pro-Nazi leanings, he found a job as a civilian member of the prosecution team prosecuting Nazi war criminals in Wiesbaden, Germany. His efforts to help the German prisoners were so blatant that he was fired. He fled Germany in 1947 abandoning a wife and two small children and went into exile in Ireland.

Yockey decided to collect his political ideas in a book. From his youth onward, he had been violently anti-Semitic and considered other minorities little better than the Jews. Yockey believed wholeheartedly in the Nazi racial program and in Nazism in general. His book, *Imperium* (1949), was a rallying cry for Nazism to reestablish itself. Yockey borrowed ideas heavily from Oswald Spengler and his *Decline of the West* in describing the ups and downs of civilizations. The major difference was that Yockey blamed the Jews for the woes of the twentieth century and World War II. He also denied the existence of the Holocaust. Yockey was harsh in his assessment of the United States and its culture. His anti-Americanism was so strong that he advocated Europe's pursuing an independent path between the United States and the Soviet Union in the Cold War.

After completing his book, Yockey looked for ways to distribute it. He approached British fascist Oswald Mosley in 1949 for help. Shortly after starting work with Mosley's British Fascist Union Movement, Yockey had a physical confrontation with Mosley at Hyde Park. After breaking with Mosley, Yockey gathered together a small group of dissident fascists and formed the European Liberation Front (ELF) in 1949.

Besides managing to get *Imperium* published, the ELF published the newsletter *Frontfighter*. The goal of ELF was to expel Jews from Europe, end the Americanization of Europe, and promote a neutral Europe. Again Yockey's behavior alienated his followers in the ELF, and he left Great Britain to advance his cause in Europe. He traveled across Europe with visits to Germany, Italy, and Egypt over the next few years promoting his book among fascists. Although authorities in various countries tried to arrest him for political agitation, Yockey was able to elude them until one of his infrequent trips to the United States. The FBI found him and arrested him in Oakland, California. After eleven days in jail, Yockey committed suicide on June 17, 1960, by swallowing a cyanide capsule. **Willis Carto**, who visited Yockey in jail shortly before the suicide, has spent the last four decades advancing Yockey's ideas and making him a martyr for the neo-Nazi and white supremacist movements. **See also** American Fascism; Anti-Semitism; Carto, Willis; Neo-Nazis; White Supremacist Movement.

Suggested readings: Martin A. Lee, *The Beast Reawakens* (Boston: Little, Brown, 1997); Martin A. Lee, "Looking Backward," *SPLC Intelligence Report* 98 (Spring 2000):30–32.

Z

ZOG (Zionist Occupation Government, Zionist Occupational Government, or Zionist Occupied Government)

ZOG, or Zionist Occupation Government, is a term used in extremist circles in the United States to describe what they claim is the Jewish domination of the U.S. government. In their view, the U.S. government is under control of a cartel of Jewish government and business leaders, who make decisions that are in the best interests of their Jewish compatriots and Israel. These extremists believe that it is the patriotic duty of all loyal Americans to fight against this conspiracy by any means possible. The main outline of the concept of the ZOG first appeared in Colonel John Beaty's *Iron Curtain over America* (1951). In this book, Beaty identifies the Khazar Jews of Russia with the communists and blames them for the Russian Revolution. **William Pierce**'s novel *The Turner Diaries* (1978), made the term ZOG popular. The hero in this novel is a leader in the struggle against the Jewish-controlled U.S. government, or the ZOG. Many of the leaders of the **militia movement** subscribe to the ZOG theory, and they have armed their militia groups to be prepared against any attempts of the federal government to take away their rights. They believe gun control legislation is the first step in a ZOG conspiracy. See also Pierce, William: *Turner Diaries, The*.

Suggested readings: Jeffrey Kaplan, ed., *Encyclopedia of White Power: A Sourcebook on the Radical Racist Right* (Walnut Creek, Calif.: Altamira Press, 2000); Cheri Seymour, *Committee of the States: Inside the Radical Right* (Mariposa, Calif.: Camden Place Communications, 1991).

Zundel, Ernst Christof Friedrich (1939–)

Ernst Zundel, Canada's leading neo-Nazi and anti-Semitic propagandist, was born on April 24, 1939, in the village of Calmback in the Black Forest region of Germany. His father was a woodcutter by profession and a veteran of the German army during World War II in which he served as a medic. Since he was only six years old when World War II ended, Zundel had little direct contact with the Nazi regime. He grew up in postwar West Germany and worked as a photo retoucher for several years in northwestern Germany before immigrating to Canada in 1958 at the age of nineteen. Soon after settling in Montreal and marrying Jeannick LaRouche, a French-Canadian, Zundel entered Sir George Williams University to study history and political science. About this time, he also became the protégé of Quebec fascist Adrien Arcand. Arcand introduced him to most of the leading **neo-Nazis** in Canada, Europe, and the United States. In the mid-1960s, Zundel moved his family to Toronto, where he associated with neo-Nazis and decided to run for public office in the Liberal Party. When he received no support from the party, Zundel returned to business affairs and soon owned a successful advertising agency and a commercial studio.

In 1976 Zundel started publishing right-wing literature. His publishing company, Samidsdat Publishing Company, specializes in publishing and republishing Holocaust denial material. Among Zundel's published works is a eulogy to Adolf Hitler entitled *The Hitler We Loved and Why* (1978). His publishing company has an income of from $60,000 to $100,000 per year. He soon found himself in legal trouble with Canadian authorities over some of his publications. Zundel wrote a pamphlet, *Did Six Million Really Die?* and a letter titled "The West, War and Islam," in which he charged that a Jewish conspiracy existed and denied that the Holocaust ever happened. In December 1983, Sabrina Citron, a member of the Canadian Holocaust Remembrance Association and a Holocaust survivor, brought charges against him for these writings citing a law against making "false news." Zundel hired a right-wing lawyer, Doug Christie, to represent him in court. He also commissioned an amateur engineer, Fred Leuchter, to travel to Poland to take samples to prove that the gas chambers never existed. In two sensational trials, in 1985 and 1988, during which testimony on whether or not the Holocaust ever happened, Zundel was found guilty and sentenced to fifteen months in prison in the first trial and nine months in the second trial. The Canadian Supreme Court overturned these verdicts declaring the "false news" law unconstitutional. These trials also allowed Zundel to pose as a champion of free speech and to increase his public exposure.

Zundel continues to travel around Canada and the United States speaking out against the Holocaust. His publishing empire includes four AM radio stations in the United States, which broadcast his message to both Canada and the United States. Another of his enterprises is his *Another Voice of Freedom* television broadcast which airs on sixty American public-access channels. He claims that his biggest market is the Rocky Mountain area. Among his recent targets has been the Academy Award–winning movie *Schindler's List*. He considers the movie to be anti-German hate propaganda and attacks it on every occasion. Zundel considers Hitler a much-maligned figure and does everything possible to rehabilitate his reputation. Zundel has had a mixed record of success in the 1990s. In the summer of 1995, he formed the Internet Zundelsite to spread his political viewpoint. The Canadian government responded by applying existing laws against hate propaganda, defamation, and obscenity on the Internet. Zundel responded to this political pressure by moving his Zundelsite to California. Germany imposed censorship on the Zundelsite in 1996 citing a law against spreading Nazi propaganda. Zundel also tried to address the Canadian Parliament in June 1999, but all political parties united to ban him from speaking. He sued Parliament in Ottawa, Canada seeking civil damages for the ban, but the court denied his suit. Also, in 1993, Zundel had unsuccessfully applied for Canadian citizenship, so in late 1999 he decided to leave Canada, and since then his last reported location was at a remote site in Tennessee. His high profile led an arsonist to burn down his home in Toronto, Canada on May 7, 1995. **See also** Holocaust Denial Movement; Leuchter Report; Neo-Nazis.

Suggested readings: Roger Boyes, "Neo-Nazis Fight to Take Over Extremist Publishing Empire," *Times* [London] (November 14, 1996), p. 1; Alan David, ed., *Antisemitism in Canada: History and Interpretation* (Waterloo, Ont., Canada: Wilfrid Laurier University Press, 1992); Seymour Diener, "Governments Need to Tackle Problem of Web Hate Sites," *Ottawa Citizen* (May 13, 1998), p. G4; Peter Hum, "Political Parties Unite to Fight Zundel Lawsuit in Court," *Ottawa Citizen* (January 19, 1999), p. A6; Mitchell Jones, *The Leuchter Report: A Dissection* (Cedar Park, Tex.: 21st Century Logic,

1995); Deborah Lipstadt, Denying the *Holocaust: The Growing Assault on Truth and Memory* (New York: Plume, 1993); Douglas Martin, "Anti-Semite on Trial, but did Ontario Blunder?" *New York Times* (February 15, 1985), p. A2; Nathaniel C. Nash, "Germans Again Bar Internet Access, This Time to Neo-Nazism," *New York Times* (January 29, 1996), p. D6: Tracey Tyler, "Top Court Rejects Zundel's Appeal of Citizenship Review," *Toronto Star* (May 1, 1998), p. A6.

Selected Bibliography

GENERAL REFERENCE WORKS

Encyclopedias and Dictionaries

Bekoff, Marc, ed. *Encyclopedia of Animal Rights and Animal Welfare*. Westport, Conn.: Greenwood Press, 1998.

Buhl, Marie J., Paul Buhle, and Dan Georg akas, eds., *Encyclopedia of the American Left*. 2d ed. New York: Oxford University Press, 1998.

Hunt, Ronald J. *Historical Dictionary of the Gay Liberation Movement: Gay Men and the Quest for Social Justice*. Lanham, Md.: Scarecrow Press, 1999.

Kaplan, Jeffrey, ed. *Encyclopedia of White Power: A Sourcebook on the Radical Racist Right*. Walnut Creek, Calif.: Altamira Press, 2000.

Lewis, James R. *Peculiar Prophets: A Biographical Dictionary of New Religions*. Saint Paul, Minn.: Paragon House, 1999.

Mather, George A., and Larry A. Nichols. *Dictionary of Cults, Sects, Religions and the Occult*. Grand Rapids, Mich.: Zondervan Publishing House, 1993.

Nash, Jay Robert. *Terrorism in the 20th Century: A Narrative Encyclopedia from the Anarchists, through the Weathermen, to the Unabomber*. New York: Evans, 1998.

Rees, Philip. *Biographical Dictionary of the Extreme Right Since 1890*. New York: Simon and Schuster, 1990.

Handbooks, Surveys, and Readings

Anti-Defamation League. *Audit of Anti-Semitic Incidents*. New York: Anti-Defamation League, 2000.

———. *Danger: Extremism: The Major Vehicles and Voices on America's Far-Right Fringe*. New York: Anti-Defamation League, 1996.

———. *The Skinhead International: A Worldwide Survey of Neo-Nazi Skinheads*. New York: Anti-Defamation League, 1995.

———. *Young Nazi Killers: The Rising Skinhead Danger*. New York: Anti-Defamation League, 1993.

Hamilton, Neil A. *Militias in America: A Reference Handbook*. Santa Barbara, Calif.: ABC-CLIO, 1996.

Lewis, James R. *Cults in America: A Reference Handbook*. Santa Barbara, Calif.: ABC-CLIO, 1998.

Miller, Timothy, ed. *America's Alternative Religions*. New York: State University of New York Press, 1995.

Moran, Sarah. *The Secret World of Cults: From Ancient Druids to Heaven's Gate*. Godalming, U.K.: CLB International, 1999.

Sargent, Lyman Tower. *Extremism in America: A Reader*. New York: New York University Press, 1995.

AUTOBIOGRAPHIES

Atkins, Susan, and Bob Slossen. *Children of Satan, Child of God.* Plainfield, N.J.: Logos International, 1977.

Breault, Marc, and Martin King. *Inside the Cult: A Member's Chilling Exclusive Account of Madness and Depravity in David Koresh's Compound.* New York: Signet Books, 1993.

Chynoweth, Rena, and Dean M. Shapiro. *The Blood Covenant.* Austin, Tex.: Diamond Books, 1990.

Covington, Harold. *The March Upcountry.* Reading, Pa.: Liberty Bell, 1987.

Cox, Mike. *Stand-off in Texas: "Just Call Me a Spokesman for the DPS."* Austin, Tex.: Eakin Press, 1998.

Davis, Angela. *Angela Davis: An Autobiography.* New York: Random House, 1974.

Davis, J. David. *Finding the God of Noah: The Spiritual Journey of a Baptist Minister from Christianity to the Laws of Noah.* Hoboken, N.J.: Ktav Publishing House, 1996.

Halevi, Yossi Klein. *Memoirs of a Jewish Extremist: An American Story.* Boston: Little, Brown, 1995.

Hay, Harry. *Radically Gay: Gay Liberation in the Words of Its Founder.* Boston: Beacon Press, 1996.

Hearst, Patricia, and Alvin Moscow. *Every Secret Thing.* Garden City, N.Y.: Doubleday, 1982.

Layton, Deborah. *Seductive Poison: A Jonestown Survivor's Story of Life and Death in the Peoples Temple.* New York: Anchor Books, 1998.

Manson, Charles, and Nuel Emmons. *Manson in His Own Words.* New York: Grove Press, 1986.

Martinez, Thomas, and John Guinther. *Brotherhood of Murder: How One Man's Journey of Fear Brought The Order—The Most Dangerous Racist Gang in America—to Justice.* New York: McGraw-Hill, 1988.

Means, Russell, and Marvin J. Wolf. *Where White Men Fear to Tread: The Autobiography of Russell Means.* New York: St. Martin's Griffin, 1995.

Noble, Kerry. *Tabernacle of Hate: Why They Bombed Oklahoma City.* Prescott, Ontario, Canada: Voyageur Publishing, 1998.

Peck, Abe. *Uncovering the Sixties: The Life and Times of the Underground Press.* New York: Citadel Press, 1991.

Phillips, John W. *Sign of the Cross: The Prosecutor's True Story of a Landmark Trial Against the Klan.* Louisville, Ky.: Westminister John Knox Press, 2000.

Radosh, Ronald. *Commies: A Journey Through the Old Left, the New Left and the Leftover Left.* San Francisco: Encounter Books, 2001.

Seale, Bobby. *A Lonely Rage: The Autobiography of Bobby Seale.* New York: Times Books, 1978.

———. *Seize the Time: The Story of the Black Panther Party and Huey P. Newton.* New York: Random House, 1970.

Shakur, Assata. *Assata: An Autobiography.* Chicago: Lawrence Hill, 1987.

Watson, Paul, and Warren Roger. *Sea Shepherd: My Fight for Whales and Seals.* New York: Norton, 1982.

Weed, Steven. *My Search for Patty Hearst.* New York: Crown Publishers, 1976.

Williams, Miriam. *Heaven's Harlots: My Fifteen Years As a Sacred Prostitute in the Children of God Cult.* New York: Eagle Brook, 1998.

X, Malcolm, and Alex Haley. *The Autobiography of Malcolm X.* Harmondsworth, U.K.: Penguin Books, 1968.

BIOGRAPHIES

Bridges, Tyler. *The Rise of David Duke.* Jackson: University Press of Mississippi, 1994.

Dyson, Michael Eric. *Making Malcolm: the Myth and Meaning of Malcolm X.* New York: Oxford University Press, 1995.

Friedman, Robert I. *The False Prophet: Rabbi Meir Kahane—From FBI Informant to Knesset Member.* London: Faber and Faber, 1990.

Goldman, Peter. *The Death and Life of Malcolm X.* New York: Harper and Row, 1973.

Halasa, Malu. *Elijah Muhammad: Religious Leader.* Los Angeles: Melrose Square Publishing, 1990.

Jeansonne, Glen. *Gerald L. K. Smith: Minister of Hate.* New Haven, Conn.: Yale University Press, 1988.

Jezer, Marty. *Abbie Hoffman: American Rebel.* New Brunswick, N.J.: Rutgers University Press, 1992.

Lesher, Stephan. *George Wallace: American Populist.* Reading, Mass.: Addison-Wesley, 1994.

Magida, Authur J. *Prophet of Rage: A Life of*

Louis Farrakhan and His Nation. New York: Basic Books, 1996.

Malu, Halsa. *Elijah Muhammad: Religious Leader.* Los Angeles: Melrose Square Publishing, 1990.

Marcus, Sheldon. *Father Coughlin.* South Bend, Ind.: Notre Dame University Press, 1973.

Massengill, Reed. *Portrait of a Racist: The Real Life of Byron de la Beckwith.* New York: St. Martin's Griffin, 1996.

Michel, Lou, and Dan Herbeck. *American Terrorist: Timothy McVeigh and the Oklahoma Bombing.* New York: Regan Books, 2001.

Pearson, Hugh. *The Shadow of the Panther: Huey Newton and the Price of Black Power in America.* Reading, Mass.: Addison Wesley, 1994.

Perry, Bruce. *Malcolm: The Life of a Man Who Changed Black America.* Barrytown, N.Y.: Station Hill Press, 1991.

Raskin, Jonah. *For the Hell of It: The Life and Times of Abbie Hoffman.* Berkeley: University of California Press, 1997.

Rose, Douglas D., ed. *The Emergence of David Duke and the Politics of Race.* Chapel Hill: University of North Carolina Press, 1992.

Rosenthal, A. M., and Arthur Gelb. *One More Victim.* New York: New American Library, 1967.

Schmaltz, William H. *Hate: George Lincoln Rockwell and the American Nazi Party.* Washington, D.C.: Brassey's, 1999.

Serrano, Richard A. *One of Ours: Timothy McVeigh and the Oklahoma Bombing.* New York: Norton, 1998.

Simonelli, Frederick J. *American Fuehrer: George Lincoln Rockwell and the American Nazi Party.* Urbana: University of Illinois Press, 1999.

Singular, Stephen. *Talked to Death: The Life and Murder of Alan Berg.* New York: Beech Tree Books, 1987.

Sloman, Larry. *Abbie Hoffman and Hey, His Turbulent Times.* New York: Doubleday, 1998.

Timmons, Stuart. *The Trouble with Harry Hay: Founder of the Modern Gay Movement.* Boston: Alyson, 1990.

Warren, Donald. *Radio Priest: Charles Coughlin the Father of Hate Radio.* New York: Free Press, 1996.

Zatarain, Michael. *David Duke: Evolution of a Klansman.* Gretna, La.: Pelican, 1990.

MONOGRAPHS

General

Abanes, Richard. *American Militias: Rebellion, Racism and Religion.* Downers Grove, Ill.: InterVarsity Press, 1996.

Able, Deborah. *Hate Groups.* Springfield, N.J.: Enslow Publishers, 1995.

Aho, James Alfred. *The Politics of Righteousness: Idaho Christian Patriotism.* Seattle: University of Washington Press, 1990.

Alnor, William M. *UFO Cults and the New Millennium.* Grand Rapids, Mich.: Baker Books, 1998.

Anderson, Scott. *The 4 o'clock Murders.* New York: Doubleday, 1993.

Ansell, Amy Elizabeth. *New Right, New Racism: Race and Reaction in the United States and Britain.* Washington, Square, N.Y.: New York University Press, 1997.

Anti-Defamation League. *Explosion of Hate: The Growing Danger of the National Alliance.* New York: Anti-Defamation League, 1998.

Aronowitz, Stanley. *The Death and Rebirth of American Radicalism.* New York: Routledge, 1996.

Bailey, Brad, and Bob Darden. *Mad Man in Waco.* Waco, Tex.: WRS Publishing, 1993.

Baird-Windle, Patricia, and Eleanor J. Bader. *Targets of Hatred: Anti-Abortion Terrorism.* New York: Palgrave, 2001.

Baker, Marilyn, and Sally Brompton. *Exclusive!: The Inside Story of Patricia Hearst and the SLA.* New York: Macmillan, 1974.

Barkun, Michael. *Religion and the Racist Right: The Origins of the Christian Identity Movement.* Chapel Hill: University of North Carolina Press, 1997.

Barrett, Stanley R. *Is God a Racist? The Right Wing in Canada.* Toronto: University of Toronto Press, 1987.

Bjorgo, Tore, ed. *Terror from the Extreme Right.* London: Frank Cass, 1995.

Blanchard, Dallas A. *The Anti-Abortion Movement and the Rise of the Religious Right: From Polite to Fiery Protest.* New York: Twayne, 1994.

Bradlee, Ben, and Dale Van Atta. *Prophet of Blood: The Untold Story of Ervil LeBaron and the Lambs of God.* New York: Putnams, 1981.

Braun, Aurel, and Stephen Scheinberg, eds. *The*

Extreme Right: Freedom and Security at Risk. Boulder, Colo.: Westview Press, 1997.

Broyes, J. Allen. *The John Birch Society: Anatomy of a Protest.* Boston: Beacon Press, 1964.

Bryan, John. *This Soldier Still at War.* New York: Harcourt, Brace, Jovanovich, 1975.

Bugliosi, Vincent, and Curt Gentry. *Helter Skelter: The True Story of the Manson Murders.* New York: Norton, 1974.

Burkett, Elinor. *The Right Women: A Journey Through the Heart of Conservative America.* New York: Touchstone Books, 1998.

Bushart, Howard L., John R. Craig, and Myra Barnes. *Soldiers of God: White Supremacists and Their Holy War for America.* New York: Kensington Books, 1998.

Cagin, Seth, and Philip Dray. *We Are Not Afraid: The Story of Goodman, Schwerner and Chaney and the Civil Rights Campaign for Mississippi.* New York: Bantam Books, 1989.

Castellucci, John. *The Big Dance: The Untold Story of Kathy Boudin and the Terrorist Family That Committed the Brink's Robbery Murders.* New York: Dodd, Mead, 1986.

Chidester, David. *Salvation and Suicide: An Interpretation of Jim Jones, the People's Temple, and Jonestown.* Bloomington: Indiana University Press, 1988.

Clendinen, Dudley, and Adam Nagourney. *Out for Good: The Struggle to Build a Gay Rights Movement in America.* New York: Simon and Schuster, 1999.

Coates, James. *Armed and Dangerous: The Rise of the Survivalist Right.* New York: Hill and Wang, 1987.

Cohn, Norman. *Warrant for Genocide: The Myth of the Jewish World Conspiracy and the Protocols of the Elders of Zion.* London: Serif, 1996.

Collins, John J. *The Cult Experience: An Overview of Cults, Their Traditions, and Why People Join Them.* Springfield, Ill.: C. C. Thomas, 1991.

Colvin, Rod. *Evil Harvest: A True Story of Cult Murder in the American Heartland.* New York; Bantam Books, 1992.

Coppola, Vincent. *Dragons of God: A Journey Through Far-Right America.* Atlanta, Ga: Longstreet Press, 1996.

Corcoran, James. *Bitter Harvest: Gordon Kahl and the Posse Comitatus: Murder in the Heartland.* New York: Viking Press, 1990.

Cozic, Charles P. *The Militia Movement.* San Diego: Greenhaven Press, 1997.

Craig, Barbara Hinkson, and David M. O'Brien. *Abortion and American Politics.* Chatham, N.J.: Chatham House, 1993.

Cruikshank, Margaret. *The Gay and Lesbian Liberation Movement.* New York: Routledge, 1992.

Daniels, Jessie. *White Lies: Race, Class, Gender and Sexuality in White Supremacist Discourse.* New York: Routledge, 1997.

Daniels, Ted, ed. *A Doomsday Reader: Prophets, Predictors, and Hucksters of Salvation.* New York: New York University Press, 1999.

Davies, Alan, ed. *Antisemitism in Canada: History and Interpretation.* Waterloo, Ont., Canada: Wilfrid Laurier University Press, 1992.

Dees, Morris, and James Corcoran. *Gathering Storm: America's Militia Threat.* New York: HarperCollins, 1996.

Dees, Morris, and Steve Fiffer. *Hate on Trial: The Case Against America's Most Dangerous Neo-Nazi.* New York: Villard Books, 1993.

Diamond, Sara. *Roads to Dominion: Right-Wing Movements and Political Power in the United States.* New York: Guilford Press, 1995.

———. *Spiritual Warfare: The Politics of the Christian Right.* Montreal, Que. Canada: Black Rose Books, 1990.

Dinnerstein, Leonard. *Antisemitism in America.* New York: Oxford University Press, 1994.

Dobratz, Betty A., and Stephanie L. Shanks-Meile. *"White Power, White Pride!": The White Separatist Movement in the United States.* New York: Twayne, 1997.

Douglas, John E. *Unabomber: On the Trail of America's Most-Wanted Serial Killer.* New York: Pocket Books, 1996.

Dyer, Joel. *Harvest of Rage: Why Oklahoma City Is Only the Beginning.* Boulder, Colo.: Westview Press, 1997.

Earley, Peter, *Prophet of Death: The Mormon Blood-Atonement Killings.* New York: William Morrow, 1991.

Eisenberg, Dennis. *The Re-Emergence of Fascism.* New York: A. S. Barnes, 1967.

Epstein, Benjamin R. *The Radical Right: Report on the John Birch Society and Its Allies.* New York: Vintage Books, 1967.

Evans, Richard J. *Lying About Hitler: History, Holocaust and the David Irving Trial.* New York: Basic Books, 2001.

Ezekiel, Raphael S. *The Racist Mind: Portraits of American Neo-Nazis and Klansmen.* New York: Penguin Books, 1995.

Fenster, Mark. *Conspiracy Theories: Secrecy and Power in American Culture.* Minneapolis: University of Minnesota Press, 1999.

Ferber, Abbey L. *White Man Falling: Race, Gender, and White Supremacy.* Lanham, Md.: Rowman and Littlefield, 1999.

Finch, Phillip. *God, Guts, and Guns.* New York: Seaview/Putnam, 1983.

Finsen, Lawrence, and Susan Finsen. *The Animal Rights Movement in America: From Compassion to Respect.* New York: Twayne, 1994.

Fletcher, Jim, Tanaquil Jones, and Sylvere Lotringer. *Still Black, Still Strong: Survivors of the U.S. War Against Black Revolutionaries: Dhoruba Bin Wahad, Mumia Abu-Jamal, and Assata Shakur.* Brooklyn, N.Y.: Semiotext (e), 1993.

Flynn, Kevin, and Gary Gerhardt. *The Silent Brotherhood: Inside America's Racist Underground.* New York: Free Press, 1989.

Forster, Arnold, and Benjamin R. Epstein. *The New Anti-Semitism.* New York: McGraw-Hill, 1974.

Frankfort, Ellen. *Kathy Boudin and the Dance of Death.* New York: Stein and Day, 1983.

Freeberg, Sydney P. *Brother Love: Murder, Money and a Messiah.* New York: Pantheon, 1994.

Freeman, Jo, ed. *Social Movements of the Sixties and Seventies.* New York: Longman, 1983.

Gardell, Mattias. *In the Name of Elijah Muhammad: Louis Farrakhan and the Nation of Islam.* Durham, N.C.: Duke University Press, 1996.

George, John, and Liard Wilcox. *Nazis, Communists, Klansmen, and Others on the Fringe.* Buffalo, N.Y.: Prometheus Books, 1992.

Golsan, Richard J., ed. *Fascism's Return: Scandal, Revision, and Ideology Since 1980.* Lincoln: University of Nebraska Press, 1998.

Graysmith, Robert. *Unabomber: A Desire to Kill.* New York: Berkeley Books, 1998.

Guillermo, Kay Snow. *Monkey Business: The Disturbing Case That Launched the Animal Rights Movement.* Washington, D.C.: National Press Books, 1993.

Guither, Harold D. *Animal Rights: History and Scope of a Radical Social Movement.* Carbondale: Southern Illinois University Press, 1998.

Gurock, Jeffrey S., ed. *Anti-Semitism in America.* 2d ed. New York: Routledge, 1998, 2 vols.

Guttenplan, D. D. *The Holocaust on Trial.* New York: Norton, 2001.

Hamlin, David. *The Nazi/Skokie Conflict: A Civil Liberties Battle.* Boston: Beacon Press, 1980.

Hamm, Mark S. *American Skinheads: The Criminology and Control of Hate Crime.* Westport, Conn.: Praeger, 1993.

Harris, David. *The Last Stand: The War Between Wall Street and Main Street over California's Ancient Redwoods.* New York: Times Books, 1996.

Haskins, Jim. *Power to the People: The Rise and Fall of the Black Panther Party.* New York: Simon and Schuster Books for Young Readers, 1997.

Helvarg, David. *The War Against the Greens: The "Wise-Use" Movement, the New Right, and the Anti-Environmental Violence.* San Francisco: Sierra Club Books, 1994.

Herek, Gregory M., and Kevin T. Berrill. *Hate Crimes: Confronting Violence Against Lesbians and Gay Men.* Newbury Park, Calif.: Sage Publications, 1992.

Herman, Didi. *The Antigay Agenda: Orthodox Vision and the Christian Right.* Chicago: University of Chicago Press, 1997.

Higham, Charles. *American Swastika.* Garden City, N.Y.: Doubleday, 1985.

Hilliard, Robert L., and Michael C. Keith. *Waves of Rancor: Tuning in the Radical Right.* Armonk, N.Y.: Sharpe, 1999.

Jacobs, James B., and Kimberly Potter. *Hate Crimes: Criminal Law and Identity Politics.* New York: Oxford University Press, 1998.

Jakes, Dale, and Connie Jakes. *False Prophets: The Firsthand Account of a Husband-Wife Team Working for the FBI and Living in Deepest Cover with the Montana Freemen.* Los Angeles: Dove Books, 1998.

Jones, Charles E., ed. *The Black Panther Party: Reconsidered.* Baltimore: Black Classic Press, 1998.

Jones, J. Harry. *The Minutemen.* Garden City, N.Y.: Doubleday, 1968.

Jones, Mitchell. *The Leuchter Report: A Dissection.* Cedar Park, Tex.: 21st Century Logic, 1995.

Josephy, Alvin M., Joane Nagel, and Troy Johnson, eds. 2d ed. *Red Power: The American Indians' Fight for Freedom.* Lincoln: University of Nebraska Press, 1999.

Juergensmeyer, Mark. *Terror in the Mind of God: The Global Rise of Religious Violence.* Berkeley: University of California Press, 2000.

Kahaner, Larry. *Cults That Kill: Probing the Underworld of Occult Crime.* New York: Warner Books, 1988.

Kaplan, Jeffrey. *Radical Religion in America: Millenarian Movements from the Far Right to the Children of Noah.* Syracuse, N.Y.: Syracuse University Press, 1997.

Kaplan, Jeffrey, and Tore Bjorgo, eds. *Nation and Race: The Developing Euro-American Racist Subculture.* Boston: Northwestern University Press, 1998.

Kelly, Robert J., and Jess Maghan. *Hate Crime: The Global Politics of Polarization.* Carbondale, Ill.: Southern Illinois University Press, 1998.

King, Dennis. *Lyndon LaRouche and the New American Fascism.* New York: Doubleday, 1989.

Kinsella, Warren. *Web of Hate: Inside Canada's Far-Right Network.* Toronto, Ontario, Canada: HarperCollins, 1994.

Kronenwetter, Michael. *United They Hate: White Supremacist Groups in America.* New York: Walker, 1992.

Lamy, Philip. *Millennium Rage: Survivalists, White Supremacists and the Doomsday Prophecy.* New York: Plenum Press, 1996.

Lang, Susan S. *Extremist Groups in America.* New York: Watts, 1990.

Lee, Martha F. *Earth First: Environmental Apocalypse.* Syracuse, N.Y.: Syracuse University Press, 1995.

Lee, Martin A. *The Beast Reawakens.* Boston: Little, Brown, 1997.

Leppard, David. *Fire and Blood: The True Story of David Koresh and the Waco Siege.* London: Fourth Estate, 1993.

Lesce, Tony. *Wide Open to Terrorism.* Port Townsend, Wash.: Loompanic Unlimited, 1996.

Levi, Ken, ed., *Violence and Religious Commitment: Implications of James Jones' People's Temple Movement.* University Park: Pennsylvania State University Press, 1998.

Lewis, James R. *Cults in America: A Reference Handbook.* Santa Barbara, Calif.: ABC-CLIO, 1998.

———. *The Gods Have Landed: New Religions from Other Worlds.* Albany: State University of New York Press, 1995.

——— ed. *Magical Religions and Modern Witchcraft.* Albany: State University of New York Press, 1996.

Lewis, James R., and J. Gordon Melton, eds., *Sex, Slander and Salvation: Investigating the Family/Children of God.* Stanford, Calif.: Center for Academic Publishing, 1994.

Lincoln, C. Eric. *The Black Muslims in America.* 3d ed. Grand Rapids, Mich.: William B. Eerdmans, 1995.

Linedecker, Clifford L. *Massacre at Waco: The Shocking True Story of Cult Leader David Koresh and the Branch Davidians.* London: True Crime, 1993.

Lipstadt, Deborah E. *Denying the Holocaust: The Growing Assault on Truth and Memory.* New York: Plume, 1993.

Long, Robert Emmet, ed. *Religious Cults in America.* New York: Wilson, 1994.

Madigan, Tim. *See No Evil: Blind Devotion and Bloodshed in David Koresh's Holy War.* Fort Worth, Tex.: Summit Group, 1993.

Manes, Christopher. *Green Rage: Radical Environmentalism and the Unmaking of Civilization.* Boston: Little, Brown, 1990.

Marks, Kathy. *Faces of Right Wing Extremism.* Boston: Branden Publishing, 1996.

Matthiessen, Peter. *In the Spirit of Crazy Horse.* New York: Viking Press, 1983.

McLellan, Vin, and Paul Avery. *The Voices of Guns: The Definitive and Dramatic Story of the Twenty-Two-Month Career of the Symbionese Liberation Army—One of the Most Bizarre Chapters in the History of the American Left.* New York: Putnam's Sons, 1997.

Mello, Michael. *The United States of America versus Theodore John Kaczynski: Ethics, Power and the Invention of the Unabomber.* New York: Context Books, 1999.

Miller, Timothy, ed. *America's Alternative Religions.* Albany: State University of New York Press, 1995.

Mintz, Frank P. *The Liberty Lobby and the American Right: Race, Conspiracy, and Culture.* Westport, Conn.: Greenwood Press, 1985.

Moore, Jack B. *Skinheads Shaved for Battle: A Cultural History of American Skinheads.* Bowling Green, Ohio: Bowling Green State University Popular Press, 1993.

Morris, David B. *Earth Warrior: Overboard with Paul Watson and the Sea Shepherd Conservation Society.* Golden, Colo.: Fulcrum Publishing, 1995.

Naipaul, Shiva. *Black and White*. London: H. Hamilton, 1980.

Neiwert, David A. *In God's Country: The Patriot Movement and the Pacific Northwest*. Pullman: Washington State University Press, 1999.

Nelson, Jack. *Terror in the Night: The Klan's Campaign Against the Jews*. New York: Simon and Schuster, 1993.

Novick, Michael. *White Lies White Power: The Fight Against White Supremacy and Reactionary Violence*. Monroe, Maine: Common Courage Press, 1995.

Nugent, John Peer. *White Night*. New York: Rawson, Wade, 1979.

Peck, Abe. *Uncovering the Sixties: The Life and Times of the Underground Press*. New York: Citadel Press, 1991.

Perkins, Rodney, and Forrest Jackson. *Cosmic Suicide: The Tragedy and Transcendence of the Heaven's Gate*. Dallas, Tex.: Pentaradial Press, 1997.

Quarles, Chester L. *The Ku Klux Klan and Related American Racist and Antisemitic Organizations: A History and Analysis*. Jefferson, N.C.: McFarland, 1999.

Reavis, Dick J. *The Ashes of Waco: An Investigation*. Syracuse, N.Y.: Syracuse University Press, 1995.

Reston, James. *Our Father Who Art in Hell*. New York: Time Books, 1981.

Ridgeway, James. *Blood in the Face: The Ku Klux Klan, Aryan Nations, Nazi Skinheads, and the Rise of a New White Culture*. New York: Thunder's Mouth Press, 1990.

Risen, James, and Judy L. Thomas. *Wrath of Angels: The American Abortion War*. New York: Basic Books, 1998.

Sayer, John William. *Ghost Dancing the Law: The Wounded Knee Trials*. Cambridge, Mass.: Harvard University Press, 1997.

Scarce, Rik. *Eco-Warriors: Understanding the Radical Environmental Movement*. Chicago: Noble Press, 1990.

Segel, Benjamin W. *A Lie and a Libel: The History of the Protocols of the Elders of Zion*. Lincoln: University of Nebraska Press, 1995.

Seidel, Gill. *The Holocaust Denial: Antisemitism, Racism and the New Right*. Leeds, U.K.: Beyond the Pale Collective, 1986.

Seymour, Cheri. *Committee of the States: Inside the Radical Right*. Mariposa, Calif.: Camden Place Communications, 1991.

Sims, Patsy. *The Klan*. New York: Stein and Day, 1978.

Singer, Margaret Thaler. *Cults in Our Midst: The Hidden Menace in Our Everyday Lives*. San Francisco: Jossey-Bass, 1995.

Singh, Robert. *The Farrakhan Phenomenon: Race, Reaction, and the Paranoid Style in American Politics*. Washington, D.C.: Georgetown University Press, 1997.

Sloman, Larry. *Steal This Dream: Abbie Hoffman and the Countercultural Revolution in America*. New York: Doubleday, 1998.

Smith, Brent L. *Terrorism in America: Pipe Bombs and Pipe Dreams*. Albany: State University of New York Press, 1994.

Smith, Jennifer B. *An International History of the Black Panther Party*. New York: Garland, 1999.

Smith, Paul Chaat, and Robert Allen Warrior. *Like a Hurricane: The Indian Movement from Alcatraz to Wounded Knee*. New York: New Press, 1996.

Snow, Robert L. *The Militia Threat: Terrorists Among Us*. New York: Plenum Trade, 1999.

Solinger, Rickie, ed. *Abortion Wars: A Half Century of Struggle, 1950–2000*. Berkeley: University of California Press, 1998.

Stanton, Bill. *Klanwatch: Bringing the Ku Klux Klan to Justice*. New York: Grove Weidenfeld, 1991.

Stern, Kenneth S. *A Force upon the Plain: The American Militia Movement and the Politics of Hate*. Norman: University of Oklahoma Press, 1996.

———. *Holocaust Denial*. New York: American Jewish Committee, 1993.

———. *Loud Hawk: The United States versus the American Indian Movement*. Norman: University of Oklahoma Press, 1994.

Stock, Catherine McNicol. *Rural Radicals: Righteous Rage in the American Grain*. Ithaca, N.Y.: Cornell University Press, 1996.

Sturgeon, Noel. *Ecofeminist Natures: Race, Gender, Feminist Theory, and Political Action*. New York: Routledge, 1997.

Teal, Donn. *The Gay Militants, How Gay Liberation Began in America, 1969–1971*. New York: St. Martin's Press, 1971.

Timothy, Mary. *Jury Woman: The Story of the Trial of Angela Y. Davis*. San Francisco: Gline Publications, 1975.

Tribe, Laurence H. *Abortion: The Clash of Absolutes*. New York: Norton, 1990.

Tull, Charles J. *Father Coughlin and the New*

Deal. Syracuse, N.Y.: Syracuse University Press, 1965.

Vaid, Urvashi. *Virtual Equality. The Mainstreaming of Gay and Lesbian Liberation*. New York: Anchor, 1995.

Van Zandt, David E. *Living in the Children of God*. Princeton, N.J.: Princeton University Press, 1991.

Vickers, George R. *The Formation of the New Left: The Early Years*. Lexington, Mass.: Lexington Books, 1975.

Wade, Wyn Craig. *The Fiery Cross: The Ku Klux Klan in America*. New York: Simon and Schuster, 1987.

Waits, Chris, and Dave Shors. *Unabomber: The Secret Life of Ted Kaczynski*. Helena, Mont.: Helena Independent Record and Montana Magazine, 1999.

Walter, Jess. *Every Knee Shall Bow: The Truth and Tragedy of Ruby Ridge and the Randy Weaver Family*. New York: Regan Books, 1995.

Walters, Jerome. *One Aryan Nation Under God: Exposing the New Racial Extremists*. Cleveland: Pilgrim Press, 2000.

Wangerin, Ruth. *The Children of God: A Make-Believe Revolution?* Westport, Conn.: Bergin and Garvey, 1993.

Warren, Donald. *Radio Priest: Charles Coughlin the Father of Hate Radio*. New York: Free Press, 1996.

Weller, Worth H., and Brad Thompson. *Under the Hood: Unmasking the Modern Ku Klux Klan*. North Manchester, Ind.: DeWitt Books, 1998.

Wheaton, Elizabeth. *Codename Greenkil: The 1979 Greensboro Killings*. Athens: University of Georgia Press, 1987.

Whitehead, Don. *Attack on Terror: The FBI Against the Ku Klux Klan in Mississippi*. New York: Funk and Wagnalls, 1970.

Wyler, Rex. *Blood of the Land: The Government and Corporate War Against the American Indian Movement*. New York: Everest House, 1982.

Zakin, Susan. *Coyotes and Town Dogs: Earth First! and the Environmental Movement*. New York: Viking Press, 1993.

Extremist Literature

Beam, Louis. *Essays of a Klansman*. N.p., 1983.

Emry, Sheldon. *Billions for Bankers, Debts for People*. Phoenix: America's Promise Ministries, n.d.

Guerrilla Girls. *Confessions of the Guerrilla Girls*. New York: HarperPerennial, 1995.

Hearst, Patricia. *Every Secret Thing*. Garden City, N.Y.: Doubleday, 1982.

Kahane, Meir. *Time to Go Home*. Los Angeles: Nash, 1972.

Keith, Jim. *Black Helicopters over America: Strikeforce for the New World Order*. Lilburn, Ga.: IllumiNet Press, 1994.

Pierce, William, and Andrew MacDonald. *The Turner Diaries*. Hillsboro, W.V.: National Alliance, 1978.

Singer, Peter. Animal Liberation: *A New Ethics for Our Treatment of Animals*. New York: Avon Books, 1975.

Yockey, Peter Francis. *Imperium*. Sausalito, Calif.: Noontide Press, 1963.

INTERNET SOURCES

Anti-Defamation League. "Poisoning the Web: Hatred Online." www.adl.org

Michaels, David. "Neo-Nazi Terrorism." www.ict.org.il

Mitchell, Terry, and Loey Glover. "About Green Panthers!" www.greenpanthers.org.

Nelson, Cletus. "The Bong and the Rifle." www.greenpanthers.org.

The Nizkor Project. "The Leuchter Report; Holocaust Denial & the Big Lie." www.nizkor.org/faqs/leuchter/.

Southern Poverty Law Center. "The Rise of the National Alliance." www.splcenter.org/intelligenceproject/alliance.html.

Index

Page numbers for main entries in the encyclopedia are set in **boldface** type.

About the Author

STEPHEN E. ATKINS is Associate University Librarian for Collection Management at the Sterling C. Evans Library at Texas A&M University. He is the author of *Historical Encyclopedia of Atomic Energy* (Greenwood, 2000), which received the Booklist Editor's Choice Award for 2000, *Terrorism: A Handbook* (1992), *Arms Control and Disarmament, Defense and Military, International Security and Peace: An Annotated Guide to Sources 1980–1987* (1989), and *The Academic Library in the American University* (1991), as well as numerous journal articles on arms control.